ENTERPRISE AND SECULAR CHANGE

READINGS IN ECONOMIC HISTORY

ENTERPRISE and SECULAR CHANGE

Readings in Economic History

EDITED FOR THE

AMERICAN ECONOMIC ASSOCIATION

AND THE

ECONOMIC HISTORY ASSOCIATION

BY

FREDERIC C. LANE, Editor

JELLE C. RIEMERSMA, Assistant Editor

1953

RICHARD D. IRWIN, INC.

HOMEWOOD, ILLINOIS

First Printing, January, 1953

PRINTED IN THE UNITED STATES OF AMERICA

Preface

Appearing as it does under the joint sponsorship of two professional associations, this collection of essays has been conceived to serve readers from several disciplines. Its subject is both theoretical and historical, and necessarily touches on basic issues regarding the study of human action. It should help economists, sociologists, and general historians to acquaint themselves with some of the problems and achievements of economic history. Above all it should provide young scholars starting on their own investigations in economic history with a collection of material in which they can find together some of the aims, methods, and results of other investigators.

We wanted to show the diversity of problems studied by economic historians, to illustrate their use of different kinds of historical sources, and to present a number of the more important concepts and methods in use. On the other hand, we also wished to include a sufficient number of essays dealing with the same problem, or set of related problems, to show what advances have been made since economic history became an independent discipline in the 1890's. Not all the essays which have been included present, therefore, the latest findings of research. Some were selected because they were cited frequently in later discussions; others because they show how a subject which is still of great interest was studied by a scholar of an earlier generation. The essays translated from German, Italian, and French present material hitherto unavailable in English. By means of our selections we intended to convey a sense of the development of economic history as an international intellectual enterprise which has an inner continuity and, in spite of many disputes, a recognizable unity of purpose.

In order to treat one or two themes intensively, it proved necessary to exclude others. Industrial history and agrarian history, for example, had to be neglected; additional volumes would be required to present them adequately. But we have chosen articles on two themes—business units (Section I) and money and prices (Section II)—in such a way as to indicate secular changes from the Middle Ages to our own times.

The division between Section I and Section II was suggested in part by the way in which political economy has been divided into micro-economics (the economics of the firm) and macro-economics (aggregates in the total economy). And the two sections complement each other in other respects. Section I illustrates the connections between economic organizations and other changing institutions in Western culture. Section II provides illustrations of the close connection between economic history and the history of economic thought.

In Section III, on methodology, the essays included were selected in order to reveal conflicting views sharply. By editorial introductions we have indicated the historical setting of each author and his relation to the others. Although some of the studies of concrete historical problems presented in Sections I and II depend largely on one method, others more largely on other methods, none of these concrete historical studies was selected for inclusion in order to serve as an illustration of the application of the method advocated in a particular essay in Section III. The final section is not in that sense directly linked to the other two. But various conceptions of economic history are implicit in the historical articles, and it seemed of value to bring together in relatively small compass rigorous statements of the main methodological positions.

Instead of the bibliography usually included in the volumes in the Series of Republished Articles in Economics sponsored by the American Economic Association, this book offers a biographical and bibliographical appendix. Our policy in regard to footnotes has not been uniform. From some articles footnotes were eliminated altogether, namely, where the nature of the sources was evident from the text or where the cited material was rather inaccessible. In some instances footnotes were very extensive, and limitations of space have been a major consideration. An editorial foreword or editorial notes occasionally serve to indicate omissions or additions. The application of uniform style rules by the publisher has had the result that in some selections the footnotes are numbered differently than in the original article.

The proposal for a volume of readings in economic history, to be sponsored jointly by the American Economic Association and the Economic History Association, originated in discussions led by Arthur H. Cole at the meetings of these associations. He was chairman of an exploratory committee which agreed on the aims to be served by the volume, as mentioned above. At the annual meeting of the Economic History Association in 1949 I was asked to serve as chairman of a committee which would proceed with the preparations. Its members were: J. B. Brebner, S. B. Clough, A. H. Cole, E. J. Hamilton,

H. Heaton, M. M. Knight, F. Machlup, B. Mitchell, F. Redlich, and H. F. Williamson. They provided me with suggestions about specific articles and about the general plan of the book. With their help I gradually arrived at the plan and contents presented here, working in consultation with Jelle C. Riemersma, whose services as assistant editor I was able to secure while he was Research Fellow in Economic History at The Johns Hopkins University. The Committee on Research in Economic History of the Social Science Research Council gave a grant which made it possible to prepare a number of translations expressly for this book.

We wish to thank the members of the committee that assisted in planning the book, and the authors who permitted us to republish their articles. Many persons in one way or another helped us with the translations or with various editorial tasks: Mrs. Eugenie Cahén, Mrs. Angela Fales, Rashi Fein, Karl F. Helleiner, Lilly Lavarello, C. D. Rouillard, H. Von Schuching, Stefan Stykolt, and Giorgio Tagliacozzo. To Raymond De Roover and Florence Edler–De Roover we are indebted for their assistance in preparing the Italian translations. Fritz Redlich worked over with us the introduction to his translation of Arthur Spiethoff's paper on method. Finally, we must express our thanks to the editors and publishers who allowed us to use their material.

F. C. L.

November, 1952

Table of Contents

SECTION I. BUSINESS UNITS

SECTION I

Business Units

1

*The Historical Development of the Enterprise**

By GUSTAV SCHMOLLER

Editors' Foreword

The series of articles under the collective title "Die geschichtliche Entwickelung der Unternehmung," which Gustav Schmoller published in his *Jahrbuch für Gesetzgebung, Verwaltung, und Volkswirtschaft im deutschen Reich* during the years 1890–93, consists of the following parts:

"Einleitendes," 1890, XIV, 735–42
"I, Die älteren Arbeitgenossenschaften," 1890, XIV, 743–67
"II, Die ältere agrarische Familienwirtschaft," 1890, XIV, 767–83
"III, Der Einfluss des Handels," 1890, XIV, 1035–43
"IV, Das Handwerk," 1890, XIV, 1053–76
"V, Die Hausindustrie," 1890, XIV, 1053–76
"VI, Das Recht und die Verbände der Hausindustrie," 1891, XV, 1–37
"VII, Die antike Grossindustrie," 1891, XV, 38–47
"VIII, Das mittelalterliche Genossenschaftswesen," 1891, XV, 635–60
"IX, Die deutsche Bergwerksverfassung von 1150–1400," 1891, XV, 660–710
"X, Die deutsche Bergwerksverfassung von 1400–1600," 1891, XV, 963–1029
"XI, Die Handelsgesellschaften des Altertums," 1892, XVI, 731–48
"XII, Die Handelsgesellschaften des Mittelalters und der Renaissancezeit," 1893, XVII, 359–319
"XIII, Die Handelsgesellschaften des 17. und 18. Jahrhunderts, hauptsächlich die grossen Kompagnien," 1893, XVII, 959–1018

The translations in the following pages represent a few selected fragments of Schmoller's vast undertaking; the extensive footnotes of the original articles have been omitted. The material has been divided, for purposes of presentation, into three sections: I. Introduction; II. Ancient Labor Associations; III. Large-Scale Enterprises of Antiquity.

Schmoller relates the structure of economic enterprise to the structure of

* Selections from Gustav Schmoller, "Die geschichtliche Entwickelung der Unternehmung," *Jahrbuch für Gesetzgebung, Verwaltung, und Volkswirtschaft im deutschen Reich* (Berlin, 1890, 1891), Vol. XIV, pp. 735–47, 749–50, 750–52, 752–54, 755–56, 762–67; Vol. XV, pp. 38, 42–45, 636–37. Translated and included by courtesy of Duncker & Humblot, publishers, Berlin.

society as a whole, by applying what may be called a comparative method of universal scope. Studying all forms of economic enterprise through history, two major forms of association stand out: (1) labor associations, which are co-operatives of equal partners, governed by customs and traditions, and (2) associations governed by authority, which have a clear-cut differentiation between the rulers and the ruled.

J. C. Riemersma is responsible for the translation.

I. INTRODUCTION

In everyday language we speak of the "enterprises" of great princes and generals. The word "enterprise" is also used for building projects, conquests, colonizations, and finally for particular ventures and speculations. Yet it has at the same time become customary to designate a very special kind of social and economic organization as an "enterprise." When we refer to an enterprise without further specification, we mean a business or economic entity, many of which exist in present-day economic life, with a certain continuity over a period of time. Using the word in this way, we contrast the economic activity of the enterprise with that of the family, club, municipality, or state. Private businesses, consumers' co-operatives, and corporations can all be regarded as enterprises, and the same holds for such organizations as municipal gas companies, city loan offices, national banks, and railroads. But nobody will use the word "enterprise" for the army, even if it incidentally produces cannon or gunpowder. Nobody calls it an enterprise when a maid regularly takes care of the family wash; but the washerwoman who today works in one household and tomorrow in another is statistically counted as an enterprise. There are doubtful cases. One may wonder whether a group of bricklayers moving from place to place, the men working with their own tools under the leadership of a foreman, can be considered an enterprise or as a group of wage laborers. One may also question whether the activity of a lawyer or doctor constitutes an enterprise. The answer is affirmative if one thinks of the financial compensation for which they work; negative if one regards their task as the performance of professional duties.

There are various secondary reasons for business transactions, but the underlying idea is always that the businessman, through these transactions, acquires a gain or at least recovers his expenditures in time, material, and other things. Thus he maintains himself by delivering goods and services. The enterprise, as a category, comprises all forms of social and economic organization which aim to provide people with goods and services on the basis of free bargains or contracts. The enterprise is a result of the division of labor in an economy characterized by markets, money, and communications. Each individual enterprise is a unit, externally and internally, whether it includes only one person or a number of persons. As a social organ it has a certain autonomy, property, and internal organization. This organization regulates the co-operation of the participants and the distribution of returns. Viewed from the outside, an enterprise is an institution held together by purposes of an enduring character, namely, the interests of the partners. It struggles for survival and expansion, competes with similar organisms, and strives for profit by selling goods to the public. An enterprise is a well-organized combination of labor power and means of production which performs a separate part of the total task of economic production. For this purpose it buys goods and services, performs technical and economic operations, and sells products; all these activities are geared to their profitability.

Ever since political economy became a science, in the eighteenth century, it has become customary to speak of the "entrepreneur" [*Unternehmer*]; he is the person, in the provisions of civil law, for whose account the enterprise is conducted. Theorists have been almost exclusively occupied with the question whether entrepreneurial income belongs in the legal and economic category of interest—capital gains—or in the category of wages. English authors have maintained the former position; French authors the latter. This scholastic debate about words has been combined with a debate about the intrinsic justification of entrepreneurial gains. Such gains were attacked by socialists, who regarded them as a consequence of private property, of capital accumulation, and of the whole existing legal order. Socialists denied the organizing and creative ability of the entrepreneur, lumped interest and profits together, and regarded them both as unjust. Interest was seen as an unearned income, as a monopoly gain; profit was condemned for similar reasons. German economic theorists in particular have attempted to oppose these arguments by making clear that entrepreneurial income was a separate kind of income, apart from interest and wages. Mangoldt attempted to prove this from the nature of economic organization, Mataja from the essential characteristics of price formation. All these authors made the error of assuming that a kind of income (and the social institutions concerned) can be justified by some cleverly devised theoretical scheme listing various kinds of income.

The concept of the enterprise has only in recent decades been subject to attempts at definition. One kind of definition has emphasized the combination of various productive forces in an enterprise (but this combination also occurred in the ancient patriarchal family). Another has given attention to production for private account and with private risk. Other definitions have related enterprise to the existence of markets and communications, i.e., to the phenomenon of goods produced for the market rather than for home consumption. All these definitions have failed to give full emphasis to the social and legal aspects involved. Every enterprise originates in the context of existing customs and legal relations and as such has a particular function and legal status. Empirical research has achieved a better approach to the problem, and more accurate results. Schäffle is the main representative of those who studied various forms of present-day enterprises. Historians have discovered older forms of associations and companies. We are in need, at the present moment, of a deeper insight into the social context of the enterprise. We ought to know where it originates, under what conditions it takes various forms, what are the psychological determinants and legal regulations that govern its existence, who are the persons and groups that play a role in it. Its function in production needs to be studied, as well as the consequences for marketing, distribution, and capital accumulation. Finally, we should discover its consequences for social and cultural life, and the interrelations of the enterprise with other organs and institutions of society.

The central concern of this study is to discover the long historical process during which entrepreneurial activity became, first, a secondary function of clans, families, and other organs of community life and, later, the sole function of independent associations. These new social units, after having become autonomous, increased in size and developed according to their own laws. Economic enterprises wedged themselves gradually between individuals and families, on the one hand, and associations, municipalities, states, corporate bodies, and churches, on the other hand. The consequent formation and strengthening of the enterprise system is the essential aspect of the development of a national economy [*Volkswirtschaft*]. Economic phenomena have acquired an independent existence in actuality as well as in thought. The backbone of the economic system is formed by enterprises, and the present attacks on the existing pattern of economic organization are therefore directed with utmost vehemence against this central core.

Our purpose is to obtain an insight into the causes which have dominated this historical process up to the present day. This aim is best served if we describe, one after the other, the typical forms of enterprise in their developmental sequence. Separate phenomena from very different times and peoples will be placed side by side on account of their inner resemblance. This comparative approach may certainly be criticized, because the descriptive material for particular times and peoples is not yet adequate for the purpose. This objection, however, would make any general study in the domain of social and economic science impossible. Attempts to arrive at a synthesis on the basis of present scientific data must be repeated over and over. Preliminary results will be valuable until better and richer materials are organized by more competent hands.

The total complex of causes dominating the development of a system of separate enterprises will appear from the particular results of our investigation. Even at this point, for the sake of a preliminary orientation, it is useful to indicate some major categories of causes.

(1) In any period the existing social conditions and, correspondingly, the nature of enterprise are dependent upon inherited forms of social grouping and co-operation. Traditional forms of organization, manifesting themselves in the legal rules applying to the family and to the association, are the building stones and the framework for new needs and institutional developments.

(2) The organizational forms transmitted from the past are the results of earlier economic conditions as well as of moral and spiritual forces. Changed conditions, especially technical and material advances, stimulate effectively the formation of new social organs, and particularly new forms of enterprise. The stimulus may derive from population increase, capital accumulation, the improvement of communications, technique, agriculture, tools, machinery, and the division of labor. All these material changes may be incorporated into social life in various ways in accordance with the spiritual factors.

(3) The spirit of an age and of a people determines how a society will use material circumstances; healthy or unhealthy forms of organization can be the outcome of similar material conditions. Everything depends upon the moral and mental energies available. Only great and energetic periods and persons create epochal achievements. Newly created forms reflect the degree and orientation of egoism and of community spirit; they are also dependent on the feelings of groups and individuals and on dominant conceptions and ideas.

(4) Existing social classes, together with the resulting distribution and organization of property, are a set of given conditions for newly arising enterprises. These conditions cannot be quickly altered but have

to be utilized as they are given. Indirectly, new forms of enterprise will then react upon social organization and the property distribution; there is a complex interplay of forces. But these reactions are, historically speaking, only aftereffects. It is quite inconceivable that social stratification in classes could be greatly improved—for instance, through social reform—*before* the new forms of enterprise had originated. During their period of formation new forms of enterprise have as yet neither a clearly defined shape nor well-known social effects. Therefore, it can only be later generations which will be able to lessen their long-range consequences for society.

The traditional class structure and property organization are the main factors determining how the form of enterprise affects income distribution. But these matters must be postponed until the end of our study.

Even in the earliest stages of human existence it is probable that occasional surpluses of goods were available for exchange or sale. There may also have been occasions when for certain services—for instance, the services of a sorcerer—a reward could be demanded. We can speak of an enterprise, however, only if such practices occurred with a certain regularity, which happened in those cases where property, division of labor, and communications were sufficiently developed to make the exchange and supply of surplus goods and of services an indispensable part of the life of individuals and groups.

This situation could arise in various ways. It could be a result of new ways of acquiring the means of subsistence, originating among certain gifted and well-organized tribes or among groups performing certain tasks within those tribes. Regular markets sprang up wherever hunting or fishing were particularly successful or where the domestication of animals and the working of stone and metal created surpluses of food, clothing, and implements. They could also be the consequence of military exploits, plundering expeditions, piracy, and cattle raids if these occasions gave rise to regular accumulations of various kinds of treasure. Finally, permanently settled tribes on fertile soil could sometimes grow more plants and fruits than they themselves consumed. It is evident from this enumeration that the earliest enterprises go very far back. We can rest content with the observation that advances in cattle raising, fabrication of metal tools, permanent settlement, agriculture, and trade (all these phenomena are known with historical certainty for the first time in relation to the Egyptians, Babylonians, Indians, and Phoenicians) were prerequisites for a clearly recognizable development of the enterprise. Another early factor which furthered the development was the replacement of natural money by metallic money and coins. The whole set of described conditions, or roughly similar ones, has persisted until as late as the seventeenth and eighteenth centuries of our era, among Indo-Europeans and Semites. The entire epoch can be treated as a unit, when we deal with the history of forms of enterprise; its conditions can be compared with the characteristics of half-cultivated races of other periods and countries. In doing this, we will have to trace certain forms down to the very present, while, on the other hand, some forms will, for the time being, be left aside, despite the fact that they appear as early as the Middle Ages. The latter are omitted because they can be dealt with more briefly and appropriately together with their modern descendants.

At the beginning of the long epoch with which we are concerned, the existing organs of social life are the tribe and the clan. The matriarchal clan is in all more advanced and wealthy tribes—already in those tribes in which wealth consists in cattle—transformed into the more loosely organized patriarchal clan. (We have briefly shown this in another connection.) Within the patriarchal clan we find a rapid increase in importance of the individual family. In the prominent agricultural and cattle-raising peoples this individual family is large and patriarchal. Elsewhere, and particularly in later times, it takes the form of a small union of parents and children: the present form of the family. In the ancient period with which we are concerned, isolated individuals hardly occur. Especially in tribes with a rather undifferentiated social life such individuals are not entirely absent, but they are still under the rule of the clan or they are made slaves. In the long run the tribal organization becomes transformed into the organization of a small state, a territorial unit. Between tribe and state an intermediate stage is the tribal league. Within small states new communal associations emerge: local units, such as the field and village communities. We also find the rise of social classes—or guilds, castes, companies, and other groupings. Modern individualism with personal freedom and independence, and with legal protection for individuals, probably originated in antiquity and was renewed in the fifteenth and sixteenth centuries. It is largely absent in the period with which we are dealing; in the earlier half of this era we hardly find society stratified into slaves, freemen, and serfs, while this division is characteristic of the later half. Slaves and serfs are then the lowest members of the extended family. They were originally regarded, within the large households, as members of the family; in later times their position became more and more dependent. Sometimes they were treated as cattle, in other cases they were permitted to live in small households and families.

What would be the form of the enterprise under these conditions? Its essential roots are twofold: clan and family. The tribe was as yet not sufficiently united to be regarded as an economic enterprise, except in certain warrior tribes.

The clan and the small and large derivatives of the clan are, indeed, not real enterprises in the modern sense. They are no more so than were the early family and household economies. However, the clan and similar associations contain origins and examples for later forms of enterprise, and therefore they deserve careful study. They might be called *semi-enterprises* because they are social organs which produce partly for their own needs and partly for the market. First we will discuss the clan and its derivatives, some of which have survived until the present time. It is true that the information about clanlike associations derives primarily from later periods in which the family had long supplanted them as the important economic unit, but these units are certainly of ancient origin.

II. ANCIENT LABORERS' ASSOCIATIONS[1]

Even in the advanced forms of tribal life, where central authority was vested in a king or in a council of chieftains and where rules for organized warfare existed—an important advance in social development—the backbone of social organization remained the clan structure. The tribe as a whole might construct defense works, carry on expeditions for plunder, and promote the welfare of its people by the efforts of strong chiefs or kings; it also sometimes accumulated hoards of goods for times of war. Nevertheless, the solid foundation of social life rested with the clans, constituting not only the warrior organizations but the early forms of economic association as well. Clans were held together

[1] [TRANSLATOR'S NOTE: The term *Arbeitsgenossenschaften* has many connotations and cannot be easily translated. In P. A. Sorokin's article in the *Encyclopaedia of the Social Sciences* on the "Artel" the author uses words like "association," "community," "comradeship," "brotherhood," "co-operative," and "gang." All these words express particular facets of what Schmoller calls *Arbeitsgenossenschaften.* I want to emphasize here that these economic units are not confined to the regulation of economic activity but also engage in productive activity itself; this is what makes them enterprises. They can therefore be distinguished from such associations as the English regulated companies, or modern trade-unions. Following George R. Lewis usage in *The Stannaries* (Boston, 1908), we will speak of "laborers' associations"; in some cases we will also use the term "co-operative."]

by communal sentiments of extraordinary strength; they united from forty to one hundred men under a rigorous moral discipline. Here we find the psychological base of all ancient forms of association. The clan members were united through common shrines, by having the same name and the same ancestors, and through common burial places. They were obliged to support each other in the necessities of life and death; they had to show solidarity in blood revenge, and they assisted each other in funeral ceremonies. Wherever it was necessary, clan members worked together. They were not greatly differentiated, physically or mentally, and they led a herdlike and fraternal existence. Each used only the simplest weapons or tools, and—to this he had been conditioned all his life—he obeyed the leader of the clan or the elected leader of smaller groups. The *Schwurgenossenschaft* as well as the group of followers who surrounded a chief had a character similar to that of the clan enterprises. Plundering expeditions, raids for acquiring slaves and cattle, were performed largely by clans or their subdivisions. Organized warfare in ancient times was always based upon the cohesion of the clans during battle. Schtscherbina is therefore certainly justified in deriving the *artel* of South Russia from the bandit-warrior organization of the Cossacks. Parallel with the associations for war and plunder there existed early organizations for peaceful labor; men co-operated in the building of houses and ships and in the clearing of forests, which resulted in the extension of the area cultivated by the women. Some peoples applied co-operation to tilling the fields. Co-operation also occurred in hunting, fishing, shipping, mining, and transportation. Custom created a number of forms of laborers' associations, some of which have persisted for centuries and millenniums, even up to the present. These groups came together, not on the basis of written contracts, but on the basis of tradition and of ceremonies which were regarded as binding. They united for the specific purpose of hunting, fishing, or other common action, and the proceeds were to be divided according to traditional rules (per capita division, or in certain numerical proportions). The fraternal bond was established by kissing the ikon, for instance, or by sharing a common drink. There existed no treasury, no common fund, no businesslike character, and no solid corporate organization. Some of those laborers' associations came together for only a few days or weeks and were often renewed; others became more permanent. Their character was that of brotherly co-operatives. While the laborers sometimes formed a meal-sharing community with common stores, nevertheless each member had the free disposal over his share of the proceeds from the undertaking. This kind of co-operative was not an enterprise in the proper sense, because there was no common sale of products. But services were performed for a reward, surpluses were produced by unified effort, and goods were then sold or bartered by the members individually.

The psychological and legal conditions which, among advanced races, led to the ancient organizations of warfare and communal agriculture were also responsible for the rise of a whole gamut of laborers' associations. The village community, the guild, the *Innung,* and similar organizations had comprehensive communal tasks, while the *artels,* fishing companies, and other co-operatives engaged in more immediate and limited performances of united effort. Both kinds of economic organization had the same social base.

The real significance of ancient laborers' associations has until recently been largely unrecognized, partly because written sources tell us little about them and partly, because in Europe only sparse remnants of this institution have survived. European scientists have now [1890], discovered the *artel* in Russia, and we have also obtained more precise knowledge of the Chinese system of co-operatives. Through the study of comparative law and through the progress of economic and cultural history, we have become cognizant of a chain of manifestations of laborers' associations, extending through various periods of history. We can find remnants of these associations even in the advanced civilizations of the present. Among other races and peoples they have sometimes been preserved to a much larger extent.

We will now make some more detailed observations. In the present context it is necessary to touch for a moment on the subject of communal co-operation. The center of our discussion will, of course, remain the free associations of workers which in part became enterprises. Communal co-operation occurred in the building of communal houses, inhabited by dozens and sometimes hundreds of people. Such houses are found in many tribes, but only in those in which social organization had reached a somewhat higher level, probably in connection with technical and social advances. They undoubtedly originated for the purposes of better defense. It is a safe assumption that they were a product of clan co-operation. According to Dargun, communal houses occurred often before the introduction of communal agriculture, and they are to be found even in the absence of such agriculture. Among some peoples, communal houses were used only for the lodging of strangers and of youthful warriors, for temporary assemblies, and, finally, also for the storage of boats on dry land. The Greeks had for every gens the *lesche* as a common house, to be used for assemblies. Among Germanic tribes such communal houses are unknown to me. But in the German Alps the original custom that all neighbors and villagers give each other voluntary aid in the building of any new house has been preserved up to the present day. And in those cases where a military or priestly despotism forced the people as a whole to build defense works, temples, roads, and ships, we may assume readily that clan customs with respect to common work were the psychological and legal foundations for these political and economic systems.

Ascertained cases of agricultural groups planting co-operatively and sharing the produce after the harvest are as infrequent as are the communal meals of large social groups, with which communal agriculture is probably associated. Only tribes with a very strong social discipline, with a highly developed group solidarity, could reach this stage. In any event, in so far as records and recent travel reports allow us a glimpse into the conditions which lead to meal-sharing and communal agriculture, the clan appears as the basis and the cause of such customs.

We may always assume that the numerous forms of later agricultural co-operation—occurring among Indo-Europeans and other groups, sometimes up to the present—are frequently mere remnants of a much stronger economic co-operation in social groups of earlier periods. Communal co-operation was gradually weakened and dissolved as a result of the growing egoism of separate families. The transformation of kinship groups into local communities; the decline of raiding, hunting, and warfare; the gradual predominance of peaceful agriculture—all these circumstances made the separate small family more independent. The co-operative labor of clan members and villagers retained, nevertheless, for a long time considerable importance. Villagers helped each other in case of fire, floods, and other disasters; the victims were helped without an expected return. The men also helped each other in clearing fields, felling trees, building roads, and constructing dams. In many activities, such as housebuilding and the harvesting of grapes or corn, villagers took turns in helping the man who needed assistance. Other tasks, such as standing guard at night and performing obligatory services for a lord, were done by the village inhabitants in turn. The shepherd served the whole village, pasturing the herd was a communal activity, and communal rules regulated the agriculture of separate families. . . .[2]

[2] Parts of Vol. XIV, pp. 747–49, omitted from the translation.

It is a well-known fact that in Germany forest labor even today is largely done by a kind of laborers' association. At least two men [*eine Säge*] will operate one saw; other tasks are undertaken by larger groups under collective agreement. The Prussian forest administrators have the duty of making sure that individual members of such co-operatives are treated equitably when the earnings are distributed.

In shipping and fishing, co-operative customs have been most energetically developed and maintained. To describe these customs we must again refer back to older clan and local associations and, at the same time, anticipate ourselves in touching upon the transformation of laborers' associations into associations of property and capital. The transformation will be more extensively discussed later on, but the coherence of the subject matter requires a few remarks at this point.

During the later development of ancient states with maritime power, the existing ships belonged partly to the state and partly to private persons like big merchants and shipmasters. This proves nothing about earlier conditions, because our information derives from a relatively much later period. Nothing, therefore, stands in the way of the hypothesis that all shipbuilding, just as housebuilding among so many tribes, was originally done by the co-operation of clans or their subdivisions. In earliest times shipbuilding was a preparation for plundering expeditions and for fishing. As far as we know, these activities were almost always undertaken by groups instead of by individuals. . . .[3]

What little we know about the earliest North Germanic shipping corresponds completely with conditions elsewhere. Kings and chieftains, commanding groups of followers, engaged in adventurous seafaring raids; but in addition to these ships we also find ships for mercantile purposes. In the latter, partners shared their meals and fulfilled in successive order the duties of watchman and cook. Usually such ships were supplied, maintained, and manned by coastal regions. Dahlmann informs us that Haakon the Good (around A.D. 950) introduced this shipping organization into Norway, but it is quite certain that his regulation points back to pre-existing customs. In Haakon's time there were 292 coastal districts which had the duty of providing an equal number of ships, with crews totaling 12,700 oarsmen. The long ships of the king and of the cities are mentioned separately from the above vessels. Ancient Swedish organization seems to have been very similar, and the same probably holds for Danish and English shipping. On the basis of

[3] Part of p. 750 omitted.

such contributions *in natura* it becomes understandable how the small Nordic states could at times operate with fleets of six hundred to twelve hundred ships. This requisition of ships can be understood only under the assumption that from earliest times the kinship and local groups of the coastal regions had been accustomed to co-operative shipbuilding and to expeditions in which every man took part. The same assumption explains clearly why so many of the great maritime peoples of ancient times had periods in which their naval power collapsed. I regard this phenomenon as a consequence of the decline of their old institutions. The duty of providing ships became a more and more onerous burden on the coastal districts, ships arrived slowly and in bad condition, and were manned by inadequate crews. They were consequently unfit to cope with well-disciplined fleets. Moreover, coastal co-operatives remained unaffected by technical advances in shipbuilding. The royal ships of more highly developed seafaring states were constructed by tax funds and manned by paid soldiers and mariners, and these ships were greatly superior. The same holds for merchant ships. In the face of such overwhelming power, the once brilliant position of maritime states based on group co-operation in shipping would disintegrate.

Apart from the co-operative shipbuilding of whole coastal districts (which here and there developed an administrative and military organization), we already find in the earliest times individuals uniting in smaller groups for the purpose of building ships and boats and for using them in common. These groups engaged in fishing, commerce, and transport; they developed a kind of fishing and shipping association which can be observed among almost all coastal peoples. Remnants of ancient co-operative systems are preserved in the custom of having seamen share in the proceeds of the voyage. In studying the preserved historical material about these things we must never forget that the evidence naturally does not give us the picture of the origin and early formation. It shows rather the decline of ancient associations and co-operatives in periods when more modern forms of enterprise are in existence.

A vivid picture of ancient shipping institutions has recently been given by Kohler, who has published and interpreted a Malayan law book dating from 1676, also containing older laws. This book shows that individual shipping was far less important than shipping by associations and co-operatives. Yet, at the same time, commerce was carried on in a purely individualist fashion; each person on the ship took goods along for his own account: the captain as well as the helmsman, sailor, and trader. Someone who lacked capital took goods in *commenda*. . . .[4]

Similar institutions probably existed in early antiquity and in the Middle Ages. The sea law of Rhodes, which was codified in late Roman times, states that seamen were paid in wages by the year, by a fixed sum per voyage, and finally also by a portion of freight receipts. Those receipts were then divided into a specified number of shares. The *patronus* or captain received two, the helmsman, carpenter, and other members got one and a half shares, every sailor one share, and the cook one-half share. The oldest medieval code of maritime law, the Rôles d'Oléron, contains the following passage (this code was written down in the south of France): "If, in Bordeaux or elsewhere, a ship is being loaded, the shipmaster should ask the sailors: 'Do you want to bring in cargo to the amount of your wages, or do you want to be paid by sharing in the freight receipts?' The sailors must announce their choice. If they want to be paid from freight returns, they will obtain the portion that is allotted to them. If they prefer to load their own goods, they must do so without delay. It is established as an old custom of the sea that, in case the sailors of a ship are paid in proportion to the freight, they nevertheless can take along a small cask of their own, free of freight charges." The Rôles d'Oléron also state that sailors were paid partly by portions of the freight and partly by a fixed hire. Laband, in discussing the maritime code of Amalfi (twelfth to fourteenth century), defines the contract *columnae communi* as an association among the following: part owners of the ship, owners of the commodities on board, capitalists investing money in the undertaking, and finally the seamen, who would serve aboard ship. All these people formed a society, and, after the voyage had been ended, they divided among themselves the gains or losses, according to fixed and predetermined proportions. Nobody, however, could lose more than he had invested. Our author thinks that in fourteenth-century Italy this kind of agreement had already been replaced by others. At any rate, in northern Europe, as late as the sixteenth century, some sailors were paid in proportion to the proceeds of the voyage, while others worked for hire. Sailors also had the right, in addition to their hire, to take along a certain quantity of goods free of charge. According to a Russian law of 1781, sailors and seamen were indeed no longer to be paid on the basis of freight received, but we find an order that the registered seamen in towns and seaports should enter, under the leadership of their seniors, into well-organized companies

[4] Part of Vol. XIV, p. 752, omitted.

[*artels*], each one of which was to perform contracted tasks conscientiously and carefully.

Apart from these shipping associations, there also existed participation of capital by outsiders in both shipbuilding and ownership. Such participation, as is evident from medieval sources of southern as well as northern Europe, I also regard as a derivative of earlier co-operative shipping and shipbuilding. . . .[5] This whole organization will be discussed further in connection with the origins of merchant associations.

Compared to fishing, sea transport required from an early date the ownership of valuable property, because relatively large ships were used. These ships could be acquired only by the well-to-do, especially since their building occurred in later ages on the basis of division of labor. It is true that fishing boats could also have considerable property value, but nevertheless all inhabitants of the seacoast were able to build them, and timber for shipbuilding would be cheap if it grew along the coast. The possession of a boat, individually or together with others, did not exempt the owner from joining in the work. Owners and nonowners of ships remained for a long time members of the same class.

In his description of ancient Nordic life Weinhold reports that fishing was carried on by co-operatives, in which harmony was preserved by the belief that quarreling would bring bad luck in fishing. The gains were divided equally, with the exception that the owner of the boat received an additional portion. Each member was required to have a proper sea outfit of sheepskin and sealskin and had to bring his own fishing equipment (fishing rod, lines, bait, and the broad knife with which the fishes were knocked on the head). Beneke tells us about the ancient fishing associations on the Island of Hela. Here the able-bodied men of the fishing villages joined together in groups of seven to twenty men for the purpose of small- and large-scale fishing. Every association furnished and maintained its own nets, boats, and the like, and shared expenses. The men worked together and shared the catch; they took some of it for their own use and sold the rest. The daily provisions were bought in quantity and then distributed among the members. The older men, the widows, and the orphans belonging to the association had to make themselves useful by spinning, repairing nets, and other activities according to their ability; in return they received one-quarter to one-half of a man's share in the catch.

Such organizations have in many places been preserved up to the present, probably because the members realized clearly that the total

[5] Parts of Vol. XIV, pp. 754–55, omitted.

proceeds depended upon the devotion and skill of every individual in the boats, and that successful fishing demanded subordination and sacrifices for the common welfare. When boats became larger and more valuable, the only change was that the real co-operative was replaced by a profit-sharing arrangement. Even in Russia the original equality of all associates has recently disappeared. The division of the catch *in natura* has, moreover, been replaced almost everywhere by joint sales. But in other respects the old pattern has been preserved; it can still be found in the regions of the North Sea and the Baltic, in England and Scotland, on the shores of the Channel, as well as on the Atlantic and Mediterranean shores of France. . . .[6]

We are speaking here about laborers' co-operatives uniting no more than two, three, or at most a few dozen men. As a rule, they work with hardly any division of labor; the partners perform the same activities, have the same strength and training, and operate with simple tools owned by the individuals themselves. These are the basic conditions of early laborers' associations. Sometimes a leader or at most a few exceptionally skilled men may rise above the others, but this happens only to a minor extent.

The inculcation of proper psychological attitudes for co-operation in distant ages was the task of the clans. In later times these attitudes were engendered by kinship and neighborhood groups, and by long periods of working together. In this way a naïve community spirit originated among uneducated men; it was combined with a primitive form of egoism and a certain carelessness about the future. These men contented themselves with the products and money that were divided equally among all and with their share in the victuals. The clan-spirit, the devotion to the small group which was fostered, is comparable to the solidarity that exists in the companies and regiments of an army. It implied a sense of honor and the expulsion or exclusion of dishonest, unfit, and unable elements. The performance and reliability of laborers' associations was strongly conditioned by their spirit.

Most co-operatives united only men; these men worked characteristically some distance away from their homes and families. Under such conditions it is understandable that, particularly among fishermen, mariners, and Italian masons, co-operatives were also meal-sharing associations. These forms of organization are to be found only as exceptions in agriculture proper and in trade. The earliest agriculture was the work of women; later it became the task of families. The extended

[6] Vol. XIV, pp. 756–62, largely omitted.

family of early times, consisting of several generations who worked together on one piece of land or farm, was indeed a kind of co-operative; but its cohesion, even allowing for the fact that new individual members could be introduced by agreement, rested on different presuppositions. From its origin onward, commerce had been carried on by individuals, by separate family heads, or by great lords. Co-operative forms of commercial organization were conspicuously absent in those times, which is the more remarkable, since co-operative trade could have been an imitation of already existing co-operatives in travel and shipping. Neither did ancient co-operatives engage to any large extent in handicrafts. The extended families that traditionally existed tended to split into smaller fragments wherever handicrafts did emerge; for most handicraft undertakings apparently one master with one or two helpers was sufficient.

There are some exceptions, but they do not invalidate the general rule. Thus Issajew has recently shown that up to seventy Russian crafts were organized in *artels:* cabinet makers, coopers, weavers, musicians, carpenters, tailors, masons, and others. To a large extent these *artels* are of recent origin. Their development is connected with the social reform ideas of Schulze-Delitzsch. *Artels* have been fostered in a deliberate attempt to counteract large-scale capitalistic enterprises, through a resurrection of ancient Russian customs. This only goes to demonstrate that widespread popular customs of ancient origin can be favorable to the rise of modern co-operative movements. But admittedly even in Russia the handicraft *artel* has hardly been prosperous, and in domestic industry the importance of *artels* is negligible. Under the combined impact of technical advances, increasing division of labor, capital accumulation, and the threatening rise of modern forms of enterprise, the importance of the Russian *artel* system has declined.

Reports exist to show that Chinese craftsmen who [during the nineteenth century] came to California were organized groupwise; these groups were located in various towns and streets and were supervised by a central board of the craft. Workers came together in such groups for one year; they operated as if they were business partners. Each member supplied capital according to his ability; his pay varied proportionately with his contribution and with his share in the work. This organization had an extraordinary degree of guildlike control and co-operative discipline, surpassing anything that is known about other races. One would still like to ask whether this kind of association would not be more likely to succeed among the Chinese abroad than among those at home. Their complete dependence upon the great shipping companies that had brought them over may have been a contributing factor. I am reminded of the medieval organization of German artisans and merchants in Bergen; they, too, formed a separate community in the midst of a settled native population. It is true, however, that the Chinese have shown great conservatism in retaining old customs and that the individualistic spirit of capitalist enterprise has affected them less than it has affected any other civilized or semicivilized people.

While there were among the ancient co-operatives described above some kinds of association which, almost from their beginning, had a common property, for instance, a boat, in others the co-operating laborers at an early date became associates of an entrepreneur who owned the capital. This kind of association survived for centuries. There were also early associations of property which owned a monopoly or which through rising land values became property associations. They received property rents aside from rewards for work. The occurrence of these forms of organization does not invalidate our assertion that the pure workers' co-operative was the form under which the system flourished. The system originated in the early beginnings of economic civilization, in a time of very simple techniques, slight division of labor, and limited influence of capital and property. Its characteristics were the dominance of custom, the continuous disappearance and reappearance of short-lived co-operatives—often uniting for no more than weeks or months—and the total absence of businesslike spirit. Laborers' associations had few written records and frequently no common fund. Specific written contracts were lacking, and there were no definite organizational rules to guide the leader, his associates, and the body of members.

Whether these ancient co-operatives should therefore be classified as real enterprises is doubtful, as we have already observed. But they were organizations with an acquisitive purpose. Some produced salable surpluses which were brought to market by individuals or by the group as a whole, while others performed services paid for by outsiders. Most of them were and remained free associations for economic purposes. They are an important phenomenon in the historical development of economic organization.

Later they disappeared to a large extent or altogether and made room for other forms. The underlying spirit could never quite vanish. It has been vigorously restored in the modern co-operative movement, in labor unions, in collective agreements, and in any large enterprise pervaded by a sense of moral responsibility. Any method of wage payment which through bonuses, premiums, profit participation, and welfare arrangements creates a moral bond among the workers follows the same principle. Laborers' associations have here and there managed to survive in a pure or modernized form, and they will also survive in the future. Examples are provided by the tile workers of Lippe, the *Drägilen* of Russia, and the fishing companies or associations of various countries. In other places, however, the natural process of history has brought about their decline. This happened wherever leadership became more difficult and had to adopt wider views, where distant markets were to be discovered, and where business demanded larger capital and more complex techniques.

III. LARGE-SCALE ENTERPRISES OF ANTIQUITY[7]

Where large properties in land and capital coexisted with cheap slaves, we find the beginnings of the transformation of the aristocratic household economies [the *oikos*] into large agricultural, industrial, or commercial enterprises.

The merchant princes of Tyre, Sidon, and Carthage exemplify how oriental monarchs became entrepreneurs. After 1500 the European conquest of colonies created a purely businesslike plantation economy wherever slavery was introduced. Our best information regarding the deeper causes of the emergence of large enterprises derives from the ancient states of Greece and Rome.[8]

The greatest and most ruthless aristocracy in the world [the ancient Roman aristocracy] had at an early date made a clear distinction between the spheres of public and private life. However, its members began to apply the talents and abilities which they acquired in public service to the affairs of their private household. The rapidly expanding household economies—"whole peoples were incorporated into the *familia*"—became models of large, well-disciplined enterprises. Their basis was slavery, more and more harshly enforced. Because of a magnificently clear-cut system of property and civil law, the aristocrats could utilize their expanding possessions in highly profitable business ventures. There existed a system of capitalistic associations. As many undertakings of the state and the community as possible were given over to these business associations, and this opened unlimited possibilities for speculation.

[7] *Jahrbuch für Gesetzgebung, Verwaltung, und Volkswirtschaft im deutschen Reich*, Vol. XV, pp. 38, 42–45, 636–37.

[8] End of the passage on p. 38.

Thus the development of any future economic enterprise was outlined in principle. It seems as if the vast possibilities as well as the social dangers of the entreprise system should be exhibited immediately in the most striking and brutal example. In the building of roads and waterways, in the construction of palaces and temples, and in the organization of mining, commerce, and credit, Roman achievements have hardly ever been equaled—given the technical conditions. Despite the slowness or stagnation of technical advance, the Romans expanded and cheapened production and greatly increased the profitability of business. Their success depended on an excellent economic organization and discipline and on a plentiful supply of capital for agricultural and other enterprises. Nothing even remotely comparable had been accomplished by the small farms and craft shops of earlier times. The associations of *publicani,* as regards their size and power, can only be compared with our modern corporations. It is also true that the exploitation of dependent labor and the ruthless utilization of property for maximum profit have never again reached the shameless extremes of ancient Rome. No other period has manifested such a disregard for conscience and ethics.

The described phenomena are in part the results of social and psychological conditions peculiar to the Roman Empire and depend on the basic principles of its culture. But in part the causes must also be sought in certain essential characteristics of economic enterprises in general. The same causes have therefore been operative in later times. It is worth while to consider the matter a moment longer.

Any large economic enterprise is a specimen of social organization, formed by a number of persons, whether few or many, who are welded together for the sole purpose of a common, co-ordinated activity. The difficulty of working together increases with the number of persons. In medieval guilds and in ancient co-operatives internal cohesion was maintained by fraternal ties, by community feelings, and by the fact that all members of the group had a clear idea of the purpose of its activity. This is not the case, or at least not necessarily the case, in large-scale enterprises. Neither do such enterprises have the kind of cohesion that exists in families through the forces of sex and sympathy and through the common concern with daily necessities of food, clothes, and living quarters. The religious or warlike spirit which holds ecclesiastical orders, bands of warriors, and brotherhoods together is also generally absent. Capital investments and trading voyages, mines, plantations, and frequently large buildings are all undertakings that become profitable only after a number of years. Production for a market is often production for complete strangers. Such remote ends of economic activity are first envisaged by uncommonly intelligent and farsighted men, striving for honor or profit. The mass of their obedient collaborators is at first indifferent or even hostile to the purpose. The problem is: How do aristocratic leaders find the many subordinates needed for the task? The lower the intellectual and moral level of their cultural environment, the more the leaders will have to rely upon force and violence to obtain their personnel. Slavery, and in part also the serfdom of later times—the harsh domination of one man by another—was the basis of the first efficient large enterprises. Even in our own day people enter lower positions in large enterprises only by force of necessity, because they have no other recourse. In these organizations the individual must submit to a disagreeable yoke of labor that stifles all his natural impulses. He must work on time, in a particular place, according to precise rules. His actions must fit a strange plan whose purpose he does not understand, and which leaves him indifferent. The worker must become a wheel in a living machine. This machine uses and consumes individuals without considering their needs, idiosyncrasies, or weaknesses, and it has no regard for their families. The stricter the discipline and the more willingly the individual subordinates himself, the better the machine works. Only economic ends determine how the workers are fitted into and taken out of the machine.

As we have seen, the Roman aristocrats were the ablest of administrators. In their families, in the army, and in the government of the provinces, they had been accustomed to absolute authority. To treat aliens as outlaws, to reduce enemy tribes to slavery by the thousands, was in those ages accepted custom. Barbaric and unskilled slaves could be used in agriculture. Besides, the Romans found in Greece and Asia a different kind of servile material; men who often were morally corrupt, used to harsh treatment, but extremely skilled in commerce and crafts. Those slaves were used in commercial, technical, and industrial tasks of a higher kind. In this way, Rome obtained a plentiful supply of cheap labor. Willingly or with much muttering, yet always without resistance, this labor force submitted to control by military and political power. The root of this submission was a feeling that the Romans were morally superior. Their control remained effective as long as they were feared and thought to be superior. The organic structure of any large enterprise is conditioned by the difference between the physical, moral, and intellectual qualities of the directing and the subordinate forces, and by the resulting mutual relations and tensions.[9]

[9] **End of the passage, pp. 42–45.**

Great cattle owners and medieval landowners with their servants and serfs have created the beginnings of modern large agricultural enterprise. In our present age, merchants and technicians who tower above the middle and lower classes through their capital and intelligence are the born leaders of enterprise. The hierarchical structure [*herrschaftliche Verfassung*] of present-day companies cannot be abolished at a stroke by any change in political or social legislation, no matter how radical.

The question why large enterprises have not generally been associations of equal partners is almost identical with the question why social organization in general has not been based upon the partnership principle. To ask such questions seriously is to betray historical naïveté, and also complete ignorance of psychology.

However, one objection is obvious. Our modern civilization was preceded by long periods in which fraternal associations and partnerships [*Genossenschaften*] were formed. Our first article discussed primitive laborers' associations in connection with this phenomenon. We know also that this system had many ramifications in historical periods. In the ancient city-states those associations of equals were rapidly overshadowed by the state, the family, and the individual; but this may have been conditioned by the more rapid cultural development in these cities. Gaps in the documentation do not permit us to observe all phenomena. In the Germanic Middle Ages, however, fraternal associations show a prolific growth, to some extent side by side with manorial and similar structures, but also spontaneously growing out of those structures. Thus manorial society included a multitude of dependent fraternal associations which later attained independence. In the period from the seventeenth to the nineteenth century, the state, the family, and the individual rose to dominance; hierarchical organizations seem to replace all fraternal associations. But in recent times the latter once again have experienced a renascence [the co-operative movement]. The legal and economic form is different, the new associations serve other purposes, but the psychological and moral basis is the same as in earlier ages.

These facts cast a somewhat different light on the victory of large hierarchical organizations in the field of economic enterprise: the importance of such organizations is not as great as might be supposed. Evidence suggests two distinct but parallel lines of development. Only under special psychological, social, and economic conditions does one or the other become the dominant form.[10]

[10] End of the passage on pp. 636–37.

2

*Medieval and Modern Commercial Enterprise**

By WERNER SOMBART

Editors' Foreword

Der moderne Kapitalismus is the synthesis of Sombart's attempts to give a historical characterization of the economic system of modern Europe. The book begins with an elaborate discussion of medieval economic life. A unified conception of the economic activity of medieval Europe served Sombart as a background against which the uniqueness of modern capitalism would be clearly revealed. Fragments of this section of his work are contained in the following pages; the translator, Jelle C. Riemersma, has divided the subject matter according to six headings.

I. The Size of Business Enterprise
II. The Precapitalist Merchant
III. Family Partnerships
IV. Occasional Partnerships
V. Capitalist Enterprise as a Form of Property Organization
VI. Systematic Bookkeeping

I. THE SIZE OF BUSINESS ENTERPRISE

A prerequisite for a correct conception of precapitalist trade is a precise knowledge of it magnitude. Especially we should know the quantities of goods or the amounts of money involved in the transactions of the individual merchant. Unfortunately, our enlightenment depends on merely occasional references in the sources. So far we have had to rely on those references, and in the future our position will probably be similarly unfavorable. At present, the information we have about

* Selections from Werner Sombart, *Der moderne Kapitalismus* (2nd ed., München, Duncker & Humblot, 1916), Vol. I, Pt. 1, pp. 280, 281–84, 291–96; Vol. II, Pt. 1, pp. 86–90, 95–98, 101–3, 118–23.

Sombart's elaborate footnotes have been omitted. Translator's notes indicate the location of passages and add a few clarifications.

Translated and included by courtesy of Duncker & Humblot, publishers, Berlin.

medieval trade is enough, however, to give us an approximate idea of its quantitative importance.[1]

Two methods may be used to give a correct idea of the size of a merchant's business in remote ages. First, we can divide the total turnover of a place by the number of merchants trading there; secondly, we can use the records of an individual merchant to discover the quantity of goods he handled.

Of course, figures for the total turnover of a place or the quantities of goods moving along trade routes are very scarce for early periods. But there are a few instructive and quite reliable statistics at our disposal, of which the following may serve as samples.

We have, in the first place, monetary figures for the exports of the major Hanse towns during the fourteenth century. In the final year for which our authority gives the figures, these amounts are:

Reval (1384) . . . . 131,085 marks lub. or 1,245,305 marks of present currency [1916]
Hamburg (1400) . . . . 336,000 marks lub. or 3,192,000 marks of present currency [1916]
Lubeck (1384) . . . . 293,760 marks lub. or 2,790,720 marks of present currency [1916]
Rostock (1384) . . . . 76,640 marks lub. or 728,080 marks of present currency [1916]
Stralsund (1378) . . . . 330,240 marks lub. or 3,137,280 marks of present currency [1916][2]

The volume of trade moving over the St. Gotthard Pass during the later Middle Ages, according to Schulte's computations, was roughly 1,250 tons per year. This equals the load of one or two freight trains of our own time.

We have quite precise information about the size of the urban grain trade in medieval and early modern times. In the grain center of Stettin 2,000–3,000 tons of grain entered the export market; in Hamburg, the quantity was 4,000–6,000 tons. Thus in the case of Stettin the whole yearly turnover in grain equaled one modern shipload.[3]

The data we have about the quantities of wool exported from England

[1] End of the passage on Vol. I, Pt. 1, p. 280.

[2] Sombart quotes his figures to bring out clearly the smallness of medieval business. For this purpose rough comparisons are perhaps justified, but it must be realized that the comparison between medieval and modern money values—the transformation of the *lübeckische* mark into modern marks of 1916—is extremely hazardous. Sombart arrived at his proportion between the two monetary units by using silver-equivalents.

[3] Sombart's views on the medieval grain trade are elaborated in his review of Wilhelm Naude's work, in *Jahrbuch für Gesetzgebung, Verwaltung, und Volkswirtschaft im deutschen Reich,* 1890, XIV, 312–17.

by foreign merchants are even better. In the year 1277–78, 14,301 sacks of wool were exported, which means somewhat less than 3,000 tons (1 ton = 1,000 kg.). The Hanseatic merchants alone exported in this year 1,655 sacks, or 330 tons. In recent years, about 200,000 tons of wool were imported into Germany! The picture is similar if we substitute monetary values for physical quantities.[4]

The figures quoted become of real interest only if we also know the number of merchants sharing in the trade. In sixteenth-century Hamburg, the number of grain exporters was apparently 6–12. The number is given by an authority who, in his own interest, would be likely to underestimate. There are other sources which lead to the conclusion that a "great" corn merchant, even as late as the sixteenth century, did not sell more than 400 last at the most.[5]

No less than 252 merchants took part in the export of English wool in the year 1277–78. The average for each was about 56 sacks of wool, or 15,000 marks in present currency. Since there were 37 German merchants in this period, the share of each was only 45 sacks, 13,000–14,000 marks in present currency.

Therefore, we may assume, in general, that the total turnover of goods in the Middle Ages was very small, while the number of active merchants was remarkably large.[6]

II. THE PRECAPITALIST MERCHANT

In precapitalist times professional merchants led the life of mere artisans; this can be deduced from the size of their business. Their way of thinking and feeling, their social position, and their work make them resemble the petty craftsmen of their time. Indeed, nothing could be more absurd than populating the Middle Ages with economically sophisticated merchants, imbued with a capitalist mentality. The artisan-like mentality of the typical medieval merchant appears clearly if we study his motivations. The merchant, like the craftsman, had no acquisitive urge comparable to the aspirations of the modern entrepreneur. The merchant of old times wanted neither more nor less than to earn the living which belonged to his position in society. His entire activity was dominated by the idea of securing a proper living—proper according to traditional standards; this idea can be designated as the "livelihood principle." It was expressed in the peculiar legal and ethical order of

[4] A short passage has been omitted from Vol. I, Pt. 1, p. 283.
[5] 1 last = 2 tons = 2,000 kg.
[6] End of the passage, Vol I, Pt. 1, pp. 281–84.

medieval trade. We may recall at this point the many penitential and reformatory pamphlets of the beginning of the modern period. In these writings the mentality which during medieval centuries had been taken for granted was, as it were, reaffirmed. The *Reformatio Sigismundi,* containing a characterization of the artisan, dealt with the merchant in similar terms: it allowed him a reward for travel and transport expenses and sought to prohibit all entrepreneurial gains. The Protestant Reformers, especially Luther, drew by instinct a correct picture of the traditional "livelihood" pattern of commerce. Witness the following passage: "Thus you should intend to strive for nothing else but your appropriate livelihood, when engaging in such a trade. Food, trouble, work, and risk can be brought into account, and then the commodity itself can be priced. The price can be raised or lowered in such a way that your labor and exertion find their reward."[7] In the same vein are the ideas contained in Christian Kuppener's famous pamphlet on usury (1558).[8] The "new men," striving for boundless gain, are here contrasted with the respectable artisanlike traders who worked for their own and their families' traditional livelihood. All these social critics have the same central conception that the merchant should regard his earnings as simply a reward for labor expended. This conception lies at the root of the idea of the "just price" that dominated the Middle Ages. The trader is or ought to be, in accordance with a venerable tradition, nothing else but a technical laborer or craftsman. The social critics who propounded this idea touched the essentials of early economic life. If we want to form a correct picture of the medieval merchant, we must first forget everything we know about modern trade and merchants.

The modern merchant is, above all, and nowadays almost exclusively, a man who is concerned with selling: the art he practices may be called "the domination of the market." This art, for reasons to be analyzed in another connection, has now been developed into a science.[9] The modern merchant sets himself the task of disposing of commodities: he must find buyers. Modern economic life has the distinctive characteristic that the performance of this task of marketing is regarded as a highly

---

[7] Martin Luther, "Von Kaufshandlung und Wucher," *Werke, Kritische Gesamtausgabe* (Weimar, 1899), Vol. XV, p. 296.

[8] Kuppener's pamphlet is contained in Max Neumann, *Geschichte des Wuchers in Deutschland bis zur Begründung der heutigen Zinsengesetze* (1654) (Halle, 1865), Beilage E, pp. 594–95.

[9] Sombart has in mind specialized techniques of marketing, market analysis, advertising.

important and lucrative function. Wherever the market is crowded, wherever two producers are after one consumer, modern mercantile activity has its true domain. The merchant then becomes the master of the situation and makes the producers dependent on him. But this necessarily requires an ability to organize, to calculate, and to speculate. Without these qualifications, one cannot be a good merchant.

Because production was undeveloped, early economic life, and particularly that of medieval times, had no knowledge of such things: marketing difficulties were absent. As a rule, two buyers were after one producer. Sales moved along well-worn grooves, within a customary scheme of things. The quantities of goods that entered into transactions were very small. How could the merchant possibly find anything on which to plan, calculate, or speculate? The opportunity did not exist.[10]

The conditions which prevented the merchant from becoming a capitalist entrepreneur also forced him to engage in many technical operations with which modern merchants are no longer concerned. The merchant of earlier times could not plan, calculate, or speculate, but he was all the more active in packaging, measuring, transporting, retailing, and sometimes even manufacturing. We know that any commercial undertaking which required transport was troublesome and often dangerous; yet transport was almost always necessary. We know also that the merchant, girding himself with a sword, had to be a traveler himself. To get his few packs safely to their destination, he was for weeks and months performing the tasks of carriage driver and innkeeper. The seller was found on the road much more than at present. The multitude of small merchants of medieval times were always dispersed over wide areas, now appearing in one town, now in another. A document of 1271 gives a characteristic picture: "Mercatores, qui de loco ad locum merces et necessaria deferre consueverunt."[11] Another example: Andreas Ryff visited thirty or more markets every year, and this merchant says of himself: "Have had little rest, few times that the saddle didn't burn my behinds."

When the merchant arrived back home, he had to stand again behind the counter of his shop. Then he had to handle the yardstick and scales, just as he had done before in foreign fairs and markets. The shopkeeper prepared his own spices out of the saffron, pepper, and ginger which he had bought. The technical skills of the spice dealer were highly

[10] This peculiar conclusion is based on Sombart's view that production is primary and commerce secondary. Many historians have brought evidence that, historically, production was often stimulated by pre-existing mercantile enterprise.

[11] "Merchants who are wont to bring commodities and necessities from place to place."

esteemed. In an ordinance of Charles VII of France (1484) a careful revision is ordered of the sugar and spice sellers' weights and scales. The ordinance reads in part: "because of the importance of the making of sugar and confectionery, the rules as to a four years' apprenticeship and the making of a successful masterpiece must be strictly enforced." These merchants were treated like pharmacists! Everywhere the precapitalist merchant had the same preoccupation with technical work. Of course, he had also the specifically mercantile task of buying and selling. The merchant, more than his colleagues behind the screw vise or the planing bench, was professionally obliged to enter the mysterious realm of numbers. But even in so far as he was a merchant in the narrower and real sense of the word, his activity must be regarded as devoid of economic rationality. His conduct in business, just like that of his artisan fellows, was quite empirical and traditionalist.

Only a small fraction of the mercantile profession knew how to read and write; this holds true for Italy until the thirteenth century and for the rest of Europe during the whole of the medieval period. To be specific, we know that few merchants in tenth-century Venice could even sign their name (20–50 per cent of the mercantile group). We may assume that the numerical proportion between literate and nonliterate merchants was not radically and suddenly altered; the change in the later Middle Ages must have been slow. We are certain that arithmetical skill, perhaps even more important for the professional merchant, remained for centuries on the lowest possible level. During the Middle Ages, arithmetic was done almost without the aid of writing. We must take into account, in this respect as in others, a time lag of two hundred years between Italy and the rest of Europe. In the late medieval period, Italy was the teacher of the north in the "ars computandi." Even in the early sixteenth century Lucas Rem went to Venice to learn arithmetic—and what kind of arithmetic! It hardly contained more than the four operations with cardinal numbers.[12] The instruction did not touch more difficult problems than arithmetic proportions and elementary commercial calculus. An ability to divide properly was considered a mark of much schooling. At the end of the sixteenth century Hieronymus Froben and Andreas Ryff are evidently rather proud that they can find the right quotient of a division problem.

The practice of arithmetic depended on clumsy devices, such as the counting board (abacus and counters). Decimals and the symbol for

[12] Addition, subtraction, multiplication, division.

zero were not used; this is true for Italy until the thirteenth century and for northern Europe until the fifteenth.[13]

III. FAMILY PARTNERSHIPS

The family is a very ancient form of economic organization. It may even be regarded as the oldest economic unit, of which traces can be easily rediscovered in all those independent craftsman undertakings which are, in part even nowadays, simply based upon the family. If, however, we designate one particular form of organized economic activity as a "family economy," at this point we mean the family partnerships or companies that flourished in the late Middle Ages and early modern period, especially in Italy and Germany. Such companies carried on what were sometimes very important commercial, industrial, and transporting enterprises. Their significance as a form of organization in the early capitalist period should not be underrated.

As a rule, family partnerships originated when, after the death of their father, the sons continued his business as an undivided inheritance. Afterward this partnership of theirs was often expanded by including other relatives and, in the long run, even members of befriended families. Under the conditions of early capitalism some of the largest enterprises in wholesale trade, large-scale industry, and especially finance were carried on by family partnerships. Considerable sums were brought together as business capital by the merging of numerous fortunes. The following are some of the best-known examples of family partnerships in Italy and Germany. In Italy we have the Bardi, Peruzzi, Alberti, Soderini, Strozzi, Acciauoli, Medici, and others, all in Florence. It is safe to assert that in Florence all important businesses were managed by family partnerships, some of which included befriended families. Thus the Alberti company, in 1322, consisted of four major associates and, apart from them, three Alberti sons and two sons of the Neri family. In 1313 the Peruzzi company included eight members of the house of Peruzzi, two of the Baroncelli, and six descendants of other houses. In 1339 the same Peruzzi company included eleven Peruzzi and nine descendants of other families. The Acciauoli partnership, in 1340, united fourteen Acciauoli and four others.

This kind of organization can be found not only in Florence but in other Italian cities as well; the Soranzo family in Venice, for instance, had a similar partnership.

---

[13] End of passage, Vol. I, Pt. 1, pp. 291–96.

The important family partnerships of Germany existed mostly in southern German towns. In Augsburg we find the Fugger, Welser, Heerwart, Neidhart, Manlich, and Baumgarten families engaged in such organizations. The Imhof, Ebner, Volkamer, and Tucher families of Nürnberg are comparable, just as the Ruland family of Ulm. Not only in the south but also in other German regions family partnerships can be found. Contrary to the opinion of certain authors, this form of business organization was not entirely absent in the area of the Hanse; I am reminded here of the Loitzen company in Stettin.

Like their Italian counterparts, some German family companies grew to considerable size. The Welser company, according to the contract of 1508, included no less than eighteen persons; members of the Welser, Vöhlin, Imhof, Heintzel, and other families.

On occasions the great merchant fellowships, like the Ravensburger Gesellschaft, have been regarded as family partnerships. This view is, however, untenable, because these fellowships developed probably from a very different origin, namely, from a guildlike organization. On the other hand, it is true that in these fellowships kinship ties were important, while their conduct in business strongly resembled that of the family partnerships.

The size and transactions of family partnerships were often very considerable: it is sufficient to recall the millions of the Medici, the Welsers, and the Fuggers. Nevertheless, it would be wrong to regard these family partnerships as modern capitalistic enterprises. I think it is misleading even to describe them as partnerships with unlimited liability. . . .[14] They differ from our present capitalistic enterprise in the following respects.

(1) In family partnerships the acquisitive tendency remained undeveloped, as a result of the particular structure of such companies. Too many other motives influenced the conduct of business. We recall an utterance of one Medici partner who was thinking of the splendor of his house rather than of unlimited gain. We also remember the particular position of Jacob Fugger, who had an American way of thinking, in the circle of his relatives. Occasional utterances like these confirm the opinion—which we also deduced from the over-all characteristics of family partnerships—that such companies differ greatly from purely profit-making enterprises. In an excellent statement, Falke drew the distinction as follows: "Trading, for these families, was not just a means

[14] Part of Vol. II, Pt. 1, pp. 88–89, omitted.

to acquire quickly and easily a fortune, after which the activity was transferred to other hands. On the contrary, commerce itself was a binding principle of these families; in a process of slow and certain increase over the centuries commerce led to the accumulation and preservation of the fortune of a large kinship group. Commerce was the solid foundation of a high social position in the civic community. It was also, for the younger members, an unfailing opportunity for instruction and honorable action."

(2) One glance over the accounts of family partnerships is sufficient to show that they were anything but economic enterprises in modern style. We do not have to base our argument on general impressions: business records make it clear that economic conduct as a whole was still essentially pervaded by fraternal and communal sentiments. In the family partnerships the individuals were "among brothers," and only slowly is this spirit later replaced by purely businesslike attitudes.

In the first place, the capital of business was not kept strictly separate from other parts of the family fortune. Neither in the existing ideas nor in the practice of accounting did such a separation exist. Every family company had originally a common purse into which entered all payments and out of which the expenses were paid. This was the fundamental idea that determined the conduct of business of even the greatest commercial houses, as far down as the sixteenth century. We will show later how the legal concept of a separate business capital is developed. At this point the absence of the concept may be demonstrated in a few examples.

About the company of the Soranzo brothers in fifteenth-century Venice we learn: "The fraterna owned the capital, the inherited houses, and the shares in the state debt. However, the expenses of the household were also borne in common. The 'spese di bocha per la fraterna,' the amount spent for food, was, between 1409 and 1418, the sum of 960 ducats. In 1424 a female slave, named Maria, was bought for the fraterna. In 1408 the fraterna donated a piece of white silk to the monastery of San Lorenzo. . . ."[15]

The accounts of the Fugger company present the same picture. The inventory of 1527 made no distinction between the private possessions of the Fuggers and their business capital. The same inventory lists clothes, beds, and the like as well as business accessories. The expenses of the household were brought together with those of business. Eco-

[15] Part of Vol. II, Pt. 1, p. 90, omitted.

nomic conduct, and its expression in the way books were kept, was patriarchal, lax, and "brotherly."[16]

IV. OCCASIONAL PARTNERSHIPS

Various forms of joint ventures, or occasional partnerships, were singularly well fitted to the artisanlike, medieval pattern of economic life. For one thing, such associations enabled the petty artisan to get the most necessary means of production without making him dependent on the services of moneylenders. Besides, these occasional partnerships provided opportunities for many people who were not regular merchants but traded only on "occasions." Again I must warn against the naïveté of regarding the medieval *commenda* and *societas* as capitalist associations. Obviously, one must not view the craftsman who borrows a few hundred marks for his workshop, or the *miles* or *notarius* who entrusts his savings to the petty merchant in a *commenda* as a capitalist entrepreneur. To do so demonstrates a poor understanding of economic essentials. Especially students of law, if they intend to understand economic conditions, must struggle toward the clear realization of the following fact: legal forms—which claim their main attention—do not correspond to economic realities. If a sum of money is lent upon a promise of repayment, a law student—from his standpoint correctly—would regard this as a *mutuum,* a particular legal relation. He makes no distinction between the case of a poor *supernumerarius* who borrows fifty marks from a usurer and the case of a loan of five millions through which a large modern corporation expands its capital. Indeed, since the formal character is the same, there is no reason to make a distinction in the legal sphere. But if one applies this naïve assumption in the case of the occasional partnerships, one must become convinced that any kind of *commenda* or *societas* can exist just as well in an artisanlike as in a capitalist economic system. A given form of association or partnership would then allow no conclusions—absolutely none—about the essential character of its economic activity.[17]

Medieval trade, according to my theory, was either occasional or artisanlike, and it had nothing in common with modern capitalism. Instead of attacking this incontrovertible thesis—a useless attempt—my critics ought to have belabored a different point. They could have argued

[16] End of the passage Vol. II, Pt. 1, pp. 86–90.

[17] Sombart suggests here the importance of size in the economic characterization of an institution like the occasional partnership. This recalls Marx's idea that quantitative changes can ultimately lead to qualitative differences; in this way one economic system is transformed into a new and fundamentally different system.

with some justification that medieval partnerships like the *commenda, rogadia, sendeve,* and *weggelinge* had nothing to do with capitalism but that they were nevertheless instrumental in the development of capitalist forms of organization. This was the effect of the ideas and intentions behind such occasional associations. The legal patterns that allowed the rise of the *commenda* and similar partnerships originated in a spirit of a new age. These partnerships had therefore inevitably a revolutionizing effect: when they kept on expanding, they would in the long run destroy the solid framework of medieval economic institutions and would prepare the way for new relations between businessmen. True, the handicrafts had for centuries used the occasional type of partnership without being damaged. However, the legal forms which the system itself had created became imperceptibly the factor that changed the craft system into a fundamentally different economic pattern. Specifically, the significance of various legal forms of occasional partnerships for the development of capitalism must be sought in their revolutionary impact on basic economic ideas.

These revolutionary principles, implicit in medieval partnerships of the occasional kind, were the following:

(1) "Strangers" were united in a common activity by contractual ties. Partners no longer had to have kinship relations, neighborly or professional affinities. It is true that originally there were limits to the extent to which they could be strangers to each other. Most statutes allowed partnerships only among citizens of one and the same town. But the first step had been taken on the road that leads from natural, historical, and organic relations to deliberate, mechanical relations among men. "Contractual partnerships" in principle had begun to replace "communal partnerships," and purposive organization replaced the community.

(2) Business activity became a separate sphere, kept clearly apart from personality as a whole. Temporary associations for a specified purpose had the result that economic action as such could begin a life of its own and develop autonomously; and, as we shall see, this is the basic principle of capitalist enterprise. All other forms of organization had traditionally affected all spheres of personal life. The guilds and brotherhoods of craftsmen as well as the family partnerships were strongly communal organizations; business was only one part of their total activity. Occasional partnerships, however, were organizations exclusively concerned with business. Between *commendator* and *tractor* no ties were necessary except their business connection. Business only, quite apart

from their personalities, created the common bond. In later times this phenomenon led to the total autonomy of business as such, and more particularly the autonomous existence of what for the time being was merely a business fund—the business capital.

(3) Unlimited accumulation of productive forces, especially of means of production, was a third important consequence of the principle of mechanical and contractual association. Simply by joining resources, large stocks could be brought together, and, apart from the purpose of the undertaking, this process of addition had no boundaries. But this signified the complete abolition of all restrictions which were inherent in the organic characteristics of other forms of association. Such restrictions as the limitations of the family fortune, the size of the guild, and the size of productive units like the ship, mine, or mill, that had affected other forms of organization no longer existed for the occasional partnerships. These partnerships, therefore, led to the free operation of boundless acquisition as a principle of economic conduct.[18]

V. CAPITALIST ENTERPRISE AS A FORM OF PROPERTY ORGANIZATION

We now wish to show the difference that exists between capitalist and noncapitalist forms of property organization, especially with reference to earlier periods. Let us ask first: What new element enters into the organization of economic conduct when capitalist enterprise appears? The answer cannot be difficult to find: the enterprise is now autonomous. What this means is the emergence of a separate economic organism, above and beyond the individuals who are engaged in economic activity: all business transactions that formerly occurred in a more or less separate way—side by side or one after the other, in various ventures—are now included in one conceptual unit, namely, the enterprise. This unit is a going concern, continuing beyond the lives of the participating individuals and appearing as the "carrier" of the economic actions. It is true that in earlier times supra-individual organizations had occurred, particularly in the economic sphere, but they were organisms binding together natural groups of human beings in all aspects of their life. The continuity of such communities or total associations was the consequence of the natural sequence of generations. Tribe, clan, family, even village community and guild, were examples of this kind of supra-individual organism, and economic actions were a part of their existence, viewed in relation to them.

[18] End of passage Vol. II, Pt. 1, pp. 95–98.

Now an abstract phenomenon, namely, "the business" or "the enterprise" as such, arises to replace the natural forms of organization. "Business" includes the sum total of all separate business transactions. Therewith economic relations were separated from particular persons and started an independent existence. Instead of regarding economic actions as personal actions, people started to view them as the performances of an abstract entity having an independent existence and moving according to its own laws. I have often referred to this phenomenon as a depersonalization [*Versachlichung*] of property relations. . . .[19]

A capitalist enterprise is a mechanism for acquisitive purposes which operates impersonally. Only in this kind of mechanism could the acquisition principle find a vehicle for its unrestricted activity; the depersonalization of economic actions was necessary before these actions could be geared solely to profit.[20]

To describe the evolution of the capitalist enterprise is the same as to give an account of how and when "business" as such became an autonomous economic entity. Only by indirect methods can one find out how this happened. No entrepreneur or other individual ever proclaimed that "from now on there exists a capitalist enterprise, in the sense of twentieth-century theory." Frequently the autonomy of business was an unintended achievement, occurring despite the insight or desires of its leaders. Only in a few cases do they show an intention to regard their own persons as something separate from their business. The necessary separation was to some extent the result of extra-economic forces, and then it was, of course, tacitly adopted rather than accepted with a clear awareness of what had happened. Our conclusions must be derived from merely external indices—ways of acting and the adherence to certain tenets of behavior.

The segregation of the business sphere occurs under the impact of three different phenomena, as far as I can judge, and the end result is the capitalist form of enterprise. These phenomena occur in jurisprudence, in accounting, and in the character of the market. Business achieves its autonomy in the form of the legal entity called "firma," the accounting entity called "ragione," and the credit entity called "ditta."[21]

VI. SYSTEMATIC BOOKKEEPING

Order heightens our powers. Organization in economic matters increases economic potentialities. This general wisdom applies in all eco-

[19] A passage on p. 102 has been omitted.
[20] End of the passage in Vol. II, Pt. 1, p. 102.
[21] End of the passage Vol. II, Pt. 1, p. 103.

nomic situations: "Order and clarity stimulate thrift and accumulation. A slovenly manager is satisfied and at ease with his ignorance; he avoids calculating his debts. But a good manager likes nothing better than to check every day on his growing wealth. Even a mishap does not frighten him; it may come as an unpleasant surprise, but he immediately realizes the advantages on the other side of the balance." This is true for the farmer and the artisan, the capitalist entrepreneur and the housewife. The truth of these maxims becomes even clearer if we think about the importance of bookkeeping. The characteristic pattern of business organization resulting from systematic bookkeeping has been of crucial importance for the development of capitalism in its most essential aspect. One cannot imagine what capitalism would be without double-entry bookkeeping: the two phenomena are connected as intimately as form and contents. One cannot say whether capitalism created double-entry bookkeeping, as a tool in its expansion, or whether perhaps, conversely, double-entry bookkeeping created capitalism. . . .[22]

The method of double-entry bookkeeping actualizes the complete separation of the funds used in profit making and the funds used for everyday life. Herewith the acquisition principle reaches its full development. There remains only one single purpose: to increase a measured amount of "value." To penetrate the mysteries of bookkeeping, one must forget the qualities of goods and services. One must no longer think of ships or shiploads, flour or cotton, but exclusively in terms of quantities, of increasing and diminishing amounts of value. The idea of organic limitations of human needs, expressed in the livelihood principle, is replaced by the principle of acquisition as an end in itself.[23]

The very concept of capital is derived from this way of looking at things; one can say that capital, as a category, did not exist before double-entry bookkeeping. Capital can be defined as that amount of wealth which is used in making profits and which enters into the accounts.

Closely connected with the preceding observations is the argument that the complete rationalization of economic life became possible only through the advent of double-entry bookkeeping. Rationalization, in one of its aspects, means dealing with economic occurrences by means of figures and numerical calculations. The acquisition principle and rationalization are evidently closely connected: the former urges toward the maximization of profit, while the latter allows the more and more

[22] End of the passage Vol. II, Pt. 1, p. 118.

[23] A passage on p. 120 has been omitted.

perfect realization of the ideal. Both principles dissolve the economic world into numbers.

Of course, double entry would promote the calculating spirit. Outside the books no economic occurrences exist: "quod non est in libris, non est in mundo." The accounts contain only things that can be expressed in money. Since amounts of money are expressed by figures, each economic occurrence is reflected in a numerical datum. Economic action consequently becomes equivalent to calculation. If this is so, all subsidiary principles of the economic system follow. Thus the concept of "exchange value" found an adequate expression only through double-entry bookkeeping. . . .[24]

Double-entry bookkeeping created not only "capital" as a concept but also "the capitalist enterprise." This particular form of economic organization aims at the turnover of a specific capital for profit purposes. The creative significance of bookkeeping is already evident in the very origin of capitalist enterprise, since the essence of such an enterprise—as an organization of property—is the autonomous existence of business. And, of course, systematic bookkeeping is most effective in separating the business capital from the other parts of private wealth.

How is the autonomy of business achieved?

(1) The business account and therewith the management of business are separated from the entrepreneur as a person and are organized for purely businesslike purposes. The accounting procedure is mechanized and made objective. This means that the procedure now becomes a general, commonly accepted one, independent of the accidental qualities of the man who directs the affairs. Everybody can understand its method. In medieval account books, only the owners could and should know their way; in books that follow a system every informed individual is at home. Already the founders of double entry demanded that books should be kept in a clear and generally understandable way. Thus Luca Pacioli writes in his twelfth chapter:

"You must enclose all journal entries—including written remarks—with a line if they are transferred [into other books]. The same must be done in the case of memorandum entries. If you transfer [an entry] from the memorandum into the journal, you will cross out the [entry] by a single diagonal line. This will signify that the entry has been transferred into the journal. And in case you do not wish to cross out the entry, you shall mark the first or last letter of the beginning of the entry by means of a little lance or some other sign. Hereby you are enabled to see that the said entry has been carried over into the journal. You may use all sorts of signs; it is best, however, to use with common ones generally used by

[24] A passage on p. 121 has been omitted.

other native merchants. Then you will not appear to deviate from ordinary commercial practice [*modo mercantesco*]."

(2) Through double-entry bookkeeping the account becomes not only objective but also mechanical: once the beginning is made, the rest follows in a specific way. This aspect has been strikingly expressed by Schär, who said that "accounting has now been brought into a compulsory frame."

The conduct of a business herewith lost its highly personal character. A strictly businesslike procedure replaced personal management. The enterprise became autonomous and moved according to its own laws. This holds in a double sense: first, the enterprise emerged as an independent entity in the accounts, represented by its capital; secondly, this business entity now stood apart from the person of the entrepreneur, who, as it were, became his own creditor.

3

*Small and Great Merchants in the Italian Cities of the Renaissance**

By GINO LUZZATTO

In one of his essays on economic history, which are admirable for their penetrating scholarship, their realism, and their critical sense, the late Von Below has tackled the problem of small- and large-scale commerce in the Middle Ages.[1] The issue revolves around the question whether during the age of the urban communes the activity of the small retail trader should be regarded as clearly distinct from the activity of the great merchant. After carefully analyzing the most important evidence, he came to the conclusion that, while there existed a broad category of persons who were nothing but small shopkeepers, one cannot cite one example of a merchant who engaged exclusively in wholesale trade. No merchants existed who did not have, directly or indirectly, an interest in some kind of retail trade. In this as well as in his other works, Von Below's conclusions refer to Germany only. He cited, however, examples from neighboring countries, and, while he did not generalize overmuch, he was clearly inclined to think that his conclusions were applicable, with few exceptions, to the whole of western Europe in the period of the town economy.

If one wants to study carefully the slow process by which the small, isolated, self-sufficient economies of the late Middle Ages evolved into the modern world economy, Von Below's problem is extremely important. Today commerce is the great regulating principle in economic life. Agriculture and industry, in so far as they do not produce for subsistence and immediate consumption but for sale, increase and reduce

* An abridged translation, with the approval of Professor Luzzatto, of "Piccoli e grandi mercanti nelle città italiane del Rinascimento," in *Saggi di storia e teoria economica in onore e ricordo di Giuseppe Prato* (Turin, 1931), pp. 27–49. The author's footnotes, which were fairly extensive, have been omitted for reasons of space. Mrs. Angela Fales made the translation. The paper appears here with the permission of Professor Luzzatto.

[1] See Georg von Below, "Grosshändler und Kleinhändler im deutschen Mittelalter," *Jahrbücher für Nationalökonomie und Statistik,* 1900, LXXV, 1–51.

their production according to market conditions. Thus the commodity exchanges of New York, London, and Hamburg direct the performance of large cotton, wheat, coffee, sugar, and rubber plantations and of metal mining in the most distant regions. How important commerce is can be seen from the extreme degree to which it is specialized. Commercial activity ranges from that of the peddler, who, with a sack of merchandise on his shoulder, visits lonely farms, to the activity of the stock-exchange tycoon, who, by cabling an order, influences prices on markets all over the world. In between these extremes an infinitely varied range of activities reflects the varied needs which commerce must satisfy. We assess the importance of retail trade within a city by the degree to which its shops are specialized. The growing importance of wholesale trade, national and international, can be measured similarly by the extent to which commercial functions and activities are differentiated, whether according to specific commodities or to different kinds of customers or to different functions. Since the growing importance of the exchange of goods accompanies a growing number of differentiated commercial activities, the degree of commercial specialization during a historical period may be taken as a sure index of economic development.

One can prove that in large Italian mercantile cities, like Venice, Genoa, and Florence, specialization was already considerable in the fourteenth century, and especially during the next two centuries, at least in auxiliary commercial activities. Without doubt there existed in those cities large groups of brokers who performed important tasks. The brokers were regulated and were explicitly recognized by the laws of the city and of the guilds. Frequently such men acted as public officials, particularly in transactions with foreigners. Secondly, we have the much more numerous *factores, nuntii,* and *commissi,* who at times were employed by merchants or merchant companies as agents in distant cities. In other cases, more frequently, men indicated by these terms were partners who had an interest in the commercial undertaking in which they served; special partnership contracts limited their activity to the branch of the company of which they were in charge. It also happened that the *factores,* etc., were commission agents; a merchant who had insufficient business in a city to warrant the opening of a branch, would often ask one of his fellow-citizens to handle his business for him on a commission basis. Finally, there were those who performed transport services over land or sea [carriers, shipmasters]. Shipping agents as a specialized group seem to have been lacking; as far as we know now, they appeared for the first time in Holland during the seventeenth century.

For our problem the existence of these different auxiliary commercial activities and of retailers specializing according to kinds of merchandise is, however, far less important than a possible distinction between wholesale and retail trade. Above all, it would be of importance to know whether there were, at least in the large commercial centers, a distinct class of great merchants, differentiated from the far more numerous group of small retailers by the nature of their business transactions, by their mentality, and by their economic and social importance.

In this as in other parts of economic history two methods can be followed in handling the problem. First, there is the impersonal and statistical method: one may study commercial and other economic activities separate from the individuals who were engaged in them. Then one deals with the kinds of goods exchanged, trade routes, commercial techniques, government measures promoting or hindering particular activities, the increase or decrease of total wealth, and the like. Second, one can follow what might be called the "individual" method, by studying the characteristics of economic development in a historical period from the life history of a single businessman or company. Clearly, to discover the trends and essential features of an economic situation, the historian must use both methods. But since we are attempting to solve the particular problem of the existence and type of activity of great merchants, the second method, based on sources concerning individuals, such as memoirs, letters, contracts, and ledgers, is not only the more important but also the only method which can yield certain and final answers.

Unfortunately, when it comes to sources, the historians do not always have much choice. About the economic history of the thirteenth and fourteenth centuries in particular, our archives are not rich in public records which could give us reliable and detailed facts regarding quantitative developments in production, transportation, and commerce. The archives are even poorer, undeniably, in private business records of merchants. Most of those records have probably been lost or destroyed. Conditions are more favorable for the fifteenth century; of this period a greater number of commercial letters, ledgers, memoirs, and diaries have been preserved. While some of these records have been briefly mentioned [in published research], complete editions of these sources, or analytical studies of their full contents, are still lacking. Only

Tuscany, as far as we know, has preserved the complete archive of a great fourteenth-century merchant,[2] as well as fragments of the archives of some large Florentine houses. Even in the absence of such major sources it will, however, be possible to reconstruct the life and activity of some of our merchants; this can be done through careful and detailed research in notarial archives and in public documents. Only by local scholars can this long and difficult task be accomplished. On the whole, and barring a few exceptions, the work has hardly been begun.

It may be of some value to determine even now which conclusions are warranted by the public and private documents of which we have knowledge, while we are waiting for publications of, or studies on, the materials that are buried in our archives. These conclusions must be summary and tentative, but we can say the following: If by "great" commerce we mean wholesale trade, and by "small' commerce retail trade, then the city statutes and the guild regulations show that Von Below's thesis [namely, that "great" and "small" commerce are not clearly distinguishable] can even be extended to the most important commercial cities of Italy during the period of their greatest development.

True, a few exceptions must be made: in the statutes of the physicians, apothecaries, and mercers of Florence, for instance, there existed from 1314 on a distinction between apothecaries who sold *in grossum,* and those who sold *ad minutum.* In a reform of the same statute the two categories are distinguished so clearly that they must have been separate branches of the guild. A similar phenomenon occurs in Siena, where there existed in the first decade of the thirteenth century two separate guilds, one of merchants and one of *piczicarii.* According to Zdekauer's interpretation, which was later confirmed by Arcangeli, wholesale merchants and bankers belonged to the former, while retail merchants belonged to the latter guild. However, in the oldest city statute, that of 1262, the two guilds already appear to have merged into one, although the two kinds of *mercanzia* still had their separate consuls. In the statute of 1310 the merger seems complete: only one *arte della mercanzia* is mentioned, the consuls of which are called *dei mercanti,* without distinction.

These exceptions to Von Below's conclusion have been derived from the wording of statutes which cannot easily be proved to have corresponded to reality. Most of the statutes, however, confirm the conclusion that the term *mercanzia* was loosely used and that no clear and definite

---

[2] Enrico Bensa, *Francesco di Marco da Prato. Notizie e documenti sulla mercatura italiana nel secolo XIV* (Milan, 1928), contains part of these records.

distinction was made between the two forms of trade which we today characterize as "wholesale" and "retail."

Wherever a guild of *mercatores* or *negotiatores* can be found—particularly within those urban communes in which international trade never became very important—it included only merchants dealing in woollen and other cloths who sold locally produced as well as foreign cloths, linens, and fustians. In cities with more intense commerce, accompanied by considerable industrial activity, there was not just a guild of *mercatores* but several mercantile guilds. These guilds were differentiated according to the trade in which their members engaged or according to the industrial activity that accompanied this kind of trade. In Verona, instead of a guild of *mercatores,* there existed a guild of drapers who controlled the production and sale of woollen cloths, a guild of *scavezzatini,* or retailers of cloth, a guild of mercers, and one of apothecaries. The *domus mercatorum,* which at first was called *communitas mercatorum* or *universitas mercatorum,* was not a guild but a civic magistracy, exercising controls and watching over productive activities. It was part of the city government and had a voice in the preparation of commercial treaties. In Milan, Cremona, Piacenza, Pisa, and, above all, Florence, the situation was apparently the same. In Florence, for instance, the *mercanzia* was neither a guild nor an association of guilds but a commercial court. This court was formed by five guilds: the Calimala, the wool guild, the guild called Por Santa Maria, the guild of money changers, and finally that which united physicians, apothecaries, and mercers.

Florentine guild organization was distinguished by its greater degree of specialization and particularly by the existence of the Calimala. Although in medieval institutional history we must always be careful not to state our conclusions too categorically, the Calimala may be adequately characterized as a great international trading guild. It is true that members of the wool guild, of the Por Santa Maria, and of the apothecaries guild also, were often to an important extent engaged in import and export trade, in industry and in home trade, wholesale or retail. But, while for the other guilds foreign trade was no more than an occasional or complementary pursuit, the Calimala guild, which in the fourteenth century numbered among its members many of the greatest Florentine capitalists, had foreign trade as its most important and customary activity. Now the Calimala, although originally formed for the trade of imported cloths from the north—Flanders, France, and England—did not prevent its members from selling at retail in the shops of the narrow Calimala street. Neither did it make a clear distinction between those who sold a few yards of cloth from their shop window or out on the street and those who were members of the large companies with branches in all the most important western European and Mediterranean markets. It must be noted that the lack of differentiation between wholesale and retail did not prevent the Calimala from being a typical organization for large-scale international trade. In fact, its statutes constantly mention the "companies" in which guild members associated. From the way they are mentioned, it is clear that these "companies" were not mere subdivisions of the guild but real commercial associations of the kind that played such an important part in the expansion of Florentine trade through the civilized world.[3]

Thus the provisions of the statutes show in Florence the existence of great merchants as a specialized group. In Genoa and Venice the very silence of the statutes on this point and the absence of a specialized merchant guild are revealing. Thus in Genoa there existed during the second half of the thirteenth century a guild of drapers separate from that of the woollen clothmakers. There was a guild of brokers and a guild of physicians and apothecaries, which probably included the mercers, as was the case in Florence and in some other cities. During the same years in Venice there were guilds of dealers in secondhand clothing and other goods, of linen sellers, of apothecaries, of food retailers, and of mercers. The mercers specialized, as they did in Florence, in the sale of gloves, belts, bags and other leather goods, ribbons, and small silk articles. But neither in Genoa nor in Venice can we find evidence of a special mercantile guild which engaged in international exchange, shipping, and banking. No guilds comparable to the Florentine Calimala or to the Florentine money-changers guild can be found; and the reasons for this will be evident from what follows.

After the Florentine commune was formed and grew strong, there existed in the city a powerful landholding aristocracy against which the bourgeoisie had to defend itself. When the bourgeoisie rose to power, there were the artisans to be reckoned with. A profound difference existed between the wealthy merchant classes and the artisans; while at times one class or the other might gain complete control, neither succeeded in retaining it. In Venice and Genoa, on the other hand, the commune itself was simply the ruling organ of the wealthy bourgeoisie. The wealth of the commune was entirely based on the activities of this class: commerce by land and sea, shipping, exchange dealings, and

[3] Passage omitted, pp. 36–39.

loans. The ruling bourgeoisie would not feel the necessity of a guild organization; especially in Venice, it rather used the guilds as a means of controlling the very numerous artisan classes. We find guilds of mercers, of apothecaries, and of retailers, but no sign of guilds of money-changers, of cloth merchants, and of shipowners. This fact clearly shows how widely and deeply felt was the distinction between the small retail merchants, who were comparable to artisans and who had no political influence, and the real merchants, who enjoyed full political rights and who personally as well as through their capital could participate in international trade. In Venice this contrast was even reflected in two different forms of citizenship. There was citizenship *de intus* for those who could engage in internal trade and citizenship *de intus et de extra* for those who could also participate in foreign trade, particularly with the Levant.

We may conclude that in the larger Italian cities small and great merchants were differentiated; this appears clearly from statutes. More completely and convincingly it could be proved from the life histories of individual merchants, if these were examined one by one. Memoirs of Florentine merchants in the fourteenth century, together with some information to be gleaned from other sources about the merchants of other Tuscan cities and those of Venice and Genoa, reveal an essential uniformity in their *curriculum vitae.* All these merchants seem to have started their career by long voyages, by land or sea, and by long sojourns abroad. In Venice such voyages by young men frequently took the form of the performance of an official function aboard the galleys or in the colonies. This was due to the peculiarities of the Venetian constitution; the main purpose of these voyages was, however, to promote the commercial interests of the family to which the young man belonged or of his partners. After wandering abroad over the then known world, some of these merchants would settle in some foreign city; the majority returned home when they reached middle age and spent the rest of their life in their city. A merchant who became sedentary did not abandon his connections with foreign markets. He might become active in public life or return to the seclusion of his family, but in either case he would still be carrying on his enterprises, alone or with partners. Now the active part of his business would be attended to by his sons, nephews, or employees, who visited the great international fairs or managed the branches of his firm in the major commercial markets—Provence, Flanders, Paris, London, Spain, the Balearic Islands, the Italian cities, and the Levant.

While it is true that all larger Italian cities had a merchant class which engaged primarily in foreign trade and which prepared for this function by long sojourns abroad, the nature of this business, its form, purpose, and extent, could vary greatly according to the city. In the Tuscan cities, particularly in Florence and Siena, great merchants primarily engaged in the business of exchange and in the import and export of cloth, and they did so preferably in associations rather than as single merchants. The question whether the cloth trade or the dealings in money were more important is difficult to answer. Probably financial transactions were most significant: the lending of money to princes, to the clergy, to cities, and similar operations. Because of such transactions, in large sums or small, "Tuscans" can be encountered in all large and small commercial centers of Italy and western Europe; their names, sometimes confused with the wider term "Lombards," had a fame rather similar to that of the Jews and Cahorsins. While Florentine companies dealt mainly in money and in cloth, they also traded actively in spices, perfumes, metals, skins, dyes, and sometimes grain. Through loans and partnerships, they took part in the management of the two largest textile industries of their country, the products of which they brought to the markets of the south and of the Levant. While associations were strong and numerous, individual personalities were not prevented from coming to the fore; such is the case of the now well-known Franceso Datini, who came from Prato and who, after having started a modest retail *fondaco* in Avignon, widened his activities to include the trade between Florence and Provence. After he returned to Italy, his affairs became more and more diversified and complex. He opened a bank in Florence, handled all kinds of imports and exports on a growing scale, had branches in Pisa, Majorca, Avignon, Barcelona, and Valencia, and participated with others in financing the industry of his native city. While he formed several companies, these associations must not be regarded as having merely the purpose of bringing capital together; from the moment he could consider himself a great merchant, Datini used these companies or partnerships to secure himself the loyalty of those who worked for him. In his various undertakings, with his associates *in partibus,* he was not just a capital-providing partner but also the leader and manager of the business.

Comparing the Tuscan cities (Florence, Siena) with Genoa and Venice, we notice a twofold difference. In the first place, financial transactions by great merchants abroad were of less importance in the latter cities, at least until the fifteenth century. Second, in Venice and

a year, a hired employee received immediately a salary of five to seven florins, which increased rapidly in accordance with seniority and services performed. To these who worked abroad and who promoted the interests of the company in the best way the highest salaries were paid, often 100 to 150 florins, even 200 florins for the men who headed the English and Flemish branches. The salaries of the two general managers who kept the accounts and prepared the budgets were exceptional: Cino del Migliore and Fetto Ubertino received 300 florins a year.

This list of Bardi personnel has been discussed at some length because it reflects the complexity, the completeness, and the high cost of business management in that time. It shows better than any other statistical material the character of a large firm in the first half of the fourteenth century. It is true that the Bardi company was for a few years the most powerful Florentine firm, but several associated or rival firms, in Florence itself and elsewhere, were not much less important. Still it is possible to insist, in agreement with Von Below's thesis, that even in the case of the Bardi, for a short time the most powerful European merchants and bankers, no clear-cut differentiation between wholesale and retail trade existed. They financed the wars of the English king in Flanders and in France, exported entire shiploads of wheat from Apulia, and at the same time still kept their *fondaco della drapperia* with, as is probable, a retail shop annex. But to conclude from this that great and small merchants were not differentiated would be to misjudge the nature of medieval commerce. The absence of a clear distinction between wholesale and retail trade does not mean that there was no distinction between small and great merchants. Indeed, there existed a class of small merchants with the "artisan mentality" which Sombart regarded as characteristic of medieval trade as a whole. The artisan who sold his products directly to the consumer and the petty merchant who retailed products from the surrounding countryside or from foreign countries had the same way of life and the same minute chances of making a fortune. Some merchants, as well as a few artisans, succeeded in making more money than they needed for their living and could consequently accumulate capital and improve their lot. But such cases were exceptional, and usually a man rose from small beginnings by practicing commerce abroad. Small-scale commerce, rigidly controlled by guild regulations, was, like any other craft, based on the balance between demand and supply and on the merchant's relations with a restricted number of clients whom he knew and whose needs he could foretell. No great risks were involved in this kind of business, but there was no chance of obtaining large profits either. It secured the man who engaged in it a reliable source of subsistence during a calm and uneventful life.

A great merchant would have a different, almost an opposite, mentality. He would leave the enclosed city and its narrow streets behind and so continue the tradition of the peddlers of earlier times, with their passion for wandering, for knowledge, and for life in distant countries and markets. He was attracted to international trade because this kind of business alone resulted in large profits; for their sake he consciously faced all kinds of danger. These dangers and hardships not only sharpened his business instincts but also developed new qualities of leadership and organization. His energy and his aspirations made Italy during the fourteenth and fifteenth centuries the teacher of all Europe, in business arithmetic and bookkeeping, in the rational organization of business firms, in commercial techniques, and in commercial law. The great Italian merchant of the Renaissance was no narrow specialist, dealing in certain kinds of goods and engaging in certain activities only. He was a businessman in the complete sense. Equipped with some personal capital but also with daring, initiative, and the gift of organization, he engaged in all kinds of ventures: trading at home and abroad, wholesale or retail; dealing in cloth, wool, spices, and other goods; financing industries; changing moneys; lending to private individuals and governments; and collecting customs duties under contract. At times he would even engage in several of these activities at once, to satisfy the ever-present thirst for gain which was the impulse behind all his efforts.

4

*The Culture of the Medieval Italian Merchant**

By ARMANDO SAPORI

1. According to Werner Sombart, the medieval merchant was not only uneducated but, as a rule, even illiterate. This well-known thesis is worthy of consideration if one is willing to accept another one of Sombart's assertions, namely, that in the Middle Ages there existed nothing but a host of small businessmen who had the mentality of mere artisans and who confined themselves to activities which afforded them no more than a modest livelihood. This class, Sombart thought, predominated to such an extent that it was characteristic of the whole epoch.

This conception does not correspond to reality, at least not in every part of Europe. It is true that research based upon documentary evidence has confirmed that artisans selling their finished products directly to consumers and storekeepers who served local needs did indeed predominate, as, for that matter, they do today. But this research has also revealed the existence, particularly in the major Italian cities, of a considerable number of business firms of medium size and of some with exceptional importance. In a single source—a small group of letters of the second half of the thirteenth century—we find references to several Sienese companies engaged in international trade in France, Flanders,

---

* An abridged translation, by Raymond de Roover and Florence Edler de Roover, of "La cultura del mercante medievale italiano," *Rivista di storia economica,* 1937, Vol. II, No. 2, and reprinted in Sapori, *Studi di storia economica medievale,* (2nd ed., Florence, Sansoni, 1946). In the present version sections 3, 9, and 10 have been omitted, as well as the very extensive footnotes. The original numbering has been retained. Professor Sapori preceded the original article by the following Table of Contents: "1. The General Culture of the Italian Merchant in the Middle Ages; the Composition of the Merchant Class." "2. The Orderly Mind of the Merchant: Notarial Protocols, Memoirs, Diaries, Chronicles." "3. [omitted] The Merchant's Knowledge of Arithmetic According to Sombart's Theory." "4. The Merchant's Knowledge of Arithmetic as Evident from His Account Books." "5. The Merchant's Education in School." "6. The Merchant's Education in the Counting House, the *fondaco.*" "7. The *fondaco* as the Center of His Life and Education." "8. The Computer's Tools: The Great Abacus." "9. [omitted] The Small Abacus, or *taboletto dei conti di ragione.*" "10. [omitted] The Merchant Manual, the *manuale di mercatura:* Contents, Origins, Its Compilation." "11. Conclusion."

The translation which follows appears here with the permission of Professor Sapori.

England, and Germany. In addition to the great Bonsignori company—by far the largest in its time—the letters mention several smaller companies, such as the firms of the Cacciaconti, the Fini, the Gallerani, the Maffei, the Marescotti, the Piccolomini, the Sansedoni, the Salimbeni, the Squarcialupi, the Tolomei, the Ugolini, the Vincenti. Sources relating to centers other than Siena refer to the following families as having extensive business connections all over Europe toward the end of the thirteenth and the beginning of the fourteenth centuries:

Asti: Alfieri, Asinari, da Saliceto, Garetti, Malabaila, Pelleta, Roveri, Scarampi, Solari, Toma.

Lucca: Barca, Burlamacchi, Calcinelli, Cenami, Corbolani, Forteguerra, Guinigi, Moriconi, Onesti, Rapondi, Ricciardi, Schiatta, Spiafame, Trenta.

Pistoia: Ammanati, Cancellieri, Dondori, Panciatichi, Partini, Simiglianti.

Florence: Alberti, Albizzi, Antella, Ardinghelli, Baroncelli, Bondelmonti, Cerchi, Del Bene, Falconieri, Frescobaldi, Gianfigliazzi, Mozzi, Pazzi, Portinari, Pulci and Rimbertini, Scali, Spini, Strozzi.

This list does not include the powerful companies of the Bardi, the Peruzzi, and the Acciaioli, called by the chronicler Giovanni Villani the "pillars of Christianity."

Granted that the small shopkeeper might get along with a single memorandum book kept by himself or by an apprentice, other merchants—and they were numerous—certainly needed quite a different setup, with more elaborate records, given the size and scope of their business. Many of the companies had branches in foreign parts, distant from the main office. Naturally, this involved an enormous amount of correspondence, as one can see from the Sienese letters already mentioned. Many other collections of business letters, no less important, buried in public and family archives, are still waiting to be rescued from centuries of oblivion.

2. It would be a mistake to state, as Sombart does, that the medieval merchant was an implacable enemy of pen and ink, loath to stain his hands with them, and writing only in cases where it could not be avoided. Supposing the merchant disliked to write, his dislike would make little difference and would not reduce greatly the volume of correspondence, if such correspondence were a necessary part of his business. But there is no basis for assuming an aversion to writing. On the contrary, we are in a position to assert that in the Middle Ages, among all epochs of the history of mankind, men were most eager to record what they did or what they witnessed. The persons who felt this desire more than any others were the merchants, founders of the middle class, who

by nature were orderly to the point of fussiness and who became, as time went on, conservative to the point of bad taste.

No matter of economic interest that was of the least importance escaped being put on paper. First of all, the merchant frequently resorted to the services of a notary, a public official who was, and still is, much more important in Europe than in the United States. Notaries were licensed to draft deeds and solemn contracts; one of them was summoned, for example, to enregister a loan secured by the pledge of some shabby bedclothes. In another instance a notary was called upon to fill pages and pages with legal formulas concerning an agreement between an artisan who promised to undertake a certain job, on the one hand, and a patron who promised to pay as the work progressed, on the other. Articles of apprenticeship also generally required the intervention of a notary as the person who had to draw up the contract.

Secondly, the merchant entered all his business transactions in his account books and, if necessary, he kept private notebooks or diaries, called *ricordi, ricordanze,* or *libri segreti.* In them he wrote down day-by-day household expenditures, family events, notices about public affairs, and even international episodes about which he happened to hear.

All this can be ascertained from surviving records. There is also adequate evidence to show that the people of the time were aware of the necessity of committing everything to paper because they could otherwise become victims of sharp practice or might be betrayed by a faulty memory. This evidence is found in a number of literary texts, ranging from the thirteenth century to the eve of modern times, in which famous as well as unknown authors repeat the same admonitions. Among the oldest, one anonymous Genoese expresses himself with a vivacity typical of his particular dialect: "But I must urge you to write down carefully your affairs, and do it immediately before they slip your mind"; "the lazy man who is remiss in writing down his dealings cannot live long without damage or mistake." And in the next century we hear the more polished words of Dino Compagni, of Paolo di messer Pace from Certaldo, of Giovanni di Paolo Morelli, of Franco Sacchetti. The chronicler of the so-called "parte bianca" [his name is Dino Compagni] ends a long list of suggestions to merchants with the following: "Keep your accounts carefully and make no mistakes." Morelli and Sacchetti must have borrowed from each other the dictum: "Never spare pen and ink." Paolo, son of Messer Pace, from Certaldo, gives in his elegant and precise language the following advice: "Every time that you enter into a contract, have a book at hand, and write down the date, the names of the notary who drafted the deed, and of the witnesses, the reason why you made the contract, and the name of the party with whom you dealt, so that, if you or your children need to look up the record, you will find it easily; and in order to forestall any possibility of deceit by men of bad faith, have the contract drafted in due form and put it away in a safe place."

Although he was compelled to write a great deal, the merchant was not content to use a rough-and-ready style but often endeavored to give an elegant form to his notes, so that not a few of the surviving account books, memoirs, and diaries are so remarkable for beauty and aptness of expression, for acuteness of observation, and for their wealth of information that they have been published for their value as philological texts or as historical sources. There have been published, for Florence alone, those of Guido dell'Antella, of Luca di Totto da Panzano, of Giovanni Morelli, of Bonaccorso Pitti, of Donato Velluti, of Oderigo di Credi, of the silk merchant Goro Dati, of Guido Monaldi, of Nado di ser Nepo da Montecatini, of the spicer Luca Landucci, of the vintner Bartolomeo di Michele del Corazza, of the kettle-maker Bartolomeo Masi, of the grain merchant Domenico Lenzi. Nor is it necessary to mention that among professional or occasional merchants we find the great story-writers Giovanni Boccaccio and Franco Sacchetti; that the major chroniclers Dino Compagni and Giovanni Villani were merchants and sons of merchants; and that Leon Battista Alberti, who came from a prominent merchant family which had engaged in trade since the thirteenth century at least, was himself an expert in business matters. He wrote the famous treatise on household management that has been a fruitful source of studies on the history of bourgeois mentality. It may be said that the major sources for the history of Florence during the Middle Ages and the early Renaissance are, in fact, the work of her merchants.

In view of what has been said, one cannot be accused of rash statement or of bias if one asserts that the medieval Italian merchant was not part of a crowd in which the ignorant and illiterate predominated. He was capable of rising above the level of the small businessman or the shopkeeper, and this fact indicates that he was a cultured individual with a precise and orderly mind. In the case of some outstanding individuals, the merchant had good literary taste. He also was curious about human affairs, which he would try to understand and to interpret. As a result, the diaries and chronicles written by merchants occasionally achieve the dignity of history.

4. Sombart's colorful characterization of the ignorance of the medieval merchant is a theoretical construction which collapses when confronted with evidence from the account books of the Middle Ages. He had the temerity to cite these books as proof for his contentions without bothering to analyze them amply and completely. A careful study of these account books, a great many of which are preserved in the Italian archives—not only those of companies with world-wide connections but also those of firms of a modest size—reveals that the Italian merchant of the Middle Ages, meticulous in recording all the episodes of his life and any interesting news that reached him, also made it a point to be accurate in his computations and clear in his bookkeeping, because he was convinced that accuracy and clarity were indispensable in the conduct of business. Besides, he took care to be equipped with a knowledge of arithmetic more than adequate for this purpose.

Concerning efficiency in bookkeeping, the necessary evidence is found in my study based upon the group of books—not just one, but an entire set—that once belonged to a rather modest company within the Calimala guild which was active during the early years of the fourteenth century. Following in the steps of the medieval bookkeeper, I checked one by one all the entries, and I arrived at the same results for the figures of profit and loss, and for the composition of assets and liabilities at the moment that the business was liquidated, as did that bookkeeper.

Concerning the merchant's knowledge of arithmetic, we learn from the same set of books that by the beginning of the fourteenth century—we may safely assume that the practice dates from an even earlier time—interest was already compounded by being added to the capital at the end of the year: the expression was *fare capo d'anno.* It appears that the merchants also knew how to calculate accurately the average maturity [*adeguato di scadenza*] of several sums due at different dates; the expression used was *aguagliare in uno di.* Discount was computed not according to our current method but according to the more refined and more accurate one of true discount. The publication of the Peruzzi account books, two large manuscripts—the only ones extant from a mass of records that are lost—has not only confirmed my previous findings but also enabled me to check an enormous number of entries made by several medieval bookkeepers in the course of many years. Thereby I was able to establish the fact that these bookkeepers, far from being satisfied with approximate results, constantly avoided rounding off figures even in transactions bearing on thousands and hundreds of thousands of pounds. Nowadays accountants of large banks do not hesitate to use this shortcut. For the sake of accuracy, medieval bookkeepers also carried their divisions to very small fractions when they converted sums of money from one currency into another.

5. If at this point we ask ourselves where the merchant got his education, we must answer: either in the public schools or elsewhere. If the former is true, we must assume that the curriculum was of a higher caliber than Sombart seemed to think. At any rate, let us consider both possibilities. An examination of the *Liber Abaci* of Leonardo Fibonacci, called Leonardo Pisano, written in 1202, and of later versions prepared for teaching purposes by fourteenth-century schoolmasters shows that medieval instruction in schools was much better and more extensive than Sombart suspected. For instance, all treatises from the end of the thirteenth century onward follow Pisano and explain the computation of compound interest and discount. According to Sombart, these subjects are found only in the manuals of the fifteenth century; he disregards the fact that they are applied, in practice, in account books dating back to the very beginnings of the fourteenth century, as we have just seen.

Public instruction did not remain exclusively on what we would call the elementary level; there was also education on the secondary level. Thus a basic education and a good foundation for further development and specialization could be acquired. It is not surprising that so much emphasis was placed on education, since the political constitution of the Italian commune required the active participation in public life of a considerable and ever-increasing proportion of the population. A majority of those who were called to public office made a remarkable record, whether as members of town councils, as members of special committees, or as envoys, experts, or auditors. They displayed maturity of thought in dealing with problems of foreign or internal policy in the town councils, and they could state their point of view with an eloquence which was sometimes overemphatic but never irrelevant. Those who sat on committees as experts or "wise men" [*savi*], as they were then called, dealt successfully with difficult, controversial, and technical questions. Others must have been capable of fulfilling their missions with honor when they were sent as envoys of their native cities to princes or to the pope. Still others were called upon to serve as auditors [*calculatores* or *rationerii*] on special committees or *sindicati,* entrusted with the task of examining the accounts of outgoing magistrates. The number of those committees was the greater because of the multitude of public officials and the brevity of their terms of office (in some cities from two to six months). Those who held public office, from the highest post in the Signoria to the lowest, were all merchants or artisans, since membership in a guild was nearly always a prerequisite for the exercise of full civic and political rights. Even in the aristocratic republics none of the nobles to whom offices were reserved stayed aloof from business [*procul negotiis*], at least in the thirteenth and fourteenth centuries. The public school had to be the object of particular interest on the part of the public authorities because it was a preparation for the honorable exercise of the coveted rights of citizenship and it also enabled people to make a success of a business career. Finally, in the public schools education was fitted into the common religious and civic background.

6. Although for some of these achievements credit must be given to the schools, we should not assume that a boy, at the age of fourteen or less, left school with all the knowledge which he would possess in later life. With the exception of a few economically or intellectually privileged young men who went on to study at one of the universities, we may be sure that the average youth, after having received a sound educational background in school, perfected and completed his education in the "school of life." Such a young person worked his way up in a *fondaco* ["countinghouse"] or in an industrial shop, which he would enter as an apprentice and frequently leave as an accomplished master of his art; another part of his education was effected through the performance of his everyday duties as a citizen.

One should insist on the importance of the schooling received in the countinghouse. Certainly this schooling was largely responsible for giving uniformity to the business practices of the Italian merchants, from their way of making deals to their way of bookkeeping, and even to their calligraphy. In this connection, we should give up the widespread idea that in the Middle Ages secrecy was carried to extremes and that business secrets in particular were closely guarded, either by distrustful individuals or by particularistic statutes. Some secrecy in business is to be expected in all periods, but it was no more prevalent in the Middle Ages than it is today. I have made some holes in this theory of medieval secrecy by exploding the legend about the alleged obscurity of medieval bookkeeping, especially the contention that it was deliberately obscured. That this theory is false can also be proved by evidence regarding the formation of mercantile and banking companies, their management by a salaried staff, their supervision by public and guild authorities, and the prevalence of associations—temporary or permanent—for the purpose of dividing the risks inherent in business ventures.

Medieval companies—"companies" [*compagnie*] is the term used in contemporary sources, although they were only partnerships—were usually founded by kinsmen, but in the long run outsiders were increasingly admitted as partners. We know that such outsiders took an active part in the management. Sometimes they would transfer to another company, and naturally they then would bring with them all the information and experience which they had acquired while serving the first firm. More frequently, information was spread by agents, factors, clerks, apprentices, and errand-boys, who moved from one company to another much more easily, since such transfers did not involve the formalities connected with breaking up a partnership agreement.

The control over business by bodies politic (communes and guilds) was exercised in accordance with the regulatory tendencies of the guild system by the members themselves. Nonetheless, this control would lead to inquiries—not to say inquisitions—which gave publicity to some of the things which went on in each company. For all these reasons, it would have been futile to try to keep everything secret. Furthermore, one must not overlook the solidarity which united all the merchants of the same city in the defense of their over-all interests. This solidarity was undoubtedly stronger abroad than at home, manifesting itself in the creation of organized colonies or "universitates," headed by a consul. Another manifestation was that several firms often pooled resources to undertake joint ventures or even formed combinations resembling present-day cartels and trusts.

7. The perusal of economic, legal, and, above all, literary sources enables us to get glimpses of the life that went on in the *fondaco.* From this evidence we can construct a picture which is valid for an important part, at least, of the mercantile classes. If we do so, we get the impression that, far from being pervaded by mystery and silence, life was animated and full of conversation. The frontal part of the countinghouse, in full view of the passers-by, served, according to the regulations of the law, for transactions with customers. The clerk's desk was in a more secluded place, so that the figures which he wrote down were protected from the indiscreet glances of the curious. In the rear of the shop an ever-changing group of merchants was engaged in animated discussion. They commented on government regulations and political events that had bearing on their interests. These meetings took place every day because couriers dispatched by this or that company were constantly arriving from some place or other and leaving for various destinations, with their pouches full of mail. In the late Middle Ages, arrivals and de-

partures already followed a fixed schedule, so that one may speak of regular mail service organized with the co-operation of the entire business community. Business letters of the time were like newspapers; they contained all sorts of information, from the rates of exchange and the commodity prices quoted at the fairs to the outcome of a battle, rumors of threatening confiscations and arrests, or the prospects of obtaining new privileges from princes and governments.

While chatting, these shrewd businessmen, with a detached air, would seek to fish out information from one another. In the midst of this hustle and bustle, which was more orderly than appeared on the surface, the merchant sharpened his mind, steeled his nerves, felt the stimulus of adventure, and remained aware of the necessity for prudence. He appears to have been, and actually was, a man worthy of our admiration and representative of the greatness of his age.

In the relatively quiet corner occupied by the clerk or bookkeeper, the future merchant completed his education and applied himself to arithmetic and bookkeeping. These matters he had learned as a boy under the influence of the persuasive voice and the perhaps still more persuasive rod of his teacher. Let us visualize for a moment, seated at the clerk's desk, a real youth who had the makings of a merchant and who might have been successful if he had not died at the age of twenty-two. He was the ill-fated son of Donato Velluti. His father wrote of him in his colorful domestic chronicle:

> When he grew up I sent him to school. Since he had a good mind and remarkable ingenuity, he quickly learned how to read and write, and he impressed everybody with his ability. Thus he made such rapid progress that he finished his grammar course in a very short time. Then he was started on the abacus, and very soon he became skilled at that also. I then took him out of school and put him in the wool business, first with Ciore Pitti, then with Manenti Amidei, where he was cashier. He kept his job for several years, without much enthusiasm at first, but later he took great interest in it and was as diligent and proficient as the best young man in town. When he was promoted to bookkeeper, he kept the ledger as well as if he had been forty years old. Because of his keen intelligence and retentive memory, he would have become one of the most successful and substantial merchants of the city.

This sketch gives us additional proof that a successful and substantial merchant was a person of intelligence, with good memory, efficient in his work, and enthusiastic about his business. From the technical point of view, he had to be skillful in the use of the abacus.

8. This expression brings us back to the countinghouse and to its most secluded corner, near the desk of the bookkeeper. In that corner

were several shelves, usually built into the wall, on which the books were kept. Their number varied according to the size and importance of the company. Books were taken from the shelves whenever they were needed by the bookkeepers, either for consultation or for making new entries. Almost always one or more books in current use were lying on the desk within easy reach. Near the desk there was always a table the top of which was divided into squares, much like a chessboard. This was the large counting board. Often there was a smaller counting board, similar to the large one, and there were several bags or bowls full of *quarteruoli,* or counters, of various sizes, shapes, and colors. Somewhere within reach would be a dog-eared manual or *pratica della mercatura.* The counting boards with the counters and other accessories taken together were called the "abacus" in one of the meanings which this word had acquired by the later Middle Ages. From the beginning of the thirteenth century, the word "abacus" meant: computation by means of Arabic figures. In a stricter sense, the word was used for "commercial arithmetic." Earlier the ἄβαξ or ἀβάκιον of the Greeks, the abacus of the Romans, and the abacus of the Middle Ages until the time of Gerbert of Aurillac (Pope Sylvester II, 999–1005) had been an auxiliary device to make computations. This instrument was arranged differently, depending on the period in which it was used, but it was always composed of a flat surface with squares marked off by heavy lines, upon which counters were thrown or cast. The large counting board and its smaller counterpart were therefore both indicated by the term "abacus."

Understandably enough, no examples of counting boards have survived, but there can be no doubt that they were extensively used as computing devices. How they were operated can be imagined if one thinks of the English exchequer which was very similar to the counting boards used by the merchants. One reason why there would be no difference is that the pound, divided into 20 shillings or *soldi,* each subdivided into 12 pennies or *denari,* was at that time used in Italy as well as in England.

Further evidence regarding the use of the abacus in the *fondachi* or countinghouses is furnished by an entry in one of the Peruzzi account books regarding the purchase of an impressive number of counters for use by the Florence *fondaco,* which was the main office. According to this entry, the Peruzzi company spent about £20 11*s.* 6*d.* affiorino for 61 pounds and 5 ounces of *quarteruoli* or counters.

According to the historian Piton, the exchequer was originally a board, or table, of about 3.30 by 1.65 meters, with a raised edge 8 centimeters in height, covered by a dark cloth which was divided by six vertical and four horizontal chalked or painted lines into 35 chequers or squares, each 47 by 33 centimeters. The counters placed in the column farthest to the right represented pennies; those in the second from the right, *soldi* or shillings; those in the third, *lire* or pounds. In the fourth column one used counters each representing 20 pounds; in the fifth, counters representing hundreds; in the sixth, thousands; and in the seventh, ten thousand pounds.

A counting board of such large dimensions was suitable to the stately office of the Exchequer or Treasurer. Exercising our imagination, we can visualize the robed Chancellor accepting the vouchers of debtors and creditors of the Crown and reading the amounts to assistants, who moved the counters on the counting board accordingly. After they had completed their computations, the Chancellor would instruct other clerks to enter the totals on the rolls.

The Italian merchant did not proceed with as much formality, nor did he have as much space. He had to be content with the help of a boy or apprentice handing him his counters, while other apprentices who had just left school were looking on, learning "the lines," i.e., the use of the abacus. A merchant's abacus, being of more manageable size than the Exchequer's, could be operated by one man. In order to deal with large amounts of money, it was, however, provided with a greater number of columns and squares than was customary in the Exchequer's office. Thus in the case of the Bardi company, the total of the general balance reached the enormous figure of £1,266,775, 11*s.* and *Od. a fiorini.* In spite of its smaller squares the mercantile abacus could be operated quite efficiently. The trick used to avoid the piling up of counters in these small squares was to use counters representing multiple units which had a particular shape, color, or thickness; they could also be placed in a special order. Otherwise one might have to accumulate up to 19 counters in the square of the soldi, but in this way the number could be much smaller.[1]

11. In this study I started out by examining the account books in

---

[1] In Section 9 Professor Sapori states that the large abacus described above, the line abacus, was mainly used to add or to subtract. "For all other operations a smaller and handier form of abacus was preferred, consisting also of a counting board divided into squares, but differently arranged." The author has included drawings of the line abacus of the Exchequer variety, and of the small abacus which is described in Pegolotti's *La pratica della mercatura.* In Section 10, the merchant manual, already referred to in Section 8, is further described. Particularly important for our knowledge of medieval business is Pegolotti's manual (see *Francesco Balducci Pegolotti, La pratica della mercatura,* Allan Evans, ed. [Cambridge, Mass., Mediaeval Academy of America, 1936]).

order to ascertain the extent of the medieval merchant's notions of arithmetic. Then I investigated how the merchant acquired this knowledge, and next I have described the tools which he used constantly in the *fondaco* or countinghouse: (1) the abacus or counting boards, which helped him in making computations, and (2) the merchant manual, which was useful as a ready reckoner but was principally valuable for the wealth of information which it furnished, indispensable in the conduct of a business of any size.

The first of these two tools, the simple abacus, in the ancient meaning of the word, may evoke a smile on the lips of modern accountants because they are accustomed to the wonders of modern machinery. But they will have to admit, to their embarrassment, that the abacus, however primitive, was the ancestor of the modern calculating machine. Such a machine actually operates much as does someone who moves counters on the squares of a counting board. The historian, on the other hand, who is acquainted with the magnitude of medieval business, will find it hard to believe that all the necessary computations were made by playing with chips, as in a child's game. In my opinion, neither the smile of the accountant nor the incredulity of the historian is justified. Both are due to misapprehension of the environment in which the medieval merchant lived.

It was formerly believed that the merchant of the Middle Ages was secretive about his business, but it has been shown in this study that the life in the *fondaco* depended on the exchange of ideas and information with partners, competitors, and clients. Neither should we imagine that the medieval merchant fumbled awkwardly with his counters. It should be observed that he spent a considerable time in the abacus school to learn "the lines," until he acquired dexterity in making computations with counters. Today we are not surprised at the speed of a typist whose fingers can scarcely be followed by the eye as they strike the keys; therefore, we should not be surprised if once upon a time people's eyes could hardly follow the computer's fingers as they threw the counters upon the abacus. In that time, as well as in our own, long practice gave speed and also astonishing accuracy. It is irrelevant that these devices appear to us as rudimentary, almost as toys. What really matters is that they made possible daring enterprises the like of which the world has seldom seen in modern times, even with the aid of very complex labor-saving machinery.

How many modern privately owned calculating machines have had the honor of adding up the astronomical amounts of the debts of sovereigns or popes? The humble medieval *quarteruoli* could boast of having been used to figure the value of many princely crowns. For example, they were used by a handful of bold and determined Italian lenders to calculate the cost of financing the wars of Edward III.

The way in which merchant manuals were compiled is no doubt impressive. Just as the study of account books gives us a better idea of the medieval merchant's knowledge of arithmetic and bookkeeping, so the merchant manuals give us a correct picture of his knowledge of the kinds of merchandise and of geography. In both respects his accomplishments were remarkable. Our attitude of polite admiration for his far-flung enterprises may change into a true estimate of his stature if, through perusing the merchant manuals, we make ourselves acquainted with all the trade centers recorded therein. If we follow the old trade routes, running all the way to Cathay, the China of Marco Polo, we may be able to judge the merchant's wisdom in the selection of his routes, and we will become aware of the careful way in which he extended his trading relations. Then we must also keep in mind the close connections between industry, banking, and trade, as complementary and interrelated branches of business.

The problem of medieval marketing could be based on research in merchant manuals. One could ask: What were the channels of trade through which goods flowed from the place of their provenance to the manufacturer or consumer? Only after answering this question and related ones can we hope to get a better idea of the volume of medieval trade, based on an adequate knowledge of the facts. The victorious conquest of foreign markets by Italian cloth, for instance, will be fully understood only after we have more information about the textile industry, about its sources of raw material and dyestuffs, the manufacturing processes, and the demand for different types of cloth.

From my data and observations we can draw the general conclusion that the supremacy of Italian merchants, preceding by at least two centuries the spread of commercial capitalism to other countries, was a result not only of the favorable geographical position of their country but also of their own achievements as organizers and managers. The Italian merchant was orderly to the point of meticulousness; he was a shrewd observer and a clear thinker. Being always willing to learn, he reached a relatively high level of strictly professional competence. But he also created, by harmoniously combining his various achievements in different spheres of knowledge, a genuine mercantile culture which was broad, solid, and magnificent.

5

Capitalism—Concepts and History[*1]

By N. S. B. GRAS

Although the system of capitalism may be very old, the concept of such a system belongs almost wholly to the last hundred years. I shall deal with only five views, thereby leaving to others such additions as they think fit.

First, there is the technological concept, namely that capitalism is a system which uses capital in the form of machinery for the production of goods and services. A century ago men were impressed with the revolution that was occurring in manufacture and transportation. The key lay in the use of capital, not of workers. While Adam Smith emphasized that part of fixed capital which consisted of machinery used in manufacture, John Stuart Mill was impressed with the part used in transportation. This emphasis on fixed capital is highly important, at least as a part of an acceptable concept. In truth, however, it should be extended to include the farmer's plow and hoe and the artisan's hammer and lathe, that is, earlier and simpler instruments of production.

Second, the ethical concept of the socialists and communists is of high importance, at least for propaganda. As Marx and others thought of capitalism, exploitation of the workers was the primary ingredient. In the Communist Manifesto of 1848, while the terms "capital" and "capitalist" are used, the term "capitalism" apparently does not occur. The expression there is "bourgeois production." This is a system in which the businessman takes unto himself the value created by the worker. Both Adam Smith and John Stuart Mill held to the theory of surplus value. Capitalism then is a system that is socially iniquitous and should be destroyed. There is something of this in Sombart, especially

* *Bulletin of The Business Historical Society,* 1942, XVI, 21–34. Reprinted by courtesy of the author and Henrietta M. Larson, editor.

[1] NOTE BY HENRIETTA M. LARSON: This article is made up of parts of a much longer paper read by Professor Gras at a joint meeting of the American Historical Association and the Business Historical Society in Chicago, on December 29, 1941.

where he places the origin of capitalism in the unearned increment of urban rent, turned into foreign commerce. This produced a system which came late in human history and should be made soon to take its exit. For most journalists, many historians, and the rank and file of citizens, whether they would fight and die for capitalism or not, this concept of exploitation has become a fixed idea and therefore like religion outside the realm of rational treatment.

Third, capitalism has come to mean individual ownership as against common ownership, regardless of the ethical element. Mingled with this distinction are sundry other ingredients according to the author dealing with the subject. It is hard to justify this use, because individual ownership might be of land and labor as well as of capital. Moreover, capital would be used in a régime of common ownership.

Fourth, capitalism is a system of production in which capital predominates. Nothing is implied as to the ethical aspects of sharing the income from production. Such is the view expressed by Sombart later in his life. It is not objectionable in its direction but is, like much of Sombart's thinking, devoid of clarity and adequacy. If we take the statement literally, production becomes capitalistic when the capital elements are more than one half of the total. This is not very helpful and yet it is suggestive of something we should not forget—increasingly, capital is coming to play a dynamic and strategic part in production. Still, capital alone is barren, a fact that Sombart would not deny if it were presented to him, as his works otherwise show.

Fifth, the concept taken here to be the most significant is that capitalism is a capitalist-administrator system. It is an organization of production in which the owner of capital enters into partnership with the administrator to produce an income for all concerned—themselves chiefly but also for workers and the owners of land and other natural resources as well as the owners of trained abilities. Of course, the owner of the capital and the administrator of production might be the same person, and in fact the two were commonly identical in early times.

The essential element of capital is something produced and then saved, not used up. Into this saving of goods to constitute capital, there goes necessarily a large amount of what is found in administration—planning, forbearance, and management. Business administration, like political administration, is made up of policy-formulation, management, and control. In reality, capitalism is basically psychological. It is production in a certain way with a certain objective. It is the work of the businessman who operates in a certain way and for a certain purpose. It is in contrast to the ways and purposes of the proletarians, the landed aristocrats, and entrenched officeholders.

Behind capitalism, then, there is a will to save, to plan, to advance, to accumulate, and to attain security (for the investing capitalists and for the administrators). All persons, including workers, may join the ranks of the capitalists, if they save part of their income and plan their lives. In fact, a large number of workers are psychologically capitalists and, in a small way, actually capitalists. This existence of small owners of capital infuriates the intellectuals who would lead the proletarians into socialism or communism. Most hated by socialists and communists, in fact, are these petty bourgeois who are many in number and firm in their faith in saving and planning and managing. There is no greater error than identifying workers with the proletariat.

If capital is something created by the administrative effort of men, large and small, and if capital to be effectively used must, like labor, be administered, then the essential element in the system of capitalism is administration.

* * *

Since no one, so far as we know, has made administration the basis of capitalism, we have to stop to explain why this has not been done. To a student of business administration, putting the doing of things into the center of the picture, or making it the hub of the wheel, seems natural and inevitable. But clearly this is not obvious to others.

A large part of the difficulty of economic analysis has lain in the disposition to stress the physical. Although the idea goes far back, it was the Physiocrats who gave pointed emphasis to the general theory. They regarded land as alone productive. Adam Smith made progress in adding labor and capital, so that in his opinion there were three agents of production. He made an effort to include the businessman but he tripped up badly when, in his analysis of the capitalist, he confused interest with profits and the investing capitalist with the businessman. He knew many categories, including artisans, retailers, wholesalers, merchants, and bankers, but the full, well-rounded organization centering in the sedentary merchant he missed completely. He saw the separate parts of the business order but not the combination or living nexus centering in the sedentary merchant. Clearly, he was most impressed with the petty capitalist whose workshop or store he was familiar with. Observing the petty capitalist at work, he emphasized labor without seeing the management involved even in a petty capitalist unit. Nowhere does Smith display an accounting sense. His life was led apart from the profit system, that is, a system wherein costs of operation must be less than sales of services and goods. Perhaps we may say that, if Adam Smith had possessed a feeling for accounting, the history of the modern world would have been somewhat different.

John Stuart Mill followed Smith in accepting land, capital, and labor as the three agents of production. Any other, such as the businessman, he set down as definitely unproductive. In truth, Mill had no term for businessmen as a class: he thought the French lucky in having the word "entrepreneur."

J. B. Say, writing in 1803 and 1814, was in some way the Adam Smith and John Stuart Mill of France, but he accepted the entrepreneur as the fourth agent of production and provides us with an interesting analysis of the businessman's functions. But when the American translator of Say's book was confronted with the term "entrepreneur," he was forced to fall back upon "adventurer," a word commonly applied to the sedentary merchant of London in the time of Elizabeth and James I.

A survival of the analysis of a century ago is found in Professor Chester W. Wright's excellent *Economic History of the United States,* published early in 1941. In this book we find a recognition of the existence of the businessman and even of business itself under the heading of the "economic order," but business as a factor in production is dealt with in chapters on labor and but briefly. We are reminded of the possible influence of the old terms "wages of labor" and "wages of superintendence" found in some of the texts of classical economists.

In economic history generally there is to this day a holdover of emphasis on the physical that can be traced right back to the Physiocrats. The things that can be seen and the efforts that lie on the surface predominate. Goods are more considered than services. Land, labor, and capital are emphasized to the neglect or exclusion of business. Agriculture, trade, commerce, transportation, banking, mining, and so on are studied with little reference to administrative effort.

By the end of the nineteenth century, economists had generally come to accept four agents or factors of production, one of which was management. But they commonly robbed management (or administration) of its real key position by putting it alongside of capital, labor, and land instead of putting it in charge of the other three. If proletarian workers should turn a nation into a communistic state, they would have to develop administrators in their midst and the people of the new state would have to save collectively the capital necessary to continue operations and expand production.

During the first part of this present year (1941) there appeared in New York a book entitled *The Managerial Revolution* by James Burnham, a former follower of Trotsky. The book attempts to show that socialism is to be the new order and that therefore stockholders and financial capitalists will disappear. In the new order, where ownership will be vested in the state, the dominant position will be occupied by the managers (engineers and business technicians) and by top executives (shorn of their prepossession with profit-making). In other words, control of business in the new order will be vested in managers and executives who will receive the highest reward and become the top social class. Russia, Germany, and Italy already exemplify this change, while America, under the New Deal, limps along in the same direction. While there is much that can be criticized in this book, it deserves attention. Confused as it is in places, it has discovered the importance of management and control, or as these might better be called "business administration." Mind you, the author does not expect to see either politicians or bureaucrats occupy the seats of the mighty but the departmental managers and top executives of units of production. This work of Burnham followed by two years my book *Business and Capitalism,* which emphasizes business administration as a key to business history.

* * *

And now we turn to the history of business itself, or rather the history of capitalism, a large part of which is occupied by the history of business. I believe that the development of capitalism can be better grasped by looking at it in a very broad way, at least at first. As I see this development, there are three types: pre-business capitalism, private-business capitalism, and public-business capitalism. The first is largely prehistoric; the second constitutes the substance of business history up to date; and the third belongs largely to the future, if indeed it is to have a future.

Pre-business capitalism is that early part of human experience which we learn about from the analogy of primitive peoples, not from history. During this era, man made tools and weapons for production and defense. He learned to save food for a difficult season. He planned his crops or his nomadic pastoral pursuits. In pastoral nomadism, indeed, primitive man was quite a capitalist. His flocks and herds were meat, drink, clothing, and defense, all in one. We do not need to stop to dwell upon this pre-business capitalism, the longest period in human history, but we can note that it saw considerable progress essential to all subsequent growth and that it lived its life entirely in the era before economic towns. It was characterized by the absence of regular exchange, market price, and high specialization in production. It did have a sense of values and fluctuating supply, as seasons helped or injured production. Such was the age when men exercised their individualism more in battle than in peaceful production. It was not so much an age of little capital as of nontechnological capital objects. Accumulations in cattle and sheep, horses, and goats were sometimes large, but there were no well-filled storage houses for trade and no well-equipped workshops.

Such was not the pre-capitalistic era of Sombart which, if understood literally, is fantastic. It was not the time when man walked with God and lived at ease with his neighbor. It was a healthy beginning of something better to come, but it was a time of little supply and scant variety. What was obtained might come with great care or even prodigious labor, but it was uneven and uncertain. Business was still unborn.

The second big type is private-business capitalism. Men saved as before but now they increased their production and therefore their capacity for saving. They produced for sale to someone else. They became specialists and therefore dependent upon others. Each man or family sought an ever larger capital for himself and in this way there was more for all. Regular exchange of goods was established and market prices gradually developed. All this took place in centers that were, or were becoming, towns. These towns were to become the centers not only of material production but of general cultural creativeness. The broad base of a material foundation was being laid for subsequent civilization. After centuries of town life, metropolitan communities were to arise, and at this point we are in the midst of our own times.

The third type is public-business capitalism, or complete socialism or communism. This may be the goal, or the doom, of society but there is no evidence of such an end. The little local communistic communities have disappeared one after another. The big experiment of Russia has been able to keep up the pretense of communism only by going over to semi-socialism, and this may be on the way out. Many have discerned in Russia a transition to private-business capitalism, as a middle class of officialdom arises ready to become a middle class of businessmen. At any rate, Russia has been eminently capitalistic throughout the experiment: only the capital, which has been scarce, has been public, and the control part of administration of the capitalistic system has been political. The top executives have been politicians and not businessmen, the chief difference in this case being that the politicians are more greedy and less qualified for their work. It has been necessary to line them up against a firing wall to bring about reform. Probably there have been fewer changes at the departmental level, where technicians predominate, than elsewhere in administration.

* * *

Obviously our interest lies in the second type—the type of private-business capitalism and the accompanying flowering of our intellectual and artistic culture. The simple formula for this dual success seems to be that, when many men specialize in business, they so increase production that many others can devote all their time to art, letters, philosophy, and science. Little need be said of this, for the fact at least is history: it is a record which anyone may read, not in unbroken flow but still with remarkable growth, as business and culture rise in or near Asia Minor and spread to the ends of the earth.

Business history is not the over-all study of the getting of a living but the study of getting a living during the private-business and public-business régimes. It rises with the businessman seeking private profit and it will go on to the politican seeking public profit. It concentrates on control, policy, and management. It works on, and from, the inside. Accounting is more to the point than economic geography. Internal organization of masters and men is more to the point than legislation or piracy.

The most summary, and I think the most fundamental, treatment of business history must concentrate on the interwoven strands of efforts by businessmen to produce a profit through service. Although local conditions may vary, there is a general pattern for types of concerted effort and for change from one type to another. I have presented this subject in a book, to which I may refer any one who is interested.[2] The essence of this presentation is that there are five stages (or succeeding phases) of business, which tend to cover shorter periods of time as they come down to the present.

* * *

The first stage in business history is petty capitalism. As we know it from the records of ancient and mediaeval towns and from its recrudescence in early American history, it was a system of small shopkeepers,

[2] *Business and Capitalism* (New York, F. S. Crofts & Company, 1939).

storekeepers, hucksters, pedlars, and traveling merchants. The capital of each was small and the emphasis of the group was on economic equality which was normal and threatened only on rare occasion until the system came near to the end. Each small businessman learned his job with or without apprenticeship and in due time became a small master in his own right. Where conditions were favorable, these small masters formed gilds for protection, mutual aid, and monopolistic advantages. The products were sold on the town market, in stores, in shops where made, or from house to house. Although wholesaling existed, it was in conjunction with retailing.

The small businessman owned the capital, had full control, formulated policies, managed everything, and was the chief workman. His records were scant and his system of bookkeeping crude though adequate. His home and place of business were under one roof, unless he was a huckster, pedlar, or traveling merchant. His wife, son, and one or two apprentices constituted his helpers. Skill was personal but technique was traditional. As time went on, in towns at least, there was leisure for banquets, public discussion, holiday parades, training of military bands, musical contests, and the like. Relative variety, specialization in small enterprises, and moderate status in life were outstanding. The existence of scores of groups of specialists characterized the petty bourgeois society of this stage.

These petty capitalists created three principal orders or disciplines: the first was the business of the town, the second the government of the town, and the third the humanistic and scientific culture of the town. All put together, these constituted urban civilization, which has been dynamic and progressive, fructifying and continuous.

* * *

The new mercantile capitalism, the longest-lived of any capitalistic régime since the ancient period, grew upon the backs of petty capitalists. It was a system of wider trade, larger amounts of capital, and unprecedented growth of control, of policy-formulation, and of management, all centering in one office—a counting house. The central figure was the sedentary merchant, a merchant too wise, too occupied, too economical to travel. His distant connections were maintained by agents, traveling or resident. This sedentary merchant grew up in the ancient period but apparently had a short life in that era. In the later period he flourished from about 1300 to 1800. The outstanding sedentary merchants were called merchant princes. Some mercantile families actually attained political power and princely status. Their tastes and culture were the object of public admiration and their friendship sought by princes and emperors far and wide. Holding the purse-strings, they were often the arbiters of considerable international contests. Those who grew to be bankers loaned money to rival princes and helped decide rivalries of lasting importance, such as the imperial election of 1519.

Sedentary merchants (mercantile capitalists) came into being because of one great paramount need that the petty capitalists were not meeting. This was the need for a wider market than the town area and the town group. On the one hand, there were products within the town economic area that needed an outlet and, on the other hand, that area could use goods from other districts far and near, particularly if they could be procured at a lower price. Of course, it is obvious that widening the market would provide the group that accomplished the feat with large rewards in the form of profits. It is an old story that the class that takes the risks earns the profits, if it is on the right track. In this case it was.

Sedentary merchants organized the existing facilities of production and marketing into a larger pattern, in which importing, exporting, and wholesaling constituted the key or center. In a general way, this meant that favorably located towns would grow into larger centers and a few, later, into metropolitan cities. This meant that just as petty capitalists became subordinated to mercantile capitalists so did small towns become subordinated to larger towns. Hand in hand with this process came the gradual extension of trade in large volume to most distant seas; finally, through discovery and exploration, completely around the world. It was only through the work of mercantile capitalists that the foundations were laid and the immediate preparations made for the discoveries of America. We think of kings, the pawning of jewels, the bulls of popes, the daring of captains, without looking under the surface to the basis on which the action of all the others depended—the construction of a deeper, stronger, and richer capitalistic system to provide a surplus large enough to support not only artists, scholars, and philosophers in large numbers but also trained navigators and explorers. I do not wish to dwell upon this point, but I believe it to be true that the civilization of the late Middle Ages and the early modern period rested on the work of sedentary merchants or, in other words, on big business.

In the early years of mercantile capitalism, the sedentary merchants openly and competitively purchased their supplies of manufactured wares from petty capitalists—artisans in the town or in the country.

Commonly it was services that were purchased, or work on material supplied, as when the master saddler employed joiners, painters, and lorimers to work on his saddles. In the towns, such artisans were protected by their craft gilds; in the country there could be no effective gilds. A conflict in ideals and attitudes soon became apparent. As a petty capitalist, the artisan was slow moving, not very ambitious, working according to routine techniques. He could be little influenced by a sedentary merchant who wanted the products of his hands and his skill. Indeed, there was a conflict of management between the two classes of business capitalists. These conflicts were long and in places they were loud. In the end, the sedentary merchant won and many petty capitalists lost their economic independence: they came to be tied to sedentary merchants and forced to work as directed. In other words, the sedentary merchant introduced into manufacture the draw of the market; enthroned demand, if you will.

The sedentary merchant was the key pin of the system. He was the great policy-formulator, manager, and controller. He laid the foundations of extended trade, big business, big cities, exploration, and general culture. This is not to say that many other workers and sundry other disciplines did not enter into the building up of the material and cultural world. It was the sedentary merchant's consummate administration that made so much of so little at a time when resources were scant and heaps of jobs lay waiting to be done—but only at the magic touch of an administrator. Workers, engineers, soldiers were all necessary but individually and collectively helpless without the sedentary merchant.

* * *

The time came, however, when the key to business lay more in manufacture and transportation. A new group of businessmen arose to create an industrial revolution, the Industrial Revolution; and this destroyed the sedentary merchant. In other words, mercantile capitalists gave way to industrial capitalists. These industrial capitalists were specialists in the new techniques of power-machine production—railroading, steamship operation, distribution in inland as well as coastal regions, and so on. With the specialization went increasing size. Capital and permanently employed workers were required in business units as never before. The old scattered, flexible, almost invisible régime of mercantile capitalism was giving way to a concentrated, rigid, and strikingly prominent industrial capitalism. Factories and railroads were two of the visible evidences of the new system of production.

For centuries, mercantile capitalists had put pressure on petty capitalists to produce more and more, to get more out of themselves and out of their workers. The effect of this on manufacture has been studied. Here we can note that it caused the petty capitalists, and some workmen capitalistically minded, to turn to mechanical devices for automatic machine production and for the use of water and later steam power. There is no need to rehearse the early part of the Industrial Revolution. Only let us *not* think of the activity of Kay, Arkwright, Hargreaves, and others as labor. Their efforts lay clearly on the management side of business turning to new productive devices. Nowadays, the manager would call in an inventor. In those days the manager, or the would-be manager, turned his own mind and fingers to work to contrive a new mechanism.

We are recovering from the past a fuller knowledge of the industrial revolution which still affects us. We are commonly more interested, however, in the temporary ill effects of the revolution on the workers than we are in the social revolution in the field of administration. In fact, the world witnessed a revolution in administration without seeing it. The long submerged or controlled class of petty capitalists found their opportunity. The new production was along their line. From tools to machines was a big but a logical jump. They could make it, and in doing so they could regain their economic independence. They could overthrow the long-hated mercantile capitalist. They could attain social justice, in fact the only kind of social justice that evolving society seems to accept. A sentimental outcry may lead to a political revolution but not to an economic revolution. It is only the substantial contribution that the broad selfish view of men, in their everyday life, accepts as a worthy basis for social justice. To be sure, times may change; I do not prophesy as to the future, merely try to sum up the past.

The new industrial capitalists, whether they came from petty capitalists or mercantile capitalists, proved to have two elements of strength—one in production, the other in marketing. Perhaps the former came from the ranks of petty capitalists, while the latter descended from the mercantile capitalists. At any rate, the industrial capitalists prospered enormously in their competition with the survivors of the older régimes which still used older techniques. When the older forms of business had disappeared—by the 1860's, then competition became more and more between industrial capitalist and industrial capitalist. The spirit of ruthless competition, when exerted against the old order, merely hastened the incoming of the new; but, when directed against other members of the industrial capitalistic group, it led to diminished profits and threatened disaster. In the deep depressions of the downward secular trend which lasted in America from 1866 to 1897, efforts were made to avert disaster by doubtful practices, such as rebates and particularly drawbacks. It was necessary to resort to consolidations to cut down excessive competition. In spite of these twists and turns, bankruptcy came to many a useful firm.

We see clearly enough now that industrial capitalists, while strong in production and distribution, were weak in private finance. They did not have adequate reserves against depressions. They had no clear-cut vision of a long-run policy as against a short-run policy. They did not distinguish between fixed capital and working capital, at least not effectively. Commonly, they were long on fixed capital and short on working capital. The latter they secured from commercial banks, which in time of depressions had to demand repayment so that depositors could be satisfied.

* * *

To many persons, Wall Street was a Trojan Horse which brought dangerous gifts. Gratitude is not a well-developed human emotion. It has little existence in business or politics. The fact that Wall Street was in New York, was rich, and contributed financial services—never well understood by a debtor people—made it an easy mark for politicians, journalists, and reformers who spent more time in denouncing than in studying.

Let there be no mistake about Wall Street. The investment bankers who led it were selfish and not public spirited. They were touched off by their own interests. They ignored the feelings of the public. They were negligent of petty capitalists, including farmers. And, for a long time, they cared little about workers, who were regarded as articles to be bought at the market. And yet, the investment bankers, who wanted profits for the buyers of the securities which they sold, were doing much for America when they provided for the effective flow of savings and earnings into business. While emphasizing the fees from the sale of stocks and bonds and their profits from buying and selling stocks, these investment bankers were serving America even more than themselves. In ignoring the feelings of the people they were undiplomatic, but future historians will show that they were more up to date in their business policy than the public in its emotional thinking. In ignoring petty capitalists and neglecting labor, financial capitalists proved themselves short sighted and without a political sense. In going beyond the bounds of ordinary competition in reaching out to get from one another large masses of property in a way that disturbed the smooth operation of business, especially the working of the money market, they uncovered weak links in policy just as the industrial capitalists had disclosed weakness in their policies. It was the financial weakness of industrial capitalists that gave to investment bankers, who represented the owners of business as against the administrators, the opportunity they seized. When Wall Street gained control, financial capitalism was born. This does not mean what has been called "security capitalism"—buying and selling securities—which has been developing since at least the fifteenth century. It does not mean simply the building up of firms with colossal assets. That is incidental, not essential. It means the influence or control of investment bankers in the interest of the owners of the securities which these bankers originate and continue to sell.

Let us briefly put down some of the major policies and methods of financial capitalists: (1) to provide adequate working capital for the firms in which they were interested, (2) to build up reserves against disaster, (3) to create integrated units in order to insure supplies at reasonable costs and to prevent squeezes from the outside, (4) to diversify products in the interest of survival during depressions, (5) to give up excessive competition where that system made profits impossible, and (6) to put profits above wages.

The heights of financial capitalism were reached in America under J. P. Morgan, Sr., about 1893–1913, and under his son about 1914–29. Wilson threatened it in 1912–14, but only the depressed years 1929–33 and the New Deal régime of 1933–39 saw its eclipse. Whether under a revised form it will ever be given another chance to operate, remains to be seen. I do not mean to question the present functioning of Wall Street, though it operates at a low ebb. I deal simply with the question of predominance in business.

* * *

The latest stage in the history of private-business capitalism began about 1920. It grew to some maturity in Italy beginning in 1922 and in Germany and America beginning in 1933—in the first instance in the primary postwar depression and in the second instance in the secondary postwar depression. There is some question as to whether it should be called national capitalism or state socialism. This issue is not wholly a matter of words but largely a matter of emphasis. The central figures are not businessmen but political leaders. So far they seem to be aiming at national capitalism. Ownership and management are vested in private individuals. Control and policy-formulation are lodged in politicians of the dominant party. True, there is some nationalization of business services, but this tendency is restricted. Although we now have national capitalism in America, there is a considerable group in the dominant party that would welcome a larger measure of state socialism.

To me, there seem to be four clear facets to national capitalism. First, there is a cardinal urge to destroy financial capitalism—international Jewry in Europe and Wall Street in America. Second, the government will co-operate, must do so in times of war, with industrial capitalists. Third, there is a real desire to aid petty capitalists whether in shops or farms, though this aid is likely to be sporadic and at times a delusion. Fourth, the cream of the benefits of the new régime is to go to the new party leaders who alone can be trusted. Fifth, these leaders will share the freshly distributed benefits with the workers—the chief electorate—either directly as in Europe or indirectly through unions as in America.

The long-run tendency is to subordinate individualism, self-reliance, and saving for risk ventures in favor of a universal dependence upon the national government. Bound up with the whole régime is a degree of financial recklessness that knows no precedence. And always inherent in such recklessness is the recourse to international war.

6

*The Commercial Revolution of the Thirteenth Century**

By RAYMOND DE ROOVER

Professor Gras makes a distinction between petty capitalism and commercial capitalism and between the traveling and the sedentary merchant. The transition from the first of these systems to the second gave rise to a "commercial revolution," which occurred about the end of the thirteenth century and which cuts the Middle Ages into two periods: an earlier period up to about 1300 and a later period which includes the fourteenth and fifteenth centuries.

By a commercial revolution I understand a complete or drastic change in the methods of doing business or in the organization of business enterprise just as an industrial revolution means a complete change in the methods of production, for example, the introduction of power-driven machinery. The commercial revolution marks the beginning of mercantile or commercial capitalism, while the industrial revolution marks the end of it.

In the twelfth and thirteenth centuries the fairs of Champagne were the great gathering place which attracted traveling merchants from Flanders and Germany on the one hand and from Provence and Italy on the other. At these fairs Flemish cloth was exchanged for spices, silk, and other luxury articles from the Levant. Historians have attributed the decline of the fairs to certain ill-advised fiscal measures of the French kings, to the beginning of regular voyages of galleys between Italy and Bruges, and to the social troubles in Flanders and the war between that country and France. None of these explanations is quite satisfactory, for reasons which we cannot stop to consider here.

The real cause for the decline of the fairs of Champagne lies in the

---

* *Bulletin of The Business Historical Society,* 1942, XVI, 34–39. Reprinted by courtesy of the author and Henrietta M. Larson, editor.

The paper contains the comments made by Raymond de Roover on the preceding paper by N. S. B. Gras, during the meeting of December 29, 1941.

fact that the Italian merchants became sedentary, established permanent agencies in Bruges, and began to buy Flemish cloth in the centers of production. This new form of business organization came into being because new techniques for control and management had been gradually developed:

(1) Instead of forming partnerships for the duration of a single venture, a new type of partnership agreement was evolved: the terminal or permanent partnership, which was to last for a number of years unless it was prematurely dissolved by the death of one of the partners.

(2) The traveling merchant knew the "letter obligatory" either given under seal ("letter close") or given under the form of a deed ("letter patent," notarial act). This instrument was inadequate when merchants ceased to attend the fairs and began to work with agents and correspondents abroad. The "letter of payment," or bill of exchange, was developed to meet the need for a more practical instrument. It made possible the transfer of money from place to place without the shipping of actual coins.

(3) The greater security along the roads made it henceforth unnecessary for the merchants to convey their goods themselves and to travel in armed caravans. Goods could safely be entrusted to specialized common carriers on land as well as on sea.

(4) The development of maritime insurance made it possible to shift the sea risk to the underwriters, and consequently it was no longer necessary to divide that risk by shipping goods on different ships and by entering into partnership with several traveling merchants.

(5) The bookkeeping of the traveling merchant had been crude, though adequate for his purpose. Accounting records were merely memorandum entries of credit transactions; no record was kept of cash or barter transactions. Accounts between partners were settled very simply by deducting the expenses from the proceeds of each venture and by dividing the rest among the partners according to the rules agreed upon. This could be done on a scrap of paper.

In the late thirteenth and early fourteenth centuries, accounting advanced with great strides. One innovation of major importance was the current account kept in bilateral form, that is, the personal account divided vertically into two columns, one for the debit and one for the credit. Later, double-entry bookkeeping was introduced by adding impersonal accounts to the existing personal accounts. Good methods of bookkeeping were essential in order to keep accounts straight when two persons, residing in different cities, had numerous business dealings with each other. Merchants had to know where they stood, and accounting served as a guide by revealing profits and losses.

All these techniques were merely tools for control and management. They did not replace intelligence and common sense in the conduct of business enterprise.

The consequences of the commercial revolution may be summarized as follows:

(1) The Italians were the first to master the new techniques just mentioned. As a result, foreign trade in Western Europe became virtually an Italian monopoly. Italian supremacy did not break down until well into the sixteenth century, long after Italy itself had declined as a consequence of the geographical discoveries.

(2) The traveling merchants of Flanders, who used to visit the fairs of Champagne, were entirely eliminated. Foreign trade was taken out of the hands of the Flemings, who ceased to play an active rôle and confined themselves to acting as intermediaries. The native upper class in Bruges, during the fourteenth and fifteenth centuries, was not made up of merchants but of brokers, innkeepers, *drapiers,* and commission agents.

(3) Any investigation into the origins of capitalism should concentrate on Italian practices. There is in America a tendency to overrate the importance of England. Until the reign of Elizabeth, England was commercially backward. (It was mainly an agricultural country with wool as its principal product for export.) One example will suffice to bring this out: the bill of exchange remained unknown to English merchants until the fifteenth century.

(4) The Italians controlled foreign trade in the Levant, in Southern Europe, in France, in Flanders, and in England. For various reasons they did not penetrate into Germany. The Baltic trade, in particular, remained the monopoly of the Hanseatic League.

ITALIAN VS. HANSEATIC BUSINESS METHODS

From an economic point of view the mediæval European world did not form a geographic unit after 1300, but was divided into two areas: one under Italian influence and the other under the sway of the Hanseatic League. The principal difference between the two areas is that business methods in the Hanseatic territory were much behind Italian methods. In 1500 there was perhaps a lag of two centuries. Sweden, for example, remained in a stage of natural economy up to the end of the sixteenth century. In other words, the Hanseatic merchants were still in a stage of petty capitalism long after the Italians had reached the stage of commercial capitalism.

Nothing brings out this fact more clearly than the crudeness of German methods of bookkeeping as compared with Italian methods. Hanseatic partnerships were formed for a single venture or were loose associations involving one merchant operating from a certain trading center and another merchant from another center. In partnerships of the latter type the settlement of accounts was sometimes postponed for years. The late Finnish historian, Gunnar Mickwitz, attributed the bankruptcy of Hildebrand Veckinchusen to defective methods of bookkeeping and control. Veckinchusen was a prominent Hanseatic merchant of the early fifteenth century, whose account books are extant in Reval and whose business correspondence has been published by Wilhelm Stieda. The Hanseatic system of keeping books was more or less satisfactory as long as only two partners were involved, but it was entirely inadequate when partnerships became three- or four-cornered affairs. Accounts would soon become hopelessly entangled and lead to lawsuits and even to more serious difficulties, as the story of Hildebrand Veckinchusen exemplifies.

NO COMMERCIAL REVOLUTION IN THE SIXTEENTH CENTURY

Some historians have expressed the opinion that there was a commercial revolution in the sixteenth century, but it seems that there is little evidence to substantiate such a view. First of all, it should be clear that a shift in trade routes does not necessarily mean a change in business organization. The discovery of America did not lead to any new methods in management and control, at least not immediately. On the contrary, since the newly discovered continent was inhabited by savage tribes, an organization had to be built up from scratch, and at first it was necessary to revert to methods in use in the thirteenth century. Lately historians have come more and more to the realization that there was no breach of continuity between Bruges and Antwerp. Italian preponderance in international trade did not abruptly come to an end either, but it is true that the knowledge of accounting, of insurance, of the law merchant, of business administration spread to other European nations during the sixteenth century. Writers like Malynes and private schoolteachers were instrumental in diffusing this knowledge.

Professor Nef has pointed out that, during the period from 1540 to 1640, England overtook the other countries and became the most industrialized nation of the time. There was a considerable increase in the amount of capital invested in industry and in the size of industrial enterprise. Methods of production were greatly improved. Such progress also required increased efficiency in management and control. A study of the literature of the time would indicate that Italian methods became known in England chiefly through the translation of French and Flemish (Dutch) works published in the Low Countries.

THE IMPORTANCE OF THE PUTTING-OUT SYSTEM

Another topic which seems important for the history of capitalism, and which is closely related to the changes brought about by the commercial revolution of the thirteenth century, is the advent of the putting-out system in the textile industries. As long as petty capitalism prevailed, the artisan sold directly to the consumer or to the merchant; that is to say, industrial production was still in the retail handicraft and independent wholesale handicraft stages. The traveling merchant, being constantly on the road, was not in a position to extend his control over manufacturing. This situation changed when the sedentary merchant appeared on the scene. He began to organize production, frequently through a hired manager or by entering into partnership with someone who knew the technique of the industry.

The most outstanding work dealing with the putting-out system is still Doren's book on the Florentine woolen industry. Doren, unfortunately, was under the influence of Marx. He overlooked the fact that the Florentine cloth manufacturer did not have any influence on the price which was offered for his product or on the price which he had to pay for wool, his principal raw material. These were determined by market conditions over which the individual producer had no control. Wages also were determined independently by supply and demand, though gild regulations may have had some influence here. In any case, the Medici Manuscripts in the Selfridge Collection at the Harvard Business School do not prove that the Florentine cloth manufacturers enjoyed monopoly profits derived from an oppressive labor policy. Frequent unemployment and low wages were apparently the result of adverse business fluctuations which affected the sale of Florentine cloth. The individual producer was not responsible. The Florentine woolen industry is an early example of competitive conditions rather than of monopoly.

The existence of a competitive market with price as the regulating factor is characteristic of the capitalistic system, a point which Doren apparently missed. Price does not, of course, play any rôle in other economic systems, such as a closed village economy and a manorial economy. Under a competitive system the main task of the capitalist administrator is to bring price and cost in equilibrium.

CAPITAL UNDER MERCANTILE CAPITALISM

From the standpoint of the economic theorist an essential difference between industrial and commercial capitalism depends upon the nature of capital accumulation under both systems. Under mercantile capitalism, capital is largely a stock in trade or a revolving fund which is used to buy raw materials and to pay wages and which is replenished by the sale of the finished product. Little is invested in productive equipment, with perhaps two notable exceptions: the shipping and the mining industries. Industrial capitalism, on the contrary, presupposes large investments in equipment before production can really start. Depreciation, maintenance, and overhead thus become important elements in figuring cost. An example will make this clear: depreciation in one of the sixteenth century Medici partnerships for the manufacture of woolen cloth was less than one per cent of cost. In other words, depreciation was practically negligible. Overhead amounted to only ten per cent. Direct costs were consequently the determining factor.

* * *

To conclude, I should like to point out that many of the statements which I have just made are generalizations and may need to be qualified, since there are always in history many exceptions to the rule. Synthesis, however, is not possible without some general concepts and a method of approach. Professor Gras provides both by his emphasis on forms of business organization and on the problems of management and control. Professor Gras is right in placing the rise of the sedentary merchant in the focus of our attention. He thereby makes a contribution of great value which, in my opinion, gives the clue to a correct interpretation of mediæval economic, social, and business history.

7

*Family Partnerships and Joint Ventures in the Venetian Republic**

By FREDERIC C. LANE

I

Corporations have been the big basic units of recent American business; in the Venetian Republic the basic units of business life were family partnerships. To be sure, since a Venetian family partnership was not an organization formed for business purposes only, it did not correspond exactly to a corporation. There were in the Venetian economy during the Later Middle Ages some enterprises which required the use of so much capital that normally several families banded together to spread the risks and for such occasions they formed joint ventures. From some points of view these joint ventures, rather than the family partnerships, corresponded in Venetian economy to the corporation in modern economy; for they were organized for strictly business purposes, they involved large capitals, and their ownership was divided into shares. But the joint ventures lacked the permanence of the modern corporation and they had quite limited objectives. They lasted only for the duration of a voyage or until a cargo had been sold. Moreover, they did not have so large capital funds as did the family partnerships which created them. Venetian business enterprise, having been fathered by the state and mothered by the family, remained subordinated to these older and stronger institutions. This fact is not surprising, for when viewed in historical perspective the modern corporation appears a parvenu of uncertain future. In most societies, at most times, it has been the great family which by its wealth, power, prestige, and presumption of permanence has been the outstanding institution in private economic enterprise.

---

* *Journal of Economic History,* 1944, IV, 178–96. All footnotes have been omitted, because of the relative inaccessibility of the sources used. Reprinted by courtesy of the author and New York University Press.

As late as the sixteenth century Venice presented a fine example of family capitalism in the *fraterna* or the family partnership. Originally *fraterne* derived their existence from the physical fact that brothers often lived together in the same house, shared the same board, and consumed together the products of their country estates. Under Venetian law members of a family thus living together and doing business as a unit automatically became full partners without any formal contract. Even after the family partnership became the dominant form of business organization in Venice, it continued to be more than a mere business partnership. All the property inherited from the father—houses, land, furniture, and jewelry as well as ships and merchandise—was entered on the books of the *fraterna* unless withdrawn from it by special agreement. Expenditures for food and household furnishings, as well as business expenses, were recorded in its ledgers along with the big sales and purchases which kept merchandise moving through Venice.

Many men prominent in Venetian politics belonged to family partnerships which were the leading business firms of the city. One example mentioned by chroniclers is the Doge Andrea Vendramin, elected in 1476. In describing him at the time of his election, Malipiero says he was very rich, worth 160,000 ducats. This may have been but the fragment of his fortune left him in his old age after he had spent very liberally on his political career. Especially noteworthy among his political expenses were the dowries of 5,000 to 7,000 ducats which he had given with each of his six daughters in order to have influential sons-in-law. In his youth, continues Malipiero, "he was a great merchant and when in *fraterna* with his brother Luca they used to ship enough merchandise from Alexandria to load one and a half or two galleys, and he had many factors who have grown rich managing his affairs; . . . ."

As late as the sixteenth century, leadership in government and in business was combined. An active politician and the leading banker of Venice between 1509 and 1528 was Alvise Pisani. He survived a number of runs on his bank, saving the situation during the most serious run in 1499 by a skillful personal appeal to the crowd on the Rialto, and at one time he concentrated in his hands nearly all the banking business of the state. When the bank of Lorenzo di Tassis in Rome failed in 1518, Alvise Pisani learned of it earlier than did Lorenzo's brother Andrea who was in Venice at the time. Consequently Pisani was able to make good his claim against Andrea di Tassis before the latter could get away. The Florentines and Genoese lost heavily, but the Venetians did not.

Like the Doge Andrea Vendramin, Alvise Pisani spent freely for political advantage. He, too, married his daughters (he had five) to members of families of political influence, and it cost him 40,000 ducats in dowries. One of his sons was a wealthy cardinal. He himself was frequently a member of the highest councils of the Republic, and although he did not attain the highest office, the dogeship, he received a number of votes in one ducal election. Even his death was in a sense a success, for he died in the service of his fatherland when the army with which Venice and her allies were besieging Naples was decimated by the plague. The solvency of his bank was celebrated four months later when his son, dressed in black and surrounded by many of the highest dignitaries of the state, came forth from the celebration of Mass in the church on the Rialto, signaled for the sounding of trumpets and fifes, and ordered the scarlet-clad public crier to proclaim that the bank was to be liquidated and that all who wished might come and receive their money.

Alvise's mercantile operations were carried on in co-operation with his brothers, Lorenzo and Almorò. They died about 1528 also and some account books of the executors and heirs of Almorò survive in the Frari at Venice. Although Venetian sources constantly refer to such *fraterne* as those of Vendramin or Pisani, no ledger of an equally rich *fraterna* or individual has been found among surviving account books. Consequently the Pisani books come as near as any that have survived to affording a glance into the organization of big business in Venice.

Another glance, from a different angle, is offered by the Journal of Lorenzo Priuli, also a holder of the highest offices beneath the dogeship and father of the well-known banker and diarist, Girolamo Priuli. The Pisani and Priuli families were connected through Vincenzo Priuli's marriage to a daughter of Alvise Pisani. Besides being an active naval officer, at one time commanding the merchant galleys of Beirut, Vincenzo was active in the business of importing wool from England. Girolamo Priuli kept his bank in his own name, but Vincenzo's operations in wool and many other transactions handled by him, by Girolamo, and by a third son, Francesco, are described in Lorenzo's book. It is the central record (1505–35) of the management of another large family fortune.

A third glimpse into big business comes from the letter book of Michele da Lezze. He was named, together with Alvise Pisani, as one of the ten richest men in Venice, but the operations recorded in his letters are disappointingly small and surprisingly simple. His letters and the Priuli Journal have the advantage of being a moving record and therefore of telling more about the methods of business operations than do the surviving Pisani books, although neither opens with any sort of inventory. They do not give an over-all view of a family fortune as do the Pisani ledgers.

II

The wealth of the three Pisani brothers once totaled close to 250,000 ducats and possibly more, for Alvise's wealth may have exceeded greatly that of the other brothers. The surviving books certainly fail to give a full indication of Alvise's property. By some earlier division of the family inheritance he had acquired title to the family palace on the Canal Grande at Santa Maria Zobenigo. This is commonly called the Palazzo Pisani-Gritti, recently a part of the Grand Hotel. Alvise's ownership is revealed incidentally through the fact that the other brothers paid him rent for an upper floor. How much else Alvise owned personally, either in real estate or in liquid funds, and how much claim if any he had on the possessions of the family partnership is not clear. Probably he had withdrawn earlier from the family estate as his share a sum at least as large as that which remained for the other, less prominent brothers.

The investment of the Pisani family wealth was widely diversified and shows the forms of investment then available to men with capital. A very sizable amount was in real estate on the mainland. At Boara near Rovigo a factor named Paul the Winehead (Paolo Capo di vin) collected rents for them from an estate valued at 20,000 ducats. At Treviso the Pisani owned the mills which stood then, as mills do today, above the streams flowing through that city. The holdings in government bonds reached an impressive total on their books. The market value of these government bonds was much less than their book value; just how much less varied greatly from year to year with the fortunes of war. Of the commercial assets taken over by the executors when the brothers died in 1528, the biggest was a shipment worth 5,378 ducats sent to Constantinople, but there were many worth between 2,000 and 4,000 ducats. Another part of the *fraterna's* capital was in merchandise *in monte,* that is, wares being held in Venice in the basement of the family palace or in warehouses. Very little was being held in bills of exchange, but this may well have been because exchange operations were left to Alvise's bank, in which the *fraterna* had a tidy balance. Perhaps the Pisani made some restrictions about what wares they would handle but no sign of it appears. Their funds moved a heterogeneous collection of commodities—cloth, wool, tin, salt, grain, spices, bow-wood, and many others.

In addition to moving wares in international commerce, the Pisani *fraterna* sold a great deal to retailers and manufacturers in Venice. They helped finance the local woolen industry, not by going into partnership with the cloth manufacturers but by supplying them with their materials. When the executors took over the *fraterna's* affairs, 5,000 to 6,000 ducats were invested in wool which was being made into cloth or was already in cloth in the finishing processes. The Pisani partnership gave out the raw materials and received in return the finished products. Yet the individuals in the woolen trade with whom the Pisani dealt were not craftsmen but gentlemen with *Ser* before their names. Perhaps there was a sort of double putting-out system in Venice. The Pisani, and other merchants who imported wool and cloth, "put it out" to merchant employers who, in turn, "put it out" to the craftsmen. But the Pisani could and did supply from their warehouses the needed dyestuffs as well as the wool or cloth.

Diversification was also evident in the investments of the Priuli family. They received rents from real estate in Venice and grain for their household from their country place. The sons traded with family funds in spices, silver, cloth, and a variety of government obligations as well as in wool. Vincenzo sold the imported wool to the *drapieri* of Venice on two or three years' credit. A balance sheet for any year from 1505 to 1510 would probably have shown a substantial portion of the Priuli's assets in this sort of commercial accounts receivable. Michele da Lezze similarly traded in spices from Egypt, wool from England, gold from Barbary, and so on.

The commercial investments of a family partnership could be supplemented by those made by brothers individually and this was done by the Pisani. While the *fraterna* owned some property and carried on some commercial operations, each of the Pisani brothers also held property in his own name and engaged in business activities on his own account. In case of bankruptcy it might have been difficult for one brother to avoid liability for the debts of the others, but the separate accounts of the brothers could certainly affect the way they assigned profits among themselves.

The money which a brother invested in his own name might be obtained from his wife's dowry or from a separate legacy. It could also be had in great amount by borrowing from the partnership. Both

Almorò and Lorenzo were in debt to the Pisani *fraterna* for about 43,-000 ducats when they died. Alvise Pisani and his son Giovanni together owed the family partnership about 10,000 ducats. Some of the sums thus drawn from the *fraterna* may have been used for personal expenses and have ceased to exist as capital. A good deal of it, however, was certainly used in commercial operations distinct from and yet somehow connected with those of the *fraterna*. This connection is evident in many partnerships which may in a certain sense be considered subsidiaries of the family partnership.

The clearest examples of such affiliated partnerships are the "Western" or London Company and the Syrian Company. "The London Company," as I shall call it, was a partnership among Lorenzo Pisani, Almorò Pisani, and Nicolò Duodo. Since this company was also referred to as "Nicolò Duodo e Cia," Duodo appears to have been the active partner. How much of the capital he contributed, if any, cannot be determined. The sum due Lorenzo and Almorò when the executors took over appeared on the books at a book value of 8,248 ducats. The assets actually consisted entirely in bills payable, presumably credit balances which were left over from many years of operation and which included many bad debts. The heirs or executors were willing to release all their claims in favor of Nicolò Duodo if he would pay them half that sum. Besides the amount which Nicolò Duodo, as manager or survivor of the London Company, owed to his partners Lorenzo and Almorò, the London Company as a whole owed to the Pisani *fraterna* 5,500 ducats. This debt did not represent the unsettled balance due on shipments from Venice to London. It was called "per conto a parte," that is, it was a special credit extended by one of the partnerships to the other. At the same time, as has been said, Almorò and Lorenzo were debtors on the books of the *fraterna* of which they were members. In brief, the situation at the liquidation of the partnership was as follows: Nicolò Duodo owed money to Lorenzo and Almorò, his partners in the London Company; these brothers owed money to their family partnership; and the London Company also was in debt to the Pisani family partnership. This network of debts justifies calling the London Company an affiliate and the Pisani *fraterna* the major company.

The affairs of the London Company show how the sums withdrawn by the brothers from the family partnership could be used to set up a branch company to act as their agent. A similar subsidiary company devoted to the Syrian voyage was managed for the Pisani by Giovanni della Riva. The subordinate position of the company is clearly implied by Della Riva's previous career. From 1507 to 1516 he was the salaried agent of the family in Syria, first at 120 ducats a year as a mere factor, and later at 250 ducats a year as branch manager in charge of the warehouse or workshop which he had built for the Pisani at Aleppo. Finally he was made a partner in the Syrian Company.

The three companies named—the parent *fraterna,* the London Company, and the Syrian Company—acted as agents for each other in buying and shipping or in receiving and selling. As we do not have the ledger of the *fraterna* itself, but merely excerpts carried from it into the executors' books, we have very few examples of how this worked in practice. One interesting entry does show, however, that the Syrian Company shipped cotton to the London Company. This probably does not imply any direct voyage from Syria to London, but it does mean that the cotton was consigned by the Syrian Company directly to the order of the London Company. When the cotton was lost by shipwreck, the London Company bore the loss.

While the relation to the *fraterna* of these two affiliates is fairly clear, a number of other associations illustrating the many ramifications of the Pisani business are mentioned without enough detail to define their position. Spanish associates were referred to cryptically in the will of Lorenzo Pisani. Giovanni Francesco Pisani e Cia in the "West" and Vincenzo Pisani in Syria appear to have been minor subsidiaries designed to give young men of the family a chance to try their skill. Of salaried factors in foreign market places there is no mention except for Giovanni della Riva who was ultimately taken into partnership. Consequently we are left to assume that these partnerships were enough to supply at key places the loyal agents needed for extensive international operations. Elsewhere ordinary commission houses may have given adequate service.

A very special affiliate of the family was the bank of Alvise Pisani. The bank had been inherited as a going concern from the father, Giovanni, who had run it with his brother, Francesco. It was clearly a separate firm. The deposit of the *fraterna* in the bank was about 2,500 ducats and those of Almorò personally were considerably larger, but since the total deposits in Alvise's bank were probably over 250,000 ducats, its debts to the Pisani family do not seem sufficiently large to place the bank in a dependent position. There is no reason to think the bank paid any interest on these deposits or that the brothers shared in any way in the profits Alvise may have made from his bank. If there was a mutually profitable relation between the *fraterna* and the bank, it was probably connected with the buying and selling of bills of exchange.

III

Besides acting through relatively permanent subsidiaries, the Pisani *fraterna* conducted its affairs through a number of strictly temporary partnerships formed for a particular purchase or a particular voyage. These temporary associations of capital were of great importance to Venetian economy. In a strict legal sense, at least in Venetian eyes, they may not have been true partnerships at all but arrangements for joint ownership and for conferring power on a common agent. In regard to joint ownership, the object owned could often be physically divided among the owners. This actually might have been done in the case, for example, of a cargo of salt which the Pisani *fraterna* and two or three other merchants jointly imported and sold to the Salt Office. In practice the cargo jointly owned was not usually divided but was sold by one of the joint owners who acted as agent for the others.

By extension, joint ownership was applied to objects which could not in a physical sense be divided. If the cost of an operation was high enough to place a strain on any single family fortune, the liability could through a temporary partnership or joint venture be divided among a number of distinct investors. The farm of the wine tax for a year usually ran to about 70,000 ducats. By holding some shares in the farm, the Pisani assumed less risk than if they had put the whole 70,000 ducats, something like a fourth of their wealth, into that one venture.

Among these temporary partnerships, or agreements for joint ownership and agency, the associations of capitalists to finance the voyages of the merchant galleys are of special interest. More capital was involved in these voyages than in any other type of enterprise in the Venetian economy. A fleet of three or four galleys employed a crew of 600 to 800 men and the voyage to Flanders took at least a year, often nearer two years. The cargo carried by a fleet of the Flemish galleys was worth about 250,000 ducats. The relatively short voyage to Alexandria required only three to six months, but the cargoes were often valued at half a million ducats. The cost of these galleys, of their fittings, of food and wages for the crews, and especially of the cargoes exceeded the resources of even as rich a family as the Pisani.

By a system of renting galleys, the state supplied an important part of the needed capital. Ever since the middle of the fourteenth century, great merchant galleys had been built almost exclusively by the Arsenal of the Republic. When the Senators decided that a fleet of galleys should sail, they stipulated the route, the size of the crew, and many of the freight rates. Sometimes the Senate offered a subsidy with the galleys. Then the galleys were put up at auction and the operation of the galleys for a specified voyage was awarded to the highest bidder, provided the successful bidder was subsequently approved by the Senate as a capable person of proper age with reliable financial backers. If approved he became galley master, the *patron.*

Because galleys were leased by the state, wealthy families such as the Pisani and the Priuli had less incentive to own ships. Without this action of the state, they would have needed galleys of their own in order to make sure of being able to send their wares. An investment in merchant galleys might have led to the maintenance of a small private replica of the Arsenal or to the financing of various shipbuilding and shipowning partnerships as relatively permanent subsidiaries. Of course, if the Pisani partnership had been interested in routes or commodities not served by the merchant galleys, especially if they had been pioneering the exploitation of a new route, then they would have needed their own ships. Since there is no mention of shipowning or shipbuilding partnerships in either the Pisani or the Priuli books, it appears that they were content to operate in well-tested branches of trade and mainly in the types of merchandise carried by galleys. Consequently they did not need to worry about the long-run overhead costs of a merchant fleet. They could rent a galley for one voyage, assume the overhead of that voyage only, and then turn the galley back to the Arsenal on which fell all the problems of overhead costs.

Although the state, by keeping galleys for rent, supplied part of the capital engaged in the voyages, most of it was private capital and was supplied by *fraterne.* One of these family partnerships might have borne practically the whole cost and risk of a galley or two, but generally costs and risks were shared among a number of *fraterne* which entered into temporary partnerships with each other or with persons of wealth. Some of these partnerships were galley partnerships, others were called *maone,* partnerships of the whole fleet.

The galley company which put up the money to rent and outfit the ship was the most basic of the partnerships centering around the individual galley. This "company of the galley" was divided into twenty-four shares (*carati*) on the model furnished by shipowning partnerships. The shareholders were commonly called *parcenevoli* and might own so much that the *patron* was really their employee. Although the surviving records of the Pisani are only excerpts from the *fraterna's* books, they show that the Pisani invested at least three times in Barbary galleys, at least once in a Beirut galley, and twice in Flemish galleys.

How much outlay of capital was involved in such investments? The ideal sources from which to answer this question would be the accounts of the galley kept by the *patron* or by the official clerk, the *scrivan.* The Pisani books and entries in the Priuli Journal supply only tantalizingly incomplete clues. Lorenzo Priuli and Sons owned eight *carati,* that is, one third, of the galley company of which Federigo Morosini was *patron.* Their galley was one of the three "Flemish" galleys which made a quick voyage, leaving Venice in September 1504 for England and returning in October 1505 with a full cargo. The *patron* reported to Lorenzo Priuli and Sons in April 1507 that the total "cost" of the galley amounted to 7,503 ducats and 7 grossi. But just what "cost" this figure represents is very hard to say. It is probably a sort of net cost in the "West," figured by the *patron* by deducting from his total expenses in England the amount of freights he had collected there. (Some freights were payable in England, others in Venice.) Figures of the same order of magnitude occur in the balances of the galley accounts in the Pisani books. Their twelve shares of a galley of Flanders in the fleet which sailed early in 1518 was debited for 4,220 ducats, and their shares in the galleys of Barbary of 1519–1521 were carried at just about the same amount. These balances appear to represent also the amounts spent on the galley in excess of the receipts collected by the *patron* from shippers during the voyage. The cost above receipts of each galley had to be advanced by its *parcenevoli.* It was paid back to them by assigning them their shares of the galley's accounts receivable, namely, their shares of the freights payable in Venice after the galley's return, and, in some cases, their shares of the subsidy which the Senate had offered with the galley. Consequently these "costs" are some indication of the amount of capital advanced for the voyage, but the total required from *parcenevoli* before and during the voyage may have been much larger. Perhaps the figures of 7,500 ducats or 8,000 ducats should be doubled or tripled to represent the full amount of the outlay above receipts which had to be paid out during the voyage of a Flemish galley. Even so, the sums involved were small compared to the wealth of a family such as the Pisani.

If the Flemish voyage had involved only the cost of operating galleys, there would hardly have been need of share-owning partnerships to spread the risk among several families. But the *parcenevoli* had other and heavier commitments at the same time. The big investment was in the cargoes. Of course, the cargo worth a quarter of a million ducats brought by a fleet of three of the Flemish galleys was made up of wares owned by a great number of different shippers who had no partnership among themselves and who did not need any such association in order to ship. The galleys were regulated by the Senate as if they were public carriers and they were obliged to load the most important items in their cargoes at rates fixed by law. But the *patroni* and *parcenevoli* of the galleys could expect some favor in the loading of their wares. At least they had assurance that their wares would not be those left behind if the galleys were crowded and would not be put where they were most likely to be wetted by the sea. If merchants were going to invest in the operation of a galley, they had incentive to invest also in its cargo. Moreover, they might need to do so to make sure that there was enough cargo and that their galley did not sail half empty. In practice, the same persons or families that financed the operation of a galley for a voyage financed also a good part of its cargo.

The investment of the Priuli in the Flemish galleys of 1504 consisted not only in their share in the galley company but also in the use of family funds to buy cargo. They purchased in three ways—individually, jointly with other members of the galley company, and jointly with all the shareholders of all the galleys of the fleet. By far the largest outlay was made directly by the family through the purchase for its account of wool, cloth, and oxhides worth about 10,000 ducats. This may be considered the center of the whole venture from the point of view of the Priuli. Collections from the sales of the wool were to be a main income of the family for some time. Their investment in the galley company was very probably a subordinate investment made for the purpose of being sure of getting the wool.

Just as desire to obtain wool led to joining in a galley company so that the galleys would sail, the ownership of shares in the galley company led in turn to other purchases. Some were for the purpose of assuring an adequate cargo. The Priuli joined for one third, the amount of their share in the galley, in the purchase of 200 *botte* of Cretan wine, *malvasia,* bought by the *patron,* Ser Federigo Morosini. Had there been enough spices to fill the outgoing galleys, there would have been no occasion to buy wine. Indeed, wine could not be loaded on the galleys until all spices that were offered had been loaded. Consequently the Cretan wine was usually sent to England by the large high "round ships." But, as Girolamo laments in his diary with all the more vehemence because his family was involved, spices were not being shipped to the West from Venice in 1504 because spices were arriving from India in Portugal. The *patroni* had to buy wine to fill their vessels.

While some joint purchases were made by the *patroni* and *parcenevoli* of a single galley, others were made jointly by all the *patroni* and *parcenevoli* of the fleet. The purchase of wine to complete the cargo for the outward voyage was arranged separately for the Morosini galley, but a purchase of lead for the return trip was made jointly for all the galleys. Such a union of all the shareholders in the ships of the fleet, of all the *patroni* and *parcenevoli* of all the galleys, was called a *maona*. Joint activity by this whole group has been little noted, and historians of Venice have seemed unaware of the existence there of any business organization called a *maona*. In truth, the Venetian *maona* may be considered more important because of its potentialities than because of what it actually was. It is an instructive case of what proved in the end to be arrested development.

A number of purposes might lead to the formation of a *maona*. Sometimes the Senatorial regulation of the voyage stipulated that the freights of all the galleys in the fleet be pooled in one fund, and in that case the *patroni* were almost compelled to make some supplementary agreement for the administration of that fund. Even when the Senate made no such rule, the *patroni* had a common interest in seeing that there was adequate cargo for the fleet as a whole. It was the common practice of merchants to split up their shipments and load part of their wares on each galley so as to lessen the danger of loss from shipwreck. Consequently no one galley could expect to go full while the others went empty, and to a certain extent good cargo for one meant good cargo for all. A way of trying to assure good cargo for all was for the *maona* to agree to joint purchases that would help to fill the galleys. The lead bought for the account of the *maona* to which Lorenzo Priuli belonged was quite possibly bought jointly to ensure that each galley had enough ballast.

Assurance of adequate cargo for the whole fleet was indubitably the purpose of a *maona* contract referred to by Michele da Lezze, the wealthy contemporary of Alvise Pisani and Lorenzo Priuli. Michele da Lezze owned a third of one of the Barbary galleys of the fleet of 1506. Writing to his son Luca who was going on the voyage as a *patron,* Michele refers more than once to the *maona* formed by the *patroni.* They had agreed, in order to have a satisfactory loading of wool in Valencia, that each of them would buy his share up to the amount of 500 sacks if that were necessary to bring the total cargo of wool up to 2,000 sacks. Although this did not necessitate joint action, it gave occasion for it, and in fact the *patroni* agreed to handle the wool as a unit.

The need of the individual galley for funds to cover operating expenses and the need of the whole fleet for cargo induced some agreements for joint action on the part of the galley company in the one case and of the *maona* in the other. Joint action was also stimulated by the desire for monopoly or for a favorable bargaining position. Merchants generally were on the lookout for ways of making agreements to effect some temporary monopoly or near monopoly. Groups that had learned to act together as a galley company or as a *maona* seeking cargo could the more easily act together to prevent competition.

Desire to avoid competitive bidding may have been one motive for making jointly the purchases of wine and of lead in which the Priuli shared, and it may have been behind the handling as a joint account of the wool bought by the *maona* to which Michele da Lezze belonged, although only as a secondary motive. It was plainly an important consideration in a contract among *patroni* and *parcenevoli* of the Flemish galleys of 1487 which provided for joint action on behalf of the *patroni* in the sale of soap in London or at ports along the way. In addition to arranging to avoid competition in the sale of soap in London, these *patroni* of the *maona* of 1487 agreed that fifty to sixty thousandweights of gallnuts should be bought jointly by a single agent in Venice and should be sold, similarly, all on a joint account, by one of the *patroni.* These agreements gave no assurance of complete monopoly, but their signers at least renounced competitive bidding among themselves.

Altogether, there were substantial motives pushing the *patroni* and *parcenevoli* of each fleet into associations and partnerships of various kinds. Desire to suppress competition among themselves gave an impetus to general merchandising agreements, but more insistent were the needs for pooling operating expenses and for making sure of full cargoes. These motives arose from the very nature of the enterprises in which the merchants were engaged, just as, in later times, trading between England and India or the building of railroads created, from the nature of those enterprises, motives for large-scale business organization.

Had the Venetian government kept its hands off the merchant marine, there would have been real need in Venice of turning the *maone* into better organized and more permanent institutions. If the state had not supplied the galleys, private merchants would have had to tie up their funds in galleys and in ships' stores. Possession of this enduring physical equipment would have given the *patroni* and *parcenevoli* reason for making more permanent combinations to assure profit on the future use of their investment. As it was, the state intervened; it supplied the galleys, determined the basic freight rates, and appointed the fleet commander needed for common protection. Thus the galley company and the agreements of the *maona* were encouraged to remain only temporary joint ventures because the government required merchant operators to charter the merchant galleys anew for each voyage. Since the state did so much, the famed Venetian galley voyages created no need for any private business institution having either the longevity of the corporation or the large capital and the large powers of command which are organized in the corporation. A variety of agreements, each temporary and each providing for only a relatively small part of the needed capital investment, sufficed to finance the voyages of the merchant galleys.

IV

Senatorial initiative and regulation, changing slightly from year to year, rich family partnerships of relative permanence, and joint ventures of a few years' duration—all three together formed the structure of Venetian business. It was a very flexible structure. Under it, Venetian mercantile capital was kept liquid and could be moved rapidly from one branch of trade to another. The family firms could invest one year in the Barbary voyage or in wool imports from England. Another year, if the trip to Barbary was too dangerous or if the Venetian market was overstocked with English wool, the funds of the great families could be used to import spices from Egypt or Syria. Under Senatorial direction the same galleys went first on one voyage, then on another; similarly, through the medium of joint ventures, investments went first into one field of trade, then into another. Neither a galley company nor a *maona* created any vested interest in a particular voyage. Each had a minimum of overhead and was dissolved as soon as it had served the special purpose for which it was created. Investment in such companies was in harmony with the efforts of the rich family partnerships to spread their risks, and their policy of diversification helped in turn to keep fluid Venetian mercantile wealth as a whole.

Diversification and flexibility were generally desiderata in the affairs of the resident merchants who were the typical capitalists of the Later Middle Ages. But these qualities were even more emphasized in Venice than in most commercial centers. This emphasis explains why Venice appears in certain respects old-fashioned in the age of the Fuggers. Although she was then a leader of Europe in many aspects of capitalistic business practice, Venice lagged behind in the development of the joint-stock company, which began to appear elsewhere in the fifteenth century, and in the sixteenth became a regular feature of the mining industry, oceanic commerce, and colonization. Compared to Florence or Genoa, Venice was behind also in the development of general business partnerships designed to live for many years independent of family ties and to earn profits on a definite fund of commercial capital. While the use of general business partnerships and embryonic forms of chartered joint-stock companies was spreading elsewhere, family partnerships continued to dominate in Venice, supplemented by short-lived joint ventures. This "backwardness" of Venice in business organization should not be considered a sign of stupid traditionalism, however; a tendency for the Venetian galley companies or the *maone* to develop into joint-stock companies of some permanence, with policy and personnel of their own, was checked by the fact that this would have introduced into the Venetian economy undesirable elements of rigidity.

Reasons why the Venetians especially should fear rigidity in business organization are not hard to find. To the best of her ability Venice made herself the universal middleman. Some cities were relatively specialized: cloth trades were the main basis of Florentine prosperity; Ulm depended largely on a particular kind of cloth, fustian; and Augsburg merchants combined the cotton and fustian trade with financing princes and handling the overland exchange between Italy and the North. In comparison, Venetian merchants had open to them an unusually wide range of commercial opportunities—in Constantinople, Syria, Spain, England, and many other regions, and in spices, cotton, wool, and many other commodities—but their group of opportunities was continually changing. While all international commerce of the time was subject to violent interruptions, the commerce of Venice was especially full of sudden vicissitudes because her geographic position had been exploited to make Venice a "world market." Consequently Venetian merchants needed flexibility.

Geography is only a permissive factor, however, not a compelling factor in history. The respect for the integrity of state power which distinguished Venice from the other medieval Italian cities was a vital element in the development of Senatorial control over navigation. Venice was also noted among the Italian cities for her patriarchal character; the family was exceptionally important in her government and society as well as in her economy. These traditions were in constant interaction with the social and geographic environment of the Venetians. Faced with an economic situation which called for business forms of great flexibility, the Venetians found in the supervisory role of the Senate, in the great family partnerships, and in short-lived joint ventures institutions that met the economic need and also were in harmony with their inherited ideals of state leadership and family solidarity.

8

*Origins of the American Business Corporation**

By OSCAR HANDLIN and MARY F. HANDLIN

I

The concentration of business enterprise in corporate structures at the end of the last century called the attention of scholars to the history of the business corporation, the chartered joint-stock company. Even those who agreed that "the honour of originally inventing these political constitutions entirely belongs to the Romans" realized that their modern economic functions were relatively recent and demanded explanation.[1] In this country, Williston's brilliant essay, the studies of Simeon Baldwin, and a number of other investigations probed into the origin and nature of the institution at about the period when it became a pressing social issue.[2]

Thinking of the corporation in terms of what they saw about them, most writers, whatever their attitude toward its impact on society, agreed that it was logically, naturally, admirably adapted to American economy. Since this form was "the greatest single discovery of modern times," without which "even steam and electricity . . . would be reduced to

---

* *Journal of Economic History,* 1945, V, 1–23. Reprinted by courtesy of the authors and of New York University Press.

[1] For Roman origins cf. William Blackstone, *Commentaries on the Laws of England,* Vol. I, E. Christian, ed. (London, 1793), p. 468; Charles C. Abbott, *Rise of the Business Corporation* (Ann Arbor, Edwards Brothers, 1936), pp. 20 ff. However, the absence of a link between Roman and modern business forms was demonstrated by Max Weber, *Zur Geschichte der Handelsgesellschaften im Mittelalter nach südeuropäischen Quellen* (Stuttgart, 1889), pp. 3–14; also Karl Lehmann, *Die geschichtliche Entwicklung des Aktienrechts bis zum Code de Commerce* (Berlin, 1895), p. 3.

[2] Samuel Williston, "History of the Law of Business Corporations before 1800," *Harvard Law Review,* 1888, II, 105ff., 149 ff.; S. E. Baldwin, "History of the Law of Private Corporations in the Colonies and States," *Select Essays in Anglo-American Legal History . . . Compiled by . . . the Association of American Law Schools,* Vol. III (Boston, Little, Brown & Co., 1907–9), pp. 236 ff.; *idem, Modern Political Institutions* (Boston, Little, Brown & Co., 1898); *idem,* "American Business Corporations before 1789," *Annual Report of the American Historical Association . . . 1902,* Vol. I (Washington, 1903), pp. 255 ff.

comparative impotence,"[3] it was self-evident that businessmen would seize its opportunities as soon as their affairs reached a stage that could use them. After the American Revolution, "banks and means of communication were imperatively needed."[4] For "many enterprises of these types it was inevitable that incorporation, with the privilege of limited liability and the conditions of more stable organization, should be sought."[5] And as soon as the establishment of a new government in 1789 offered a "fair field . . . for the permanent investment of capital in large operations, with such an assurance of safety as could command general public confidence," people recognized that "there is but one mode in which such operations can be conducted with lasting success . . . through some form of corporate organization."[6] As the economy of the nation expanded in the three decades after the Revolution, charters of incorporation issued forth at an ever accelerating rate from the chambers of state legislatures.[7]

To account for this quick popularity in the United States, the standard authorities have endowed the business corporation even of 1789 with three attributes. It was the natural organization for new business enterprise because the creation of a fictitious personality simplified the management of large accumulations of capital contributed by many shareholders; because the liability of participants was limited; and because the corporation was free, within the terms of a perpetual charter or contract with the state, from the interference of government. Yet examination will show that in the eighteenth century these characteristics were not so clearly defined and so inextricably related to corporateness that the practical businessman, seeking a mode of organizing his affairs in England, on the Continent, or in America, would inevitably turn to the government for a charter of incorporation.

II

The test of experience had not yet proved that corporations were "business bodies of enviable efficacy," or that they offered the most

[3] Cf. Nicholas Murray Butler, *Why Should We Change Our Form of Government?* (New York, Charles Scribner's Sons, 1912), p. 82.

[4] Julius Goebel, Jr., *Cases and Materials on the Development of Legal Institutions* (New York, 1931), p. 652.

[5] Joseph S. Davis, *Essays in the Earlier History of American Corporations,* Vol. II (Cambridge, Mass., Harvard University Press, 1917), pp. 6, 7.

[6] Baldwin, "American Business Corporations," *loc. cit.,* pp. 256, 257.

[7] Cf. also Abbott, *Rise of the Business Corporation,* pp. 3 ff.; J. S. Davis, *Essays,* Vol. II, p. 329; G. S. Callender, "Early Transportation and Banking Enterprises of the States in Relation to the Growth of Corporations," *Quart. Jour. Econ.,* 1902, XVII, 146.

suitable form for the management of capital.[8] European developments to match those across the Atlantic had to wait at least fifty years. Although English business organization was far more complex than American, the older forms seemed to permit satisfactory adaptation to new conditions. Partnerships of many degrees were unaffected by the restrictions of the Bubble Act; by 1800, unincorporated joint-stock companies, though conducted as partnerships and lacking the legal characteristics that could be obtained only by a special charter, "had reached the point where the financial interest was almost if not entirely as liquid as it was with the incorporated companies."[9] One need only think of the company mills in the woolen industry or of the Banking Company of Aberdeen, in which 446 partners got on without incorporation, to measure the flexibility of the old forms.[10] Turnpike building, which in the United States occasioned extensive corporate activity, in England was undertaken by trusts acting as local public agencies.[11] That was likewise true of many improvements in river navigation.[12] In spite of the favored position of the incorporated Royal Exchange and London Assurance companies, the bulk of underwriting remained private.[13] Life insurance was entirely so.[14]

Throughout the whole of the eighteenth century England chartered some half-dozen corporations for manufacturing purposes, and hardly more in any other business sphere. Until well into the nineteenth century the corporation was used extensively only in the organization of canal companies.[15] Not until the Companies Act of 1844 did it become

---

[8] Shaw Livermore, *Early American Land Companies: Their Influence on Corporate Development* (New York, The Commonwealth Fund, 1939), p. 258.

[9] Cf. Armand B. DuBois, *The English Business Company after the Bubble Act, 1720–1800* (New York, The Commonwealth Fund, 1938), pp. 36, 38; H. A. Shannon, "Coming of General Limited Liability," *Economic History,* 1931 (Suppl. to the *Econ. Jour.,* Vol. II), pp. 270 ff.; William R. Scott, *The Constitution and Finance of English, Scottish, and Irish Joint-Stock Companies to 1720,* Vol. I (Cambridge, Eng., The University Press, 1910–12), p. 247.

[10] J. H. Clapham, *An Economic History of Modern Britain,* Vol. I (Cambridge, Eng., The University Press, 1930–38), pp. 195, 267, 268.

[11] Cf. Frederick Clifford, *History of Private Bill Legislation,* Vol. II (London, 1885–87), pp. 12 ff.; Clapham, *op. cit.,* Vol. I, p. 93; DuBois, *op. cit.,* p. 229.

[12] Clifford, *op. cit.,* Vol. I, pp. 39 ff.

[13] Clifford, *op. cit.,* Vol. II, pp. 430, 571, 591 ff.; Clapham, *op. cit.,* Vol. I, pp. 288 ff.

[14] Clifford, *op. cit.,* Vol. II, pp. 601 ff., 615, 616; Clapham, *op. cit.,* Vol. I, pp. 292 ff. Cf. also, in general, Bishop C. Hunt, *The Development of the Business Corporation in England 1800–1867* (Cambridge, Mass., Harvard University Press, 1936), pp. 11, 12, 22 ff.

[15] Cf. Leone Levi, *History of British Commerce* (London, 1880), p. 16; Hunt, *op. cit.,* pp. 5, 10.

common, and full growth awaited the coming of limited liability after 1855 and the enactment of the Consolidated Statute of 1862.[16]

Development across the Channel was no more rapid. The Code de Commerce of 1807 systematized the law of commercial associations, partnership and corporate, for the French empire, and ultimately served as a model for most of the Continent. Yet the number of charters increased only gradually thereafter. For railroads and other special purposes the corporation entered into use in the 1830's. But wider application did not come until the enactment of general incorporation laws after mid-century.[17] Here new devices involving many degrees of individual liability and diverse types of internal organization met the varying needs of a changing economy. By and large, the dominant forms, ranging from the *société en nom collectif* to the *société en commandite,* were partnerships rather than corporations.[18]

[16] Clapham, *op. cit.,* Vol. II, pp. 135, 138 ff., 351; Hunt, *op. cit.,* pp. 50, 56 ff., 82 ff., 96 ff., 133 ff., 144; Shannon, "Limited Liability," *loc. cit.,* Vol. II, pp. 279 ff., 289; Levi, *op. cit.,* pp. 340–45. On the assumption that the corporate form was logical and natural, English historians face the problem of accounting for this tardy development. Some, like Hunt (*op. cit.,* p. 9), blame it on the Bubble Act, though that should not have restricted incorporations, since it aimed only at the unincorporated companies. DuBois' excellent study shows, as a matter of fact, that the unincorporated company did develop in spite of the act. But he in turn must reconcile the unwillingness of the government to permit company activities under the legal corporate form with its willingness to tolerate the same activities under the illegal joint-stock form (DuBois, *op. cit.,* pp. 39, 436 ff.; cf. also Shannon, *op. cit.,* p. 269).

[17] For Prussia, cf. Kurt Bösselmann, *Die Entwicklung des deutschen Aktienwesens im 19. Jahrhundert* (Berlin, 1939), pp. 67 ff., 179, 189 ff.; Richard Passow, *Die Aktiengesellschaft eine wirtschaftswissenschaftliche Studie* (2nd ed., Jena, 1922), p. 17. For other parts of Germany, cf. Alfred Strauss, *Die Aktiengesellschaft nach altem bayerischen Recht* (Munich, 1931), pp. 28 ff., 36 ff.; Otto Sehrt, *Die niederrheinischen Aktiengesellschaften unter dem Code de Commerce* (Cologne, 1912), pp. 9–28. For Holland, cf. E. Tekenbroek, *De Verhouding Tusschen de Aandeelhouders en de Bestuurders bij de Publieke Naamlooze Vennootschap in Nederland* (Delft, 1923), pp. 17 ff. Cf. also J. H. Clapham, *The Economic Development of France and Germany 1815–1914* (Cambridge, Eng., The University Press, 1928), pp. 130 ff., 395 ff.; Karl Lehmann, *Recht der Aktiengesellschaften,* Vol. I (Berlin, 1898–1904), pp. 68–72; *idem, Lehrbuch des Handelsrechts* (Leipzig, 1912), pp. 374 ff.; Rodolphe Rousseau, *Des sociétés commerciales françaises et étrangères,* Vol. I (4th ed., Paris, 1912), pp. xi–xxxi, 706 ff.; Arthur K. Kuhn, *A Comparative Study of the Law of Corporations* (New York, Columbia University Press, 1912), p. 65; A. A. Berle and G. C. Means, "Corporation," *Encyclopaedia of the Social Sciences,* Vol. IV (New York, 1931), p. 416.

[18] We see no foundation for the assertion that the Code Savary (1673) endowed the *société en commandite* with "the status of a corporate entity."—Livermore, *Land Companies,* p. 71. For the text of Section 4, cf. *Recueil général des anciennes lois françaises,* Vol. XIX, Isambert, Decrusy, and Taillandier, eds. (Paris, 1829), pp. 96 ff. Cf. also Charles W. Cole, *Colbert and a Century of French Mercantilism,* Vol. I (New York, Columbia University Press, 1939), pp. 327, 360. On the origins of these forms, cf. William Mitchell, "Early Forms of Partnership," *Select Essays in Anglo-American Legal History,* Vol. III, pp. 191, 192; Weber, *op. cit.,* pp. 15 ff., 34, 35; Lehmann, *Lehrbuch,* pp. 287 ff.;

Yet by contrast to English and Continental experience, the less advanced economy of the United States produced almost 350 business corporations between 1783 and 1801.[19] By 1799, if not earlier, Massachusetts even had a general incorporation law.[20] Nor is it enough to point to the relative ease of incorporation in America without answering why it was less difficult to secure charters in the New World. If the weight of common-law inertia was not quite so heavy on one side of the ocean as on the other, and if independence freed colonial merchants from some imperial restraints, it nevertheless would be rash to claim that after 1776 enterprisers in the United States had more influence in government than did their European counterparts.[21]

But whatever one's judgment on these debatable questions, there remains still unsolved the problem of why American investors whose business experience was similar to that of Europeans should have anomalously stressed the corporate form, of why "the collective desire of the business community for effective organization" should have focused here.[22] While incorporation, with the capacity for suing and being sued, and for holding and transmitting property, offered some advantages in the contact of companies with the law, unincorporated associations everywhere had contrived numerous strategems to achieve the same ends.[23] Even before the Revolution, large-scale enterprises in many fields—mining, manufacturing, banking, and trade—used the forms prevalent throughout the Western world, the unchartered joint-stock company and co-partnership.[24] In 1741, the extension of the Bubble

---

Rousseau, *op. cit.,* Vol. I, pp. 243 ff.; W. S. Holdsworth, *A History of English Law,* Vol. VIII (London, Methuen & Co., 1903 ff.), pp. 104, 195 ff. For attempts to account for the absence of these forms in Anglo-American law, cf. *infra,* footnote 45.

[19] J. S. Davis, *Essays,* Vol. II, pp. 8, 22.

[20] For aqueduct corporations, St. 1798, Ch. 59 (Feb. 21, 1799), *General Laws of Massachusetts,* Vol. I, Stearns, Shaw, and Metcalf, eds. (Boston, 1823), pp. 571 ff. Baldwin, "American Business Corporations," *loc. cit.,* Vol. I, p. 274, cites an earlier North Carolina general incorporation law for canals; but J. S. Davis, *Essays,* Vol. II, pp. 17–19, denies that it referred to corporations.

[21] For the effect of the Revolution, cf., e.g., Abbott, *op. cit.,* p. 39. It is important to note in this connection, however, that there were no legal impediments to colonial incorporation. The Act of 1741 applied only to joint-stock companies, not to corporations. Cf. Andrew M. Davis, "Provincial Banks: Land and Silver," *Publications of the Colonial Society of Massachusetts,* Vol. III (Boston, 1900), pp. 26 ff. For the power to incorporate, cf. material in J. S. Davis, *Essays,* Vol. I, pp. 8, 18, 27, 28; Baldwin, "American Business Corporations," *loc. cit.,* Vol. I, pp. 257 ff.

[22] Livermore, *Land Companies,* pp. 1, 4 ff.

[23] DuBois, *op. cit.,* pp. 216 ff.

[24] For many examples, cf. S. E. Baldwin, "History of the Law of Private Corporations," *loc. cit.,* Vol. III, pp. 243–45; J. S. Davis, *Essays,* Vol. I, pp. 92–97; Andrew M. Davis, *Currency and Banking in the Province of the Massachusetts-Bay,* Vol. II (New York, Macmillan Co., 1901), pp. 75 ff.

Act to the colonies in consequence of the operations of the Massachusetts Land Bank had put a halt to some of the more prominent developments. But independence removed that restraint and thereafter there were few legal limits to the activities of such enterprises.[25] In addition, American law had at hand all the while the extremely flexible concepts of uses and trusts, concepts which in the 1880's were to furnish the instruments of the widest and most intense American industrial concentration, until the antitrust movement made necessary a reversion to the corporate structure.[26]

These methods of organizing and managing capital seemed adequate; in many fields they persisted long beyond the period of corporation growth. In some of the most important phases of post-Revolutionary economy, in shipping and in trade, in land speculation and in the fisheries, joint-stock companies were prominent; there was only one small, short-lived corporation.[27] This was doubly curious because in European experience mining and overseas trade were the first and most profitable fields of corporate activity.[28] Why should not the adventurers trading from Boston and Salem to Russia, China, and India have formed themselves into corporations?[29] In such spheres as insurance and banking, all the business types—corporations, joint-stock companies, partner-

[25] Baldwin, "History of the Law of Private Corporations," *loc. cit.*, Vol. III, p. 246; *idem, Modern Political Institutions,* p. 187; A. M. Davis, *Currency and Banking,* Vol. II, pp. 152, 161 ff.; Livermore, *Land Companies,* p. 66, note 72.

[26] Cf. Frederic W. Maitland, *Collected Papers,* Vol. III, H. A. L. Fisher, ed. (Cambridge, Eng., The University Press, 1911), pp. 271 ff., 336 ff., 356 ff., 372 ff., 389 ff., 394. For the origins of these concepts, cf. Holdsworth, *op. cit.,* Vol. IV, pp. 410 ff., 439, 476 ff.; Vol. V, pp. 304 ff. Excellent comparative studies may be found in Robert Liefmann, *Beteilungs- und Finanzierungsgesellschaften in Deutschland, den Vereinigten Staaten, der Schweiz, England, Frankreich und Belgien* (4th ed., Jena, 1923), esp. pp. 205 ff.; Fritz E. Schmey, *Aktie und Aktionär im Recht der Vereinigten Staaten* (Marburg, 1930), pp. 453 ff., 509 ff. For recent developments, cf. Remo Franceschelli, *Il "Trust" nel diritto inglese* (Padua, 1935), pp. 3 ff.

[27] In Connecticut, J. S. Davis, *Essays,* Vol. II, p. 289. Cf. also Livermore, *Land Companies,* pp. 39–41.

[28] Cf., for example, Weber, *op. cit.,* pp. 15 ff., for southern Europe; the companies discussed by C. W. Cole, *op. cit.,* Vol. I, pp. 116 ff., for France; Jacob Strieder, *Studien zur Geschichte kapitalistischer Organizationsformen* (Munich, 1925), pp. 110 ff., for northern Europe; and Scott, *op. cit.,* Vol. II, also Lehmann, *Recht der Aktiengesellschaften,* Vol. I, p. 51; *idem, Geschichtliche Entwicklung,* pp. 7 ff.

[29] Cf. Samuel Eliot Morison, *The Maritime History of Massachusetts, 1783–1860* (Boston and New York, Houghton Mifflin Co., 1921), pp. 41 ff. The fact that shipping was generally financed for individual voyages should have been no greater obstacle to incorporation for merchants in the United States than for the East India Company, or, for that matter, than individual ship underwriting was for the sponsors of marine-insurance corporations. Discussions in the constitutional convention questioned the power of Congress to incorporate commercial companies, but not that of the states. *The Records of the Federal Convention of 1787,* Max Farrand, ed. (New Haven, Yale University Press, 1911), Vol. II, pp. 615 ff.; Vol. III, pp. 375 ff.

ships, and individual ownership—continued to serve.[30] Projects here, refused incorporation, got along perfectly well without it.[31] On the other hand, despite Adam Smith's injunction, corporations arose to rival the older structures in manufacturing.[32] Furthermore, there seemed no consistency among incorporators. The same undertakers sought charters for some projects but not for others. Duer incorporated his ventures in manufacturing but not in land; John Brown in canals but not in manufacturing; and Mackay, Craigie, Swan, Gorham, and Higginson similarly divided their interests.[33] Yet if the corporate form was so adaptable and so advantageous in the management of capital, it should have been equally irresistible for all types of large-scale enterprise.[34]

In any case, there is no correlation between the rate of incorporation and the number of new enterprises launched by the fresh spirit of post-Revolutionary business activity. The areas of most intense economic development were not the areas where the most corporations appeared. Fully 60 per cent of all charters were in New England while only 15 per cent were in New York and Pennsylvania; New Hampshire alone granted more than either of the two central states. Was the need for this device for accumulating and managing capital more urgent in New Hampshire than in Pennsylvania?[35] Nor was there a correlation between the scale of enterprise and organization under charters. The unincorporated Ohio and Scioto land companies, for instance, involved a larger

---

[30] The spread of private banking in Massachusetts, for instance, provoked a restrictive law, St. 1799, Ch. 32. Cf. also Edward R. Hardy, *Account of the Early Insurance Offices in Massachusetts* (Boston, 1901), pp. 47–51; J. S. Davis, *Essays,* Vol. II, pp. 232 ff.

[31] Cf., for example, J. S. Davis, *Essays,* Vol. II, pp. 44 ff., 78.

[32] For Adam Smith on the role of the corporation, see *Wealth of Nations,* Vol. III (London, 1786), pp. 146 ff.

[33] Cf., in general, Robert A. East, *Business Enterprise in the American Revolutionary Era* (New York, Columbia University Press, 1938), pp. 308 ff.

[34] Shaw Livermore neatly evades this dilemma by asserting that there was no significant difference between incorporated and unincorporated companies, that "incorporation was not highly prized in the business world" before 1800, and that land companies voluntarily "passed by" the corporate form. *Land Companies,* pp. 61, 69, 73, 137, 245; "Unlimited Liability in Early American Corporations," *Jour. Pol. Econ.,* 1935, XLIII, 674 ff. Aside from the fact that contemporaries thought a difference existed, this assertion still leaves unanswered the question of why some companies should, and others should not, have gone through the process of incorporation. The argument that limited liability was less necessary "in the merchandising of land" than in other enterprises (*Land Companies,* p. 215) would hardly have convinced Duer, Morris, and Macomb, the most prominent adventurers in that sphere, whose residence in debtors' jails was a consequence of land speculation (limited liability is discussed *infra.* pp. 109–18). In any case, there is evidence that at least one company attempted successfully, and another unsuccessfully, to secure a charter. *Land Companies,* pp. 136, 137; *supra,* footnote 27.

[35] Computed from J. S. Davis, *Essays,* Vol. II, p. 22. Davis' explanation (Vol. II, p. 296) may stand when New England is contrasted with the southern, but not with the central, states.

capital, on paper at least, and more complicated finance with interstate and international ramifications than any Massachusetts corporation of the same period, and the Tontine Association of Boston in 1791 marketed 100,000 shares without benefit of charter.[36] In this connection, many have misread the early acts, which specified not the capital stock but the maximum value of the property that could be held, two figures between which there was no connection.[37] Factories were small; $10,000 was a substantial investment for building and equipment.[38] Even in banking, which needed substantial sums to begin with, the number of participants and the amounts involved were not significantly larger than in other enterprises. The Massachusetts Bank, for instance, whose 50 to 100 stockholders were almost all related by family and business tie, was not far different in size and scope from the great associations that sponsored the oriental trade.[39] Early practice, European and American, certainly supports the conclusion of the historians of another period that "large commercial enterprises may be conducted . . . by aggregates of men that are not incorporated. The law of tenancy in common and joint tenancy, the law of partnership, these have been found equal to many heavy and novel demands."[40]

III

If the corporation possessed few structural advantages, it is still supposed to have held out the attraction of limited liability, safeguarding the investor from the responsibilities of corporate obligations beyond the amount of his original commitment, and thus offering special inducement for organization under the corporate form. Indeed, to some, limited liability seems the very essence of the institution.[41]

But other forms would have satisfied as well the demand for limited liability. When the desire to protect investors became important, the

[36] J. S. Davis, *Essays,* Vol. I, pp. 131 ff., 278; Vol. II, pp. 70 ff.

[37] Thus a North Bridgewater factory in which $8,000 was invested secured an act of incorporation in 1813 which limited its property to $150,000. Bradford Kingman, *History of North Bridgewater* (Boston, 1866), pp. 377, 378.

[38] Cf. examples cited by J. S. Davis, *Essays,* Vol. I, pp. 369, 479; Vol. II, p. 271. Henry Wansey, *Journal of an Excursion to the United States* (Salisbury, 1796), p. 85. Cf. also Caroline F. Ware, *The Early New England Cotton Manufacture* (Boston and New York, Houghton Mifflin Co., 1931), p. 20.

[39] Cf. J. S. Davis, *Essays,* Vol. II, pp. 47, 67, 192–94; East, *op. cit.,* pp. 255 ff., 260, 261.

[40] Sir Frederick Pollock and Frederic W. Maitland, *History of English Law before the Time of Edward I,* Vol. I (Cambridge, Eng., The University Press, 1899), p. 488. For a comparative study of some ultimate developments within these forms, cf. Fausto Ardigo, *La società per azioni nel diritto inglese* (Padova, 1939), Ch. 1, 2.

[41] Cf., for example, J. S. Davis, *Essays,* Vol. II, p. 317.

Continent ultimately developed a wide array of unchartered organizations; the Kommanditgesellschaft and the Kommanditgesellschaft auf Aktien, the stille Gesellschaft and the G.m.b.H. satisfied the desires of the business community for restrictions on the responsibility of shareholders.[42] In the very years of corporate beginnings in America, the Irish Parliament set up a system of limited partnerships.[43] And there were traces of the tendency even in America; in New York in 1786 an unincorporated association of iron manufacturers was granted limited liability for a term of years.[44] That this precedent was not followed, and that a half century passed before the limited partnership emerged in America, points not to the essential nexus between corporateness and limited liability, but to the slight importance of limited liability.[45]

That factor entered the minds of a few businessmen, of course. It was a special privilege included in some eighteenth-century English charters, but not in all.[46] Before 1800 one New York company petitioned for the

[42] Cf. Lehmann, *Lehrbuch*, pp. 339 ff., 355 ff., 460 ff., 467 ff.; Rousseau, *op. cit.*, Vol. I, pp. 268 ff., 682 ff.; Passow, *op. cit.*, pp. 558 ff. Among more specialized studies, cf. Otto Bundschuh, *Die wirtschaftliche Entwicklung der deutschen Kommanditgesellschaften auf Aktien* (Berlin, 1914), pp. 17 ff.; August Saenger, *Die stille Gesellschaft* Vol. VI (Die private Unternehmung, Mannheim, 1924), pp. 28–44, 118–26.

[43] 21–22 Geo. III, Ch. 46, *Acts and Statutes, Made in a Session of Parliament at Dublin* (Dublin, 1782), pp. 949 ff.; Hunt, *op. cit.*, p. 52. Cf. also E. Lipson, *The Economic History of England*, Vol. III (London, Macmillan & Co., Ltd., 1929–31), p. 218. For attempts by English unincorporated companies to secure limited liability, cf. Scott, *op. cit.*, Vol. I, p. 344; Vol. III, p. 276.

[44] Baldwin, *Modern Political Institutions*, pp. 201 ff.; Livermore, "Unlimited Liability," *loc. cit.*, XLIII, 683; J. S. Davis, *Essays*, Vol. II, p. 260.

[45] Scott's explanation that the failure of the Anglo-Italian banks before the period of commercial expansion in England prevented the Italian partnership forms from entering English law is hardly convincing, particularly in view of the persistence of the Italian firms in Scotland (*op. cit.*, Vol. I, pp. 2, 13). Livermore's attempt (*Land Companies*, p. 10, note 3) to account for it on the basis of their origin in Roman law is unconvincing because their origin was not in Roman law (cf. *supra*, footnote 1) and because this would still not explain why Anglo-American law should not have adopted them in the eighteenth century, as it ultimately did in the nineteenth. On Italian law in England in general, cf. also Holdsworth, *op. cit.*, Vol. V, pp. 67 ff.

[46] For English petitions and bills without mention of limited liability, cf., for example, British Cast Plate Glass (1773), 13 Geo. III, Ch. 38, *Statutes at Large*, VIII, 222; *House of Commons Journals*, XXXIV, 64, 149 ff., 190; Globe Insurance (1799), *ibid.*, LIV, 595, 697, 740. For those with mention, cf. Winchelsea Cambrick and Lawn (1764), *ibid.*, XXIX, 752, 785; Northumberland Fisheries (1789), *ibid.*, XLIV, 163, 167, 487; Sierra Leone, 31 Geo. III, Ch. 55; London Flour (1800), *ibid.*, LV, 599 ff., 626, 632 ff. Cf. also Hunt, *op. cit.*, pp. 10–12; DuBois, *op. cit.*, p. 76. Some students (for example, Hunt, *op. cit.*, p. 25; Scott, *op. cit.*, Vol. I, p. 270) have read limited liability into another provision. Many prospective investors in England were deterred by fear that stock ownership would make them and their lands liable to the onerous bankruptcy laws, often involving felony, which applied only to traders. Cf. Holdsworth, *op. cit.*, Vol. I, pp. 256 ff.; Vol. VIII, p. 205; Adam Anderson, *Historical and Chronological Deduction of the Origin of Commerce*, Vol. III, Coombe, ed. (Dublin, 1790), pp. 232, 237; S. W. Dunscomb, *Bankruptcy: A Study in Comparative Legislation* (New York, 1893), pp. 17 ff. Saving clauses beginning with 13–14 Charles II, Ch. 24, therefore exempted them. Cf., for example, Linen and

exemption,[47] and after the turn of the century limitation appeared sporadically in other states.[48] But in the first thirty years of Massachusetts development no grant or petition for an act of incorporation mentioned it.[49]

Examination of contemporary Anglo-American law, with particular reference to Massachusetts, strikes at the very roots of the common assumption that limited liability was always an essential attribute of corporateness, like the power to sue or the possession of a seal, and could be taken for granted without specific statement in the charter.[50] It had long been established that the corporation, like the joint-stock company, had a common purse, and that its debts were, in the first instance, chargeable only against the common purse.[51] But what are the grounds for

Cotton Cloth (1779), *House of Commons Journals,* XXXVII, 108; *Succinct Digest of Laws Relating to Bankrupts* (Dublin, 1791), p. 18; James Chalmer, *Remarks upon the Scots Bankrupt Bill* (Edinburgh, 1782), pp. 2 ff. That the bankruptcy provision was completely distinct from limited liability is shown by the fact that some charters like the Winchelsea Cambrick and Lawn and the Northumberland Fisheries contained both (cf. 4 Geo. III, Ch. 37, *Statutes at Large,* pp. 485 ff.), as did the Irish limited partnership act (21–22 Geo. III, Ch. 46, *loc. cit.,* pp. 949 ff.). A conflation seems to have occurred later. Compare, for instance, the act incorporating the London Flour Company (1800), 39–40 Geo. III, Ch. 97, *Statutes at Large,* pp. 448 ff., with the comments of Tierney and Perceval, *Hansard's Parliamentary Debates,* XXXV, 455, 460, and similarly the comments on the Gas and Coke Bill (1810), *Hansard,* XVII, 231 (cf. also *House of Commons Journals,* XXXVII, 147). DuBois, *op. cit.,* p. 156, note 92, cites even earlier instances. The bankruptcy exemption seems historically similar to the privileges given the French nobility (Cole, *op. cit.,* pp. 249, 384).

[47] The Bank of New York petition may have carried the clause as a special attraction to compete with the projected land bank. Cf. Henry W. Domett, *History of the Bank of New York 1784–1884* (2nd ed., New York, 1884), pp. 6 ff., 14, 19, 34, 126 ff.

[48] Cf., for example, Joseph G. Blandi, *Maryland Business Corporations, 1783–1852* (Baltimore, Johns Hopkins Press, 1934), pp. 16, 39, 43, who is troubled by these developments because he assumes limited liability already existed in the eighteenth century.

[49] A grant to the Exchange Coffee House illustrates the exceptional nature of the privilege. The company charter (June 20, 1807) specifically affirmed individual liability (St. 1807, Ch. 32, Sec. 7), but a supplementary act (March 3, 1808) permitted the corporation to raise a mortgage "without personal responsibility" (St. 1807, Ch. 78). Livermore, "Unlimited Liability," *loc. cit.,* XLIII, 678, cites the Newburyport Company as having limited liability. Cf., per contra, its charter, St. 1793, Ch. 27.

[50] Cf., for example, J. S. Davis, *Essays,* Vol. I, pp. 5, 383; Shannon, "Limited Liability," *loc. cit.,* Vol. II, p. 267; Goebel, *op. cit.,* pp. 636 ff.; Hunt, *op. cit.,* p. 41 (citing a case of 1891); Livermore, "Unlimited Liability," *loc. cit.,* XLIII, 676. Corporations were far more numerous in Massachusetts than in any other state between 1782 and 1800. Even within the limits of a rather narrow definition, fully eighty-three, one-quarter of the total in the United States, were chartered there (cf. table in J. S. Davis, *Essays,* Vol. II, pp. 22–23).

[51] Lehmann, *Geschichtliche Entwicklung,* pp. 51, 52, defines this concept as *beschränkte Haftung nach aussen.* That is the only point involved in Lord Kenyon's famous decision in 1788 in *Russell v. the Men of Devon*—a case sometimes cited as upholding limited liability. 2 T.R., 672, *English Reports* (Edinburgh, 1909), C, 362. The verdict dealt with the question whether an English county was a corporation and held that the absence of a corporate fund was evidence it was not. Cf. also C. T. Carr, "Early Forms of Corporateness," *Select Essays in Anglo-American Legal History,* Vol. III, p. 163.

believing that members were free of obligation if the common purse proved not long enough? Certainly, there was no clear precedent from Roman law,[52] and, on the Continent, that freedom was not expressly defined until the Code de Commerce of 1807.[53]

Early English law knew nothing of limited liability. Pollock and Maitland, finding no trace of it in the period they studied, concluded: "The non-liability of individual corporators for the debts of the corporation can not be regarded as of the essence of a corporation."[54] As far as boroughs were concerned, it remained clear for a long time, as Madox noted, that distraint could be had upon the lands and chattels of the burgesses as well as upon those of the corporation. And in the seventeenth century Chief Justice Rolle held: "If a summe of money be to be levied upon a corporation, it may be levied upon the mayor or Chief Magistrate, or upon any member of the corporation."[55] These rulings were frequently upheld in the Massachusetts courts as far as towns were concerned, and remained law throughout the period of corporate growth.[56]

In respect to limited liability, an eighteenth-century businessman could find no legal basis for drawing a distinction between towns and

---

[52] Ulpian's much quoted statement in the *Digest,* Vol. III, 4.7 (Milan ed., 1931), p. 98, has often been interpreted as maintaining limited liability. Cf., for example, Pollock and Maitland, *op. cit.,* Vol. I, p. 487; Goebel, *op. cit.,* p. 575. But it merely distinguished between individual and corporate obligations, without reference to liability for the debt of an insolvent corporation. Some evidence exists that in that event individuals might be liable. —Lehmann, *Recht der Aktiengesellschaften,* Vol. I, pp. 15 ff.; Williston, "Business Corporations," *loc. cit.,* II, 160; Baldwin, *Modern Political Institutions,* pp. 156 ff. In any case, the paucity of material and the uncertainty concerning the general character of Roman corporations render the drawing of analogies hazardous. Cf. W. W. Buckland, *Manual of Roman Private Law* (Cambridge, Eng., The University Press, 1939), pp. 34 ff., 294 ff.; M. Rostovtzeff, *The Social and Economic History of the Roman Empire* (Oxford, Clarendon Press, 1926), pp. 532, note 22, 602, note 20; Fritz Schulz, *Principles of Roman Law* (Oxford, Oxford University Press, 1936), pp. 25, 72.

[53] Special provisions in the charter, as in the case of the Compagnie des Indes Orientales, were needed until then (cf. Cole, *op. cit.,* Vol. I, p. 481). Cf. also Lehmann, *Geschichtliche Entwicklung,* pp. 23, 24, 54; *idem, Recht der Aktiengesellschaften,* Vol. I, pp. 1, 2; Bösselmann, *op. cit.,* p. 62; Kuhn, *op. cit.,* p. 56. For the earlier character of the *société anonyme,* cf. Baldwin, *Modern Political Institutions,* pp. 181 ff.

[54] Pollock and Maitland, *op. cit.,* Vol. I, p. 493. However, they did say that limited liability developed in practice if not in theory afterwards in the fifteenth century (Vol. I, pp. 492 ff.). Cf. also John P. Davis, *Corporations; a Study of the Origin and Development of Great Business Combinations,* Vol. I (New York, G. P. Putnam's Sons, 1905), p. 26.

[55] Cf. Clifford, *op. cit.,* Vol. II, p. 211; Amasa M. Eaton, "First Book in English on the Law of Incorporation," *Yale Law Journal,* 1903, XII, 372. For Rolle, cf. Holdsworth, *op. cit.,* Vol. V, pp. 375 ff.

[56] Cf. *Chase v. Merrimack Bank* (1837), 19 Pickering, 569 ff.; Nathan Dane, *General Abridgment and Digest of American Law,* Vol. V (Boston, 1824), p. 158; Samuel M. Israeli, *Nature of the Liability of Shareholders of a Corporation* (Philadelphia, Avil Printing Co., 1901), pp. 3 ff.

other corporations. When the legislature passed on problems common to all, such as the payment of damages for lands taken for improvements, it treated them alike. In bridge and canal corporations, for instance, it frequently affirmed that "the bodies of any of the . . . Proprietors shall be . . . liable to be taken in execution . . . in the same manner the inhabitants of any town are liable."[57]

On the general question of limited liability in any type of corporation, English law had, by the period of the American Revolution, gone no further than to distinguish between individual and corporate obligations and had not passed on the question of liability when the corporation was unable or unwilling to pay.[58] In that event, convincing though negative evidence points to the conclusion that stockholders were personally liable. On the two occasions when Coke described the qualities of a corporation (*Sutton's Hospital; Mayor of Stafford v. Bolton*) he failed to mention limited liability.[59] Similarly, Shepherd in 1659 said nothing of it when discussing "declaratory or explanatory" attributes.[60] And in this respect, the eighteenth-century writers, Blackstone and Kyd, were also expressively silent.[61] Both significantly mentioned limited liability only in connection with the members of dissolved bodies.[62] In

[57] Cf., for example, West Boston Bridge Corporation (March 28, 1793), St. 1792, Ch. 87, Sec. 3; Proprietors of the Locks and Canals on the Connecticut River (February 23, 1792), St. 1791, Ch. 32; Ten Mile Falls Canal (March 11, 1797), St. 1796, Ch. 93. As late as 1884 Justice Field, discussing legislation on unlimited liability in the early period, pointed out that it followed "the analogy of inhabitants of towns" (*Child v. Boston & Fairhaven Iron Works,* 137 Mass., 517). Cf. also *infra,* p. 116.

[58] Three fifteenth-century cases have been cited to the contrary (cf. Holdsworth, *op. cit.,* Vol. III, p. 484; Hunt, *op. cit.,* p. 3). But these do not go beyond the mere distinction between corporate and individual purse. Cf. Y.B. 8 Hen. VI, Mich., pl. 2; Y.B. 19 Hen. VI, Pasch. pl. 1; Y.B. 20 Hen. VI, Mich., pl. 19 (London, 1679), I, 64, 9. The seventeenth-century case of *Edmunds v. Brown and Tillard* cited by Holdsworth (*op. cit.,* Vol. VIII, p. 203) refers to liability *after* the dissolution of the corporation, a problem that is completely different. Cf. 1 Lev. 237, *English Reports,* LXXXIII, 385; also *infra,* footnote 62.

[59] Cf. Williston, "Business Corporations," *loc. cit.,* II, 113, 115, 116, 160. Cf. also Edward Coke, *First Part of the Institutes of the Laws of England or, a Commentary upon Littleton,* Vol. III, 6, 413 (Philadelphia, 1853); Vol. II, 250a.

[60] Eaton, "Law of Incorporation," *Yale Law Review,* XII, 281. Cf. also the most popular of the law dictionaries, John Covvell, *Interpreter or Booke Containing the Signification of Words* (London, 1637); [John] Cowel, *Law Dictionary* (London, 1708). On Cowel and Shepherd, cf. Holdsworth, *op. cit.,* Vol. V, pp. 20 ff., 391 ff.

[61] Cf. Blackstone, *op. cit.,* Vol. I, pp. 467, 468, 474 ff.; Stewart Kyd, *Treatise on the Law of Corporations* (London, 1793–94), particularly Vol. I, pp. 2 ff., 13, 69 ff.; Williston, "Business Corporations," *loc. cit.,* II, 116–18.

[62] Blackstone, *op. cit.,* Vol. I, p. 484; Kyd, *op. cit.,* Vol. II, p. 516. We are disposed to give heavy weight to Kyd's evidence, despite recent attacks upon him, for example, Goebel, *op. cit.,* p. 610. The charge of medievalism hardly comports with his political activity in the Society for Constitutional Information and his sympathy with the French Revolution that brought him to trial for treason. Cf. *Dictionary of National Biography,* Vol. XXXI, S. Lee, ed. (London, 1892), p. 348. In any case the substance of these criticisms, as of

England the concept that limitation was inherent in corporateness was foreshadowed earlier, but even after the turn of the nineteenth century it had not yet emerged completely from its fuzzy chrysalis.[63]

Until well into the eighteenth century in England, and through the whole period of origins in the United States, the internal organization of the corporation made unlikely the raising of the question. Generally, there was no specific capital stock and no par value for shares. Funds were collected by assessments against the shareholder, and there was, at first, no legal limit to the total number of assessments. "Leviations" could, as in the case of the Middlesex Canal, come to fully a hundred.[64] As first organized, therefore, corporations could replenish their coffers by drawing without limit on the resources of all their members.[65] Chartered associations could not voluntarily dissolve and were not subject to bankruptcy proceedings; there was no way legally to evade creditors.

The question of stockholder liability would arise only in the case of recalcitrant corporations that refused to assess their members. Here the question was one of procedure—how might a plaintiff who had entered into a contract with a collective body that refused or was unable to pay bring suit against an individual member? As early as 1628, the case of the Muscovy Company created precedent for relief.[66] The principle was definitely written into law in the famous case of *Dr. Salmon v. the Hamborough Company* (1671), which held that a creditor could find a remedy in equity against the personal effects of members of an assetless corporation by forcing the corporation to assess a "Leviation upon every member."[67] This decision remained law throughout the eighteenth century. Mr. Williston, after a diligent search, found no case "inconsistent

---

similar strictures against the "solemn inanities of Blackstone," is that they threw together an "aimless array of cases . . . under the rubric 'corporations,' "—Goebel's introduction, DuBois, *op. cit.*, pp. viii, ix. Whether their conception of the institution is intrinsically sounder than that of their modern critics is less important than the fact that eighteenth-century jurists saw the corporation in terms of the century which preceded rather than of the century which followed.

[63] For continued resistance to limited liability, cf. material in DuBois, *op. cit.*, pp. 94, 96, 146, 150, note 67; Hunt, *op. cit.*, pp. 25 ff.

[64] Christopher Roberts, *Middlesex Canal, 1793–1860* (Cambridge, Mass., Harvard University Press, 1938), p. 179; J. S. Davis, *Essays*, Vol. II, pp. 167, 168, 170–73. For origins and English precedents, cf. Scott, *op. cit.*, Vol. I, pp. 45, 447; Anderson, *op. cit.*, Vol. III, p. 177.

[65] *Haftung nach innen,* according to Lehmann, *Geschichtliche Entwicklung,* pp. 53 ff.

[66] *House of Lords Journals,* III, 864 ff.

[67] I Chan. Cas., 204, 206 (*English Reports,* XXII, 763 ff.). Cf. also Holdsworth, *op. cit.*, Vol. VIII, pp. 203, 204; A. L. Oliver, *Brief Inquiry into the Origin and Nature of Corporate Privileges* (Cincinnati, 1850), p. 26; Israeli, *op. cit.*, p. 4.

with the theory that members of a corporation [were] . . . thus liable."[68]

In Massachusetts, persistent refusal to create a court of chancery or some other formal equity jurisdiction befogged the question.[69] The English remedy could not be relied upon as, from time to time, changing conditions raised the issue.[70] This deficiency affected not the corporation alone, but every sphere where business met the law under new conditions. Story pointed out in 1808 how frequently the growth of "commerce and manufactures" raised cases "in which no remedy for wrongs" existed at a common law "bound by settled forms of proceeding, and by a rigid adherence to rules of decision."[71]

In the absence of equity the legislature had to work out new procedures in each instance. Failing to reach solutions on a general basis, it devised provisions when some immediate question incidentally brought up the matter of procedure. But even here, the vagaries of individual bill drafters were more weighty than considerations of consistency, for the lawmakers were casual and haphazard about including even clauses the principles of which were universally accepted. The power to assess and to sell the shares of delinquents at auction, like the method of at-

---

[68] Williston, "Business Corporations," *loc. cit.*, II, 161, 162; Kyd, *op. cit.*, Vol. I, p. 272 ff. Per contra, Livermore, *Land Companies*, pp. 280 ff., but on the basis of later cases. The procedural difficulties to which Livermore refers arose out of the doctrine that a corporation could not be imprisoned (Holdsworth, *op. cit.*, Vol. III, p. 488) and the consequent limitation on chancery action, not out of a question on the merits of the principle. The whole case from the original petitions in 1667 to the aftermath in 1674 may be traced. —*House of Lords Journals*, XII, 198, 214, 224, 348, 359, 361, 404, 409 ff., 563, 564, 572, 583, 630, 640; Historical Manuscripts Commission, *Eighth Report*, App., p. 147; *idem*, *Ninth Report*, App. II, pp. 29, 47.

[69] On the problems of chancery, cf. *Journal of Debates and Proceedings in the Convention . . . to Revise the Constitution of Massachusetts . . . 1820* (Boston, 1853), p. 136; E. B. Gager, "Equity, 1701–1901," *Two Centuries' Growth of American Law 1701–1901 by Members of the Faculty of the Yale Law School* (New York, Charles Scribner's Sons, 1901), pp. 131, 136. On the ill repute of equity in the eighteenth century, cf. Holdsworth, *op cit.*, Vol. I, pp. 230, 231.

[70] This deficiency was mentioned in petitions (cf., for example, Massachusetts Archives, H.D. 9244, S.D. 5875) and in tangential cases as late as 1819 (cf., for example, *Vose v. Grant*, 15 Tyng 521, 522; *Spear v. Grant*, 16 Tyng 15). Significantly, the question raised in these cases was ultimately settled in the federal court of equity, *Wood, et al. v. Dummer*, 3 Mason 308, *Federal Cases*, Vol. XXX (St. Paul, 1894 ff.), pp. 435 ff. In South Carolina where equity existed the principle of the Hamborough Case was reaffirmed in *Hume v. Winyaw* and *Wando Canal Company* in 1826–28, in which the court pointed out that "without the aid of the extraordinary power of the Court of Chancery" the plaintiff "would be without a remedy."—*Carolina Law Journal*, 1831, I, 228. There was no explicit reversal anywhere until 1844. Cf. *American Law Magazine*, 1843, I, 96 ff.; *ibid.*, 1845, IV, 363 ff.; Israeli, *op. cit.*, pp. 4, 5, 7 ff.; Blandi, *op. cit.*, p. 40.

[71] Cf. Massachusetts Archives, H.D. 6265, H.D. 6413, H.D. 7232; G. S. Hillard, "Memoir of Joseph Story, LL.D.," *Proceedings of the Massachusetts Historical Society*, 1868, X, 180.

taching stock for private debts, sometimes appeared, sometimes did not; successive acts bestowing identical other privileges upon the same types of companies showed no uniformity. Thus an act amending the charter of the Proprietors of the Locks and Canals on the Connecticut River granted the power to make assessments; but the Middlesex Canal, incorporated a few months later, exercised the same power without specific authority.[72]

In the same way, as other problems brought the question of shareholder liability to the consciousness of the legislators, they hit upon means to implement the accepted principle. For corporations that exercised the right of eminent domain, a remedy against individual members often crept in among the regulations on damages. In canal companies, bridges, and turnpikes the obligation was sometimes direct, sometimes created by analogy with towns.[73] In banks and insurance companies, the question arose out of the problem of securing creditors against fraud or mismanagement. Without mentioning liability in the event of ordinary losses, which presumably fell on stockholders, the charters established the individual liability of directors for those losses that derived from the overissue of notes or the underwriting of excessive risks.[74] The general aqueduct incorporation act of 1799 which codified the principles in sixteen earlier special acts dealt with the question in connection with dissolution which, by common law, would have relieved both corporation and members of liability. The law provided that

> all contracts . . . shall remain in full force, and the last proprietors . . . shall be capable and liable, in and by the same name and capacity as before . . . to sue and be sued . . . and if no corporate property can be found to satisfy any judgment . . . it shall be lawful for the judgment-creditor to satisfy his judgment . . . out of the private estate of such proprietors.[75]

The question of liability during the life of the corporation was taken for granted here, and also in the earlier acts.[76]

---

[72] St. 1792, Ch. 39 (February 25, 1793); St. 1793, Ch. 21 (June 22, 1793).

[73] Cf. Connecticut River Canal (St. 1791, Ch. 32), and *supra,* footnote 37.

[74] Cf. Massachusetts Bank (March 9, 1792), St. 1791, Ch. 65, Sec. 1; Maine Fire Insurance (February 7, 1800), St. 1799, Ch. 42. The banking acts seemed to follow some precedents of the Bank of England. Cf. A. Andréadès, *History of the Bank of England,* C. Meredith, trans. (London, P. S. King & Son, 1909), p. 73; Anderson, *op. cit.,* Vol. III, p. 143. Mutual fire insurance company provisions were more complex, since the same individuals were both creditors and stockholders. Cf. Massachusetts Mutual Fire Insurance (March 1, 1798), St. 1797, Ch. 67. Cf. also Edwin M. Dodd, Jr., "First Half Century of Statutory Regulation of Business Corporations in Massachusetts," *Harvard Legal Essays* (Cambridge, Mass., Harvard University Press, 1934), pp. 72, 79, 84, 86.

[75] St. 1798, Ch. 59, Sec. 9.

[76] For judicial interpretation of a similar provision in New York law, cf. *Slee v. Bloom et al.,* 19 Johnson 456 ff.; *infra,* p. 117.

Manufacturing corporations offer the clearest indication that the whole trend of legislation on unlimited liability was procedural rather than substantive. The first and third charters granted in this field included no provisions for assessments, for the auction of the shares of delinquents, or for attachment for the private debts of the stockholders. The second contained such clauses.[77] The fourth added to the clause on attachments, a matter completely disconnected from the question of corporate indebtedness, the provision that

> in any judgment to be rendered against said Corporation, the plaintiff not being able to find any property of the Corporation to attach on *mesne process,* or whereon to levy his execution, shall have the right of attaching or levying his execution on any . . . individual members of the Corporation, in the same manner as if the action had been brought and the judgment rendered against them in their individual capacity.[78]

This passage reappeared in the next three manufacturing charters and was finally embodied in the general law regulating such corporations of March 3, 1809.[79]

The history of the general act challenges the assumption of Dane in 1824 and of some recent students that the liability clause was new and embodied a substantive change.[80] The precedents already cited controvert the charge of newness; the circumstance of enactment that of innovation. The provision occasioned no discussion. A search of contemporary newspapers and private materials has unearthed not one word of the debate that would inevitably have followed a radical change. That this clause formalized the principle of unlimited liability for one class of corporations at the very moment when broader forces were breaking it down in others does not obscure the fact that the same principle originally applied to all. Indeed, as late as 1822 the New York Court of Appeals, passing on whether certain acts dissolved a corporation, in which case its members were liable by statute for its debts, pointed out that the same liability would exist even if it were not dissolved "upon the principles of the case of *Dr. Salmon v. the Hamborough Company.*"[81]

The full consequences of applying the traditional rule of unlimited

[77] Cf. Beverly Cotton (February 3, 1789), St. 1788, Ch. 43; Newburyport Woollen (January 29, 1794), St. 1793, Ch. 27; Calico Printing (February 25, 1796), St. 1795, Ch. 58.

[78] Salem Iron (March 4, 1800), St. 1799, Ch. 80, Sec. 8.

[79] St. 1808, Ch. 65, Sec. 6; also Dodd, *op. cit.,* pp. 88 ff.

[80] Nathan Dane, *A General Abridgment and Digest of American Law,* Vol. I, p. 472; Livermore, "Unlimited Liability," *loc. cit.,* XLIII, 674 ff.

[81] *Slee v. Bloom et al.,* 19 Johnson 484.

liability to the new areas of corporate activity remained unclear for some decades. The very nature of the undertakings in which corporations were first formed made it unlikely that such questions should reach the courts. Corporations entered spheres that were at first thought to involve relatively little risk. They emerged not in land speculation or in trade where failure was likely, but primarily in fields where success seemed almost certain. And the disappointed took for granted the assistance of generous governments which came to their aid with lotteries, grants of land, and increased tolls when profits slackened.[82] As long as stockholders recognized their responsibility for risks and as long as no creditors suffered from the insolvency of corporations, the question of liability could hardly have been important. For more than twenty years it was not raised by litigation and consequently not adjudicated.[83]

The operation of the new enterprises did bring to the fore certain peripheral questions. Did the creation of shares with a par value specified in the charter set a limit to assessments?[84] Could the corporation contract with its members to call no more than a fixed sum?[85] What recourse did it have to enforce collections beyond the sale of shares?[86] Did the fixing of liability on the part of directors for mismanagement diminish or eliminate the liability of stockholders, as James Sullivan claimed?[87] In the first three decades of the nineteenth century, judicial decisions ultimately supplied the answers and, in the process, set a limit to the liability of stockholders. But the nature of those answers could not have been known or predicted on the basis of precedents and principles that existed in 1800. And, certainly, even the most perspicacious businessmen could not have envisioned the total mosaic eventually pieced together from collateral opinions and random dicta. As a matter of fact none of the changes in law or interpretation had any discernible effect upon the rate of incorporation, a significant indication of the unimportance of limited liability in the minds of incorporators.[88]

[82] Cf., for example, Middlesex Canal (January 25, 1800), St. 1799, Ch. 35; Andover Bridge (February 27, 1796), St. 1795, Ch. 79. For English precedents, cf. Scott, *op. cit.*, Vol. II, p. 19.

[83] On the absence of creditor losses, cf. J. S. Davis, *Essays,* Vol. II, p. 294.

[84] In this period fixed value for shares appeared only in banks and joint-stock insurance companies and then only after 1792.—J. S. Davis, *Essays,* Vol. II, pp. 105, 242 ff. For English precedents, cf. Scott, *op. cit.,* Vol. II, p. 28; DuBois, *op. cit.,* pp. 99 ff.

[85] Cf. Holdsworth, *op. cit.,* Vol. VIII, pp. 204, 205.

[86] Cf., for example, *Worcester Turnpike Corporation v. Willard* (1809), 5 Tyng 80.

[87] Cf. [James Sullivan], *Path to Riches* (Boston, 1792), pp. 37, 48, 51.

[88] Cf. the tabulation by William E. Rappard, *Les corporations d'affaires au Massachusetts* (Paris, 1908), p. 244. Herein we agree with the general conclusion of Eli F. Heckscher, *Mercantilism,* Vol. I, M. Shapiro, trans. (London, G. Allen & Unwin, 1935), pp. 367, 368. Cf. also Dodd, *op. cit.,* p. 92; Ware, *op. cit.,* p. 147.

IV

A third supposed attribute of the corporation, stable freedom from interference by the state, likewise rests upon a misconception of the early character of the institution.[89] To the enterprising businessman of the 1780's a charter brought no such freedom; on the contrary, it introduced new restraints. English precedents were not reassuring, for Parliament was even then putting the East India Company on trial. Not until Marshall and Story held in 1819 that the charter was a contract protected by the Federal Constitution was a sturdy bulwark against legislative interference erected around the corporation.[90]

The decision in the Dartmouth College case was no token of the earlier acceptance of the theory. That Sam Adams and the Revolutionary theorists had used the compact argument against England[91] undoubtedly helps to explain the veneration for the contract clause when it ultimately entered the service of the corporation, but there is little evidence that Adams' theory was thus applied or that the act of incorporation was thus conceived in the forty years before the Dartmouth College case.[92] On the contrary, legislatures took substantial liberties with charters. In 1792, for instance, the General Court altered that of the Massachusetts Bank; and the corporation, while protesting, failed to appeal to the judiciary.[93] Twenty years later, an attorney argued with success that "the

[89] For a contemporary statement of the idea of noninterference, cf. Thomas Paine, *Political Writings,* Vol. I, G. H. Evans, ed. (Middletown, 1837), pp. 412 ff. For a recent interpretation, cf. Livermore, *Land Companies,* pp. 259 ff.

[90] The question of contractual protection was significant because it was generally agreed that the legislature, like Parliament, unless bound by such restrictions, was free to revoke a charter. Cf. Kyd, *op. cit.,* Vol. II, p. 446; [*Outline of the Argument on Part of the Plfs, in the Cause between the Trustees of D. College & William H. Woodward*] (s.l., n.d., Webster's copy, H.C.L.), 77 ff.; 4 Wheaton 643 (ed. B. R. Curtis, Boston, 1864). For a discussion on the case, cf. Benjamin F. Wright, *Contract Clause of the Constitution* (Cambridge, Mass., Harvard University Press, 1938), pp. 28 ff., 39; [C. H. Hill], "Dartmouth College Case," *American Law Review,* VIII, esp. 211 ff.; Carl B. Swisher, *American Constitutional Development* (Boston, Houghton Mifflin Co., 1943), pp. 157 ff.; John M. Shirley, *Dartmouth College Causes and the Supreme Court of the United States* (St. Louis, 1879), pp. 411 ff.

[91] Cf. Thomas Hutchinson, *The History of the Colony and Province of Massachusetts-Bay,* Vol. III, L. S. Mayo, ed. (Cambridge, Mass., Harvard University Press, 1936), pp. 258, 406; Baldwin, "History of the Law of Private Corporations," *loc. cit.,* Vol. III, pp. 252 ff.; Homer C. Hockett, *The Constitutional History of the United States,* Vol. I (New York: Macmillan Co., 1939), pp. 8, 94. For contemporary use of the argument, cf. Paine, *op. cit.,* Vol. I, pp. 372, 378 ff., 397.

[92] Even James Wilson, who argued in 1784 that a charter was a contract, seemed prepared to admit the authority of Congress, but not of the states, to modify or revoke.—*Selected Political Essays of James Wilson,* R. G. Adams, ed. (New York, Alfred A. Knopf, 1930), p. 148 Cf. also Wright, *op. cit.,* pp. 18 ff.; *American Law Review,* VIII, 195 ff.; Shirley, *op. cit.,* pp. 213 ff., for the development of the contract clause.

[93] J. S. Davis, *Essays,* Vol. II, pp. 68 ff.; N. S. B. Gras, *The Massachusetts First National Bank of Boston, 1784–1934* (Cambridge, Mass., Harvard University Press, 1937), p. 63.

notion of a contract between the government and a corporation" was "too fanciful to need any observation."[94] And in 1812, when the legislature changed the Harvard College charter without the consent of the corporation, the Board of Overseers acquiesced, voting it was "not disposed to bring its rights to the test of judicial decision."[95]

Nor did Marshall's decision close the question; in the very same year Webster himself argued for a restricted application.[96] Two decades later the validity of the verdict was still challenged,[97] and even thereafter saving clauses reserved the state's freedom of action.[98] Certainly the post-Revolutionary enterprisers could not have assumed that an act of incorporation carried privileges which would be forever after beyond the reach of the legislature.

Aware of this circumstance, Story rested his defense of the charter upon a distinction between public and private corporations, a classification he had already made in *Terrett v. Taylor* (1815).[99] In this respect he followed the lead of James Wilson and Thomas Paine who had, in defense of the Bank of North America in 1784, attempted to draw a line between public laws and legislative "acts of agency or negociation . . . of the nature of a deed or contract," transactions in which "the state stands as an individual, and can be known in no other character in a court of justice."[100] But neither the division into public and private laws nor the distinction between public and private corporations was accepted by eighteenth-century law. Parliamentary practice differentiated between public and private acts, and Massachusetts followed to some extent in distinguishing between acts and resolves. But that classification did not rest on the basis set up by the Pennsylvania theorists, for in Massachusetts and often in England acts of incorporation were public laws in this period.[101]

---

94 *Brown v. Penobscot Bank* (1812) 8 Tyng 448; Shirley, *op. cit.*, p. 185.

95 Josiah Quincy, *History of Harvard University*, Vol. II (Cambridge, Mass., 1840), pp. 301 ff.

96 *Foster v. Essex Bank* (1819) 16 Tyng 266 ff.

97 Cf., for example, [David Henshaw], *Remarks upon the Rights and Powers of Corporations* (Boston, 1837), pp. 5 ff.

98 Cf. Rappard, *op. cit.*, p. 45.

99 9 Cranch 52 (Curtis ed., 1865); cf. also 4 Wheaton 664, 667 ff.; Wright, *op. cit.*, p. 38; H. W. Rogers, "Municipal Corporations," *Two Centuries' Growth*, p. 253.

100 Cf. Paine, *op. cit.*, Vol. I, pp. 373 ff.; also Adams, *op. cit.*, pp. 138 ff.; Wright, *op. cit.*, p. 17; Lawrence Lewis, *History of the Bank of North America* (Philadelphia, 1882), pp. 65 ff.; J. S. Davis, *Essays*, Vol. II, pp. 310 ff.

101 English private laws were first issued in series in 1798. For their nature, cf. introduction to Thomas Vardon, *Index to the Local and Personal and Private Acts: 1708–1839,—38 Geo. 3—2 & 3 Vict.* (London, 1840). For American law, cf. Rev. St., Ch. 2, Sec. 3; James Kent, *Commentaries on American Law* (Boston, 1884), p. 459; Henshaw, *op. cit.*, pp. 7, 11.

Story's distinction between public and private corporations had as little validity. It broadened the scope of the latter to include any body involving private rights, a position difficult to maintain and later considerably modified.[102] But in any case it was a differentiation completely unknown before 1800.[103] Until then corporations were either clerical or lay, with the latter further divided into eleemosynary and civil.[104] There is no doubt that at their origin business corporations like universities came under the heading of civil. Both Kyd and Blackstone put the Bank of England, the East India Company, and the insurance and manufacturing companies in the same category as boroughs, universities, and the College of Physicians; and even Justice Holt in *Phillips v. Bury,* a case much cited by Marshall's court, adopted the same classification.[105]

To support its position the court argued that towns, the status of which the legislature could clearly alter at will, were quasi corporations, different from others.[106] That contention disregarded the fact that eighteenth-century quasi corporations possessed the same attributes as others except for their origin which was in prescription rather than in charter.[107] In Massachusetts all towns arose in this manner before 1684 because the common law kept the central government, itself a corporation, from creating others.[108] After the Province Charter of 1691 even that difference disappeared; towns thereafter chartered were in law like

[102] Cf. 4 Wheaton 659 ff., 669 ff., *American Law Review,* VIII, 220 ff.; Shirley, *op. cit.,* p. 364. Chief Justice Richardson of New Hampshire in the state decision against the trustees had drawn another distinction between public and private corporations, more logical in 1819, but equally invalid as applied to the law of the eighteenth century. Cf. Timothy Farrar, *Report of the Case of the Trustees of Dartmouth College against William H. Woodward* (Portsmouth, 1819), pp. 211 ff.

[103] Modern writers who have drawn that distinction for the eighteenth-century corporation have done so despite the fact that it was "a distinction then unrecognized." Cf., for example, J. S. Davis, *Essays,* Vol. I, pp. 49, 75.

[104] Kyd, *op. cit.,* Vol. I, pp. 12 ff., 25 ff.; cf. also William Shepherd (1659), quoted in Eaton, *op. cit.,* Vol. XII, p. 264; *American Law Review,* VIII, 216 ff. It is worth noting that Webster himself accepted this distinction in his first argument.—*Outline of the Argument,* p. 13; Shirley, *op. cit.,* pp. 176 ff. The *Law of Corporations* (1702) divided the lay into general, such as cities, and special, such as trades and charities.—Williston, "Business Corporations," *loc. cit.,* II, 110.

[105] Kyd, *op. cit.,* Vol. I, pp. 28 ff.; Blackstone, *op. cit.,* pp. 470 ff.

[106] For the argument that a town is not a corporation, cf. J. S. Davis, *Essays,* Vol. I, pp. 61, 62.

[107] Cf. *Dillingham v. Snow* (1809), 5 Tyng 547; 13 Mass. 193; Oliver, *op. cit.,* p. 5; J. S. Davis, *Essays,* Vol. I, p. 7. James Sullivan's memorandum to the legislature (1802), Massachusetts Archives, S.D. 2957/5, rested the distinction upon the absence of a common seal, but eighteenth-century law held that unimportant, following Coke in *Mayor of Stafford v. Bolton,* in the position that corporations "when they are incorporated may make or use what seal they will."—Williston, "Business Corporations," *loc. cit.,* II, 116–18; Kyd, *op cit.,* Vol. I, p. 268. Cf. also H. W. Rogers, *op. cit.,* p. 219.

[108] J. S. Davis, *Essays,* Vol. I, p. 20.

other corporations.[109] James Sullivan clearly expressed the opinion of this period when he wrote of the Massachusetts Bank:

There is no lawyer in the state, who is disinterested, that will give it as his opinion, that the legislature has not a right to repeal the act of incorporation of that society . . . it is on the same foot of other legislative acts, such as incorporating towns and proprietors, which laws may be repealed at pleasure. Here was no contract between these people and the government.[110]

Neither Story nor Marshall took cognizance of another fundamental problem that had troubled thinkers little more than a decade earlier. Whether a charter was a grant or a contract, public or private, had once seemed less significant than the question of what was the life of the corporation. Marshall, in 1819, spoke glibly of its immortality.[111] But to an eighteenth-century lawyer like Kyd, that was a manifest absurdity: "That a body framed by the policy of man, a body whose parts and members are mortal, should in its own nature be immortal . . . seems beyond the reach of common understandings."[112]

Only in a very limited sense was perpetuity "regarded as a *sine qua non* of the common law corporation."[113] That word had a narrow meaning in eighteenth-century charters. Sometimes, as when Blackstone said that corporations "maintain a perpetual succession,"[114] it referred to the privilege of co-opting new members and holding property as if the components of the group remained unchanged, "just as with flocks of sheep, the flock remains the same though the sheep die."[115] When applied to the corporation itself, it meant that the body was "*capable* of an indefinite duration."[116] But even if the flock remained the same, there was

---

[109] For the corporateness of towns, cf. the opinion of the solicitor of the Board of Trade, 1774, cited *ibid.*, Vol. I, p. 61; *Wrentham Proprietors v. Metcalf* (1763), in *Reports of Cases . . . between 1761 and 1772*, Josiah Quincy, Jr., ed. (Boston, 1865), pp. 36 ff.; the state constitution of 1780, Ch. 1, Sec. 3, C1. 2; St. 1785, Ch. 75, Sec. 8. It is interesting that in the first argument before the New Hampshire court, Marsh, of counsel for the trustees, accepted and used the similarity between corporation and town.—Shirley, *op. cit.*, pp. 159, 178.

[110] Sullivan, *op. cit.*, p. 57.

[111] Cf. 4 Wheaton 636.

[112] Kyd, *op. cit.*, Vol. I, p. 15; *American Law Review*, VIII, 213 ff.

[113] Livermore, *Land Companies*, p. 260.

[114] Blackstone, *op. cit.*, Vol. I, pp. 467, 474.

[115] Pollock and Maitland, *op. cit.*, Vol. I, p. 508; Kyd, *op. cit.*, Vol. I, pp. 2 ff., 69; James Wilson, *Works*, Vol. II, Bird Wilson, ed. (Philadelphia, 1804), p. 427. Cf. also cases cited in Carr, *Select Essays in Legal History*, Vol. III, pp. 174, 175.

[116] Kyd, *op. cit.*, Vol. I, p. 17. Thus a seventeenth-century treatise spoke of actions: "I call those perpetuall . . . which have not any set time expressly allotted for their continuance." [John Cowell], *Institutes of the Lawes of England*, W. G., trans. (London, 1651), p. 238.

nothing to suggest it was immortal.[117] If it was not, and if the charter contained no explicit provision of time, what were the limits of its life? Whatever the nature of the charter, was not the state free, in the absence of express time limits, to terminate it at any moment?

That problem faced the Attorney General of Massachusetts, asked by the legislature in 1802 to interpret the 1784 charter of the Massachusetts Bank.[118] In 1802 as in 1792 Sullivan could find no legal obstacle. Yet he was no longer willing to face the consequences of assuming that position. For to concede that power to the legislature was to recognize an omnipotence seemingly harmless in 1792, but dangerous after a decade of business development in which the new institution had reached out into many spheres where property rights were closely involved and widely spread. Personally interested in many corporations, the Attorney General wished to believe that the state did not have the right, but failed to convince even himself and finally refused to answer categorically. His reply to the committee nevertheless pointed to the dependent position of the corporation and to its lack of freedom from governmental control: "There have been no decisions on the point in the country, and it is therefore out of my power to answer the question. . . . There is no legal decision, no precedent established in the government on which to predicate an opinion, or to form decisive answers."[119] A new concept of perpetuity arose soon after; but in the period of corporate growth it did not exist.

V

The attributes of peculiar economic efficiency, of limited liability, and of perpetual freedom from state interference were thus not present at the birth of the American business corporation. Divested of these characteristics, the form assumes a new significance. At its origin in Massachusetts the corporation was conceived as an agency of government, endowed with public attributes, exclusive privileges, and political power, and designed to serve a social function for the state. Turnpikes, not trade, banks, not land speculation, were its province because the community, not the enterprising capitalists, marked out its sphere of activity.

[117] Thus an English statute (1719) 6 Geo. I, Ch. 18, Sec. 1, *Statutes at Large,* p. 197, described a grant as both perpetual and revocable. Cf. also J. P. Davis, *op. cit.,* Vol. II, p. 121.

[118] Gras, *op. cit.,* p. 80.

[119] Massachusetts Archives, S.D. 2957/5. Sullivan's hesitancy is particularly significant in view of the fact that he had been chairman of the legislative committee that approved the bank charter in 1784. Cf. T. C. Amory, *Life of James Sullivan,* Vol. I (Boston, 1859), pp. 146, 387.

The explanation for its development in this period lies in the impact of the economic ideas and the economic interests of the last two decades of the eighteenth century upon legal doctrines developed in the previous century and a half. It was a slow process which cannot be described well except as part of a general study of the role of government in the economy of Massachusetts.[120] Seen in its historic background, the multiplication of corporate bodies, at a time when they did not possess the attributes which later became their best-known characteristics, resulted from forces inherent in the American democratic conceptions of the state. Creation of many corporations spread the benefits of this aspect of government among many citizens, instead of confining them to a favored few as in Europe, and thus transformed the old institution. The privileges that went with the charter lost their previous meanings and new interpretations adjusted old forms to unaccustomed activities. In the process, the business corporation acquired its modern character.

[120] We are preparing such a study which will present the positive aspects of this question, under the auspices of the Committee on Research in Economic History of the Social Science Research Council. [EDITOR'S NOTE: See Oscar Handlin and Mary F. Handlin, *Commonwealth, a Study of the Role of Government in the American Economy: Massachusetts, 1774–1861* (New York: New York University Press, 1947).]

9

*The Growth in the Relative Importance of the Large Corporation in American Economic Life**[1]

By GARDINER C. MEANS

Very large corporations with gross assets over $80,000,000 occupy an increasingly dominant position. Estimates indicate that this class controls 80 per cent of assets of corporations having stocks regularly traded on the New York Stock Exchange and that the 200 largest non-financial corporations in 1927 controlled over 45 per cent of the assets of all non-financial corporations, received over 40 per cent of corporate income, controlled over 35 per cent of all business wealth and between 15 and 25 per cent of national wealth. Between 1909 and 1927 the assets of the 200 largest increased more than twice as fast as the assets of other non-financial corporations. They reinvested a larger proportion of their earnings, secured a larger proportion of new capital in the open market and increased in size through mergers. If recent rates of growth were to continue, 80 per cent of non-financial corporate wealth would be in the hands of 200 corporations by 1950.

The huge corporation has come to be a commonplace in American economic life. There are few major industries which cannot boast of at least one corporation with assets over a hundred million dollars. Six industries can boast of one or more "billion dollar" companies. A merger creating such a billion dollar concern results in little public discussion. The individual has almost daily contact with one of these great companies. If he is not actually employed by one of them he at least uses the telephone, rides in the railway, drives an automobile, buys gasoline. And it is extremely difficult to do any of these, as well as countless other things, without dealing directly or indirectly with a huge corporation.

* *American Economic Review,* 1931, XXI, 10–42. Reprinted by courtesy of the author and of the American Economic Association.

[1] The following study is one outgrowth of a project in combined legal and economic research conducted at the Columbia Law School under the auspices of the Columbia Social Science Research Council. Certain important conclusions have been based on income statistics for 1927 or prior years. After the material was in type the statistics of income for 1928 became available. They clearly support the conclusions based on the earlier years. Where relevant they have been attached.

In spite of the general familiarity with individual large corporations, there has been little exact information available to indicate the extent to which the large corporations as a group have come to dominate industry. We know that particular corporations have grown with amazing rapidity but others have declined in size. Industry as a whole has grown. Have the large corporations as a group kept pace? Have they increased even more rapidly? Are they coming to absorb a larger proportion of industry? Shall we regard them, not, as in the past, in the light of monopoly, combination, and the trust problem, but as forms of enterprise through which most of the economic activity of the future will be carried on?

It is the purpose of the present article to examine the large corporations in the light of these questions and quite apart from any trade restraining influence which they may have; to present a picture of the extent to which they pervade industry today; and in particular to furnish evidence that the large corporations are already so important and are so rapidly increasing in importance that if this growth continues at its present rate, most of the industrial wealth and activity of the country will soon be in the hands of a few huge units.

Before measuring the importance of the large corporation, it is necessary to select a measure of size. For this purpose the gross assets[2] controlled by a corporation have been employed, though, where possible, the results obtained have been checked by the use of a second measure of size—net earnings.[3] Other measures could undoubtedly be used with equal justification, but the available materials allow greater accuracy with the two chosen.

It should be noted that both these measures are roughly measures of wealth, though wealth would be differently defined in each case. While accounting practice varies widely with different companies and with the same company at different times as to the mode of determining gross assets and net income, the major differences in accounting presumably cancel out where one large group of companies is compared with another large group. Gross assets are then roughly proportional to wealth based on its depreciated cost. Net income, on the other hand, is roughly

---

[2] Gross assets less depreciation. In some balance sheets depreciation is subtracted from assets and in others it is included as a liability. Both practices are legitimate, but the latter results in a larger figure for gross assets. An adjustment has, therefore, been made where necessary to obtain gross assets exclusive of depreciation.

[3] Statutory net income as compiled by the Treasury Department. This consists of the untaxed net income derived by a corporation directly from its business operations.

proportional to the market value of these properties since market value is based primarily upon income-producing capacity.[4] If we chose to base the definition of wealth not on cost but on market value, net income would then be roughly proportional to wealth. Both definitions of wealth are widely current, and no effort is being made here to choose between them. It is sufficient to point out that if groups of corporations are graded in size by gross assets or by net income, they will be grouped roughly according to wealth.

In addition to a measure of size, it is necessary to have in mind what lies behind the concept "large corporation." A company having assets of a million dollars would be considered large by many people. In 1927 (the most recent year for which income tax data have been published) two-thirds of all the corporations reporting net income earned less than $5,000.[5] The average non-financial corporation in that year had an income of only $22,000[6] and gross assets of but $570,000.[7] In comparison with the great modern corporations, these median or average corporations are pygmies. Based on assets, the American Telephone and Telegraph Company would be equivalent to over 6,000 average sized corporations; the United States Steel Corporation to over 4,000; the Pennsylvania Railroad (exclusive of the Pennroad Corporation) to over 4,000. A hundred million dollar company would be equivalent in assets to nearly 200 average corporations. If, then, we restrict our study of the large corporations to those with 80 to 100 million assets or more, it is apparent that we will be dealing only with super-corporations, with corporations far separated, at least in size, from the average, many of them so large as to be almost beyond imagination. It is with such huge corporations that we have to deal.

The study is further restricted to non-financial corporations. The inclusion of banks, insurance companies, etc., would involve consider-

[4] This takes no account of the wealth represented on the liability side of the balance sheet by bonds, notes, etc. The tax data used in this study do not make possible the inclusion of the income from this wealth. If, for each group of corporations compared, the interest paid on borrowings were proportional to net income, then the latter would be proportional to wealth. To the extent that interest paid is not proportional to income, the latter would be inaccurate as a measure.

[5] *Statistics of Income, 1927,* p. 19.

[6] *Ibid.,* pp. 16 and 17. Net income of all non-financial corporations reporting net income divided by total number of non-financial corporation tax returns. If the net income minus net deficit of all such corporations had been divided by the number of corporations, the average would have been $16,000. If the net income of all corporations reporting net incomes had been divided by the number of corporations reporting net income, the average would have been $41,000.

[7] *Ibid.,* pp. 371 and 372.

able duplications, since an important part of their assets are composed of securities of other companies. On the other hand, all organizations such as Massachusetts trusts, which are classed as corporations for income tax purposes, are included.

In seeking to present a picture of the relative position of these large corporations, four economic areas will be examined: (1) the New York stock market; (2) all corporate wealth; (3) all business wealth; and (4) the national wealth.

THE LARGE CORPORATION IN RELATION TO THE NEW YORK STOCK MARKET

In the New York stock market there can be no question of the dominant position of the large corporation. Taking the list of stocks published weekly by the *Commercial and Financial Chronicle* and covering all but the most inactive stocks traded on the New York Stock Exchange in a normal week, 130 out of the 573 independent American corporations represented can be classed as huge companies, each reporting assets of over one hundred million dollars.[8] These 130 companies controlled more than 80 per cent of the assets of all the companies represented. In the following table, these corporations are grouped by size showing the total assets held by each group and the per cent which this represents of the assets of all the corporations covered:[9]

Size Measured by Gross Assets	Number of Companies	Gross Assets Held by Group	Per Cent of Total Assets
Under $50,000,000	372	$ 7,325,000,000	10.9
$50–$100,000,000	71	4,950,000,000	7.4
Over $100,000,000	130	54,714,000,000	81.7
Total	573	$66,989,000,000	100.0

Besides showing the overwhelming importance of the huge corporation, this table shows what is perhaps of even greater significance, the relative

[8] The stocks of 678 corporations were included in the list published by the *Commercial and Financial Chronicle* in the issue selected, that of the typical week of March 9, 1929. Of these 76 were subsidiaries of other corporations on the list, 21 were foreign corporations and 8 were financial corporations. When a corporation listed on the exchange was a subsidiary of a corporation not listed, the parent was regarded as represented on the exchange. The assets of the listed corporations were obtained in *Moody's Manuals* for 1928 and 1929.

[9] A similar study was made for the independent companies listed on the New York Curb Exchange, using the curb transaction list from the same issue of the *Commercial and Financial Chronicle.* Unfortunately the study was first made for a different purpose which involved only the companies in existence in 1927 and a compilation of assets as of

unimportance of the medium-sized corporation having assets between $50,000,000 and $100,000,000 and as a group controlling less than 8 per cent of the total assets represented. The small corporations—and in this day of industrial giants the reader must not be shocked by the reference to all corporations with assets less than $50,000,000 as small—though numerous, do not hold an important position. It is noteworthy, however, that practically half the corporations included had less than $30,000,000 assets and as a group controlled less than 6 per cent of the total. Table I shows the companies distributed in more detail according to size.

THE LARGE CORPORATION IN RELATION TO ALL CORPORATIONS AS MEASURED BY ASSETS

While the large corporation bulks so important among corporations listed on the stock exchange, this is no indication that it plays such an important rôle in comparison with all corporations. To discover its importance in this larger field a list was compiled of the two hundred American corporations reported in *Moody's 1928 Industrial, Public Utility,* and *Railroad Manuals* as having the largest gross assets.[10] This list included 45 railroads, 58 public utilities, and 97 industrial companies each with assets of over $85,000,000 at the end of 1927. The combined assets of these two hundred largest non-financial corporations amounted to $67,165,000,000.

This figure represents the gross assets directly controlled by these corporations, except for two partially counterbalancing factors. Examina-

that date. For this reason it does not include many companies which should be added. As the correction would probably not make a radical difference in the set of percentages, the uncorrected results are given below:

Size Measured by Gross Assets	Number of Companies	Gross Assets Held by Group	Per Cent of Total Assets
Under $50,000,000	371	$ 3,731,000,000	24.3
$50–$100,000,000	31	2,308,000,000	15.0
Over $100,000,000	37	9,338,000,000	60.7
Total	439	$15,377,000,000	100.0

[10] In the 26 cases where a consolidated balance sheet was not given in *Moody's* an estimate was made based on the assets of subsidiaries and the assets of the parent corporation minus its investments in affiliated companies. These estimates, while they cannot be perfectly accurate, are sufficiently so for the present purpose. In two cases, no balance sheet of the parent was given but a very rough estimate of the assets controlled was made, based on the bonds and stocks of the parent company and the assets of certain of its subsidiaries. See Tables IIa to IIe in Appendix.

tion of the consolidated balance sheets of various companies shows part of these assets to consist of the securities of other corporations. These must be securities either of independent companies or of subsidiaries whose accounts are not consolidated with the accounts of the parent. (It is customary to consolidate only subsidiaries which are controlled by a 95 to 100 per cent stock ownership.) In the former case the gross assets

TABLE I

SIZE OF CORPORATIONS REPRESENTED BY STOCK LISTED AND ACTIVE ON THE NEW YORK STOCK EXCHANGE[1]
(573 Independent Corporations)

Gross Assets in Million Dollars	Number of Corporations	Gross Assets in Million Dollars	Number of Corporations
Under $10	100	$100–$200	49
$10– 20	115	200– 300	22
20– 30	70	300– 400	18
30– 40	56	400– 500	7
40– 50	31	500– 600	12
50– 60	21	600– 700	4
60– 70	16	700– 800	3
70– 80	17	800– 900	4
80– 90	10	900–1000	
90–100	7	Over 1000	11
Total under $100	443	Grand total	573

[1] Derived from *Commercial and Financial Chronicle*, (*Mar. 9, 1929*) Vol. CXVIII, No. 3324 pp. 1514–23 and *Moody's Railroad, Public Utility* and *Industrial Manuals* for 1928 and 1929.

appear greater than are actually controlled. In the latter case they usually appear less than are controlled since as a rule the gross assets of the subsidiary are greater in value than the stock held by the parent. These two factors must in some measure cancel each other. It is difficult to say with certainty which factor dominates, but there are many indications that the securities of subsidiaries play the more important rôle. For this reason there appears to be little danger of overestimating the assets controlled by the large companies if the assumption is made that these two items just cancel each other and that, for the group of companies as a whole, the assets reported are exactly equal to the assets controlled.

In order to measure the percentage of all corporate assets which this figure represents, an estimate of the gross assets of all non-financial corporations was derived from income tax figures. In 1927, the gross assets of all non-financial corporations whose balance sheets were tabulated by the Treasury Department amounted to $174,600,000,000.[11] This figure is not, however, immediately comparable with that for the two hundred

[11] Gross assets of all corporations minus the gross assets of financial corporations, *Statistics of Income, 1927,* p. 372. The Treasury Department requires that depreciation should be subtracted from assets.

largest corporations. Two sets of adjustments must be made. First, the balance sheets tabulated do not include all corporations. Ninety-nine and one-half per cent of the corporations reporting net income over $5,000,-000 are included and 99 per cent of the corporations reporting a net income between $10,000 and $5,000,000; but only 89 per cent of corporations reporting no income or income less than $10,000 are included.[12] Presumably the companies in the last group whose balance sheets were not tabulated were, for the most part, small and would not appreciably increase the total even if included. It is, therefore, reasonable to assume that 99 per cent of the assets of all corporations are included in the total. On this basis the gross assets of all corporations would have been increased one per cent to $176,400,000,000.

One further correction must be made. An important portion of these assets are represented by the securities of subsidiaries and other corporations whose assets are also included. To make the figure comparable to that of the two hundred corporations, this amount, covering both stocks, bonds, and loans, should be deducted if duplication is to be avoided. Non-financial corporations paid $5,354,800,000 in cash dividends and received from domestic corporations $1,098,600,000 in dividends, thus indicating that they owned approximately 20.5 per cent of the stocks of other corporations.[13] The capital stocks of all non-financial corporations were carried on their own books at $76,200,000,000.[14] Assuming that corporations carry the stocks of other corporations at the same value as the issuing corporation (par in many cases), 20.5 per cent of this figure, or $15,600,000,000, would be the amount of duplication in total assets to be subtracted due to the holding of the stocks of one corporation by another.[15]

A similar adjustment must be made for loans to other corporations, either through the purchase of bonds, or, more frequently, by direct loans to subsidiaries. In 1927, non-financial corporations reported the receipt of $768,300,000[16] in interest exclusive of that received from

---

[12] *Statistics of Income, 1927,* pp. 380 and 383. For each group the number of returns filed and the number of balance sheets compiled were calculated by subtracting the financial corporations from all corporations.

[13] *Statistics of Income, 1927,* pp. 312 and 315. This assumes that the volume of stocks of financial corporations owned by non-financial corporations was negligible.

[14] *Statistics of Income, 1927,* p. 373.

[15] In many cases, the stocks of other corporations are carried by the owning corporation at a figure higher than that recorded by the issuing corporation, particularly in the case of no par stock where part of the capital realized from the sale of stock has been attributed to "paid in surplus." Only occasionally are stocks carried at a figure below that of the issuing corporation. This tends to minimize the figure for stocks owned by corporations.

[16] Derived from *Statistics of Income, 1927,* pp. 312 and 315.

federal, state and municipal bonds. This item included interest on bank deposits, notes, mortgages and corporation bonds. The total cash and bank deposits of non-financial corporations amounted to $7,131,000,000[17] which, at 3 per cent, would yield $214,000,000 of interest, probably a figure larger than was actually received. Assuming it to be correct, however, there would remain $554,300,000 of interest derived from loans to individuals, partnerships and other corporations. Since only financial corporations make a wide practice of loaning to individuals, it seems reasonable to attribute at least three-quarters of this interest, or $415,800,000, to loans to other corporations. Capitalized at 5 per cent[18] this would give a capital sum of $8,300,000,000 as the amount of duplication included in the figure of gross assets as a result of loans to other corporations.

When correction is made for these two factors, the resulting figure for the gross assets of all non-financial corporations, 302,993 in number, is $152,500,000,000. Since the 200 largest non-financial corporations were found to control gross assets of $67,165,000,000, they would appear to control 44 per cent of all non-financial corporate wealth.[19]

In the opinion of the present writer, this is a conservative figure. It seems probable that more nearly half of all corporate assets, excluding those of financial corporations, were controlled by the 200 largest non-financial corporations in 1927.

THE LARGE CORPORATION IN RELATION TO ALL CORPORATIONS AS MEASURED BY NET INCOME

A partial check on this figure was obtained by estimating the proportion of the net income of all non-financial corporations which was received by the 200 largest. This estimate was based on the Treasury Department's compilations of the net income of corporations in 1927 as reported for different income groups. Unfortunately for the present purpose, subsidiaries which filed separate income tax returns were tabulated as separate corporations. All corporations, even subsidiaries, were required to file separate returns, except where 95 per cent or more of

[17] *Statistics of Income, 1927,* pp. 312 and 315.

[18] Dr. King reports .0568, .0401 and .0533 as the ratios of interest paid to funded debt in 1925 for factories, railroads and electric light and power companies respectively. (National Bureau of Economic Research, Inc., *The National Income and Its Purchasing Power* [New York, 1930], p. 201.) Short term unfunded debt was presumably paid at a lower rate.

[19] The corresponding figure for 1928 is 45.5 per cent. This assumes that 97 per cent of the corporate assets were tabulated. (*Statistics of Income, 1928,* pp. 318, 321, 380, and 381.)

the stock (or of the voting stock) was held by a parent corporation.[20] Even in such cases they were allowed to file separate returns if they so desired. It is therefore apparent that frequently the net income reported by a corporation did not include all the net income derived from property under its control. For instance, the American Telephone and Telegraph Company was presumably represented in income tax returns as four companies, the parent company with assets over $3,000 million in 1928, the Pacific Telephone and Telegraph Company with assets over $379 million, the New England Telephone and Telegraph Company with $268 million assets and the Mountain States Telephone and Telegraph Company with $80 million assets.[21] Even dividends received from these subsidiaries were not included in the statutory net income of the parent, which, therefore, appears smaller in the income tax compilation than would be warranted by the amount of net income derived from property under its control. Many other large corporations were in the same situation. For this reason the earned income reported by the large companies is frequently less than the earnings of property under their control.

A second factor tending to minimize the apparent importance of the large corporation, is the greater proportion of its income which is paid out as interest and therefore is not included as "statutory net income." It is fairly certain that large companies, particularly railroads and public utilities, tend to have a larger indebtedness in proportion to their size than small companies.

Keeping in mind the fact that the income tax figures therefore tend to minimize the importance of the large corporations, just what do they show? In 1927, the two hundred largest non-financial corporations, each with an income over $4,000,000, received 38.4 per cent of the income of all such corporations.[22] If the net income of all subsidiary corporations

[20] Revenue Act of 1926, Sec. 240 (a), (c) and (d). In case 95 per cent or more of the stock or of the voting stock of each of two or more corporations was owned by "the same interests" the corporations could file a consolidated return and would, therefore, appear as a single corporation in the statistics of income. Such a situation arises so infrequently that it need not be regarded here.

[21] Subsidiaries of the American Telephone and Telegraph Company presumably filing income tax returns separate from parent in 1928 (*i.e.*, less than 95 per cent owned). Derived from *Bell Telephone Securities-Reference Tables and Descriptions, 1929,* published by the Bell Telephone Securities Company, a subsidiary of the American Telephone and Telegraph Company. Figures as of December 31, 1928:

Gross Assets in Millions	*Name*	*Per Cent Stock Owned by A. T. & T. Co.*
$ 80.1	Mountain States Tel. & Tel. Co.	72.82
268.6	New England Tel. & Tel. Co.	61.98
379.6	Pacific Tel. & Tel. Co.	82.00

[22] The corresponding figure for 1928 is 40.4 per cent. See Table III.

had been included in the net income of parents, and if income had included amounts paid out as interest, it is probable that the two hundred largest would have received well over 40 per cent of the net income of

TABLE III

GROWTH OF LARGE CORPORATIONS AS MEASURED BY STATUTORY NET INCOME[1]

	Net Income of All Non-financial Corporations (Million Dollars)	Estimated Net Income of 200 Largest Non-financial Corporations (Million Dollars)	Per Cent by Largest 200 Corporations	Estimated Net Income of 800 Next Largest Non-financial Corporations (Million dollars)	Per Cent by Next Largest 800 Corporations
1920	$6,899	$2,307	33.4	$1,305	19.0
1921	3,597	1,354	37.6	708	19.6
1922	6,076	1,958	32.2	1,151	19.0
1923	7,453	2,445	32.8	1,386	18.6
1924	6,591	2,378	36.0	1,247	19.0
1925	8,060	2,993	37.1	1,522	18.9
1926	8,337	3,335	40.0	1,564	18.7
1927	7,459	2,865	38.4	1,360	18.2
1928	8,646	3,493	40.4	1,618	18.7
Average 1920–1923	$6,006	$2,015	33.5	$1,137	18.9
Average 1924–1927	$7,611	$2,888	37.9	$1,425	18.7

[1] Derived from *Statistics of Income* for the respective years. Net income of all non-financial corporations equals statutory net income of all corporations reporting net income less that of financial corporations reporting net income. Income for the largest 200 was estimated by taking the net income of all non-financial corporations reporting income over $5,000,000 including nearly 200 companies and adding to this an estimate of the income of additional companies to make the total of 200. In each case the few additional companies were assumed to have a net income of $5,000,000. (If the average income of the added companies had been $4,500,000 it would have lowered the estimate in 1927 only from 38.4 to 38.2 per cent. In other years the change would have been very much less. As in each year there were approximately 800 companies having incomes between $1,000,000 and $5,000,000, it is unlikely that the average income of the few companies necessary to make up the 200 largest would have been below $4,500,000 and was probably closer to $5,000,000. The assumption of the latter figures would not, therefore, lead to appreciable error.)

Income for the next largest 800 was estimated by taking the income of all non-financial corporations reporting statutory net income of over $1,000,000 (approximately 900 corporations in each year) and adding an estimate of the income of additional companies to make a total of 1,000, the extra companies being assumed to have an income of $1,000,000. From the resulting figure the estimated income of the largest 200 was subtracted. (Error due to the probability that the additional companies had an average income of somewhat less than $1,000,000 would be negligible. If the average in 1927 had been $900,000 it would have reduced the percentage only from 18.2 to 18.1. As there were nearly 1,000 corporations having incomes between $500,000 and $1,000,000, the average income of the added companies must have been more nearly $1,000,000 than $900,000. In other years the error would be even less.

all corporations. This figure would tend to give support to the figure derived on the basis of gross assets.

The income figures also give support to the conclusion that the medium-sized corporation is not a particularly important factor. The 800 non-financial corporations next in size (according to net income) after the largest 200, received only 18.2 per cent of the net income of all corporations. This figure covers all corporations reporting income of over one million dollars and less than four and one half million dollars, income representing assets ranging roughly from 18 to 80 million dollars. If all corporations had filed consolidated income accounts, the 800 corporations would have reported a still smaller proportion of corporate income since that of many important corporations would have been shifted into the higher group and only a slight balancing would come through addition from below.

In contrast to the medium-sized, the small corporation, reporting an income under one million dollars, makes an important showing. Such corporations accounted for 43.4 per cent of all corporate income, due, in large measure, to the sheer weight of numbers among the smallest units. Over 28 per cent of the net income of all corporations was received by the 178,273[23] corporations, each reporting net income of less than $250,000 and in the main, having assets of less than four million dollars. This would seem to indicate that the bulk of corporate wealth was represented either by huge units having assets running into the hundreds of millions or by relatively small corporations having assets under four million dollars.

THE LARGE CORPORATION IN RELATION TO ALL BUSINESS WEALTH

There appears to be no adequate basis for determining the exact relation of corporate wealth to all business wealth. It is possible, however, to make a very rough approximation on the basis of the net income of corporations and the net income of non-corporate business. The statutory net income of all non-financial corporations, exclusive of interest received, amounted in 1927 to $6,886,700,000.[24] The statutory net income of private business can be estimated as follows: All individuals and partnerships having a gross income of $5,000 or over from business or professional activity were required to file tax returns. Since no appreciable business can exist without gross sales of over $5,000, we may be sure that practically all the income from private business is included. The total income from private business and the professions amounted to $5,042,500,000.[25] To make this figure comparable to the income of corporations, two deductions must be made: first, the professional income; and, second, an amount to compensate for the direct labor of the

[23] *Statistics of Income, 1927,* pp. 365 and 369.

[24] Statutory net income of non-financial corporations minus interest other than that from government bonds. Derived from *Statistics of Income, 1927,* pp. 316 and 319.

[25] Business $3,287,400,000 and partnership $1,755,100,000, *Statistics of Income, 1927,* p. 8.

proprietors, an item which is included as a cost in the case of the corporations.

No direct division of this income into business and professional can be made, but it can be roughly divided on the basis of figures which have been compiled by the Treasury Department for all returns reporting a net income over $5,000 and covering over one-third of private business and professional income. Forty per cent[26] of this income was received in the occupations classed as "service" and including all professions, amusements, hotels, etc. The bulk of this amount must have been professional, since, to a very important extent, hotels and amusements are incorporated if at all large. If three-quarters of this amount was professional, then 30 per cent of the sample must have been professional and 70 per cent business income. Applying this percentage[27] to the total private business and professional income would give $3,500,000,000 as the net income from private business. This income was received by approximately 1,000,000 individuals.[28] How much should be subtracted to account for the labor of the proprietors? No basis is available for estimating this amount, yet the figure used would markedly affect the results. An average labor return per proprietor of $1,500 would seem to be a conservative estimate. Using this figure, the part of the net income of private business which should properly be attributed to labor would amount to $1,500,000,000, leaving $2,000,000,000 as the net income derived from private business comparable to the $6,886,700,000 business income of non-financial corporations. The total net income of all business would then amount to $8,886,700,000, 77.5 per cent of which would have been corporate. This probably underestimates by a wide margin the proportion of business wealth controlled by corporations.

We found that the 200 largest corporations controlled roughly 44 per cent of all non-financial corporate wealth. If corporate wealth amounted to only 77.5 per cent of all business wealth, the two hundred largest corporations would have controlled 34.2 per cent of all business wealth. This final figure is, at best, only a rough approximation tending to minimize the importance of the large corporation. It is the writer's belief that the two hundred largest corporations controlled between 35

[26] *Statistics of Income, 1927,* p. 11.

[27] It is probable that a smaller proportion of business and professional income was professional for individuals reporting income under $5,000 and that a larger proportion of partnership income was professional.

[28] The number of individuals was not reported in 1927 but in 1925, 700,000 individuals (*Statistics of Income, 1925,* p. 8), received the non-service income, while the partnership income amounted to approximately one-half that of individual business. In 1927, the total income from both sources was approximately the same as in 1925.

and 45 per cent of all business wealth—excluding from business wealth that of government, agriculture and the professions.

THE LARGE CORPORATION IN RELATION TO NATIONAL WEALTH

The comparison of the wealth of the 200 largest corporations with the national wealth involves no tedious analysis; but, as all estimates of national wealth can only be very rough, the results are necessarily only approximate. The National Industrial Conference Board has estimated that the national wealth in 1927 amounted to $346,399,000,-000;[29] while the gross assets of the 200 largest corporations amounted to only $67,165,000,000[30] or 19.4 per cent of the total wealth of the country. The lower relative importance of the large corporation is due, in the main, to the importance of agricultural land and improvements, residential real estate, personal property, including automobiles, and the large volume of government property.

To recapitulate, the following table gives the results of the foregoing analysis:

PROPORTION OF VARIOUS ECONOMIC AREAS COVERED BY LARGE CORPORATIONS ON OR ABOUT JANUARY 1, 1928

Controlling Unit	Actual Figure Obtained by Computation (Per Cent)	Probable Limits (Per Cent)
All non-financial corporations		
200 largest (gross assets over $85,000,000)	44.0	45–50
200 largest (net income over $4,500,000)	38.2*	40–50
All non-financial business activity		
200 largest corporations (net income over $4,500,000)	34.1*	35–45
National wealth		
200 largest corporations (gross assets over $85,000,000)	19.4	15–25

* Unadjusted for unconsolidated subsidiaries.

It is apparent from these figures that a very considerable portion of the industrial wealth of the country has been concentrated under the control of a relatively few huge units. There were over 300,000 non-financial corporations in the country in 1927. Yet 200 of these, or less than seven-hundredths of one per cent, control nearly half the corporate wealth.

It must further be remembered that the influence of one of these huge

[29] National Industrial Conference Board, *The Conference Board Bulletin,* No. 38 (February 25, 1930), p. 303.

[30] The error due to including bills receivable in gross assets is not sufficiently large in comparison to the probable error in the estimate of national wealth to warrant making an adjustment.

companies extends far beyond the assets under its direct control. Smaller companies which sell to or buy from the larger companies are likely to be influenced by them to a vastly greater extent than by other smaller companies with which they might deal. In many cases the continued prosperity of the smaller company depends on the favor of the larger, and almost inevitably the interests of the latter become the interests of the former. The influence of the larger company on prices is often greatly increased by its mere size, even though it does not begin to approach a monopoly. Its political influence may be tremendous. Therefore, if roughly half of corporate wealth is controlled by two hundred large corporations and half by smaller companies it is fair to assume that very much more than half of industry is dominated by these huge units.

THE GROWTH OF LARGE CORPORATIONS AS MEASURED BY GROSS ASSETS

Of even more importance than the relative position of the large corporations is the question of their growth. Are they growing more rapidly than other corporations and than national wealth; or, more exactly, are they coming to control a larger proportion of industrial wealth and to receive a larger proportion of industrial income? To answer these questions two studies were made, the first based on gross assets and the second on net income.

For the years 1909, 1919, 1927 and 1928 the gross assets of the 200 largest corporations in the respective years were computed by the method already described for 1927. For each year between 1919 and 1927 a method was employed which gave a figure practically equivalent to the gross assets of the 200 largest corporations.[31] The assets of the 153 identical corporations included in both the 1919 and 1927 list were compiled for each intermediate year. To the resulting figure were added the gross assets of the 47 largest corporations not already included. This gave a total which was almost identical with the figure which would have been obtained if the gross assets of the 200 largest in each year had been compiled. The results of the compilation are given in Table IV, column (a). The assets of the 200 largest corporations increased in the ten years from 1909 to 1919 from $26.0 billion to $43.7 billion, an increase of 68 per cent. In the next ten years from 1919 to 1929 they increased to approximately $78.0 billion,[32] an increase of 78 per cent.

[31] It would be identical if none of the 153 corporations became so small in the intermediate period as not to be included among the 200 largest.

[32] Making a rough extension of trend by adding to the figure for 1928 the average annual gain for the previous three years.

TABLE IV

COMPARISON OF GROWTH OF LARGE CORPORATIONS WITH GROWTH OF ALL CORPORATIONS

	200 LARGEST NON-FINANCIAL CORPORATIONS		ALL NON-FINANCIAL CORPORATIONS	
YEAR	Gross Assets as of December 31[1] (Million Dollars)	Annual Rate of Growth[2] (Per Cent)	Estimated Wealth as of December 31 (Million Dollars)	Annual Rate of Growth[2] (Per Cent)
	(a)	(b)	(c)	(d)
1909	$26,063		$63,300[3]	
1919	43,718			
1920	48,436	5.1		3.0
1921	47,762		90,507[4]	
1922	49,729	4.1		4.3
1923	51,886	4.2		
1924	54,337	4.7	102,658[5]	
1925	58,317	7.2		4.8
1926	63,404	8.7	112,435[6]	
1927	67,165	5.9	117,693[7]	4.5
1928	73,139	8.6	124,334[8]	5.7
1909–1927		5.3		3.5
1921–1927		6.0		4.4
1924–1927		7.3		4.7

[1] For method of obtaining figures see text.

[2] Where an interval of more than a year intervenes between successive figures, the annual rate of growth is figured on a basis which gives a rate compounded annually.

[3] Estimate obtained by determining the per cent growth in the capital stocks and indebtedness of all non-financial corporations between December 31, 1909 (*Annual Report of the Commissioner of Internal Revenue, 1910*, pp. 69 and 74) and December 31, 1924 (*Statistics of Income, 1925*, pp. 31, 43 and 46). In the latter year the fair value of all capital stocks was used, as it was somewhat larger than total par value even for those corporations reporting par value. This percentage was then applied to the estimated wealth of non-financial corporations on December 31, 1924.

[4] Estimate of non-financial corporate wealth made by the Federal Trade Commission and based upon the capital stock tax returns for approximately December 31, 1921, as compiled by the Treasury Department. (Federal Trade Commission, *National Wealth and Income*, p. 134.) This figure includes real estate, buildings, and equipment as reported and estimates for cash and inventory. Figures cover all corporations.

[5] Figures for real estate, buildings, equipment, cash, and inventory of all non-financial corporations as tabulated by the Treasury Department (*Statistics of Income, 1925*, p. 40) plus an adjustment for wealth of corporations whose balance sheets were not tabulated. Adjustment was made by assuming the wealth of corporations whose assets were not tabulated was in the same proportion to the fair value of their stock as the wealth of corporations tabulated to the fair value of their stock (*ibid.*, p. 31).

[6] Real estate, buildings, etc., of non-financial corporations (*Statistics of Income, 1926*, pp. 360 and 390) adjusted for corporations whose balance sheets were not tabulated. This adjustment was made on the basis of the proportion of balance sheets tabulated in each income class. As over 99 per cent of all but the very smallest corporations appear to have been tabulated, the error in estimation cannot be large (*ibid.*, pp. 356, 358, 360, and 398).

[7] Same basis as (6) (*Statistics of Income, 1927*, pp. 371, 372, 380 and 382).

[8] Same basis as (6), except that 97 per cent of balance sheets were assumed to be tabulated. (*Statistics of Income, 1928*, pp. 32, 380 and 386.)

Table V gives the growth of 153 identical corporations included in the largest 200 in both 1919 and 1927. The assets of 45 identical railroads increased from $18 billion in 1919 to $22 billion in 1927 or 21 per cent; 72 identical industrial corporations increased from $14 billion to $21 billion in the same period, a growth of approximately 50 per cent in eight years. In the public utility field, as is well known, the rate was vastly more rapid. In the same eight years the assets of 36 identical utilities grew from $6 billion to $15 billion, or two and one-half times. The more rapid growth of the utilities approximately compensates for the slow growth of the railroads, and the total for the 153 corporations shows a growth from $39 billion to $59 billion, or an increase of practically 50 per cent, the same as that shown by the industrials.

TABLE V

Gross Assets of 153 Identical Corporations Common to Both 1919 and 1927 List of 200 Largest American Corporations

	Gross Assets (Million Dollars)			
On or about December 31	45 Railroads	72 Industrials	36 Public Utilities	Total 153 Corporations
1919	18,616	14,364	6,107	39,088
1920	20,691	16,263	6,485	43,439
1921	20,328	15,665	6,839	42,834
1922	20,776	16,039	7,850	44,665
1923	20,557	17,249	8,846	46,653
1924	20,986	17,779	9,921	48,688
1925	21,423	19,181	11,627	52,231
1926	22,034	20,645	13,684	56,364
1927	22,619	21,084	15,702	59,405
	(Per Cent)	(Per Cent)	(Per Cent)	(Per Cent)
Increase 1919–1927	21.4	46.7	157.0	52.4
Annual rate of growth[1] 1919–1927	2.3	5.0	12.3	5.3
Annual rate of growth[1] 1924–1927	2.6	5.8	16.5	6.9

[1] Compounded annually.

Though the growth of the large corporations shown in these tables is rapid, it is truly significant only if it has been more rapid than that of all industrial wealth. We have already discussed the difficulty in estimating the total industrial wealth for each year; but, as we have seen, more accurate material is available with reference to the wealth of corporations. Here again the distinction between financial and non-financial corporations is necessary, especially in view of the rapid growth of financial companies in more recent years. Where industrial activity is concerned, there is reason to exclude such companies from consideration.

In examining the growth of the 200 largest corporations, the increase in their gross assets has been accepted as a reasonable measure of growth. In measuring the growth of all non-financial corporations, no accurate figures for gross assets are available. For certain years, notably 1921, 1924, 1926, and 1927, a figure which the Federal Trade Commission has designated as "wealth used in corporate business" can, however, be employed as a satisfactory measure of growth. This item includes only cash, inventory, land, buildings and equipment. In each of these years the figure is based upon the data supplied from tax returns, and, to be made comparable for the different years, must be slightly adjusted, as indicated in the footnotes of Table IV. With these adjustments the figures for different years become reasonably comparable and should indicate with a fair degree of accuracy the rate of increase of all corporate wealth exclusive of that of financial corporations. For the year 1909 less satisfactory material was available; but an estimate, involving a very much larger margin of error, was made for that year.[33] The rates of growth of the wealth of all non-financial corporations, the assets of the 200 largest corporations, and, except for 1909, the assets of the 153 corporations which were among the 200 largest both in 1919 and in 1927 are given in Tables IV and V.

These figures indicate that the large corporations as a group are growing very much more rapidly than all corporations. For the period from 1909 to 1927 their annual rate of growth has been 5.3 per cent, while that of all corporations (assuming the estimates are reliable) has amounted to only 3.5 per cent, and for corporations other than the largest 200 only 2.0 per cent. The large corporations would thus appear to be increasing in wealth over 50 per cent faster than all corporations or over two and one-half times as fast as smaller corporations. From 1921 to 1927 the annual rate of growth of the large corporations has been 6.0 per cent compared with 4.4 per cent for all corporations or 3.1 per cent for the smaller companies. From 1924 to 1927, a period of most rapid growth, the annual rates were respectively 7.3 per cent for the large, 4.7 per cent for all, and only 2.3 per cent for corporations other than the largest 200, indicating that the large corporations were growing more than half again as fast as all corporations and three times as fast as smaller corporations.[34]

THE GROWTH OF LARGE CORPORATIONS AS MEASURED BY INCOME

To check this study of growth, a second study was made based on the net income of corporations as reported by the Treasury Department. By the same method employed for the year 1927, the statutory net in-

[33] See note 3, Table IV.

[34] Assuming that the large corporations controlled 45 per cent of all corporate assets in 1927, and increased their assets from 1909 to 1927 at the annual rate of 5.3 per cent as against 3.5 for all corporations, the rate of growth of the smaller corporation representing 55 per cent of corporate wealth would be 2.0 per cent. The annual rate of growth of smaller corporations in the periods 1921–1927 and 1924–1927 were calculated in the same manner.

come of the 200 largest non-financial corporations, as reported in income taxes, was calculated for the years from 1920 to 1927. The results are given in Table III. For 1921 the results are misleading as in that year, the year of depression, the net income of all corporations was extremely low, and on purely statistical grounds, one would expect the proportion received by the corporations reporting the largest income to be very much greater than normal. In the remaining years, however, there is no reason to think that the figures are not reasonably comparable for different years. The results run closely parallel to those obtained when the growth in assets was examined. Thus, the years from 1920 to 1923 show no noticeable growth in the proportion of net income received by the 200 largest. From 1924 to 1927, however, there is a very marked increase in the proportion of all corporate income going to the 200 largest, increasing from 33.4 per cent in 1920 to 38.4 per cent in 1927 or from an average of 33.5 in the years 1920–1923 to an average of 37.9 in the years 1924–1927.

This increase in the proportion received by the large companies could theoretically be explained on two grounds other than the actual growth of the large corporations. If they had obtained an increasing rate of return on their capital in comparison with the smaller companies, the increase in the proportion of income could be explained. It could likewise be explained on the ground that for a large number of subsidiary corporations the net income was not consolidated with the parent in the earlier years and was so consolidated in the later years. This latter explanation, however, could at most account for only a very small part of the increase, since approximately the same proportion of all non-financial corporate dividends were reported as received by non-financial corporations in 1927 as in 1922,[35] indicating that subsidiaries were reported as separate corporations to approximately the same extent throughout the period.

It is quite conceivable that an important part of the increase is explained by the greater profitableness of large corporations; but the fact that the change coincides roughly with the change shown for corporate wealth tends to strengthen the conclusion that the large corporations increased both their proportion of the wealth and their proportion of the income of all corporations.

Since it seems fair to assume that an increasing proportion of all in-

---

[35] 20.3 per cent in 1922 and 20.5 per cent in 1927. Derived from *Statistics of Income, 1922,* pp. 18, 19 and 22, and *Statistics of Income, 1927,* pp. 312 and 315.

dustrial activity has come under corporate sway,[36] the growth of the 200 largest in relation to corporate wealth may be accepted as an indication that they have been absorbing all industrial wealth at a rate at least as rapid.

THE GROWTH OF LARGE CORPORATIONS IN RELATION TO GROWTH OF NATIONAL WEALTH

The relative growth of the wealth of the large corporations and the national wealth can be roughly calculated. As we have indicated, national wealth is a difficult concept to define, and all estimates of national wealth must be, at best, approximate; so that too much reliance should not be placed on any comparison of the growth of corporate wealth with that of national wealth. The most recent estimate of national wealth for the period of years under consideration is that made by the National Industrial Conference Board.[37] Between 1922 and 1928, their estimates indicate a growth in national wealth of 12.5 per cent compared with the growth in assets[38] of the 200 largest corporations of 45.6 per cent, or annual rates of growth of 2.0 per cent and 6.3 per cent respectively.[39] While the estimates based on the 1930 census may be considerably higher than those of the Conference Board, the estimates of the latter for 1928 would have to be increased by over 30 per cent to make the rate of increase in the national wealth equal to that of the 200 corporations. There can, therefore, be little doubt that the wealth of the large corporations has been increasing at a very much more rapid rate than the total national wealth.

To summarize the conclusions with relation to growth:

(1) On the basis of gross assets, the large corporations appear to have been growing between two and three times as fast as all other non-financial corporations.

(2) This conclusion is supported by the figures of corporate income.

[36] The 1899 census reported 66.7 per cent of all manufactured products are made by corporations, as against 87.0 per cent in 1919. An extension of trend based on the log of the figure for the per cent of manufactured products not made by corporations according to the census figures of 1899, 1909, and 1919 indicates that in 1929 approximately 94 per cent of all manufactured products were made by corporations. Basic figures obtained from 14th census of the U.S., Vol. VIII, pp. 14 and 108.

[37] National Industrial Conference Board, *Conference Board Bulletin* No. 38 (February 25, 1930), p. 303.

[38] The use of the gross assets of corporations rather than their tangible wealth is reasonable, since the comparison is primarily for noting changes in relationship rather than an absolute relationship.

[39] Compounded annually.

(3) Since an increased proportion of industrial wealth presumably continues to come under corporate sway, the proportion of industrial wealth controlled by the large corporations has been increasing at a rate even faster than the proportion of corporate wealth controlled by them.

(4) Since estimates of national wealth are extremely approximate it is not possible to determine the growth in the proportion of national wealth controlled by the large corporations, but there can be little question that the proportion has been increasing at a rapid rate.

THE MANNER OF GROWTH

To check further the conclusion that large corporations have been growing more rapidly than all corporations, a study was made of the ways in which corporate growth takes place. A given corporation can increase the wealth under its control in three major ways: by reinvesting its earnings, by raising new capital through the sale of securities in the public markets, and by acquiring control of other corporations by either purchase or exchange of securities. While there are numerous other ways by which an increase could take place, such as private sale of securities to individuals, these three so far outweigh other methods that they alone need to be considered. Each of these three ways of increase has been examined to discover the relation of the activity of the large corporations with respect to that of all corporations.

A. Growth by Reinvestment of Earnings

A comparison of the savings of large corporations with those of all corporations indicates that the big companies as a group save a larger proportion of their net income. In the six-year period from 1922 to 1927 inclusive, 108 corporations (all of the 200 largest for which consolidated statements could be obtained for each year) saved 38.5 per cent of their net income available for dividends. [See Table VI.] In the same period, all corporations combined saved only 29.4 per cent of their net income.[40] While the figure for the savings by the 108 corporations does not necessarily represent the proportion of income saved by all the two hundred largest companies as a group, there is no reason to think that a bias exists in the large sample chosen. We can therefore conclude

---

[40] This difference in rate of savings is probably not an indication of greater liberality in paying dividends on the part of the small corporations but an indication of their greater liability to loss. For both groups, the net income for the group included the net income of those making a profit minus the losses suffered by the remainder.

TABLE VI

COMPARISON OF SAVINGS BY LARGE CORPORATIONS AND BY ALL NON-FINANCIAL CORPORATIONS 1922–1927

Calendar Year	Proportion of Net Income Saved	
	By 108 Identical Large Corporations[1] (Per Cent)	By All Non-financial Corporations[2] (Per Cent)
1922	33.8	33.7
1923	41.5	37.8
1924	37.5	26.6
1925	39.9	36.3
1926	42.2	28.2
1927	35.2	14.8
Total for 6 years	38.5	29.4

[1] 108 identical companies, (39 railroads, 31 public utilities, and 38 industrials) included at one time or another between 1922 and 1927 in the list of 200 largest corporations. Information was obtained from *Moody's Railroad, Public Utility,* and *Industrial Manuals* covering net income available for dividends and cash dividends paid. Any loss reported was treated as negative income. Savings were recorded as net income less cash dividends.

[2] Ratio of savings to net profits after taxes for all non-financial corporations as reported in *Statistics of Income* for the respective years.

that the large corporations gain in relation to the smaller corporations as a result of savings.

B. Growth through Public Offering of Securities

In the second field, the increase in corporate wealth through sale of securities in the public markets, the large corporation plays a most important rôle. The *Commercial and Financial Chronicle* publishes for each month a list of the new corporate securities offered to the public. This list may be accepted as including practically every public offering.[41] For the six years from the beginning of 1922 to the end of 1927, the offerings of every third month (March, June, September, and December) were classified according to (1) those offered by one of the 200 largest corporations (1927 list) either directly or through a subsidiary, and (2) those offered by companies independent of the largest 200. In making the classification all offerings amounting to two million dollars or more not made directly by one of the big companies were checked to determine whether or not they were made by a subsidiary of the latter. Smaller offerings not made by a big company were classed with the lat-

[41] A representative of the company publishing the *Commercial and Financial Chronicle* writes—"Bond and investment houses all over the country report to us all their offerings, sending us complete details so as to get a notice in our paper, and in addition we have virtually all the newspapers of the country searched for information regarding bond and stock offerings of every kind. We have a very extensive clipping service of our own, subscribing for hundreds of newspapers, and in addition get clippings from numerous regular clipping agencies. In the circumstances we do not see how we could fail to learn of any offerings of consequence and therefore our offerings of corporate securities may be regarded as practically complete."

ter only where the offering company was recognized as a subsidiary. It is therefore possible that a few smaller issues were classified wrongly as offerings of small companies. The total volume of such errors could not have been great; but to the extent that they existed they would tend to minimize the proportion of offerings by the large companies.

Further examination shows the dominance of the large corporations. Of all the bonds offered, the proportion issued by the big companies varied from 50.2 per cent to 68.2 per cent in different years while the percentage of stocks varied from 28.1 to 82.5. There is no clear indication of a trend one way or the other. For the whole period, however, 63.6 per cent of all securities were offered by the big companies.

Two important adjustments should be made to obtain the proportion of new capital going into the large corporations. A certain proportion of these securities was offered by financial corporations and therefore involved a duplication of investment. When the issues of financial corporations are subtracted from the total issues, the proportion of securities offered by the large companies is increased, amounting in the maximum year to 78.6 per cent and for the period as a whole to 71.8 per cent. That such a large proportion of all public financing should involve financing by the 200 largest corporations is indeed striking. It is fair to assume, however, that an important amount of the issues by these large and established companies involved refunding rather than the actual raising of new capital. It is not possible to segregate the refunding from the new issues by the large corporations; but the total volume of refunding for all non-financial corporations is reported separately by the *Commercial and Financial Chronicle.* If we arbitrarily attribute 90 per cent of this refunding to the large corporations, a minimum estimate of the proportion of new capital raised by them should be obtained. The estimate obtained by such a method indicates that 74.7 per cent of new capital procured by the floating of securities in the public market was obtained by the 200 largest companies in 1927, the year of maximum proportion, and that, for the six years from 1922–27 inclusive, 66.5 per cent of new capital obtained by this method was received by the large corporations. This must account, in a considerable degree, for the more rapid growth of the large corporations in relation to all corporations.

C. Growth through Mergers

The third and more spectacular method of growth of the large corporations is by consolidation or merger. In considering this growth, it

TABLE VII

Mergers of Big Companies[1] 1922–1929

Companies on List of 200 Largest Companies at Some Time During Period Which Have Been Acquired by Another Company on the List

Year	Company Acquired	Acquiring Company	Assets of Company Acquired at About the Time of Acquisition (Million Dollars)
1919	None		
1920	Associated Oil Co.	Pacific Oil Co.	$ 68.1
1921	Midwest Refining Co.	Standard Oil Co. of Ind.	85.9
1922	Lackawanna Steel Co.	Bethlehem Steel Corp.	89.6
1923	Toledo, St. Louis & West. Rd. Co.	N.Y., Chi. & St.L. R.R. Co.	59.5
	Chile Copper Co.	Anaconda Copper M. Co.	151.4
	Midvale Steel & Ordnance Co.	Bethlehem Steel Corp.	285.4
	Morris & Co.	Armour & Co.	95.0
	Steel & Tube Co. of America	Youngstown Sh. & T. Co.	94.0
	Utah Copper Co.	Kennecott Copper Co.	66.0
1924	Carolina, Clinchfield & O. Rd. Co.	Atl. Coast Line R.R. Co.	78.7
	Internat. Gr. Northern Ry. Co.	Mo. Pac. R.R. Co.	77.5
	Chicago Elevated Rys. Co.	Commonwealth Ed. Co.	97.4
1925	Kansas City, Mex. & Or. Ry. Co.	At., To. & S. Fe Ry. Co.	88.0
	Alabama Power Co.	Southeastern Pr. & Lt. Co.	86.0
	New Orleans Public Service Co.	Electric Pr. & Lt. Co.	69.3
	Ohio Fuel Supply Co.	Columbia Gas & Elec. Co.	78.9
	Utah Securities Corp.	Electric Pr. & Lt. Co.	100.0[2]
	Western Power Corp.	North American Co.	96.4
	Magnolia Petroleum Co.	Standard Oil Co. of N.Y.	212.8
	Pan Am. Pet. & Trans. Co.	Standard Oil Co. of Ind.	179.5
1926	Penn. Electric Corp.	Ass. Gas & Elec. Co.	88.1
	Standard Power & Light Co.	Ass. Gas & Elec. Co.	300.0[2]
	United Rys. Investment Co.	Standard Gas & Elec. Co.	250.0[2]
	Pacific Oil Co.	Standard Oil Co. of Calif.	181.0
	General Petroleum Corp.	Standard Oil Co. of N.Y.	102.0
	Pacific Petroleum Co.	Standard Oil Co. of Calif.	95.3
1927	Georgia Ry. & Power Co.	Southeastern Pr. & Lt. Co.	76.5
	San Joaquin Light & Power Co.	Western Power Corp.	75.0
1928	Northwestern Pacific Ry. Co.	At., To. & S. Fe Ry. Co.	70.0
	Pere Marquette Rd. Co.	Allegheny Corp.	157.0
	Texas & Pacific Rd. Co.	Missouri Pacific R.R. Co.	140.0
	American Light & Traction Co.	United Lt. & Pr. Co.	128.5[2]
	Brooklyn Edison Co.	Cons. Gas Co. of N.Y.	153.3
	Mackay Companies	Internat. Tel. & Tel. Co.	93.4
	Montana Power Co.	American Pr. & Lt. Co.	106.0
	National Electric Power Co.	Middle West Utilities Co.	123.0
	National Public Service Corp.	Nat. Electric Power Co.	174.7
	Philadelphia Electric Co.	United Gas Imp. Co.	278.4
	Puget Sound Power & Light Co.	Eng. Public Service Co.	122.2
	California Petroleum Co.	Texas Corp.	102.2
	Dodge Bros. Inc.	Chrysler Corp.	131.5
1929	General Gas & Electric Co.	Associated Gas Co.	175.0
	Massachusetts Gas Companies	Koppers Co.	89.6
	Mohawk Hudson Power Co.	Niagara Hudson Pr. Co.	190.0[2]
	New England Power Assoc.	Internat. Paper & Pr. Co.	216.8
	Northeastern Power Corp.	Niagara Hudson Pr. Co.	131.4
	Penn-Ohio Edison Co.	Com. & So. Pr. Co.	153.3
	Southeastern Power & Lt. Co.	Com. & So. Pr. Co.	507.2
	Greene Cananea Copper Co.	Anaconda Copper M. Co.	56.2

[1] Merger is used here to refer to the acquisition of control of one company by another either involving a consolidation of properties or simply stock control.
[2] Estimated.

is necessary to treat separately mergers between two companies already included in the list of two hundred companies and mergers in which one of these companies absorbs a company not included. In the six-year period under consideration 26 companies included in the list of 200 largest at one time or another during the period were acquired by another large corporation.[42] This concentration of the 200 large companies in 1922 into a smaller group in 1927 required the addition of other companies to take the place of those absorbed if the total of 200 independent companies was to be maintained. The mergers therefore increased the assets of the 200 corporations in the latter year by the amount of the assets of the companies added. Since this involved the addition of smaller companies having average assets in 1927 of approximately $90,000,000, the increase in the assets of the 200 largest in 1927 over the 200 largest in 1922 would amount to roughly $2,340,-000,000 (26 times $90,000,000). This is the amount of the increase in assets which should be attributed to mergers between companies already included in the 200 largest.

The addition to the assets of the 200 largest companies through the acquisition of smaller companies is extremely difficult to estimate. It is safe to say, however, that it is large, perhaps involving an addition of as much as $2,000,000,000 for the six-year period.[43]

It is evident that mergers may result in a growth in the importance of the large companies with a reduction in the sum of the assets of small companies. No merger between corporations can bring about an increase in the assets of the group of small companies. This form of growth must therefore make for increased relative importance of the large corporation.

So far we have considered the three most important ways in which the large corporations could increase their proportion of total corporate assets. We find that as a group they saved a larger proportion of their net income, that as a group they received a very much larger proportion of new capital obtained in the public markets than their relative assets would warrant, and finally that to a very considerable extent they increased their assets through merger or consolidation at the expense of the corporate assets not included in the large companies.

[42] See Table VII.

[43] In 1928 and 1929, two years of phenomenal merger activity, sixteen important acquisitions added $724,000,000 to the assets of the large companies. This number doubtless omits the acquisition of many small companies which must have occurred; and it only includes industrial companies. It is, however, suggestive of the extent to which the acquisition of smaller companies can build up the wealth controlled by the larger companies.

It must not be concluded, however, that this necessarily proves the more rapid growth of the large corporations. There are two ways by which the assets of the group of smaller corporations might be increased which would have little effect on the larger companies. First, corporations frequently obtain new capital from private sources. As the largest companies almost invariably obtain their new capital by public offerings, the addition to assets from private sources would redound almost entirely to the smaller companies. Second, the incorporation of a business previously private would add to the total of corporate assets; but, since such a new corporation is unlikely to be included among the largest 200, the gain would fall entirely in the group of smaller corporations. The increase in the assets controlled by smaller corporations from these two sources might, therefore, more than counterbalance the more rapid growth of the larger companies in the fields already considered.

Unfortunately it has not been possible to discover the extent to which corporate assets have been increased by either of these methods. It is possible, however, to determine roughly the amount of increase from these two sources which would have been necessary if the growth of the large corporation had not been more rapid than that of all corporations. If this amount should turn out to be improbably large, the conclusion that the large corporations have grown more rapidly than all corporations would have further support.

The first step in making this estimate is to complete the picture of the growth of large corporations. In addition to the three major ways of growth already considered, changes in their assets can result from certain minor sources. For instance, their gross assets could be increased or decreased by a change in the volume of bank borrowing or by retiring securities without refunding. It is also possible for a corporation to change its assets by marking up or marking down the value of assets on the balance sheet in such a way as not to affect the net profits reported. No effort has been made to discover the exact importance of each of these practices. Marking down of inventories and assets immediately after the depression of 1921 may have accounted for some reduction in assets. Bank borrowings presumably remained constant or decreased slightly. Some securities must have been retired without refunding. In total, however, these items do not appear to have been of serious magnitude.

An additional difficulty arises from the possible duplication involved where a merger was brought about, not through the issue of new securities of the acquiring corporation, but through the direct expenditure of part of its assets. In such a case the actual assets expended in bringing about the merger would have to be subtracted from the increase in assets which would otherwise be attributed to the merger. Thus the four to five billion dollars of assets added to the total of the 200 corporations between 1922 and 1927 would presumably have involved a smaller actual addition. These unknown factors make it extremely difficult to approximate the growth due to the different items, but a rough approximation can be made.

Assuming that mergers brought a bona fide increase of $4,000,000,000 to the assets controlled by the large corporations in the six-year period, their total growth would be derived from the following sources:

Savings out of earnings[1]	$ 5,748,000,000
New capital from sale of securities	11,820,000,000
Growth as a result of mergers	4,000,000,000
Total additions to assets	$21,568,000,000
Actual growth as compiled	19,561,000,000
Loss in assets from reappraisal, retirement of securities other than refunding, etc.	$ 2,007,000,000

[1] Estimated on the assumption that the savings by the largest 200 corporations bore the same relation to the savings of the sample of 108 of their number as did the gross assets of each group in each of the six years.

While at best this is only an approximate compilation, it is worth noting that more than half of the growth of the large corporations, not as individuals but as a group, arose from new capital obtained in the public markets, somewhat more than a quarter came from savings, and less than a quarter as a result of mergers and consolidations. At the same time this increase was in some measure counterbalanced by a decrease in assets through reappraisal and through the retiring of securities other than refunding.

On the basis of this compilation it is possible to make an estimate of the increase in the assets of all corporations which must have occurred if large and small had increased at the same rate. Two additional assumptions are necessary, first that reappraisal, retirement of securities, etc., accrued to the same extent with both large and small corporations and can therefore be disregarded; and second that 45 per cent of the assets of all corporations in 1927 were held by the largest 200 companies. If the large companies with 45 per cent of all corporate assets added $21,568,000,000 to their assets in the six-year period, the remaining corporations with 55 per cent of all assets would have had to add $26,360,000,000[44] to their wealth if they were to grow at the same

[44] $21,568,000,000: 45%::X:55%.

rate as the large companies. The addition to assets through saving, public offerings, private offerings, and incorporation of new companies must have amounted to this figure plus $4,000,000,000 to replace the estimated assets of small companies absorbed into the 200 largest as a result of mergers. Of this $30,360,000,000, savings could account for $6,509,000,000[45] and public offerings $5,795,000,000,[46] leaving $18,056,000,000 of new assets which must have been added in six years through private sale of securities and through incorporation of previously unincorporated businesses if the small companies were to keep pace with the larger ones.

This figure is so large as to be extremely improbable. The volume of unincorporated business which is incorporated each year is not large, probably not adding over half a billion at the most. The volume of new capital obtained by private offerings is probably somewhat greater, particularly through the launching of new enterprises, but even this is unlikely to average more than a billion a year. It is probably very much less. Therefore, while no accurate figures can be advanced to indicate beyond doubt that very much less than $18,000,000,000 was added to the assets of smaller companies through private sale of securities and through incorporation of private businesses, the magnitude of this sum lends considerable support to the previous conclusion that the large corporation as a group has been growing at a more rapid rate than other corporations.

Since the studies of net income and methods of growth both support the general conclusion derived from the study of gross assets, we can accept the results of that study with greater confidence and seek to discover their significance. The most important of these findings were: first, that for the 18-year period from 1909 to 1927 the annual rate of growth for the largest 200 corporations amounted to 5.3 per cent as against 3.5 per cent for all corporations; second, that in the three years from 1924 to 1927 the rates of increase were respectively 7.3 per cent and 4.7 per cent; and third that between 1922 and 1928, the large corporations increased at the annual rate of 6.3 per cent, while the national wealth increased (on the basis of very approximate estimates) only 2.0 per cent a year.

The exact significance of this more rapid growth of the large corporations can be better understood when these rates are projected into the future. If all non-financial corporations and these 200 largest cor-

[45] Total savings by all non-financial corporations less estimated savings by 200 large corporations.

[46] Six-year total of new financing by all non-financial corporations less that by big companies.

porations should increase in the next twenty years at the rates indicated for the period from 1909 to 1927, by 1950 two-thirds of non-financial corporate wealth would be held by 200 huge units.[47] If the more rapid rate of growth from 1924 to 1927 were maintained for the next twenty years, 80.5 per cent would be held by the largest 200 in 1950. If the indicated rates of growth of the large corporations and of national wealth were to be effective in the future, within twenty years virtually half of the national wealth would be owned by the 200 giant corporations.

Whether the relative growth of the large corporations will continue in the future as in the past, there is no means of knowing. In the years 1928 and 1929 for which the data are as yet incomplete there are many indications that they have gained even more rapidly than in the previous three years. Some important mergers occurred in 1930 and others are now in progress. The consolidation of the railroads into a few major systems promises to concentrate industrial wealth still further. The extension of chain, group, and branch banking tends to concentrate the banking resources into larger aggregates which are better able to assist the further expansion of the huge companies. The technique of larger scale administration is improved by experience and makes still larger aggregates possible. The sheer economic weight of "big business" tends to dissolve any popular resistance to its concentration. There appear to be few forces in action which would tend to retard its development. There are many which would accelerate it. The trend is unmistakable.

CONCLUSION

In conclusion, then, the huge corporation, the corporation with $85,000,000 of assets or more, has come to dominate most major industries if not all industry in the United States. A rapidly increasing proportion of industry is carried on under this form of organization. There is apparently no immediate limit to its increase. It is coming more and more to be the economic unit with which American economic, social, and political life must deal.

What are the implications involved in these conclusions? Only a few of the myriad implications can be suggested here, a few of particular importance to the economist.

(1) Most fundamental of all, the economist must think, to a very

[47] Assuming 45.0 per cent of non-financial corporate wealth was held by the largest 200 in 1927.

important extent, in terms of these huge units rather than in terms of the multitude of small competing elements of private enterprise. For most fields Marshall's "representative firm" has ceased to be a useful tool of thought, since the great companies which dominate one industry after another are in no sense "representative." The emphasis must be shifted to that very great proportion of industry in the hands of a relatively few units, units which can be studied individually and concretely. Such studies will reveal the operation of half of industry and what is more important, that half which is likely to be more typical of the industry of the future.[48]

(2) Competition has changed in character and the principles applicable to present conditions are radically different from those which apply when the dominant competing units are smaller and more numerous. The principles of duopoly have become more important than those of free competition.

(3) An increasing proportion of production is carried on for use and not for sale. With the increase in the large companies, a larger proportion of goods is consumed by the producing organization in the process of making further goods. To this extent the calculus of cost versus quality would presumably be solved in the interests of producing a product which would yield the maximum use per unit of cost rather than the maximum profit per unit of investment. Under the latter incentive the consumer is only incidentally offered the product which will give him the most use per unit of cost unless he himself is easily able to measure usefulness. Adulteration, shoddy goods, and goods of lower quality than would be economically desirable are frequent under the incentive for profit. To the extent that production is for use by the producing organization there is no such incentive.[49]

(4) The nature of capital has changed. To an increasing extent it is composed not of tangible goods, but of organizations built in the

---

[48] For instance it seems likely that a study of the directors and senior officers of the 200 largest companies, their training, social background, and other characteristics, would reveal more of vital importance to the community than a study of those at the head of thousands of smaller companies. The same would be true of the ownership of the large companies, their labor policies, their price policies, their promotion practices, etc. This is not to suggest that the practices of the large companies would be typical of the smaller companies, but rather that they would be factually more important.

[49] For instance, it is to the advantage of the American Telephone and Telegraph Company to have its subsidiary, the Western Electric Company, make the best possible vacuum tubes for the innumerable repeater sets in use on its long distance lines. On the other hand, it might be to the advantage of a corporation making tubes for sale to the public to make second-grade tubes which would wear out quickly and allow a second sale at a second profit to be made.

past and available to function in the future. Even the value of tangible goods tends to become increasingly dependent upon their organized relationship to other tangible goods composing the property of one of these great units.

(5) Finally, a society in which production is governed by blind economic forces is being replaced by one in which production is carried on under the ultimate control of a handful of individuals.[50] The economic power in the hands of the few persons who control a giant corporation is a tremendous force which can harm or benefit a multitude of individuals, affect whole districts, shift the currents of trade, bring ruin to one community and prosperity to another. The organizations which they control have passed far beyond the realm of private enterprise—they have become nearly social institutions. Shall we then regard these men as seekers for private gain or as economic statesmen serving the commonweal?

---

[50] Less than 2,000 men were directors of the 200 largest corporations in 1927. Since an important number of these are inactive, the ultimate control of nearly half of industry was actually in the hands of a few hundred men.

Appendix

TABLE II*a*

72 Industrial Corporations in List of 200 Largest Companies in 1919 and 1927

Name	Gross Assets on or About Dec. 31 (Million Dollars)	
	1919	1927
Allied Chem. & Dye Corp.	$ 59.6	$ 250.4
Aluminum Co. of America	85.0[5]	300.0[5]
American Can Co.	135.0	167.9
American Car & Foundry Co.	177.7	125.9
American Locomotive Co.	97.4	111.3
American Smelt. & Refining Co.	215.2	227.7
American Sugar Refining Co.	147.4	180.0[5]
American Tobacco Co.	206.1	210.5
American Woolen Co.	125.9	124.6
Anaconda Copper Mining Co.	236.5	620.0[5]
Armour & Co. (Ill.)	490.8	471.2
Atlantic Refining Co.	95.4	138.8
Bethlehem Steel Corp.	357.2	651.7
Chrysler Corp.[1]	66.9	103.8
Consolidation Coal Co.	135.1	97.2
Corn Products Refining Co.	138.0	118.7
Crane Co.	58.0	101.3
Crucible Steel Co. of America	123.1	115.6
Cuba Cane Sugar Corp.	109.9	111.1
Deere & Co.	84.1	84.9
Drug, Inc.[2]	58.0	149.0[5]
Du Pont de Nemours & Co. (E. I.)	240.9	322.4
Eastman Kodak Co.	88.7	125.2
Firestone Tire & Rubber Co.	73.7	100.9
Ford Motor Co.	332.9	742.0
General Electric Co.	276.7	428.1
General Motors Corp.	446.6	1,270.0[5]
Goodrich Co. (B. F.)	175.7	115.2
Goodyear Tire & Rubber Co.	163.2	213.3
Gulf Oil Corp. of Penn.	218.4	347.3
Inland Steel Co.	59.3	89.0
International Harvester Co.	266.6	325.5
International Mercantile Marine Co.	268.6	161.4
International Paper Co.	86.4	290.5
Jones & Laughlin Steel Corp.	130.0[5]	201.0
Kennecott Copper Corp.	135.6	278.3
Lehigh Coal & Nav. Co.	76.0	87.7
Liggett & Myers Tobacco Co.	151.4	181.0
Lorillard Co.	88.3	99.6
National Biscuit Co.	77.7	109.6

[1] Changed from Maxwell Motor Corp. to Chrysler Corp. in 1925.
[2] Changed from United Drug Co. to Drug Inc.

TABLE IIa (*Continued*)

Name	Gross Assets on or About Dec. 31 (Million Dollars)	
	1919	1927
National Lead Co.	88.0	102.2
Ohio Oil Co.	81.7	104.4
Phelps Dodge Corp.	$ 147.2	$ 127.5
Pittsburgh Coal Co.	159.7	157.9
Prairie Oil & Gas Co.	117.9	186.3
Procter & Gamble Co.	93.7	84.9
Pullman, Inc.	190.0[5]	302.8
Pure Oil Co.	115.0	188.8
Republic Iron & Steel Co.	125.8	120.6
Reynolds Tobacco Co.	100.0[5]	154.4
Sears, Roebuck & Co.	154.8	184.7
Sinclair Cons. Oil Corp.	232.2	400.0[5]
Singer Mfg. Co.	100.0[5]	182.5
Standard Oil Co. of Calif.	174.3	579.3
Standard Oil Co. of Ind.	200.0[5]	775.0[5]
Standard Oil Co. of N.J.	853.3	1,426.6
Standard Oil Co. of N.Y.	234.0	678.0
Studebaker Corp.	88.1	135.8
Swift & Co.	489.5	337.2
Texas Corp.	230.8	324.6
Tide Water Associated Oil Co.[3]	59.9	248.9
Union Carbide & Carbon Corp.	200.0[5]	213.1
Union Oil Associates[4]	89.6	213.7
United Fruit Co.	147.6	208.2
United Shoe Machinery Corp.	76.1	92.7
U.S. Rubber Co.	319.5	339.9
U.S. Steel Corp.	2,365.8	2,433.5
Vacuum Oil Co.	79.6	158.7
Westinghouse Elec. & Mfg. Co.	184.8	222.6
Wilson & Co.	127.0	95.6
Woolworth Co. (F. W.)	89.5	137.7
Youngstown Sheet & Tube Co.	90.0[5]	216.9
(Total 72)	$14,364.4	$21,084.6

[3] Changed from Tide Water Oil Co. to Tide Water Associated Oil Co. in 1926.
[4] Changed from Union Oil Co. of Calif. to Union Oil Associates.
[5] Estimated.

TABLE II*b*

45 Railroads in List of 200 Largest Companies in 1919 and 1927

Name	Gross Assets on or About Dec. 31 (Million Dollars)	
	1919	1927
Atchison, Topeka & Santa Fe	$ 876.9	$ 1,041.5
Atlantic Coast Line	620.0[2]	886.8[2]
Baltimore & Ohio	823.3	1,003.4
Boston & Maine	219.0	243.3
Chesapeake Corp.[1]	342.9	441.1
Chicago & Alton	139.0	130.3
Chicago Burlington & Quincy	581.8	630.3
Chicago & Eastern Illinois	114.4	96.2
Chicago, Great Western	131.4	149.9
Chicago, Milwaukee, St. Paul & Pacific	735.0	743.2
Chicago & North Western	491.0	550.9
Chicago Rock Island & Pacific	385.3	474.2
Chicago & Western Indiana	100.8	86.6
Chicago Union Station Co.	60.0[2]	101.0
Delaware & Hudson	164.0	174.9
Delaware Lack. & Western	269.8	180.4
Denver & Rio Grande Western	241.8	233.6
Erie	492.1	521.7
Florida East Coast	61.6	127.9
Great Northern	723.1	806.1
Illinois Central	459.5	681.6
Kansas City Southern	117.1	153.7
Lehigh Valley	215.3	215.7
Missouri Kansas Texas	219.9	302.5
Missouri Pacific	433.3	561.4
N.Y. Central	1,209.5	1,450.8
N.Y. Chicago & St. Louis	86.3	227.9
N.Y. N.H. & Hartford	515.6	538.6
Norfolk & Western	381.5	460.0
Northern Pacific	737.2	795.5
Pennsylvania	1,807.6[2]	2,400.0[2]
Pere Marquette	136.4	157.0
Reading Co.	302.1	382.5
Seaboard Air Line	222.4	275.1
Southern Pacific	1,619.6	2,105.5
Southern Ry.	549.1	638.1
Spokane, Portland & Seattle	128.3	135.7
St. Louis–San Francisco	314.0	420.8
St. Louis Southwestern	118.7	136.0
Union Pacific	775.9	1,114.0
Virginian	109.9	153.1
Wabash	231.4	319.7
Western Maryland	148.8	162.3
Western Pacific	115.6	116.7
Wheeling & Lake Erie	88.6	102.4
(Total 45)	$18,616.8	$22,619.7

[1] Changed from Chesapeake & Ohio to Chesapeake Corp. in 1927.
[2] Estimated.

TABLE II*c*

36 Public Utilities in List of 200 Largest Companies in 1919 and 1927

Name	Gross Assets on or About Dec. 31 (Million Dollars)	
	1919	1927
American Pr. & Lt. Co.	$ 100.0[7]	$ 520.9
American Tel. & Tel. Co.	1,530.1	3,457.4
American Water Works & Elec. Co.	140.0[7]	355.7
Boston Elevated Ry. Co.	73.8	113.2
Brooklyn-Manhattan Transit Corp.[1]	225.7	271.2
Brooklyn Union Gas Co.	56.2	106.6
Buffalo, Niagara & Eastern Pr. Corp.[2]	61.2	210.2
Chicago Railways Co.	107.3	115.0
Cities Service Co.	531.6	735.2
Columbia Gas & Elec. Corp.	74.3	393.4
Commonwealth Edison Co.	130.1	314.4
Commonwealth Power Corp.[3]	70.0[7]	313.8
Consolidated Gas Co.	176.1	842.9
Con. Gas Elec. Lt. & Pr. Co. of Baltimore	65.6	123.9
Detroit Edison Co.	75.4	234.2
Edison Elec. Ill. Co. of Boston	62.8	168.0
Elec. Pr. & Lt. Corp.[4]	90.3	350.0[7]
Hudson & Manhattan R. R. Co.	127.1	131.5
Interborough Rapid Transit Co.	406.0	527.9
Middle West Utilities Co.	90.0[7]	970.0[7]
National Pr. & Lt. Co.	75.0[7]	500.0[7]
North American Co.	230.0[7]	655.4
North Am. Lt. & Pr. Co.[5]	88.0	243.3
Pacific Gas & Elec. Co.	167.8	337.6
Peoples Gas Lt. & Coke Co.	102.1	162.6
Philadelphia Rapid Transit Co.	56.9	93.0
Portland Elec. Pr. Co.[6]	69.8	93.9
Public Service Co. of No. Illinois	60.7	151.2
Public Service Corp. of N.J.	167.0	615.4
Puget Sound Pr. & Lt. Co.	89.7	122.2
Southern Calif. Edison Co.	100.4	295.2
Standard Gas & Elec. Co.	200.0[7]	983.2
Third Av. Ry. Co.	80.2	90.9
United Gas Improvement Co.	104.8	681.9[7]
United Rys. & Elec. Co. of Baltimore	92.0	95.4
Western Union Telegraph Co.	229.6	326.2
(Total 36)	$6,107.6	$15,702.8

[1] Changed from Brooklyn Rapid Transit to Brooklyn-Manhattan Transit Corp. in 1923.
[2] Changed from Niagara Falls Power Co. to Buffalo, Niagara & Eastern Pr. Co. in 1925.
[3] Changed from Commonwealth Pr. Ry. & Lt. Co.
[4] Changed from Utah Securities Corp. to Electric Pr. & Lt. Corp. before 1926.
[5] Changed from Illinois Traction Co. to North American Lt. & Pr. Co. before 1924.
[6] Changed from Portland Ry. Lt. & Power Co. to Portland Elec. Pr. Co. in 1924.
[7] Estimated.

TABLE II*d*

25 Industrials in List of 200 Largest Corporations in 1927 but Not in 1919

Name	Gross Assets on or About December 31, 1927 (Million Dollars)
Amer. Radiator Co.	$ 100.6
Borden Co.	90.6
Cuban Dominican Sugar Co.	88.4
Dodge Bros., Inc.	131.5
Glen Alden Coal Co.	244.5[1]
Gt. At. & Pac. Tea Co. of America	113.2
Gt. Western Sugar Co.	86.3
Internat. Match Corp.	189.4
Internat. Shoe Co.	97.1
Koppers Co.	150.0[1]
Kresge Co. (S. S.)	87.3
Loew's Inc.	103.5
Long-Bell Lumber Corp.	114.9
Marland Oil Co.	117.9
National Dairy Products Corp.	91.1
Paramount Famous Lasky Corp.	156.9
Phila. & Reading Coal & Iron Corp.	127.9
Phillips Petroleum Co.	143.4
Pittsburgh Plate Glass Co.	89.6
Prairie Pipe Line Co.	129.1
Richfield Oil Co.	149.0[1]
Shell Union Oil Corp.	348.2
Tobacco Products Corp.	117.0[1]
U.S. Realty & Imp. Co.	100.0[1]
Wheeling Steel Corp.	120.4
	$3,287.8

[1] Estimated.

TABLE II*e*

22 Public Utilities in List of 200 Largest Corporations in 1927 but Not in 1919

Name	Gross Assets on or About December 31, 1927 (Million Dollars)
Amer. Elec. Pr. Corp.	$ 96.9[2]
Amer. Gas & Elec. Co.	407.0[2]
Amer. Lt. & Traction Co.	128.5[2]
Amer. States Securities Corp.	125.0[2]
Assoc. Gas & Elec. Co.	338.8
Duke Power Co.	180.9
Elec. Bond & Share Sec. Corp.[1]	353.8
Empire Power Corp.	133.0[2]
Engineers Pub. Serv. Co.	177.3
Federal Water Serv. Corp.	149.0
General Gas & Elec. Corp.	151.2
Internat. T. & T. Corp.	232.7
Midland Util. Co.	128.9
Mohawk Hudson Pr. Corp.	182.9[2]
New England Pr. Assoc.	192.4
Northeastern Pr. Corp.	150.0[2]
Pacific Lighting Corp.	122.5
Penn. Ohio Edison Co.	113.0[2]
Southeastern Pr. & Lt. Co.	474.4
St. Louis Pub. Serv. Co.	113.0[2]
United Lt. & Pr. Co.	278.4
Utilities Pr. & Lt. Corp.	240.8
	$4,470.4

[1] Assets of America & Foreign Power Co., only.
[2] Estimated.

10

*Railroads as an Economic Force in American Development**[1]

By LELAND H. JENKS

I

Any attempt to discuss the way in which railroads have promoted the rise of the American economy must assume some theory of economic evolution. The following analysis is based upon Schumpeter's theory of innovations.[2] Briefly this theory holds that economic evolution in capitalistic society is started by innovation in some production function, that is, by new combinations of the factors in the economic process. These innovations may center in new commodities or new services, new types of machinery, new forms of organization, new firms, new resources, or new areas. As Schumpeter makes clear, this is not a general theory of economic, much less of social, change. Innovation is an internal factor operating within a given economic system while the system is also affected by external factors (many of them sociological) and by growth (which means, substantially, changes in population and in the sum total of savings made by individuals and firms). These sets of factors interact in economic change. "The changes in the economic process brought about by innovation, together with all their effects, and the response to them by the economic system" constitute economic evolution for Schumpeter.[3]

Railroad development has had three phases or moments which have

---

* *Journal of Economic History,* 1944, IV, 1–20. Reprinted by courtesy of the author and of New York University Press.

[1] This article is an elaboration and extension of a paper delivered at the meeting of the Mississippi Valley Historical Association, Washington, D.C., December 28–31, 1938.

[2] Joseph A. Schumpeter, *Business Cycles,* Vol. I (New York and London, McGraw-Hill Book Co., 1939), esp. Ch. 3 and 7; *idem, The Theory of Economic Development* (Cambridge, Mass., Harvard University Press, 1934), Ch. 2 and 6; *idem,* "The Instability of Capitalism," *Econ. Jour.,* 1928, XXXVIII, 361–86. Cf. the theory of Allyn A. Young, "Increasing Returns and Economic Progress," *ibid.,* 527–42.

[3] *Business Cycles,* Vol. I, p. 86.

involved innovation in distinctive ways. I shall consider (1) the railroad as an idea, (2) the railroad as a construction enterprise, and (3) the railroad as a producer of transportation services.[4]

II

By the railroad as an idea is not meant the original design of steam locomotion on rails. It pertains to the inception in particular areas of particular projects, conceived as likely to be appropriate opportunities for business enterprise. In this sense the idea of any major innovation, such as the railroad, is a potent economic force. For once railway projects have been conceived and plans for their execution elaborated, it becomes easier for other innovating ideas to be entertained.[5] On the one hand, the socio-psychological deterrents against entering upon new ways are lowered. On the other, the characteristics of the prospective future are altered; they assume an aspect more favorable to men and firms with new plans than to men and firms whose position is established. Thus early railway projects were attended by a retinue of satellite innovations.

The first railway projects emerged in the United States in the thirties in a situation in which the psychological risks had already been appreciably lowered by the general passion for internal improvements displayed in a plethora of projects for canals, turnpikes, plank roads, bridges, banks, and other enterprises.[6] The earliest railways paralleled, supplemented, or improved transport systems that were already in being.[7] The real railway revolution dates from the forties, prior to the California gold discoveries, in projects to cross the Appalachians, to link the seaboard with the interior, the Ohio Valley with the Great Lakes, and, breaking away from the contours of water transport, to unite distant points by more direct routes.[8] It was the determination to build

[4] These distinctions are hinted at but not developed in Schumpeter, *Business Cycles,* Vol. I, pp. 130–36. They are not to be construed precisely as stages or periods, although each was relatively more conspicuous in certain decades than in others.

[5] Three types of obstacles to innovation are distinguished in Schumpeter, *Business Cycles,* Vol. I, p. 100: hostility to the new idea, absence of facilitating economic functions, and inhibitions against entering upon a relatively incalculable course. Young, *op. cit.,* p. 534, stresses the need to remake human material in terms of new skills and habits and in terms of redistribution of population.

[6] Carl Russell Fish, *The Rise of the Common Man* (New York, Macmillan Co., 1927), Ch. 4 and 5.

[7] One thinks of the Boston & Lowell, New York & New Haven, Philadelphia & Columbia, Allegheny Portage, the original Baltimore & Ohio, and the lines connecting Albany with Buffalo.

[8] The most dynamic set of American innovations consisted in plans to build railways in anticipation of traffic. Lewis Henry Haney, *A Congressional History of Railways in the United States to 1850* (Madison, University of Wisconsin, 1908), p. 31. Congressional

railroads in advance of traffic that gave the "railroad idea" prolonged force in American economic life. The conviction that the railroad would run anywhere at a profit put fresh spurs to American ingenuity and opened closed paddocks of potential enterprise.

Innovations are the work of enterprisers. For the railroad as idea, the role of entrepreneurship was pretty much identical with promotion; and the promoter was rarely limited in outlook to the railroad itself. In action, he was omnicompetent and omnipresent. His imagination leaped readily from the concrete problem of securing authority for a right of way to visions of a countryside filled with nodding grain, settlements of industrious families, and other evidences of progress and civilization. Each railway project involved the sanguine judgment of enterprising individuals and groups in particular, local situations that a certain line would be of direct or indirect pecuniary advantage to themselves. It was linked to specific plans for town promotion and real-estate speculation, to combinations for contracting services and supplies or for exploitation of resources, in anticipation of the actual movement of traffic by rail. But as projects multiplied they collectively acquired a symbolic function, dramatizing broader purposes. The railway projector became an exemplification of the power of steam, of the advantages of the corporate form of business organization, of the ability of man to master his environment. The early railway promoter was not only a potential economic agent; he embodied the dream of developing communities, regions, the continent.

Thus, as the barriers to new projects were periodically lowered by the inception of new railway systems, the first moment of the railroad as an economic force was manifested in a wavelike profusion of new enterprises of many sorts. Moreover, its effects in the United States were not exhausted in a decade or so, as they were in England. The railroad idea was periodically renewed for region after region and route after route, as national development, at least facilitated by the earlier railroads, widened the horizons of enterprise.

---

land grants were a factor, as in the case of the Illinois Central, the first large system built through sparsely settled territory. Paul Wallace Gates, *The Illinois Central Rail-road and Its Colonization Work* (Cambridge, Mass., Harvard University Press, 1934). Canal building had, however, in the old Northwest, anticipated the railroad less successfully in building ahead of population. Frederic L. Paxson, *History of the American Frontier 1763–1893* (Boston and New York, Houghton Mifflin Co., 1924), Ch. 30. For early systems and projects, cf. Caroline E. MacGill *et al., History of Transportation in the United States before 1860,* Balthasar Henry Meyer, ed. (Washington, D.C., Carnegie Institution of Washington, 1917); J. L. Ringwalt, *Development of Transportation Systems in the United States* (Philadelphia, The Author, 1888).

III

The second moment of the railroad as an economic force came with the actual construction of new lines. The statistics of net mileage added in each year from 1837 to 1937 give a quantitative measure of this contribution of the railroad to development, as appears on the accompanying charts. Two general statements are strikingly supported by these data.[9] In the first place, railway building proceeded in an undulating pattern, paralleling closely the general contours of major business cycles until the First World War. From 1850 to the nineties, omitting the years of the Civil War, the rise and fall in new construction in fact led by a perceptible interval most other indices of business conditions.[10] In the second place, there was a long-run trend in new railway construction, which was predominantly upward in absolute figures from the late 1840's to about 1890. The rate of this upward trend tended to slacken with the aggregate movement approximating graphically a logistic curve, but, for the whole period, expansion of railway plant averaged about 10 per cent a year. The trend since 1890 has been irregularly downward, bearing the aspect of a reversed logistic curve. The early persistent succession of fresh waves of railway construction, arising largely in the development of new areas in the American West and South, must be regarded as one of the basic phenomena in the total economic growth of the United States, while the logistic curve of total experience presents in outline a picture of an industry passing from youth through adolescence to maturity.

But how did railway construction as such act as an economic force? How could it be a pace setter? The answer is broadly that it operated directly to create a demand for various factors of production. In response to this demand there were rises in prices or increases in supply or both. Increase of supply could come only from some sort of further innova-

---

[9] The data for these charts are derived from the United States Treasury Department, Bureau of Statistics, *Statistical Abstract of the United States, 1900* (Washington, D.C., U.S. Government Printing Office, 1901), *ibid., 1914,* p. 637; and *ibid., 1937,* p. 379. Chart II is adapted from Simon S. Kuznets, *Secular Movements in Production and Prices* (Boston and New York, Houghton Mifflin Co., 1930), pp. 191, 526–27.

[10] This correlation was initially based upon inspection of the mileage data in comparison with the chart in Schumpeter, *Business Cycles,* Vol. II, p. 465, and the analyses of business conditions in Willard Long Thorp, *Business Annals* (New York, National Bureau of Economic Research, 1926) and National Bureau of Economic Research, *Recent Economic Changes,* Vol. II (New York, McGraw-Hill Book Co., 1929), p. 892. More decisive support is provided by John E. Partington, *Railroad Purchasing and the Business Cycle* (Washington, D.C., The Brookings Institution, 1929). As Partington includes orders for replacements as well as for original basic construction, he finds that orders of railway capital goods led business-cycle changes as late as 1907. Throughout this period, he finds, railway earnings followed, instead of preceded, changes in purchases.

tions, such as the drawing of fresh increments of land, labor, or capital into economic uses or the transfer of such factors to more effective combinations. This process meant the periodic dislocation of the economic

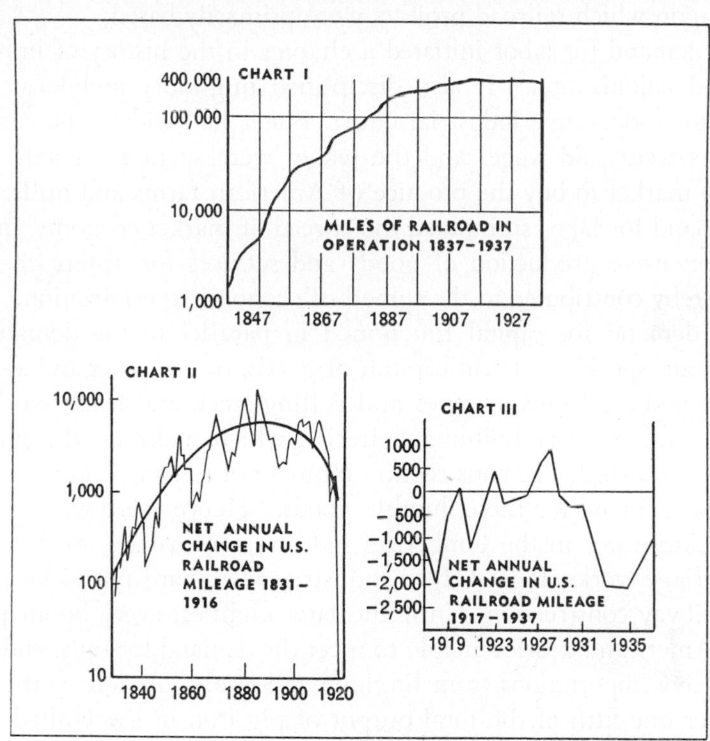

structure as well as the disruption of the activities of individuals and communities. At the same time it enhanced the opportunities for enterprisers having a high degree of flexibility, pioneering individuals and groups, the agents of innumerable innovating firms and procedures.

The land for railroad construction was largely new land, previously not of economic use. It cost virtually nothing to the railway companies, and not very much to anyone else.[11] Socially the land devoted to railroad purposes more than paid for itself by the increment in productivity of adjacent land. This was so obvious to everyone connected with railway building that periodic land booms came to communities even before the rails were laid. The speculative activity thus diffused in anticipation of

[11] Frederick A. Cleveland and Fred Wilbur Powell, *Railroad Promotion and Capitalization in the United States* (New York, Longmans, Green & Co., 1909), pp. 199–200. "In the Southern States, and the Mississippi Valley . . . all the real estate required for way, and for depots, stations, etc., are generally gratuity to the roads." *American Railroad Journal,* Jan. 3, 1852, XXV, 13. Cf. James Blaine Hedges, *Henry Villard and the Railways of the Northwest* (New Haven, Yale University Press, 1930), *passim.*

railroad construction may have brought many creative innovations in its wake. But, by distracting labor and enterprise from productive to parasitic activities, it frequently delayed the realization of the plausible hopes upon which railroad projects were primarily based.

The demand for labor initiated a chapter in the history of immigration and colonization.[12] It also disciplined migratory and local labor power to co-operative industrial effort. But it had wider repercussions. Laborers were paid wages and the wages were spent for goods. They went to market to buy the produce of American farms and mills. Thus the demand for labor stimulated the spread of market economy and the more extensive production of goods and services for distant markets, and thereby contributed to the spread of economic specialization.

The demand for capital functioned in parallel to the demand for labor. I am speaking of real capital, of goods, of the picks and shovels, sleepers and steel rails, engines and rolling stock and bridgework and culverts and ordinary building material, which make up the physical plant of a railroad. The construction moment of railway history brought an initial demand for these durable goods.[13] Hence there was a chance for the innovator in the lumbering industry, in quarries, in iron mills and carriage works. Indeed these industries were hard put to keep pace with railway construction. Until the later eighties, every boom period found American factories unable to meet the demand for rails, and there were heavy importations from England and Wales. As late as the nineties, over one fifth of the total output of pig iron in the United States was being rolled into railroad bars.[14]

Much of this demand for durable goods turned eventually into a demand for labor in mine and quarry and mill, into wage payments to labor. And these wages too were spent for consumers' goods and meant

---

[12] Gates, *The Illinois Central Rail-road,* pp. 89, 94–98. Despite its crucial importance, the subject of labor supply has been too frequently neglected by railway historians. Adequate data for labor employed in new construction are available only for a few large lines such as the Central Pacific, Union Pacific, and the Illinois Central. On each of these, upward of 10,000 men were employed at the peak of construction. Probably a thousand men were needed for every hundred miles. Assuming that twice as many miles were in progress as were completed in any given year, the figure of 200,000 men is reached as the maximum employed at any one time in the construction of these railways. This figure was not attained until the eighties, by which time the census reported 250,000 officials and employees of railroads, presumably engaged directly or indirectly in transportation service.

[13] Cf. files of railway periodicals for advertisements of manufacturers and dealers in railway materials and supplies. Ringwalt, *Development of Transportation Systems in the U.S.,* pp. 132–36, 210.

[14] For details, cf. *Statistical Abstract of the U.S., 1902,* p. 380, and corresponding tables in earlier volumes.

widening markets, increased specialization, and, presumably, greater productivity.

Thus the initial impetus of investment in railway construction led in widening arcs to increments of economic activity over the entire American domain, far exceeding in their total volume the original inputs of investment capital. To this feature of modern capitalism, John Maynard Keynes and others have applied the term "multiplier."[15] It is believed that for present-day England the efficiency of the multiplier may suffice to double the impact of a new investment in construction. For nineteenth-century United States, its efficiency seems to have been considerably greater than that.

I have spoken of inputs and investment. In our economy the demand for land and labor and capital has meant another demand, a demand not for an independent factor of production, but for something equally essential, a demand for money capital.[16] In fact, without a supply of money capital there could have been no effective demand for any of the real factors, no railways, and no stimulus from them for economic development. Hence it is convenient to think of the building of railroads as an investment of money capital. To this investment there corresponded in the long run the accumulation of savings. That saving came first and investment in the railroads afterwards is a proposition for which there is little historical evidence, at least in the United States. It is true that the practice of thrift as an individual and family responsibility was built into our social system by the Puritans. But the savings thus made in the middle of the nineteenth century went largely into land, into improvements on the farm, into the mill, the private business, and, in relatively small amounts, into public securities. Few railroads were originally financed by direct subscription of the shareholders at par in ready cash.[17]

---

[15] John Maynard Keynes, *The General Theory of Employment, Interest and Money* (London, 1936), Ch. 11; R. F. Kahn, "The Relation of Home Investment to Unemployment," *Econ. Jour.*, 1931, XLI, 173–98.

[16] Admittedly "money capital" constitutes merely a vehicle or instrumentality, the means of acquiring command over the several factors of production. More commonly it is spoken of as long-term credit or capital funds. But sometimes an instrument becomes so important that it exerts influence by itself and requires consideration on its separate account.

[17] These were chiefly railroads built in the thirties and forties. Cf. Frank Walker Stevens, *The Beginnings of the New York Central Railroad* (New York and London, G. P. Putnam's Sons, 1926). Even in these cases, as we know from accounts of the crises of 1854 and 1857, the subscribers carried their shares on bank loans. Cf. Schumpeter, *Business Cycles,* Vol. I, pp. 325–30.

In final analysis, the funds for railway construction came from the extension of credit by American banks and from foreign exchange supplied by European investors. This was accomplished by many devices which called into play the charitable cupidity of contractors and iron manufacturers on both sides of the Atlantic, and the lively anticipations of property owners in the area which the railroad was to develop.[18] Some of the shares were sold at a heavy discount to local residents, but more were given outright for land, for legal and legislative services, for banking accommodation, or as a bonus to promote the sale of bonds. Frequently there was a construction company, analogous to the Crédit Mobilier, which took all the securities in payment for the road and operated it pending the completion of construction. Since the books of these organizations have been conveniently mislaid, it will always be impossible to ascertain what our railroads really cost originally in money capital. The construction companies turned over whole blocks of securities to manufacturers and contractors in payment for goods and services. These enterprisers usually seem to have pledged the securities with banks for working capital in the process of supplying the goods. In New York and elsewhere, speculators and specialists in railway finance, operating also on bank loans, facilitated this inflationary process by their dealings in stocks and bonds and daily risked the credit of the railway companies in their furious contests of bulls and bears.

The American banking mechanism did not have to bear this periodic strain alone. Every burst of new railway construction, in the thirties, in the fifties, at the close of the Civil War, through the eighties, and again from 1904 to 1907, meant new investments from abroad by British, Dutch, and German capitalists.[19] Schumpeter states that the boom from 1866 to 1873, which doubled our railway mileage, was entirely financed by an estimated two billion dollars of capital imported during those

[18] Cleveland and Powell, *Railroad Promotion and Capitalization,* is still the most adequate account for aspects before 1900. Cf. William Z. Ripley, *Railroads; Finance and Organization* (New York, Longmans, Green & Co., 1915), pp. 10–52; Cleveland and Powell, *Railroad Finance* (New York, D. Appleton & Co., 1912), Ch. 2–4 and the very rich bibliography; Charles F. Adams, Jr., "Railroad Inflation," *North American Review,* 1869, CVIII, 138–44.

[19] This paragraph is based upon original research in London and the United States, made possible by a sabbatical from Wellesley College and a grant from the John Simon Guggenheim Memorial Foundation. An introduction to the subject is available in Cleona Lewis, *America's Stake in International Investments* (Washington, D.C., The Brookings Institution, 1938), Ch. 2; Ripley, *Railroads; Finance and Organization,* pp. 1–10; and Leland H. Jenks, *The Migration of British Capital to 1875* (New York and London, Alfred A. Knopf, 1927), Ch. 3 and pp. 169, 255–59 and notes. Before the Civil War the share of foreign investors was smaller than it became later. In only a few cases was it an initiating factor in railroad development.

years.[20] It is incorrect to suppose, as he apparently does, that any such amount of foreign money was at that time invested directly in the railways. British, Dutch, and German investors were then buying nearly half of the Civil War debt, chiefly in 5–20's and 10–40's, to the amount of more than a billion dollars par. The railroads obtained directly only about half a billion. The purchase of government bonds by foreigners, however, released savings and bank resources for railway, industrial, and commercial promotion in the United States. In no subsequent period was the impact of foreign capital as momentous; but it is easy to exaggerate its importance. Although something like one fifth of the nominal value of American railroads was foreign-owned in 1873, the whole volume of foreign claims amounted to only 6 or 7 per cent of national wealth.[21] While in the course of subsequent fluctuations foreign ownership of railroad securities may have reached the proportions of one third in 1890 and nearly as much just before 1914, yet at these later dates it constituted a smaller proportion of the total national wealth than it had in 1873. According to the estimates, foreign investments did not keep pace with the growth of the national wealth.

It would be desirable to measure more precisely the investment of money capital at successive periods. Available figures of railway capitalization are entirely unsatisfactory for historical purposes. Apart from the obscurities of early railroad finance already mentioned, tabulations and estimates do not carefully and regularly include net floating debt or exclude intercorporate securities. The pathology of early stock watering has no necessary connection with the "overcapitalization" from which most railroad systems have suffered in recent years. This overcapitalization is entirely compatible with real historical investment as large as the nominal capitalization. But the available statistics give no adequate clue, before the last few decades, when such amounts actually were invested.

Whatever the source or timing of the application of money capital, the financing of railroad construction encouraged innovations in financial enterprise: the development of stock exchanges and their techniques; the specialization of firms, old and new, in investment banking and in security brokerage; the specialization of banking institutions (especially trust companies) as trustees and registration agents for securities, and as agents for distributing capital and interest payments; the rise of legal firms specializing in corporation law and in adjusting con-

[20] Schumpeter, *Business Cycles,* Vol. I, p. 335.

[21] Lewis, *America's Stake in International Investments,* p. 560.

struction activities to the intricacies of the American political system.

New financial techniques and innovations in corporate structure were involved when established railway companies became agents in the flow of capital. By the early fifties the Pennsylvania was using its credit to supply funds for the building of western connections which it only informally controlled.[22] With the establishment of the Pennsylvania Company in 1869, the holding company became a permanent feature of the American scene. In many cases initial construction was of the sketchiest sort and by the seventies it was an established practice, of which foreign security holders bitterly complained, for companies to invest their earnings in necessary improvements and extensions. This financing of corporate growth from within may fairly be claimed to be an American innovation in capitalistic technique, which has only recently been diffused to the British Isles.

With financial innovation came a transformation of the role of the enterpriser in connection with particular railway systems. In the initial moments of construction, the typical enterpriser was still pretty much the omnicompetent pioneer, the individual of imagination, daring, and energy. Like General W. J. Palmer of the Denver and Rio Grande, he considered himself an agent of civilization, an embodiment of collective purpose.[23] No aspect of the task of railway building was too technical for his consideration and none too petty. In looking for the enterpriser of particular lines, official titles should not deceive. There was usually one man or a small informal group of unspecialized associates who could get things done, who could deal effectively at the same time with laborers, suppliers, politicians, and the local citizenry, and could command the confidence of sources of credit. At the construction moment, administration of a large formal organization was not necessarily involved. The mechanism of subcontracting provided a pattern for the cooperation of innumerable lesser enterprisers of a similar type.

Such enterprisers were rarely able, however, to cope with recurrent financial involvements. The elaboration of the superstructure of railroad securities sooner or later compelled a more formal division of tasks and responsibilities in the continuance of construction. In some cases this involved a shift of the center of decision from the engineer-promoter to financial and legal experts either within or outside the railroad organiza-

---

[22] Pennsylvania Central R.R. Co., *Annual Reports, passim.*

[23] William J. Palmer, *The Westward Current of Population in the United States* (London, 1874) and Glenn Chesney Quiett, *They Built the West* (New York and London, D. Appleton-Century Co., 1934), Ch. 2–6, throw light upon the career of this neglected enterpriser.

tion.[24] The financier-enterpriser assumed many guises, now entering upon new construction to win stock-exchange battles, now basing a program of calculated expansion upon a re-ordering of company accounts, now entering belatedly, as did William Rockefeller in Northwestern, the race for competitive bigness.[25] There was inescapably a narrowing of horizon; the financier-enterpriser could decide freely only problems stated in financial terms, and he focused his attention chiefly on relations with potential intermediaries and rivals for the supply of capital.

Thus the second moment of the railroad as an economic force came with a demand for the factors of production in new construction, accompanied by the rise of new techniques and institutions of finance, by the aggregation of capital in mobile forms, and by the gradual displacement of the omnicompetent type of enterpriser.

IV

The third moment to be surveyed is that of the railroad as a going concern, a complex of tracks and engines and cars and managers and employees engaged in the business of carrying passengers and freight. By rendering this transportation service, the railroad in operation has doubtless added directly to the real income of the United States, and indirectly to economic expansion.[26] There appears to be no satisfactory technique for giving a precise measure to the extent of this contribution. It seems that the railways carried irregularly increasing ton-miles of freight until 1929, while the aggregate of passenger-miles expanded until 1920. The quanta involved, said to be from 13 billions of freight

[24] N. S. B. Gras, *Business and Capitalism* (New York, F. S. Crofts & Co., 1939), pp. 246–59, 272–75, indicates the "normal" process by which financial capitalists became involved in industry. He is correct, I believe, in implying that the opportunity and need have not been confined to late phases of the construction moment. From the standpoint of innovation, the emergence of the financial enterpriser in the railroads is not to be identified with the rise of special departments within the organization. The latter, or their heads, may be simply parts of a formally established group functioning as management-enterpriser. See Section IV below.

[25] Max Lowenthal, *The Investor Pays* (New York, Alfred A. Knopf, 1933).

[26] Ringwalt, *Development of Transportation Systems in the U.S.*, pp. 382–85, and Henry V. Poor, *Influence of the Railroads of the U.S. in the Creation of Its Commerce and Wealth* (New York, 1869), are representative of early discussions. "Our new railroads increase the value of farms and open new markets for their products. They lessen the time and cost of travel. They give a value to commodities otherwise almost worthless. They concentrate population, stimulate production, and raise wages by making labor more efficient. Our existing railroads are computed to create more wealth every year than is absorbed for the construction of new railroads." *Commercial and Financial Chronicle*, Jan. 11, 1873, XVI, 41.

in 1870 to 450 billions in 1929, are certainly enormous.[27] But the available figures, at least before 1890, are neither accurate nor complete. There have been important changes in the composition of traffic. As Pigou points out, any attempt to measure differences in real income between situations involving substantial variations in the use of productive factors and in the composition of demand is theoretically at least precarious.[28] For contemporary comparison, Holmstrom has worked out a technique by which "virtual costs" (operating and maintenance charges plus interest on replacement cost of ways and works plus depreciation and profits) are equated with "direct benefits" on the one hand and "consumer costs" plus public subsidies on the other.[29] In view of the defective character of the data and the violence of price fluctuations in the United States, there is little hope of applying these means of measurement to the historical problem.

It is commonly assumed that the great contribution of railroad transportation came from the reduction of shipping costs. As compared with pre-motorized forms of highway transportation, the advantage of the railroad has always been obvious. There is no convincing evidence, however, that railways have ever carried freight at lower costs either to shippers or to society than canals or waterways.[30] The advantages that early railways showed over canals, such as speed, flexibility of service,

---

[27] Attempts to use railway data in connection with the study of changes in real income and "productivity" are exemplified by Arthur F. Burns, *Production Trends in the United States since 1870* (New York, National Bureau of Economic Research, 1934), and Spurgeon Bell, *Productivity, Wages, and National Income* (Washington, D.C., The Brookings Institution, 1940). A brief factual summary of the role of the railways in the economic system after the First World War is provided by the Bureau of Railway Economics, *The Railways and Economic Progress,* Miscellaneous Series No. 50 (Washington, D.C., 1929). The theory there suggested that the "economic contribution" of the railways is measured by the volume of their expenditures of all kinds is, however, at variance with the premises of this paper. Incidentally, this is an unusual place to find a theory popularly associated with New Deal economics. On railroad expenditures, cf. Partington, *Railroad Purchasing and the Business Cycle.*

[28] A. C. Pigou, "Comparisons of Real Income," *Economica,* New Series, May 1943, X, 93–98.

[29] J. Edwin Holmstrom, *Railways and Roads in Pioneer Development Overseas* (London, P. S. King & Son, 1934), Ch. 1. Cf. E. A. J. Johnson, "New Tools for the Economic Historian," *The Tasks of Economic History,* 1941 (Suppl. to the *Jour. Econ. Hist.,* Vol. I, pp. 30–38.

[30] General treatments of the economic significance of improved transportation are also found in D. Philip Locklin, *Economics of Transportation* (Chicago, Business Publications, 1938), Ch. 1, and Cleveland and Powell, *Railroad Finance,* Ch. 1. On comparative costs of service, cf. MacGill, *History of Transportation in the U.S. before 1860,* pp. 574–82; Haney, *Congressional History of Railways in the U.S.,* Ch. 3; Charles H. Ambler, *A History of Transportation in the Ohio Valley* (Glendale, California, Arthur H. Clark Co., 1932), pp. 358 ff.; Harold Kelso, "Waterways versus Railways," *Am. Econ. Rev.,* 1941, XXXI, 537–44.

and special adaptability to short hauls, are analogous to those of modern highway transport over the railroad. It was far more important that the railroad brought transportation to areas that without it could have had scarcely any commercial existence at all. At a later epoch, the motor highway provides means to achieve this result, at least in British colonial areas, at lower initial social cost. But historically, the very existence of most American communities and regions, of particular farms and industrial firms and aggregates, was made possible by the railroad.

Holmstrom's study of the cost characteristics of various forms of transportation brings other considerations to the forefront of analysis. He shows that the traffic potential of the railroad per unit of installation is even now far greater than that of any other form of transportation that he considers. For colonial areas in the early 1930's, for example, he computes that human porters could carry a maximum of 1,450 ton-miles of freight per annum; heavy animals, 3,600; "horsed wagons," 118,800; tractor trains, 1,000,000; and broad-gauge railways, 3,613,-500.[31] Thus an initial and continuing potential contribution of the railroad has come from the volume of traffic it has been able to carry.

The converse of this proposition is the fact that the railroad constitutes a case of increasing return, with special features that give a decisive bent to its impact upon economic structure. Its social costs per unit of traffic decrease rapidly with traffic density.[32] A familiar manifestation of this condition was the well-known shift from passengers and light traffic as principal sources of revenue in the early railroad days to bulk traffic. Any isolated railroad system would tend to expand along those lines. But as new railroads in the United States became linked to previously existing lines, and as the innovation of freight-car interchange was established after the Civil War, a principle of acceleration was manifested enabling newer lines to begin farther along the cost curve. Between 1890 and 1941 the average actual haul of each ton of freight became 50 per cent longer (increasing especially during the First World War and the 1930's); there was an increase of more than 100 per cent during the same period in the distance traveled by the average passenger. These are revealing data about the long-run function of the railroad in the economic system.[33] Such expansion is, however, not a measure of in-

[31] Holmstrom, *Railways and Roads in Pioneer Development Overseas,* p. 56. Palmer, *The Westward Current of Population in the U.S.,* relates that in 1866 the stage line from the terminus of the Kansas Pacific in Topeka carried six passengers daily to Denver. Two years later, daily trains carried westward one hundred to five hundred passengers daily.

[32] Holmstrom, *op. cit.,* pp. 104–12.

[33] United States Interstate Commerce Commission, *Statistics of Railways in the United States, 1941* (Washington, D.C., U.S. Government Printing Office, 1943), pp. 159–60.

novation; the recent increase reflects to no small degree adjustments by railroads to other innovations in the economic system. What is significant about the principle of increasing return in the railroad is that it indicates directions in which railway transportation affects the economic structure.

That the railroad tends to attract factors of production to its right of way needs no comment; this perception lay at the heart of the American railroad innovation. As Holmstrom points out, however, this supply of potential traffic does not distribute itself at random. It is polarized first about line terminals, and secondarily about traffic intersections.[34] There is a further tendency. Irrespective of rate differentials, the service of the railroad is of greatest advantage to large shippers requiring a fairly regular flow of traffic.[35] Thus railroad transportation provides a considerable addition to the external economies that firms can realize from large-scale operations. Such phenomena as the ecological structure of wholesale trade, the localization and concentration of primary processing establishments, and the vertical integration of production units in spite of their geographical separation are thus functionally related to railroad transportation service. In more concrete terms, attention may be directed to the initial localization of the textile industry in New England, the development of the factory system in some other industries at points remote from water power and dependent upon rail supply of coal, the establishment of stockyards in Chicago and other terminals, the rise of assembly plants, and generally the concentration, at terminals convenient to the source of supply, of industries processing and reducing the bulk of raw materials. In all these respects, railway transportation has worked in the same direction as, but in different areas from, water transport. It has functioned differently from the realized and probable tendencies of highway traffic.

The organization of railway enterprise itself early displayed the same tendencies to differentiation that it encouraged in other industries. On the one hand, the railways transferred to other enterprises part of their business. First in individual railway lines, and gradually on a more national scale, came the innovation of express companies, specializing in the rapid transmission of small items of high value. Opportunity arose for Pullman and other specialists in high-cost passenger service. On the other hand, individual railways themselves engaged in other

[34] Holmstrom, *op cit.*, pp. 265–66, 273.
[35] *Ibid.*, pp. 271–72.

business activities. If their land departments developed in order to implement construction, they proved of more value in augmenting traffic density to remunerative levels. Reading and other companies acquired anthracite fields in the interest of controlling the supply of bulk traffic between terminals. A great deal of change in the internal structure of railway organizations was merely a function of their expansion, involving innovations of a highly derivative and adaptive character; but other changes involved the positive quest of increasing return. The extension of particular systems by purchase, lease, and contract did not invariably contemplate development, but often aimed at controlling for the benefit of original main lines the supply of traffic at terminal points. The consolidation movement and much resistance to it on the part of particular companies may be interpreted from this point of view.

It must be clear that to yield real income and participate in expansion are not the same as to be a force for economic development. On the economic structure, the impact of the railway as a going concern was most decisive in the early years of the expansion of each system and in many respects came from the network as a whole rather than from any particular part. In time many other forces reinforced the polarizing tendency of the railroad. Urban centers tended to generate conditions that made for their own growth into metropolises. The returns to railways from increasing density tended to increase at slackening rates. Change in the railways gradually became more a matter of adjustment to external innovations than a primary source of disturbance to the economic structure.

As early as the eighties, railway systems that had been daring ventures only a decade before found themselves embarking on extensions and improvements, not as acts of innovating faith, but to enable them to handle traffic that had been offered them or to keep somebody else from getting the business.[36] In region after region development initiated by the railroad outran the plans of the projectors. The business of the railroad came increasingly to consist not in starting something but in keeping pace with what others were doing. That the railway would carry freight at known rates and with gradual change in the quality of service came to be part of the normal expectations of every business firm, a stable part of an environment which, of course, might still be disturbed

[36] For instance, new financing was sought by the Grand Trunk of Canada in the seventies and the Norfolk & Western in the eighties to make it possible to handle traffic already being offered. It was not always an extension that was involved but more often double-tracks, sidings, rolling stock, and improvements in the right of way.

by other innovations.[37] While the real income accruing to society from railway transportation probably continued to grow until 1929, the railroad functioned decreasingly as a pace setter or as an inciting force in the expansion of which it was a part.

By the time of the financial reorganizations of the nineties, many American railways manifested signs of belonging to an industry that has reached maturity.[38] The signs became more widespread in the first decade of the present century with the completion of the last cluster of new systems. For enterprises in general, Oxenfeldt thinks "newness of economic consequence" can be assumed to have worked itself out within a year of establishment.[39] This seems too short a period for the railroad. Although the bulk of improvement in the early years of American railway systems is properly classed as "construction," the leverage of increasing return in this field involves such extensive relocation of productive forces that opportunity for major business decisions may recur for several years after "completion" of the system.[40]

That some innovations have been made by railroads since 1910 must be conceded. Both technological and organizational changes are involved in the recent rapid increase in ton-miles of freight handled per employee and per unit of capital, in the increased capacity of cars, in speed of train units, in locomotive efficiency, etc. The National Resources Planning Board, however, takes the view that potentialities in this direction are thus far more an idea than an actuality.[41]

Consolidation looms as the source of the most important innovations in the near future. In 1933 only 16 per cent of the time of a typical freight car from shipper to consignee was consumed in hauling; 37 per cent of the time was attributable to railroad terminal movement; and a total of 84 per cent was spent in terminals.[42] Co-operation among carriers could improve this condition, but changes of innovational consequence seem to wait upon government action.

---

[37] Schumpeter, *Business Cycles,* Vol. I, Ch. 2, presents a representative theoretical analysis of this "equilibrium" position to which railway enterprises have been approximating.

[38] E. G. Campbell, *The Reorganization of the American Railroad System, 1893–1900* (New York, Columbia University Press, 1938).

[39] Alfred R. Oxenfeldt, *New Firms and Free Enterprise* (Washington, D.C., American Council on Public Affairs, 1943), p. 75.

[40] The degree to which in recent decades public regulation has restricted this opportunity as far as pricing of services is concerned has been the subject of a suggestive inquiry by the National Resources Planning Board. *Transportation and National Policy* (Washington, D.C., U.S. Government Printing Office, 1942), esp. pp. 87–128.

[41] *Ibid.,* pp. 60–65.

[42] *Ibid.,* p. 41.

But what has been the role of the entrepreneur in the railroad as a going concern? What is the source of innovation in an enterprise almost wholly concerned with rendering transportation service? The rise of a line organization with few staff features was an early aspect of railway operations, and was well established by the eighties. The Pennsylvania Central seems to have led the way in the practice of promotion from within, a practice that developed rapidly into seniority policies at all levels and the establishment of railroading as a career. For a couple of decades after the Civil War, the training thus afforded made the Pennsylvania an important source from which new companies drew top executives who often developed entrepreneurial talents as individuals. Thomas A. Scott, who rose from the ranks to the presidency of Pennsylvania, was of pioneering quality. As horizons of opportunity narrowed, however, selection from within tended to bring competent administrators of a more routine sort to top executive positions, men who had spent so many years mastering the complexities of detailed management along established lines that they had little interest in changing those procedures. This tendency has been marked in many railroad systems, and is associated with the shift to adaptive change as the principal relation of the railroads to economic expansion in recent years.

Nevertheless, some innovation has taken place, and it can occasionally be traced to pioneering leadership. Large organizations as such, however, apart from their degree of maturity, set up certain hazards to innovation. To continue operations they require the delegation of specialized authority and responsibility to a considerable number of individuals. An innovation disturbs their tasks and their relations with each other quite as much as it does economic relations and activities outside the organization. This disturbance to internal equilibrium is not adjusted through market mechanisms and bargaining transactions. It involves planning activity. Decisive importance can scarcely be allowed to attach to individuals who conceive new ideas, even when this duty is delegated to them as a specific task. The locus of decision tends to spread to a group that includes persons in a position to know and deal with prospective internal disturbances which are only partially of an economic character.[43] It is not clear that this development has explicitly gone far in

[43] An introduction to the sociological theory of organization can be found in Chester I. Barnard, *The Functions of the Executive* (Cambridge, Mass., Harvard University Press, 1938). Cf. T. N. Whitehead, *Leadership in a Free Society* (Cambridge, Mass., Harvard University Press, 1936), Ch. 6 and 8. The problem at a lower level of enterprise structure is analyzed in F. J. Roethlisberger and William J. Dickson, *Management and the Worker* (Cambridge, Mass., Harvard University Press, 1939), Ch. 24 and 25.

railroad organization. As an innovation in the role of entrepreneurship itself, it is emergent in some newer large-scale industries. The extent to which the management-enterpriser type, as we may call it, has actually functioned in railroads informally and without explicit recognition deserves inquiry.

V

This general interpretation of the role of the railroad as an economic force suggests what might be undertaken in greater detail to apply the innovation theory to the history of particular companies and of the railroad system as a whole. What was the impact of the railroad upon technological, locational, structural, and organizational alterations in particular firms, industries, and regions? Parallel inquiries could be made regarding the part played by other major innovations, such as the more recent rise of the electromotive industries. It is not a question of applying the facts of economic history to verify an economic theory. It is a question of using a theory as a tool to coherent understanding of the facts. Economic historians seem increasingly willing to make use of conceptual aids for this purpose. It is one of the most prominent symptoms of what may be a wider tendency to employ analytical procedures in historical studies.

For the study of long-run change, the innovation theory stresses two important aspects of historical process: (1) the distinction between innovating (disturbing, inciting, evolutionary) change and various types of adjustment (including expansion), and (2) the distinctive role of entrepreneurship. The first of these aspects provides the framework for systematic exploration of the relation between changes in several sectors of the economy, in so far as these can be interpreted in economic terms. The breakdown of the railroad innovation into three "moments" is only a convenience that may be peculiar to transportation. In any case, the distinction between innovating and adaptive change is a device that should become more serviceable to the historian as it is sharpened by application to a number of particular situations. It does not necessarily require the economic historian to take into account other than economic events and processes. Indeed, its logical adequacy can only gain from rigorous limitation to the items that are considered to be a part of an economic system.

The emphasis upon entrepreneurship as the crucial factor in capitalistic evolution involves both theorist and historian in considerations that go far beyond the limits of economics. Schumpeter is explicitly aware of this fact, and insists that in his conception the economy is not isolated but functions in a larger universe which requires in the first instance sociological analysis for its interpretation. The theory of innovations is neither a "great man" nor a "better mousetrap" theory of history. The innovator is a person whose traits are in some part a function of his sociocultural environment. His innovation is a new combination of factors and elements already accessible. It relates in every phase to previously developed business and monetary habits, technological skills, and variable tastes, none of which can be regarded as functions of economic activity alone. Thus Schumpeter's theory involves the question of the sociological factors favorable to the emergence of entrepreneurship. In a recent work he has presented a partial analysis of such factors.[44] Further analysis seems to be called for, at least so far as American capitalism is concerned, analysis that will come to closer grips with the special features of American social structure and the various influences which made for a strong entrepreneurial bias in the "social character" of the nineteenth-century American.

Despite his sociological sophistication, however, Schumpeter tends to think of his entrepreneur pretty much as a deviant person—a particular individual or at most a family. This approach tends to make highly problematical the existence of any entrepreneurship in a bureaucratic enterprise such as the railway, whether under private or public ownership. It must be recognized that innovations in a socialist economy would work themselves out by mechanisms other than under capitalism. But not all of such differences would be peculiar to socialism. Practically, large-scale organization offers a new type of social resistance to innovation. At the same time, as Schumpeter himself vigorously argues, the large organization offers real support to technological change, at least, by mobilizing resources for its systematic planning.[45]

It is possible that there is a real social lag in conceptions of the entrepreneurial function. The question deserves to be considered whether policy formation by group action is an obstacle to innovation, not inherently, but only because of certain peculiarities in our culture. Is the entrepreneurial role in large organizations increasingly the function of a co-operating group? Is it true that this tendency is not absolutely new but can be discerned in earlier phases of modern industry; that it is

[44] Joseph A. Schumpeter, *Capitalism, Socialism, and Democracy* (New York, Harper & Bros., 1942), Ch. 11–14.

[45] *Ibid.*, pp. 96–98. Schumpeter seems to regard this change as more than adaptational. In so far as it is innovational, however, it functions less to develop capitalist structure than to further its incipient transformation into something else.

less important in entrepreneurial studies to single out the contributions of one individual than to ascertain the personal composition of the group with which he usually interacted and the way in which the members compensated for their respective shortcomings and were adjusted to each other? In so far as there is validity in affirmative answers to these questions, a practical problem of much importance falls upon the large organizations of the present day, that of cultivating social techniques for facilitating innovations. But there would be a broader social problem, that of developing personalities whose practical imagination and responsibility for decision will be stimulated rather than frustrated by membership in policy-determining groups. This would be a task for the family and other educational institutions and for socializing processes in the wider society.

11

*An Approach to the Study of Entrepreneurship**

By ARTHUR H. COLE

Twenty years ago Edwin F. Gay gave the Phi Beta Kappa Commencement address at Harvard. He entitled it "The Rhythm of History," and not infrequently in his later years he referred to the theme that he embodied in it:

> The amount of permissible free competition . . . varies with the social need. In differing degree it must always be active—this is what the socialists fail adequately to recognize—but it must always be subject more or less to group control, for the interest of the group predominates, and each member of the group consciously or unconsciously acknowledges this. The self-centered, active individual is a disruptive force, and there are periods in the rhythm of history when the cake of custom must be broken, when that disruptive, innovating energy is socially advantageous and must be given freer opportunity. But the social or group motive is even then latently powerful, while for normally longer periods of the rhythm the motive of social stability and order enjoys the more marked social approval. It then becomes active in building and defending social institutions and in seeking security for its members.[1]

Perhaps Mr. Gay liked to recall this thesis long after its first formulation because he could observe its increasing confirmation as the years and decades passed. Surely with him we can note the ever rising aspirations toward economic security and the continuing development of group organizations. Possibly we are also justified in thinking that this tide has begun to turn, the rhythm reached another turning point—with the rebuff to totalitarianism, with the moderation of English socialist beliefs, and with the prevailing contentment of American labor unionists to get along without Communist aid. Of course, the future direct

---

* *Journal of Economic History,* 1946, VI, Supplement, pp. 1–15. Reprinted by courtesy of the author and of New York University Press. This paper with an additional, opening tribute to Edwin F. Gay, was presented as a Presidential Address at the annual meeting of the Economic History Association, Baltimore, Md., September 13, 1946.

[1] Edwin Francis Gay, "The Rhythm of History," *Harvard Graduates' Magazine,* 1923–24, XXXII, 12.

and indirect influence of Russia constitutes the largest present question mark.

As historians, however, we may be allowed to take a longer view. Whether we stand at a turning point or must watch the trend toward socialization proceed yet further, surely we can look back upon and examine critically the extended period when "disruptive, innovating energy" was breaking through the "cake" of pre-existing customary forms, and "social need" appears to have condoned, even supported, a high degree of "permissible free competition" on the part of "self-centered, active" individuals. Surprisingly enough, this aspect of economic life has attracted less scholarly attention than it has deserved.

Reasons can be found for this relative neglect. Possibly the conjuncture of a rising interest in economic history with an evolving socialized economy may be a factor. The novel elements in recent history have been the new regulatory bodies or the new social groupings. The restless, innovating businessman could be taken for granted, a wholly familiar figure, even as, a hundred years ago, McCulloch thought that free trade was a self-evident truth.

A factor yet more potent may well have been the course of economic thought. Here the villain of the piece is David Ricardo. Building upon Adam Smith, but in important ways altering the scientific method, he influenced processes of thinking in that area, which, transmitted through Mill and Cairnes and Marshall, have not wholly lost their potency to the present day. Economists since Ricardo have been largely preoccupied with "long-run" conditions, "static" analysis, and the like, and thereby have tended to distract attention from short-run, but repetitive, forces that are productive of change.

But my quarrel with the eminent stockbroker is more specific. In the construction of his economic principles, Ricardo failed to pursue the suggestion supplied by Cantillon and Jean-Baptiste Say that the entrepreneur be distinguished clearly from the other agents of production. This failure is somewhat difficult to understand, since Say had formalized the term "entrepreneur" and given it definition some fifteen years before Ricardo's *Principles* appeared, and he had repeated the notion several times in the interim, at least one version of which was available to Ricardo in English translation. Not merely is the term itself absent in Ricardo's writings, but no concept of business leaders as agents of change (other than as shadowy bearers of technological improvements) is embraced in his treatment of economic principles. In neglecting to follow Say, Ricardo seems to me to have rendered a great disservice to economics, and secondarily to economic history.[2]

Say had presented a characterization of extraordinary insight and imagination. The entrepreneur is the economic agent who

> unites all means of production—the labor of the one, the capital or the land of the others—and who finds in the value of the products which result from their employment the reconstitution of the entire capital that he utilizes, and the value of wages, the interest, and the rent which he pays, as well as the profits belonging to himself.[3]

This person, this entrepreneur, must have special personal qualities:

> . . . judgment, perseverance, and a knowledge of the world as well as of business. He is called upon to estimate, with tolerable accuracy, the importance of the specific product, the probable amount of the demand, and the means of its production: at one time, he must employ a great number of hands; at another, buy or order the raw material, collect laborers, find consumers, and give at all times a rigid attention to order and economy; in a word, he must possess the art of superintendence and administration . . . . In the course of such complex operations, there are abundance of obstacles to be surmounted, of anxieties to be repressed, of misfortunes to be repaired, and of expedients to be devised.[4]

This appraisal seems to me exceptionally full, as I have already suggested. Indeed, after a perusal of more modern authors—Walker and Knight, Schumpeter, Chamberlin, and divers others—I am inclined to paraphrase Say in an effort to blueprint the individual or institution that exhibits and has for centuries exhibited the "disruptive, innovating energy," of which Mr. Gay wrote. Say's analysis does fail to emphasize the spirit of adventure and the element of innovation, without which, it seems to me, a complete formulation of the entrepreneurial function is impossible.

I

Entrepreneurship may be defined in simplest terms as the utilization by one productive factor of the other productive factors for the creation

[2] Moreover, when the "entrepreneur" had been adopted in English (and American) economic theory, he was a colorless personage, and he remained colorless and unchanged down to Marshall and Keynes, perhaps because economic theorists have known so little economic history, and economic historians have paid so little attention to economic theory.

[3] Jean-Baptiste Say, *Catechism of Political Economy* (London, 1816), pp. 28–29. The first French edition appeared in 1815.

[4] Jean-Baptiste Say, *A Treatise on Political Economy,* Vol. I (London, 1821; 1st French ed., 1803), p. 104.

of economic goods. But such a definition means little until we have answered a barrage of questions: Why? How? Through what institutions and instrumentalities? With what concessions to the prevailing political and social environment? Elaborated as a result of such a catechism, entrepreneurship may be described as follows: the integrated sequence of actions, taken by individuals or by groups operating for individual business units, in a world characterized by a large measure of uncertainty, such actions being modified in greater or less degree by contemporary economic and social forces. This sequence of actions is intended to increase the residual element in business income for those business units, namely, profits, or to achieve some other business gain, for example, power, efficiency, or the survival and growth of these units (or the avoidance of loss). Thereby an advantage or satisfaction is hoped for (directly or indirectly, immediately or shortly) by those planning and executing these actions either for themselves or for the institutions with which they are affiliated and have identified themselves. At this point, it becomes essential to fragmentize the problem.

Obviously, we are concerned primarily with individual business units, with their creation, their preservation, and their demise, in whatever portion of economic and business life they may chance to be concerned, and in whatever form—proprietorship, partnership, or corporation—they chance to be organized. Also we are interested in the one person or in the several or many persons who alone, counseled by external advisers, or as a joint undertaking carry the destiny of each enterprise in his individual or in their co-operating hands. In the case of group entrepreneurship, such as we find in many large corporations, our concern is primarily with the so-called "top executives" or "top management"; but the diffusion of authority seems often so great that sovereignty may be no less difficult to locate than in the British form of government. I am inclined to think the lower edge of entrepreneurial power in group executive situations to be more like an uneven fringe than a neat clear line.[5]

In the promotional and survival purposes which entrepreneurship serves relative to individual business units, three processes alone seem important: innovation, management, and adjustment to external conditions, with the last including the imitation by some enterprises of the

[5] Parenthetically I might observe that quite obviously my analysis does not follow that of James Stauss (and of Frederick Hawley before him), who want to identify the corporation as "the entrepreneur." See James H. Stauss, "The Entrepreneur: The Firm," *Jour. Pol. Econ.*, 1944, LII, 112–27; Frederick B. Hawley, *Enterprise, and the Productive Process* (New York, G. P. Putnam's Sons, 1907).

innovations initiated by other business units that are directly or indirectly competing, and the utilization by enterprises in one industry of innovational services provided by ancillary concerns.[6] Innovation and adjustment, in turn, are the resultants of business decisions—business decisions motivated, as just suggested, by a purpose of increasing some differential business advantage or some satisfaction, or avoiding some differential or positive business disadvantage or unpleasantness.[7]

Under such a concept, risk bearing and profit receiving obviously become mere negative or passive elements. The real purpose of business strategy is to minimize risks and uncertainties and, if possible, to pass them off upon other business units; while the distribution of profits within business enterprises is a function of law, custom, and internal pressures, and, except in simple business oganization, has no close relation to the active derivation of profits.[8]

Since adjustment to forces external to given business units—economic, business, or social forces—may be regarded as a sort of necessary evil (inasmuch as no single enterprise can enjoy a monopoly of business talent and since business cannot generate its own environment), entrepreneurship boils down in basic functions to innovation upon a solid operational base achieved through the medium of business decisions. Innovation without a solid base tends to be ineffective—as witness the thousands of concerns that yearly die before their first birthdays; while management without innovation gives a poor prognosis, being the "dry rot" of enterprises on the way toward ossification and extinction.

In turn, these activities—and the decisions behind them—relative to innovation, management, and the adjustment to external forces may be conceived as directed along a half-dozen channels, which together, in fact, comprehend all the important phases of purpose in the individual

[6] Admittedly there is overlapping among these three elements. For example, innovations are possible in the business operations commonly looked upon as management; or innovations may be stimulated by efforts to adjust to external conditions; or some adjustment to external conditions of the cyclical character may become a part of business routine. Yet I believe the threefold division of entrepreneurial function—innovation, management, and adjustment to external change—to be defensible.

[7] Possibly one could use relative to all lines of innovation the apparatus of secondary and subsequent repercussions that Leland Jenks suggested in a recent article pertaining to railroads.—*Jour. Econ. Hist.*, 1944, IV, 1–20. As an imaginary case, one might think the creation of a "bargain basement" to have led to the development of a new purchasing policy or practice, and this in turn to an experiment with evening store hours. In addition, there would be cases in which innovations within older branches of business led to the erection of new, service institutions.

[8] Under this concept, the problems posed by Ripley, Berle, Means, and Burnham become almost side issues. They relate to the pressures and strategies in corporate government—much as pressures and strategies in the sharing of public benefits relate to political government.

business unit, whether it be large or small, or concerned with commercial, industrial, banking, or other business activities. Of course, the proportionate importance of the several phases will differ with size and with the nature of the business unit, as well as with some other factors. The half-dozen spheres of action are:

1. The determination of the business objectives of the enterprise, and the change of those objectives as conditions require or make advantageous;
2. The development and maintenance of an organization, including efficient relations with subordinates and all employees;
3. The securing of adequate financial resources, the retention of them, and the nurture of good relations with existing and potential investors;
4. The acquisition of efficient technological equipment, and the revision of it as new machinery appears;
5. The development of a market for products, and the devision of new products to meet or anticipate consumer demands; and
6. The maintenance of good relations with public authorities and with society at large.

In any of these phases of entrepreneurial activity there is constant need for decisions, and in any of them there is opportunity for innovation, management, and the adjustment to external conditions, including alterations of public opinion. It is through these avenues of operation that entrepreneurial power functions.

Thus, in brief, we have at the base of our pyramid a half-dozen lines or avenues of activity—from organizing the enterprise to getting along with the general public—in following which entrepreneurship really does things. Then we have three objectives or purposes which occasion activities along these several lines: innovation, management, and the imposed adjustments. The actions for these three purposes along any of the six lines are the resultants of executive decisions; these decisions are the acts of a real person, or a real, but variantly composed, group of persons at or near the top of individual business units; and these decisions are made in response to divers psychological imperatives and are conditioned by various and changing environmental forces.

II

The economic significance of such business phenomena is patent, although infrequently adumbrated. Economic advance, at least insofar as it springs from business and not from governmental or other forces, is largely a consequence of innovations by individual enterprises copied by competing business units. These innovations may be of any sort, from the organization of a business unit itself—the launching of an enterprise novel in product, place, or form—to a new method of packaging a manufactured item. They may be innovations of technological equipment and productive processes, or they may be purely innovations of management.[9] Also, one may properly conceive of innovations pushing out, first in one sector of operations and then in another, first by one enterprise and then by another, like the advancing front of a long battle line. Advantageous innovations, made effective by efficient management, are copied by other enterprises; the differential advantages of the innovating institutions are repeatedly lost; marginal expenses are reduced; and the phenomenon of economic progress—greater productivity at lower human cost—is attained. Such surely is an adequate social reason for studying entrepreneurship.

The central position of entrepreneurship in other economic relations is suggested by consideration of the fact that entrepreneurial decisions (including those of banking "entrepreneurs") constitute the chief element in business cycles. Albert Hart and George Shackle have paid special attention to this situation in their analyses of "anticipations"; Sumner Slichter and others have studied businessmen's reactions in their examination of "turning points" in business cycles; while, of course, to Joseph Schumpeter, innovations and other entrepreneurial phenomena are pivotal. Again, one may say that entrepreneurial policy has been half (or more) of the problem of industrial relations; and it forms an equivalent proportion of public relations. In short, entrepreneurship cannot, it seems, be regarded as other than a potent change-producing force in a free or relatively free economy.[10] To study the "entrepreneur" is to study the central figure in modern economic history, and, to my way of thinking, the central figure in economics.[11]

---

[9] The responsibility of choice by entrepreneurship among possible innovations applies quite as much to technological changes as to others. After a choice is made, there is the need of adjusting new techniques into a pre-existing system of operation, with possible alterations in nearly all phases from wage scales to marketing.

[10] What the relative importance may be among entrepreneurship, technological invention, and the discovery of new natural resources is difficult to say, especially if one function of entrepreneurship be conceded to be that of making practical the new techniques and bringing to market the new resources.

[11] We are not directly concerned with theories of profit, which indeed seem too inadequately developed to serve as guides in the exploration of entrepreneurship. Quite obviously, however, my approach derives from that of Joseph Schumpeter, insofar as a theoretical schema is involved. A full-blown theory of profits would need to take into account not merely the phenomena of entrepreneurship (as it has never done sufficiently heretofore), but also the effects of the legal system (for example, patents), monopolistic or quasi-monopolistic positions, conjunctural gains, and the like.

Such strong statements may well demand support, and I offer a few brief explanations. Entrepreneurship seems to me central in economics for a number of important reasons, some of which are of significance for economic historians. I agree with my friend G. Heberton Evans that the development of sound theory in dynamic terms and the forging of links between aggregative economics and the economics of the individual firm are urgent present-day problems in economic theory, and that here the study of entrepreneurship should be productive. Again, the hypothesis—almost invariably taken as self-evident—that the aim of all businessmen is and always has been the maximization of profits has been a primary element in economic theory over many decades, but actually no one has collected evidence to establish the truth of this contention. Undoubtedly other forces have had influence, while also without doubt the strength of the lure of profits has varied among time periods. For instance, there is good reason to believe that few entrepreneurs have really made decisions on the grounds of "the public be damned"—while probably there are still fewer who have operated on the policy of "my church, my family, my friends, my social and business relations be damned." Joan Robinson, with a liberty appropriate to her sex, speaks of the "horrors of inflation" being "sucked up with the milk of the mothers of bank presidents";[12] and surely—with more seriousness—other, less specific attitudes are derived by entrepreneurs from their family and social or business milieus. Again, one may quote Sir Sidney Chapman who, at the end of a long experience, has ventured recently to assert that "in nine cases out of ten" the assumption of crass money seeking would not be true: chiefly the entrepreneur strives for efficiency and assumes an enhanced pecuniary gain only as a related consequence.[13] And do we not know that men have frequently measured their success by the growth of the enterprises with which they have identified themselves, that others have kept active at business after they had more wealth than they could themselves utilize, that still others—in mutual savings banks or similar institutions—have long operated with a feeling for social service? Actually we know precious little about the motivations of entrepreneurs or the changes in motivations over time. Success in entrepreneurship may itself actually prevent the maximization of profits, as was suggested by my predecessor in office, Harold A. Innis, in his presidential address: "Large-scale effective mechanization of distribution

[12] Joan Robinson, *Essays in the Theory of Employment* (London, Macmillan & Co., Ltd., 1937), p. 26.

[13] Sir Sidney Chapman, "The Profit Motive and the Economic Incentive," *Econ. Jour.*, 1946, LVI, 51.

necessitated a single price and the search for devices to prevent outbreaks of competitive warfare. The price system weakens the profit motive by its emphasis on management."[14]

On the other hand, it may be contended that a study of entrepreneurship in its historical setting provides an opportunity to synthesize the work going forward in economics and in business administration, in economic history, business history, and social history, in the history of entrepreneurial thought and the history of social thought. It is not without significance that economists like Taussig or Schumpeter or Gordon, psychologists like Thorndike and Katona, political scientists like Dimock, historians of social thought, business historians, and divers others have paid some, if inadequate, attention to entrepreneurship and its characteristics.

III

For those economic historians concerned with the development of a logical framework of our subject, I would suggest the potentiality of devising "stages" of economic evolution—or, as I prefer to think of it, plotting the longitudinal segments of change—which would have greater pertinence to basic conditions in a world of private economy, even for business history (and would have greater logic), than the "commercial capitalism," "industrial capitalism," "financial capitalism," etc., which now have broad acceptance among us.[15] I have no intention of belittling such categories. However, one may fairly ask whether these conceptual tools are sounder than "commercial initiative," "industrial initiative," "financial initiative," and the like—even "commercial," "industrial," and "financial" law.

I should propose the analysis of business and economic evolution in terms of the "disruptive, innovating energy" which over recent centuries has been a continuingly important factor in evoking change; and, until some more imaginative and more profound student devises a superior formulation, I suggest the categories of empirical entrepreneurship, rational entrepreneurship, and cognitive entrepreneurship. Somewhat less elegant terms might be rule-of-thumb, informed, and sophisticated en-

---

[14] Harold A. Innis, "On the Economic Significance of Culture," *The Tasks of Economic History,* 1944 (Suppl. to the *Jour. Econ. Hist.,* Vol. IV), p. 93.

[15] The differentiation intended between "stages" and "longitudinal segments of change" is between a word that seems to mean action or conditions in specific periods of time, and a phrase which, it is hoped, conveys the sense of continuing action or conditions throughout a long river of time. Early forms often do not wholly disappear, but they become less wide currents in a stream of experience.

trepreneurship. However, I have yet to find any set of appellations that conveys the full concepts at each level.

I do not believe that the character of the decision-making organ—whether singular, plural, or institutionalized—is a crucial element, although rational entrepreneurship would be likely to be less individualized than the itinerant peddler or the primitive textile proprietor, while a cognitive entrepreneurship would usually coincide with the multiple leadership of which Robert Gordon has written.[16] Again, I do not find that the business form—whether proprietorship, corporation, international cartel, or what not—is a determining force. Nor does it seem to be vital for differentiating change in this social institution whether entrepreneurship be concerned with commercial or industrial pursuits or be temporarily (and partially) linked to a set of financial advisers.

What seems most important for economic evolution is a composite of elements which together condition efficiency of entrepreneurial activity. First there must be a favoring environment: the prevalence of an adventurous spirit either in men or in organizations; the existence of potent incentives, whatever their nature; an opportunity to reap rewards adequate to continued initiative; and, if entrepreneurship is to have sustained development, provision for succession and the training of successors to those who launch new enterprises. Then within that general climate of beneficence, the significant factor appears to be the growth in skill of making wise decisions relative to innovation, management, and the adjustment to external forces. Here the most noteworthy changes over time seem to pertain, first, to knowledge of what really is going on within and outside the individual business unit (where entrepreneurship draws on accountancy, statistics, systematic business information, and the like); secondly, to the rise of advisers—away from the local lawyer or general storekeeper to well-chosen boards of directors, and to permanent administrative staffs; and, thirdly, to the development of ancillary business agencies and institutions, by aid of which some of the uncertainties of the individual business unit are passed to other shoulders, and some of the rule-of-thumb expedients eliminated, or through which increased knowledge or superior advisors come to its service.[17]

To be sure, the criteria just suggested are two dimensional, if not

[16] Robert Aaron Gordon, *Business Leadership in the Large Corporations* (Washington, The Brookings Institution, 1945).

[17] By "ancillary" institutions, I have in mind those that are not directly concerned with the production of consumable goods and services: banks, insurance companies, labor exchanges, advertising agencies, machine builders, and so forth.

three. The business leader of modern decades not only must know more facts about more subjects than his eighteenth-century counterpart, synthesize more appraisals of experts and advisors, and be cognizant of more services from more service institutions, but he must relate his decisions to a longer time space of past and future. Also he tends to approach or handle his greater body of data for his longer range decisions in a different manner—with an attitude more akin to that of the so-called "learned professions," with more awareness of the data that he does not possess, and with higher appreciation (at least in larger situations) of the repercussions of his actions upon the various parts of his own business unit, upon his direct and indirect competitors, upon the customers whom he desires to influence, or upon the public or the governmental officials with whom he seeks to maintain amicable relations. Ideas along these lines are implicit—some explicit—in much of the recent literature on monopolistic competition; while other aspects of the development arc suggested by Mr. Barnard's stimulating study of the executive in operation.[18]

While those segments of entrepreneurship—empirical, rational, and cognitive—all persist today; while, like the use of snuff, empirical businesses are quantitatively more important than they were two hundred years ago; and while empirical procedures can still be found in business units of the most advanced quality, yet I do not believe the statement likely to be challenged that empirical or rule-of-thumb entrepreneurship prevailed universally in this country (and with few exceptions elsewhere) until the nineteenth century; that informed entrepreneurship, waxing steadily in its rationalizations, grew to prominence a hundred years ago and especially after about 1860; while, evolving particularly since 1890 or thereabouts, a cognitive entrepreneurship has come to characterize the leading, and some medium-sized business units of the present day. In short, I offer you the concepts of empirical, rational, and cognitive entrepreneurship as a growth sequence, and offer them in the hope that they may be improved and refined as research progresses.

Such a series of evolutionary phases, though obviously defined by business criteria, does have an economic basis and possesses an economic significance of no small moment. Even as, in other connections, man's progress is measured by his increasing knowledge of and control over nature, so the terms tendered here express (or are intended to express) a varying, increasing degree of effectiveness in the utilization of eco-

[18] Chester I. Barnard, *The Functions of the Executive* (Cambridge, Mass., Harvard University Press, 1938).

nomic factors by that fourth factor in production: entrepreneurship. Thus we come back finally to our starting point, the simple definition of entrepreneurship as the employment of other productive factors by the fourth.

IV

For those who find little satisfaction in system framing, the study of entrepreneurship offers a rich opportunity from the fact, suggested in my earlier definition of this economic function, that in entrepreneurship "an individual or group operating for an individual business unit" takes an "integrated sequence of actions." The entrepreneur, whether individual or multiple, does not "decide" in the abstract, "adjust" in the abstract, innovate, or maintain an organization in the abstract. Always such actions are taken relative to concrete living institutions, and therefore they can best be examined in concrete historical settings. Again, not only are decisions arrived at, and indeed conditioned by an environment of social, political, and economic factors (including contemporary thought), but one decision in some measure conditions all subsequent decisions. Moreover, one phase of entrepreneurship as a whole conditions subsequent phases. Accordingly there seems to be a rich opportunity for business history—as Thomas Cochran has emphasized in other connections[19]—to provide the necessary data for broad generalizations respecting business behavior. In this regard, N. S. B. Gras has had a proper intuition, and we can welcome the spread of interest in the field which the latter has done so much to establish. Out of the work that N. S. B. Gras's group, and now a host of research workers, are providing may yet be evolved a new emphasis in economics and business administration and a new outlook in economic history.

Sometimes, though with limited objectives, it will be possible to indulge in studies cross-sectional in time. For example, we could learn a good deal about the Colonial merchant entrepreneur by an intensive examination of those men who were active in the later pre-Revolutionary days: Hancock, Laurens, Morris, and the rest. To the data that Robert East purveyed to us this afternoon,[20] I can add a few facts as yet unassimilated. In this early environment, men could and did set them-

---

[19] Thomas C. Cochran, "The Economics in a Business History," *The Tasks of Economic History,* 1945 (Suppl. to the *Jour. Econ. Hist.,* Vol. V), pp. 54–65.

[20] Robert G. East, "The Business Entrepreneur in a Changing Colonial Economy, 1763–1795," *The Tasks of Economic History,* 1946 (Suppl. to *Jour. Econ. Hist.,* Vol. VI), pp. 16–27.

selves up in independent business or entered partnerships in the first years of manhood: Hancock at twenty, Laurens at twenty-three, Christopher Gadsden (of Charleston) at twenty-two, and Robert Morris at twenty—a considerable contrast to the ages at which men in recent years have reached the top executive positions in large modern enterprises. Again, I know that Thomas and John Hancock made (or had made) annually an average of 950 credit entries in their ledgers in the period 1755–70—or about three transactions per working day,[21] while the number of daily transactions at country stores seem to have been not much greater. On the other hand, a typical department store in Boston is confronted annually with the job of handling 1,700,000 transactions, or better than 5,000 per day. And the daily transactions of a large grocery "chain" must approach or exceed 100,000 per diem. What do such contrasts mean as far as entrepreneurial history is concerned?

Similarly we could study the plantation owners of the 1850's, the railroad executives of the 1870's, or the investment bankers of the 1890's. We would, of course, want to know much more than their entering ages or volumes of transactions: their origins, their burdens of uncertainties (with the collateral facts regarding their accountancy, controls, etc., or regarding ancillary institutions), the sources of their business information, the availability of counselors, or their attitudes toward business and economic problems of their times. The investigator would here be dealing more with the externals of entrepreneurship than with motivations or personal characteristics or specific business decisions, into which business biographies and company histories can hope to penetrate; but he would be blazing trails through what is now largely terra incognita and often he would be doing all that is possible to do with situations so far removed in time. Perhaps we would wind up with a historical sociology of entrepreneurship—comparable possibly with existing studies of the church or the immigrant or the public school.

Again, there is opportunity for longitudinal studies of particular entrepreneurial functions or relations: the use of the corporate form, trends in personnel policies, employment of accountancy, and the like.

In a few instances, the investigator can survey even broader areas, areas toward which perhaps all narrower studies should trend, and areas that bring once more to mind Mr. Gay's thesis. One such inquiry is re-

---

[21] William T. Baxter, *The House of Hancock; Business in Boston, 1724–1775* (Cambridge, Mass., Harvard University Press, 1945), p. 159. Actually the years 1757–59 and 1762–64 are omitted because of insufficient data.

ported in E. Lipson's effort to apply economic history to the solution of current problems: his *Planned Economy or Free Enterprise.*[22] Here in words that Mr. Gay might have used, "the entrepreneur" is viewed as "the powerful dissolvent of a communal regime which had been organized on the basis of craft gilds and village courts."[23] And he suggests the manner whereby this result was achieved when he notes how "the richer members" of the guilds could begin the breakdown of these units by gathering "into their hands a monopoly" of the business; or how the "large traders [in regulated companies] . . . managed to squeeze out the 'young beginners' and men of 'lower estates.' "[24] Surely these "pushing" individuals (as Mr. Gay used to characterize the corresponding figures of a later period) were entrepreneurial in type—innovating businessmen squirming like unborn chicks to break out of the shell of communal life.

Here in England from the later Middle Ages onward, or in the entrepreneurs of "hard cutting edge" in the Industrial Revolution (again to employ a favorite phrase of Mr. Gay), in the "robber baron" period of our post-Civil War days (of which Chester Destler told us today), or in the growth in social responsibility whch various observers think to detect in the American business leaders of the past few decades—here one can work closely indeed in the theorem that Mr. Gay propounded.

In short, there are opportunities for factual investigations as diverse as the differences among us of temperament and intellectual values—from the intensive examination of a company's or an individual businessman's career to a wide-ranging effort at co-ordinating known facts into fruitful hypotheses.

V

The area of entrepreneurial history stands open to the present generation of research workers, almost as unworked as the "significance of the frontier" when Frederick Turner first voiced his hypotheses. Some tools of analysis—some ploughs and harrows, if you will—have been fashioned, although we do not know but what they will "foul" as did the cast-iron ploughs in prairie land. A few specimens of the soil have been treated scientifically. A few uncertain maps have been sketched. But the main rich territory awaits the intellectual explorers and exploiters who will locate and develop the more valuable sections—explorers and

[22] E. Lipson, *A Planned Economy or Free Enterprise; the Lessons of History* (London, A. & C. Black, 1944).

[23] *Ibid.*, p. 86.

[24] *Ibid.*, pp. 159, 129.

exploiters who, it is to be hoped, will maintain contacts with the older parts of the country—in this case, the parts of the historical world that Mr. Gay described. Thus in the end the new may be achieved by reaching out from the old: we can honor our distinguished first president by examining systematically a hazy segment of his "rhythm of history" and offering our new facts and theories as tributes to his memory.

SECTION II

Money and Prices

12

*The Role of Money in Economic History**

By WESLEY C. MITCHELL

The role money has played, and still plays, in the evolution of social organization and individual behavior remains a dark area though some corners besides price history have been studied intensively. You know better than I how much has been written by anthropologists, numismatists, and historians about such matters as the different forms of money men have used, the evolution of coinage, the relation of gifts and piracy to the rise of regular trade and organized markets, the commutation of dues in kind and services into money payments, the transformation of an agricultural peasantry into an industrial proletariat, the changing methods of governmental finance in war and peace, the development of credit and banking, the spread of bookkeeping and its refinement into accounting, the diverse forms of business enterprises, and the interrelations between making goods and making money. Some of the monographs I have read upon these and related topics are admirable pieces of work. But monographs are flashlights; they do not give general illumination. What we do not yet have, what we need, and what economic historians should supply is a coherent story of how monetary forms have infiltrated one human relation after another, and their effects upon men's practices and habits of thought. I am well aware that the spadework desirable for this job is far from completed; but even now well-equipped students could draw an authentic sketch of the process as a whole. By so doing they would both stimulate detailed research and enlighten the thinking of all who are concerned with social organization, past and present.

I

Perhaps I can make my plea for undertaking this task more poignant by recalling some of the many ways in which the use of money has in-

* *Journal of Economic History,* 1944, IV, Supplement, pp. 61–67. Reprinted by courtesy of New York University Press.

This paper was presented at the meeting of the Economic History Association, September, 1944.

fluenced the fortunes of successive generations and conditioned their minds.

When money is introduced into the dealings of men, it enlarges their freedom. For example, when a personal service is commuted into a money payment, the servitor has a wider choice in the use of his energy and the lord a wider choice in the use of his income. By virtue of its generalized purchasing power, money emancipates its users from numberless restrictions upon what they do and what they get. As a society learns to use money confidently, it gradually abandons restrictions upon the places people shall live, the occupations they shall follow, the circles they shall serve, the prices they shall charge, and the goods they can buy. Its citizens have both a formal and a genuine freedom in these respects wider than is possible under an organization in which services and commodities are bartered. Adam Smith's "obvious and simple system of natural liberty" seems obvious and natural only to denizens of a money economy.

But economic freedom, like its sister, political freedom, brings responsibilities and dangers as well as opportunities. As personal relationships between master and man were transformed into a cash nexus, frequent laments were heard over the hard lot of the many who did not know how to profit by their larger opportunities. Living by making and spending a money income requires mental and moral abilities of a kind not inculcated by a system of personal mastery and dependence, and far harder to acquire than most moderns realize. In grasping the advantages of a money economy, society was unwittingly subjecting itself to a harsh new discipline which compelled people to become more calculating, more self-reliant, and more provident, that is, to acquire what the finished products of this discipline came to call "economic virtues."

Individuals who possessed superior aptitude for making money came to the fore in all walks of life, gradually giving society a new group of leaders to compete and combine with those whose eminence derived from high birth, skills in war or intrigue, or the qualities that won preferment in the church and success in the arts. The old aristocracy, as well as the old peasantry, had its unadaptables to the new order, and they suffered a romantic decline. The new leaders found many chances to exploit others and took advantage of them; but, broadly speaking, men who are trying to make money are the servants of consumers—that is, of the whole society. For to make money, a man has to sell goods, and not very often can the seller force people to buy. Usually he must depend upon persuasion—he must offer goods people want at prices they are ready to pay. In this sense, the money economy gradually put the task of making goods under the direction of men who provided most efficiently what solvent consumers wished to buy, and whose continued leadership depended on maintaining their efficiency.

The increasing use of money accelerated changes in the methods of producing and distributing goods, and changes in the character of products. Through the impersonal mechanism of the market, successful innovators could put pressure upon less enterprising businessmen to adopt improved methods. Forced change is an uncomfortable, sometimes a cruel, readjustment, and a society unaccustomed to it puts obstacles in its way. But the money economy offered such incentives to the ingenious and energetic, and the effects of their innovations were often so pleasing to consumers that opposition to change could do no more than retard the reorganization of trade, farming, fabrication, and transportation. The time came when public opinion, which had condemned breaches of tradition in economic matters, began to take pride in them as "progress."

To nations as to individuals money economy brought trouble as well as gain. It exposed a nation to a novel set of dangers arising from the technical exigencies of monetary systems. Men had to learn how to keep coins of different denominations and coins of different metals in concurrent circulation; how to prevent counterfeiting, clipping, and sweating of the coinage by private persons, and how to prevent depreciation of coins by the sovereign authority; how to get precious metals for coinage and how to guard against the depletion of the monetary circulation through export. Later came the host of problems connected with the use of paper money of various sorts. These technical problems were urgent because in a money economy livelihood itself depends upon the orderly functioning of an intricate system of production and distribution, which in turn depends upon price margins, and prices are affected in bewildering ways by money. Even the nations that had the best monetary systems were gravely disturbed by fluctuations in the supply of silver and gold flowing into Europe from dim outer regions. Nor is this entirely a story of the past. We have not yet fully mastered the monetary systems we set up. They still do unexpected and unpleasant things to us. Witness the difficulties our own country has in preventing its war effort from being hampered by fluctuations in commodity prices at wholesale and retail, in wage rates, and in rents. Nor do our experts agree about the best way to design monetary systems, as reactions to this summer's conference at Bretton Woods sufficiently prove [1944].

A more subtle difficulty is that our minds become obsessed by monetary illusions. An individual gets rich by making money. Why does not the aggregate of individuals called a nation do the like? I need not dwell upon mercantilist ideas about the peculiar importance of gold and silver as items of national wealth, or Adam Smith's refutation of this teaching, or the flaws modern students find in his critique. Perhaps there is more likelihood of neglecting the many schemes of "money magic" that have been presented for enriching mankind, and the laments of moralists that money corrupts our sense of values. Certainly the age-old "desire for distinction" gets a pecuniary twist in a money economy, as Veblen demonstrated to our discomfort.

These subjective effects have their objective counterparts. Production in a money economy is directed towards wares that promise a profit to the makers, not toward goods that will be most beneficial to the consumers, whatever that should be taken to mean. Money economy fosters inequality in the distribution of income, and where inequality is marked no one contends that what pays best is what the community needs most. A subtler effect, though less noticed, may be scarcely less important in directing, or misdirecting, our energies. As denizens of a money economy we are prone to pay far more attention to the relatively few factors that influence our money incomes in a way we can readily trace than to the host of factors that influence our money expenditures. This twist in perspective explains, for example, why protectionist promises of larger markets, fuller employment, and higher wage rates win our votes, despite free-trade demonstrations that high tariffs reduce "real incomes" by diverting enterprise from the lines for which a nation is relatively best equipped. In general, the highly technical character of money-making enables us to be far more rational in carrying on that process than we can be in spending money to satisfy competing desires, which we cannot reduce to a common denominator.

I think money economy is responsible also for business cycles. So far as I have been able to trace them, these recurrent alternations of expansion and contraction in economic activity occur only in communities where the production and distribution of goods are carried on mainly by business enterprises managed for profit, and where most people get their livings by making and spending money incomes. Communities otherwise organized undergo fluctuations in fortune, and may not enjoy so high a standard of living as the most fortunate money economies; but they seem to be exempt from cyclical contractions in employment.

II

Money economy has also a profound effect on man's efforts to know himself. By giving economic activity an immediate objective aim, and by providing a common denominator in terms of which all costs and all gains can be adequately expressed for business purposes, the use of money provided a technically rational scheme for guiding economic effort. It thereby paved the way for economic theory; for technically rational conduct can be reasoned out, and in that sense explained. But money economy does this job of rationalizing conduct only in a superficial sense, and unwary observers of human behavior fell into the trap it had set. Thoroughly disciplined citizens of the money economy readily assumed that all economic behavior is rational, and when they tried to penetrate beneath the money surface of things they found no absurdity in supposing that men do psychic bookkeeping in pains and pleasures as they do pecuniary bookkeeping in outgo and income. On this basis they could go to the length of declaring, as Mill did, that money merely enables men to do more easily what they would do without it. Following the money-making pattern, economic theory became, not an account of actual behavior such as historians attempt to provide, but an analysis of what it is to the interest of men to do under a variety of imagined conditions.

Fascinating systems of thought have been excogitated in this fashion. They are not wholly lacking in verisimilitude in a nation where money economy is highly developed, and pecuniary accounting is the guide of many actions. But, after all, money economy has not made human nature over in its own image. We cannot explain our economic behavior in terms of a calculating pursuit of self-interest if for no other reason than because much of our behavior is not guided by calculations. So patent has this fact become that economic theory now virtually rejects the theory of value, which used to be considered the cornerstone of the entire structure. Today's fashion is to assume demand schedules or curves of indifference, without inquiring what men's preferences really are, how they are arrived at, or how they are changed. But knowledge of economic behavior remains exceedingly schematic, superficial, and technical when it rests on confessed ignorance of what men are striving to get and what they are striving to avoid. To say merely that men have scales of preference lays a foundation for speculations that apply logically to Esquimaux and London bankers, to men of the tenth and men of the twentieth centuries, to peoples at war and peoples at peace. The very generality of the conclusions that can be deduced from such assumptions prevents them from fitting the facts of any place and time. Pretty much all that economic historians try to learn is barred from economic theory of the current abstract type.

Not only did the money economy make it plausible to explain economic behavior as a calculating pursuit of self-interest, it also long kept a more scientific treatment very difficult. Even in the first decade of the nineteenth century, a realist like Malthus could find data for testing speculations about the growth of populations. But Ricardo could not have found adequate data for testing his "laws" of distribution, however hard he tried. The humdrum processes of producing and exchanging goods, of paying and receiving money were recorded in private account books, but students had no access to these basic sources, and virtually no summaries of them were compiled. As Mr. Hamilton points out, until Jevons published his index numbers in 1863, economists did not even know whether the trend of wholesale prices of commodities was rising or falling. No method of inquiry into most economic problems other than speculative reasoning from assumptions of uncertain factual validity was feasible so long as observations of what occurred were scanty and the methods of using such observations as could be had were crude. But in the course of their expansion, the money economies reached a stage where businessmen, investors, and officials needed economic information more extensive than their predecessors had. How operating requirements led to the collection and publication of an ever-expanding array of data is a development that economic historians should not neglect. One consequence was that it became possible to test a wider range of explanatory hypotheses. And that possibility encouraged economists to formulate their hypotheses with an eye to empirical testing. Nowadays we can begin laying the foundation for a type of economics that will have a demonstrable relation to the actual conditions with which men have to deal, because it can be based upon an analytic study of actual behavior. This empirical science, whose birth pangs we are witnessing, will be as definitely a by-product of a later phrase of money economy as mercantilism and the speculations of Ricardo were by-products of earlier phases.

III

To the best of my knowledge and belief, I have said nothing new. What I have tried to do is to suggest how diverse are the cumulative changes to which the adoption of monetary institutions has led. For that purpose, familiar items are the most telling illustrations. I have one more remark to make, and that is as familiar as its predecessors. All the developments I have mentioned, and many others you might add to my short list, are interrelated. That is, their historical evolution cannot be adequately accounted for piecemeal. Monographs we need, more than we now have. They are indispensable. But however many we may accumulate, monographs will not give us understanding of the organization we received from our forefathers and shall pass on with modifications to our grandsons. Economic theory makes a valuable contribution to the understanding of this institutional complex; but it will not give us insight into the way our organization has changed through the centuries and is changing today. And such insight into the way social organization evolves is imperative now that we are striving more consciously and daringly than ever to readjust our economic organization to the larger opportunities opened before us by the application of science to the work of the world.

While serving society by focusing attention upon this theme, economic historians would at the same time be meeting one of their own professional needs. They are painfully aware how hard it is to organize the vast array of materials that have to be crammed into their general treatises. To cite examples: readers of Cunningham's and Clapham's great books can hardly see the forest for the trees. What I have been saying leads to a suggestion for overcoming this difficulty. The nations with which economic historians are chiefly concerned organize their economic activities under the form of making and spending money. This practice supplies the basic framework for economic theory. Cannot economic history be organized most effectively around the evolution of pecuniary institutions? If the activities studied have a definite scheme of organization, should not a history of them follow that scheme?

If this suggestion merits serious consideration, the first step toward trying it out in practice would be to frame the best account now feasible of the way men came to organize their dealings with one another on the basis of money payments, the way this scheme spread from one sphere to another, the material and cultural consequences to which it led, the rationalizations and condemnations it evoked, and the further changes it seems to be undergoing in our day. Not only would such a sketch contribute toward effective dealing with the large problems of social organization that are impinging upon us, it would contribute also toward the planning of research in economic history and the effective presentation of its findings.

13

Natural and Money Economy As Illustrated from Swedish History in the Sixteenth Century*

By ELI F. HECKSCHER

The concepts of natural and of money economy, which have become common property through an article published by Bruno Hildebrand in 1864, are among the most useful within the whole sphere of economic history. A fresh attempt to illustrate the problem by a wealth of facts taken from all countries and periods has just been made by one of the leading scholars of medieval history, Professor Alfons Dopsch;[1] and it may be well to refer to his book in the following, though no general criticism is intended in this place. One of the editors of this *Journal,* Professor N. S. B. Gras, a short time ago gave its readers an interesting study of economic stages generally;[2] that will also have to be taken into account.

I

It is a remarkable fact that economic history and economic theory have remained poles asunder. Most representatives of the so-called Historical School of economists, who have very often been looked upon by historians as representatives of economic thinking proper, have either deprecated the use of economic theory on principle, or, if not, have remained largely out of contact with the trend of thought followed by theorists ever since the days of Ricardo, if not of Adam Smith. Now, if economic theory is at all what it ought to be, its reasonings should apply to economic life as such, and consequently to that of all ages. No doubt much remains to be done in the field of economic theory; but an attempt

* *Journal of Economic and Business History,* 1930–31, III, 1–29. Reprinted by courtesy of the author and Harvard University Press.

[1] *Naturalwirtschaft und Geldwirtschaft in der Weltgeschichte* (Vienna, L. W. Seidel & Sohn, 1930), pp. xii, 294.

[2] "Stages in Economic History," *Jour. Econ. and Bus. Hist.,* May 1930.

might at least be made to utilize economic theory for the work of economic history. Our subject will illustrate the need for that.

With regard to the general concepts of economic history it appears to be useful to distinguish between periods, on one side, and what I should like to label aspects, on the other. Periods are simply convenient chronological partitions, and for them different criteria may very well be used in different cases, so that, for example, labor conditions are considered characteristic of one period and money conditions of another. Aspects, on the other hand, must be consistent throughout. The object of making use of them must be to show how a distinct side of economic life, a distinct economic category, was constituted; and to that extent the basis may be found in economic theory. Aspects will never be able to embrace all that is important in a period; but they will still be able to throw a great deal of light upon the actual working of economic life. If possible, they should be arranged in some sort of logical, instead of chronological, order. For the same features come up in different order of time in different societies, and may even come back several times in the history of the same society, as Professor Gras has pointed out.

The aspects of economic history may be arranged according to each of the fundamental sides of economic life. You may start from the character of supply and base the aspects upon, say, natural conditions, or population, or labor, or capital, or business organization; you may base them upon the character of demand, or upon that of the price system, or on that of exchange. All these groups of aspects are not only possible but very fruitful, as I have tried to show elsewhere;[3] but in this place they are pointed out only in order to create the proper background for our subject, natural and money economy.

The aspects of natural and money economy are based upon the use or non-use of a particular medium of exchange, called money. They consequently belong to that particular side of economic life called exchange. It is true that money is also to some extent used outside of exchange proper; but even those uses of money are closely enough related to exchange to make exchange the dominating consideration. The character of exchange and of money in its turn influences economic life throughout, and in so far as that is the case, natural and money economy may be made use of to explain economic conditions as a whole, or the general character of different periods. But it must never be lost sight of that economic life is then looked at from a particular angle, which is more

[3] "Den ekonomiska historiens aspekter," in the Swedish *Historisk tidskrift,* Vol. L (1930), pp. 1 ff.

important in some respects and at some periods than in others, and that periods may be alike from that point of view but different in other respects.

As to the aspects of exchange, the first question which arises is whether any exchange exists in a given society at all. Properly speaking, only a Robinson (without his Friday) is quite outside the range of exchange, for services and goods are exchanged inside every household. But it may be convenient to consider the household as the smallest economic unit; if there is no exchange between different households, we shall look upon it as a total absence of exchange. Here it is enough just to mention this much debated "closed household economy" of Karl Bücher and others, only adding that it probably remained a predominant feature in the life of the majority of many European peoples well into the nineteenth century.

Next comes the existence of exchange (including gifts and other deliveries) between different families and households. The question then will be how that should be subdivided. From an economic point of view nothing in the domain of exchange is at all comparable in importance to the use or non-use of a medium of exchange. We then arrive at two new aspects. The first is direct exchange, also called barter, in which the goods and services required are directly exchanged against those given away, no third commodity coming between them. The second of these aspects clearly is indirect exchange, making use of an intermediate commodity.

If we are then to subdivide indirect exchange in its turn, the important consideration will be the character of the intermediate commodity. If the medium of exchange is one chosen at random, differing in different cases and not accepted as a general solvent, or currency—sometimes iron, sometimes corn, sometimes cattle—you get indirect exchange without the use of money. But if, on the other hand, the medium of exchange is a generally accepted one, you get money exchange. Money exchange, in its turn, presents many different forms; but they may be left aside in this connection.

What is called natural economy will then be found to contain no less than three different aspects, held together only by the absence of a generally accepted medium of exchange, or currency: absence of exchange, direct exchange, and indirect exchange without money. It must then be asked whether the whole conception of a natural economy is a useful one, as it embraces three distinct aspects. The answer is that it certainly is, because the influence of money upon economic life is so great that its absence creates considerable unity, irrespective of other differences.

So far I have concentrated attention upon the character of exchange itself. Closely allied to exchange is the existence of one-sided payments, such as taxes and the like. It need not detain us, however, as it represents the same idea: if money is used for one-sided payments it may still be called currency. But it is otherwise with another use of money, namely, that as a standard of value. The use of such a standard is common also in cases when exchange itself is carried on without money; we have then the type called by Professor Gras money barter. Lastly, money is also used as a standard of deferred payments, which comes near to a standard of value, also in the respect that different sorts of money are often used for currency, on the one hand, and for the two purposes now under consideration, on the other. All these possibilities should certainly be kept in view; but it appears most convenient to base the distinction between natural and money economy upon the use of money for purposes of exchange (and one-sided payments), so that the use of money for other purposes only is not considered to create cases of money economy.

It should be superfluous to add that all exchange in the last resort is one in kind, goods and services being always taken and given for goods and services. The difference between natural and money exchange refers only to the machinery through which this ever-present result is effected. A remarkable passage in Professor Dopsch's book appears, however, to be at variance with this. In order to show the continued existence of natural economy—as to which I agree with him—he says, *inter alia:* "Also in the world's commerce of to-day commercial debts still are liquidated without cash, through deliveries in kind, even beyond the confines of each single State"; as an instance, "given in the most recent literature," he mentions sugar exported from Bohemia to England and paid for by English woolen exports to Bohemia by way of bills of exchange.[4] As will be seen, there is no more delivery in kind in this case—which is a very simplified instance of the general working of foreign trade—than what is necessary for exchange as such. As a matter of fact, modern foreign trade belongs to money economy of a high order, all goods and services on each side being lumped together and exchanged against one another, without any reference to their individual features. This is ef-

[4] Dopsch, *op. cit.,* p. 254.

fected, as between the countries, through bills of exchange, acting as a generally accepted intermediate good, or money. Unless the economic functions of exchange and money are taken into account, little appears to be gained by making any distinction between natural and money economy.

Even if correctly stated, this distinction, however, to a great extent remains in the air, unless it is possible to show how each of the different forms of exchange and uses of money was working in actual economic life at different times, as well as how they worked into each other. Having now attempted to clear the ground for such a description, the following review will illustrate our subject from Swedish sixteenth-century conditions. My intention consequently is, not to make a contribution to the economic history of Sweden as such, but to make use of Swedish materials for a problem of general economic history. I hope to be able to show that these materials have some features which make them particularly serviceable for our purpose. The most interesting part of the subject will be found to be the implications and consequences of the methods of exchange.

II

What makes Swedish economic life in the sixteenth century so useful in this case is the combination of remarkably "backward" or "early medieval" conditions with a no less remarkable "modern" fulness of information on most sides of economic activity. This is due to the double fact that the political founder of modern Sweden, Gustavus Vasa, altogether belonged to the old economic order of things but knew his country better than most rulers knew theirs and also had his knowledge transmitted to posterity. His long reign, from 1521 or 1523 to 1560, therefore, presents exceptional opportunities to the student of economic history. He was not only the principal landowner, but also the principal farmer; he was the all-important foreign merchant and the ablest trader within the country, being in fact past master in every sort of acquisition, often none too scrupulous; and he conducted personally the reformation of iron-smelting and refining, directing also such manufacturing processes as there were outside of pure handicraft. Consequently his activities take us into the heart of economic life itself, instead of only showing attempts at directing it from the outside, as is usually the case with state measures. When it is added that he had almost a passion for having everything put upon paper and brought to account, himself writing—or rather dictating—singularly outspoken letters which fill twenty-nine stout volumes in print,[5] it is clear that our opportunity to learn the economic life of Sweden in the sixteenth century is good.

As a background for the description of those conditions from the point of view of natural and money economy, it will be enough to say a few words on the population of the country.

The principal modern authority for this period, Hans Forssell, on the basis of assessments for an extraordinary tax in 1571, found a population for Sweden proper, that is exclusive of Finland, within its boundaries of that time, of something between 427,000 and 531,000 inhabitants.[6] Investigations, made by the historical department of the General Staff of the Swedish army and so far unpublished, have shown, however, the probability of the population of Finland at the beginning of the seventeenth century being considerably greater than would have been possible if the figures used by Forssell had been correct. This conclusion is corroborated both by the fact that assessments for taxation purposes are almost invariably too low and that a comparison with the figures at the beginning of Swedish vital statistics in 1750 would give an improbably great increase of population in the intervening period, if the figures of Forssell were accepted. Though it is impossible to make much more than a guess at the present moment, when the facts for Sweden proper have not yet been investigated on the new basis, it may be said that a figure of something like 900,000 for the then territory of Sweden and Finland together in the second half of the sixteenth century does not appear improbably high. The present population within the same boundaries is about eight millions.

More important for our purposes than figures for the total population is, however, the relation between town and country. The figures of Forssell would point to the conclusion that the town population was barely five per cent of the total in Sweden proper; and in Finland the towns were even less important. As the relation as late as in 1800 had hardly increased to ten per cent with regard to Sweden proper, Forssell's percentage figure for the towns probably is not too low. The field of our study is consequently a country where the numerical importance of towns was almost negligible.[7]

[5] *Konung Gustaf den Förstes registratur* (Stockholm, 1861–1916). As this publication is chronological throughout, it has been found sufficient to give the dates of the letters quoted. When other sources (or the few undated papers of this series) have been used, full references have been given. All quotations have been translated, unfortunately not without destroying a great deal of their flavor.

[6] Hans Forssell, *Sverige 1571* (Stockholm, 1872, 1883), especially p. 348.

[7] A few details must also be given about the monetary system of the country. The leading denomination in Swedish money was called mark, or *mark örtug;* it sank in weight

III

When coming to our proper subject, we may begin by considering what was used as a standard of value and of deferred payments in the time of Gustavus Vasa. As a typical instance of the standard in deferred payments, a transaction, recorded in a letter of April 17, 1559, between the King and six Swedish merchants may be noted. His subjects had taken over 45 *last* of butter from him, "and have promised to us for each *tun* of butter 36 marks good and honest payments next Michaelmas, in the form of good cloth, that is, English, Brabant, Westphalian, or other commodities which may be convenient to us, and making such a reasonable bargain as we might be able to make with other chapmen for the same goods." Here we have barter in a credit operation; but the basis for it is a distinct money price for the goods tendered at the date of the agreement, and at least the possibility of such a price for those to be given in return in the future. There is a great number of cases of the same character. The use of money as a standard at this time is not surprising, for already the imposing series of old Swedish provincial laws, none of which are later than the thirteenth century, stipulated fines in money, although probably in ninety-nine cases out of a hundred they were actually paid in kind. On the other hand it is far from being true that all credit transactions in the sixteenth century created a debt to be expressed in money.

In spot deliveries, that is, when there was exchange in kind, it appears probable that the use of money as a standard of value was less common. It occurs extremely often that the value of herring, for instance, was expressed in that of rye or barley, salmon in iron, cloth or salt in butter or malt, or the reverse, without money values being introduced at all. The very character of payments in kind, in such cases where it did occur,

---

of pure silver from 8.78 grams in the period from 1572 to 1535, to 6.02 grams in the years 1540–61, that is, during the latter part of the reign of Gustavus Vasa. Under his sons it fell to almost nothing, containing only 0.47 grams in 1593. The coined mark must be kept altogether distinct from the weighted mark, or *mark lödig,* from which it must have had its origin. During the period 1527–35, twenty-four marks in coin were equivalent to one mark in weight of fine silver; during the second part of the reign of Gustavus, the corresponding number was thirty-five. Outside this system was the *daler,* or Swedish dollar, an adaptation of the German *thaler;* from 1540 onward it held the weight of 25.6 grams of fine silver (corresponding to $1.07). It was mostly used in international payments, as a substitute for silver bullion.

For the monetary system of Sweden see, especially, Hans Forssell, *Sveriges inre historia från Gustaf den Förste,* Vol. II (Stockholm, 1875), and K. A. Wallroth, *Sveriges Mynt 1449–1917* (*Numismatiska Meddelanden,* Vol. XXII [Stockholm, 1918]). The details about Swedish monetary conditions given in Ferdinand Friedensburg, *Münzkunde und Geldgeschichte der Einzelstaaten des Mittelalters und der neueren Zeit* (Munich and Berlin, 1926), are unfortunately almost entirely lacking in economic interest.

often made a valuation in money curiously left-handed. To illustrate, early in his reign, on October 28, 1526, the King wrote about one of his captains in the War of Liberation: "We wonder that he did not make known to us, how highly the butter and iron were valued which he received as an assistance from the Chapter of Scara, which they gave to us, and likewise the iron he got out of Wermland . . . so that we might find out how highly priced each piece of English cloth has been." The cloth clearly had been exchanged for the butter and the iron. In another letter, dated July 23, 1550, he wrote that "you have given for each *last* of salt as much corn as amounts to eight dollars." In money economy it would have been said eight dollars the *last* had been paid for salt, but there the price had first to be expressed in corn, the payment really being made in corn, and that amount afterwards expressed in money value. So much for the standard of value.

As to the character of exchange itself, there can be no doubt that it was effected in the majority of cases without the use of money or currency. It is true that a statistical presentation of the different forms of exchange in sixteenth-century Sweden is impossible until the enormous unprinted accounts of the warehouses of Gustavus have been worked up; they show how he disposed of his taxes in kind and generally carried on his trading in different directions. But enough appears from his correspondence to show that the use of money in exchange did not prevail. This holds good not only with regard to internal trade. Even foreign trade was apparently carried on chiefly without the use of money.

In foreign trade, natural economy must have meant that each transaction involved both an import and an export; and this had important consequences for the direction of trade. As is illustrated by a letter of June 26, 1551, Gustavus Vasa had an ineradicable belief in the virtues of passive trading, that is, in the profit to be gained by "the foreigners coming to us after those things which we formerly always used to drag into their own hands at their own door." As far as can be seen, the King's will in the majority of cases prevailed in that respect, for exchange took place mostly in the Swedish ports. It was far from being exclusively so, however; ships were also sent out to the Hansa towns and, to a less extent, to Holland.

It would be difficult to find a more characteristic example of the working of natural economy than the treatment of the great debt of the state to Lübeck, which power had financed the War of Liberation; this debt dominated the whole political situation during the first decade of the reign of Gustavus. According to a letter of August 9, 1532, the debt was paid in kind, in one case in butter. In another instance it was paid in different victuals; and a postponement of the payment in 1527 had to be given up for the very cogent reason that the victuals collected for that purpose in Stockholm were in danger of becoming tainted.[8]

It must not, however, be inferred from what has now been said, that all this trade, inside and outside the country, constituted direct exchange. Irrespective of money being used as a standard of value—a question which is quite unrelated to our problem—barter clearly to a great extent had given way to indirect exchange in kind. And that was only to be expected, little as economic historians have until now been interested in this development. On the one hand, the difficulties of barter in a community where private trading prevails are clear. Each of the two parties to an exchange must hold the peculiar position of being at the same time able to offer what the other party wants and wanting what the other party is able to offer, all this at a rate agreeable to both. On the other hand, the introduction of money is often a difficult operation. Consequently both direct exchange and money exchange are in many cases out of the question.

It is this which paves the way for indirect exchange in kind. Such exchange occurs almost unconsciously, because in outward character differing little from pure barter. It may even be described as a double barter. For what takes place is that the person who wants to sell and to buy begins by selling his own commodity for one which he does *not* want, in order to be able, by selling that commodity in its turn, to arrive at what he really wants. Evidently the well-known difficulty of pure barter, just pointed out, can be obviated through this system; and it might have been foreseen without any evidence at all that such exchange was common. But evidence is not wanting. Already the enormous interest—mostly of a repressive character on the part of rulers—which the middleman's trade awakened in earlier times appears to have been due to this situation; for indirect exchange in kind is particularly suitable to the trade of a middleman. When the only method for a man to get at what he really wanted was, not to sell and buy for money but to sell for goods and buy for the goods received, the trade of a middleman became a necessity to which we have no counterpart in our own days.

With regard to Swedish sixteenth-century conditions, the hundreds of decrees against peddling, or country trading, bring out the prevalence

[8] Gottfrid Carlsson, "Wulf Gyler i svensk tjänst," *Historisk tidskrift,* Vol. XLII (1922), p. 302.

of indirect exchange in kind, in so far as more or less professional transactions are concerned. It may be enough to give two cases of that sort.

A good instance is the famous proclamation of Gustavus Vasa of April 4, 1546, concerning the high prices or "hard times"; there he thunders against the people who "go with corn into mining districts and in other places, and exchange that corn for iron, huckstering afterwards that iron about, just as they had done with corn before." During the reign of his second son, John III, one of the most detailed decrees against country trading (1589) spoke about all sorts of people who visited unlawful harbors and other places, where they "not only exchange for corn the fish which they have produced themselves, but also buy fish, butter, linen, frieze, and such-like traders' commodities of others; and after having exchanged them for corn, sell it to the inhabitants of the skerries and to other poor people for fish and butter again and practise peddling in that way."[9] But the most important cases are those in which it can be shown that indirect trading in kind was used for the purposes of procuring what the persons themselves needed. The following cases will make it clear.

A citizen of Arboga, according to a letter of August 29, 1544, procured permission to buy oxen in the southern provinces in order to sell them in the mining districts, "exchanging these oxen for iron, with which he can furnish his forge," in order that he might become more diligent in erecting new forges. Here oxen are the intermediate commodity, not as a general solvent, but simply as something which can be bought and sold again, in an exchange between the citizen's own goods, on the one hand, and iron, on the other. Another case in a letter of January 29, 1547, is even more characteristic. The "necessities" of the peasants of the province of Dalsland, in the West Country, consisting of "salt fish and such-like things," could not be procured through pure barter. They therefore received permission with regard to their own products, "which are butter, cheese, and other victuals, to travel into the [adjacent] Crown mining district in Wermland and there exchange it for iron; and then take that iron into the Norwegian places [on the West Coast, then in Norwegian hands], in order to fetch there their necessities in exchange for that iron." In this second case it is particularly clear what had to be done when pure barter could not take place, but money was out of the question. Iron had to serve as a medium of ex-

---

[9] *Samling utaf konglige bref, stadgar och förordningar etc., angående Sweriges rikes commerce, politie och oeconomie,* Vol. I, A. A. von Stiernman, ed. (Stockholm, 1747), p. 350.

change between butter and other commodities, on the one hand, and fish, on the other; but it was not in the least in the nature of a currency or a generally accepted commodity, any more than was the case with oxen in the previous instance. The system retained the characteristics of natural economy but was none the less different from pure barter.

It is consequently quite clear that natural economy played a very great part in Swedish sixteenth-century life. But this must not be understood to mean that there were no money transactions at all. The belief in a pure natural economy is, at least with regard to historical times, the result of the unfortunate confusion between the periods and the aspects of economic history; as I have said already, Professor Dopsch appears to me to be quite right in repudiating it. Even in our money-economy system of today there are important relics of natural economy. So far from money being absent from the period now under discussion, it is very usual to find money payments and payments in kind inextricably interwoven; and in many cases it is impossible to explain why the one or the other form of exchange was preferred.

Very often one gets the impression that money and commodities were used just as they happened to be at hand; and the mixture of both in the same payment was particularly common. A few illustrations from the domestic trade will show how the system worked. On one occasion, April 17, 1548, a servant of the King received 300 marks in money and some butter with which to buy oxen; on another, August 10, 1558, the citizens of three towns were to have both salmon and money with which to buy iron in the mining districts. But transactions in which payment was entirely in money also occurred rather often; this was when the King purchased at a fair, for instance, wrought or old copper for export (January 18, 1551) or herring (November 19, 1544), as well as when he sold the innumerable commodities which he received as taxes in kind. An item from the last-named is of special interest, namely, the stipulation, repeated several times in a short period, that the sale of corn at the Sala silver mine should be for money.[10] This was one of the channels through which money flowed out into the country, a matter of significance in view of Sweden's not unimportant position as a silver producer just before the great influx of precious metals from America.

In foreign trade the situation was not very different. The mixture of goods and money as a payment was perhaps even more common in that case, and luxuries seem to have been paid for in money more often than other goods. What must be emphasized particularly with regard to the

[10] July 31 and August 4, 1543, and two undated letters in May, 1544.

forms of payment in foreign trade is, however, that each transaction was as isolated and as individualized in the foreign as in the home trade, even if money was used. The absence of bills of exchange in foreign trade is particularly significant, for they would have created a connection between different trade operations. It is well known that the bill of exchange was slow to penetrate into Northern Europe.[11]

One instance will speak more clearly than lengthy descriptions of the character of operations in active foreign trade, in spite of its showing even more inter-relations between different operations than usually occurred. This particular instance, as described in a letter of April 7, 1532, was concerned with the bringing to Sweden from Danzig of an unusually imposing vessel, called the *Great Caravel*. Payment was to take the following form. First should be used what remained of three *last* of butter sent out in the previous autumn, principally to pay for wine which had been received earlier. Next, seven or eight *last* more were ordered sent to Danzig as payment. Thirdly, the King's emissaries had received 135¼ weighted marks (*mark lödig*), that is, very nearly 28½ kilograms, silver bullion. Fourthly, "in the case of this butter and silver not sufficing for the payment of all the aforesaid commodities, and some of His Grace's burghers might now be staying in Danzig, then the emissaries may borrow from them as much as the difference amounts to, which His Grace will readily and promptly pay back to them, and give them a gain from it, according to what they can get for salt and hops here in the city of Stockholm; or otherwise [borrow] from somebody else, and His Grace well keep them indemnified." This shows how parcels of commodities and monies had to be brought together for the payment of each imported item. In the later years, when the King's finances became excellent, there was not even a need for recourse to borrowing from prospective importers, as in this case; and the isolated character of each operation became consequently even more complete.

All these illustrations bring out with great clearness what has always rightly been considered the most characteristic feature of natural economy, that is, its want of elasticity, or, to use a better word, fungibility. In pure barter, what one can procure through one's own efforts depends entirely upon what the other party in a transaction has to offer; one's

[11] See, for instance, Josef Kulischer, *Allgemeine Wirtschaftsgeschichte des Mittelalters und der Neuzeit,* Vol. I (Munich and Berlin, 1928), p. 335. It follows from the text that one of the leading ideas of Dopsch's book, namely, that the difference between natural and money economy usually is one between districts and branches of economic life (*op. cit.*, pp. 47, 51, 94 f., 181, 248, etc.), is partly disproved but partly corroborated by the materials here used.

whole mode of life is decided by what can be gotten, instead of by what is desired. At the present day this comes out with particular clearness with regard to the most important relic of natural economy, the remuneration of domestic servants; their upkeep costs their masters much more than it is worth to the servants themselves. This situation is improved by indirect exchange in kind; but another difficulty then remains. Since there does not exist anything which everyone will accept in payment, a buyer must still be found in order to make it possible to purchase what is wanted. In foreign trade this worked out in such a way that a purchaser of the export goods had to be found at the place where the imports came from, in order to have the means with which to pay for the imports. Consequently there was little more than the alternative between, on the one hand, selling exported commodities at the places where imports could be bought, and, on the other hand, making foreigners bring their goods to trade at Swedish ports. The predilection of Gustavus Vasa for the second alternative—the passive trade—was quite natural in these circumstances.

The non-fungible character of trade in general extended even to money, the most non-individual or most fungible of all goods. The characteristics of natural economy, in other words, come to light even in those cases where money was actually used. Otherwise expressed, money was also in the nature of a commodity. This is shown, first, by the fact that different kinds of money were not interchangeable—it is the system called *Sortengeld* by Karl Helfferich. With currency proper, the mark, and its more or less variable subdivisions, the *öre*, *örtug*, and *penningar,* this was the only difficulty, and even that was not a serious one. But innumerable other sorts of coins were not only not interchangeable but were also looked upon as commodities. This was the case even with the *daler,* or Swedish dollar, in spite of its being coined within the country; the foreign gold and silver coins, such as the German *thaler, Engelotts,* Hungarian *gulden, Portugalese,* Spanish *ducats,* and so on, could then of course not be seen in any other light than that of other goods.

It is worth noticing that all sorts of foreign coins were continually imported and exported in the days of natural economy, in spite of the insignificance of foreign trade; while at the present time, in spite of an enormous trade between countries, foreign monies practically are confined to tourist traffic. This shows the fundamental "natural-economy" character of both money and foreign trade in earlier times, and the opposite in our own day.

This want of fungibility in money in the sixteenth century also explains the character of the royal accounts of coin and bullion. To a modern eye they look not only incredibly detailed, but also altogether lacking in unity. Each amount received from mines, churches, or subjects, or received in payment for goods, is specified by itself; in some accounts the use to which it was put is also recorded. In other accounts inventories are made of the different silver chambers, of which the King had several; the contents of each particular numbered chest and keg are given, in many cases even minute subdivisions of the chests in numbered "weights," which probably meant satchels, most of which held the same amount. When payments had to be made, it was specified from which of these satchels and chests they were to be taken, so that it would be possible for the King, or one of the few whom he trusted, to find out exactly what should remain in each small compartment.

Two instances will show how this worked. Out of 5,000 uncoined marks of silver bullion from the mines, kept at the Castle of Stockholm, "the Antwerp jeweler" received, in 1561—the year after the death of Gustavus, in payment for some gems which he had delivered for Lady Anne's wedding, weights number one to twenty-three, weighing in all some 1,151 uncoined marks in bullion and amounting to 9,212 dollars. In an undated account which is at least ten years older, the inventory of the silver chamber in the northern tower of the Castle of Gripsholm is given. Three chests delivered to one man were said to contain 97,784 dollars; 31 kegs delivered to someone else amounted to 61,221 dollars. From these were taken out, among other things, a sealed sack containing 2,880 dollars; three kegs amounting to 5,729 dollars in all; and 2,880 dollars, with which the jeweler, George of Nuremberg, was paid; and so on.[12]

What has already been said will show that this remarkably consistent treatment of economic life along the lines of natural economy did not exclude the use of credit. This is so much in the nature of things that there would be no need of pointing it out, except that Bruno Hildebrand had unfortunately added the stage of credit economy to the two, in his view, earlier ones of natural and money economy. It is indeed difficult to understand how a scholar, who had made such an outstanding contribution to economic history as the creation of the two last-named categories, could put forward something so much at variance with

[12] This is taken from the different unprinted accounts in the Treasury Record Office (*Kammararkivet*) in Stockholm, the series relating to the Silver Chambers of the Kings of the House of Vasa, as well as the provisionally arranged records, called Red Number Series, No. 19.

historical fact and clear theoretical thinking as this so-called third stage of credit economy. He explicitly says that "a credit economy can arise only when an organized system of money transaction is completely set up" and that in earlier times "credit transactions are only exceptions from the rule and the consequence of temporary inability to pay,"[13] whereas in truth there probably never existed a period of history when those intervals in time between two parts of an exchange which constitute a credit operation have not existed in a number of cases.

In sixteenth-century Sweden, as in many other countries existing under natural economy, even interest was sometimes stipulated in kind. An illuminating document, dated December 29, 1597, stated that peasants had borrowed seed-corn and had "been forced to give back double the amount which they had received, and part of them even more," while others had promised the lenders part in the harvest in exchange for the loan—a sort of *métayage* based on a credit operation.[14] The sources are full of these and other credit operations in kind.

It is obvious that a people dominated by natural economy to the extent here shown must have paid most of its taxes in kind. It may be postively affirmed that such was the situation; more perhaps than any other country with a similar economic and political development, Sweden retained the idea of state finances based upon natural economy. Gustavus Adolphus and his Chancellor, Oxenstierna, in the first half of the seventeenth century, were greatly in favor of changing this system, it is true; and they made some efforts to bring it about. A reversal to the old régime occurred, however, towards the end of the seventeenth century, and that order of things held on for centuries—the most characteristic part of it was not completely abolished before the dawn of the present century.

IV

We now come to the question of the ideas entertained in Sweden during the sixteenth century. As very little is known about opinions on economic questions in wider circles, we must confine ourselves to the King himself. But about his attitude there can be little doubt.

Generally speaking, Gustavus Vasa was altogether unprejudiced and realistic in his choice between money and payments in kind; and upon this particular point he showed a clearness of vision which people during

[13] Bruno Hildebrand, "Naturalwirtschaft, Geldwirtschaft und Creditwirtschaft," *Jahrbücher für Nationalökonomie und Statistik,* Vol. II (1864), p. 4.

[14] Von Stiernman, ed., *op. cit.,* Vol. I, pp. 446 f. Cf. Dopsch, *op. cit.,* pp. 52, 141, 143, 188, 198.

the following centuries might well have envied him. This does not mean that he was not at times eager to have money. On one occasion, as indicated in a letter of December 9, 1544, he objected to contributing in money his share in a mining enterprise, for the reason that he could better supply the victuals and such-like things needed; this was due, not to his unwillingness to part with the money, but to the fact that he had commodities to dispose of. The king chose certain coins in preference to others, and seems to have preferred gold to silver and, possibly, foreign coins, or at least dollars, to Swedish coins.[15]

The nature of this interest in money points to the conclusion that the money was not needed for purposes of circulation or payment within the country. This is borne out by statements which show the other side of the shield. In the majority of cases the King preferred taking payments in kind, he himself paying in money. To the factors of the foreign merchants he paid more willingly in dollars than in corn, in order not to strip the country of this commodity. With regard to payments in the opposite direction, he expressed himself with remarkable openness. In a letter of June 19, 1547, he said: "We do not much care for ready money, dollars or other coin. But we had rather (as we have a big crowd of naked people down there) that they were at diligent pains to procure for us a heap of Naarden, Aalst, and other coarse cloth, and exchange for that a heap of our butter, so that the soldiers we have just enlisted can get something with which to cover themselves." Concerning the payment of a fine in a case of treason, the King wrote to the governor of a province on July 16, 1546: "Could you procure oxen for that amount also, we will then take them willingly and even rather than money, *as* peradventure awaits us in this autumn a stupendous expenditure in fitting out of ships and such things."

The "as," italicized by me in this last statement, gives the idea in a nutshell: when you foresee expenditure, you stand in need of commodities and not money. The counterpart of this point of view comes out in the instances given before, in which Gustavus desired money for treasure or for ornament. This may be said to be only natural, and it certainly shows a keen perception of economic realities. But the contrast to the opinion of the mercantilists is clear; for mercantilist statesmen believed that money was required precisely in order to enable the state to spend it. Colbert, the foremost, the most consistent, as well as the most outspoken of mercantilist statesmen, in a memorandum to Louis XIV devoted some twenty pages to showing that there must be a definite

[15] A more than usually high-handed proceeding comes out in a letter of June 23, 1550.

ratio of circulating money within a country to the amount of "money" the king wanted in taxes.[16]

The fundamental reason for this difference in attitude, as can be seen from what has already been shown, is the contrast between natural and money economy. This is an extremely important consideration, for it gives the nucleus of the explanation not only of the mercantilist attitude on its most characteristic side—what distinguishes merchantilism from almost everything that went before—but also of the point of view which has remained the instinctive one to this day.

For, serious as were the obstacles which natural economy presented to an efficient and plastic economic life, it still had one great advantage over money economy. Under natural economy, economic life showed its proper working to the dimmest eye, as real conditions had not been overlaid by the most deceptive of all appearances—the cloak of money. When money had once been introduced and had become the indispensible medium of every transaction, the confusion between money and what it represents, between Juno and the cloud, became unavoidable; and all the efforts of economists since the days of Hume to eradicate the "Money Illusion," as Professor Irving Fisher calls it, have met with small success. While natural economy still showed economic life in its nakedness, no such efforts were necessary.

This applies to foreign trade as well. When each international transaction palpably implied giving away as well as getting back commodities, it was next to impossible to believe that the advantage of foreign trade should consist in giving more away than you got back. Crude protection, in the sense of being afraid of commodities, is therefore out of the question under a natural economy. You are then much nearer to the opposite extreme, that is, of trying to hamper exports in order to retain as many commodities as possible. This contrast is at the bottom of the great change from medieval to mercantilist ideas, as I have tried to show in different writings in Swedish and hope to have an occasion to explain in English also.

From Swedish sixteenth-century conditions it is easy to see that Gustavus Vasa, with extremely few exceptions, favored imports and looked upon them as the whole aim of economic life, and was, therefore, bent on hampering exports far more than imports. The best view of economic policy from that angle is usually got by comparing export and

[16] "Mémoire au roi sur les finances" (1670), in *Lettres, instructions et mémoires de Colbert,* Vol. VII, Pierre Clément, ed. (Paris, 1870), pp. 233 ff., especially p. 238. Numerous utterances to the same purpose on the part of English mercantilists might be added.

import prohibitions. In a lengthy study of Swedish sixteenth-century economic policy I have given a detailed table of these,[17] and I shall confine myself to the general results in this place. Import prohibitions were simply nonexistent, while export prohibitions—those referring to money excepted—are found in the King's printed correspondence, to the imposing number of 112. It is true that the number of export licenses, ninety-seven, is not much smaller, but it is invariably found that they go together with export prohibitions, not with import prohibitions, for they are not needed unless the rule is to hamper exports. To what extent this holds good in the present case is shown in a curious way through the fact that even commodities "not prohibited of export" were in need of a license. Besides, the license is often given with an addition such as "though only moderately," or something similar. And the list includes not only all sorts of food and cattle, but also horses, iron and copper, lumber goods, and hides, all normal Swedish exports of the period.

A few quotations will suffice to show the attitude of Gustavus. The citizens of a town in Finland got permission to export, October 22, 1533, "but upon the condition that they bring into the country salt, hops, and other things of which there is a need." "You should also think of bringing some good goods into the country in exchange," runs a letter of March 20, 1545, "from which the country and good people may have some further profit, use and favor." And lastly about a citizen of Reval, April 8, 1546, who sold his cargo and wanted to take away the lumber he had got in exchange as well as some fats, against the promise of returning with sixty *last* of corn and other useful things: "Then, we can say nothing else about this, but only that, *if it can in truth be found that he has brought solid goods into this country and will bring in more henceforward,* as he has here promised, *we will well suffer that he may ship out of the country in exchange fats and other goods,* which may be profitable to him." What is considered a benefit to the country and what to the foreign merchant could not be shown more clearly than in this sentence.

The realistic sense of Gustavus Vasa in this respect went, however, even further than that of most sovereigns during the reign of natural economy, for he did not even object to the sending away of money, the export of which was in most countries prohibited from an early date during the Middle Ages. It is true that he fulminated, November 23,

[17] "Det äldre Vasakonungadömets ekonomiska politik och idéer," *Historiska studier tillägnade Ludvig Stavenow* (Stockholm, 1924), pp. 109 ff.

1538, and January 15, 1539, against those of his subjects who exported money. But the reason given was that they were unable to procure such terms as he considered reasonable. This opened the door for his own export of money, which was altogether impartial and included uncoined silver, foreign coin, and Swedish dollars; the traditional Swedish coin, the mark, probably found no good market outside the country. His own merchants were to a great extent furnished with silver—an instance of that has already been given—and he often preferred to pay the foreign merchants coming into the country in the same way, as has also been said. It is no less characteristic that in a list which he made out in 1550 of import and export goods to be used in trade with different countries, he explicitly inserted Swedish dollars among those native commodities which should normally be sent to Russia, Portugal, Lisbon, and "Prouos" (Brouage, on the French Atlantic coast).[18] Few statesmen before the nineteenth century had the courage to do that.

As far as I have been able to learn, there is only one exception to this Olympic view of money on the part of Gustavus. The exception is no less characteristic than the rule. It occurred in the early 1540's, when there was a serious uprising, in the south of Sweden, with which to contend. During the first part of 1543, especially, a spirit, unknown both before and afterwards, spoke from the King's letters. The official in charge of the Treasury was told on January 22, 1543, about the imperative necessity of "collecting in our Treasury the greatest amount of money which is by any means procurable, especially as we discern clearly that money will now verily be needed, if anything shall be achieved at this time." His assistant is ordered to "bring and scrape together the most money which you are able to do by any means, should you even have to borrow for that purpose," so that 200,000 marks in ready money be immediately available. In a later letter, dated March 19, 1543, the King as strongly urged the coining of money, this time giving as his reasons that he was daily expecting new troops; he even raised his demands, saying that 300,000 marks in ready money was too little "for such a crowd." Shortly afterwards, May 21, 1543, he insisted on an increase in silver mining to meet the enormous expenditure; and still later, July 31, 1543, he asked for sixty or seventy thousand marks in money and fourteen or fifteen thousand Swedish dollars, with the same breathless reminder that as much money as possible should be brought together in order to pay the large army.

What Gustavus Vasa experienced during these few months was the

[18] *Konung Gustav den Förstes registratur,* Vol. XXI, pp. 56 f.

normal situation of Continental rulers. The reason was the same in both cases. This was the only time when Gustavus had to use mercenary troops in any great numbers, except in the War of Liberation which procured him his throne. On the Continent, on the other hand, mercenaries had to be used as a normal thing. Richard Ehrenberg has shown in his famous book, *Das Zeitalter der Fugger* (1896), that this was exactly what created an insoluble financial problem and made governments incessant—and usually insolvent—borrowers of the Fuggers and other financiers, since troops had to be paid in money while taxes were largely paid in kind. In most countries on the Continent the need for money is easily explained and has a great deal to do with general policy and economic views. That an uprising was able to change the very different attitude of the Swedish King, points to the explanation that he owed his unromantic views of money in ordinary times largely to the fact that he was free from the incubus of mercenaries.

Gustavus Vasa's usual indifference to money, with the exception of the time of the uprising, indicates that he had a great deal of ready money in excess of his needs, though it is not possible to give the figures at present. A large part of this excess money income was stored in the silver chambers. This is very characteristic of natural economy, though it has usually been overlooked. The idea that mercantilism was to any appreciable extent concerned with hoarding in the proper sense of the term, plausible as it is, must be said to be demonstrably wrong; mercantilists cared for circulation, not for the hoarding of the precious metals. Though the amounts collected by Gustavus cannot be given in their completeness, one detail will show that they were considerable for the time. In 1559 he refused a loan to Livonia of 200,000 Swedish dollars, not because he did not have the money but because of the risk involved.[19]

From this instance it appears that the King, late in his reign, was lending ready money as well as commodities. There is a great deal of information in his correspondence with regard to loans to merchants. different industrial establishments, and handicrafts. In a letter of February 11, 1557, the different coins used for the loans were specified.

These details show the influence of a factor which was likely to extend money economy, for the borrowers certainly did not hoard the money they got, and on which they, at least in some cases, had to pay interest. This is probably the only feature in the activity of the King which tended in that direction. It is especially noticeable that he had no wish at all to increase the amount of circulating money, but rather the

19 Letters of June 1, 1559, and following.

reverse. He objected strongly to "wastefulness" in coining, an objection which tended to neutralize, as time went on, the influence of the debasement of money. After he had reduced the money by 28 per cent in 1540, it is true, he had to recoin the old currency in the following two years. Besides, he went on coining silver from the mines until 1545. But, as has been shown by the principal authority on the subject, Hans Forssell, an all but complete stoppage of the mint occurred in the ten years which followed.[20]

This led to the very remarkable result that the national Swedish money, the mark, towards the end of the King's reign began to appreciate as compared with the silver it contained and, therefore, also as compared with the Swedish dollars. In trade the dollar came to be exchanged at the rate of 1 for 3½ marks, while in silver weight it was equivalent to not less than 4; this meant an appreciation of the mark by some 14 per cent as compared with its silver content. Again, this is the explanation of the additions to the silver chambers, for they became the recipients of the silver Gustavus saved out of the earlier heavier coins. He, unlike most princes, reduced the money, not to get more to spend but more to hoard.[21] Gustavus likewise hoarded much of the silver taken from the mines; according to a rough estimate which I have made for the period, 1538–50, the coinage of new silver was less then half the proceeds of the mines.

Generally speaking, the efforts of Gustavus Vasa were concentrated upon keeping together and bringing into an unprecedented order the economic system with which he was so thoroughly familiar. In spite of his perspicacity in economic matters he had not much imagination in things economic. This observation is applicable to most statesmen, for nothing is more rarely met with in the history of economic policy than imagination; the consequence has been that the conscious contribution of statesmen to economic development has usually not been of primary importance. Into almost every phase of economic life Gustavus brought order, without changing the foundations of medieval conditions: he felt no desire to break up the system with which he had grown up. But, from the point of view of the study of economic history, it is this very feature in the character of Gustavus Vasa which makes him of singular interest; for, because of it, we have been able to get a full-sized picture

---

[20] Forssell, *Sveriges inre historia,* Vol. II, Pt. 2, p. 64.

[21] See Alf Johansson, "Penningväsendet under Gustav Vasas regering," and, by the present writer, "Gustav Vasas myntpolitik," both in the *Historisk tidskrift,* Vol. XLVI (1926).

of a system which had reigned more or less unrecorded and haphazardly for many centuries before his time.

V

This study of natural and money economy may seem to imply that the former has preceded the latter. That precisely was the idea held by Bruno Hildebrand; and there can be no doubt that money economy has been on the increase in Sweden since the second half of the sixteenth century. But in order to prevent an over-emphasis on this view it must in conclusion be said that economic development, like development in other fields, shows a devious and irregular tendency, so that every general statement about chronological sequence must be very largely qualified.

What reverses the direction which matters might be expected to take with regard to money is, first and foremost, the habit of rulers to debase money. This creates a distrust which battles in the long run against its use as a medium of exchange. During the period which we are now studying, there were at least a couple of instances of this attitude. In his proclamation of April 4, 1546, concerning "hard times," Gustavus thundered against a group of wandering agricultural laborers, for the reason that they were unwilling to be paid in money, "taking wages for their threshing only in corn, not money, through which they practise usury with regard to a great deal of the grain of the peasant." Even more directly he, unintentionally, touched on debasement in an open letter of January 9, 1549, to a community assembled at a fair, his usual way of influencing public opinion: "The coin of the realm is here so much in mutual contempt, that neither the one nor the other will receive it, but all are clamoring for, and wanting to have, commodities, though it is not the custom and habit in any realm or province that he who possesses the coin of the realm should be unable to receive for it what he wants."

But even so, the debasement which took place during the reign of Gustavus Vasa was, comparatively speaking, so small that his reign came afterwards to be considered the very paragon of monetary virtue. His tampering with money was as nothing when compared with the practice of his sons. The tendency culminated in 1592–93. There is evidence that the relation between exchange in kind and the state of the circulation was, at this time, clear even to contemporaries. In the records of Stockholm for that period the following sentence appears: "At this time Swedish coin was so corrupt that nobody was willing to take money for his goods; but those who were careful, they exchanged goods for goods."[22] This was not confined to subjects either. The unwillingness of Swedish rulers at different periods to accept the change of payments in kind into money payments came in part from a distrust of the money which they had themselves been instrumental in debasing.[23] What took place in this respect during and after the World War has consequently had many precedents, as is the case with most of the experiences in the field of money.[24]

NOTE BY THE AUTHOR: Most of the subjects touched upon in the paper given above have been treated more fully in Swedish in the first two half-volumes of my economic history of Sweden since Gustavus Vasa (*Sveriges Ekonomiska Historia från Gustav Vasa* [Stockholm, 1935–36]).

---

[22] Printed in *Historisk tidskrift*, Vol. XXX (1910), p. 277.

[23] Most of the subjects treated in this article have been studied by the present writer in an article, "Svensk natura- och penninghushållning i äldre tid," in the *Ekonomisk tidskrift*, Vol. XXV (1923).

[24] The tendency of Dopsch to belittle the relations between relapses into natural economy and debasement of money (*op. cit.*, pp. 243 ff.) is consequently in contradiction with Swedish experience and does not appear to me to be convincing in other respects either.

14

*The Theory of Imaginary Money from Charlemagne to the French Revolution**

By LUIGI EINAUDI

1. If one reads the books on monetary subjects that were written in the period from the sixteenth to the eighteenth century, one frequently encounters the concept of "imaginary money." Other terms used are "ideal money," "political money," *moneta numeraria,* "money of account." What these terms meant was not very clear even to contemporaries. The most authoritative writer among the historians of French monetary vicissitudes, François Le Blanc, resigned himself to defining as imaginary any kind of money which, "properly speaking, is but a collective term comprising a certain number of real moneys." The imaginary money which almost everywhere was called "pound" or an equivalent term like "livre," "lira," "pond," was, in Le Blanc's words, "never changing in value; in fact, we have used it since the time of Charlemagne, and it has always been worth 20 sous (shillings), and each sou, 12 deniers (pence)."[1] It is called "imaginary" because of the fact that

* A translation, by Giorgio Tagliacozzo, of "Teoria della moneta immaginaria nel tempo da Carlomagno alla rivoluzione francese," *Rivista di storia economica,* 1936, I, 1–35. The essay is printed here with the permission of President Einaudi, who has approved the translation. The editors acknowledge the valuable assistance of Raymond de Roover in the preparation of the manuscript.

With the approval of the author, paragraphs 31, 32, 33, and 35 were omitted from the translation. Paragraph 34 of the original is number 32 in the present version; to preserve the continuity of the argument President Einaudi has made a brief addition to this paragraph. The notes of the original article have been included and a few notes added by the translator.

[1] [TRANSLATOR'S NOTE: Up to the time of the French Revolution the pound system, which still survives in Great Britain and parts of the British Commonwealth of Nations, existed in most countries of western Europe, including France, Italy, and the Low Countries. The pound (Fr. *livre;* It. *lira;* Dut. *pond*) varied in name and value from one country to another. In England, it was called the "pound sterling"; in France, the "pound of Tours" (*livre tournois*); in the Low Countries, the "pound groat" (*livre de gros* or *pond grooten*). In Italy there was a great variety of pounds: *lire di grossi, lire di imperiali, lire di piccioli,* etc. Everywhere 12 pence (Fr. *deniers;* It. *denari*) were equal to 1 shilling, and 20 shillings (Fr. *sous;* It. *soldi*), to 1 pound. The universally used abbreviations for these three units were £, *s., d.* The different pounds should not be confused any more

it has never been coined; "because we have never had a real species which has consistently been worth 20 sous or one worth 12 deniers." Although from time immemorial men have neither seen nor touched any imaginary money, nevertheless, in the remote past it was something real, "since if we go back to the time when in France people began to count in pounds, shillings, and pence, we shall find that these imaginary moneys owe their origin to a real thing." According to Le Blanc, Charlemagne really coined silver shillings, 20 of which weighed a Roman pound of 12 ounces.[2] Thus the silver shilling was a real currency, and 20 of them weighed 1 pound, while each of them was divided into 12 pennies. The pound, however, was never coined; yet from then onward people acquired the habit of counting in pounds of 20 shillings with each shilling divided into 12 pence. Later on, according to Le Blanc, the shilling, along with the penny, deteriorated more and more, so that it ceased to be the twentieth part of the pound-weight; but the public went on counting in pounds, shillings, and pence despite the fact that the pound tale, as Le Blanc observed, weighed in his time (1690)—or was supposed to weigh—only 7 pennyweights and 3 grains, less than 3 per cent of the original weight at the time of the restored Roman Empire (800).

"These changes, I [Le Blanc] admit, are surprising because if there is anything in the world which ought to be stable, it is money, the measure of everything which enters the channels of trade. What confusion would there not be in a state where weights and measures frequently changed? On what basis and with what assurance could one person deal with another, and which nations would care to deal with people who lived in such disorder? Nevertheless, this has not prevented money, which is the most precious and most important of all standards, from changing its value in France almost as often as our clothes change in fashion."

2. The practice of counting in pounds, shillings, and pence—already sanctioned by the glory of Charlemagne—became even more venerable

---

than American, Canadian, and Mexican dollars are. During the period under consideration, the relation between real and imaginary money was always closer in England than on the Continent. The reader should bear in mind that the expressions "pounds, shillings, and pence" as used in this study do not refer to English money only, but to money of account in general, unless otherwise specified in the context.]

[2] [TRANSLATOR'S NOTE: The truth is that Charlemagne never coined a silver shilling but only a silver penny or *denarius*. Two hundred and forty of such pennies were cut from a pound weight. Originally, the pound weight and the pound tale were thus the same, since they both contained the same number of pennies. The shilling or solidus was uncoined and was merely a numerical expression for twelve pennies.]

when, in 1226, Saint Louis coined the groat, or *gros tournois,* which had a weight and fineness equivalent to that of the sou or shilling of the imaginary pound. For a time the sou, instead of being imaginary, became real, visible, and tangible. "This is the great epoch for the value of our sou and consequently for that of the *livre.* The people became so strongly attached to that established value that in subsequent reigns, whenever the money was debased . . . they always asked that it be restored to the same goodness as it had formerly in the time of Saint Louis." Perhaps "it was an effect of the veneration which the French had for everything this saintly monarch had done."[3]

3. The idea of a form of money which for centuries remained invisible, exerted a powerful influence on the human mind: "Two kinds of money," wrote Dutot, "are the soul and the moving force of Trade: one Real and the other Ideal. Real money is of gold and silver. It was introduced to facilitate commercial intercourse, and it caused sales to replace barter by becoming the price and measure of everything which is the object of trade. But since the shipping of specie from one country to another was so embarrassing as to constitute a serious obstacle to trade, bills of exchange were resorted to as a means of transferring funds from place to place. To facilitate the making of bargains and computations, people invented moneys of account or of exchange, such as the livre, the sou, and the écu in France; the penny, the shilling, and the pound sterling in England; the groat, the shilling groat, and the pound groat in Holland. This kind of ideal or imaginary money which, properly speaking, consists of collective terms comprising also a certain number of real moneys, will be called Political Money."[4] He speaks of a "collective term," evidently regarding ideal money as if it were some kind of compound, equivalent to a certain number of real moneys. His strange definition does not specify the kind and the number of real coins that the imaginary money is supposed to represent.

4. The Italian writers are no more helpful than the French. According to the Italian economist, Giovanni Antonio Fabbrini, "money is called imaginary in so far as it has no substance, being a mere idea or product of our imagination. It is called 'of account' because it is helpful in keeping accounts and, unlike real coins, it stands firm and cannot

---

[3] François Le Blanc, *Traité historique des monnoyes de France* (Paris, 1690), pp. xxi, xxv, and *passim.*

[4] Dutot, *Réflexions politiques sur les finances et le commerce* (The Hague, 1754), Vol. II, pp. 4–5.

arbitrarily be cried up or down. Since real coins are all variable, imaginary money performs for coins the same function which money in general performs for other goods, that is, it expresses the idea of a fixed value."[5]

Although Ferdinando Galiani (1728–1787) did not believe that "in this world, one can hope for . . . perpetual stability and stagnation" and, although he was convinced that "a constant and unchangeable measure need not be desired or sought," since perpetual stability "is wholly repugnant to the ordering and genius of nature itself," still he did not deny the logical possibility of an imaginary money that would be stable. He wrote: "If imaginary money were a term for a definite number expressing an idea of price, and if this idea were fixed in our minds and so detached from everything that it would not be affected by any disturbances, then it would certainly be invariable and constant."[6]

5. An idea, a product of imagination liberated from the legislator's arbitrary action, a numerical expression, an idea detached from everything and unaffected by any disturbances—all such terms and concepts were, according to the stern verdict of the impeccable Messedaglia, "evidently the consequences of rather inaccurate and confused notions on the subject."[7] Luigi Valeriani had an easy time discrediting and denying the concept that money of account was something "impassive, independent of all human values." This absurd notion grew out of the fact that people, as they played with the words "imaginary," "ideal," "of account," "fixed," came to believe that money of account was a mere idea, whereas "it is very improperly called imaginary or ideal, there being nothing imaginary in it but its derivation, by mental division or multiplication, from moneys which are said to be real."[8]

6. No, money of account was not the mere idea of money, as Fabbrini believed. An idea cannot be a standard of value, or an invariable term of comparison for evaluating commodities, even if, as Galiani corrected, the idea is fixed in our minds. In that case we must assume not only that this idea is detached from everything and from all disturbances but also that man himself is invariable in his wants and in his tastes and that the

[5] Giovanni Antonio Fabbrini, *Dell'indole e qualità naturali e civili della moneta* (Rome, 1750), p. 93.

[6] Ferdinando Galiani, *Della moneta* (Naples, 1750), pp. 99 and 101 (ed. Niccolini, Bari, 1915, pp. 87–88).

[7] A. Messedaglia, *La moneta e il sistema monetario in generale* (Rome, 1882), Ch. 7, p. 1.

[8] Luigi Valeriani, *Ricerche critiche ed economiche . . . sulle monete di conto* (Bologna, 1819), Pt. I, pp. 150–51.

goods themselves are invariable in quantity and quality. But neither was the money of account an uncoined multiple or fraction of a coin in actual circulation, as Valeriani contended, since a double or half of a gold florin, even though it did not happen to be coined, would be real money no less than the florin itself.

7. Pompeo Neri, the clearest among the Italian monetary writers of the eighteenth century, finally identified the imaginary pound as equivalent to the result obtained by dividing or multiplying a specific current coin by a given number. In order to express a valuation, one even could use a number without specifying the unit which was used; for instance, by saying "that a philippus dollar was worth seven and a half, the sequin fourteen and a half, the dobloon twenty-five and a fourth, and so on," except that "the public was accustomed to the words" pound, shilling and penny, "and was scrupulous in preserving the identity of the word *pound* in sound rather than in value." The number in question did not remain unchanged, mainly because it was not related to a stable currency. Because of men's malice and princes' needs, the pound was at any time linked to the worst moneys in circulation. "The unit of value designated by the name of pound having steadily decreased in the estimation of the public, a forever greater number of these units became necessary to evaluate the same quantity of metal. In the same way, to ascend a tower, it is necessary to climb more steps if the steps are low than if they are steep, although the height of the tower does not increase, as some naïvely believe. They are deceived by the same illusion which misleads the eyes of anyone who, leaving the shore in a boat, thinks that the shoreline is moving rather than the boat."[9]

Even though Neri's definition, "imaginary money is the result of dividing or multiplying a real coin by a given number," comes closer to reality, it is still unsatisfactory. This definition contradicts what it is supposed to define. The pound, quotient of the division of the gold florin by a variable number, is indeed variable, but it is no less real than the florin. Why then call it imaginary and oppose it to the florin, a real currency, as if it had an entirely different nature?

8. The difficulty in finding a satisfactory definition for "money of account" results from its history. Money of account was not created by decree but grew almost spontaneously out of men's habit of keeping accounts in monetary units, some of which corresponded in the time of

---

[9] Pompeo Neri, "Osservazioni sopre il prezzo legale delle monete," in *Scrittori classici italiani di economica politica,* Vol. VI, Custodi, ed., pp. 109–10 and 154–56.

Charlemagne to real coins.[10] Later on it happened from time to time that the money of account was pegged to a real coin which was equivalent to a pound, shilling, or penny. Such a correspondence was accidental or, if deliberate, did not last long. Except for the penny, the name given to the real coin was different. The coexistence over long periods of time of a penny in money of account and a penny in coin, one equal to the other, does not prove, as Landry (*Essai,* p. 13) rightly observes, that the two systems, that of imaginary and that of real money, were linked or soldered together. It is not correct to say that through the penny both currency systems were based on a real coin. In addition to the money of account—the pound of 20 shillings and the shilling of 12 pence—were there not also coins like the gold *mouton,* the silver groat (*gros tournois*), and the silver penny? It was possible that at a given moment one silver penny was equivalent to one penny in money of account. But the relation between the mouton, the silver groat, and the silver penny was not so stable as that between the pound, the shilling, and the penny, since, in terms of money of account, a pound was always 20 shillings and one shilling was always 12 pence. Besides, even when the groat was rated 1 shilling, it does not follow that it contained twelve times as much silver as did the penny.[11] Little by little—and this happened during the fourteenth and fifteenth centuries—the penny in coin lost its equivalence with the penny in money of account and was coined first in vellon (that is, an alloy composed mainly of copper mixed with a little silver) and then in pure copper.

9. Sooner or later, but generally at the beginning of modern times, the different monetary systems in various European countries reached a state in which they were governed by a seemingly very odd principle, very different from our modern conception.

Today each country has only one monetary unit: the lira, franc, mark, pound sterling, or dollar. This is the system established by the French assemblies at the end of the eighteenth century. In Italy, for example, the present monetary unit is the lira, defined as a given weight of pure gold, namely (1936), 0.07919113 grams.

It is possible that a real coin containing that quantity of pure gold, and having the legal fineness of 90 per cent, is not in actual circulation.

[10] Not in all three denominations: pounds, shillings, and pence. According to Le Blanc (*Traité,* p. xxii), as we have seen, only silver shillings were coined; according to Adolphe Landry, *Essai économique sur les mutations des monnaies dans l'ancienne France de Philippe le Bel à Charles VII* (Paris, 1910), p. 11, only the penny (*denarius*) was coined.

[11] [TRANSLATOR'S NOTE: This was especially true in the Low Countries, where weight, alloy, and seigniorage varied from one denomination to another.]

If such is the case, its multiple of 20 or 50 or 100 lire will exist. If not, the fact does not change the principle. The silver coins or bank notes in circulation are representative money, convertible in gold because the owner of silver or paper money is entitled to have it exchanged for gold at the central bank, or for drafts on a foreign bank which will deliver the same quantity of gold. Furthermore, if in the country in question convertibility is temporarily suspended, such a suspension does not cause the monetary unit to lose its quality of real currency. The note of the Bank of Italy today (1936) is a promise to pay, at an indefinite time in the future, 0.07919113 grams of pure gold for each lira. Perhaps the market will cause that promise to be valued at a discount in order to transform it into present gold. The fact remains that the monetary unit is defined as a real physical quantity of gold, silver, some other metal, or perhaps even another commodity. On the basis of that monetary unit or on the basis of representative coins or notes, we make bargains, accept obligations, and settle debts. We promise to pay 100 lire and discharge this obligation by delivering a note of 100 lire. The note of 100 lire is real money.

10. Prior to the French Revolution, the monetary system of most European countries was based on altogether different principles. Contemporary authors could take these principles for granted and did not have to explain them to others. Their strange terminology causes us, who live in another world, to wander for a while in a dark forest.[12] By and by, we finally understand the tacit assumptions of their discourses. The key, needed to interpret the apparent confusion of the monetary treatises written prior to the eighteenth century, is the distinction between a monetary unit used as a standard of value and of deferred payments and another monetary unit used as a medium of exchange.

11. There was, then, a monetary unit used only as a standard of deferred payments (promises to pay) or for the purpose of keeping accounts. This was the function of a money of account, an imaginary or ideal money. The public made contracts, kept books, established mortgages, or stipulated rents in pounds, shillings, and pence. In the time of Malestroit and his "Paradoxes" (1565), an ell of velvet was valued at 10 pounds *tournois;* a measure of wine, at 12 pounds; a pair of shoes,

[12] A typical example of a tangle is Marquis Girolamo Belloni's *Lettera in riposta ad un quesito propostogli sopra la natura della moneta immaginaria* (Rome, 1727), p. 27, which the complacent editors, the Paglierini, praise as written "with such method and clarity" that it leads "the reader easily and gradually to a true understanding of imaginary money." The letter is reprinted in Vol. II of the collection, *Scrittori classici italiani di economica politica, parte moderna,* edited by Custodi.

at 15 sous; the daily wage of a laborer, at 5 sous; the annual rent of a gentleman, at 500 pounds; and a town-house or farm, at 25,000 pounds.[13]

Although it was possible to make contracts or to keep accounts in imaginary money—that is, in pounds, shillings, and pence—it was impossible to make actual payments in these monetary units, since they had not been coined for several centuries. Payment was made in real currency, that is, in gold coins, white money or silver coins, black money or low-grade silver, vellon or copper coins.

The coins in circulation had a great variety of names:

Gold: florins, ducats, sequins, angels, nobles, crowns, sovereigns, French and other écus, moutons, gold louis, doblons, guilders.
Silver: Philippus and other dollars, pieces of eight, reals of Spain, silver louis, testoons, blanks, guilders (originally gold), ducatoons, etc.
Vellon and black money: farthings, obols, Dutch stivers, French *douzains,* Tuscan *crazie,* etc.

In the time of Malestroit, a customer could pay a shopkeeper for an ell of velvet, priced £10 *tournois* in money of account, by giving him 4 écus du soleil rated at £2 10*s.* each. Similarly, the buyer of a barrel of wine, costing £12, could give in payment 20 testoons current at 12 sous per testoon. A shoemaker would be satisfied if he received 15 douzains in black money, at 12*d.* per douzain, for a pair of shoes selling at 15*s.* In the same way, a journeyman, whose wage was 5*s.* per day, would be content with 5 douzains in currency. A gentleman would collect his rent of £500 *tournois* in the form of 200 écus du soleil; and the one who had sold a house or a farm for £25,000 would give quittance to a buyer who had paid him 10,000 écus at £2½ per écu. If there was a change in the ratio between real and imaginary money—for example, if the rates of the currency in terms of money of account were doubled or reduced by half—the number of coins to be paid in discharge of a debt would vary inversely. For example, if we assumed that prices remained the same, either 2 or 8 écus, respectively, instead of 4 would be needed to pay for an ell of velvet priced at £10 *tournois.* The workman would receive either 2½ or 10 douzains instead of 5; the gentleman would collect

[13] The present study was undertaken as a result of the recent publication of a hitherto unedited memoir by the Seigneur de Malestroit, author of the paradoxes made famous by the *Response de Bodin.* For the convenience of the reader, the text of the "Paradoxes" and a second reply by Alexandre de la Tourette to the memoir of Malestroit are republished in the same volume; *Paradoxes inédits du Seigneur de Malestroit touchant les monnoyes avec la response du Président de la Tourette,* Luigi Einaudi, ed. (Turin, G. Einaudi, 1936).

either 100 or 400 écus instead of 200; and the seller of a house would receive either 5,000 or 20,000 écus, instead of 10,000.

12. The essence of the concept of imaginary money is not, therefore, the idea of a collective term (Le Blanc and Poulain), or of a fixed value (Fabbrini and Galiani), or even of a result obtained by using a variable divisor or multiplier (Neri). Early writers were correct in making a distinction between imaginary and real money, but their definitions of the former show that they were not sure of the basis of that distinction.

Imaginary money—here is my thesis—is not money at all. It is a mere instrument or technical device used to perform some monetary functions.

13. Let us assume the monetary unit to be the gold franc weighing 0.29 grams of pure gold (0.32 grams at the fineness of 90 per cent). Let us further assume that gold pieces of 10, 20, and 100 francs were coined; for medium-sized and small transactions, silver species of 5, 2, and 1 franc; nickel coins of 50 and 20 centimes, and copper coins of 10 and 5 centimes. However, the silver, nickel, and copper coins contain so little metal that, if melted, they cannot be sold at a price equal to the nominal value inscribed on the coin. Therefore, those coins circulate only as representative money, as tokens of the gold coins into which they are legally convertible. Let us further assume that only gold coins can be minted freely and are full legal tender for all debts. The other coins are minted by the state only and are legal tender up to a certain amount, which is somewhat larger for the silver coins than for the inferior nickel and copper coins.

In this system, that of the pure monometallic standard, there is no place for imaginary money, even if the monetary authorities should wish to introduce imaginary money for the purpose of stabilizing the currency. Keeping accounts and stipulating contracts in imaginary livres and at the same time making payments in real francs would not present any advantages and, besides, would necessitate the establishment of a legal ratio between the livre and the franc. If this ratio were 1 to 1, the two denominations would be identical. If another ratio were chosen, for example, 2 to 1 or 1 to 2, the livre would become either a fraction or a multiple of the franc. The introduction of an imaginary money would in this case only complicate matters and would serve no purpose, not even that of keeping the subsidiary coins in circulation. They would stay in circulation simply because melting them down is unprofitable, their value as bullion being so much less than their monetary value.

The device of an imaginary money is also unnecessary to prevent the overvalued subsidiary coins from driving the gold out of circulation.

They cannot do so as long as they are not coined in excessive quantities and are not full legal tender. If the rules are not observed, disturbances may occur, but they will be the result of the government's monetary policy, and the creation of imaginary money will not prevent their occurrence. This analysis, of course, presupposes the existence of rational rules and their rational application.

14. Now let us assume that the monetary system is that of the bimetallic standard. The monetary unit is still the franc, defined as being equivalent to either 0.29 grams of pure gold or 4.5 grams of pure silver. The denominations actually coined are gold pieces of 10, 20, and 100 francs and silver pieces of 1, 2, and 5 francs. Let us disregard for the moment the existence of token coins for the smaller denominations, since the remarks made above would apply to them. If left to themselves, the two kinds of francs—gold and silver—would be two different monetary units. There is no reason why the market should permanently consider 0.29 grams in gold, the weight of the gold franc, as the exact equivalent of 4.5 grams in silver, the weight of the silver franc. Such an equivalence, if it existed, would be merely accidental and ephemeral. As a natural consequence, a double standard is accompanied by a double price system: the same commodity may have one price in gold francs and another price in silver francs. Thus one hundred loaves of bread may conceivably sell for 40 gold francs or for 38 silver francs. This is not bimetallism, but duometallism, and it would be extremely cumbersome.

15. A duometallic standard with two monetary units and two price systems can be changed into a bimetallic standard with only one monetary unit and only one price system, if certain requirements are fulfilled. These requirements are: (1) that both gold and silver coins are full legal tender; (2) that there exists free coinage for both metals, so that anyone bringing gold or silver bullion to the mint will receive the same weight in gold or silver coins of the desired denominations (in order to avoid minor complications, let us assume that this transaction involves neither expense nor delay);[14] (3) that there exists a fixed legal ratio between gold and silver. For example, this legal ratio was 1 to 15½ in the countries adhering to the Latin Monetary Union, which means that 100 silver francs weighed 15½ times as much as 100 gold francs.

16. For the bimetallic standard to operate properly, it is further nec-

[14] In fact, today the cost of minting is very small, little more than two per thousand in those countries that still charge seigniorage. In the countries, such as the United States, that have free coinage, there is still the loss of interest for the time required by the minting. For the importance of these charges, see below, paragraph 18.

essary that the market ratio be equal to the legal ratio or, in other words, that the price ratio between gold and silver ingots or bars in the bullion market be the same as that established by the mint. As long as this requirement is fulfilled, it is indifferent to a debtor whether he effects payment in gold or silver francs, because they have the same value in bullion as in currency. For this reason, both kinds of currency will remain in circulation, and one will not have the tendency to drive the other out.

17. The accidental identity of the legal and the market ratio may last for a long time. If the mints absorb most of the gold and silver bullion offered on the market, the mint price (that is, the amount of currency supplied by the mints in exchange for a given weight of bullion) tends to dictate the market price for industrial uses, so that the bimetallic system sometimes gives the impression of lasting stability. If, however, there should be an appreciable change in the production of either one of the two metals, or in the tastes of the public for jewelry and plate, or in the preference of hoarders for gold or silver, or in the demand for gold rather than for silver coins, then the market ratio would tend to deviate from the legal ratio. While the latter remains fixed at 1 to 15½, the former may rise to 1 to 16 or drop to 1 to 15. In the first case, gold is worth more as bullion than as coin. Silver, being overvalued by the mint, will be delivered by the public to be coined. The silver coins thus obtained will be exchanged for gold at the legal ratio of 1 to 15½. This gold will then be resold at a profit on the bullion market, with the result that all the gold coins will soon disappear from circulation and their place will be taken by heavy and inconvenient silver coins. In the second case, silver instead of gold is at a premium and is worth more as bullion than as coin. Therefore, it is now silver that will be hoarded or exported or sent to the melting pot. The country will be reduced to using gold coins, beautiful, indeed, but inconvenient for petty transactions. Soon the public will complain about the lack of small change, and the officials will resort to makeshifts: they will be forced to allow the circulation of tokens or of dirty scrip, having the disadvantage of conveying contagious diseases.

Thus the bimetallic standard is bound to become an alternating monometallic standard, swinging from gold to silver and from silver to gold, to the great annoyance of the public.

18. To prevent these swings, it is possible to use two devices, while still keeping the bimetallic standard in operation. One of them is seigniorage, but it is effective to a limited extent only. The reason is that seigniorage in recent times has been very moderate. In Italy the mint

charges are only 2 per thousand to cover the expense of coinage. At any rate, seigniorage is to a certain extent a check against the practice of selling coins in circulation for their value as bullion, whenever the market price of bullion has risen above the mint price. On the other hand, let us assume that silver has fallen in price because of an increase in production. If the coinage were free of charge and not subject to delay, it would be profitable to take silver to the mint as soon as the price of the quantity of bullion contained in 100 francs dropped, even by a very small percentage, below the amount of 100 francs. If there is a coinage charge of 2 per thousand, the price of the same quantity of bullion has to fall below 99.80 francs before it becomes remunerative to bring bullion to the mint. As long as the drop in the price of bullion on the market does not exceed the seigniorage, it is unprofitable to coin more silver and to melt down the gold coins.

19. It must be admitted that today seigniorage, because it is either nonexistent or insignificant, can hardly be considered an effective check against the disruption of the bimetallic standard. This was not true of former centuries. From Charlemagne to the French Revolution, seigniorage was much higher than it is today, although it varied greatly from one country to another, from one period to another, and from one denomination to another. But in those times seigniorage did not always serve as an effective device of monetary policy, stabilizing the existent standard. The rulers considered the mint as a source of income, and in a period of financial stress increased seigniorage in the hope of thereby increasing their revenue, whether or not such a measure was called for to protect the standard at that particular time. The rulers also were reluctant to increase seigniorage on gold coins. The gold coin was a symbol of their sovereignty, and rulers rarely tampered with it; they were more inclined to make seigniorage high for the silver coinage and still higher for black money and vellon. It happened that they increased the seigniorage when they should have lowered it; they sometimes lowered it inadvisedly for the very coins which were being culled out to be sent abroad or to the melting pot. Accordingly, seigniorage cannot be used today and was not used in the past as an effective instrument of policy to prevent the breakdown of the bimetallic standard.

20. The second device available to governments to preserve the bimetallic standard is to change the legal ratio in accordance with the variations of the market ratio. Unfortunately, this device, too, is clumsy and difficult to use. If the market ratio increased from 1:15½ to 1:16, gold would disappear from circulation unless the legal ratio was also

changed and made to conform to the market ratio. This might be done in two ways, either by increasing the weight of the silver franc from 4.5 to 4.645 grams of pure silver, while the contents of the gold franc (0.29 gram) remained unaltered, or by reducing the weight of the gold franc to 0.28 gram without changing the weight of the silver franc. In both cases a recoinage, either of all the gold or of all the silver that was in circulation, would be necessary. If changes in the market ratio were frequent and appreciable, one recoinage would follow on the heels of another, and the currency would always be in a state of flux and confusion. As Ferdinando Galiano stated with reference to the disequilibrium between good and bad money, "to withdraw it [one of the two, and he was thinking of the good money rather than of the bad], to recoin it and to put it back into circulation, takes too much time" (*Della moneta,* ed. Niccolini, p. 181).

21. In past centuries the device used to remedy monetary disturbances was precisely the money of account or the imaginary pound. It was an instrument of extraordinary flexibility which had been slowly developed in the ten centuries after the reign of Charlemagne. Its full possibilities were realized neither by the Revolutionary Assemblies, which eventually abandoned it, nor by the monetary authorities, who during the ten preceding centuries had failed to take full advantage of it and had diverted it to dangerous uses. Apart from the imaginary pound or livre, divided into shillings (sous) and subdivided into pence (deniers), in which prices were set and contracts established, there were also real moneys. These real moneys could not be reduced to two types (with their several denominations), as is the case with the bimetallic system; on the contrary, there were several types, and each of them was a unit or denomination independent from all the others.

At the time of Cesare Beccaria (1738–1794), a famous economist and criminologist of the eighteenth century, the following coins were current in the Duchy of Milan:

GOLD

National Milanese: doblon (25.5.—)[15]

Foreign

Spanish: doblon (25.10.—), another doblon with two columns (25.—.—)

---

[15] The figure between parentheses, after the name of each coin, indicates the current rate in Milanese *lire di imperiali.* Thus, "doblon (25.5.—)" means that the coin called doblon was rated currently, or officially, £25 5*s.* 0*d. di imperiali,* the imaginary money used in Milan.

French: the old louis (25.10.—), the doblon called *merliton* (24.12.6), another coin with the sun and two shields (31.—.—), another coin with the cross of the Holy Spirit (37.2.6), another coin with four escutcheons (26.2.6)
Venetian: sequin (14.10.—)
Genoese: doblon (25.7.6)
Florentine: doblon (25.15.—); sequin (14.10.—)
Roman: doblon of Clement XII (25.—.—)
Savoy: doblon (25.—.—); sequin (14.7.6)
Mantua: doblon (25.5.—)
Portuguese: *old lisbonina* (41.—.—), new doblon with effigy and border (110.—.—)
Viennese: *ongaro* (14.5.—)
Chemnitz: *ongaro* (14.7.6); Roman sequin (14.15.—); Genoese sequin (15.—.—)

SILVER
National Milanese: ducatoon (8.12.—); philippus dollar (7.10.—)
Foreign
Roman: ducatoon of Clement XI (8.2.6); new testoon (2.5.—); new paolo (—.15.—); half-paolo (—.7.6)
Savoy: ducatoon (8.9.—); new écu of Piedmont (7.12.—); old lira of Savoy (1.10.—)
Venetian: ducatoon (8.8.—); *giustina* (7.7.6)
Florentine: ducatoon (8.7.6); *livorina* with the tower (6.19.—); same with the rose (6.12.6)
Mantua: ducatoon (8.9.—)
Genoese: *genovina* (10.5.—)
French: old écu (6.19.—); écu with the three fleurs-de-lis (17.11.—); écu with the two L L (6.—.—); écu with three crowns (7.16.—); écu *del popone* (6.5.—)
Burgundian: ducatoon (8.7.6)
German: ducatoon (8.5.—)
Bologna: écu (6.4.—)
Spanish: piece with the arms of Castile (6.17.6); half-piece (5.8.9); another piece with column and globes (6.16.—); half-piece (3.8.—); écu of St. John the Baptist of Genoa (6.—.—)[16]

Beccaria does not list the black moneys and copper coins which circulated at the same time. Their inclusion would only have strengthened the impression that the currency of the small Milanese duchy was in a disorderly state. Disorder did reign, but not because of the multiplicity of monetary types in circulation; there circulated no less than 22 gold

[16] Cesare Beccaria, "Del disordine e de' rimedi delle monete nello stato di Milano nell' anno 1762" in *Le opere*, Vol. I (Florence, Le Monnier, 1854), pp. 470–71.

coins and 29 silver coins, most of which were foreign. What really matters, however, is that all these types, with one or two exceptions, were independent monetary units. Table 1 shows how they may be classified according to their value in money of account.

TABLE 1

RATES OF THE GOLD AND SILVER COINS CURRENT IN MILAN (1762)

GOLD

Number of Coins	Rate in Money of Account	Number of Coins	Rate in Money of Account	Number of Coins	Rate in Money of Account
	£ *s. d.*		£ *s. d.*		£ *s. d.*
1	110. 0. 0.	2	25.10. 0.	1	14.15. 0.
1	46. 2. 6.	1	25. 7. 6.	2	14.10. 0.
1	41. 0. 0.	2	25. 5. 0.	2	14. 7. 6.
1	37. 2. 6.	3	25. 0. 0.	1	14. 5. 0.
1	31. 0. 0.	1	24.12. 6.		
1	25.15. 0.	1	15. 0. 0.		

SILVER

Number of Coins	Rate in Money of Account	Number of Coins	Rate in Money of Account	Number of Coins	Rate in Money of Account
	£ *s. d.*		£ *s. d.*		£ *s. d.*
1	10. 5. 0.	1	7.11. 0.	2	6. 0. 0.
1	8.12. 0.	1	7.10. 0.	1	5. 8. 9.
2	8. 9. 0.	1	7. 7. 6.	1	3. 8. 0.
1	8. 8. 0.	2	6.19. 0.	1	2. 5. 0.
2	8. 7. 6.	1	6.17. 6.	1	1.10. 0.
1	8. 5. 0.	1	6.16. 0.	1	0.15. 0.
1	8. 2. 6.	1	6.12. 6.	1	0. 7. 6.
1	7.16. 0.	1	6. 5. 0.		
1	7.12. 0.	1	6. 4. 0.		

SOURCE: Cesare Beccaria, "Del disordine e de' rimedi delle monete nello Stato di Milano nell'anno 1762," in *Le opere*, Vol. I (Florence, 1854), pp. 470–71.

As the table shows, there was only one instance in which three coins were current at the same rate. There were only eight instances in which it happened that two pieces were rated the same. Except for these few cases, no other two coins had the same value. Moreover, none of the fifty-one coins listed by Beccaria, with one single exception, had multiples or submultiples. The exception refers to the case of the *paolo* rated 15*s.* and the half-paolo rated 7*s.* 6*d.* There are a few other instances of coins which were double the value of other coins, but this is purely accidental, since the types in question were issued by different foreign mints without any attempt being made to issue doubles or halves.

How could a coherent system be built with different monetary units? How could they be counted, and in which of the fifty units? This difficult problem was solved by using the imaginary livre. This was the abstract unit which was used to evaluate all the coins in actual circulation and to bind them into one system. By saying that the Spanish doblon "with the two columns," the Roman and the Savoyard doblons—all three of them gold coins—were worth £25 *di imperiali,* one stated simply that they were equal in value; and by saying that the sequin of Genoa, actually coined in Chemnitz, was worth only £15, one stated that this coin was worth three-fifths of the doblons mentioned above and was rated twice as high as the Milanese phillipus current at £7.10*s.* *di imperiali.*

22. It was possible that wrong rates were set for coins of the same metal, as, for example, when two coins having different gold or silver contents were made current at the same rate in money of account. In fact, Beccaria shows that, of the three doblons, all rated £25, the Spanish doblon contained $117\frac{9}{16}$ grains of fine gold, the Roman doblon $117\frac{13}{96}$ grains, and the Savoyard doblon only $112\frac{6}{16}$ grains. The Savoyard doblon, being much lighter than the other two, was consequently overrated to that extent. Such errors in rating, once they were ascertained by assaying, could easily be adjusted when the coins in question were all of the same metal, be it gold or silver.

23. The problem of setting accurate rates and of establishing a workable monetary system was much more difficult and complex when the coins in circulation were of two or more different metals. In this case, the setting of proper rates in money of account for all the current coins depended not only on the skill of the assayer but also on the ability of the mint officials to keep in touch with the conditions prevailing in the bullion market and to follow closely any changes in the price ratio between the metals that had monetary uses.

24. In order to simplify matters, let us assume that there are only two coins—gold florins and silver scudos—which are full legal tender and to which the mint extends the privilege of free coinage. Let us further assume that the market ratio between gold and silver is 1 to 12, which was actually the ratio in the second half of the sixteenth century, a fact recognized by both contenders in the famous Malestroit-Bodin controversy. With these assumptions in mind, let us suppose that the gold florin, weighing 120 grains of fine gold, is current at the rate of £24 in money of account. What, then, should be the rate of the silver scudo having the same weight of fine silver? Evidently, £2, or one-twelfth of the rate given to the florin. For our monetary system of florins and scudos to be in equilibrium, the proportion between the rates, £2

and £24, set by royal proclamation, has to be the same as the ratio, 1 to 12, existing in the bullion market between the price of a silver ingot and that of a gold ingot of equal weight.

Now let us suppose that the market ratio changes from 1:12 to 1:11½. In the case of the bimetallic system, as it existed during the nineteenth century in the United States and in Europe, adjustment would have been difficult to achieve unless all the gold or all the silver in circulation were recoined. Before the officials of the mint had even begun to make the necessary arrangements, all the undervalued coins would most likely already have been sent abroad or to the melting pot. In former centuries, however, an adjustment could have been made very promptly. It would have sufficed to issue a royal proclamation crying up the silver scudo from £2 to £2. 1*s.* 9*d.*, that is, to a number obtained by dividing £24, the rate of the florin, by 11½ instead of by 12.

And what if the market ratio changed from 1:12 to 1:12½? In such a case, the normal procedure would have been to cry down the silver scudo from £2 to £1 18*s.* 5*d.*, that is, to a figure obtained by dividing £24 by 12½.[17, 18]

25. The function of imaginary money in a country that had adopted the bimetallic standard was consequently that of keeping the monetary system in equilibrium. This objective was achieved by the simple process of crying the currency up or down, that is, by increasing or decreasing the current rates in money of account of the real coins. If this were done carefully, the legal rates would at all times be in accordance with the ratio between the prices of gold and silver, as determined by market conditions.

The instrument called "imaginary money" has the following connotations:

(*a*) Expressions in "imaginary money" are abstract numbers, notwithstanding the denomination in terms of pounds, shillings, and pence. People used these terms in their enumerations in remembrance of the historical fact that, in the past, pounds, shillings, and pence had actually existed in concrete form.

(*b*) Expressions in "imaginary money" are not absolute numbers.

---

[17] In decimal fractions, those new values corresponded, respectively, to £2.087 and £1.92. The old system of counting in pounds, shillings, and pence allowed the use of figures which corresponded more closely to currencies in actual circulation.

[18] [TRANSLATOR'S NOTE: These adjustments are based on the assumption that the monetary authorities did not wish to alter the rate of the florin. Otherwise, the same result might have been obtained by crying down the florin from £24 to £23, if the market ratio changed from 1:12 to 1:11½, or by crying up the florin from £24 to £25, if the market ratio changed from 1:12 to 1:12½.]

Instead of saying: the gold florin is worth £24.—, it is possible to assign to the same coin another value, provided that other coins got new rates accordingly. The rate, in "imaginary money," of the silver scudo should be a function of the rate of the florin; and, to be precise, this functional relationship should reflect the market ratio between gold and silver.

(*c*) It is a matter of indifference which coin is chosen as the one whose rate is fixed, while the value of all others may vary. Both can conceivably be allowed to vary, but only on condition that the rates reflect the market ratio between gold and silver.

(*d*) According to historical experience, it was, however, more expedient to keep the rates of gold coins fixed, while the rates of silver coins might, if necessary, be altered. Since gold coins were regarded as a symbol of sovereignty, rulers were reluctant to damage the prestige of this symbol by alterations. Not only the rulers but also the subjects believed that gold coins should circulate at stable rates; they were convinced that an invariable archetype should serve as the standard of value. Both myths, that of the royal symbol and that of the unvarying standard, were the outcome of unfortunate experiences; the current rates of the real coins, as expressed in terms of money of account, were often manipulated for purposes other than the preservation of the bimetallic standard.

26. The discovery of "imaginary money" as an instrument of monetary policy was not the work of a theorist, but the result of a long process of historical change (see paragraph 8 above). However, if, among many contingent factors, one wanted to indicate which one came closest to being determined by deliberate choice, one should mention the longing of medieval men for the eternal, the immutable, the universal, accompanied by an abhorrence of the transitory, the mutable, and the particular. They stubbornly looked for an invariable standard of value and called it the pound; they pretended that it was immutable in the monetary chaos in which abraded, clipped, and adulterated foreign as well as domestic coins circulated side by side. Eventually they discovered that imaginary money could be used as an instrument of monetary policy, in order to obtain certain results. Legislators and economists after 1789 scorned this discovery. Far from realizing its potentialities, they failed to see its true import, considered only its passing attributes (cf. below, paragraphs 43 ff.), and then forgot all about it. If the great advocate of universal bimetallism, Enrico Cernuschi, had meditated upon the solution offered by the age-old experience of European nations, he would have exclaimed: "Eureka!"

27. Another reason why legislators and economists misunderstood, despised, and forgot this monetary device is that the concept "imaginary money" was surrounded by the thick mist of a strange terminology, repellent to the layman and conducive to deceitful practices. We have already pointed out how difficult it is in times of monetary devaluations and revaluations to persuade men that prices have not changed but that the monetary yardstick has become longer or shorter. Yet today the terms of comparison are only two: the monetary unit, e.g., the lira (in Italy), and one unit of a given commodity, e.g., a kilogram of bread; and there is only one ratio: between the monetary unit and the unit of a commodity. Whether a change in this ratio occurs because of a change in one or the other of the two variables should therefore be easily ascertainable. At the time of imaginary money three units had to be correlated: the imaginary monetary unit (the pound), the real monetary unit (the scudo), and a unit of an economic good (e.g., a kilogram of bread). As a result, there were also three ratios: pound to commodity, pound to scudo, and scudo to commodity. Upon reflection it is a simple proposition; yet it is apt to confuse casual observers as well as more profound thinkers. When individual or class interests were at stake, endless disputes were certain to arise. The point of the great controversy between Malestroit and Bodin was that Malestroit contended that a change in the pound-to-commodity ratio had been canceled by a contrary change in the pound-to-scudo ratio, with the result that the scudo-to-commodity ratio had remained constant. On the other hand, Bodin considered only the scudo-to-commodity ratio and declared that it alone had changed.

If we assume that the price of bread had increased from £1 to £2 and that, at the same time, the rate of the scudo had increased from £2 to £4, then the price of bread had remained unchanged at ½ scudo. The public, used to counting in pounds, shillings, and pence, complained about the rise in prices, but Malestroit demonstrated that "the general rise in prices, about which everyone today complains, is only a delusion, a way of counting without consistency or substance" (Malestroit, *Paradoxes,* Einaudi, ed.). The learned man was right, because the pound was a mere numerical expression, and the scudo a real silver coin. However, the people whose incomes were fixed in imaginary pounds, shillings, and pence were not wrong either. They were damaged if they did not succeed in getting their "abstract" incomes raised, because only then did they receive the same number of scudos as before. After the great monetary devaluations following the First World War we have become accustomed to the idea of variability in the monetary standard. Since prices are sticky, either because it is their natural tendency or because they are regulated by the government, we all suffer or benefit, as the case may be, whenever there is a change in the symbols of wealth without a change in the reality. Today monetary devaluations or revaluations attract immediate notice only through the fluctuations of the foreign exchanges in which only those few who have dealings abroad are directly interested. But this was not so in the past; then the public became immediately aware of monetary disturbances because of fluctuating *domestic* exchange rates, indicating current rates of real coins in terms of money of account. If the ratio between the precious metals changed from 1:12 to 1:11½, the market, being very sensitive, often anticipated the ruler's proclamation. The rate of the silver scudo priced officially at £2 (as compared to the gold florin priced at £24) rose little by little in the market until it reached £1 1*s.* 9*d.* Such an unofficial quotation was called in Italy "in abusivo" because it was an abuse of the law, and hence strictly prohibited; coins were supposed to be current at the rate fixed by the monetary ordinances. Nevertheless, it frequently happened that the change in the market rate, although illegal, was only a prelude to a change in the official rate, to be proclaimed sooner or later, depending upon the alertness of the monetary authorities.

28. With reference to monetary matters, the language used in former centuries was so confusing that the public was befuddled as to what was actually going on. Today this same terminology is so unfamiliar to economists that it constitutes a serious obstacle to the understanding of early monetary literature.

Prior to the French Revolution, the expression "enhancement of the currency" (Fr. *augmentation;* It. *aumento* or *alzamento*) meant that the real coins were cried up, that is, that their rates were raised by proclamation, as, for instance, the silver scudo from £2 to £2 1*s.* 9*d.* However, in so far as people reckoned and stipulated contracts in pounds, shillings, and pence, such a rise of the current rates corresponded to a weakening (Fr. *affaiblissement;* It. *indebolimento*), deterioration (It. *peggioramento*), or debasement of the money of account. By "crying up" the money, a single legislative act devalued the money of account and revalued the currency, that is, the real coins. Usually the result was that, after a while, prices were raised as expressed in pounds, shillings, and pence, although they remained constant if measured in revalued gold and silver currency. Contrary to what a modern economist would expect, "crying up" (Fr. *hausser la monnaie;* It. *alzare*) was synonymous with debasement or with a shift from what was called "strong" money (Fr. *monnaie forte;* It. *moneta forte*) to "weak" or "base" money (Fr. *monnaie faible;* It. *moneta debole*).

29. Conversely, the expression "abatement of the currency" (Fr. *diminution;* It. *sbassamento*) indicated that the current coins were cried down, that is, that their rates were decreased, as, for example, when the silver scudo was called down by proclamation from £2 to £1 18*s.* 4*d.* Consequently, "abatement of the currency" was synonymous with an improvement or strengthening (Fr. *renforcement;* It. *rinforzamento*) of the imaginary money of account, which was the standard of value. By such an act, the money of account was revalued, and the currency devalued. After a while, prices in pounds, shillings, and pence tended to fall, although they often remained on the same level if measured in gold or silver. "To abate the currency" (Fr. *diminuer les monnaies;* It. *sbassare*) was, therefore, a shift from weak to strong money. Often it meant a return to good money (Fr. *retour à la forte monnaie*) which had been allowed to deteriorate.

30. As today, so also between A.D. 800 and 1800, people had their minds fixed on the mirage rather than on reality. Therefore, they protested especially against the enhancements of the currency and approved of abatements. Those who complained the most—and they formed the majority—were wage earners, pensioners, and all recipients of revenues fixed in pounds, shillings, and pence. They were hurt by enhancements, and the resulting curtailment of their purchasing power, through the rise in prices as expressed in money of account. This same group naturally gave its support to the abatements, which tended to lower the price level.

31. In a monetary system based on the use of imaginary money, the banks did not and could not issue notes promising to pay in money of account instead of in real currency. What would it have meant for a bank to be a debtor of 24 million pounds toward the bearers of circulating banknotes? In so far as people used imaginary money as a standard of deferred payments, but made payments in scudos and other real coins, the said bank, in case of enhancement of the scudo from £2 to £4, could have discharged its obligations with 6 million scudi instead of 12 million, thereby gaining the difference. On the other hand, if the scudo were cried down from £2 to £1, the bank would have been compelled to repay with 24 million scudi the original 12 million for which it was obligated, and thus would have been reduced to a state of bankruptcy. Perhaps it is possible to find a bank which failed for this reason,

but, if so, it was an accident due to a mistake in the conduct of business. This mistake must then also be attributed to the halo of mystery which for a thousand years surrounded the concept of imaginary money and caused it to be mistaken for something different from what it really was. Even the careful Pompeo Neri missed the truth—as so many other writers did—when he listed the pound-banco (*lira di banco*) among the imaginary moneys. As a matter of fact, his own description contradicts this classification.

According to Pompeo Neri, the pound-banco (*lira di banco*) was created "by taking as its measure a given weight of silver, or even an unadulterated coin, and by determining its contents in pure gold or silver, without giving any consideration to subsequent adulterations introduced by custom or law. Then the values of the imaginary pound-banco and scudo-banco would be fixed, so that they would be regulated by a standard independent of arbitrary legislation or public catastrophies. As a result, contracts would be made stable, and this standard of value, being perpetual and incorruptible, would be a convenient yardstick for measuring the value of all sorts of merchandise and real money" ("Osservazioni," *loc. cit.,* p. 153). Thus the pound-banco was a promise made by a bank which had received, let us say, 10 grains of pure gold, defined by the bank itself as a "pound," to restore to the owner an ingot of identical weight and fineness. However, this was not imaginary money but real money, and even the best of the real moneys, since it was immune from clipping and from frauds in weight or fineness. It was easily transferable from person to person, or even from place to place, and independent of variations in the name, the substance, or the rates of other currencies.

32. During the thousand years of its history the monetary system based on the coexistence of the imaginary pound and real moneys could and actually did perform the following functions in a more or less efficient way and with more or less comprehension on the part of princes, bankers, and contracting parties:

(*a*) This system allowed every state to have its own unit of account, the pound, which might be equal to the unit of other states, but not necessarily so; in most instances equality soon disappeared.

(*b*) This system also allowed every state to coin one or more real moneys: of gold only, of silver only, or of both metals. A state might even have no mint of its own, if it pleased the ruler to give currency to foreign coins. Beccaria—and Verri agreed with him—gave excellent reasons for advising a prince, especially a small one, against minting his own currency. Except in some particular cases, "the coinage of money is but a comedy of transformations accompanied by an unnecessary waste of metal in minting; it is a public burden which only profits the projectors, men who conceal their gains under the cloak of a pretended benefit to the sovereign, and hence to the entire nation" (*Del disordine,* Florentine ed., p. 478).

This single unit of account—the pound and its fractions—made it possible to use for payments any number of coins or real moneys—gold as well as silver, domestic as well as foreign—upon the sole condition that their rates were fixed in proportion to the gold or silver contents of the coins; moreover, the official ratio and the market ratio between gold and silver bullion had to be equal.

The principal shortcoming of this system was that the official rates set by proclamation were slow in adapting themselves to changes in the market ratio. In order to overcome this defect, Ferdinando Galiani, by far the best Italian economist of the eighteenth century, proposed in his book, *Della moneta* (written in 1750, when he was twenty-three years of age) a practical remedy: the current or proclamation rates should no longer be compulsory. Instead, the current rate was simply to become an optional price (*prezzo di voce*), effective only in the absence of any agreement to the contrary. Does the state fix the prices of commodities in general? It does not. Why, then, should it fix the price of currency? "The prices of wheat, of wine, and of oil are much more important [than the currency rates]. Those of land, of buildings, of rents, of interest, and of foreign exchange are still more important, and yet those prices are not regulated by any other law than 'the consensus of the public' " (*Della moneta,* ed. Niccolini, pp. 159–60).

Ferdinando Galiani's proposal to make the unofficial rate legal would have compelled the prince to revise promptly the proclamation rates whenever they were out of line with those practiced in the market. By following this policy, he would have avoided the inconveniences and the lack of stability inherent in the modern bimetallic system and would have supplied the public with currency in the desired quantity and of the desired denominations.

Since each state was already provided with its own standard of value or imaginary pound and since the creation of paper money representing mere numbers is and was inconceivable, a bank, even if it were a national bank, necessarily assumed in those times a supranational character. The pound-banco, representing a given weight of pure gold or silver, was itself a universal currency, which, like any other of the real currencies, could be rated in the money of account of each state and which was more suitable than hard coin for the purpose of making international transfers. The bank moneys of Venice, Genoa, and Amsterdam were used in traffic all over Europe, owing to the confidence which these moneys enjoyed, because of their convertibility into invariable weights of gold and because they could easily be made current abroad. In the Christian community of medieval Europe it was possible for each nation to adopt any foreign currency as its own, by simply giving it a rating in domestic money of account.

33. If these were the functions which actually were or might be filled by imaginary money, it does not seem that a conscious effort was ever made to use it as a means to achieve a purpose—supposing this purpose were desirable and possible—for which it was particularly well suited. That purpose is the utopian idea of price stability, which must be called "utopian" for a number of reasons.

(1) An acceptable definition of the concept "the general level of prices" does not exist, since it is uncertain which goods should be included in the preparation of a satisfactory index: Only finished products, or also raw materials and unfinished products? Only tangible goods or also services? Only consumer goods or also capital goods? Furthermore, economists and statisticians are not in accord as to the criteria which should be used in constructing an index for measuring the price level itself, and all are skeptical about the possibility of adhering to those criteria, once they are chosen.

(2) The idea that it is desirable to stabilize the general level of prices—a naïve and undemonstrable idea—does not have to be accepted. Why should invariability of prices exist in a world where everything else continuously changes? Should we also aim at the invariability of each single price, which is manifestly absurd? Why intend the invariability of something as abstract as the general level of all prices? One should, however, recall that medieval man was inclined to look at the world in the light of eternity and immobility. The modern popular desire for a general price level that would be constant may be a fossil remnant of that medieval state of mind.

(3) The possibility of reaching that end by means of a monetary policy which consists in decreasing or increasing the volume of money in circulation, as prices go up or down, especially if those variations are undesirable, is questionable. The success of such a policy depends en-

tirely upon the assumption that everything else remains equal. If it is true that nothing, absolutely nothing, changes in the economic world except the quantity of money, then prices, by definition, will vary with this quantity. If nothing varies, except that the quantity of money is doubled, the person who has £10 instead of £5 will spend £10 instead of £5, because, if he is not willing to do so, his desire to build up monetary reserves will have changed, which is contrary to our assumption. If nothing varies, the same amount of economic goods is offered for £10, no more and no less. Consequently, one unit of an economic good priced at £5 must necessarily go up to £10. The assumption that other things remain equal is extremely useful for purposes of analysis, but does not work out very well in practice. Everything changes with the change in the volume of money in circulation: the cash reserves of the individuals, and consequently the velocity of circulation; the production of economic goods, and consequently also their supply. Monetary policy has to operate with a very delicate and complex mechanism. In order to be successful, the policy-maker must combine an analytical mind with a quick appraisal of the imponderable factors.

34. Whether one considers stability of the price level possible or utopian, desirable or naïve, does not matter much; what I wish to emphasize is that the attainment of this goal might have been, and still might be, greatly facilitated by using imaginary money as a tool of monetary policy.

Today such a policy, intended to counteract undesirable price fluctuations, requires that the monetary authorities take either one or the other of the following steps if, let us suppose, prices go up and are to be brought back to their former level: (1) either the volume of bank credit and the circulation of bank notes has to be contracted, or (2) the metallic currency has to be withdrawn and recoined with a higher content in fine per monetary unit, whereby, as a result, the number of units that can be coined from the existing stock of precious metal is reduced.

On the other hand, if prices fall and the monetary authorities want to raise them to their former level, the appropriate measures to be taken are: either (1) an expansion of the volume of bank credit and the circulation of bank notes or (2) a devaluation of the monetary unit by reducing its gold or silver content, whereby the number of units that can be coined from a given stock of precious metal is increased.

The trouble is that all these measures are very cumbersome and slow and that they are liable to cause violent and unpredictable reactions which will disturb equilibrium conditions, if such exist, in other sectors of the economy.

The use of imaginary money as a tool of policy, on the other hand, offers a tempting solution of the difficulty. Let us assume that the index of general prices is at 100; that the gold florin is current at £24 and the silver scudo at £2. Let the index now rise to 111.11. In order to adjust the matter, all one need do is to cry down the currency by one-tenth, to reduce the rate of the florin from £24 to £21 12*s.*, and that of the silver scudo from £2 to £1 16*s.* The transaction resembles what is called "a monetary deflation." The amount of currency in circulation is unchanged, but its purchasing power is automatically cut down by one-tenth. Everyone owns the same number of florins and silver scudi as before the proclamation, but everyone has one-tenth less in imaginary pounds. Since buying and selling is done in money of account, the reduction of its volume by one-tenth, by virtue of the quantity theory of money, will bring prices down again from 111.11 to 100.

And what to do if the price level drops to 90? In order to raise it again, all that the monetary authorities have to do is to issue a proclamation crying up the currency by one-ninth: the florin from £24 to £26 13*s.* 4*d.* and the silver scudo from £2 to £2 4*s.* 5⅓*d.* Such a transaction resembles what is called a "monetary inflation." Although the volume of currency remains the same, its purchasing power is raised by one-ninth by legislative fiat. Everyone now possesses one-ninth more in money of account, and, since this is the standard of value, prices must go up again from 90 to 100.

35. It is conceivable that the normal sequence of events may be the following:

(1) The production of precious metals increases.

(2) As a result, the volume of currency in circulation, florins and scudi, increases too.

(3) This increase automatically causes another increase in the number of imaginary pounds, as long as the current value of the florin and the scudo remains fixed at £24 and £2, respectively.

(4) Since the quantity of economic goods that are offered for sale remains steady, as do all the other data of the problem, except the volume of money, prices tend to increase.

(5) However, the prince, by crying down the currency at the opportune moment, prevents an increase in the volume of imaginary money, despite any increase in the volume of actual currency.

(6) Therefore, prices, too, are prevented from rising. The problem

created by a decrease in the production of precious metals and by a tendency of prices to fall, while the production of economic goods continues to grow, is solved by reversing the procedure described above.

36. It is not easy to understand why Irving Fisher, who examined with such care the historical precedents for his managed and invariable dollar, failed to mention the system of imaginary money. To those princes of past centuries who were eager to secure for their subjects the benefits of price stability, this system could have rendered great service. Illusory stability, to be sure, because stable prices in imaginary pounds would nevertheless result in the payment of a greater or lesser quantity of florins or scudi. But did Pompeo Neri not teach that "the public was scrupulous in preserving the identity of the word pound in sound, rather than in value" ("Osservazioni," *loc. cit.*, p. 110)?

37. In the same formal way, another troublesome problem of modern times, that of foreign exchange, might have been considered solved. But it would have been solved by being transferred from the international to the national scene. The monetary advisor, anxious to preserve the prestige of the domestic currency, could have reasoned as follows: "In the system of imaginary money, by hypothesis, two national moneys exist side by side, one imaginary and the other real. Among the latter, we have supposed that there was a gold florin weighing 120 grains of pure gold and having a value of £24 in money of account.

"If the prince was careful to maintain the weight of the florin at 120 grains, the foreign exchanges, expressed in florins, would remain stable. A foreign prince might reduce the weight of his sequin from 120 to 100 grains of pure gold; in that case the domestic florin would be at a premium of 20 per cent over the sequin: a perpetual reason for national pride and prestige.

"If, later on, the prince decided to cry up the florin by one-tenth and to increase the current rate from £24 to £26 8*s.*, this was a domestic matter which affected only the 'internal' exchange, or the relation existing between the 'national' moneys: the real florin and the imaginary pound. The foreign exchanges between the real currency of one country and the real currency of another country were unaffected. What did it matter to foreigners, if someone chose to modify the basis for the settlement of debts between citizens of the same state?"

This analysis leads to one important observation: whereas the present system of real money is likely to arouse emotions, because it creates the false impression that foreigners are to blame for any devaluation of the national currency, the ancient system of real and imaginary money made it clear to everyone that monetary devaluation was mainly a domestic matter, important only in the relations between classes and individuals within the same nation. In domestic trade, contracts were stipulated and accounts were kept in imaginary money, while in foreign trade prices were usually fixed in gold florins.

38. The rate at which a coin was officially allowed to circulate was called "corso di grida," the current rate by proclamation. There existed also a "corso di voce" or "corso in abusivo" which, as the names suggest, was the unofficial or market rate. These two conceptions, curious as they are, are to be found at every step when one goes through the monetary tracts, treatises, and proclamations before 1800. At first, one is perplexed by these terms, then the matter becomes somewhat clearer, and finally one is attracted. Is it possible that the legislators of the French Revolution were, through their eagerness to return to the true and simple, actually opening the road to mystery and complication? What they wanted to make clear to the public was that the monetary unit was a disc of silver weighing 4.5 grams, or a disc of gold of 0.29 grams. Thereby, they erroneously assumed, people would never again fall into the error of looking at the monetary unit as perpetually endowed with a fixed value of its own. That these enlightened legislators were wrong is shown by the fact that in our days the link between various monetary units, such as the mark, lira, and franc, has again been broken. From these monetary names all precise connotations disappeared when it became no longer possible to convert the corresponding units into specific weights of precious metal; and at present convertibility is neither unconditional, prompt, nor certain. Thus, after one and a third century of fixed metallic equivalents, people are again debating attempts to give a fixed meaning to the monetary names which correspond to nothing but signs or tokens.

Legislators before 1800 had solved the problem by clearly separating money as a token or sign and money as a commodity (metal). The former was called "imaginary money," the other was the real currency. Now the *theory* of "imaginary money" could lead to the *reality* of dealing with money as a marketable good, not different from other commodities. While their contracts were made in pounds, shillings, and pence, people thought of the gold florins or silver scudi in which they would be paid; and by thinking in this way they were constantly reminded of the fact that florins and scudi had no miraculous virtues of their own. These coins, therefore, in spite of their name, had no permanent value or other characteristics but were priced as were, for instance, wine, wheat, or a farm. From the Middle Ages down to the end of the eighteenth century, men saw much better than we do that money is a negotiable commodity like any other. Because we exchange money only at national boundaries, it appears to us, at least inside a country, to be a supercommodity whose value is stable: One lire is always one lire, one franc is always one franc, and one mark is always one mark. In former times, because of the existence of money of account, men every day set a price on the florins, scudi, écus, doblons, sequins, and testoons which they received and paid out. Every day, in every single transaction, it was made clear to their minds that the money with which they paid, even bank money or paper money, was a commodity like any other, that its price was governed by the market and, like any other price, was the result of an infinite number of economic and noneconomic forces which determine the general equilibrium of all prices.

39. In the language of the Enlightenment, my present essay would have been called "an apology for imaginary money." After this attempt, which I believe to be the first one of its kind, a "philippic against imaginary money" seems superfluous. Such attacks, virulent as philippics usually are, can be found in all writings dealing with debasements and monetary disturbances, as, for example, in the historical summary given by Francesco Ferrara in one of his classic introductions.[19]

40. The myth of the immutability of the monetary unit, which could be used in the harmless game of keeping the price level stable in terms of imaginary money (but variable in terms of real money), or of stabilizing the foreign exchange (while allowing fluctuations in the domestic exchange), lent itself also to other, less innocent uses. The influence of what was a pure ideal allowed the sovereigns to engage in counterfeiting.

41. A sovereign often could not resist the temptation to tamper with the coinage, especially when through the expenses made in foreign and civil wars he was under compulsion to raise additional revenue, without being able to collect larger taxes from his subjects. One favorite method was recoinage: the sovereign decried or banned the old coins and forced the public to bring them to the mints so that he could deduct the seigniorage for the coinage of the new moneys.[20] The seigniorage was usually deducted in kind from the bullion or from the decried coins brought to

---

[19] "Della moneta e dei suoi surrogati," Introduction to Vol. VI of the Second Series of the *Biblioteca dell'economista,* pp. xxxv–liv; republished in F. Ferrara, *Esame storico-critico di economisti,* Vol. II, Pt. I, pp. 324–44.

[20] It should be observed that seigniorage was not necessarily higher on coins of base metal. There could be a low seigniorage on an inferior coin with much alloy and little silver, if it were not overvalued according to its current rate in money of account. On the other hand, there could be a high seigniorage on a fine coin of nearly 24 carats, if it were overvalued and made current at a high rate (in money of account).

the mint. This procedure allowed the prince to take away 10 or 20 per cent of the precious metals owned by the public. He was able to get more revenue without having to ask for a benevolence from the Estates General, who gave financial aid only grudgingly. It is no wonder that the mint was regarded as a source of revenue in a time when an adequate tax system had not yet been established and when revenues from the royal domain were no longer sufficient.

The system of the imaginary pound was useful in making the tribute somewhat less felt. If it had been the practice of the mint to pay 7 ounces in coin for one mark of precious metal, consisting of 8 ounces, it would have been obvious to the public that the prince retained one ounce for seigniorage. But such was not the practice. Let us suppose that the mint price was £480 for a mark of pure gold. A merchant who delivered bullion to the mint would consequently receive £480, or 20 florins of £24 each, for one mark of bullion. From this one mark of bullion the mint coined 22.85 florins instead of only 20 florins, current at the rate of £24. In so doing, the mint gained 2.85 florins on each mark, a seigniorage of exactly one-eighth. Afterward the price of bullion, expressed in new florins of £24, was likely to increase and to rise even above the mint price. If the operation was not too frequent and if the public had time to forget previous experiences, it could succeed.

High seigniorage, open or concealed, fell into disuse at the beginning of modern times. It was less easily concealed, and, when in later ages regular taxes were established, princes were no longer impelled to use this device.

42. Accusations of counterfeiting, such as the one which Dante hurled at Philip the Fair, King of France (1285–1314), were in many cases justified by the facts. The prince surreptitiously coined florins or scudi which were reduced in weight, in fineness, or in both, while he continued to call these adulterated coins by the same name as before and continued to make them current at the same rate: £24 for the florin and £2 for the silver scudo. By weighing and assaying the new coins, the public soon discovered them to be deficient in weight and fineness, and then became offended.

43. Instead of tampering with the real coins, princes could perform their operations through the instrument of the "imaginary money." A florin which hitherto had circulated for £24, or a newly coined florin of the same weight and fineness, could simply be "called up" to £30. Thereby nothing was changed, except that the circulating medium was raised one-fourth in nominal value. This would please large numbers of

people because with the same number of florins in their purses they had become richer by one-fourth; in imaginary pounds, it is true. A prince who had received 24 million pounds in the form of a million florins of £24 each could now repay his debt with only 0.8 million florins of £30 each. His debt was diminished, and he consequently gained, by 2 million florins.

44. Ferdinando Galiani justified enhancement of the currency in his theory by defining it as follows: enhancement is "a profit which the prince and the state derive from the slowness with which the majority of people change their ideas with regard to the value of money and the prices of goods." Even at present no better definition of devaluation, today's name for "enhancement of the currency," could be given. Galiani insisted that his definition had no malicious intent: "Are not the sale of noble titles, the award of honors, and a large number of other customs actually based simply on deep-rooted associations which cannot easily be changed?" And Galiani continued: "If a prince ennobles *all* his subjects, he does not give them added honor but takes away some honor from the word 'nobility.' The meaning of 'nobility' is changed. Similarly, if in establishing a new decoration for merit he does not confer this decoration first upon people who are already admired and illustrious, which fixes the value of the order in peoples' minds, but gives it to his lackeys, then the decoration will simply be regarded as a livery for servants, whatever its design." Similarly, "enhancement of the currency" does not produce a change of things but merely of words. The prices of commodities, in order to remain the same in reality, must consequently be changed in name. If this occurs on the same day on which the currency is enhanced and if everything is changed simultaneously and proportionately, then enhancing the currency will have no more effect than would a law giving Latin, Greek, or Hebrew, instead of Italian, names to the different coins. If there is a change in the words by which prices are expressed, and nothing else, things remain as they were. If, on the other hand, the words remain unchanged, then things themselves change. We are being told that an enhancement of prices is a remedy for enhancement (of the currency). When everything has been readjusted, the effects of the "enhancement" may be said to have vanished as the morning mist is dissipated by the rays of the sun. Disturbing effects of any enhancement of the currency must therefore be the result of the fact that prices are slow in adjusting themselves. The delay occurs because people who are accustomed to paying one ducat for a certain dish expect to be able to buy the same dish

as long as they pay something called a ducat. They complain about the avarice of whoever denies the dish to them, or they foolishly accuse others of having caused the dearth of all things. It must be noted that a prince who would repeat enhancement every month would necessarily destroy any association between a given commodity and its price, and thereby the device of enhancement would become perfectly useless and ineffective (as an instrument of monetary policy). What normally could be accomplished by an enhancement of the currency would subsequently have to be done by other means" (*Della moneta,* ed. Niccolini, pp. 186–87).

45. Galiani had already demonstrated that enhancing the currency favored debtors, by lessening the burden of private and public debts. It would bring about a temporary reduction of wages and salaries and taxes, thereby encouraging industry. Galiani was impatient with the defenders of those who were hurt; "Nor should one call for help and try to arouse pity with the words 'orphans,' 'widows,' 'virgins,' 'pupils,' because they are very few. The true orphan, the true pauper, is the industrious peasant, the craftsman, the mariner, the merchant. These should be pitied, and they are those who, being accustomed to paying on leases and rents, will benefit from enhancement of the currency" (*ibid.,* p. 209.)

46. Galiani's subtle praise is more devastating than the virulent philippic of Ferrara. In the long run, people prefer security; they prefer it to the advantage obtained at the expense of others. Through monetary devaluation or through the invisible reduction of wages owing to the fixity of popular associations regarding the value of money and the prices of commodities, debtors obtained, as in a Hebrew jubilee, partial remission. Imaginary money was a splendid instrument invented during the infancy of European nations for performing certain tasks of public policy which today are performed by other methods. However, this instrument destroyed all certainty. Instead of a crude but certain monetary unit like the grain or gram of pure gold, it established an abstract unit which the public fancied to be stable. Princes could manipulate this monetary device for their own advantage, although they acted as if it were for the benefit of the public. When the instrument was misused, the drawbacks outweighed the advantages. The device of imaginary money was consequently discarded at the end of the eighteenth century and was replaced by a real monetary unit which was fixed beyond doubt to a weight of fine gold; thus the gram of gold became the standard of value. Under this principle people lived and throve for more than a

century. But with the coming of a universal monetary deluge (since World War I) the monetary universe entered into a period of fluidity in which the long-forgotten imaginary money made its reappearance, namely, in the writings of those who proposed what in effect amounted to a pallid imitation of the device of earlier days. What has been attempted in these pages is not the advocacy of its reintroduction. We only have tried to demonstrate that what certain modern authors advocate is a monetary device which, after having been perfected over the centuries, was abandoned in the period of the French Revolution.

15

The Origins of Banking: The Primitive Bank of Deposit, 1200–1600[*1]

By ABBOTT PAYSON USHER

I

The study of the origins and early history of banking raises a broad problem of definition. What is the simplest credit agency that can legitimately be called a bank? It is clearly important to draw some distinction between isolated credit transactions and organized banking. The lending of coined money, with or without interest, merely transfers purchasing power from one person to another. The mere acceptance of deposits of coined money involves no banking activity, even if the money is used in trade. In such a case, too, there is merely a transfer of purchasing

* *Economic History Review,* 1934, IV, 399–428. Reprinted by courtesy of the author and of the Economic History Society.

[1] The source materials from Barcelona upon which the present study is largely based were collected in 1929. Travelling expenses and the costs of more than two thousand photostats were covered by grants made by the Committee on the Milton Fund of Harvard University, and by the Committee of the Social Science Research Council on Grants in Aid. These original grants also covered the costs of clerical expenses involved in preparing translations of about one-third of the material. The Committee on Research in the Social Sciences has assisted, in the years 1932–3, and 1933–4, with grants to meet certain clerical expenses of work upon these materials and the published sources available for the study of banking in Italy. Careful study of these Italian and Catalan sources shows clearly that the Catalan material must be regarded as the controlling source for the period prior to 1500. The material at Barcelona is more abundant and more varied in character than for any single region in Italy. In Sicily, relatively few ordinances are available prior to 1500. At Venice, there are ordinances, but no accounts or business documents. The lack of accounts is serious. Printed inventories for Italy contain no indication of additional bank accounts prior to 1500, except at Genoa. These Genoese accounts seem to be the only known material, prior to 1500, not already utilized or published *in extenso.* The records at Barcelona contain a large number of ordinances, many registers of accounts for the critical period 1370–1450, and large masses of business documents. Additional material is available at Valencia. The Italian material becomes much more abundant after 1500, but new interests are involved. The development of the cheque and of the doctrine of negotiability dominates the period 1500–1700. Failure to recognize the extent of these changes has led to many errors in the interpretation of the earlier documents. The present paper is a preliminary statement of the general conclusions that have emerged from an intensive study of these materials. The work is now far advanced, but the preparation of the full text is a laborious task that will require no little time.

power. Banking begins only when loans are made in bank credit. This is possible only when deposits nominally payable in specie on demand can be used effectively by a system of book transfer and clearance. The banker can then use some of the deposits to make loans or engage in trade without depriving the depositors of the free use of their deposits. The deposits become a means of payment that is independent of specie to the extent that the transactions involved can be offset by book clearance without using specie. Deposits thus become bank money, and are consciously recognized as an independent means of payment as early as the fifteenth century. In Venice, an ordinance of 1421 uses the expression *contadi di banco,* in antithesis to *denari contadi.*[2] These phrases can be adequately rendered only as "bank money" and "cash." The phrase "payment in bank," or its equivalent, appears at least as early both in Barcelona and in Sicily. These expressions indicate a somewhat tardy recognition of the essential character of banking, and the effective practice of banking must be recognized as having been already long established.

Although the lending of credit is the essential function of the banker, it is not always possible to secure specific evidence as to the nature of loans in the early historical period, and for purposes of historical criticism it is best to use more objective tests. The lending of credit becomes an assured possibility as soon as a considerable number of current deposit accounts can be drawn together in one enterprise. We may therefore presume that banking begins when we are able to find separate accounting units handling some appreciable number of current accounts. Even if the proprietors of the business are engaged in other affairs, we are entitled to speak of a bank if a separate set of books is kept for the banking business.

In studying the twelfth and thirteenth centuries, practical historical problems require us to distinguish banking from dealings in domestic and foreign coin or from the casual credit transactions that would necessarily appear in any mercantile business. Money-changing involved no use of credit in any form, and though some of the money-changers became bankers, the enlargement of function was usually recognized by some distinguishing qualification. In Catalonia, the bankers were called bonded money-changers, or public money-changers. Dealers in coin were called petty money-changers. In many parts of Italy the term "banker" appears at an early date, but, unfortunately, without assured accuracy

[2] E. Lattes, *La libertà delle banche a Venezia dal secolo XIII al XVII* (Milano, 1869), p. 47.

in usage. These terms are, thus, a peculiarly unsatisfactory basis for the establishment of the beginnings of banking. Whenever it can be established that these money-changers or bankers are actually holding deposits on current account we may safely presume that the characteristic banking functions are being exercised.

Merchants were inevitably engaged in various credit transactions. Many of them were involved in various partnerships for particular ventures or for the activities of a continuing enterprise. If the funds were furnished by a silent partner, they were, in a sense, deposited with the active partner for use in trade. Such deposits were not sharply distinguished in contemporary law from the deposits held by bankers on current account, but it is obvious that a distinction must be drawn for purposes of any functional analysis. Then, too, the merchant might purchase or sell foreign exchange, or loans might be granted to various parties. A few isolated credit transactions would hardly justify the inclusion of such a merchant in the list of bankers. If, however, there were many transactions, and separate accounts were kept of these banking activities, we must recognize the emergence of a bank. In such enterprises the independence of the accounting unit is the more significant of the two criteria.

All early banks were banks of deposit, similar in essential functions to any modern bank of deposit, but, for two centuries at least, many features of banking business assumed special forms because these early banks made no use of cheques and found no negotiable commercial paper available as a means of placing their loans. They may be characterized as a primitive type of the bank of deposit. Almost every basic feature of their operation presents itself in a form unfamiliar to us, by reason of these important differences in the legal and administrative details of handling their credit. The whole credit structure was jeopardized by the absence of a satisfactory type of short-time paper. The banks were forced to engage directly in trade, and disastrous losses in Italy in the sixteenth century led to a demand for regulation which resulted in some undesirable curtailment of the credit activities of the banks.

II

Banks of deposit do not appear in mediæval Europe, even in their primitive form, until the close of the twelfth century or the beginning of the thirteenth.[3] Precise dates vary somewhat in different regions, and

[3] Cf. Pietro Rota, *Storia delle banche* (Milano, 1874). Aurelio Martin Alonso y Agustin Blasco Cirera, *La banca a travès de los tiempos* (Barcelona, 1926). These useful

documentary material is so capriciously preserved that it is not wise to place much reliance upon any single piece of evidence. It was not a new form of economic activity, in any strict sense, because it is fairly clear that there were some deposit banks in Rome from the late years of the Republic. Banks were also to be found in the Near East both before and after the rise of Mohammed.[4] The legal basis of early banking was thus fully developed in Roman law of the period of the jurists, and these doctrines were not significantly modified until the concept of an implied contract appeared in the opinions on commercial law given by the Post glossators in the fourteenth century. The development of banking in the Middle Ages was, thus, a revival of an older institution rather than a new beginning. It is not impossible that some kind of contact may be established between banking in Imperial Rome and mediæval banking, but there is nothing in evidence now available to indicate any direct continuity in practice. Some have believed that the Jews played an active and important part in the maintenance of banking throughout the early Christian period, but recent studies indicate that the development of banking among the Jews began at a relatively late date.[5] It is not impossible that Syrian merchants coming to Europe from the Near East exercised some banking functions, but, on the whole, the presumption is against any specific continuity in the practice of deposit banking.

The legal principles upon which deposit banking was based never lost their validity, for the elementary principles were definitely embodied in all the shorter codes of Roman law that were drawn up during the period of the migrations. The revival of the study of the full text of the Digest in the twelfth century was not a necessary prelude to the revival of banking. There was no period in which it would not have been law-

---

general books are untrustworthy in many details, most especially in the critical period of the fourteenth, fifteenth, and sixteenth centuries. The chapters contributed by Pierre des Essars to the *History of Banking in all Nations,* Vol. III (New York, 1896) are unreliable.

[4] W. L. Westermann, "Warehousing and Trapezite Banking in Antiquity," *Jour. Econ. and Bus. Hist.,* 1930, III, 30–54. Rudolph Herzog, *Aus der Geschichte des Bankwesens im Alterthum* (Giessen, 1919). L. Mitteis, "Trapezita," *Zeitschrift der Savigny Stiftung,* XIX, 198–259. Georges Platon, "Les banquiers dans le legislation de Justinien," *Nouvelle Revue de Droit Français et Étranger,* 1909, XXXIII, 5, 137, 289, 434. Friedrich Preisigke, "Zur Buchführung der Banken," *Archiv für Papyrusforschung,* 1907, IV, 95. G. Petra, "La tavolette cerate di Pompeii Rinvenuti ai 3 e 5 Juglio 1875," *Atti della R. Accademia dei Lincei (Roma),* Ser. 2, 1875–76, III, 155. C. Freundt, *Wertpapiere im antiken und frühmittelalterlichen Rechte* (Leipzig, 1910).

[5] Moses Hoffman, *Der Geldhandel der deutschen Juden während des Mittelalters* (Leipzig, 1910). Staats- und Sozialwissenschaftlichen Forschungen, G. Schmoller und Max Sering, No. 152. Ignaz Schipper, "Anfänge des Kapitalismus bei den abendländischen Juden im frühen Mittelalter," *Zeitschrift für Volkswirtschaft, Sozialpolitik und Verwaltung,* XV, 501–64.

ful for a money-changer to accept a deposit of funds which he might employ in trade or lend to others, subject only to the obligation to repay the depositor on demand in coin of equivalent value. As there can be little doubt of the continuance of dealing in domestic and foreign coin, it is eminently possible that deposits were occasionally received, but this practice would not warrant the assumption that there was a sufficient volume of funds on deposit in current accounts to make credit creation possible.

There is a phase of credit development that immediately precedes the emergence of true banking. This stage is characterized by the occurrence of individual transactions in credit at such infrequent intervals that no significant development of clearance is possible. The general character of these activities appears clearly in the Low Countries in the late thirteenth century. In the last quarter of the century the Italian merchants were allowed by the authorities to establish "loan offices" (*tables de prêt*) in specified towns. The earliest dated grant is of 1280, but there is no reason to suppose that this grant for the town of Hulst was in fact the first. In the next two decades the institution was rapidly generalized.[6] In the larger towns more than one loan office might be authorized, but for the most part the privilege was held to confer some exclusive rights. Deposits were accepted, loans were made, and some of the funds were at times used in trade by the merchant-banker. Many, but not all, of the loans were pawnbroker's loans on goods. Offices of this general type continued in this region until after 1450. In the course of this period some of them doubtless came to exercise banking functions, but the volume of their business at the close of the thirteenth century must be taken into consideration. There are documents giving records of the loans made at Tournai for the years 1260–1289, though the records for many years seem to be incomplete. For 1272 and 1273, however, the returns appear to be fully representative. There were 20 transactions in 1272 amounting in all to £1,384 11*s.* 6*d.* (Paris). The records for Nivelles in 1362 show 99 transactions, but the average for the years 1356 to 1388 is only 40.[7] Even if some allowance is made for omissions, it is evident that these loan offices did not regularly carry current accounts, and that the actual number of credit transactions was so small that these activities must be recognized as incidental and discontinuous.

[6] Georges Bigwood, *Le régime juridique et économique du commerce de l'argent dans la Belgique du moyen âge,* Vol. I, pp. 319–79. Académie Royale de Belgique, Classe des Lettres et des Sciences Morales et Politiques, *Memoires,* Ser. 2, Vol. XIV (Bruxelles, 1921).

[7] Bigwood, *op. cit.,* Vol. I, p. 368; Vol. II, pp. 103–261.

The earliest positive evidence of the holding of current accounts by these loan offices is for the years 1390, 1410, and 1418, when the office at Namur acted as fiscal agent for the town in collecting certain forced loans.[8] Even in this instance the banking activity seems to be distinctly less developed than it was in the Mediterranean countries at a much earlier date. But it is not necessary to attempt to fix any positive date for the development of the use of the current account in Belgium. For the moment, our chief concern is to show the importance of making a distinction between organized deposit banking and the mere making of loans and the acceptance of casual deposits.

In Latin and in the vulgar tongues, there are terms that must be literally translated as *money-changer* and *banker.* In some parts of Italy a real distinction ultimately develops between these terms, and we find in fact that the money-changer is indeed a dealer in domestic and foreign coin, whereas the banker holds deposits and lends credit. But these terms are by no means a safe guide in tracing the early history of banking. In Florence, in Catalonia, and in France the term *money-changer* was frequently, if not generally, applied to the private bankers. In parts of Italy, the terms *money-changer* and *banker* were used indiscriminately, at least as late as the fourteenth century.[9]

The references to bankers in the notarial documents of Genoa possess some special significance, however, because these documents throw light on various supplementary activities of these bankers. The printed extracts from the earliest of the notarial note-books, covering the years 1155 to 1164, contain references to thirteen bankers.[10] In some instances, the references appear only in the lists of witnesses to contracts, but in several instances the bankers are parties to contracts of partnership for trade. It would seem likely, therefore, that they were banker-merchants, accepting deposits which they utilized directly in trade. But even though it is evident that these bankers had extended their activities beyond dealings in domestic and foreign coin, there is no basis for an inference that they held current accounts on any appreciable scale. Unless we go beyond the documents, they must thus be classed with the

[8] *Ibid.,* Vol. I, p. 434.

[9] Saverio La Sorsa, *L'organizzazione dei cambiatori fiorentini nel medio evo* (Cerignola, 1904), p. 133, Statutes of 1299, Art. 78. Alessandro Lattes, *Il diritto commerciale nella legislazione statutaria delle città italiane* (Milano, 1884), pp. 198–99. Vito Cusumano, *Storia dei banchi delle Sicilia,* Vol. I (Roma, 1887), pp. 44 ff., 71 ff.

[10] *Historiae Patriae Monumenta,* Vol. VI; chartae, II (Torino, 1853), pp. 293–989. The names are: Alberton, Amicus, Baldo Baldus, Donaldeus, Gilbertus, Ingo Ingone, Hugo, Martinus, Museus, Nubelotus Nubeletus, Poncius, Raimundus, Sorleon. The references appear in the index under these names under the word Januensis.

Belgian money-lenders, some of whom were likewise engaged in trade, and who were certainly accepting deposits. At Siena, there are references in 1156 to bankers who accept deposits, but without more details we cannot accept these references as evidence of the emergence of deposit banking.[11]

The financial activities of the Templars in England and in France disclose more explicitly the development of the current account in the later years of the twelfth century. Henry II of England deposited funds with the Temple in 1182 and 1188 for use in the Crusade, and Philip Augustus deposited funds with the Templars and with the Knights of St. John. An account of 1202 shows that the Templars held the general receipts of the French Crown and were acting generally as the disbursing agency on royal account.[12] It seems evident that these activities continued, and that the scope of the banking business of the establishments of the Temple in France increased steadily. By 1250 accounts were held for Blanche of Castile and for various peers. The itemized records of some of these accounts which have survived show overdrafts, so that we must assume that the Templars were definitely financing the larger expenditures of the Crown and some of the Peers.[13] In the second half of the twelfth century the King of Aragon and several of the Catalan nobility were given loans by the Prior in Catalonia upon the security of stated revenues. There is no evidence that the Templars held current accounts for the King.[14] By 1212, the Templars at Paris were assisting in the collection and remittance of papal revenues. There is no specific evidence that these activities were continuously maintained thereafter, but the enlarged scope of financial activity on the part of the Temple is indicative of a development of new facilities.

For Italy, too, there is unmistakable evidence of the use of current accounts in the early years of the thirteenth century. We have two sheets from the ledger of a Florentine banker for the year 1211.[15] These sheets were used as guards in the binding of a codex of the Digest, and although they were somewhat damaged on some of the edges and badly

[11] Q. Senigaglia, *Le compagnie bancarie Senesi nei secoli XIII e XIV,* in Studi Senesi (1907–8), Vols. XXIV, XXV; Vol. XXV, p. 24.

[12] L. Delisle, *Mémoire sur les opérations financières des Templiers,* pp. 27, 40. *Mémoires de l'Institut National de France, Académie des Inscriptions et Belles Lettres,* Vol. XXXIII (Paris, 1889), Pt. 2.

[13] Delisle, *op. cit.,* pp. 32–33, 99.

[14] Joachim Miret y Sans, *Les Cases de Templers y Hospitallers en Catalunya* (Barcelona, 1910), pp. 107–9.

[15] P. Santini, "Frammenti di un libro di banchieri fiorentini," *Giornali Storico della Letteratura Italiana,* 1887, X, 161–96.

worn in places, it has been possible to recover nearly the whole of the text. The entries are in Italian. They are one of the earliest extant documents in the Florentine dialect, and the interest of the editor was primarily philological. The sheets were used on both sides, and the entries were made in two columns, but this division was merely a matter of convenience. Debtor and creditor items are not carefully separated. The amounts are not drawn off in the margins, nor are any balances given at the end of each account. The book thus represents the basic elements of the ledger, in as far as it is a statement of the accounts of particular individuals or partners with the banker. But it represents a transitional stage in the development of double entry bookkeeping, because the accounts are never presented in the form of an equation or balanced statement. There are references to other books, but only in such vague terms as "the old register" (*libro uekio*) or the "new memorandum" (*quaderno nuovo*). It is difficult to identify the journal under either of these terms.

This prototype of the bank ledger shows conclusively, however, that the use of the current account was definitely established. The accounts cover parts of May and June, 1211. In some instances the entries relate to the last two weeks in June; a few items relate to transactions in May. Even with so small a fragment it is clear that there was much greater activity than in the loan offices in Belgium. The transactions, too, are specifically banking transactions: loans for a few months or for a year, on personal security; transfers of funds in bank; receipts and payments of specie. Some of the items are not dated, so that it is not possible to balance any of the accounts. It would seem, however, that some of them were definitely overdrawn.

III

The materials described above indicate clearly that banking functions were exercised by more than one kind of enterprise, even in the beginning. The Templars were active until the suppression of the order in 1312. Some of their activities in France were taken over by the Knights of St. John, but there is little to indicate that the order was an important factor in international finance in the fourteenth century. The great Italian trading companies became conspicuously important in the course of the thirteenth century, but early references to them are not very explicit in respect of their banking activities. It is significant, however, that loans made by Italians to German ecclesiastics were repaid at the Fairs of Champagne as early as 1213. By 1233, Sienese bankers were acting as fiscal agents for the Pope and a body of special privileges was rapidly built up. The bankers were authorized to lend to ecclesiastics such sums as might be necessary to meet the donations and grants customary at the time of induction into the various ecclesiastical offices and dignities.[16] Closely associated with this class of business was the general trade of northern France and Flanders centring in the fair systems of Champagne and Flanders. The Italian companies played an important part in the business of these fairs, finance as well as general trade. Their services as agencies for the remittance of funds were deeply involved in the fair trade and seem to have furnished some means for the establishment of a primitive form of interregional clearance.[17]

The fairs also attracted a class of Italians and Jews who acted as money-changers and bankers. They constitute a special type, closely similar to the resident money-changers and bankers, but they possessed a number of special functions closely associated with the fairs. In the twelfth century, their activities were largely confined to dealings in domestic and foreign coin. Then two new functions appear. Descriptions of the fairs in the early thirteenth century show that many of the transactions were cleared by book transfers. When a merchant made purchases which he was not at the moment able to cover in specie, he took his creditor to a money-changer and promised payment through the money-changer at the close of the fair. It was assumed that the merchant would then be in funds through the sale of goods. In so far as payment through the bankers took the place of specie, some proportion of the total transactions were doubtless settled by clearance. This type of transaction was not uncommon in general commercial practice, but the effect was not the same. At the fairs there was no positive obligation to pay until the end of the fair. The promise to pay through the banker, thus, did not involve any loan on the part of the banker. The banker merely guaranteed payment. The effect was about equivalent to the endorsement of a modern promissory note.

This business, however, carried the bankers towards true credit activities. In some instances merchants found that their commitments for the close of the fair exceeded the receipts from the sale of goods. In this event they found themselves facing legal action for default, unless

[16] Aloys Schulte, *Geschichte des mittelalterlichen Handels und Verkehrs zwischen Westdeutschland und Italien mit Ausschluss von Venedig,* Vol. I (Leipzig, 1900), pp. 231–35. Senigaglia, *op. cit.,* Studi Senesi, Vol. XXIV, pp. 163–64.

[17] F. Bourquelot, *Études sur les foires de Champagne et de Brie,* Vol. II, p. 103. *Mémoires de l'Académie des Inscriptions et de Belles Lettres* (Paris, 1865). The use of the fairs as a term of payment can be traced continuously from 1159. The loans and remittances of the great trading houses were built up on this practice in the course of the following century.

they could borrow funds to meet their immediate requirements. Loans repayable at the next fair appear in the records at the Champagne fairs as early as 1218, though the practice was not definitely established until the close of the century. The loan for the interval between fairs became a characteristic feature of commercial life that persisted in some centres, such as Lyons, until late in the eighteenth century. This highly important type of short-time loan constituted the chief form of loan on the part of fair bankers. In the early period it was based on the letter of the fair, or perhaps even on a book entry. In the fifteenth and sixteenth centuries such loans were made on bills of exchange, drawn in favour of the lender.[18]

Finally, there were the sedentary money-changers and bankers who had an office only in one town. In some localities this type of banker appears as early as any of the others, but they became more important in the fourteenth and fifteenth centuries. After the failures of the great Italian trading companies in the fourteenth century, the sedentary bankers became the dominant factor in banking in Italy, Spain, and France. Conditions in Central Europe were different. The rise of the great Austrian banking houses in the fifteenth century certainly reduced the small local bankers to a distinctly secondary rôle, but we do not hear enough about them to give us any precise notion of their significance in that region. Offices for dealings in domestic and foreign coin were established at Augsburg, Lübeck, Hamburg, Aachen, Dortmund, Erfurt, Nürnberg, Frankfort-am-M., and Strassburg.[19] One would infer, therefore, that

[18] Bourquelot, *op. cit.*, Vol. II, pp. 118–46. P. Huvelin, *Essai historique sur le droit des marchés et des foires* (Paris, 1897), pp. 544–69.

[19] A. Lattes, *op. cit.*, pp. 217–19; Cusumano, *op. cit., passim.* E. Lattes, *op. cit.*

References in Spanish ordinances apply primarily to sedentary bankers and money-changers: A. Diaz de Montalvo, *Ordenanzas reales de Castilla,* Lib. V, Tit. VIII, L. 1 (1445, 1455), in *Codigos Españoles,* Vol. VI, p. 410. *Novissima, Recopilacion,* Lib. IX, Tit. III, L. 1 (1435, 1436, 1455); *loc. cit.*, L. 2 (25 Julio, 1499). *Codigos Españoles,* Vol. IX, p. 183; *ibid.*, Lib. XI, Tit. XXXII, L. 1 (1548); *loc. cit.*, L. 7 (18 Julio, 1590). Cristobal Espejo y Julian Paz, *Las antiguas ferias de Medina del Campo* (Vallodolid, 1912), pp. 71–128.

For France, see Marcel Vigne, *La banque à Lyon* (Paris, 1903), pp. 50–52. Paris, Archives Nationales, KK, 5, *Livre des changeurs du Trésor, 1335–1343;* KK, 15, *Livre des changeurs du Trésor, 1397–1405,* Z 1*b*, 286–90, *Registres des changeurs du Royaume, 1456–1601;* AD, XI, 1, *Agents de change et banquiers, 1572–1789.* These materials were hurriedly examined in 1927 and 1929. They indicate roughly the general character of the development of private banking in France, but without the letters and accounts of banking firms the study could not be carried very far.

For Germany, R. Ehrenberg, *Das Zeitalter der Fugger,* Vol. I (Jena, 1896 [1922]), pp. 85–90, 186–97. See also the later literature on the Fuggers by Max Jansen, Jacob Strieder, and A. Schulte. J. Kulischer, "Warenhandler und Geldausleiher im Mittelalter," *Zeitschrift für Volkswirtschaft, Sozialpolitik und Verwaltung,* 1908, XVII, 202–4, 217–19. Paul Jacob Marperger, *Beschreibung der Banken* (Wien, 1717).

private money-changers were not very active. As in other regions, the functions of these offices were extended by the acceptance of deposits and, in some instances, deposit banks may have developed.

Public banks of deposit were established at Barcelona in 1401, and at Valencia in 1407. These institutions did not displace the private banks, but as they served as fiscal agents for the towns and provinces they restricted in some measure the scope of the activities of the private bankers. Some writers have classified these public banks as "giro" banks, assuming them to be similar in function to the banks established at Venice in 1584, 1587, and 1619, and to the Bank of Amsterdam of 1609. The banks at Barcelona and Valencia were, however, true banks of deposit, identical in all their general features with the private banks of deposit in Catalonia,[20] Spain, Italy, and France. As they were administered conservatively they exhibit the primary features of the primitive bank of deposit even more clearly than the private banks. At Barcelona, the Bank of Deposit retained its original form until 1609, though both the private and public banks in Italy introduced new features in the sixteenth century, which created some circulating credit. The Bank of Saint George at Genoa exercised banking functions during the years 1407 to 1445, and again after 1586, but these activities of the Bank have not been extensively studied, despite the abundance of material.[21]

Deposit banking developed rapidly in all the more important commercial centres of Europe in the course of the thirteenth century. The wide extent of this development was, undoubtedly, fostered by the influence of the Templars and the Italian merchants following the fairs. The relative uniformity of practice was also fostered at this time, and later by the influence of Roman Law upon the commercial law. Although the amount of material varies considerably in different regions, there is no reason to doubt the actual existence of important banking activities throughout the greater part of Europe. The dearth of material in France for the fourteenth and fifteenth centuries is especially unfortunate.

The early history of banking is in all regions dominated by a highly characteristic form of deposit bank, which differs in a number of particulars from the practice of the modern bank of deposit as well as from

---

[20] Abbott Payson Usher, "Deposit Banking in Barcelona," *Jour. Econ. and Bus. Hist.*, 1931, IV, 121–55.

[21] H. Sieveking, *Genueser Finanzwesen vom 12 bis 14 Jahrhundert,* Vol. II (Freiburg, 1898), pp. 1–75 in Volkswirtschaftliche Abhandlungen der Badischen Hochschule, Vol. I, 3e Heft. E. Marengo, C. Manfroni, and G. Pessango, *Il banco di San Giorgio* (Genova, 1911), pp. 193–217.

the modern bank of deposit and issue. Full analysis of the functions of the primitive bank of deposit requires more material than is available in many of the localities where we know banking was carried on, but a general description of the primitive bank of deposit can be given if careful use is made of the large masses of material available in Florence, Venice, Sicily, Naples, and Barcelona.

Important material is available in some other places, notably at Genoa and Valencia, and the resources of Florence, Venice, and Barcelona have not been exhausted, but material now at hand is sufficient to establish the primary features of the primitive bank of deposit. Local variations from the general type are not of great significance for the fourteenth and fifteenth centuries.

IV

The distinctive features of the primitive bank of deposit were largely derived from the predominant use of the verbal contract.[22] Written contracts were valid, but until the sixteenth century the use of the the written contract was restricted and it was regarded as a means of dealing with a number of situations that could not readily be provided for by the usual verbal contracts. In order to facilitate the establishment of the content and authenticity of contracts, the notarial system of Rome was developed and extended. The verbal contracts of mediæval commerce were thus made before a notary and witnesses. The transaction was recorded in the register of the notary and became a matter of public record. The record was accepted as competent evidence of the content of the contract, unless it could be shown that the record was incorrect. The most effective defence against the record was the establishment of an alibi. If the party alleged to have made the contract could prove that he was not in town on the day stated, the record would be overthrown,

---

[22] The critical establishment of the views presented rests primarily upon the interpretation of a number of technical terms. Some of these terms acquire new meanings in the sixteenth and seventeenth centuries, others have misleading connotations to the modern student. The wide differences of opinion about early banks have been due to the different readings given these terms. The present study is based upon a glossary of Catalan terms constructed upon rigidly historical principles. The interpretation of each term has been determined by dated passages in which the context affords an absolutely unambiguous clue to the meaning. The more difficult terms have been discussed with Prof. J. M. D. Ford, and with Jacme Llorens, a native Catalan, now studying economics at Harvard. The interpretation of Italian terms is based upon the glossary of mediaeval Italian business terms which is being prepared by Miss Florence Edler for the Mediaeval Academy of America. Problems of translation are merely incidental, for the terms used in the documents themselves must needs be rendered into modern Spanish, Catalan, or Italian. The Catalan glossary will be published with the completed text. Miss Edler's glossary will appear shortly.

because the contract required the presence of both parties to make the formal statement of the contract and to accept the contract.[23] Great pains were taken to make the notarial registers absolutely trustworthy, but, like the records of our modern registries of deeds, they were merely evidences of the actual contract.

The Journals of the early banks were given the legal status of a notarial register. Private bankers were required to swear that their Journals were a faithful record of all the transactions of the bank.[24] At Barcelona, the Journals of the Bank of Deposit were kept by notaries and thus were merely a special notarial record. The entries in the Journal were required to be made without intervening blank spaces, no erasures or cancellations might be made unless duly described in the margin, and no leaves might be torn out. These rules have left traces in modern commercial law, but the background has changed. In the Middle Ages, the Journal contained the only legally valid written record of most of the contracts between the bank and its customers. It was much more than an account book, and for this reason it was considered essential that the Journal entry should contain a full statement of the details of the transaction. The private bankers were at times lax, and in Italy there was a strong disposition to reduce the entry to the simplest possible form, but the basic facts must needs be stated. The Journal entry of a bank differed from the ordinary notarial record in the omission of all record of witnesses. The Florentine ledger of 1211, however, preserved a record of witnesses for certain types of transactions. This is the most impressive single indication of the extremely primitive character of that bank register. Because the Journal was a legal record in which cancellations could not lightly be made, it was not a book of original entry. In the Bank of Deposit at Barcelona, the account in the Ledger was ordinarily checked if any funds were to be transferred, or if any loan were to be made. If a private bank were large enough to have separate bookkeepers for the two books, the Journal entry would be made only after an appropriate memorandum had been received from the keeper of the Ledger.

These legal attributes of the Journal tended to simplify the details of paper work at the bank. It was not necessary to require separate promis-

---

[23] Freundt, *Wertpapiere,* Vol. I, p. 69. Justinian, *Institutes,* III, xix, 12.

[24] A. Lattes, *op. cit.,* p. 205. Covers specifically Genoa, Piacenza, Milan, Bologna, and Venice. Cusumano, *op. cit.,* Vol. I, p. 131. *Constitutions y altres drets de Cathalunys, compilats en virtud del cap de las corts . . . celebrados en la vila de Montso, 1585* (Barcelona, 1587; hereafter cited, *Constitutions de Cathalunya*). James II at the Cortes at Barcelona, 1299, c. vi, p. 384.

sory notes from customers who were granted a loan, because the Journal entry was itself competent legal evidence of the contract. It was not necessary to provide the customer with a pass-book or with any certificate of deposit, because the Journal was a public register of contracts that was open to the inspection of the customer. It soon came to be regarded as a breach of confidence to allow other persons to inspect the account of a customer of the bank, but in the early period it is fairly certain that the information in the Journal could not be kept confidential.

All bankers kept a ledger or some book that was a prototype of the ledger. The fragments of the accounts of the Templars at Paris and some of the records of Père des Caus and Andreu d'Olivella in Barcelona suggest that the early bankers were likely to keep a large number of separate records. The defect of their bookkeeping consisted in having too many records of particular accounts and no general analysis of the business as a whole. There is not enough material now extant to make it possible to establish the details of development during the thirteenth and fourteenth centuries. Cash accounts or separate accounts of receipts and expenditures appeared at an early date.[25] Balances and analyses of the enterprise as a whole, if made at all, were commonly separate documents and few have survived. There were considerable differences in the practices of the various regions in all these respects. At Barcelona, there is no evidence that there was any general analysis of the affairs of the bank, until late in the sixteenth or early seventeenth century. Italian practice may have been better, but the descriptions in the texts afford no basis for any positive statement. The officials of the Bank of Deposit at Barcelona were obliged to balance the accounts every two years, when new Administrators took office, but the extant record of such an audit for the year 1433 shows that it was no more than a general check on the accuracy of the arithmetic.[26] We have all the elements from which a

---

[25] Barcelona, Archivo del Real Patrimonio (hereafter ARP), 2380. Libre de Père des Caus e d'en Andreu d'Olivella . . . datas e rebudes. Cusumano, *op. cit.,* Vol. I, p. 129. E. Bensa, *Francesco di Marco da Prato* (Milano, 1928), pp. 194–208, 448–66. Marengo, Manfroni, Pessango, *op. cit.,* p. 198.

[26] Archivo Historico Municipal de Barcelona (hereafter AMB), Llevament fet per en Marti Gariera, 1433. There is no formal provision in the ordinances for any audit of the books of the Bank of Deposit earlier than 1513, but examinations of the bank were made twice each year after 1476. AMB, Reg. d'Ordinacions, 1510–18, f. 67*v; ibid.,* 1471–79, f. 111.

The fragments of accounts studied by Cusumano are largely of the sixteenth century. The accounts of private banks available at Genoa have not been studied with reference to these aspects of accounting, though the brief notes of Marengo, Manfroni, and Pessango imply that there was some general analysis at an early date.

balance sheet can be constructed, but the officers did not themselves draw up any comprehensive statement of the affairs. The private bankers may have made some audit when they started a new ledger, but there is abundant ground for doubt. For the most part, they merely copied off the individual balances of the open accounts. It is hardly surprising that there were many failures. The average banker had no exact summary statement of his commitments. We must assume that banking policy consisted chiefly in keeping some actual cash in hand, extending loans to promising customers, and making some investments in trade.

Deposits fell into two classes: general deposits and conditioned deposits. The general deposits were demand obligations on current account comparable in all respects to the deposit in a modern bank. The depositors fell into three general classes: individuals and corporations owning real property, or holders of funded debts; public bodies who carried current accounts covering all, or at least a part, of their general receipts and expenses; lastly, the business men and merchants. The deposit accounts of these early banks thus exhibit the diversities of expenditure and interest characteristic of the modern community. Public authorities and merchants carried active accounts, and were usually applicants for loans. The holders of the less active accounts were the landed gentry, widows, orphans, and ecclesiastical corporations. Their revenues were paid into the banks and drawn down gradually for personal expenditure. This group was the great resource of the state for loans, though the mercantile community must not be excluded. Long-time loans were common throughout Europe on the basis of the sale of a rent. The legal concept was readily assimilated to feudal law, and because it was in essence a sale of property there could be no infraction of the usury laws. As these rent charges could be redeemed at pleasure in most jurisdictions after the early thirteenth century, they were, in effect, mortgage bonds without a fixed date for redemption. These instruments present special features in many regions, wherever the revenues were collected directly by the mortgagee. In Spain and in France the rent charges were scarcely distinguishable from a modern mortgage bond. A fixed income was paid the mortgagee during the life of the bond. The property remained under the control of the owner, and in the case of pledges on revenues of state the state collected its revenues at its discretion.

In Barcelona, all borrowing by the city or province took the form of the sale of incomes guaranteed by pledges of specific revenues. Non-negotiable documents were issued, and in nearly all instances, after 1401, the Bank of Deposit acted as the fiscal agent of the city in selling or redeeming these securities, and paying the semi-annual interest charges. At Genoa, the loans were handled in a somewhat more primitive fashion, as the syndicates who lent the money assumed direct charge of the collection of revenue. Venetian practice was varied. Forced loans were levied on many occasions in the fifteenth and sixteenth centuries. At times, banking privileges were associated with these loans.[27]

Conditional deposits were a characteristic feature of the primitive bank of deposit. In their simplest form they consisted of actual deposits of specie to be paid to a designated party at a fixed date or after the performance of some definite act.[28] Funds to be paid on the transfer of property, sums to be paid over on dowries or marriage settlements, sums due in settlement of judgments in the courts, the price of merchandise to be delivered at a later date, might all give rise to conditioned deposits. The payor placed the funds in the hands of the banker with an explicit undertaking that they would be transferred to the payee when the conditions of their agreement had been fulfilled. Such funds did not constitute a part of the ordinary current account of either party. The payor was obviously barred from diverting such funds to other uses, and the payee could not use them because they did not become his property until the final transfer was made. In their primitive form conditioned deposits did not lead to any use of credit, but small changes made them useful in an important type of credit transaction. The banker might allow a customer to overdraw his demand account in the ledger on the security afforded by a credit due from a third party in the record of conditioned deposits, or against an engagement of the borrower to repay the banker at a stated time. This operation would have the same effect as the discounting of a negotiable bill of exchange or promissory note, although different in form. There is evidence of such transactions in the audit of the books of the Bank of Deposit at Barcelona in 1433, and in the Journals of Père des Caus and Andreu d'Olivella. Such transactions

[27] H. Sieveking, *Genueser Finanzwesen mit besonderer Berücksichtigung der Casa San Giorgio* (Freiburg, 1898). *I Prestiti della Repubblica di Venezia* (Padova, 1929) in R. Accademia dei Lincei, Documenti Finanziari della Repubblica di Venezia, Ser. 3, Vol. I, Pt. I. E. Lattes, *op. cit.,* pp. 41–44.

[28] ARP, 2375. Manual de Père des Caus e Andreu d'Olivella, ff. 1–30*v, passim.* AMB, Libre Major de la Taula de Cambi, 1403–1404. AMB, Reg. d'Ordinacions, 1519–1530, October 27, 1527, f. 175. AMB, Llevament . . . 1433, ff. 31–48*v,* 53*v.* Cusumano, *op. cit.,* Vol. I, p. 163. E. Lattes, *op. cit.,* ordinance of 1421, pp. 47–48. A. Lattes, *op. cit.,* p. 224, n. 53, covers Novara, Milan, Como, Genoa, Piacenza, Florence, and Ferrara.

continued to be a significant feature of banking until the doctrine of negotiability was fully established and simpler means of effecting the same end were available.[29]

The loans made by these early bankers commonly resembled the modern overdraft. The loan was created by transfers or withdrawals from the ledger account in excess of the credit. When the entries were in the ledger, we have no means of knowing what charges were imposed, but it is evident that no interest would be paid on any sums not actually used. The transaction differed from the modern overdraft by cheque, because each operation must needs have the consent of the banker.[30] Transfers from the current account of the primitive bank could regularly be made only in the presence of both parties, and, consequently, the client could not overdraw without the knowledge and consent of the banker, or the connivance of a clerk. The record in the Journal had sufficient legal status to make a formal promissory note superfluous, and the use of supplementary documents was confined to special cases involving the Crown, or loans to the City or Province.

The non-negotiable bill of exchange, which came into extensive use in the second half of the fourteenth century, was an important factor in the credit business of banks. A bill could not be discounted in the modern fashion, but exchange could be bought and sold. The essential objects of the modern transaction could be accomplished in various ways, though it is impossible to trace all these operations specifically in the accounts. We know, positively, that the proceeds of many loans made to the Crown by P. des Caus and A. d'Olivella were given the King in the

---

[29] AMB, Manual de la Taula, 1602. Balans del llibre de deposits, 1611–1612. See also material cited by A. Lattes; the statutes of the Italian towns remained in force, and in some instances the revisions of the statutes are of the sixteenth century.

[30] This discussion of the overdraft rests mainly upon study of the early Ledgers of the Bank of Deposit and the Llevament . . . of 1433. There are so many references to the ordinances that it is evident that the references cited below for 1435 and 1437 are characteristic of a continuous practice. AMB, Clavaria de la Ciutat . . . 1472, Oath of 1435, f. 5*v;* Reg. de Deliberacions, 1433–1437, November 19, 1437, f. 192. The Journals of P. des Caus and Andreu d'Olivella imply that their loans to the Crown were secured by formal notes and assignments of specific revenues, so that they were not overdrafts in the sense of a loan unsecured by any supplementary document. We can thus draw no inferences from the mere fact that there were debit balances in the accounts of the King of France and various French nobles with the Templars. Cusumano pays no attention to this problem in his study of the Sicilian material, though there must be conclusive evidence in the fragments of ledgers available. The Venetian ordinance of June 2, 1524, describes the practice explicitly (E. Lattes, *op. cit.,* p. 87), and Contarini (1584) clearly regards the practice as the most characteristic mode of lending (E. Lattes, *op. cit.,* p. 125). Although the evidence outside of Barcelona is less adequate than one would desire, the deficiency is due primarily to the inattention of the text writers and to the neglect of even the bank ledgers that survive. In this respect the Italian sources have been very inadequately utilized.

form of bills of exchange on Sicily. We know, too, that exchange could be purchased with bank credit. Bills might also serve, indirectly, as a basis for a loan. The characteristic transaction at the fairs was the loan of present purchasing power against a bill payable to the lender at a designated fair, either in the same town or elsewhere. A merchant could not, however, raise money directly on an accepted bill, but a banker could permit the merchant to overdraw his current account, with or without a supplementary engagement as to the details of repayment. Bills play a large part in mediæval and early modern credit operations, because at an early date the interest charges were admitted to be outside the prohibitions of canon law. The purchase and sale of currency of a different jurisdiction required no explicit recognition of interest as such, and most early bills merely state the amount of money given and the sum to be paid. In some regions, the rate of interest was openly stated, and inter-fair loans were definitely legitimated by civil statutes at an early date.

Although the bankers had several important avenues for commercial loans, they were closely associated with trade throughout the period.[31] In some instances, the mercantile interests were more important than their banking interests, and in nearly all regions bankers commonly had considerable sums invested in trade. These investments were the greatest single source of weakness to the banking houses of the early period.

The absence of cheques made inter-bank relations somewhat complex, but some contacts existed from an early date. Bankers kept accounts with each other. They could thus make some use of each other's facilities, though the authorities always distrusted such relationships.[32] In some instances, it amounted to an evasion of the banker's liability to meet the requirements of depositors on demand. It was not quite right to take the client around to other bankers to get the money. The Bank of Deposit at Barcelona feared lest the private bankers should deliberately attempt to use the reserves of the Bank of Deposit as a means of expanding their own activities. There were thus repeated prohibitions of

[31] AMB, Caja: documentos notariales y lettres de cambio, *passim*. AMB, unclassified sheets; articles of partnership for a bank, March 15, 1460. AMB, Reg. d'Ordinacions, 1433–45, fol. 63. A. Lattes, *op. cit.*, p. 208. Cusumano, *op. cit.*, Vol. I, pp. 137, 143–48.

[32] This direct use of accounts in other banks is frequently described by modern writers as if cheques were drawn. The Barcelona material is most explicit. ARP, 2375, Manual de P. des Caus e A. d'Olivella, *passim*. AMB, Libre Major de la Taula, 1403–4, *passim*. At Venice, in 1527, even when some use was being made of cheques, the ordinance reads, "when a person comes to demand his money, the bankers often take him to another bank and transfer credit to him in that bank." E. Lattes, *op. cit.*, p. 91.

the acceptance of the accounts of private bankers at the Bank of Deposit.

V

Commercial law exhibits a positive bias in favour of verbal contracts all through the fifteenth century, but exceptions were made. Some transactions in the banks were accompanied by written documents, and in some instances the written document soon became the controlling element in the transaction. The modern cheque grows out of this gradual development in the use of written orders drawn against current accounts. It is important to distinguish between the recognition of written orders in special cases and the frank acceptance of the cheque as a general means of effecting transfer or payments. The transition from a limited use of cheques to their general recognition occupied nearly a century and a half.

An exception to the rule, requiring the personal presence of the client, was frequently made by recognizing servants or messengers as agents of the client. Such a practice was not inconsistent with the concepts associated with the system of verbal contracts. Agency was recognized at an early date, and, although a formal power of attorney was required for many kinds of transactions, much business could be done by agents whose quality rested upon less rigorous proof. The Journals of Père des Caus and Andreu d'Olivella of Barcelona disclose withdrawals by servants or messengers in four instances in the period between July 20 and August 4, 1377. The sums involved were respectively: £60 10*s.* 0*d*; £3 6*s.* 0*d*; £72 0*s.* 0*d.*; £36 0*s.* 0*d.* In the same interval deposits were received by messenger in three instances; for sums as follows: £165 0*s.* 0*d.*; £643 10*s.* 0*d.*; £400 0*s.* 0*d.*[33] It is unfortunate that we have none of the papers that must have been used in such cases, as it would be interesting to know to what degree they possessed the external features of the modern cheque. It must be evident, however, that we cannot classify as a cheque an order which merely gave the bearer authority to act as agent for the client.

This problem of the legal significance of a written order or assignment is conspicuously involved in the documents printed by Bensa from the Datini archives at Prato. The papers of Francesco di Marco, an international merchant and banker of the late fourteenth century, include

[33] ARP, 2375. Manual de P. des Caus e A. d'Olivella, ff. 16, 18, 22, 23*v*, 26, 27*v*, 28*v*, 30*v*.

a considerable number of assignments on the current accounts held by the banker. In their general form, they present an extraordinary resemblance to the modern cheque, and Bensa has not hesitated to classify them as cheques. It must be recognized, however, that these documents precede by a wide interval any general use of a cheque by *private* persons. It is difficult to accept them as cheques when there is so large a body of material that indicates serious resistance to the acceptance of the concept in any form and especial resistance to any general use of such a device by private persons.[34] These documents, however, are not without special features that might easily justify their use as exceptions to the general rules in favour of verbal contracts. Three of the documents published were drawn upon the banking office by a client not at that time in town.[35] An instrument of this general character might well have been recognized as a kind of bill of exchange. The general features of the instrument correspond closely with the contemporary bills. The banking house did a considerable business with bills and might well have been willing to recognize an instrument of this general character. The other documents, drawn in favour of a party in town by a client in town, present a problem which cannot be solved without more material. In all probability these documents possessed no certain status in court. They imply a relationship that extended beyond mere agency, but we have no evidence that any court would have recognized these implications. These documents were thus prototypes of the modern cheque, rather than true cheques.

The private bankers at Venice, at the beginning of the fifteenth century, permitted non-residents to use cheques. "It has been the custom of the banks of deposit," runs the ordinance of 1421, "to make transfers for non-residents up to the amount of their deposits on the presentation of written orders, because they can only use their funds in the form of credits in the bank. . . ."[36] The privilege led to some abuses. Credits

---

[34] Bensa, *op. cit.*, pp. 164–66, 352–58.

[35] *Ibid.*, p. 352. See also Bigwood, *op. cit.*, Vol. I, pp. 648–49; Vol. II, p. 316, an isolated text of 1306.

[36] E. Lattes, *op. cit.*, p. 47. The interpretation given by E. Lattes cannot be sustained if the critical terms are read with the meanings established by other documents of the period. Important discussions of this ordinance are furnished by A. Lattes, *op. cit.*, p. 233, and by F. Ferrara, "Gli antichi banchi di Venezia," in *Nuova Antologia di Scienze,* Lettere ed Arte, Vol. XVI, p. 453. The translation given above follows these commentaries. Unfortunately the commentary accompanying the text has been uncritically copied, and some writers declare without qualification that the Venetian banks issued demand notes. This ordinance is the only passage upon which such a statement could be based. Cf. C. F. Dunbar, "The Bank of Venice," *Quart. Jour. Econ.*, 1892, VI, 316.

in the banks were being bought and sold at a discount, as compared with specie. Such purchases and sales were prohibited, and the prohibition was reiterated subsequently. Without some study of bank journals it is impossible to be certain of the nature of these transactions. It is clear, however, that the practices arose out of concessions made to non-residents, and the basic privilege seems to have continued in force.

Among residents, written instruments first came into use in the transaction of official business, but the practices of the public officials require some distinctions to be made. In some instances, the written instruments were merely orders and memoranda for accounting purposes. Even though they were required, they were not the legal authority for the payment made by the bank. In 1435, the Administrators of the Bank of Deposit were forbidden to transfer any funds on order of the City Treasurer unless he presented "a warrant from the Councillors addressed to the Administrators of the Bank and sealed with the seal of the City. In this warrant . . . there shall be given the name of the party in whose favour the Treasurer wishes to transfer funds, and the amount to be assigned and recorded in the books, in order that the Administrators may be required to file these warrants and that they may be produced when their accounts are examined."[37] It must be noted that the accounts of the City stood in the name of the Treasurer, so that his verbal order was no less necessary than this accompanying document. Such a document must thus be classified as an accounting memorandum, although it was in form an order on the Bank, which, without this text description, might erroneously be identified with a cheque.[38]

The accounts of the Province of Catalonia in the Bank of Deposit presented a different problem. When these deposits were first authorized in 1413, it was stipulated that no payments might be made from the account except upon presentation of a warrant signed by all three of the deputies who had charge of the affairs of the Province.[39] In such a case, we must regard the written order as the primary authority for the transfer. The account stood in the names of the three deputies. The order signed by all three was the only valid authority for transfer of funds. The person presenting the order was merely a messenger or agent of the Committee of three deputies. Later, when unanimous consent was no longer required, the Bank was allowed to recognize a warrant signed

---

[37] AMB, Clavaria, f. 7.

[38] Even in 1553 the Treasurer was required to transact business in person at the bank. AMB, Reg. d'Ordinacions, 1549–59, f. 101.

[39] *Llibre dels Quatre Senyals del General de Cathalunya* (Barcelona, 1634). Cort del any, 1413, c. 12, p. 22.

by a single deputy, if the payment had been duly voted by the commission.[40]

The City of Palermo, likewise, used written orders in handling City funds, from an early date in the fifteenth century. These orders were signed by the Prætor, the chief executive officer, or by one or more of the three deputies who assisted him.[41] Cusumano assumes that these documents had the status of cheques. Royal officials in various regions also used written documents, but no bank assignments are available for the fifteenth century.

The Sicilian documents of the late fifteenth century contain a formula which Cusumano assumes to refer to the cheque (*polissa*), but we have no clear references to the use of cheques until the early sixteenth century. There is evidence of general use of cheques prior to 1530, in Sicily, in Barcelona, and in Venice, and a strong presumption in favour of early use in Naples. In Sicily and Naples the practice developed continuously without interference from the authorities. In Venice, the use of cheques was absolutely prohibited, November 6, 1526. In Barcelona, the Bank of Deposit was allowed to recognize only the cheques drawn by the City Councillors, but the private bankers were allowed to recognize them.[42] The text of the ordinance in Barcelona states explicitly the objection to general acceptance of the cheque. "Inasmuch as experience has shown that there have been in the past many abuses by reason of the fact that many parties able to come in person to the said bank make transfers and entries in the bank by orders signed with their name directed to the keeper of the Journal which seems to lead to the discredit of the said bank: Therefore the Honourable Councillors and Syndics establish and ordain that henceforth the keeper of the Journal of the Bank of Deposit shall not be allowed to record any transfer by reason of any cheque or warrant drawn by any individual, unless such person . . . be present in person at the bank or be represented by his lawful attorney; excepting only in the case of some Councillor of the City, during the year of his Councillorship, who, by reason of the dignity of his office, ought not and is not permitted to come like other individuals to the bank."[43] Although provision was made for a

[40] AMB, Reg. de Deliberacions, 1596, f. 19, January 8, 1596.

[41] Cusumano, *op. cit.,* Vol. I, pp. 273–76. The earliest text cited is of 1443.

[42] Cusumano, *op. cit.,* Vol. I, pp. 233, 280–89. E. Lattes, *op. cit.,* p. 91. P. Ajello, *I depositi, la fade di credito e le polizi dei banchi di Napoli,* in Filangieri (1882), Vol. VII, pp. 646–47. AMB, Reg. d'Ordinacions, 1519–30, f. 179*v,* October 29, 1527. AMB, Reg. de Deliberacions, 1530, ff. 26*v*–27, July 11, 1530.

[43] AMB, Reg. d'Ordinacions, 1519–30, ff. 179*v*–180, October 29, 1527. Many written documents were, however, received from the Treasurer of the City, the Treasurer of

bank messenger to take statements of transfers at the homes of the clients of the bank, there were attempts to make use of cheques at the Bank of Deposit. Depositors, at times, gave a power of attorney to the keeper of the Journal or to some other officer of the Bank, but the authorities prohibited these practices in 1567. Finally, in 1609, a new public bank was established, which was authorized to accept cheques.[44]

VI

Banks of deposit retained some of their primitive characteristics, even after the cheque came into use, for some of the special features of their operations were due to the lack of negotiable paper. The investments of the bank were necessarily different in character from what they are to-day, and the details of many credit operations were affected. The development of the doctrine of negotiability was thus of critical importance to the history of banking. The emergence of true negotiable paper transformed deposit banking and made possible the bank of issue. Most of the present confusion in the treatment of the early history of banking is due to the failure of many writers to recognize the intimate relationship between the history of banking and the history of commercial paper. Although extensive use had been made of "order" clauses and "bearer" clauses in the remittance contracts of the Middle Ages, these clauses merely set up an agency which differed in vital respects from the full transfer of rights embodied in a mature concept of negotiability. In external form these early documents seem to resemble our modern commercial paper, but in actual legal properties they were profoundly different. They constitute only a preliminary step towards modern commercial paper.[45]

Upon the general introduction of the written contract in the thirteenth and fourteenth centuries a bill of exchange emerged which presented none of the superficial elements of resemblance to modern paper. This was due to the explicit inclusion in the new instrument of all the

---

Majorca, the Deputies of the province, and from attorneys. On various special days the bookkeepers were required to enter these transactions outside of banking hours. *Ibid.*, f. 176*v*.

[44] AMB, Reg. d'Ordinacions, 1519–30, f. 177, October 29, 1527. AMB, Ordinacions de la Taula, 1567, f. 3. AMB, Reg. d'Ordinacions, 1608–15, f. 38*v*, October 10, 1609.

[45] The present account is based on the later German writing: C. Freundt, *Das Wechselrecht der Postglossatoren,* 2 vols. (Leipzig, 1899, 1909). Georg Schaps, *Zur Geschichte des Wechselindossaments* (Stuttgart, 1892). Felix Hecht, *Ein Beitrag zur Geschichte der Inhaberpapiere in der Niederlanden* (Erlangen, 1869). These works supplant the older German writing to such an extent that references to the extensive earlier literature would serve no useful purpose. A fairly adequate account of these matters is furnished by W. S. Holdsworth, *A History of English Law,* Vol. VIII (London, 1922–26), pp. 113–70.

four parties involved. The typical bill of the fifteenth century designated by name: (1) the party addressed—the payor; (2) the party who would present the bill for payment—the presentor or payee; (3) the party who had given consideration for the bill—the remittor; and, lastly (4), the maker of the bill. In the earlier remittance contracts the presentor was not named. The maker contracted to pay the stated amount to the remittor, or his duly constituted agent. The "order" clause was the most general form used to cover this appointment of an agent to receive the funds, but, despite its suggestiveness to the modern mind, this clause was never more than an authorization for one formal appointment of a specific presentor or recipient of the funds. The inclusion of this presentor in the mercantile bill of the fourteenth and fifteenth centuries made the order clause unnecessary. For many kinds of transactions, too, it was not necessary to arrange in advance for the appointment of an agent.

The position of the presentor at this time differed from that of the modern endorsee in three respects: his agency was automatically extinguished by the death of his principal, the remittor; his agency might be revoked; and, if legal proceedings were necessary, suit must needs be brought in the name of the principal. For promissory notes, rather than for bills of exchange, considerable use was made of a "bearer" clause. Possession of the instrument was sometimes interpreted as sufficient evidence of appointment as agent of the principal, but the lawyers became more rigid in their doctrine and came to insist upon independent proof of an appointment as agent. The "bearer" clause thus became less useful in the course of the fourteenth and fifteenth centuries. The development of the doctrine of negotiability brought about important changes in the legal relationships among the parties to these commercial contracts. Without extensive changes in the forms of these documents there was an important transformation in their legal attributes, which made possible extensive revisions and developments of commercial practice.

There is no explicit evidence of any real break with older practices and doctrines until the second quarter of the sixteenth century, and it is equally clear that the new legal doctrines were not fully established in any country earlier than 1650. But only in 1700 can we assume that the primary types of commercial paper are fully negotiable. A critical period in the history of banking is thus complicated by this slow transition from non-negotiable to negotiable paper. If we are to avoid serious errors in the interpretation of banking practice, it is essential to have some appreciation of the timing of this process of development.

The change in the law followed changes in business practice, so that we must look to the activities of the traders and bankers for the initial impulses in this remarkable development of commercial law. In Europe, as a whole, there were three new practices which led towards full negotiability. In Naples, and perhaps in Sicily, the banks began to make use of certificates of deposit that were partially negotiable. The practice developed most explicitly in Naples among the banking departments of the public pawnshops and hospitals. There is no documentary evidence prior to 1573, because the records of the banks prior to that date were destroyed by fire, but it is presumed that the practice came into use at the time of the establishment of these banking activities in 1539, or shortly after. The extended discussion of the legal attributes of these Neapolitan instruments played a vital part in the development of the Italian theories of negotiability. By analogy, this mode of transferring rights was extended to the bill of exchange in Naples and in other parts of Italy.

In the early sixteenth century, too, there appeared in France and Holland promissory notes and bills of exchange made payable to bearer. These notes and bills circulated rapidly from hand to hand, unlike the Neapolitan certificates, which were supposed to effect only one transfer. The northern practice, therefore, brought up all the major issues of negotiability. Finally, actual use of the bill of exchange was found to present some variety of circumstance. In some instances, the remittor and the presentor were the same person. At times the remittor was, in fact, the agent of the party who became the presentor. Occasionally, it was inconvenient to name the presentor when the bill was drawn, and the space was left blank, or provision made for subsequent appointment of the presentor by the inclusion of an order clause.

These various practices made bills and notes more flexible commercial instruments than was recognized by the lawyers, and the business men placed the lawyers under a positive pressure to make some provision for various problems. After much hesitation the law was made an effective instrument for the protection of the interests of business. The earliest of these legal steps that can be accurately dated is the recognition as a properly constituted agent of any bearer of bills or notes having a bearer clause. This doctrine was recognized as mercantile custom at Antwerp prior to 1535, and in 1537 it was embodied in an ordinance of Charles V. applicable to the low countries. It appears also in the statutes of Mechelen (1535), Utrecht (1550), Dordrecht (1570), and South Holland (1571). In the revised statutes of Antwerp, of 1580–81, the bearer was authorized to bring suit in his own name.

We cannot date as adequately the legal recognition of an order written on the face or the back of a document. In Italy notations of various kinds were commonly made on the face of the document, and, as a natural result, the orders of transfer of the Neapolitan certificates of deposit were written on the face of the instrument. The precise locus of these orders is a matter of indifference, and it is thus necessary to deal only with the legal content of the practice that we now properly describe as endorsement. In France and Holland orders were written on the back of the instrument. The practice is of uncertain origin, though references in Dutch treatises indicate that it became customary to note on the back any change in the relations of the parties to the original document. Thus, the appointment of a substitute by a duly constituted agent was noted on the back of the instrument of agency. It is desirable to note that the recognition of the order did not, at first, give the party any new legal rights. The party designated by the order was merely recognized as a duly constituted agent. The document thus contained all the material facts, and it ceased to be necessary to produce independent evidence of agency. These changes can be roughly identified with the second half of the sixteenth century, though the evidence is not very satisfactory in respect of dates.

The basic legal innovation is the concept of the *adjectus in rem suam* (the agent in his own affair). This new concept was first evolved in connection with various exceptional cases in respect of the bill of exchange. If the remittor and the presentor were, in fact, the same person, it was obvious that the presentor was, in truth, a principal and not an agent. Insofar as analogous cases occurred, the courts were willing to allow a party to bring forward proof that he was acting in his own behalf and not as agent for another party. Schaps holds that this curiously expressed concept laid the foundations for the modern doctrine of negotiability. The *adjectus in rem suam* could not have his agency revoked, his rights were not contingent upon the life of another, and legal procedure was instituted in his name. The doctrine appeared in Italy and in France in the late sixteenth century, but it was at first strictly limited in application.

Freundt holds that the sixteenth century merely registered progress towards full endorsement, and that only in the seventeenth century do we find positive evidence of the establishment of the new doctrines. The Neapolitan ordinance of November 8, 1607, is the earliest explicit recognition of negotiability in Italy, but it was designed to be restrictive in effect. It speaks of the inconveniences that arise in connection with several transfers, and limits the use of the order clause to a single transfer.

There is a similar ordinance for Lucca in 1610, but for Venice and Florence we have evidence that such transfers were not recognized at all. It is significant, too, that even the Neapolitan legists Scaccia, Peri, and Turri ignore the emergence of the concept of negotiability. It would seem, therefore, that the new doctrine made its way very slowly, and that this unwillingness to recognize it led to the continued use of much "bearer" paper. In 1649 the commentator Laganarius recognized the endorsee as having the rights of a principal (*procurator in rem propriam*), and Italian doctrine assumed its mature form towards the close of the century in the writings of Casaregis.

In France and Holland evidence is not adequate for the first half of the seventeenth century. We have only a brief description of French practice that indicates a wide use of bearer paper. It is commonly held that bearer paper likewise dominated Dutch practice. Then, rather suddenly, endorsement was fully recognized. There is a series of ordinances at Amsterdam beginning in 1651, which establishes the basic principles of modern Dutch law, and Phoonsen, a writer on business law (1677), gave wide currency to the doctrine. In France these doctrines were embodied in the ordinance on commerce of 1673 and given wide currency by the writings of J. Savary and Bornier. The details of law and practice differ in several particulars from Italian custom, so that we may infer that the French and Dutch jurists were not entirely dependent upon the Italians, despite the priorities that appear at some points.

In Germany, several of the great fair towns attempted to prevent the introduction of endorsement, but beginning with the revised ordinance of Frankfort-am-M., September 18, 1666, legislation was favourable; but legal recognition was not general until the beginning of the eighteenth century. In England, the practice of endorsement was first described by Marius (1651), but legal recognition came only with the statutes of 1698 and 1704 (9 and 10 Will. III., c. 17; 3–4 Anne, c. 9).[46] In Spain, the new doctrines were not fully recognized prior to the revision of commercial law embodied in the Ordinances of Bilbao in 1737.

VII

The development of the cheque and even the early advances towards negotiable paper made many changes in the details of banking practice and gradually gave deposit banking its modern aspect. These changes inevitably resulted in greater differentiation than had existed during the fifteenth century. There were wide variations in the rate of change in dif-

[46] R. D. Richards, *The Early History of Banking in England* (London, 1929), pp. 45–46.

ferent localities, and the public authorities looked upon the new business practices with varying degrees of sympathy. In Naples, new practices were frankly recognized; in Venice the senate pursued an ultra-conservative policy and prohibited all change. Furthermore, general economic conditions were unfavourable to the development of trade in the Mediterranean countries. Even if there were no absolute decline, it is fairly certain that there was little growth. The banking system was thus subject to severe strains on account of the losses of commercial firms, and extensive banking failures occurred in all sections of Italy. The attempt of the authorities to meet these difficulties added appreciably to regional differentiation of banking practice.

Unfortunately, the sources available for the history of banking in the sixteenth century are not sufficiently extensive to enable us to describe conditions in Europe as a whole. For France we have only the merest indications of banking activity, and there are no unused source materials known to be available in the major public archives.[47] Much light is thrown upon conditions in the Low Countries by the activities of the great international bankers like the Fugger, and by the exchange operations of Thomas Gresham.[48] But these materials have not yet furnished us with any comprehensive description of the general character of banking practice. The Fugger archives are likewise the most important single source of information for Austria and Germany, but it is, of course, important to have more knowledge of the operations of the local banking firms.[49] We are thus largely dependent upon Italian material for detailed description of banking. For many towns of the north we have only brief indications in the statutes, and the abundant material at Genoa has not been effectively utilized. Significant knowledge of detail is confined to

[47] Marcel Vigne, *La Banque à Lyon du XVe au XVIIIe siècle* (Lyon, 1903). Although the text shows that careful use has been made of MS. material available in Lyons the description rests primarily upon printed material. The extensive bibliography includes the basic material available for France as a whole. No important MS. materials were brought to light by careful searches made by the writer in the printed inventories of the Departmental and National Archives, nor by exploratory work in Paris at the Bibliothèque Nationale and the Archives Nationales. The critical jurisdictions are the Cour des Aides and the Cour des Monnaies. The extant series are obviously very incomplete, and of the materials that would have served for work on banking only seven registers remain—Z1b, 286–90, and KK 5, 15. When and how these materials disappeared we have no means of knowing.

[48] George Unwin, *Studies in Economic History* (London, 1927), pp. 145–67. Ehrenberg, *op. cit.*, Vol. II, *passim.*

[49] Max Jansen, *Jakob Fugger der Reiche* (Leipzig, 1910). Translation by Mildred L. Hartsough, *Jacob Fugger the Rich* (New York, 1931). E. Reinhardt, *Jakob Fugger der Reiche* (Berlin, 1926). Jakob Strieder, "Die Inventar der Firma Fugger aus dem Jahre 1527," *Zeitschr. f. die Ges. Staatswiss.*, Ergänzungsheft, 1905, Vol. XVII. K. Häbler, *Die Fugger in Spanien* (Weimar, 1897). Alfred Weitnauer, *Der Venezianische Handel der Fugger* (Leipzig, 1931).

Venice, Naples, and Sicily. In the sixteenth century, Sicily was profoundly influenced by Catalan practice, so that Catalonia and Sicily constitute together a single region. Even with these limited materials it is evident that regional differentiation became conspicuous in the course of the sixteenth century.

In Venice, the private banks were subjected to much more rigid regulation than in other parts of Italy, and towards the close of the century a new type of public bank was created whose functions were so narrowly prescribed that scarcely any use was made of credit.[50] Venice in the sixteenth century was ultra-conservative. Commissioners were appointed on June 2, 1524, to supervise the private banks, and to enforce the obligation to meet the demands of depositors. On November 6, 1526, the use of the cheque was prohibited, and some additional regulations were made. Even in Barcelona a limited use of the cheque was permitted in the Bank of Deposit, and the private bankers were allowed to use them freely. Venice alone stood out against this important development. The anxiety to make the banks safe was offset in large measure by the desire to utilize their resources for loans to the state. The amount of loans to the city was made the limit of investments in trade. Despite the reserve of 500 ducats deposited by each bank with the Commissioners under the law of 1524, the regulations failed to check the evils of excessive expansion. At all events, increasing regulation did not avert serious failures of banks. The average length of life was short, and Contarini gives the impression that practically all banks came to a bad end. This growing distrust of deposit banking led to the establishment of the famous Giro Banks: the Bank of the Rialto (1587) and the Giro Bank (1619). In 1637, the Giro Bank absorbed the Bank of the Rialto. These banks were hardly more than institutions for centralized clearance, actual credit operations were prohibited. The abolition of all private banking that was originally contemplated proved to be impossible, and a number of private banks were established.

In Naples, the private banks suffered many reverses during the sixteenth century. They were subjected to some regulation, but were not as severely handled as in Venice. Beginning about 1539 with the establishment of the *Monte della Pietà,* the banks met with competition from the banking departments of these charitable foundations. The banking business was developed in order to furnish funds for the loans on pledge, or for the hospitals. The distinctive feature of these banks was the issue of certificates of deposit which were partially negotiable from an early

[50] E. Lattes, *op. cit., passim.* Ferrara, *op. cit., passim.* Dunbar, *op. cit., passim.*

date. They subsequently became an important element in the circulation of the region and must be recognized as the prototypes of modern credit currency. These banks also permitted the use of cheques. The *Monte della Pietà* (1539?) and the *Sacro Monte dei Poveri* (1563) maintained banking departments under their own name. The hospitals and charitable foundations that established banks treated their banks as separate institutions, and gave them separate names. Thus, the hospital, *Casa Santa dell' Annunciata,* established the bank *Ave Gratia Plena* in 1587. The hospital of the *Incurabili* established in 1589 the *Santa Maria del Popolo.* An orphan asylum established in 1591 the *Banco dello Spirito Sancto,* and other hospitals established the banks of *Sant Eligio* (1592), *Santi Giacomo e Vittoria* (1606), and *Santi Salvatore* (1640).[51] Although these banks have attracted little attention outside Italy, they played a more significant rôle in the history of banking than the better-known giro banks.

Sicily and Catalonia were conservative. Private banking continued with little change in the amount of regulation, but new public banks were established after the models furnished by Barcelona and Valencia. There are vague allusions to the establishment of a public bank at Trapani in 1459, but there is little evidence of an active bank. In the next century, public banks were established at Palermo (1552), Messina (1587), Gerona (1568), Saragossa, and Vich. There are general statements that would imply a much larger number of public banks in Catalonia, but particulars are not forthcoming. In general form, these banks show little modification of the original type until the first decade of the seventeenth century. Their statutes were then modified, or, as in Barcelona, a new bank was established, so that cheques could be freely used. The distinctive feature of the Catalan system was the reservation of the credit facilities of the public bank to the city and other public authorities. The public banks acted as fiscal agents for the public authorities and supplied them with all credit needed. The private banks served the needs of trade. The contacts between public and private banks presented a number of difficult problems of policy, which were never settled in a wholly satisfactory manner. Even after the reorganization in the early seventeenth century, Catalonia and Sicily thus retained a system of pure deposit banking, modernized by the introduction of the cheque and the development of negotiable paper.

---

[51] Eugenio Tortora, *Nuovi documenti per la Sotoria del Banco di Napoli* (Napoli, 1890), pp. 16, 17, 45, 61–62, 65–69, 82–83, 93–94, 97.

16

Prices and Industrial Capitalism in France and England, 1540–1640[*1]

By JOHN U. NEF

Throughout Western Europe during the second half of the sixteenth century, peasants, craftsmen and shopkeepers, as well as princes and bishops, all shared one novel experience of some importance for their daily lives. In each decade they found that any standard coin, even if it contained precisely the same quantity of precious metal as in the previous decade, would buy less of almost any commodity bought and sold.

This "price revolution," as it has come to be called, was caused mainly by the abundant supplies of precious metals which poured into Europe from South and Central America. Prices—measured in silver—rose in the various European countries, we are told, from two- to more than three-fold between 1520 and 1650.[2] The prices which people actually paid rose much more, because princes everywhere were debasing the currency.

For some time historians and economists have been disposed to regard the price revolution as an important cause for the rise of modern capitalism. But, until recently, no one attempted to show concretely how the inflow of American treasure promoted the development of large-scale enterprise in industry, commerce and finance. In 1929 Professor E. J. Hamilton, to whom we owe our exact knowledge of the price revolution in Spain, suggested that the rapid increase in prices stimulated the growth of capitalism mainly by cheapening labour costs, and thus mak-

---

* *Economic History Review,* 1937, VII, 155–85. Reprinted by courtesy of the author and of the Economic History Society.

[1] The essay contains the substance of a paper read in July, 1936, at the Economic History Section of the Anglo-American Historical Conference in London.

[2] Georg Wiebe, *Zur Geschichte der Preisrevolution des 16. und 17. Jahrhunderts* (Leipzig, 1895), pp. 376–77, 379, 382; Earl J. Hamilton, *American Treasure and the Price Revolution in Spain* (Cambridge, Mass., 1934), pp. 205–10, 403. Cf. François Simiand, *Recherches anciennes et nouvelles sur le movement général des prix du XVI*[e] *au XIX*[e] *siècle* (Paris, 1932), pp. 167–68.

ing possible exceptionally large profits during a period of many decades.[3] These profits brought about an unprecedented accumulation of wealth in the hands of enterprising merchants and other rich men, who could afford to invest in large-scale enterprises, and who were tempted to do so by the prospect of abnormally large returns. Later, in his *Treatise on Money,* Mr. Keynes used his great authority to support and interpret Dr. Hamilton's thesis.[4]

Dr. Hamilton observed that the effect of the price revolution upon the material welfare of the wage earner was not the same in all countries. In Spain, he found, rising wages did not lag behind rising prices anything like as much as they apparently did in England.[5] He concluded that the differences between the course of wages in the two countries provided a very important explanation for the greater progress made by capitalist enterprise in England than in Spain, especially during the first two or three decades of the seventeenth century. At that time wages caught up with prices in Spain, and the Spanish wage workers regained all they had lost in earning power during the previous eight decades.[6] But in England wages apparently lagged farther than ever behind prices, and the wage workers were able to buy only about half as much with the money they received as at the beginning of the sixteenth century.[7] The greater fall in the standard of living of the English labourer was a part of the cost the country had to pay for great national progress.[8] Without the price revolution, an extensive and prolonged decline in real wages could hardly have occurred. Therefore, according to this theory, the price revolution was the principal driving force behind large-scale enterprise during the late sixteenth and early seventeenth centuries.[9]

---

[3] E. J. Hamilton, "American Treasure and the Rise of Capitalism," *Economica,* 1929, XXVII, 338–57.

[4] J. M. Keynes, *A Treatise on Money,* Vol. II (New York, 1930), pp. 152–63.

[5] Dr. Hamilton's calculations concerning the course of real wages in Spain, as announced tentatively in his article in *Economica* (*loc. cit.,* pp. 253–54), were borne out by his further researches (*American Treasure and the Price Revolution in Spain,* p. 273).

[6] *Ibid.,* pp. 273, 279–82.

[7] Hamilton, "American Treasure and the Rise of Capitalism," *loc. cit.,* pp. 350–52.

[8] Cf. Keynes, *op. cit.,* Vol. II, p. 163.

[9] Hamilton, "American Treasure and the Rise of Capitalism," *loc. cit.,* pp. 338, 344, 349. Cf. Keynes, *op. cit.,* Vol. II, p. 159. Hamilton's argument about the influence of the discoveries in promoting capitalism was not concerned exclusively with the rôle played by the price revolution in reducing the cost of labour. He also wrote of the phenomenal profits made by merchants in the East India trade, and of the probable decline in the real cost of renting land, as further factors which increased the accumulation of capital and encouraged investments in large-scale enterprise ("American Treasure and the Rise of Capitalism," *loc. cit.,* pp. 347–50). But it was to the fall in real wages that he attached the most importance (*ibid.,* pp. 349, 355–56), and it was to this aspect that Keynes drew attention.

I. THE PROGRESS OF LARGE-SCALE INDUSTRY DURING THE PRICE REVOLUTION

A comparison of French with English industrial history during the century from 1540 to 1640 suggests that there is a danger of exaggerating the rôle played by the price revolution, and the decline of real wages that it made possible, in stimulating the progress of capitalist enterprise in industry.[10] When Dr. Hamilton wrote it was assumed that large-scale industry was developing rapidly in France as well as in England.[11] But it now seems that there were important differences. In England the rate of industrial change from 1540 to 1640 was much more rapid than in any other period before the late eighteenth century. But in France it was probably slower between the death of Francis I and the accession of Louis XIV than during the previous hundred years, when the inflow of treasure from America had hardly begun. There was no growth in the output of coal, glass, salt, alum, building materials, metal wares and ships comparable in rapidity to that which raised England from an industrial backwater to the foremost industrial country in the world. Technical changes in the methods of mining and manufacturing which greatly increased the amounts of capital needed to set up in industry were less widely introduced. The number of new, large-scale industrial enterprises started must have been much smaller, relative to population, than in England.[12] What we have to explain in the case of France is not, as in that of England, why industrial capitalism made so much progress in the age of the price revolution, but why it made so little.

The explanations arrived at for France have a special interest, because the case of France was more representative of European countries generally than the case of England. In Italy, southern Germany, and the Spanish Netherlands, the age of the price revolution was, as compared with the age of the Renaissance, a period of slow industrial development. Only in Holland, and perhaps in Sweden and the Principality of Liége, was there a speeding-up in the rate of industrial development resembling to some extent that which occurred in England.

Were there any differences between the course of wages in England and France from 1540 to 1640 which help to account for the great differences in the progress of industrial capitalism? The only index num-

[10] In this article we are not concerned, as Hamilton was, with the influence of the price revolution upon commercial and financial, as well as industrial, organization.

[11] *Ibid.*, pp. 338, 356.

[12] J. U. Nef, "A Comparison of Industrial Growth in France and England from 1540 to 1640," *Jour. Pol. Econ.*, 1936, XLIV, 289–317, 505–33, 643–66.

bers of wages and commodity prices in the two countries available when Professor Hamilton wrote his article in 1929, were those compiled in 1895 by Georg Wiebe, who used the voluminous records of wages and prices, collected by Thorold Rogers[13] and the Vicomte d'Avenel,[14] as a basis for the first comprehensive inquiry into the price revolution.[15] Dr. Hamilton reprinted these index numbers in order to compare the course of real wages in Andalusia and in England and France.[16] Mr. Keynes derived from them tables of what he called "profit inflation." These tables give for successive periods during the sixteenth and seventeenth centuries the ratio of commodity prices to costs of production, on the assumption that in both England and France money wages accounted for half the costs of production, and that the other half rose exactly as commodity prices.[17] For the convenience of the reader in following our argument, Mr. Keynes' tables are reproduced below.[18]

Mr. Keynes' Tables

England			France		
Period	Price/Costs Ratio		Period	Price/Costs Ratio	
1500–1550	...	100	1500–1525	...	100
			1525–1550	...	103
1550–1560	...	116			
1560–1570	...	112	1550–1575	...	110
1570–1580	...	116			
1580–1590	...	120	1575–1600	...	139 √
1590–1600	...	137			
1600–1610	...	139 √	1600–1625	...	118
1610–1620	...	135			
1620–1630	...	141			
1630–1640	...	134	1625–1650	...	128
1640–1650	...	133			

His results suggest that the behaviour of real wages in the two countries was similar. The standard of living among labourers apparently fell in France nearly, if not quite, as much as in England.[19] On Wiebe's

[13] *A History of Agriculture and Prices in England,* 7 vols. (Oxford, 1866–1902).

[14] *Histoire économique de la propriété, des salaires, des denrées et de tous les prix,* 7 vols. (Paris, 1894).

[15] Wiebe, *op. cit.,* pp. 374–79.

[16] Hamilton, "American Treasure and the Rise of Capitalism," *loc. cit.,* pp. 352–54.

[17] Keynes, *op. cit.,* Vol. II, pp. 159–60.

[18] Taken from Keynes, *op. cit.,* Vol. II, pp. 159–60.

[19] Wiebe compiled two sets of index numbers for commodity prices in England, based on different methods of weighting the commodities (*op. cit.,* pp. 374–76, 383). If Hamilton had reprinted not the first but the second set, which shows prices rising a

showing, there were at least two generations of French workers whose wages would buy only about half the quantity of commodities that the wages of their ancestors in the late fifteenth century would have bought.[20] While France belongs, like Spain, to the group of countries where industrial capitalism made comparatively slow progress from 1540 to 1640, it seems to belong, as England does, to a group of countries where the fall in real wages was much greater and more prolonged than in Spain.

As can be seen from Mr. Keynes' tables, Wiebe's index numbers were worked out by decades for England and by twenty-five-year periods for France. If we are to study the relations between price changes and industrial development, it is important to know not only that industrial capitalism made much slower progress in France than in England during the century from 1540 to 1640 as a whole, but also to know in which portions of the century the contrasts were greatest.

For the purpose of comparing the growth of industrial capitalism in the two countries, the century can be divided into four fairly well-defined periods.[21] The first ran from 1540 into the sixties of the sixteenth century. In France this period was probably marked by some slight slowing down in the rate of industrial growth, which had been rather rapid since the end of the Hundred Years War. In England it was marked by a speeding-up in the rate of growth. The rapid increase in the output of cloth, which had begun in the reign of Henry VII, was accompanied after the dissolution of the monasteries, in 1536 and 1539, by a rapid increase in the output of other industrial commodities, such as beer, coal and iron. Blast furnaces, costing with their water-driven bellows and hammers thousands of pounds, multiplied in Sussex, and large foundries for casting iron cannons were introduced from the Continent. The amount of capital invested in new mines and small factories was probably much larger—relative to population—than in France.

The differences between development in the two countries during this first period were slight compared with those during the next, which began in the sixties and ran into the nineties of the sixteenth century. During the seventies and eighties in England many new industries, like the

good deal more slowly, it would have appeared that the workers' standard of living fell more in France than in England.

[20] Hamilton, "American Treasure and the Rise of Capitalism," *loc. cit.,* p. 353.

[21] What follows is derived mainly from material referred to in my article, "A Comparison of Industrial Growth in France and England" (*loc. cit.*). It is intended to be a tentative statement, which I hope to correct and amplify with the help of a study of further documents.

manufacture of brass, paper, sugar, alum and copperas, were introduced, and the output of older industries, like mining, smelting, shipbuilding, salt and glass making, grew at a more rapid rate than during the forties and fifties. The phenomenal growth in industrial output, together with the widespread adoption of costly horse and water mills, hitherto little employed except in parts of southern Germany and the Low Countries, produced an unprecedented demand for industrial capital. Hundreds of new mines and small factories were started. But in France the seventies and eighties were decades of religious warfare and civil strife. While the effects of the wars upon economic life have been represented by contemporary writers and even by modern historians as more disastrous than they were, they did hold back investments in new enterprises. Much less capital was probably invested in large-scale industry during the seventies and eighties than during the forties and fifties. This was the period when the contrasts between industrial progress in the two countries were greatest.

The third period began in the nineties of the sixteenth century and lasted until about 1620. In England it may be regarded from the point of view of industrial history as a continuation of the previous period. The rate of growth in industrial output after 1604 was possibly even greater than during the seventies and eighties of the sixteenth century. New inventions cheapened the products and increased the scale of enterprise in industries like glass and steel making. Horse- and water-driven engines and large furnaces and kilns, which had been adopted in many ventures during Elizabeth's reign, replaced the older more primitive tools and ovens even more extensively, both in manufacturing and mining, in centres of population like London and centres of industry like the Tyne valley. Except in Sussex, Surrey and Kent, where the exhaustion of the forests stopped the progress of the iron and glass manufactures, more capital found investment than during the previous period in new mines and small factories and in the expansion of old ones. But, unlike the seventies and eighties, this was also in France a period of expanding industrial output and of marked technical development. A large number of new enterprises were started in many French provinces, especially after the publication of the Edit of Nantes in 1598 had brought to an end the most destructive phases of the religious wars. In comparison with the twenty-five years from 1570 to 1595, those from 1595 to 1620 were a bright period for the progress of manufactures in France. Though progress was slow compared to that in England, the contrasts were much less remarkable than during the religious wars.

The fourth period, from about 1620 until the outbreak of the English Civil War and the death of Louis XIII, was marked in both countries by a pronounced slowing down in the rate of industrial development. In England the rapid growth in the output of iron, which had begun with the dissolution of the monasteries, finally came to an end.[22] As is well known, the cloth manufacture underwent, especially during the early twenties, one of the most serious depressions in its history. Coal-mining in Durham and Northumberland suffered after 1625 from an over-supply of capital.[23]

In France the depression in the Levant trade, which began about 1620, proved a serious blow for industry at Marseilles and elsewhere in the south. Throughout Provence and Languedoc many enterprises in such manufactures as soap-boiling, shipbuilding, iron and glass-making shut down for lack of markets. Nor was the depression confined to the south. Manufacturing was on the decline in Poitou, and, at least in so far as the building of merchant ships and the production of iron was concerned, in Brittany and Champagne.

The depression of the twenties was not followed in France, as it was to some extent in England, by a substantial recovery during the early thirties. We can find nothing in France to rival the rapid expansion which occurred at that time in English merchant shipbuilding, in the manufacture of alum in Yorkshire and Durham, and in the building trades of London. The depression in the French Levant commerce, which began in the twenties, was followed by a collapse in the thirties. While the output of iron in England did not increase after the twenties, new and larger furnaces were built during the thirties in the Midlands and the Forest of Dean to replace the older ones in south-eastern England. It was not until the reign of Louis XIV that a similar development of great new blast furnaces and forges occurred in central and western France to offset the decline of the iron manufacture in Champagne and the Cévennes. The picture painted by Voltaire of the deplorable condition of French industry and trade at the great King's accession, while overdrawn, contains much truth.[24] Notwithstanding the depression which beset the English textile and iron-making industries in the two decades preceding the Civil War, England's lead over France with respect to the investment of new capital in large-scale industry may have

[22] J. U. Nef, "Note on the Progress of Iron Production in England," *Jour. Pol. Econ.*, 1936, XLIV, 402–3.

[23] J. U. Nef, *The Rise of the British Coal Industry*, Vol. II (London, 1932), pp. 75–76.

[24] Voltaire, *Le siècle de Louis XIV*, Ch. 2.

been greater than during the previous period of booming trade and industry.

When we consider the progress of large-scale industry in England and France during these four periods in relation to the course of profit-inflation as shown in Mr. Keynes' tables, what do we find? While there is nothing in the tables to account for the depression which came in England at the end of James I's reign, there is certainly a remarkable coincidence between profit-inflation, which reflects the fall in real wages, and the growth of industrial capitalism in England during the first three of the four periods. Conditions appear to have been increasingly favourable for exceptional profits between 1550[25] and 1620. Except for two decades, 1560–70 and 1610–20, the openings for profits were greater in every decade than they had been in the previous one. With these figures before us, there is a temptation to regard the price revolution as the principal explanation of the early English industrial revolution. There is a temptation to believe that the new shipyards, the hundreds of new mines, smelting furnaces and forges, the numerous soap, starch and sugar houses, the glass furnaces, breweries, brick and lime kilns, and the alum and copperas factories were built, equipped, supplied with raw materials and staffed by workmen, largely because the exceptional profits obtained by the wealthy as real wages fell had created great new reservoirs of capital awaiting investment, and because the cheapness of labour made investments exceptionally attractive.

But in France, after 1550, according to the tables, labour was hardly less cheap than in England; yet no industrial revolution occurred. It is true that from 1550 to 1575, according to the table, profit-inflation was slightly less in France than in England. But from 1575 to 1600 profit-inflation reached its zenith in France, and was even greater than in England. Theoretically this was the period in France when conditions seem to have been most favourable for investments in new enterprises; it was a period when they were more favourable in France than in England. But, in fact, this was of all four periods (with the possible exception of the last) the one during which the least new capital flowed into large-

[25] Keynes' tables give the impression that in England prices began to rise more rapidly than wages only after 1550. But Wiebe's index numbers show that the fall in real wages began much earlier, as soon as prices started upward. Prices actually began to rise in the second decade of the sixteenth century, and the rise became rather rapid during the forties. The real situation has been obscured because Wiebe's index numbers, which give prices in terms of their silver values, make it appear that prices *fell* during the forties (Wiebe, *op. cit.*, pp. 70, 376–77; cf. below, pp. 310–11). This point was called to my attention by John Saltmarsh.

scale industry in France. It was the period during which English development was in most striking contrast to French.

According to the tables, real wages in France were a good deal higher in the first quarter of the seventeenth century than in the last quarter of the sixteenth. Theoretically this should not have been as good a time for industrial progress as either the preceding or the succeeding period. But, in fact, it proved to be a much better time.

Some years ago Monsieur André Liautey, now the Under-Secretary of State for Agriculture, wrote in his study of the price revolution in France, that a rise in prices "is . . . compatible with the most dissimilar economic conditions."[26] The same thing seems to be true of a fall in real wages. Periods of profit-inflation coincided with periods of industrial expansion; they also coincided with periods of industrial depression.

II. THE COST OF INDUSTRIAL LABOUR DURING THE PRICE REVOLUTION

Since Wiebe compiled his index numbers, several sets of price and wage records, not contained in the volumes of Rogers and d'Avenel which he used, have been published. A brief examination of these records and of new data collected by the International Scientific Committee on Price History,[27] together with the old data on which Wiebe's work was based, suggests that the decline in the material welfare of the English workers from 1500 to 1642 was much less than Wiebe's index numbers suggested. Before the studies of Thorold Rogers were published, some writers claimed that the mechanic could get more wheat for a day's work on the eve of the Civil War than at the beginning of Elizabeth's reign.[28] Rogers' transcription of thousands of price and wage records made that position untenable. But he and some other scholars who used his volumes seem to have exaggerated the losses which the workers suffered from rapidly rising prices almost as much as ill-informed persons, who had no reliable statistics to establish their case, once exaggerated the gains which the same workers obtained from increases in wages.

To begin with, wage-rates apparently rose appreciably more than

[26] André Liautey, *La hausse des prix et la lutte contre la cherté en France au XVIe siècle* (Paris, 1921), p. 337.

[27] Made possible through the generosity of Sir William Beveridge, the Chairman of the English Price Committee. My work was greatly facilitated by the kind help of Miss M. E. Rayner, the Secretary of the Committee, who not only found for me the relevant material, but made some calculations of the price averages for timber purchased by the Royal Navy. I am much indebted to both of them.

[28] E.g., William Playfair, *A Letter on Our Agricultural Distresses* (London, 1821), charts facing pp. 50 and 44, and also pp. 48, 29. I am grateful to my colleague, Professor Jacob Viner, for calling my attention to this tract.

Rogers' data indicated. His data do not concern the wages of mechanics like smiths or cutlers, or the wages of spinners and weavers, or those of miners, smelters and workers in other rising manufactures. They relate entirely to the wages of labourers in the building trades, such as masons, carpenters, tilers and bricklayers. According to the averages worked out from Rogers' tables by Wiebe and others, wage-rates rose a shade less than two-and-a-half-fold between the first decade of the sixteenth century and the decade preceding the Civil War.[29]

We now have a number of new, rather complete series for the money wages paid to the same kinds of workmen in connection with building enterprises at several places in southern England. Three are for London.[30] The others are for Eton, Winchester, Dover, Canterbury, Cambridge and Exeter.[31] The new data indicate that—on the average—wage-rates rose nearly, if not quite, threefold between 1510 and 1640, or something like 20 per cent. more than Wiebe's tables show. It is mainly for the sixty years from 1580 to 1640, the period during which according to Wiebe's index numbers the building workers suffered most from rising prices, that his figures understate the increase in their money wages. According to these figures, wage-rates rose about 39 per cent. between the period 1571–82 and the decade 1633–42.[32] The new data suggest that they rose more than 50 per cent.[33]

If we are to estimate the effects of the price revolution upon the labourers' standard of living, we ought to know whether unemployment

---

[29] If we take the average wages in the decade 1501–10 as 100, then, according to Wiebe, the average in the decade 1633–42 (not in silver, but in English money) was 248 (Wiebe, *op. cit.*, pp. 377, 70). According to Steffen, the average was 237 (Gustaf E. Steffen, *Studien zur Geschichte der englischen Lohnarbeite,* Vol. I (Stuttgart, 1901). Professor Knoop and Mr. Jones have worked out from Rogers' data separate averages for Oxford and Cambridge. The result for the decade 1633–42 is 200 for Oxford and 266 for Cambridge (Douglas Knoop and G. P. Jones, *The Mediaeval Mason* [Manchester, 1933], p. 236).

[30] From one of these—the London Bridge series—averages have been derived and published (Knoop and Jones, *op. cit.*, p. 236). The other two—for the Royal Works and for Westminster College and Abbey—are among the MSS. of the Price Committee at the London School of Economics.

[31] MSS. of the Price Committee at the London School of Economics. The Committee has not yet worked out index numbers from these records.

[32] Wiebe, *op. cit.*, pp. 377, 70. According to Steffen's averages, also obtained from Rogers, wages rose only about 27 per cent (Knoop and Jones, *op. cit.*, p. 236).

[33] According to the averages worked out by Knoop and Jones, the wages paid for building work at London Bridge increased between the decades 1501–10 and 1633–42 practically threefold—from 8*d.* to about 23*d.* a day. Between 1571–82 and 1633–42 wages increased from about 14*d.* to about 23*d.* (Knoop and Jones, *op. cit.*, p. 236). My examination of the new records collected by the Price Committee indicates that these averages are more typical than those worked out by Thorold Rogers and used by Wiebe and Steffen (Rogers, *op. cit.*, Vol. IV, pp. 518–23; Vol. V, pp. 664–67).

among the building workers increased or diminished. We ought to know exactly what the workers bought with their wages. We ought also to know whether they made their purchases from the same kinds of tradesmen and on the same terms as did the Crown and the municipalities, and the colleges, hospitals, and other institutions, since practically all the price records that have been collected have been taken from the account books of such authorities and establishments. No satisfactory answer can be given to these questions. But, in dealing with them, certain rather misleading assumptions have been made by nearly all the authorities who have discussed the standard of living among wage workers during the period of the price revolution. It has been assumed that money wages were all that workmen received for their labour, and that these wages were spent almost exclusively on the purchase of certain foodstuffs and foods.

First of all, we have to consider whether the foodstuffs and foods have been selected in such a way as to give a true picture of the rise in the cost of diet among the labouring classes. Englishmen early in the seventeenth century were fond of saying that bread, and after bread, ale or beer, were the chief "stay" of the poor. But cereal products were not by any means the only nourishment of working people, as has been often assumed in attempting to determine the standard of living. Since Rogers' time authorities who have tried to estimate the rise in the price of food during the sixteenth and seventeenth centuries have never been able to include in their computations the prices of either bread or beer. They have got around this difficulty by substituting the prices paid in towns for the various grains from which bread and beer were produced. But in the principal towns at the beginning of the seventeenth century home-brewing had largely disappeared, and even home-baking was of less importance than it had been before the Reformation.[34]

Can we assume that the prices of drink, bread, and meal were rising as much during the price revolution as the prices of the grains from which they were produced? The matter is of importance, because the prices of grains, grain products, and grasses rose almost twice as much between the first decade of the sixteenth century and the decade preceding the Civil War as the prices of most foods. Wheat increased about six-and-a-half-fold in price, oats and malt between seven- and eight-fold, hay and straw more than eight-fold.[35] Meanwhile peas increased about

[34] Cf. Sylvia Thrupp, *A Short History of the Worshipful Company of Bakers* (London, 1933), pp. 74–75, 79.

[35] These figures are taken from Sir William Beveridge's MS., "Provisional Index Numbers of Food and Fuel—1500–1800" (London School of Economics, 1932).

five-fold in price, butter about four-and-a-third-fold, hens and eggs a shade under four-and-a-third-fold, and pigeons about three-and-a-third-fold.[36] There was at least one food—herrings—which apparently increased in price somewhat less rapidly than the wages of building craftsmen rose. It is possible that, with the enactment of laws to encourage fish-eating, herrings came to occupy an even more important place in the diet of the common people than before the Reformation. We have not as yet any index numbers for the prices of meat until the reign of Elizabeth. But between the decades 1580–9 and 1630–9, when the price of grain almost doubled, the price of beef and mutton rose less than 50 per cent.,[37] hardly more than the wages of carpenters.[38] During this half-century the price of foods, other than cereal products, appears to have risen only about as rapidly as wage-rates in the building trades.

The prices of bread and drink were determined by the cost of making them as well as by the prices of the grains and grain products from which they were made. When it is assumed that bread and drink rose in price as rapidly as wheat, oats, rye, barley, malt and hops, it is also assumed that the price of labour and the price of materials other than grain employed in milling, baking, malting, and brewing increased as rapidly as the price of grain, and that there was no reduction in the quantity of either labour or grain used in these processes. It seems to me that none of these assumptions is warranted.

To judge from conditions in the building trades, wage-rates rose only about three-fold between the first decade of the sixteenth century and the decade preceding the Civil War.[39] The cost of labour in baking and brewing probably increased somewhat more than these figures indicate, because the workmen were frequently supplied with food in addition to their wages,[40] but it could not have increased anything like as rapidly as the price of grain.

Firewood alone among the materials needed in making bread or beer, rose in price more than grain.[41] But in brewing, coal, which was cheap, was widely substituted for wood fuel during the reigns of Elizabeth and her two successors, so that by 1637 only one of the five brewhouses in

---

[36] As Sir William does not have index numbers for these foods covering the whole period from 1500 to 1640, I have used Steffen's ten-yearly average prices (Steffen, *op. cit.*, Vol. I, pp. 254–55, 365–66).

[37] Beveridge, "Provisional Index Numbers." Cf. Steffen, *op. cit.*, Vol. I, pp. 255, 366.

[38] As these are shown in the records of the Price Committee at the London School of Economics.

[39] See p. 301.

[40] See pp. 305–6.

[41] See p. 316.

Westminster had a log-burning furnace.[42] In baking, coal was still little used,[43] but even as late as 1619, when logs and faggots were extremely dear, wood accounted for only about one-tenth of the costs of the baker in London.[44] It is unlikely that any of the other costs increased as rapidly as the price of grain.

Nor can we assume that the quantity of labour or of grain which went into making a loaf of bread or a gallon of drink remained constant during the sixteenth and early seventeenth centuries. Although the equipment and the staff of the London baker, with his small oven and his three or four journeymen, did not alter much between the reigns of Henry VII and Charles I,[45] the equipment of the miller improved. More efficient mills for grinding corn were introduced throughout the country, especially towards the end of the sixteenth century,[46] and a new class of capitalist millers, upon whom the bakers were coming to depend for their meal and even for their flour, arose in the neighbourhood of London.[47] The growing use of better machinery and the increase in the scale of operations undoubtedly reduced the labour required in milling. The price of bread probably rose appreciably less rapidly than the price of wheat.[48]

If the course of grain prices was an imperfect guide to the course of bread prices during the sixteenth and early seventeenth centuries, it was no guide at all to the course of drink prices. Technical changes in methods of production affected the costs much more in brewing than in bread making. As a result of the introduction of hop cultivation in Henry VIII's reign and the discovery of improved methods of drying malt,

[42] Nef, *Rise of the Coal Industry,* Vol. I, pp. 213–14; *Calendar of State Papers Domestic, 1636–37,* p. 415.

[43] Nef, *Rise of the Coal Industry,* Vol. I, p. 216; Thrupp, *op. cit.,* pp. 17, 115.

[44] *Ibid.,* p. 17.

[45] *Ibid.,* pp. 98–99.

[46] This is an impression I have derived from the calendars and indexes of the Exchequer Special Commissions, the Exchequer Depositions by Commission, the Chancery and Star Chamber Proceedings.

[47] Thrupp, *op. cit.,* p. 27.

[48] In 1619–20, when wheat was selling in London for between 25*s.* and 28*s.* a quarter (Rogers, *op. cit.,* Vol. VI, p. 32), the expenses of converting this quantity into bread—including apparently the miller's charge—was estimated at 13*s.* (Thrupp, *op. cit.,* p. 17). We may perhaps infer that the expense of milling and baking accounted for nearly, if not quite, a third of the price of white bread on the eve of the Civil War. If, as seems possible, the expense of making meal and bread did not increase more than fourfold between the first decade of the sixteenth century and the decade preceding the Civil War, then the price of bread would not have increased, like the price of wheat, six-and-a-half-fold, but only about five-and-a-half-fold. In the conversion of inferior grains into bread, milling and baking doubtless accounted for a larger proportion of the cost. Bread made from rye or maslin probably rose in price slightly less rapidly than bread made from wheat.

small beer replaced ale during the sixteenth century as the common beverage of the English people.[49] In Elizabeth's reign, for the first time, Englishmen could take pride in their native beer. It had come to rival in quality the best continental brews.[50] The quantity obtained from a given amount of grain had increased, for small beer was not as strong as medieval ale had been, and the use of hops was a great economy in malt.[51] Costs of brewing had been further reduced by the growth in the scale of enterprise, and the substitution of coal for wood fuel. Some large breweries, with expensive copper boilers, brass siphons and new coal-burning furnaces, were built in London at a cost of many hundreds of pounds.[52]

These changes in manufacturing methods prevented the price of the cheapest brews from rising anything like as rapidly as the price of malt between 1500 and 1640. In every town and in many large villages by the beginning of the seventeenth century poor workmen obtained a part of the daily nourishment for themselves and their families by purchase of small beer from brewers, innkeepers and victuallers.[53] They probably drank much more beer than their descendants in the age of Dickens and Thackeray. This they could hardly have done if it had been expensive, and they appear to have seldom paid more than 3*d.* a gallon for small beer before the Civil War.[54] As the cheapest ale had rarely cost less than a penny a gallon in the last half of the fifteenth century,[55] the rise in wage-rates during the price revolution seems to have covered the increase in the price of drink.

If bread was rising in price appreciably less rapidly than wheat, and drink hardly as rapidly as the wages of masons and carpenters, it is misleading to work out costs of living mainly or even partly on the basis of

---

[49] Cf. Nef, "A Comparison of Industrial Growth in France and England," *loc. cit.*, pp. 647–48.

[50] Michael Combrune, *The Theory and Practice of Brewing* (London, 1762), p. x.

[51] Cf. Rogers, *op. cit.*, Vol. IV, p. 550.

[52] Nef, "The Progress of Technology," *loc. cit.*, p. 20; cf. Rogers, *op. cit.*, Vol. V, pp. 705–6.

[53] Cf. *Calendar of State Papers Domestic, 1637–38,* pp. 580–81.

[54] The indications are that small beer usually cost about 2*d.* a gallon during Elizabeth's reign, and that under her two successors the normal price was 2*d.* or 2½*d.* (Sir George Shuckburgh Evelyn, in *Philosophical Transactions,* Vol. LXXXVIII [1798], p. 176—a reference for which I am indebted to my colleague, Professor Jacob Viner—and Michael Combrune, *An Inquiry into the Prices of Wheat, Malt . . . etc.* [London, 1768], p. 107). Sixteen inhabitants of the villages of St. Neots and Eynesbury, west of Cambridge, claimed in 1638 that they had been accustomed to buy small beer from local innkeepers and victuallers at a penny a gallon and a farthing a quart (*Calendar of State Papers Domestic, 1637–38,* pp. 580–81).

[55] W. Fleetwood, *Chronicon Preciosum* (London, 1745), pp. 88–89, 92; Rogers, *op. cit.*, Vol. III, p. 249.

grain prices. By doing so, all authorities since Rogers' time have exaggerated the rise in the price of subsistence during the sixteenth and early seventeenth centuries. Men did not eat hay or straw, or even oats or wheat. In the towns seven or eight times as much money may have been required to feed a horse in the reign of Charles I as in the reign of Henry VII. But it would be surprising if even five or four and a half times as much was needed to nourish a man.[56] Except for green vegetables, which were probably little eaten by town labourers, and bread, there was apparently not a single article in the poor man's diet which rose in price as much as four-and-a-half-fold. As the price of bread apparently increased more than that of other foods, it is possible that the poor replaced bread, cakes and porridge to some extent by other kinds of nourishment, such as herrings, beef, mutton, eggs, cheese and small beer, which, unlike bread, could be had for much less money in Shakespeare's time than to-day.[57] While there was a marked decline in the purchasing power of the building craftsman's wages in terms of food until the sixties of the sixteenth century, it is by no means certain that this decline continued thereafter.

But the decline in the English labourer's standard of living would still be exaggerated by comparing the course of wage-rates with the course of town food prices, even if we were able to substitute the prices of bread and beer for the prices of grain, and to determine what changes took place in the diet of the workers. In the first place, the practice of feeding workers was common in the sixteenth and seventeenth centuries. Journeymen bakers in London were provided by their masters with their meat and drink in addition to their money wages.[58] Coal miners also frequently had an allowance for food and drink.[59] We cannot be sure that money was all the reward received by the building artisans.[60] Professor Knoop and Mr. Jones think it conceivable that the practice of providing these craftsmen with some nourishment in addition to their money wages became more common in the sixteenth century than it had been before.[61] In so far as an employer supplied his workmen with food, the rise in the price of diet bore down on him. His costs of prodution increased more than we should infer from a study of wage-rates.

[56] Cf. Knoop and Jones, *op. cit.*, p. 213.

[57] A. V. Judges, "A Note on Prices in Shakespeare's Time," in *A Companion to Shakespeare Studies,* H. Granville-Barker and G. B. Harrison, eds. (Cambridge, Eng., 1934), p. 384.

[58] Thrupp, *op. cit.*, pp. 17–18.

[59] Nef, *Rise of the Coal Industry,* Vol. II, p. 187.

[60] Cf. Rogers, *op. cit.*, Vol. IV, p. 501; Vol. V, pp. 637–38.

[61] Knoop and Jones, *op. cit.*, p. 212.

Nor is it probably that wage workers engaged in industrial occupations, particularly in rural districts, had to buy all their food, even when their employers did not provide it for them. Men lived closer to the earth in the sixteenth century than to-day. Most labourers—particularly the multitudes who spun or wove or forged metal wares in their cottages under the putting-out system, and even many of those who found work in the new mines and metallurgical plants—held a plot of land capable of furnishing them with a part of what they needed to live.[62]

The prices of such foodstuffs and foods as the village labourer had to buy could hardly have risen as fast as the prices of the same articles in the towns. Town prices were forced up partly by the need which arose during the Elizabethan age to draw on the supplies of distant farms. London was growing from a large town of some 50,000 or 60,000 people to a metropolis of more than 300,000.[63] Its inhabitants, nourished before the Reformation almost entirely by the produce of the home counties, became increasingly dependent on grain, meat, milk, butter, cheese and salt brought by wagon, packhorse and small ship from more remote parts of the realm.[64] The increase in prices in the capital and in some other growing towns must be attributed partly to the cost of driving livestock and carrying foodstuffs and foods greater distances, and also to the multiplication of the profit-making middleman through whose hands the commodities passed on their way from the husbandman to the consumer. On the whole the industrial labourer in rural areas escaped paying many of the new charges which fell heavily upon some items in the diet of his fellow in the largest towns.[65]

Three main points emerge from this discussion of food prices. In the first place, the index numbers hitherto compiled exaggerate the increase in the cost of subsistence during the price revolution. Secondly, the increase in the cost of the workmen's diet was borne to some extent not by them but by their employers. Thirdly, many workmen held small plots of land from which they obtained some of their necessary supplies. It follows that they were probably able to spend a more than negligible

---

[62] Cf. R. H. Tawney, "The Assessment of Wages in England by the Justices of the Peace," *Vierteljahrschrift für Sozial- und Wirtschaftsgeschichte,* 1913, XI, 535–37. Knoop and Jones tell us that some of the masons must have had agricultural holdings (*op. cit.,* p. 214).

[63] N. S. B. Gras, *The Evolution of the English Corn Market* (Cambridge, Mass., 1915), p. 75.

[64] F. J. Fisher, "The Development of the London Food Market, 1540–1640," *Econ. Hist. Rev.,* 1935, V, 46–51.

[65] Cf. A. P. Usher, "The General Course of Wheat Prices in France, 1350–1788," *Rev. Econ. Stat.,* 1930, XII, 165.

portion of the money wages they received on commodities other than food.

Were the prices of these commodities rising faster than wage-rates? After food, fuel was the most costly item in common housekeeping. But not all workers had to buy their fuel. The practice of granting fire coal to coal miners was universal, and the number of regularly employed coal miners increased many-fold between 1540 and 1640.[66] It is impossible to determine whether the majority of the workers who had to buy their own fuel were worse off on the eve of the Civil War than industrial workers had been on the eve of the Reformation, because coal replaced logs and charcoal in the housekeeping of a great number—perhaps the majority—of Englishmen during the reigns of Elizabeth and James I.[67] The change was brought about chiefly by the phenomenal rise in the price of firewood.[68] Up to the time when a workman installed an iron grate in his home and adopted a coal-burning fire, the price of his fuel undoubtedly rose much more rapidly than his wages. But once he had made the change, the price of his fuel rose more slowly than his wages. According to some provisional index numbers worked out by the Price Committee, coal in the south of England was not appreciably dearer in the decade 1620–9 than in the decade 1570–9, and was only about 15 per cent. dearer in the decade before the Civil War.[69] Wage-rates in the building trades had risen during these sixty years 50 per cent. or more. This is just the period when it has been assumed, from comparisons between the course of grain prices and wage-rates, that the workers' standard of living fell precipitately.

We know nothing about the costs of lodging. But it is by no means certain that industrial workmen had to spend a larger proportion of their wages on housing in the reign of Charles I than in that of Henry VII. Employers in the new capitalistic industries often built cottages for their workmen, many of whom had migrated from distant counties.[70] The costs of building must have risen very rapidly during the price revolution because of the phenomenal increase in timber prices.[71] But in the Elizabethan Age, all observers were struck by the widespread substitution of brick and stone for wood as building materials. To judge from conditions in the building trades, wage-rates rose during the reigns of

---

[66] Nef, *Rise of the Coal Industry,* Vol. II, pp. 187, 136–40.
[67] *Ibid.,* Vol. I, pp. 196–98.
[68] See p. 316.
[69] Beveridge, "Provisional Index Numbers."
[70] Cf. Nef, *Rise of the Coal Industry,* Vol. II, p. 187.
[71] See p. 317.

Elizabeth and her two Stuart successors at least as rapidly as the prices of bricks and lime.[72] If grain prices are not a satisfactory guide to the cost of subsistence during the price revolution, neither are timber prices a satisfactory guide to the cost of housing.

What was happening to the cost of such manufactured commodities as workers and their families were likely to need? While the price of candles rose more rapidly than wage-rates in the building trades between 1540 and 1640,[73] the price of ordinary textile wares, nails and paper rose much less rapidly,[74] the price of some kinds of glass apparently did not rise at all[75] and the price of smokers' pipes fell a great deal, at least after 1601.[76] While wage-rates increased less rapidly than the prices of most foods, they increased more rapidly than the prices of most industrial products. If a workman was able to spend as large a proportion of his wages upon manufactured commodities on the eve of the Civil War as on the eve of the Reformation, he could in all probability have bought substantially larger quantities.

Without more knowledge concerning yearly earnings as distinct from wage-rates, and concerning the items which money wages covered, prices in rural districts and wages in other industries than building, we cannot hope to make an accurate comparison between the standard of living among industrial workmen at the beginning of the sixteenth century and on the eve of the Civil War. No doubt their real earnings fell with each rapid rise in prices. But there was also a persistent tendency throughout the period for earnings to overtake prices during the intervals between these rapid rises. The indications are that this tendency was especially marked after the accession of Elizabeth. Starting with the second decade of the sixteenth century, the general trend of the wage workers' standard of living was certainly downward until at least the sixties, and the fall in their real earnings was probably most rapid during the forties and fifties. But it is doubtful whether, as has been generally believed, the downward trend in their standard of living persisted during the four or five decades of most rapid industrial expansion from about 1575 to 1620. Changes were introduced both by the Statute of Artificers of 1563 and by a later Statute of 1603, in the principles and the methods used by local authorities in assessing wages. The new legislation, and the policy

[72] MSS. of the Price Committee, "Chairman's Report on English Navy Stores," September 1933. Cf. Wiebe, *op. cit.*, p. 375.

[73] Beveridge, "Provisional Index Numbers."

[74] Wiebe, *op. cit.*, pp. 375–77, 383.

[75] MS. "Chairman's Report on English Naval Stores."

[76] *Hist. MSS. Com., Reports on the MSS. of the Duke of Rutland,* Vol. IV, pp. 437, 526, 542.

followed until the Civil War by the Privy Council in enforcing it, made the raising of wages by law, especially in the textile industry, more easily possible than it had been. And when, as was often the case, the regulations under the Statutes were evaded, the market rate of wages was usually above the legal rate.[77] Partly perhaps as a result of the new government policy, wage workers seem to have been at least as well off materially in the reign of Charles I as on the eve of the Armada. During the half-century preceding the Civil War, their wages had probably risen on the average less rapidly than the price of bread, but about as rapidly as the prices of other foods and drink, and more rapidly than the prices of coal and the products of manufactures. The contrasts between the movements of real wages in England and Spain throughout the period of the price revolution were much less striking than Wiebe's index numbers suggested.

In considering the influence of labour costs upon the progress of industrial capitalism, we are more interested in the wages paid to workmen in mines, at smelting furnaces and forges, and in other small factories than in those paid to masons, carpenters and other workmen in the building trades.[78] And we are more interested in the prices obtained for the products of these mines and factories than in the prices paid for grains, grasses, livestock and foods, commodities which were given heavy weight in Wiebe's index numbers. The fact that wage-rates in the building trades rose more slowly than the town prices of foodstuffs and foods, did not offer any special inducement to draw an enterprising country landlord to sink shafts to his coal seams or a wealthy city merchant to enter a partnership for smelting iron ore or manufacturing glass or paper.

Wage-rates could hardly have risen much less in the new industries than in the building trades. It is even possible that special bait in the form of good pay had to be sometimes offered to induce men to enter novel and disagreeable occupations like coal mining and sheet-glass manufacturing.[79] As wage-rates in the building trades rose much more rapidly between 1560 and 1640 than the prices of coal, ordinary textile wares, and most manufactured articles, wage-rates in other industries probably also rose more rapidly. But if wage-rates were rising in most industries more rapidly than the prices of the products, how could industrial ventures have been exceptionally profitable during the reigns of Elizabeth and James I?

[77] Tawney, *op. cit.,* pp. 311, 321, 534–35, 542–52, 561–64.

[78] Cf. Wiebe, *op. cit.,* p. 240.

[79] Cf. Nef, *Rise of the Coal Industry,* Vol. II, pp. 192, 194.

When, more than forty years ago, Wiebe advanced our knowledge of the price revolution by publishing his book, he warned us against assuming that the cheapness of manufactured goods could be explained entirely, or even primarily, by the slow rise in wages. Further investigation, he believed, might show that mechanical improvements were a more important factor than cheap labour.[80] We now know that labour was dearer in England than his calculations suggested, and that the improvements in industrial technology were more sweeping than he suspected.[81] The openings for profits arose mainly because costs of production were reduced by the widespread adoption of better machinery and improved kilns and furnaces, by the increase in the scale of industrial enterprise, and by the discovery and use of new supplies of raw materials such as calamine, alum stone, and, above all, coal.

Labour in France, as well as in England, was no doubt dearer than Wiebe's index numbers indicate. These index numbers were worked out in terms of silver in order to show the effects of the inflow of treasure upon prices. But during the century from 1540 to 1640, the *livre tournois* lost about half, and the shilling between a third and a fourth, of its silver content.[82] Prices rose rather more in France than in England, not less as might be supposed from a glance at Wiebe's tables. If, in these tables, we substitute prices and wages actually paid for prices and wages in terms of silver, the absolute spread between prices and wages which occurs as we proceed through the sixteenth and early seventeenth centuries is increased considerably more in the case of France than in that of England, but the ratio between the two remains the same. In the case of England, as we have seen, that ratio greatly exaggerates the decline in the real earnings of the wage worker during the sixteenth and early seventeenth centuries. Is this equally true in the case of France?

The most important work done on French wages and prices since Wiebe wrote is the study of Poitou by the late Monsieur Raveau.[83] Comparisons are difficult between his results and those which Wiebe obtained from d'Avenel's data, partly because the periods selected by Raveau are

---

[80] Wiebe, *op. cit.*, pp. 239–43.

[81] Cf. Nef, "The Progress of Technology," *loc. cit.*

[82] A. Dieudonné, *Manuel de numismatique française,* Vol. II (Paris, 1916), pp. 314, 351; H. Hauser, Introduction to *La réponse de Jean Bodin à M. de Malestroit* (Paris, 1932), pp. xxvii ff.; Wiebe, *op. cit.*, pp. 30 n., 70. (Cf. A. E. Feavearyear, *The Pound Sterling* (Oxford, 1931), esp. pp. 56–65, 78–79.

[83] P. Raveau, "La crise des prix au XVIe siècle en Poitou," *Revue historique,* 1929, CLXII, 16–24. Cf. his *L'agriculture et les classes paysannes dans le haut Poitou* (Paris, 1926), p. xxxii.

not the same as those selected by Wiebe, and partly because Raveau's averages are computed from wage records for a single province, while Wiebe's are computed from a miscellaneous mixture of sparse records for several provinces.[84] But the two results do not differ widely. Both show that although money wages rose rapidly, their purchasing power in terms of food, fuel and some other commodities fell continually from the accession of Francis I, in 1515, down to the passage of the Edict of Nantes, in 1598, when they were worth hardly half as much as at the beginning of the sixteenth century. Both suggest that real wages rose at the beginning of the seventeenth century. They rose in Poitou more than they are represented by Wiebe's index numbers as rising, but even in Poitou the wage workers were still much worse off in the reign of Louis XIII than their ancestors had been in the reign of Louis XII.

The results obtained by the Commandant Quenedey for Rouen suggest that workmen in the building trades fared better there than in Poitou throughout the period of the price revolution.[85] While food prices apparently rose less in Normandy than in Poitou during the sixteenth century,[86] wage-rates rose more. In Poitou, masons were apparently earning about twice as much money in 1578 as during the last half of the fifteenth century; at Rouen they were apparently earning appreciably more than twice as much.[87] After the Edict of Nantes, the workmen in Poitou gained on their fellows at Rouen. In both cases money wages continued to rise. But food prices were apparently rising in Normandy more than in Poitou,[88] where there was a sharp fall in the price of grain and wine at the end of the sixteenth century.[89] In spite of the gain made by the labourers in Poitou during the second half of Henri IV's reign, they were probably still somewhat worse off under Louis XIII than those at Rouen.

The new wage data collected by the Price Committee for the Ile-de-France are too scanty to serve as a basis for generalisation. So far as they go, they suggest that during the sixteenth century the course of real

84 Wiebe, *op. cit.*, pp. 378–79, 417–19. Cf. d'Avenel, *op. cit.*, Vol. III, pp. 491 ff.

85 R. Quenedey, *Les prix des matériaux et de la main-d'œuvre à Rouen* (offprint from *Bulletin de la Société du commerce et de l'industrie de la Seine-Inférieure*) (Rouen, 1927), pp. 23–25.

86 For Normandy: Quenedey, *op. cit.*, p. 26; Wiebe, *op. cit.*, p. 378; R. Jouanne, "Report on Prices at Caen," among the MSS. of the Price Committee at the London School of Economics. For Poitou: Raveau, *L'agriculture et les classes paysannes*, p. xxxii, and *passim*.

87 Raveau, "La crise des prix," *loc. cit.*, pp. 17, 20–21; Quenedey, *op. cit.*, p. 24.

88 Jouanne, "Report on Prices at Caen"; Wiebe, *op. cit.*, p. 378; Quenedey, *op. cit.*, p. 26.

89 Raveau, *L'agriculture et les classes paysannes*, p. xxxii.

wages in the neighbourhood of Paris differed from that at Rouen as well as from that in Poitou. Workmen appear to have suffered nearly if not quite as much as in Poitou, but the fall in the purchasing power of their wages seems to have been more pronounced during the first half of the century and less pronounced during the second.[90]

It is even more difficult to generalise concerning the material welfare of wage workers in France than in England, not only because we have much less data, but because conditions apparently varied more from region to region.[91] This is not surprising in view of the economic self-sufficiency that persisted in French provinces during the sixteenth and early seventeenth centuries, when it was breaking down in England.[92] What little we know suggests that Wiebe's index numbers exaggerate the decline in the material welfare of the wage workers in most French provinces, as well as in England, but probably not quite as much.

As in England, wage-rates in the building trades appear to have risen nearly everywhere between 1540 and 1640 appreciably more than has been supposed. As in England, they rose more slowly than the prices of foodstuffs and food. We have no means of knowing whether employers provided their workmen with food and drink, in addition to wages, less frequently in France than in England. The French workman who had to support himself and his family mainly out of his wages seems to have suffered more from rising prices than the English workman, in at least two respects. Technical improvements designed to reduce the costs of manufacturing were less widespread in France than in England during the century from 1540 to 1640. It is therefore probable that the costs of milling were not reduced as much to offset the great rise in grain prices common to both countries. When it came to drink, the French workmen, except to some extent in northern France, continued to depend on wine as their ancestors had done from time immemorial. And the price of wine, like that of food, but unlike that of the Englishman's common drink, was rising in some provinces substantially more rapidly than wage-rates.[93]

That was also true of the price of logs and faggots, which remained almost the only fuels burned in hearths and stoves throughout France. Until the period of the religious wars the French workman had an ad-

[90] Reports by Yvonne Bézard and Jean Mallon among the MSS. of the Price Committee at the London School of Economics.

[91] Cf. Usher, *op. cit.*, p. 165.

[92] Cf. Nef, "A Comparison of Industrial Growth in France and England," *loc. cit.*, p. 313.

[93] Raveau, *L'agriculture et les classes paysannes*, p. xxxii.

vantage over his English fellow, because firewood was rising in price more slowly in most parts of France than in England.[94] But after the English workman had substituted coal for logs and faggots, the advantage lay with him, because the price of coal in England increased much more slowly than the price of wood in France. It is not possible to say in which country the workman had to spend a larger proportion of his wages on fuel at the eve of the English Civil War, but for at least half a century in England the proportion had been diminishing.

In France as in England, manufactured articles, such as plain cloth, were rising in price more slowly than wage-rates in the building trades. If the French workman in the reign of Louis XIII had as large a portion of his wages as the English workman to spend in buying these wares, he could have got almost as much for his money.[95] But we know that the output of mines and manufactures was increasing between 1540 and 1640 at a much more rapid rate in England than in France, and it is probable that on the eve of the Civil War the volume of cloth, metal wares, tobacco pipes and perhaps even window panes produced was greater, relative to population, in England.[96] The English manufacturer excelled in the making of plain cloth and other homely wares, which found some sale even among the poorer subjects. This suggests that the purchases of the workmen may have increased more in England than in France, and that by the reign of Charles I the Englishman may have been able to lay out a larger part of his wages than the Frenchman upon the products of the rising industries.

The effects of the price revolution upon the poor man's standard of life were similar in the two countries. Such differences as we have found seem to have been mostly unfavourable to the French workmen. Their real earnings had almost certainly fallen more than those of English workmen by the last quarter of the sixteenth century, as Wiebe's own figures indicated.[97] During the next twenty years their position improved somewhat in many provinces. But it no longer seems likely that the English workmen lost ground in the half-century preceding the Civil War.

---

[94] See p. 319.

[95] It might be supposed that the cost of manufactured goods would have risen more in France than in England, as technical improvements which reduced the quantity of labour needed in manufacturing were less widespread. But the advantage which the English employer enjoyed in this respect was offset by the fact that the prices of the lumber and firewood (and possibly the price of the labour) needed in industry were rising more in England than in France (see pp. 318–19).

[96] Nef, "A Comparison of Industrial Growth," *loc. cit.*, pp. 661–63.

[97] See p. 300.

Wiebe's index numbers did not indicate that the fall in real wages favoured the English much more than the French employer of labour.[98] The new evidence collected since Wiebe's time suggests that the cost of hiring workmen may have decreased more, not less, in France than in England. If cheaper labour had been the principal driving force behind the flow of capital into large-scale enterprise, the pace of industrial change should not have been very much slower in France than in England; it should have been as fast or even faster.

III. THE COST OF TIMBER DURING THE PRICE REVOLUTION

Money wages, Mr. Keynes rightly pointed out, formed only a part of the expenses of carrying on an enterprise in the sixteenth and seventeenth centuries. In constructing his tables of profit-inflation in France and England, he assumed that money wages accounted for half the expenses of production. He further assumed that in both countries all other expenses rose just as rapidly as, according to Wiebe's index numbers, general commodity prices rose. Is this second assumption justified? Did the materials needed in mining and manufacturing rise in price no more and no less rapidly than the average price of all commodities? Were the costs of materials rising equally rapidly in France and in England, or were there differences in the behaviour of these costs which help to explain why more capital should have been invested in large-scale industrial enterprises in England than in France?

After wages, the chief expenses borne by the owners of mines and small factories in the sixteenth century were the sums spent on timber, firewood and charcoal. In the development of large-scale industry at this time, wood largely took the place occupied during the nineteenth century by both iron and coal. Metal was used only for the cutting or striking face of tools, for the gears and axles of machinery, and for the cauldrons and boilers in which various raw materials were heated. Stone and brick were commonly used only for the furnaces and kilns. In spite of the poor resistance wood afforded to the frequent fires, the rest of the plant was nearly all of timber.[99] And, in many industries, the plant was extensive. The clusters of alum and salt houses and the metallurgical works often formed so impressive a phalanx of buildings that contemporaries compared them to villages and even to small towns. At the larger mines, the houses and barns were no less numerous than at the

[98] See pp. 295–96.

[99] Cf. W. Sombart, *Der Moderne Kapitalismus,* Vol. II (1916), pp. 1138–40; Nef, *Rise of the Coal Industry,* Vol. I, p. 191.

alum works, and hundreds of pounds were often spent to obtain the additional deal boards and oaken bars required to timber the shafts. By the middle of the seventeenth century, and possibly even earlier, payments for lumber and planks of various sizes accounted for more than half the cost of building and launching a ship.[100]

Logs, faggots, and charcoal were almost the only fuels used in manufacturing in France throughout the period of the price revolution. In England they were the principal fuels until at least the reign of James I, for it was not much before the end of the sixteenth century that coal began to replace wood extensively in processes other than forging of crude metal wares and the calcining of limestones, for which it had served to some extent even in the Middle Ages. The cost of fuel was considerable in most manufactures; in some, such as glass making and the smelting of ores, it greatly exceeded the cost of lumber for construction work. Scores of acres of woods were consumed every year in supplying one of the large blast furnaces. Farmers of iron works in the Forest of Dean were legally entitled in 1639 to an annual wood supply of 13,500 cords,[101] and they probably used a much larger quantity.

In some industries, therefore, more was spent for lumber, charcoal, and firewood than for labour at the plant. In very few industries did the costs of obtaining wood form a negligible proportion of the costs of production. If we are to discover whether price conditions were more favourable for the development of large-scale industry in England than in France, we must consider the course of timber prices as well as the course of wages.

Everywhere in England the manufacturer was concerned during the reigns of Elizabeth and the first two Stuarts over the phenomenal rise in the price of firewood and lumber. In county after county trees were felled in such profusion to feed the rising industries, that lands once thick with forests could be converted into runs for sheep and cattle, or broken by the plough to supply the new demands for grains. Lumber, logs, and faggots, once available in abundance just beyond the town gates, had to be hauled or carried by wagon and packhorse for miles over rough ground and along miserable pathways full of ruts, or brought in ships from the Baltic countries. Between the decade following the dissolution of the monasteries and the decade preceding the Civil War, while the price of grains increased little more than four-fold and the price of textile wares and various other manufactured goods much less

[100] R. G. Albion, *Forests and Sea Power* (Cambridge, Mass., 1926), p. 94.

[101] *Calendar of State Papers Domestic, 1638–39,* p. 557.

than doubled, the price of firewood increased almost seven times over. Before the second decade of Elizabeth's reign had ended, firewood was already more than twice as dear as it had been in the last decade of her father's reign. By the second decade of Charles I's reign, it was nearly three times again as dear. About eleven pounds were needed at this time to buy as many logs and faggots as had sold for a pound in the first decade of the sixteenth century.[102]

The rise in the price of some kinds of lumber was no less startling, as is revealed by the accounts of the Admiralty for the purchase of naval stores. Continuous records of these purchases do not go back beyond the first decade of Elizabeth's reign. But between this time and the outbreak of the Civil War, planks and timber, mainly of oak, were growing dearer as rapidly as firewood. Four-inch planks cost the Navy more than four times as much in 1632 as in 1567, and timber more than three times as much. In 1637 timber was almost five times, and in 1641 four times as dear as in 1567.[103] Meanwhile the prices of ordinary textile wares and some manufactured goods remained practically stationary,[104] and the price of coal increased only about 20 per cent.[105] Scattered figures covering a longer period[106] suggest that the Navy paid at least fifteen times as much for oak in Charles I's reign as at the accession of Henry VIII. Meanwhile the general price level, according to Wiebe, had not risen much more than fourfold.[107] In spite of these rising costs of the basic material used in shipbuilding, the shipyards grew in number and importance. The tonnage of the royal navy doubled and that of the merchant marine nearly quintupled.[108] A great many other conditions, besides cheap labour, favourable to the progress of industry must have been present to produce an expansion in shipbuilding under such unfavourable price conditions.

With firewood and timber mounting in price much more rapidly than any other commodities, it is natural to suppose that charcoal followed suit. But, in fact, charcoal prices do not seem to have increased more rapidly than the average prices for all commodities. Charcoal was scarcely four times as dear on the eve of the Civil War as at the be-

[102] Wiebe, *op. cit.*, pp. 70, 375.

[103] The data on which these statements are based was kindly supplied by Miss Rayner, who worked out for me, from the Admiralty Accounts (Treasurers' Ledgers), five-year samples of the average price paid for timber and planks from 1567 to the Civil War.

[104] Wiebe, *op. cit.*, pp. 383, 375.

[105] MS. "Chairman's Report on Naval Stores."

[106] Collected by Albion, *op. cit.*, p. 91.

[107] Almost exactly fourfold if we take Wiebe's second set of index numbers rather than his first (see above, footnote 19 on p. 295).

[108] Nef, "A Comparison of Industrial Growth," *loc. cit.*, pp. 308–9.

ginning of the sixteenth century.[109] At first sight this is very puzzling. The price of charring wood was of course an important element in the price of charcoal. It is certain that the price of charring wood rose very much more slowly than the price of timber, probable that as a result of technical improvements in the process it rose less than fourfold. But this can hardly provide an adequate explanation of the great differences between the course of charcoal and timber prices. A more important one is possibly to be found in the fact that charcoal was cheaper to transport than logs. Our prices for both firewood and charcoal are town prices. The rise in timber prices in the towns was undoubtedly caused more by the necessity for hauling wood from greater and greater distances than by the rise in the prices paid where the trees were felled. Costs of transportation were of less, costs of production of more, importance in determining the price of charcoal than in determining the price of logs.

But charcoal was not widely used for fuel by any manufacturer save the smelter, and the prices he paid were not town prices. He bought or leased large tracts of woodlands and hired colliers to char his logs. His blast furnaces and forges exhausted the neighbouring supplies of timber, and the local price of charcoal rose nearly as fast as the local price of firewood.[110] The inevitable result was to force the smelter eventually to move to another wooded site at a greater distance from the chief markets for metal and metal wares. While this kept the price of his fuel from rising rapidly, it made it necessary for him to invest large sums in new furnaces and forges and in water-driven machinery to operate the bellows and the hammers. The rise in charcoal prices in the towns is a poor guide to the rise in the costs of producing metal caused by the exhaustion of the forests.

In the Age of Elizabeth, England was faced with a timber crisis, brought about partly by the increase in population but mainly by the remarkable growth of industry. This crisis increased the expenses of mining and manufacturing so much that the average rise of commodity prices is no index to the rise in the costs of industrial materials.

The course of wood prices, like that of grain prices and wages, varied more from region to region in France than in England. But except in a few regions such as the densely populated Ile-de-France,[111] firewood did

[109] Wiebe, *op. cit.,* pp. 70, 375.

[110] Cf., e.g., *Hist. MSS. Com., Report on the MSS. of the Marquis of Salisbury,* Vol. XII, pp. 20–23.

[111] Reports of Yvonne Bézard and Jean Mallon among the MSS. of the Price Committee at the London School of Economics.

not become conspicuously dearer than other commodities during the price revolution. Wiebe's index numbers for France, which were compiled from data collected by d'Avenel for several provinces, show no very great deviation between the trend of firewood and general commodity prices.[112] Raveau's more recent and more detailed work shows that in Poitou between 1515 and 1598 the price of firewood rose less than the price of grain and about as much as that of wine.[113] We have a new series of prices from 1558 to 1640 for logs and faggots bought at Château-Gontier, on the Mayenne.[114] While faggots were about three and a half times as dear in the last decade of Louis XIII's reign as in the decade preceding the religious wars, logs were rather less than two and a half times as dear. They had not risen in price more than such commodities as beans, butter, salt and red wine. In most French provinces, the rise in the price of wood is explained almost entirely by the increase in the supply of silver and the debasement of the currency.

The costs of fuel and doubtless also of lumber, the principal materials needed in mining and manufacturing, were rising in England much more than in France until at least the beginning of the seventeenth century. After that coal replaced firewood and charcoal in many English industries so extensively that most English manufacturers, except the smelters, began to have an advantage in the costs of fuel. Their disadvantage probably increased when it came to the purchase of lumber.

If industrial enterprise proved less profitable in France than in England during the price revolution, this cannot be explained on the ground that wood or labour were dearer. In fact wood, and probably also labour, were cheaper. The immediate explanation seems to be that in France technical changes which reduced the quantity of labour required in mining and manufacturing were less frequently made than in England, that there was no such growth in the scale of enterprise, and no such exploitation of new supplies of raw materials, like calamine, alum and coal, the widespread use of which cheapened production in many industries.

Neither the sweeping changes in technique and in the scale of indus-

---

[112] Wiebe took 100 as the price of all commodities during the last half of the fifteenth century. With this base, his index numbers for the first half of the seventeenth century—which express prices in terms of silver—show firewood at 212.5, general commodity prices at 216 in France. For England, they show firewood at 554 and general commodities at 282, or 245 if Wiebe's second, differently-weighted table is the basis of comparison (Wiebe, *op. cit.*, pp. 278–79, 375, 377, 383).

[113] Raveau, *L'agriculture et les classes paysannes,* p. xxxii.

[114] Report of René Gauchet among the MSS. of the Price Committee at the London School of Economics.

trial enterprise, nor the exploitation of new raw materials, were an inevitable result of the inflow of American silver, or of the decline in real wages that accompanied it. If they had been, an early industrial revolution would have occurred in France to match the one in England.

IV. CONCLUSION

A comparison of prices and industrial capitalism in France and England from 1540 to 1640 does not prove that the price revolution failed to stimulate industrial development. It shows that the influence of price changes was complex rather than simple, and it warns us against the tempting assumption that the remarkably long period of rising prices, common to all European countries, was of compelling importance for the rise of industrialism.

By raising prices, the inflow of treasure from America helped to keep down the costs of the labour and the land[115] needed for mining and manufacturing, and thus encouraged the investment of capital in large-scale enterprise, as Professor Hamilton and Mr. Keynes pointed out. But the decline in the real earnings of wage workers was nothing like as great as has been supposed since the time of Rogers and d'Avenel. Had the standard of living among the English working people really fallen by anything approaching half, the advantages which employers derived from hiring labour cheaply might have been offset by the reduction in the amount workmen could have spent on manufactured goods. The expansion of the mining, the metallurgical, the glass and the textile industries in Elizabethan England was brought about to some extent by the growth of home markets among the common people. If the earnings of nearly all wage workers had been cut to the bare minimum required for subsistence according to medieval standards, the demand for grates, window panes, cloth, bedding, tobacco and crude table ware could hardly have grown as rapidly as it did.

The moderate fall in real wages that occurred in England with every

[115] As I remarked above (see p. 293), Professor Hamilton suggested that cheap land as well as cheap labour probably stimulated investments in industrial enterprises. We do not know whether land rents rose more slowly than did the prices paid to mine owners and manufacturers for their products. In any case, the price revolution probably kept the costs of rent lower in every country than they would have been but for the inflow of American treasure. But the dissolution of the monasteries, which occurred on the eve of the early English industrial revolution, was probably of as great importance in England as the inflow of silver and the debasement of the coinage in making it possible for adventurers to acquire land for mining and manufacturing on favourable terms (cf. Nef, *Rise of the Coal Industry,* Vol. I, pp. 133–56). Unlike the price revolution, the dissolution of the monasteries helps to explain why industrial development in England should have been more rapid than in France.

rapid rise in prices tended to increase profits, to promote the accumulation of wealth and to encourage the investment of funds in mining and manufacturing, especially during the forties and fifties of the sixteenth century, the only period of considerable duration in which wage-rates may have risen more slowly than the prices of manufactured products. But the discoveries had little to do with the rise in prices which made possible the decline in real wages before the accession of Elizabeth. The rise in prices during the first half of the sixteenth century was caused by debasement of the coinage, and more commodities could be bought with the same quantity of silver when Edward VI became King, in 1547, than in the reign of his grandfather, Henry VII.

The rapid rise in the real costs of the indispensable supplies of timber provided a stimulus of a different kind from the fall in real wages. It helped to bring about improvements in industrial technique, which might have been less widespread had the need for them been less urgent. Without these improvements, the increasing costs of materials must have checked the growth of English industries, no matter how cheaply labour could have been hired.

French history shows that a prolonged decline in the real wages of labour, while undoubtedly an incentive to enterprise, was not by itself a sufficiently powerful influence to cause an industrial expansion, or even to prevent an industrial depression. It is possible that during the last quarter of the sixteenth century the fall in the workmen's standard of living in France was so great as to stop the growth of the demand for some industrial products and that the misery of the poor hindered more than it helped the progress of manufactures during the religious wars.

Industry was responding in different ways in the various European countries to the strains and the stimuli provided by the inflow of American treasure and the debasement of the coinage. Whether or not the response took the form of greatly increased activity in sinking mining shafts and setting up new manufacturing enterprises, depended mainly on conditions independent of the price revolution. Further comparisons between French and English history will help to reveal these conditions.

17

*Profit Inflation and the Industrial Revolution, 1751–1800**

By EARL J. HAMILTON

The evolution of machinery began at the dawn of civilization; and complex machines driven by water power had been perfected in Italy, particularly in the silk industry, long before the close of the Middle Ages. Practically every country in Europe had achieved substantial technological progress before 1750; but at no time or place were the advances sufficiently rapid, sweeping, pervasive, or permanent to appear *revolutionary* to succeeding generations. Despite a strong reluctance to fix precise dates for broad economic movements and a general recognition that the Industrial Revolution was essentially a sharp acceleration of progress already under way, most economic historians have placed its beginning in or near the decade, 1761–70, that witnessed the birth of the modern steam engine and the emergence of the great textile inventions.[1] Although many of the important new machines and processes were not generally adopted until the nineteenth century, by 1800 the inventions of Watt, Cort, Crompton, Cartwright, and a host of lesser lights had clearly demonstrated their potential superiority. Textile, engineering, and metallurgical progress in England during the second half

* *Quarterly Journal of Economics,* 1942, LVI, 256–73. Reprinted by courtesy of the author and Harvard University Press.

[1] See, for examples: Paul Mantoux, *La Révolution Industrielle au XVIIIe Siècle* (Paris, 1906), pp. 1, 5–6, 16, 199; Karl Marx, *Das Kapital* (3d ed.), Vol. I, p. 335; G. W. Daniels, *The Early English Cotton Industry* (Manchester, 1920), p. 1; J. A. Hobson, *The Evolution of Modern Capitalism* (London, 1906), pp. 71–72; Élie Halévy, *Histoire du Peuple Anglais au XIXe Siècle,* Vol. I (Paris, 1912), p. 260; C. R. Fay, *Great Britain from Adam Smith to the Present Day* (London, 1928), p. 303; T. H. Marshall, *James Watt* (London, 1925), p. 9; T. S. Ashton, *Iron and Steel in the Industrial Revolution* (Manchester, 1924), p. 60; Witt Bowden, *Industrial Society in England Towards the End of the Eighteenth Century* (New York, 1925), pp. 12–13, 73, 207; Arnold Toynbee, *Lectures on the Industrial Revolution of the 18th Century in England* (London, 1906 ed.), pp. 27, 32; W. Cunningham, *The Industrial Revolution* (Cambridge, 1908), pp. 609 ff.; George Unwin, *Studies in Economic History* (London, 1927), p. 339; N. S. B. Gras, *Industrial Evolution* (Cambridge, Mass., 1930), p. 99.

of the eighteenth century insured the eventual triumph of machine technique and the rise of the modern factory system.

That profit inflation through a lag of wages behind prices, a factor hitherto overlooked by economists and historians, facilitated the Industrial Revolution during the second half of the eighteenth century, the critical incipient stage, is the chief thesis of this article; but I specifically recognize that a favorable price-wage ratio was neither the sole nor the only important cause. Without a conjuncture of liberal institutions, public and private stimuli to mechanical research, expansion of commerce, epoch-making advances in pure science, progress in agriculture, rich natural resources, a favorable climate, insular protection against military invasion, and many other factors, the Industrial Revolution could not have occurred.

To ascertain the rôle of profit inflation, comprehensive records of commodity prices, money wages, man-hour output, and business profits are needed for every important industry and locality. Unfortunately, we can only guess at variations in man-hour output; and data on profits are meager and unreliable. Continuous index numbers of both commodity prices and money wages can be computed for very few regions from series now available. Although the price series obtainable for London are incomplete and fail to include important groups of consumption goods, and despite the regional discrepancies in English wage movements, index numbers of prices and wages at London furnish the best available gauge of relative price and wage movements. The capital and by far the largest consuming center, the metropolis was in close economic and political contact with the remainder of the country. Commodity prices and money wages at London reflected the forces that influenced their movements throughout the realm.

Chart I presents index numbers of commodity prices and money wages at London in 1729–1800 on 1729–33 as a base. The price indices have been computed from series supplied by Sir William Beveridge[2] from the account books of the Greenwich and Chelsea Hospitals. Sixteen commodities[3] are included. Since Sir William has deferred the publication of wage rates to a later volume, I have relied upon data found in Dr. Elizabeth Waterman Gilboy's *Wages in Eighteenth Century England.*[4] My index numbers of wages represent equally weighted me-

[2] *Prices and Wages in England from the Twelfth to the Nineteenth Century* (London, 1939), pp. 291–98, 313.

[3] Beer, bread, butcher's meat, butter, candles, cheese, coal, hats, hops, malt, milk, oatmeal, peas, salt, shoes and stockings.

[4] (Cambridge, Mass., 1934), pp. 254–58.

dians of the rates for craftsmen and laborers employed by the Greenwich Hospital and Westminster Abbey until 1787, when the Westminster series end, and by Greenwich Hospital alone in 1788–1800. The wage

CHART I

Prices and Wages at London (Base – 1729–33)

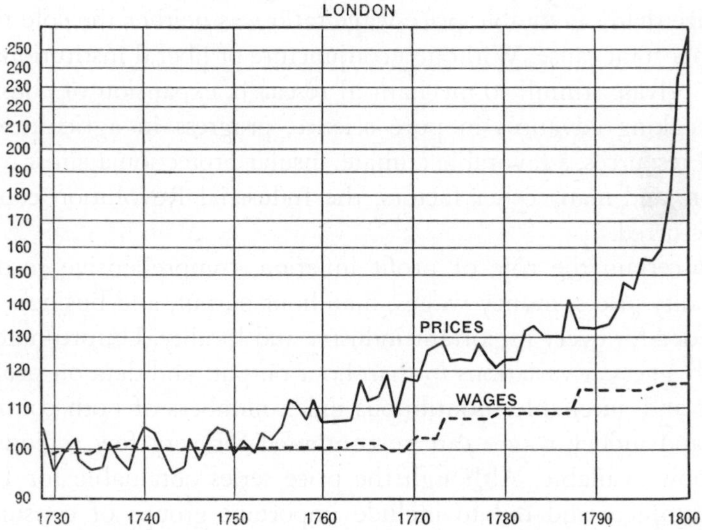

series comprise four classes of unskilled labor and six of craftsmen at Westminster Abbey and six classes of each at the Greenwich Hospital. All the classes at both institutions represent the building trades exclusively; but there is reason to believe that even in later periods characterized by greater economic flexibility and craft diversification the rates of pay of artisans and laborers engaged in building have proved to be representative of general wages.[5]

The chief factor in the failure of wages to keep pace with soaring prices in the second half of the eighteenth century was the "natural" inertia of wage movements in both directions. History records few instances of wage movements in unison with rapidly changing commodity prices. A considerable increase in the supply of labor through a large growth of the population and a heavy immigration of Irish workers, with low living standards, also obstructed wage increases. A marked acceleration of enclosures had a similar effect. Many cottagers lost their

[5] Professor Bowley found this to be the case in his investigation of British wages in the nineteenth century (*Wages in the United Kingdom in the Nineteenth Century* [London, 1900], p. 63), and Dr. Gilboy concluded that wages in the building trades "may be taken, therefore, as representing average London rates among the laborers in a 'middling' position, neither of the highest nor the lowest groups" (*op. cit.*, p. 19).

customary rights to the soil in the process, and not all free- and copyholders escaped the same fate. The legal expenses involved and the cost of draining, fencing, and adapting the land to a new type of agriculture immediately displaced many peasants of moderate means and forced others to incur debts that later swept away their holdings. As the expropriation of peasants was swelling the ranks of labor, the conversion of arable into pasture, the elimination of waste through the consolidation of land parcels, and the economies achieved through scientific farming were curtailing the demand for workers. The weakening of remaining guild restrictions and effective public opposition to nascent trade unionism at a time when Adam Smith tells us that "masters are always and everywhere in a sort of tacit, but constant and uniform combination, not to raise the wages of labour above their actual rate"[6] enhanced the natural advantage of employers in wage bargains.

The lack of unemployment statistics makes it impossible to measure real incomes, and the want of data on house rents and shifts of consumption in response to changes in relative prices render real wage indices inaccurate. It seems certain, however, that daily real wages dropped considerably in London during the last five or six decades of the eighteenth century.[7] In a very thorough study of "Real Wages of Artisans in London, 1729–1835,"[8] Dr. Rufus Tucker's index shows a decline from 58.6 in 1741–50 to 43.3 in 1791–1800. Benevolence born of moral philosophy, combined with necessity resulting from the drop in real wages, forced larger and larger grants of charity from public and private sources;[9] and the regularity and the volume of employment, windfalls through opportunities to work overtime, and the chance for women and children to supplement family earnings doubtless increased with business prosperity. A part of these gains was neutralized by the migration of

[6] Adam Smith, *Wealth of Nations,* Vol. I (Cannan ed.), pp. 68–69.

[7] In her scholarly *Wages in Eighteenth Century England,* Dr. Gilboy argues that real wages remained stable in some parts of England and rose in others, but this conclusion rests upon a comparison of money wages with wheat prices and upon the observations of contemporary writers. From William Petty to Alfred Marshall eminent British economists have estimated real wages in terms of the ratio of money wages to wheat prices, but one must not forget that men have never eaten wheat. Wheat was not the sole or even the chief component of bread prices, and man did not live by bread alone. The contemporaries who reported declining real wages (that is, stable money wages in the face of rising prices) in the second half of the eighteenth century are at least as impressive as those who held the contrary opinion. But this evidence is worth little. In judging few economic or natural phenomena is the naked eye as unreliable as in estimating price and wage movements.

[8] *Jour. Am. Stat. Assoc.,* XXXI, 73–84.

[9] Dorothy Marshall, *The English Poor in the Eighteenth Century* (London, 1926), pp. 51–56, 76–77, 153, 159–60.

textile processes into factories, which decreased the opportunity for workers and their families to earn something at home during periods of unemployment or slack business, and by enclosures, which extinguished valuable rights to pastures, garden plots, and forests.[10] The annual real incomes of workers probably fell much less than the daily rates of real wages measured by Dr. Tucker's indices. But to some workers charity was demoralizing and unpalatable, and to many a loss of leisure entailed genuine disutility.

The wage series for Lancashire compiled by Dr. Gilboy[11] rose slightly more in the second half of the eighteenth century than the price series used in the present study and as much as the price indices for London constructed by Dr. Tucker. This was at least partially due to the mechanical improvement in this area, which raised the output of labor. A given rate represented a lower efficiency wage in the north of England than in other districts. If money wages had not remained low in the rest of the country, presumably they would have risen still more in Lancashire. Because of the heavy influx of workers, house rents and the price of food probably rose a great deal more than at London. Consequently, it is by no means certain that an index of real wages for Lancashire based upon a satisfactory index of the cost of living would not show a decline.

Technological unemployment did not actually depress wage rates and even may not have intensified the lag behind prices by preventing a rise. Wages rose more in the Midlands, the seat of the Industrial Revolution, than in other parts of England in the last four decades of the eighteenth century. The demand for labor in the urban districts caused a scarcity of agricultural workers in Lancashire,[12] and Peter Stubbs experienced considerable difficulty in obtaining an adequate supply of laborers for his file works at Warrington.[13] So keen was the competition for labor in the silver plate trade of Sheffield that "masters were continually enticing the workmen from each other's houses, giving them money to *hire* with them, and letting them get into debt as a kind of security."[14] In November, 1769, Josiah Wedgwood complained of inability to find " 'hands to finish so much building in so short a time,' "[15] and in the same year

---

[10] E. S. Furniss, *The Position of the Laborer in a System of Nationalism* (New York, 1920), pp. 218–19; Cunningham, *op. cit.*, pp. 16–17.

[11] *Op. cit.*, pp. 280–87.

[12] Gilboy, *op. cit.*, p. 188.

[13] T. S. Ashton, *An Eighteenth-Century Industrialist* (Manchester, 1939), pp. 23–26.

[14] *The Songs of Joseph Mather,* Introduction, p. xvii, cited by Ashton, *ibid.*, p. 35.

[15] Ralph M. Hower, "The Wedgwoods: Ten Generations of Potters," *Journal of Economic and Business History,* IV, 289.

he reported that there "is not a hand loose in the country to be hired."[16] Despite the Act of Settlement and the restrictive force of the Poor Laws, laborers migrated into the industrial Midlands in large numbers. The liberation of purchasing power through a relative decline in the prices of the goods produced under the new technique, continuous expansion of the capital goods industry, agricultural improvements, and public works apparently more than counterbalanced the technological displacement of labor.

In a period of rising prices such as England experienced in the last half of the eighteenth century, inventory appreciation raised normal business profits; but this gain was insignificant in comparison with the windfalls accruing from a lag of wages behind prices. Under present conditions wages represent from 60 to 70 per cent of the total cost of producing most consumers' goods. In all probability they represented a considerably greater share in the eighteenth century, when much less machinery and other forms of capital were in use.[17] If we assume that the efficiency of labor remained constant and that wages accounted for 70 per cent[18] of the expenses of production of the articles in Chart I (practically all of which are consumers' goods) and make the extremely unlikely assumption that the remaining 30 per cent rose as much as prices, we find that the lag of wages tended to raise a hypothetical average of 10 per cent profits in 1741–50 to 14 per cent in 1751–60, 19 per cent in 1761–70, 22 per cent in 1771–80, 24 per cent in 1781–90, and 42 per cent in 1791–1800.[19] Inasmuch as the rent of land and mines,[20] leased under long-term contracts, also tended to lag behind prices, these figures may underestimate the inflation of profits. Furthermore, the enhanced man-hour output of labor due to technological im-

[16] *Ibid.*, p. 299.

[17] "Those who live upon the wages of labour, unproductive as well as productive, receive and expend much the greatest part of the annual produce . . ." (T. R. Malthus, *Principles of Political Economy* [London, 1820], p. 423).

[18] "In 1798 direct labour cost at Wedgwood's was 40 per cent of the value of Useful ware, and 67 per cent of the value of Ornamental" (V. W. Bladen, "The Potteries in the Industrial Revolution," *Econ. Hist.*, 1926–29, I, 125). Of course, the indirect labor costs, in the purchase of tools and materials, for example, were also considerable.

[19] The price and wage indices compiled by Tucker ("Real Wages of Artisans" *loc. cit.*, XXXI, 73–84) to measure real wages at London show a significantly greater lag of wages than do the indices used in this article.

[20] Long leases of coal mines were typical in the eighteenth century, but in some cases there was provision for profit sharing and for an increase in rents and royalties in the later years. When such arrangements were lacking, heavy profits were made from rising prices. For example, a colliery let by the Duke of Norfolk in 1737 at "£400 a year was relet (with, it is true, a slight increase in the acreage) for £6000 a year in 1805." (T. S. Ashton and Joseph Sykes, *The Coal Industry of the Eighteenth Century* [Manchester, 1929], p. 191.)

provement tended to accentuate the rise in profits and doubtless more than counter-balanced the decrease in efficiency resulting from a rise in the volume of employment and from the lower standard of consumption accompanying the fall in real wages. The high level of profits raised large incomes, which always have supplied practically all the savings in a capitalistic society. As Professor J. M. Keynes has pointed out,[21] savings without investment not only would have proved fruitless but would have depressed business and thus limited saving. By keeping the normal rate of profit far above the prevailing rate of interest, the lag of wages behind prices stimulated the investment of savings as they took place. According to one estimate, in 1740–1800 the supply of capital in Great Britain, exclusive of land, more than quintupled.[22]

An outburst of mechanical invention accompanied this growth of capital. The English patents issued jumped from 82 in 1740–49 to 92 in 1750–59, 205 in 1760–69, 294 in 1770–79, and 477 in 1780–89. Impressive as these figures are, they tend to underestimate the volume of invention; for the quality rose with the quantity, and a progressively smaller proportion of effective contrivances was patented. As the century advanced, the procedure for obtaining patents grew longer and more elaborate and expensive. Drawings and models replaced vague descriptions, and specifications became more definite and difficult to formulate. Before 1760 the government, private industry, and the various associations for the encouragement of useful arts made few grants to inventors in lieu of patents; but after this date inventors often accepted bonuses from one or more of these groups to waive their patent privileges.[23]

Many other material and intellectual factors played a part in the swift growth of inventions, but the increased capital supply was of paramount importance.[24] Most of the inventors lived upon hope and thin air instead of drawing support from capitalists while pioneering their devices; but the development of practically all inventions to the point of economic usefulness required heavy investments. It seems that the mechanical genius of James Watt, the greatest inventor of all, eventually saved the enterprise of Boulton from bankruptcy;[25] but without

---

[21] *The General Theory of Employment, Interest, and Money* (London, 1936), pp. 52–85.

[22] John Lord, *Capital and Steam-Power* (London, 1923), pp. 182–84.

"The amount of capital in this country is immense, and it certainly received very great additions during the last twenty-five years . . ." (Malthus, *op. cit.*, p. 421).

[23] Bowden, *op. cit.*, pp. 13–14, 28, 32.

[24] "If Science is the mother of invention, Finance is its father" (Marshall, *op. cit.*, p. 84).

[25] J. E. Cule, "Finance and Industry in the Eighteenth Century: The Firm of Boulton and Watt," *Econ. Hist.*, 1938–40, IV, 319–25.

years of substantial financial assistance from Dr. Black, Roebuck, and Boulton,[26] Watt's steam engine might never have pumped a gallon of water or turned a factory wheel.[27] The spinning jenny of Hargreaves, in reality a household instrument that temporarily strengthened the domestic system, was unique among the great inventions in requiring little experimentation, waiting, or investment for its introduction.[28]

The plowing back of earnings provided a large part of the capital required for the development of the factory system;[29] but, although the new machinery was generally crude in the beginning, almost invariably substantial sums were necessary in advance for its purchase, installation, and operation during initial periods of loss.[30]

The inflation of profits through the lag of wages behind prices facilitated the accumulation of funds for investment in new enterprises and widened the margin of earnings to be plowed back. Various types of agricultural improvements, the construction and improvement of highways, an orgy of canal building, the increased depths of mines, imperial expansion, and the provision of housing and other accommodations for a growing population were making heavy claims upon English capital

---

[26] Marshall, *op. cit.*, pp. 54–55, 87–90, 95–97, 126, 132–33; Fay, *op. cit.*, p. 254; Mantoux, *op. cit.*, pp. 329–32; Lord, *op. cit.*, pp. 76, 80.

[27] A lack of capital deprived the spinning machine of Paul and Wyatt, patented in 1738, of value in their hands; and this was an important factor in the several failures of Thomas Highs to exploit his water frame (Mantoux, *op. cit.*, pp. 206, 224). Unable to secure sufficient funds to utilize or even to patent the mule, the most important of all the textile inventions, Samuel Crompton gave up his secret in return for a voluntary subscription which yielded only £67 7*s* 6*d* (J. L. and Barbara Hammond, *The Skilled Labourer, 1760–1832* [London, 1920], p. 52). The skill of Richard Arkwright in obtaining financial backing was hardly less important than his managerial ability in putting the water frame into actual industrial use (cf. Daniels, *op. cit.*, pp. 221, 228; Hammond, *op. cit.*, p. 222).

[28] Gras, *op. cit.*, pp. 96–98; Mantoux, *op. cit.*, p. 309.

[29] L. H. Jenks, *The Migration of British Capital to 1875* (New York, 1927), p. 15; Ashton, *Iron and Steel in the Industrial Revolution,* pp. 46–48, 226; Ashton and Sykes, *op. cit.*, p. 6; Unwin, Introduction to Daniels, *op. cit.*, pp. xxix–xxx.

[30] George Unwin, *Samuel Oldknow and the Arkwrights* (Manchester, 1924), pp. 57, 115.

"According to Arkwright's statement, 'it was not till upwards of five years had elapsed after obtaining his first patent, and more than £12,000 had been expended in machinery and buildings, that any profit accrued to himself and partners' " (Daniels, *op. cit.*, p. 100). Cort exhausted all of his resources in starting the new iron processes that he had invented and then pledged his patents to Adam Jellicoe, who advanced him £50,000 of his own and the Government's funds (Ashton, *Iron and Steel in the Industrial Revolution,* p. 94; Fay, *op. cit.*, p. 271). It has been estimated that Boulton invested £47,000 in the development of the steam engine before any profits were realized, and "any business that could afford the initial cost of one of Boulton's and Watt's engines [which covered only the actual cost of manufacture and installation without any royalties, which were derived from the fuel economies obtained from the engine] must have possessed a large amount of capital" (Lord, *op. cit.*, p. 147; Mantoux, *op. cit.*, pp. 335–37).

and might have curbed industrial progress if the supply of investment funds had not increased rapidly enough to meet all demands.[31]

Although steadily increasing after 1750, the number of banks in England was not large until after the Bank suspension in 1797; and inasmuch as joint-stock companies or associations with more than six partners were excluded by an Act of Parliament, the banks necessarily remained small. London was the only city where they had control over significant capital.[32] There is little evidence that bankers were in a position to finance the exploitation of inventions and still less evidence that they were willing to do so.[33] A steady stream of capital accumulated in industry flowed into banking in the eighteenth century,[34] and it may well have exceeded the current in the reverse direction.[35]

In at least one respect the lag of wages behind prices, giving a low relative wage, tended to retard the Industrial Revolution. If wages had kept pace with prices, the inducement to invent and utilize labor-saving

---

31 M. M. Postan has attributed the difficulty experienced in financing new enterprises at the beginning of the Industrial Revolution to the specific nature of savings and to the imperfect investment market rather than to an absolute scarcity of capital ("Recent Trends in the Accumulation of Capital," *Econ. Hist. Rev.*, 1935–36, VI, 1–5). But Gras (*op. cit.*, p. 96) and Fay (*op. cit.*, pp. 128, 174) have recognized an absolute scarcity.

32 "English banks at this period [end of the eighteenth century] were small, private concerns and their notes circulated generally only within a limited area" (Ashton, *An Eighteenth-Century Industrialist*, p. 103).

33 Postan, "Recent Trends in the Accumulation of Capital," *loc. cit.*, p. 2.

"Nevertheless in Watt's day the financing of a new enterprise was a very difficult operation. The banks were mostly small affairs without substantial resources, and as has always been the practice in England, were not prepared to take any of the risks of business" (Marshall, *op. cit.*, p. 86).

A provincial banker supplied Arkwright with some credit but withdrew his support after one year; and only after securing the assistance of Need and Strutt, both industrialists, did he move forward. The repeated refusal of bankers to accommodate Watt and Boulton attests their reluctance to take the risks inherent in the utilization of inventions. Josiah Wedgwood, of pottery fame, advanced "£5000 to tide Matthew Boulton over his financial difficulties at Soho, during the experimental stages of the manufacture of the steam-engine" (John Thomas, "The Pottery Industry and the Industrial Revolution," *Econ. Hist.*, 1931–32, III, 407–8).

34 Cf. Ashton, *Iron and Steel in the Industrial Revolution*, pp. 227–31.

"In November, 1799, John Highway of Shrewsbury sent a 'Broasley five guinea Bill No. 447'—probably a note of a bank set up by the ironmaster, John Wilkinson" (Ashton, *An Eighteenth-Century Industrialist*, p. 102). "Some time in the early [17] 'eighties Lyon and Kerfoot had joined with a sugar-boiler, Joseph Parr, to set up the Warrington Bank, then known as Parr, Lyon & Co. (and later simply as Parr's) which is now merged in the Westminster Bank" (Ashton, *ibid.*, p. 113).

35 As Ashton has pointed out (*An Eighteenth-Century Industrialist*, p. 116), "we are shamefully ignorant of . . . the part played by the banking system in the financing of the Industrial Revolution"; but it appears that banks had "little to do with the inception of business." Although there may have been some interaction, the rise of English banking on a considerable scale seems to have been more nearly a result than a cause of the Industrial Revolution (cf. A. E. Feavearyear, *The Pound Sterling* [Oxford, 1931], p. 152).

machinery would have been somewhat greater. But even the crude machinery of the eighteenth century could do some work that the laborer could not perform with tools; and no wage, however low, would have permitted men to compete with machines in many lines of work.[36] The lag of agricultural rents behind prices reduced the real incomes of large landowners, the chief exponents of high farming, and thus diminished the resources available for agricultural experimentation. Rising prices also tended to deter long leases, which were advocated by Arthur Young and other farm leaders and which undoubtedly promoted agricultural improvement. But these tendencies were partially counterbalanced by the inducement that lagging rents offered to progressive landowners to consolidate their holdings and exploit them with hired labor directly or indirectly under their supervision.

Depression of the market for consumers' goods by a low daily rate of real wages, so greatly feared in many quarters of the globe today, did not obstruct the Industrial Revolution in its early stages. Economic historians agree that a sellers' market prevailed in the second half of the eighteenth century, when real wages were falling steadily—that the great problem was to make goods as fast as they could be sold.[37] There is general recognition that the pressure of demand upon existing modes of production was a major factor in the adoption of the new technique.[38]

To test the thesis that the Industrial Revolution resulted partially from rising prices and lagging wages, let us turn to other countries and periods.

Chart II portrays the movement of price indices for New Castile, the great central region of Spain, in 1729–1800 and of wage indices in 1737–1800 on 1726–50 as a base. The price indices include 103 commodities and the wage indices thirteen grades of labor. Both series have been taken from contemporaneous account books in the public, private,

---

[36] The mechanization of industry in such low-wage areas as the southern part of the United States and the Orient illustrates the inability of labor to compete with machinery.

[37] Malthus, *op. cit.*, pp. 402, 407–12; Unwin, *Samuel Oldknow and the Arkwrights,* pp. 9, 57, 103; Mantoux, *op. cit.*, p. 210; Bowden, *op. cit.*, pp. 66–68, 119; Daniels, *op cit.*, p. 133.

[38] Cf. Herbert Heaton, "Benjamin Gott and the Industrial Revolution in Yorkshire," *Econ. Hist. Rev.,* 1931–32, III, 54; Bladen, "The Potteries in the Industrial Revolution," *loc. cit.,* 117–119; Hower, "The Wedgwoods," *loc. cit.*, pp. 300–301.

Even Sismondi recognized that the market was too brisk for existing productive capacity in the early days of the Industrial Revolution. "Le travail, père de toute production, manquait encore, il y a soixante ans, [i.e. 1777] aux besoins du monde. Ni les bras, ni le capital, ni la science appliquée aux arts, ne suffisaient aux demandes de la consommation . . ." (J. C. L. Simonde de Sismondi, *Études sur l'Économie Politique,* Vol. I [Paris, 1837], p. 59).

and ecclesiastic archives of Madrid, Toledo, and Alcalá de Henares.[39]

The lag of wages behind prices was even more pronounced than in England, and there is general agreement among scholars that Spain arose from the ruin and decadence into which she had fallen in the

CHART II

PRICES AND WAGES IN NEW CASTILE (Base=1726–50)

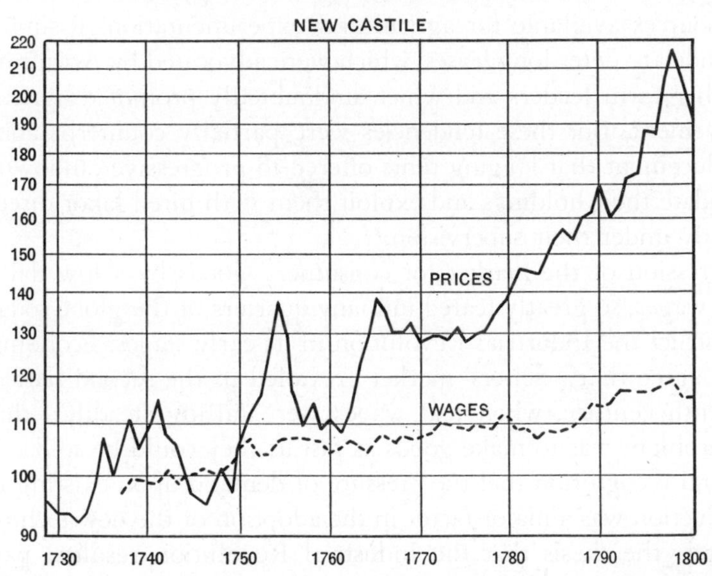

seventeenth century, when prices lagged behind wages,[40] and built a substantial and diversified industry. During the eighteenth century "many ancient manufactures revived; new ones were created under royal privileges, and certain ones of them succeeded perfectly. Industries such as the construction of iron stocking frames, silk printing, and the manufacture of tin plate, until then unknown in Spain, were born."[41] The manufacture of cotton began at Barcelona in 1746; and "it is to the cotton industry that one must attribute the modern prosperity of Catalonia, which dates from the middle of the eighteenth century."[42] At the end of the eighteenth century travelers reported that the linen, silk, woolen, hemp, cotton, potash, glass, and cutlery manufactures had made rapid strides in recent decades, and that in some instances they were in

[39] For complete information concerning the indices, see my forthcoming book on *Money, Prices, and Wages in Spain, 1651–1800,* to be published by the Harvard University Press in 1942.

[40] Earl J. Hamilton, "The Decline of Spain," *Econ. Hist. Rev.*, 1937–38, VIII, 178.

[41] André Mounier, *Les Faits et la Doctrine Économiques en Espagne sous Philippe V: Gerónimo de Uztáriz, 1670–1732* (Bordeaux, 1919), pp. 122–23.

[42] Mounier, *ibid.*, p. 129.

a position to compete in foreign markets with the best that Europe could offer.[43] Steam engines were in use at Cartagena, and a water frame of the Arkwright type was spinning American cotton at Barcelona.[44] Canal projects rivaling any in existence were under construction. The climate, resources, educational system, and institutions of Spain prevented her from challenging the industrial advances of England; but at least one English traveler could report in 1786 that "in every country a traveller can pass through, he will find some mechanical contrivances, some modes of expediting work, which are of late invention, or at least new to him; and I am inclined to think, that no country, if thoroughly examined, would furnish more than Spain."[45]

Particularly significant is the fact that Dr. André Mounier,[46] who attributed the economic recovery of Spain to the mercantilism of Gerónimo de Uztáriz[47] and the policies introduced by Philip V (1701–46), and Manuel Colmeiro,[48] who ascribed the economic revival to the influence of the *Wealth of Nations,* the first Spanish translation of which did not appear until 1794,[49] agreed that Spain achieved her greatest material progress in the second half of the eighteenth century—a date much more convenient for the present writer than for either Mounier or Colmeiro!

Despite the rich price and wage records awaiting investigation in the French archives, the published data available for every historical period are notoriously weak. With all their defects, the price and wage series compiled by Professor C. E. Labrousse,[50] largely from the reports of the *intendants* (which may or may not correspond with market quotations), seem to be the best now in print for the eighteenth century. According

---

[43] J. F. Bourgoing, *Tableau de L'Espagne Moderne* (3d ed., Paris, 1803), Vol. I, pp. 108–12, 209–14, 323–24; Vol. III, pp. 126, 155–56, 216–17, 230–37, 339–41; Joseph Townsend, *A Journey through Spain in the Years 1786 and 1787* (3d ed., Dublin, 1792), Vol. I, pp. 90–91, 153, 326; Vol. II, pp. 239–40, 323–24. Cf. Mounier, *op. cit.,* pp. 101–35; Manuel Colmeiro, *Historia de la Economía Política en España,* Vol. II (Madrid, 1863), p. 221, note 3.

[44] Townsend, *op. cit.,* Vol. I, pp. 90–91; Vol. II, p. 235.

[45] Townsend, *op. cit.,* Vol. I, p. 93.

Cf. F. -A. de Christophoro d'Avalos, *Essai sur le Commerce et les Intérêts de l'Espagne et de ses Colonies* (Paris, 1819), p. 45; Alvaro Florez Estrada, *Examen Imparcial de las Disensiones de la América con la España* (London, 1811), p. 211.

[46] *Op. cit.,* pp. 110, 122–23, 129.

[47] *Theórica y Práctica de Comercio y de Marina* (2nd ed., Madrid, 1742).

[48] *Op. cit.,* Vol. II, p. 221.

[49] According to John Rae (*Life of Adam Smith* [London, 1895], p. 360), the translation was made in 1792; but the publication was delayed for two years by the Inquisition on account of the "lowness of its style and the looseness of its morals."

[50] *Esquisse du Mouvement des Prix et des Revenus en France au XVIIIe Siècle* (Paris, 1933).

to M. Labrousse, commodity prices were 63.7 per cent higher in 1785–89 than in 1726–41. But in the same period wages rose only 22 per cent.[51] From 1715 to 1789 the foreign trade of France "increased fourfold, and in this direction the development of France was even more rapid than that of England."[52] Germain Martin tells us[53] that from 1740 to 1775 "the great manufacturing centers which constituted the industrial strength of France during the nineteenth century were founded or developed. It was especially in 1740 . . . that factories attained an incontestable importance."

A revolutionary rise in prices occurred in the second half of the fourteenth century, but the economic stimulus was largely nullified by the Black Death and other pestilences which forced wages upward at an equal pace.[54] Sweeping advances in English industry, commerce, and finance in the second half of the sixteenth century and the first half of the seventeenth synchronized with a lag of wages behind prices during the Price Revolution precipitated by the great influx of Mexican and Peruvian treasure. In Spain, where the Price Revolution was the most violent but where wages lagged only slightly, distinctly less material progress was achieved; and Florence, where wages apparently rose as much as prices, suffered economic stagnation.[55] Wages also lagged far behind prices in France; and, despite the protracted religious wars and the civil strife during the minorities of Louis XIII and XIV, genuine industrial and commercial progress was achieved. Colbertian prosperity rested partially upon the capital formed during this period.[56]

---

[51] *Ibid.*, Vol. II, pp. 362, 492.

[52] Henri Sée, "The Economic and Social Origins of the French Revolution," *Econ. Hist. Rev.*, 1931–32, III, 3.

[53] *La Grande Industrie en France sous le Règne de Louis XV* (Paris, 1900), p. 118.

[54] Earl J. Hamilton, *Money, Prices, and Wages in Valencia, Aragon, and Navarre, 1351–1500* (Cambridge, Mass., 1936), p. 185.

[55] Amintore Fanfani, *Indagini sulla Rivoluzione dei Prezzi* (Florence, 1940), p. 146.

[56] This thesis was advanced for the first time in my article on "American Treasure and the Rise of Capitalism" (*Economica,* Vol. VII, November 1929, 338–57). In a scholarly article on "Prices and Industrial Capitalism in France and England (1540–1640)" (*Econ. Hist. Rev.,* 1936–37, VII, 155–85) Professor J. U. Nef criticized my thesis on the ground that the index numbers taken from Wiebe (*Geschichte der Preisrevolution des XVI. und XVII. Jahrhunderts*) exaggerated the disparity between prices and wages in England, and that largely owing to the fact that English wood and timber prices advanced more rapidly than general prices, thus stimulating technological advance, England made more industrial progress than France, where wages lagged far behind general prices and the price of wood remained in line. But Professor Nef accepted my main thesis that "by raising prices, the inflow of treasure from America helped to keep down the costs of the labor and the land needed for mining and manufacturing, and thus encouraged the investment of capital in large-scale enterprise." (*Ibid.*, pp. 183–84). Whether the indices I took from Wiebe in fact exaggerated the lag of wages will be seen when Sir William Beveridge publishes his final volume on English prices, which will contain his wage data. Professor Nef, a careful

Since economists often experience difficulty in distinguishing between cause and effect, it is not strange that innovation and other types of economic progress, which tend to accompany rising prices, have been regarded as their cause. If ever tenable, this thesis is clearly not so for the periods 1351–1400, 1551–1650, and 1751–1800. In each instance the rise in prices synchronized with, and largely resulted from,[57] an increased output of the precious metals not caused by technological innovation. The chain of causation could not have run from innovation to higher prices to increased production of specie. For the costs of mining soar with the commodity index, and the prices of gold and silver remain fixed at the levels prescribed by the mints.

Great inventions would have materialized in the second half of the eighteenth century, and the factory system eventually would have emerged, if prices had not forged ahead of wages. Once in operation, a mechanical improvement tends to lower costs and to provide profits, savings, and capital, even when the ratio of wages to prices is advancing. The mechanization of industry invariably increases the output of labor and tends to raise the wage-price ratio without increasing the efficiency rate of wages. The new technology kept the wheels of industry turning in 1819–48 and 1873–96, for example, when commodity prices were falling and money wages were either lagging or actually rising. But the invention and utilization of the eighteenth-century machinery was accelerated by the abundance of capital and the incentive to invest result-

---

scholar with qualitative data, based a thesis concerning the rise of industrial capitalism upon the fragmentary prices of such heterogeneous articles as timber, firewood, logs, and brush, quoted in terms of such uncertain measures as loads and bundles, compiled for France by d'Avenel, Raveau, and Hauser and his assistants under the Committee on Price History and for England by Sir William Beveridge and his assistants. In Professor Hauser's *Recherches et Documents sur l'Histoire des Prix en France de 1500 à 1800* (Paris, 1936) and Sir William Beveridge's *Prices and Wages in England from the Twelfth to the Nineteenth Century* (London, 1939), the price histories of France and England published the most recently and produced under the most favorable conditions, the quotations for firewood begin after 1550; and I find no clear evidence that prior to 1650 the prices of wood rose faster, either absolutely or relatively to other prices, in England than in France. As Professor Nef recognized, the advances of charcoal prices in England did not exceed those of commodities in general. Charcoal is the only wood product in Sir William Beveridge's series that is both homogeneous and quoted in terms of an inherently reliable measure. I am not convinced that England outstripped France in industrial progress by more than the bitter wars of France against Charles V and Philip II, the fratricidal religious conflicts, and the civil strife during the minorities of Louis XIII and XIV will explain. Unless this can be shown, the comparative development of England and France can afford no conclusive evidence against my thesis.

[57] The French Revolution and the Napoleonic War were the chief cause of the rapid advance of prices in the last decade of the eighteenth century, but the upswing in Mexican silver production (A. Soetbeer, *Edelmetall-Produktion und Werthverhältnis zwischen Gold und Silber* [Gotha, 1879], p. 55) was also a factor.

ing from the lag of wages behind prices. Without profit inflation, the industrial progress would hardly have been *revolutionary* in character.

One must not forget, however, that the profit inflation, through a lag of wages behind prices, which implemented the Industrial Revolution entailed a loss of real wages to a large proportion of the poorest subjects in England, and that the economic and social adaptations to rapid changes were extremely painful. Society might well have reaped greater advantages from industrial *evolution.*

18

Treasure and Trade Balances: The Mercantilist Problem*

By CHARLES WILSON

Editors' Foreword

In a vigorous criticism of this article Eli F. Heckscher proved (1) that it cannot be maintained that, in general, trade in the seventeenth century was bilateral and (2) that there is no ground for believing that the Baltic region was "a sort of second India where precious metals were amassed." (*Econ. Hist. Rev.*, 2nd Ser., 1950, III, 219–28.) In counter-rebuttal Charles Wilson conceded that multilateral international payments by means of bills of exchange were quite common in the seventeenth century; but he continued to defend the thesis, presented below, that English commerce with particular regions, the Baltic in particular, did long retain its bilateral character (*Econ. Hist. Rev.*, 2nd Ser., 1951, IV, 231–42).

I

When the late Lord Keynes came to write his *Notes on Mercantilism* some thirteen years ago,[1] he felt bound to conclude that the Classical School of economists had been unfair to those writers who for 200 years had seen "a peculiar advantage" to their nations in a favourable balance of trade. ". . . we, the faculty of economists," he wrote, "prove to have been guilty of presumptuous error in treating as a puerile obsession what for centuries has been a prime object of practical statecraft."[2] His argument, put briefly, ran as follows. The only practical inducement to investment (and therefore to the fuller exploitation of the economic resources of the nation) in the period in question was a reduced rate of interest. That, in turn, depended on increasing the quantity of precious metals in a particular country, which in turn depended on

* *Economic History Review,* 2nd Ser., 1949, II, 152–61. Reprinted by permission of the author and the Economic History Society.

[1] J. M. Keynes, *The General Theory of Employment, Interest and Money* (1936), Ch. 23, p. 333.

[2] *Ibid.*, p. 339.

a favourable balance of trade. Lord Keynes was, of course, primarily interested in his inquiries in the relationship between state policy and employment. What he examined was an important aspect of mercantilist thought, though it is doubtful whether it was the most immediate one to those who wrote on these matters in the seventeenth and eighteenth centuries. Rereading the works of the mercantilists, one cannot avoid an uneasy feeling that employment was seen as a means to increasing bullion supplies rather than vice versa.

At the same time, others were working on the broader aspects of mercantilism in greater detail. Professor Heckscher's work had appeared in English translation a year or so earlier, and had done much to modify the older view that mercantilist arguments were based—as Lord Keynes put it—"from start to finish, on an intellectual confusion."[3] On the particular aspect of mercantilism with which this note is concerned, and which is generally agreed to be of central importance to the whole argument—the importance of precious metals—Professor Heckscher was less satisfied than Lord Keynes with mercantilist logic. In particular he pointed out that little interest was shown in contemporary literature in the practical use of the precious metals, "i.e. with regard to their final export."[4] It is the object of this note to suggest that nevertheless there were indispensable practical uses to which precious metals were put in international trade in the mercantilist period, that these uses were sufficiently well known to practical men of trade and government, that they were more or less taken for granted, and that they do in fact form an assumption, largely unspoken and far from clearly stated, in much contemporary discussion. As Professor Clark has remarked,[5] "the explanation of the mercantilist attitude seems to lie in the commercial conditions of the time, and especially in the needs of traders for capital in a solid and ponderable form." This argument can be reinforced by reference to such figures and facts as are available concerning the structure and composition of Britain's overseas trade in the period. We have been warned, and rightly so, of the inadequacies of the so-called "statistics" of trade and the warnings must be heeded.[6] Nevertheless, on certain points relevant to this inquiry, the evidence is so unanimous and the margins so wide that certain basic facts can perhaps be established. We may take

[3] *Ibid.*, p. 334. Keynes's conclusions were largely based on evidence provided by Heckscher's study.

[4] E. Heckscher, *Mercantilism* (1935), Vol. II, p. 215.

[5] G. N. Clark, *The Seventeenth Century* (Oxford, 1947), p. 27.

[6] G. N. Clark, *Guide to English Commercial Statistics, 1696–1782* (R.H.S., 1938), pp. 33–42.

Thomas Mun as the starting-point in the inquiry. Chapter IV of *England's Treasure by Foreign Trade*[7] is entitled "The Exportation of our Moneys in Trade of Merchandise is a means to encrease our Treasure." One of the two prime examples he quotes is the East Indies trade and the facts are too well known to call for more than a brief recitation. The nature of this trade was such that the vent of available exports was insufficient to pay for the quantity of goods available for return. Export of goods therefore must be supplemented by export of bullion, and the answer to criticism of the policy was that re-export brought in more bullion than was needed for the initial process of "lubrication."[8] What has received less notice is Mun's inclusion in the same paragraph of a similar case from the Eastland trade. "For I suppose," he writes, "that 100,000 *l.* being sent in our Shipping to the East Countreys, will buy there one hundred thousand quarters of wheat clear aboard the Ships, which being after brought into *England* and housed, to export the same at the best time for rent thereof in *Spain* or *Italy,* it cannot yield less in those ports than two hundred thousand pounds to make the Merchant but a saver, yet by this reckning wee see the Kingdom hath doubled that Treasure."[9]

We need not take Mun's word alone in this matter. The difficulties of the Baltic trade were notorious to all seventeenth-century traders. They were especially acute for the English who, whether they were trading to the Arctic or to the tropics, to civilized or to primitive communities, had virtually only one great export commodity to offer—cloth. Even the Dutch had the same problem of balancing their own trade to the Baltic. Their control of the North Sea fisheries, their grip on the Biscay salt trade and their range of colonial commodities might well have seemed to give them the key to world trade, but it was still difficult to find trading cargoes sufficient to pay for their Baltic purchases—largely grain and timber—and there is little doubt that the Baltic was the drain down which disappeared much of the American silver which Spain mortgaged to Amsterdam for Dutch imports. The ultimate destination of much of the contents of the Silver Fleets was the Sound.[10] Dutch dollars were a familiar currency in the Scandinavian and Baltic areas and "very much esteemed."[11] At the time Mun was writing, there was probably much to be said for the contention implied in his example

[7] Blackwell edition, 1933.

[8] *Ibid.,* pp. 15–16.

[9] *Ibid.,* p. 15.

[10] See A. E. Christensen, *Dutch Trade to the Baltic about 1600* (Copenhagen, 1941), pp. 367, 428.

[11] P. D. Huet, *Memoirs of the Dutch Trade (1700)* (Amsterdam, 1718), p. 50.

that bullion export to the Baltic could be justified along the same lines as bullion export to the East Indies—as a sprat to catch a mackerel. But there was an awkward catch in the argument. The Baltic trade was not a smooth or regular business. Baltic imports—grains, timber, iron and copper—were apt to be matters of emergency. It was an old story. Dearth was one problem. ". . . if we should have great scarcity of corn within the realm. . . . Then our commodities were in a notable scarcity to counter-value it . . . ," wrote the author of the *Discourse of the Commonweal.* The reference can scarcely be to anything but imports from the Baltic, and under these conditions, re-export to recoup losses of bullion was, in the nature of things, out of the question. There was the other emergency—war. From the sixteenth to the nineteenth century, the demands of the Navy might call for imports of timber for purely home consumption: and from the sixteenth to the eighteenth century import of Swedish iron for ordnance was a familiar necessity. The query of the *Discourse* must have been repeated by a long line of succeeding generations of men concerned with matters of national defence. ". . . if both war and dearth should come together . . . how should we do? Surely we should be in a very hard case, and much in danger of strangers."

Now by the time Mun's work was printed in 1664[12] (almost certainly as part of the deliberate propaganda campaign against the Dutch which preceded the outbreak of war in 1665) some changes had overtaken the Baltic trade. Dearth was less a danger, war a greater one. With the agricultural expansion, grain imports were less likely, but the imports of timber and naval stores had become a vital necessity. From Danzig, Riga and Memel came the bulk of the naval timber and masts —oak and fir. From St Petersburg came fir, from Stettin oak. Norway contributed spruce spars and fir timber, while mast fleets came regularly from Gothenburg.[13] These were the main areas, and in the ports the "factories" or "colleges" of British agents fought for commercial supremacy with their Dutch rivals. The strategic importance of the Baltic trade was questioned: control of the Baltic—*dominium Maris Baltici* —was a prime issue in the Dutch wars. The standing danger was that Denmark and the control of the Danish Sound would pass to the Dutch. "If they can shut us out of the Baltic Sea, and make themselves masters of that, where is your trade? Where are the materials to preserve your

---

[12] It was of course written more than thirty years earlier.

[13] See the account in R. G. Albion, *Forests and Sea Power, 1652–1862* (Harvard, 1926), Ch. 4.

shipping? Where will you be able to challenge any right by sea or justify yourselves against a foreign invasion on your own soil?" Cromwell's questions to Parliament in 1659 were not mere rhetoric: they were founded on a shrewed appreciation of a very dangerous strategic situation. Mr. Albion has shown the perils which followed from the interruptions of the Baltic supply line in the seventeenth century,[14] and the anxiety with which Pepys at the Admiralty followed the fortunes of the Gothenburg fleet during the Second Anglo-Dutch War.

This situation helps to explain the strenuous but largely unsuccessful efforts to provide an alternative source of supply of timber from the North American colonies. The policy of obtaining pitch and tar from North America was apparently somewhat more successful.[15] But the Baltic remained the Achilles heel of British strategy, the one area where a trade vital to British defence was wide open to foreign attack. With the shift of the principal menace from the Low Countries to France, the danger abated somewhat, and all through the eighteenth century the Navy drew an ever increasing supply of naval materials from the Baltic.[16]

The strategic disadvantage of the Baltic situation should not be allowed, however, to obscure the peculiar economic difficulties of trade in the Baltic area. Mun's argument about re-export wore thin when the Baltic trade came to consist almost solely of naval materials. Observers were not lacking to pour disapproval on a branch of trade where imports regularly exceeded exports. In his *Trade and Navigation England Considered* Gee wrote:

> Norway and Denmark take from England guineas, crown pieces and bullion, a little tobacco, and a few coarse woolens of small value.
>
> England takes from Norway and Denmark vast quantities of deal boards, timber, spars and iron; we pay them a very great balance which is greatly increased by the late establishment of ships in the navigation and freight of their timber.[17]

When an inquiry was ordered into the Accounts of the Inspector-General of Imports and Exports, the situation was hardly reassuring. On the basis of the years 1696–9, the entire Baltic area was found to figure in the list of trades where the value of imports normally exceeded exports. Denmark and Norway showed deficits of £93,637; the East

[14] *Ibid.*, Ch. 5.

[15] See the "Essay" attributed to Oxenford in Clark, *Guide to English Commercial Statistics*, p. 131.

[16] Albion, *op. cit.*, p. 160.

[17] *Ibid.*, p. 159.

Country a deficit of £149,940; Russia £176,373; Sweden £506,677.[18] Culliford, the Inspector-General, himself pointed out that "Upon the several trades of Sweden, Denmark and Norway, East Country and Russia, the excess is very much on the importation side (which is a demonstration these trades are less profitable to us) and the same may reasonably be supposed to arise from their clandestine carrying away of our milled money instead of our manufactures." (The export of bullion was of course taken for granted.) The trouble was accentuated, as Gee pointed out, by the fact that a great deal of the trade was carried in foreign bottoms. In the Norwegian trade, for example, "from Michaelmas 1691 to Michaelmas 1696, there were entered on the Customs House at London 1070 foreign ships from those parts and but thirty-nine English."[19] The drain resulting from payments for these freight charges to foreign shipowners was clearly recognized from the time of the Navigation Acts onwards.

The result of these disturbing revelations was a recommendation by the Board of Trade that England should be rendered less dependent on the Baltic by turning to Ireland and New England, but the solution was not easy; throughout the eighteenth century, the visible adverse balance of trade with the Baltic remained an intractable problem, and when Oxenford came to write his *Essay* in 1723 he stated that in the reign of Charles II "as well as ever since, we paid a considerable balance to our sugar and tobacco plantations, to Denmark and Sweden, Russia and the East Country . . ." and went on to inquire pertinently ". . . and from what country then were we repaid these several ballances?"[20]

The mercantilist argument did not rest only on the peculiar characteristics of these "difficult" trades. It was also rooted in the views of individual merchants about the requirements of their business. Trading capital *in money* was regarded as an indispensable link in the exchange of goods. The bill of exchange, even in the limited uses permitted by the circumstances of international trade, was conceived as a substitute for coin rather than as a clearing mechanism. For a long time merchants held coined money in higher esteem than pieces of paper which might be (and were) subject to abuse by unsound speculation. In the age of "Leviathan" it was not unnatural that the analogy should be carried into the whole sphere of political economy.[21] There seemed to be no more reason to dispute the fact that a state with bullion reserves was

[18] House of Lords MSS. (N.S.), Vol. IV, pp. 430–36, 455–57.
[19] Quoted by Albion, *op. cit.,* p. 159.
[20] Clark, *Guide,* p. 122.
[21] Christensen, *op. cit.,* pp. 399–400. See also Heckscher, *op. cit.,* Vol. II, pp. 217 ff.

better off than one without than there was to dispute the fact that a man with a sovereign in his pocket was better off than a man without.

This examination seems to suggest that throughout the period commonly described as "mercantilist" there were two main branches of trade—the East Indies and the Baltic—where bullion export was a permanent, though an unpleasant necessity. (There were others such as the Irish, Turkey, Italian and some of the Plantation trades where the argument applied, though with less force.) In the first area the trade was defended on the grounds of its ultimate greater profitability through re-export. But the Baltic trade could be defended on no such principle. The defence had to be conducted on the ground of sheer hard strategic necessity. Now given the basic assumption of the mercantilists—and it remained substantially unchallenged from at any rate the time of Mun to the time of Oxenford (roughly a century)—that a visible trade deficit could only be covered by an export of coin or bullion, certain conclusions followed as a matter of course. Overseas trade divided into two types: those in which exports exceeded imports and those in which imports exceeded exports. Clearly the former had to carry the latter. It was therefore necessary to increase to the maximum the yield of precious metal which could be squeezed from the favourable trades in order to provide the bullion or coin necessary to finance the unfavourable. In the Eastern trade the need was for a flow of cash to bridge the gap between purchase and sale—a kind of working capital: in the Baltic, it was to provide cash for purchases without which national security was imperilled. And evidently the necessity was held to excuse the unpalatable fact that the transaction was, from any short term or purely economic point of view, a dead loss. Fortunately for the imperial future, the seventeenth and eighteenth centuries did not believe in purely economic points of view.

Given this natural anxiety about trade in those areas which to-day would no doubt be designated as "hard currency" areas, the line of argument which followed was a fairly obvious one. Mun had outlined it, in 1702 Brewster was still enlarging on it, and when Oxenford reviewed the position in retrospect he concluded that in the reign of Charles II the nation had lived beyond its means. "It was the unrestrained liberty in that reign of everyone to consume foreign as well as Empire manufactures which prevented any ballance coming to England." Indeed, it was clear to him that the bullion neccessary to finance the "hard currency" areas trade must have been borrowed from strangers (which can only mean the Dutch). All this has a familiar ring. If the

Baltic and other deficits were an unavoidable necessity, could unnecessary imports from other areas be reduced? Were, for example, wine, or gold and silver lace, really necessary to the national well-being? What could be done to improve the state of Ireland's trade and the deplorable idleness of that nation? Finally, and in general, how could exports which earned favourable balances be increased? Such was, for example, Brewster's thesis: "That the full employment of all Hands in the Nation, is the surest way and Means to bring BULLION into the kingdom."[22] Modern as this may sound it was not the policy of full employment in the modern sense so much as an intermediate stage in a policy which balanced social welfare in the same scales as national defence. Similar considerations had lain behind the seventeenth-century attempts to wrest control of the herring fisheries and the colonial trades from the Dutch. There was shrewdness as well as jealously in Sir George Downing's observation that "The herring trade is the cause of the salt trade and the herring and salt trade are the causes of that country (i.e. Holland) having, in a manner, wholly engrossed the trade of the Baltic Sea. . . ." The Baltic countries might not be good customers for cloth: they were usually ready to take fish.

II

Always bearing the "hard currency" areas in mind, the mercantilists turned to another aspect of the problem. The appointment of the first Inspector General of Imports and Exports proceeded from consideration of "the Great usefulness of Keeping a Distinct account of the Importation and Exportation of all Commodities into and out of this Kingdom; and to and from what places the same are Exported or Imported, *in Order to make a Ballance of the Trade between this Kingdome and any other part of the world. . . .* "[23] The last phrase has been italicized because it is important to note that the idea of individual areas of trade with individual balances, favourable or unfavourable, was carefully preserved. Like their descendants in the 1940's, the mercantilists had more reason than the classical economist to know that overall trade balances are not always a satisfactory answer to the problem of international payments; to know that an account of a nation's trade which *in toto* shows a favourable balance may yet contain within itself hard cores of individually unbalanceable trades. The solution to the problem lay then, as now, in the formation of a system of multilateral payments,

[22] F. Brewster, *New Essays on Trade* (London, 1702), p. 45.
[23] Clark, *op. cit.*, p. 3.

but that entailed an international credit and currency structure which was unthinkable to seventeenth-century Englishmen. Until that became practicable, a store of precious metals remained the principal and often the only link between a series of channels of trade each of which was essentially bilateral. If the link was missing, imports from any area of trade might well be limited to an amount which could be paid for by direct export of commodities.

Nor was this the only reason for looking askance at the overall trade figures revealed by the Inspector General's inquiries. When Brewster came to examine the figures for exports and imports from Michaelmas 1697 to Michaelmas 1698[24] he found that the balance stood as follows:

Exports . . . . . .£6,361,108. 10*s.* 7*d.*
Imports . . . . . .£4,732,360. 5*s.* 6*d.*

The favourable balance on visible trade thus came to £1,628,748. 5*s.* 1*d.* and, as Brewster very reasonably observed ". . . if it did, this kingdom would be like *Solomon's*, have Silver as plenty as the stones of the Street." But he was not so easily deceived. The question of real (as distinct from official) values he ignores. He does, however, note the effects of smuggling, and, more important, he raises the question of foreign borrowings. Rejecting the notions of those who regarded *Foreign Money in our Publick Funds* as clear gain, he points out that these foreign proprietors had to receive interest on their money. "But suppose here may be," he continues, "but *five* or *six* Millions of Foreign Money, when *that* and the *interest* is carried *out* of the kingdom, it will make a great hole in our 12 Millions." (His estimate of the money in the kingdom.)

Brewster may have exaggerated the amount of English borrowings from abroad but he was quite correct in drawing attention to the facts. Throughout the war, the government was borrowing fairly extensively from Dutch lenders on the security of malt tickets, salt tallies and tallies on impositions. It was the beginning of the Dutch stake in the national debt, which was to grow to considerable proportions in the course of the century.[25] He was probably right also in arguing that these borrowings brought in no bullion. For most of the expenditure financed in this way went on military charges on the Continent. Government expenditure abroad was another item which (just as to-day) had to be borne in mind

[24] Brewster, *op. cit.*, p. 29.

[25] Charles Wilson, *Anglo-Dutch Commerce and Finance in the Eighteenth century* (Cambridge University Press, 1941), pp. 88–95.

as a debit against the visible trade balance. Most interesting of all, Brewster quotes Baltic purchases as amongst those financed by foreign borrowing. "We cannot think," he writes, "that all our imports (of naval stores) especially from the *Baltick,* are on Englishmens' Accompts."[26]

It was presumably in answer to this kind of charge that Oxenford[27] wrote the long-winded and obscure, but very important *Essay towards finding the Ballance of our whole Trade Annually from Christmas 1698 to Christmas 1719.*[28] That England had borrowed heavily from the Dutch he admits freely. The procedure was for correspondents to subscribe to "lotteries, annuities, or other publick funds," paying by bills of exchange. In this way some £10 million may have been raised. The obligations outstanding for the war he calculates at £14 to £15 million, and he concludes that the difference was met by the overall favourable annual balance which worked out at between half a million and a million.[29] Upon this balance rested one permanent charge—the bullion necessary to "lubricate" the trade with "hard currency" areas.

That this much was recognized is quite clear. Smuggling, freight charges, the cost of foreign wars, and the interest charges on money borrowed for those wars, made nonsense of arguments based on the so-called "statistics" of visible trade. Other "invisibles" do not appear to have been so clearly recognized. (It would be interesting, for example, to know what the cost of the upkeep of foreign embassies and Company "factories" abroad amounted to. What, too, was the cost in bullion or foreign currency of the Grand Tours, of gentlemen's purchases of *objects d'art* in Italy or of the residence of Scottish and English Nonconformist students at continental universities?) The balance on visible trade was in better fettle by 1700 than it had been in the dark days of the mid-seventeenth century, when the value of imports was calculated to be almost twice the value of exports,[30] but the margin was throughout the eighteenth century a slender one to bear the burden of all these assorted charges, most of which can never be accurately calculated. It is not really surprising that foreign borrowing continued to be necessary up to the last quarter of the eighteenth century.

All this is evidence that until well into the eighteenth century Brit-

[26] Brewster, *op. cit.,* p. 22.

[27] I am accepting Clark's suggestion that Oxenford was the author of the "Essay." Clark, *op. cit.,* p. 25.

[28] Printed in Clark, *op. cit.,* pp. 69–134.

[29] *Ibid.,* pp. 118–19.

[30] B.M. Add. MSS. 36785.

ain's financial position remained far more critical than the apparently favourable "statistics" of visible trade would seem to suggest. It was, above all, the demands of war finance which kept statesmen nervous and maintained a general respect for precious metals. It remained as true in the eighteenth as it had been in the sixteenth century that, as the *Discourse* put it ". . . money is, as it were, a storehouse of any commodity you would have."[31] Bills of exchange might grow in use, but there were many who, Cobbett-wise, preferred the more solid forms of purchasing power—and, on the whole, with good reason.

That the broadly bilateral character did give way to some kind of multilateral system of trade and payments in the eighteenth century seems to be undeniable. Its centre was not yet London but Amsterdam. In the early seventeenth century trade with the Netherlands seems to have been regarded as labouring under some of the disadvantages later attributed to the trade with the Baltic. That at any rate was the opinion in 1618 when the Privy Council was in favour of compelling Dutch merchants to employ their balances to buy British goods under the terms of the Statute of Employment. This, it was held, was the most likely means of redressing the scarcity of coin.[32] More than thirty years later the situation still remained unfavourable and an Amsterdam correspondent could observe: ". . . your expense for foreign goods is twice as much as the goods you export and this in a few years will drain all your stock and not leave you a penny. We have more English gold in Amsterdam than you have."[33] That this particular mercantilist nightmare did not materialize may have been due to an increasing willingness amongst Dutch merchants after 1660 to leave their balances invested in London. Goldsmiths and bankers were alleged to have in their charge considerable quantities of Dutch money lent out to other merchants at from 5 to 7%.[34] Here in embryo may be seen the beginnings of a mechanism of international finance which in time was to relieve the pressure on capital in its "solid" forms. For at the same time there was growing up at Amsterdam a highly organized system for international investment and acceptance credit which was no less useful to Britain than

---

[31] The idea is far from dead in the twentieth century. Addressing the T.U. Congress at Southport on 3 September 1947, Ernest Bevin referred to "this balance of payments business," and to America's failure to redistribute the Fort Knox gold. "I am quite sure," he went on, "that is one of the readiest ways to assist in increasing the purchasing power of the devastated areas of the world."

[32] A. Friis, *Alderman Cockayne's Project and the Cloth Trade* (1927), p. 215.

[33] S.P. Dom. 1651–52.

[34] Hist. MSS. Comm. Appendix to 8th Report, p. 133.

it was to the continental nations. For example, no exchange rate was quoted between London and St. Petersburg until 1763: payments for Anglo-Russian trade were made through Dutch banks.[35] It was common knowledge that a large part of the volume of bills in circulation in Europe issued from Dutch merchant bankers and ran at a commission of ½%. It would perhaps be permissible to discern the early use of this system from Brewster's remarks about foreign participation in Britain's Baltic purchases. Britain's direct trade with Holland normally showed a large visible favourable balance, and it may well be that this was used as a basis for credit in the unfavourable areas such as the Baltic and the Mediterranean. When this proved insufficient—and war expenses were apt to render it so—resort was had to loans at Amsterdam. The Dutch advanced credit for the maintenance of British forces abroad and took payment in various forms of government stock, most frequently in annuities. These loans, estimated in 1776 to account for £59 million out of a total national debt of £143 million, represent the extent to which the British Government of the day was enabled by a new system of international lending to live beyond Britain's own resources. Where their predecessors had been limited in their ambitions by the amount of hard cash they could raise, the governments of the period after the Glorious Revolution exploited with increasing success the possibilities of living beyond their income. With the borrowed profits from Holland's Golden Age, Britain gambled on an imperial future, and gambled successfully.

The advent of a system of international lending and credit, and of multilateral payments, may help to explain the lessening of anxiety about bullion resources in the course of the eighteenth century, though the anxiety was only lessened and not wholly removed.[36] The new machinery creaked continually and from time to time broke down completely—as in 1763 and 1773.[37] These periodic revelations of weakness in the credit mechanism may well have had the result of prolonging the life of the old prejudices. Certainly they died hard, and even the coming of fully convertible currencies and multilateral payments did not entirely banish them. As Lord Keynes observed: "The majority of statesmen and practical men in most countries, and nearly half of them

---

[35] J. G. van Dillen, "De Beurscrisis te Amsterdam van 1763," *Tijdschrift voor Geschiedenis,* 1922, p. 253.

[36] I cannot entirely agree with Heckscher that the need for reserves was of little consequence to seventeenth-century mercantilists. It is certainly implicit even in Oxenford's *Essay* in the eighteenth century.

[37] See Wilson, *op. cit.,* Ch. 6.

even in Great Britain, the home of the opposite view, have remained faithful to the ancient doctrine."[38] If, in the interval since those words were written, a high proportion of the dissident half have been converted, the reason must be sought in the disturbing tendency of international trade to revert to conditions which in some ways resemble those of the seventeenth rather than those of the nineteenth century.

[38] Keynes, *op. cit.*, p. 333.

19

*The Bank of England in the Eighteenth Century**

By SIR JOHN CLAPHAM

As the eighteenth century unrolls there begins to appear, and in the second half very clearly, evidence of that recurrent flow and ebb of economic activity which to-day is called the trade cycle. The years 1753, 1763, 1772–3, 1783, 1793 are all marked by some culmination, usually amounting to a danger point or crisis, in English or European economic affairs. For the earlier part of the century any apparent rhythmical sequence is much less clear. The Bank itself came into existence in the boom of the 1690's which ended in the crisis of 1696, when it suspended cash payments. After a spell of bright peace time trade, trouble recurred in 1701, with "depression and even panic." There was dragging discomfort from 1704 to 1708, due mainly to the strain of war, friction between England and Scotland over the Union, and scares of invasion. The years 1710–11 saw something more economic, an insurance boom, a "gambling in life contingencies," the floating of more than seventy insurance companies and, with them, that of the Company of the South Seas.[1] And the country was still at war. After some ups and downs in the years that follow, comes 1720, the classic Bubble year. For the next two decades there is nothing so definite, though the Act of 1733 directed against "the infamous practice of stock jobbing"[2] reflects some rather unwholesome financial activities of the early thirties.

Long ago, Stanley Jevons, looking at the rhythmic movement of the later century, and selecting his years in the earlier at a time when its economic history had been little examined, argued in favour of some

---

* Selection from Sir John Clapham, *The Bank of England. A History,* Vol. I (1945), pp. 224–36, used with permission of the Macmillan Company.

[1] Scott, *Joint Stock Companies,* Vol. I, pp. 361, 365, 367, 384–85.

[2] Usually known as "Sir John Barnard's Act" (7 Geo. II, c. 8). Barnard, who was Lord Mayor in 1737, sat in Parliament from 1728 to 1761, and was very active. Cf. Clapham, *Bank of England,* Vol. I, p. 93.

natural nine to eleven year trade cycle. He tried to connect it with a harvest cycle and that with the cycle of spots on the sun.[3] It was with this brave venture that modern study of these difficult problems began. Since Jevons' day they have taxed the observation and ingenuity of whole tribes of economists and statists.

Seen from close quarters, however, the suggested cycle of the eighteenth century loses much of its superficial appearance of inevitability and obedience to obscure natural law. Three crises of a very familiar sort, occurring when the financial and banking system was assuming its modern form—those of 1763, 1783, 1793—were demonstrably connected with, if not solely due to, the beginning or ending of a war. No one has yet suggested that natural law makes wars begin or end rhythmically.[4] There may be, there probably is, a tendency for confidence leading to overconfidence and then disappointment and perhaps disaster to recur at fairly regular intervals in commercial societies. In modern industrial societies there is apt to be some rhythm of equipment and re-equipment with durable capital goods. Spells of such confidence and such equipment or re-equipment tend to coincide. But the composition and environments of the societies, both economic and political, vary so much from time to time that quite regular results are hardly to be expected. For the early eighteenth century, down to the year of the South Sea Bubble, the closest study ever given to a rather remote problem of this sort led to the conclusion that the nine to eleven year rhythmical cycle could not be traced, nor indeed any other.[5]

As for the Bank of England, whether boom and slump are rhythmical or not, it was the product of a boom. Its early days were speculative —a part of that boom. It over-lent and it over-issued. But the crisis in which it finally had to suspend cash payments, that of the recoinage, was not its immediate fault and not a necessary part of the boom conditions in which it was born, although those conditions had been en-

[3] "On the Study of Periodic Commercial Fluctuations" (1862); "The Solar Period and the Price of Corn" (1875); "Commercial Crisis and Sun Spots" (1878–79), in Stanley Jevons, *Investigations in Currency and Finance* (1884).

[4] Sir William Beveridge argues ("The Trade Cycle in Britain before 1850," *Oxford Economic Papers* [1940]) that the cycle "at least from 1785, and possibly before this" . . . "cannot be explained away by external accidents of war or domestic politics." His attention is concentrated on industry, and he suggests, very plausibly, that the cycle begins to take its modern form when industry does the same, that is late in the eighteenth century. Sir William is not exactly arguing for a 9–11 year cycle. His suggested industrial peak years are 1792, 1803, 1810, 1818, 1825, etc. which fit the contemporary view that 7–8 years is "normal." I have no wish to "explain away" the cycle by reference to such "external accidents" as war; but economists are rather apt to write about it without adequate consideration of these "accidents."

[5] Scott, *Joint Stock Companies,* Vol. I, p. 468.

couraged by its own rather reckless infantile staggerings. Perhaps its indiscretion had complicated the problem of recoinage by driving up the sterling price of silver;[6] but the direct cause of trouble was official blundering and mismanagement.

Between the Peace of 1697 and the first blowing out of the great Bubble in 1720, nearly all the Bank's most difficult moments can be explained without calling in the help of rhythmical economic fluctuations—short or long. The explanation is usually political or half-political. In 1701 the Bank is pressed in connection with the struggle between the two East India Companies, and we hear of an organized run on it. These stories of organized runs are not all certainly authentic.[7] The more trustworthy of them have often a political background. There is a scare of a French invasion or a Jacobite landing, and the Bank's domestic enemy takes the occasion to make his thrust, if he really made one. Or someone says that Queen Anne is dead when she is not. A well-dressed galloping horseman shouts the false news and there is a short scramble for money. During the Jacobite rising of 1715 the Bank was not in grave distress[8]—the Bank of Scotland stopped payment as one might expect—and for what distress there was the political explanation is fully adequate.

But the Bank ledgers do contain at least a suggestion that the "bubbling" years 1710–11, in which so many insurance projects were floated—and the South Sea Company—may have put an economic boom strain upon its resources. Whereas at the end of August 1709 there was £352,000 in the "Treasury or Vault" and £290,000 of "cash"; and at the end of August 1711, £654,000 in the Treasury and £182,000 of cash; at the end of August 1710, though the cash stood at £200,000 the Treasury was down to £96,000.[9] Whether the cash was all coin of the realm we cannot be sure: we do know that twenty years later most of it was in the form of the Bank's own unissued notes.[10] That may have

[6] This is only a perhaps. The problem is very complex. The latest discussion, in an unpublished London thesis of 1940 by Mr. Ming Hsun Li, argues against the view that there was inflation in 1696. Cf. Clapham, *Bank of England,* Vol. I, p. 36.

[7] Cf. *ibid.,* Vol. I, p. 62.

[8] It was in a very strong position when rebellion started. The Pretender's standard was raised on 3 Sept. The battles of Preston and Sheriffmuir were fought in November. On 31 Aug. the Bank had £725,000 in its "Treasury or Vault," £276,000 of "cash" and £97,000 in its "account of gold." Its liabilities were £948,000 of "specie and cash" notes, £31,000 of "accountable notes" and £179,000 of drawing accounts (General Ledgers, V, f. 711). Whatever the "cash" was, there was excellent cover for the liabilities in case of a run. A year later the position was even better—Treasury, cash and gold £1,972,000; notes and drawing accounts £1,891,000 (General Ledgers, VI, f. 265).

[9] General Ledgers, IV, ff. 247, 428, 623.

[10] See Clapham, *Bank of England,* I, p. 293.

been so in 1710,[11] when it probably also included some goldsmiths' notes. Whatever the composition of the cash, the Treasury was very empty.

The government was pressing for advances to carry on the war. The Bank was trying to influence political appointments by the threat that changes in the cabinet might impair credit. Anderson the chronicler says that the changes which nevertheless came, especially the dismissal of Godolphin in August, "had occasioned the Bank to be much run upon."[12] Certainly balances in the drawing accounts were abnormally low at the end of that month.[13] So perhaps the emptiness of the Treasury is to be explained by circumstances that were primarily political; but there remains the possibility of a drain connected with the promoting and gambling activities of a year in which the Statute Book contained a law—not the first—against "assurances on marriages, births, christenings and services"; and against unlawful lotteries.[14]

The Bank of the early years was a speculation with an uncertain future; the Bank of the mid and late eighteenth century was an institution. The turning-point in its life history came with the South Sea Bubble and Walpole's administration. Half a century later Adam Smith, who disliked joint-stock companies, spoke of them as only suited to routine businesses such as banking. But in fact all the early companies from the East India Company to the Bank were ventures, working in fields where precedents had to be set and experiments made.[15] No doubt the Bank took over a good deal of well-developed banking routine from the goldsmiths. But there were no set precedents for the conduct of what was at once a national and a profit-making bank. It was combative, adventurous, a part of each speculative movement in succession, not that "Capitol of old Rome," that rock of refuge around which the waves of speculation might beat, to which an admirer compared it in 1720—when in fact it was only just getting out of the fight for life and place.[16]

It had fought the Land Bank project; taken sides, though discreetly, in the struggle between the two East India factions; tried its strength in

[11] This is not very likely however: notes with printed values were not issued till 1725 (Acres, *The Bank of England from Within,* Vol. I, p. 157).

[12] Anderson, *History of Commerce,* Vol. II, p. 4; for the political situation see Clapham, *Bank of England,* Vol. I, p. 74.

[13] Only £126,000 (General Ledgers, IV, f. 428). In no other year between 1707 and 1715 were they below £153,000 and the average for those years, excluding 1710, was £174,000.

[14] 9 Anne, c. 6.

[15] Adam Smith, *Wealth of Nations,* Vol. II, p. 246. Smith's view was decisively refuted by Scott, *Joint Stock Companies,* Vol. I, pp. 448 ff.

[16] See Clapham, *Bank of England,* Vol. I, p. 84.

the highest politics when it attempted to influence Queen Anne's choice of ministers; and manœuvred cautiously from the first against its rival for public favours and privileges, the South Sea Company. Combative and adventurous, it was not above joining in speculative activities. Its early dividend policy had been daring, sometimes unsafe. It divided all it could, and more. No one then called it a part of the British Constitution as Lord North did two generations later. In those elderly, sober years, when Adam Smith wrote and North spoke, there is no doubt a routine in all its ways. The forces of commercial activity and speculation play on it. They may be affected by its now traditional methods of business; but there is little chance that it will take any deliberate part in speculative movements; stimulate unwholesome activity; or do consciously any of the things that prepare the way for the crisis of the trade cycle.

It was precisely in the Great Bubble year that for the last time the Bank took an active, and misguided, part in that keen competitive finance which, in some form, normally precedes a crisis. It bid against the South Sea Company. Fighting for position with it and perhaps blinded by some current delusions on capital and credit, from May to October 1720 it lent money freely, very freely, on its own stock. At the August balance these loans stood at £948,000.[17] No doubt members of the Court of Directors, all necessarily large stockholders, realized that stock which carries borrowing rights will appreciate. The price was already too high, at 200: the highest was 265. Fortunately for its reputation and its future, the Bank was never betrayed into the far wilder, and absolutely dishonest, finance of the Company.

In spite of this free lending, there was still on 31 August 1720, when deflation of the Bubble had just set in, £991,000 of treasure in the Bank's Vault and some hard cash in the tills.[18] No doubt the loans had been mostly made in paper. There were over £1,000,000 more notes out at that time than there had been a year earlier. And in spite of its £991,000, the Vault was emptier by nearly £250,000 than it had been in August 1719. Yet in August 1718 it had been lower than it was in August 1720; so that on the whole the state of the balance in the latter year may be taken as a sign of strength.[19]

---

[17] General Ledgers, VII, f. 2. Cf. Clapham, Bank of England, Vol. I, p. 84. R. D. Richards, *The First Fifty Years of the Bank of England,* p. 251, mentions the April–May votes but not the October vote.

[18] General Ledgers, VII, f. 2. See Clapham, *Bank of England,* Vol. I, Appendix C.

[19] Notes, 31 Aug. 1720, £3,033,000; 31 Aug. 1719, £1,939,000. Vault, 31 Aug. 1720, £991,000; 31 Aug. 1719, £1,239,000; 31 Aug. 1718, £841,000. Only the figures for the

From 1721 the Vault was filled up again. Its content rose intermittently to a maximum for the twenties of no less than £2,939,000 in 1727, besides a small "account of gold." The notes had risen too, by £1,985,000 on 1720.[20] But the ratio between the contents of the Vault and the notes had greatly improved. The Bank was enjoying the solid if coarse gains of life in Walpole's England.

Even Walpole was involved in a war, with Spain, in 1726–8. But it was not a costly war, and everything suggests that the years from 1729 to 1739 were as quiet and comfortable for the Bank as for the country. On the average of the August balances for the three years 1739–41, every note in circulation had a full bullion backing. Since 1721 the Directors had pursued a cautious dividend policy, keeping a larger balance in the profit and loss account and declaring the same dividend for years together. From 1721 to 1727 inclusive the rate was 6, in equal half-yearly 3's. For 1728–9 it was 5½; from 1730 to 1732 5¾. In 1733 it reverted to 5½; and it did not vary again until 1747.[21] All through the thirties therefore prices of Bank stock remained, as a rule, very steady, dropping a little with the dividend in 1733 but recovering as market rates of interest fell in subsequent years. With the 5½ per cent dividend of the late thirties, the price normally stood between 140 and 150.[22]

In the annual statements of the thirties the Vault is never credited with less than £2,000,000; and for the year 1739 the figure is £3,125,-000.[23] The distinct entries of the "account of gold" or the "account of bullion" show that the Vault was for British coin only, though whether the coin was gold or silver is never stated. Although a good deal of treasure passed through these other accounts, either to the Mint or for export, there were seldom large balances in them before 1729. From that year balances become larger, continuous and more varied. In 1731,

---

Treasury or Vault are given in the text because of some uncertainty about the "cash" (see Clapham, *Bank of England,* Vol. I, p. 140, n. 3, and Appendix C). The "cash" in these three years was 1718, £331,000; 1719, £359,000; 1720, £553,000. This 1720 figure is abnormally high and puzzling. The references are 1718, General Ledgers, VI, f. 521; 1719, General Ledgers, VI, f. 665; 1720, General Ledgers, VII, f. 2, as above.

[20] General Ledgers, VIII, f. 365. See Clapham, *Bank of England,* Vol. I, Appendix B.

[21] Dividends voted are in the General Court Books of Minutes: they are set out in Appendix B. It is apparently the larger balance kept from 1722 which started the legend that the "Rest" was formally established in that year. Cf. Clapham, *Bank of England,* Vol. I, p. 154. The dividends up to 1720 are given in Scott, *Joint Stock Companies,* Vol. III, p. 245. They had kept fairly steady since 1709.

[22] The prices are in several newspapers and, from its foundation in 1731, in *The Gentleman's Magazine;* but before 1747 the *Magazine* gives only monthly, not daily quotations.

[23] From 1729 we have the balances from the *G.L.* summarized in the vol. *Yearly Accounts,* 1729–62, and its successors.

for instance, we get "silver bought for coinage," "gold bought," "silver bought" and "gold bought for coinage," to an aggregate of £477,000. In other years appear "silver ingots," "foreign gold coin," "gold bars," "foreign silver coin" and, from 1735 onwards, frequent and large entries of pieces of eight, the Spanish dollars. The British coin in the Vault might not legally be melted or exported. This law was broken, but not by the Bank. The rest of the treasure could be minted—as the gold normally was—or exported at the Bank's discretion. In August 1739, besides the £3,125,000 in the Vault there were a few thousand pounds worth of silver ingots and "bullion at the mint for coinage"—probably also silver; no less than £649,000 of "foreign gold coin," most likely moidores; £40,000 of "gold for coinage," possibly in bars; and £254,000 of pieces of eight—a fine varied stock of treasure.

If in the early thirties there was any dangerous excess of "stock jobbing" it was connected with active trade—of which we have some evidence[24]—and did not lead to anything that can be called a crisis. The Bank was comfortable. A fall in the funds begins in the summer of 1733. It sets in rather earlier and continues rather longer than the contemporary fall in the prices of Bank stock. The two low series suggest a gentle recession of business activity, but nothing more. Then comes that spell of high prices for "gilt-edged"—Bank stock ranging from 146 to 151—which was the occasion of Sir John Barnard's campaign to secure a general 3 per cent basis for British credit.[25]

War began with Spain in 1739 and continued, with Spain and France, from 1744 to 1748. During all these years there was no real commercial crisis, though the very sharp political crisis of the rebellion of 1745 came when national resources, and with them the resources of the Bank, had been strained by six years of war taxation and borrowing. The strain had only become acute after France joined in the fighting. Before that the leisurely conflict with Spain had hardly affected the prices of government securities. With France's entry they slid away until the peace, and there was a special plunge—followed by recovery—in 1745.

In Threadneedle Street, as might be expected, the war years show pressure on the ultimate reserve of treasure. In 1740 the Vault is still very full—£3,771,000. After that it fluctuates, but downwards. It is

---

[24] Jevons collected a very little (*Investigations,* p. 212). There is more in J. H. Wilson, "Industrial Activity in the Eighteenth Century," *Economica,* 1940.

[25] See Clapham, *Bank of England,* Vol. I, p. 93.

never again anywhere near £3,000,000. In 1745 (31 August) it is so low as £617,000 and the bullion of all sorts stands at only £808,000; though there is recovery later. The fall is no doubt connected with the contraction of the note circulation that accompanied the slackened commercial activity of war-time. Between 1740 and 1747 the circulation dropped by nearly £800,000, and between 1740 and 1745 by nearly a million. There was not need for so large a stock of hard cash to back it. Yet the figure for 1745 was dangerously low.[26]

As significant as the fluctuations in the Vault are those in the free treasure, directly available for use abroad, or not easily to be got thence when the trade balance is unfavourable, as it is apt to be in war-time. In 1740 the Bank had held no less than £956,000 of foreign gold coin, with another £164,000 of gold bars, gold for coinage, dollars and "bullion"—presumably silver—at the Mint. By 1745 the foreign gold coin was down to £173,000 and all the rest to less than £9000.

With a small sum in the Vault, at 31 August, and this much reduced stock of free treasure, the Bank entered a month of September, and an autumn, which were to prove very difficult. The Young Pretender had landed in July. On 21 September he beat General Cope at Preston Pans. When the news came to London the Bank declined to discount any bills or promissory notes that had more than a month to run, and those only for its regular clients.[27] Its own notes fell to a discount, and the run began in which, as we are told, they were cashed in sixpences to slow up the pace and save the guineas; perhaps also to prevent guineas being taken out to send to the rebels.[28] The device would hardly have served to prop the credit of the notes, had not more than eleven hundred City men pledged themselves to take Bank notes whenever offered and pay in them so far as possible.[29] How effective this was the prices of Bank Stock for the next two months show. They fell, of course, but only from 141 to 133½. A further fall came in December when the Pretender's army was at Derby. The Bank, short of cash, made a 20 per cent call on the subscribers to "the Circulation," and refused to discount any promissory note that had more than fifteen days to run or was drawn to "take

[26] Figures from the *Yearly Accounts,* as above. From 1729, at latest, we are justified in assuming that there was not more than about £10,000 of coin in the "cash"; the rest being unissued notes. See Clapham, Bank of England, Vol. I, p. 140, n. 3 above and Appendix C.

[27] Court Books O, 26 Sept. 1745.

[28] The story appears in T. Fortune, *A Concise and Authentic History of the Bank of England* (1797), p. 12. It comes from Magens, *Universal Merchant* (1753), p. 31: as Magens was in London at the time, and was not a gossiping pamphleteer, it is almost certainly true. Cf. Clapham, *Bank of England,* Vol. I, p. 71, n. 1.

[29] *Gentleman's Magazine,* 1745, p. 499.

up" another already discounted.[30] The call did not fill the Vault so full as had been hoped. The market price of "the Circulation" collapsed. Yet the price of Bank stock stood up remarkably well. There was a December quotation so high as 127. With a rebel army in the Midlands this is remarkable, even though before this particular quotation was made the Prince's men had faced about for Scotland.

More remarkable still is the way the Bank managed to improve its reserve of treasure during the next eight months. This was probably helped by the call on capital made in Jan. 1746, when the call on "the Circulation" had miscarried.[31] By August the note circulation had risen by nearly £400,000. The Vault was returned at £1,925,000. This is a very large rise on the previous year; it is even above the figure for 1744. Foreign gold coin also was up, and there chanced to be £150,000 of pieces of eight in hand when the balance was struck. This item in the account fluctuated most of all, and the return at any given date is not significant. Silver was always being bought in the market and sold again for use in international trade. Sometimes it is entered as held for the East India Company, always one of the principal buyers throughout the eighteenth century; sometimes it is held against a loan to the Mocattas or other dealers in the precious metals.[32]

For the remaining months of a war which ended in April 1748 the Bank continued in reasonable comfort, although during 1747 the Vault was not kept at the level of 1746 and the dividend dropped from the 5½ at which it had stood since 1733 to 5. Peace brought a rapid expansion of the free treasure, especially of the gold, which points to a revival, direct or indirect, of the trade with Portugal; for it was through Portugal that the new gold came into England from Brazil, the Rand of the mid-eighteenth century. A great deal of this gold was minted into guineas. The passing of gold through to the Mint was going on rapidly during the years 1749–52.[33] By October of 1752 the account of gold in bars was empty. That it had often been before: there was not a permanent stock of bars. But it is very remarkable and most unusual to find that the annual statement of August 1753 contains no free gold at all, only the British coin in the vault. Though free gold had often been low, the last time that none at all had been registered in the annual statement

[30] Court Books O, 12 Dec. 1745. For "the Circulation" see Clapham, *Bank of England,* Vol. I, p. 68.

[31] Clapham, *Bank of England,* Vol. I, p. 97.

[32] *Ibid.,* p. 137.

[33] The *Yearly Accounts* contain heavy entries of "gold for coinage" and "gold for the mint," besides the foreign gold coin.

was 31 August 1730. In 1753 the account of gold for coinage was empty by May—the metal had gone to the Mint—and that of foreign gold coin by June. There is every reason to think that the foreign coin had gone abroad as the result of an external drain, the cause of which can be suggested with some confidence, if not absolute certainty. The Dutch were important holders of British funds, East India stock and Bank stock. During the war these securities had been cheap and Dutch trade prosperous. After the war Dutch trade was abnormally depressed for some years.[34] Meanwhile British securities rose fast, the 3 per cents to their absolute maximum price of over 106 in December 1752. Dutchmen needed free capital and English prices were increasingly attractive. Steady realization and withdrawal of the proceeds by foreigners would explain what is found in the Bank's ledgers and mentioned by a foreign contemporary. "England," he says, "being obliged to pay abroad what balances were against her, species became so scarce in 1753 and 1754 that at the bankers of London you could scarcely obtain a payment of one hundred pounds in the lawful gold coin of the country."[35]

This explanation is supported by the still low level of the free gold at the Bank in August 1754 (£123,000) and its sudden rise in 1755 to £665,000; for between August 1754 and August 1755 there had been a sharp fall in the 3 per cents, of over ten points. The temptation to realize and withdraw no longer existed; and the Bank was in a position to replenish its reserves.

---

[34] C. H. Wilson, *Anglo-Dutch Commerce and Finance in the Eighteenth Century* (1941), p. 19.

[35] Quoted in Jevons, *Investigations,* p. 214.

20

*Ricardo and the Bullion Report**

By NORMAN J. SILBERLING

In the previous article[1] it was shown that the British government financed its requirements in the wars against France (1793–1815) with a remarkable degree of restraint and a praiseworthy fiscal effort; and that the heavy foreign remittances involved by the conduct of hostilities not only made necessary a suspension of specie payments by the Bank of England, but operated as an important factor in producing the abnormal variations in the price of bullion and the rates of foreign exchange during that Suspension. This portion of the study will be devoted to a critical analysis of a type of monetary philosophy which developed during the War period and culminated in the influential pronouncements and recommendations of David Ricardo and of the "Bullion Committee" of the House of Commons.

The outbreak of the first French War in 1793 was accompanied in England by a severe commercial crisis. Toward the end of 1794, and throughout 1795 and 1796, there was continued financial strain, owing to unprecedented foreign military and political expenditures and the necessity of importing considerable quantities of naval stores and foodstuffs. This strain was especially felt by the country's banking reserves held in the Bank of England; the Bank directors were forced to meet persistent and unexampled demands for advances to the Exchequer at the same time that their commercial loans were necessarily heavy, while their specie was being alarmingly depleted by the growing foreign indebtedness and also by a tendency within the country toward the hoarding of coins. Repeated appeals to Pitt by the Bank for moderation brought no hope of relief, and at length, upon urgent representations by

* *Quarterly Journal of Economics,* 1924, XXXVIII, 397–439. Reprinted by courtesy of Harvard University Press.

The chart reproduced on page 361 and referred to in footnote 4 is taken from a previous article, "Financial and Monetary Policy of Great Britain during the Napoleonic Wars; I. Financial Policy," *Quart. Jour. Econ.,* 1924, XXXVIII, 231.

[1] See *Quart. Jour. Econ.* for February 1924.

BRITISH WAR EXPENDITURE ON THE CONTINENT; PERCENTAGE DEVIATIONS IN THE PRICE OF SPANISH DOLLARS FROM PAR; BANK OF ENGLAND RESERVES; FROM 1793 TO 1820

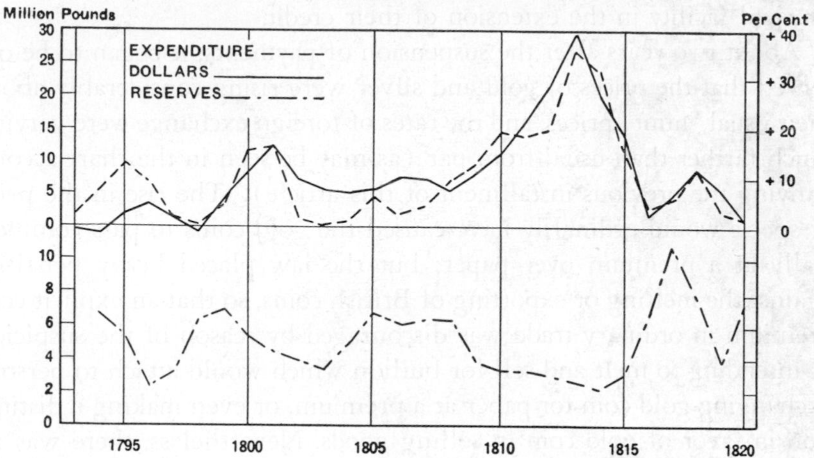

the Bank as to their condition, it was arranged by Pitt that an Order-in-Council be issued enjoining the Bank from further payment of their obligations in cash. The Suspension became effective on February 27, 1797, and saved the Bank from a state of chronic insolvency which would have demoralized public as well as private credit. While introduced as a tentative measure, with a hesitancy which seems remarkable in the light of modern practices, the Order-in-Council was presently confirmed and continued by an act of Parliament,[2] which, by subsequent renewals, prolonged the Restriction until 1821. It should be borne in mind that the Bank Restriction did not make the notes of the Bank legal tender; but so great was general confidence in the Bank that their notes circulated with the same freedom as would have been the case with legal-tender government paper.[3] Nor did the Suspension provisions apply to institutions other than the Bank of England: the country banks were technically under obligation to continue payments in cash; but it is an interesting fact that none of them actually did so, and that this policy is known to have been contested in but very few cases of a trivial nature. The country banks customarily redeemed a large proportion of the demands against them in London drafts, drawn upon balances with London correspondents. The reserves of the latter were wholly uncontrolled by law and had never been more than very moderate sums; and

[2] 37 Geo. III, c. 45.

[3] Immediately upon the public announcement of the Suspension, "a great meeting of merchants and bankers was held, which passed a resolution undertaking to accept Bank notes, and eventually 4000 signatures were attached to this." Cannan, *The Paper Pound of 1797–1821,* p. xii. For text see Cobbett, *Paper against Gold,* p. 168.

their ability to create credits was now but very little controlled by the Bank of England. In general, the country banks found the door open to unusual facility in the extension of their credit.

About two years after the suspension of payments, it began to be observed that the prices of gold and silver were rising considerably above their usual "mint" prices, and the rates of foreign exchange were varying much farther than usual from par (as may be seen in the chart accompanying the previous installment of this article).[4] The rise in the price of specie would ordinarily have caused the gold coins to pass commercially at a premium over paper; but the law placed heavy penalties against the melting or exporting of British coins, so that an explicit coin premium in ordinary trade was discouraged by reason of the suspicion of intending to melt and sell for bullion which would attach to persons exchanging gold coin for paper at a premium, or even making a distinction in favor of gold coin in selling goods. Nevertheless, there was an extensive illicit trade in melting coins for sale in the bullion market, and the gold coins, which were in better condition than the silver, very soon disappeared from circulation. Their place was taken by small notes of one and two pounds (the previous minimum denomination having been five pounds) which the Bank of England and the country banks had been permitted to issue by special legislation. While the paper currency as a whole, and particularly that of the Bank, commanded general confidence, there were random instances in business transactions of double prices (lower in specie than in paper), some of them known to have arisen from deliberate intent for petty personal reasons or for political effect. Not until 1812 did the government explicitly declare double prices illegal, by a curious law which at the same time refrained from declaring notes legal tender; nevertheless it exerted some moral effect in discouraging attempts in certain quarters to discredit Bank of England notes as a subtle means of impugning the administration of public affairs generally.

Even before the Bank suspended payments, the quasipublic functions of the Bank of England were being exploited by those who sought to make the matter a political issue and a means of attacking the conduct of the War. Thomas Paine, animated by his successful exploits on behalf of the revolutionist parties in America and in France, proceeded to develop the sombre forebodings and subtle innuendos of his earlier *Prospects on the Rubicon* (1787). In the famine year 1796, Paine pointed to the rising cost of living and denounced the British system of credit and

[4] See *Quart. Jour. Econ.*, February 1924, p. 231 [chart reproduced here on p. 361].

banking in a bitter and cynical tract—*The Decline and Fall of the English System of Finance*—which was widely circulated. England's pyramid of bank credit, the bulwark of her political strength and her foreign diplomacy, was doomed, he dolefully reiterated, to follow the way of the *Assignâts,* then in the throes of their tragic collapse. The War against the French liberals would, he thought, eventually cause the mounting extravagance of the State to sink the country in a sea of "diluted" currency, while France, with an ample reserve of the precious metals, would emerge triumphant. British paper had already "pulled down the value of gold and silver to a level with itself"; but, he added in a prophetic tone, "gold and silver will, in the long run, revolt against depreciation and separate from the value of the paper; for the progress of all such systems appears to be, that the paper will take command in the beginning, and gold and silver in the end." Thereupon people would, and should, strive to get gold into their possession, with the result that the Bank of England must suspend—as it had done before; and with suspension would come the end of the existing political régime. "The stability of the government is equal to that of the Bank and no more." All this Paine designed as encouragement and suggestion to all disaffected elements, with the thought that thereby he had "revenged the piratical depredations committed on the American commerce by the British government."[5]

Upon the Bank suspending payments, as Paine had predicted, the collapse of public credit for which he hoped failed to materialize. But the same tactics were carried forward with surprising boldness in the pamphlet press and particularly in the debates in Parliament. The Suspension furnished apt rhetorical material for assailing, not only the government's borrowings, but its remittances of treasure to the Continent to finance the allied states.[6] Charles James Fox immediately seized the opportunity to place the ministry in an awkward position by demanding a full inquiry into the reasons for the Bank Suspension, declaring ominously that this state of affairs had definitely "destroyed the credit of the

[5] Such challenging and irritating sentiments did not pass unobserved. From all sides sober business men and loyal citizens pointed out Paine's real objects and his erroneous inferences. "By attacking Lombard Street," one pointedly observed, "a revolution is attempted at St. James." ("Gresham," *Letters on the Solidity of Commercial Bills* [1796].)

[6] A special act was passed in May 1800 (39–40 Geo. III, c. 33), providing as follows: "It shall be lawful for the Governor and Company of the Bank of England to advance for the Public Service, in cash and bullion, any such sums to be remitted abroad as they shall judge expedient, from time to time, not exceeding in the whole the amount which has been, or shall be, granted in this session of Parliament on account of foreign subsidies or services abroad." (Public General Acts, 1800.) It will be recalled that Pitt sent funds to the Continent in the early years of the War without consent of Parliament.

Bank." Pitt was forced to acquiesce; but the inquiry was somehow carefully steered away from matters which would have revealed such pertinent facts as any state at war would zealously guard from public knowledge. The Committee of Inquiry therefore conveniently found the chief explanation of the Bank's difficulties in the innocuous fact that country people, fearing an invasion, had run upon their bankers, who, in turn, had hastily called in their reserves from London.[7]

Fox and Sheridan constituted themselves the leaders of a persistent tirade against the Bank Suspension, not upon grounds of financial principle, but because the Suspension permitted that institution to support the activities of what they regarded as a militaristic, reactionary, and withal bankrupt administration. On March 9 and 10 (1797) they concentrated their eloquent invective against this alliance of Bank and State which was productive of "robbery and fraud"; and they urged that the Bank be divorced forthwith from their public responsibilities and their participation in the War. Let the Ministry repay the debts to the Bank (if it could!), and let the Bank resume the honest payment of their notes. "The Bank," Fox dramatically exclaimed, "should have but one object: that of performing their engagements and discharging their debts. We have heard of the phrase 'perish commerce, let the Constitution live'; the exclamation of the Bank should be 'perish commerce, provided we pay our debts.' "[8] This clearly struck the keynote for the immediate-resumption and anti-Bank agitation, which continued for years thereafter and which forms the main theme of this paper.

Sheridan formally moved on April 4, 1797, that all financial assistance to the Continent be stopped. To Pitt's striking reply, in which he pointed to the obvious dangers of a separate peace between the German Emperor and the French, were the subsidies to be discontinued, Fox

[7] The Duke of Bedford, speaking in the Lords on May 15, 1797, pointed out that the Committee of Inquiry "was composed not only of the zealous supporters of ministers, but of members of that very Cabinet upon whose conduct they were appointed to decide." (*Hansard,* 33, pp. 517 ff.) The effect of this sidetracking of the main causes was to place in the hands of one group of subsequent controversialists an official statement which could be cited in attempting to prove that it was not the balance of foreign payments that affected the bullion and exchange quotations.

[8] *Hansard,* 33, p. 44. In concluding, Fox denounced the Cabinet for their persistence in "continuing this destructive war" at the cost of that "fatal injury" to the country's credit which was evidenced in the alleged run on the Bank and the "depreciation" of Bank notes. All this went far afield from the tolerant and practical views of Adam Smith, who, in his chapter on "Public Debts," had looked at the problem of war financing sincerely and dispassionately: "An immediate and great expense must be incurred in that moment of immediate danger which will not wait for the gradual and slow returns of the new taxes. In this exigency government can have no other resource but in borrowing." (*Wealth of Nations,* Bk. 5, Ch. 3.) This was, of course, the view to which the majority of the Lords and Commons subscribed.

offered the astonishing rejoinder that the outcome of the War was a matter of little consequence compared with the immediate restoration of "public credit." *Fiat justitia, ruat cœlum!*

While the currency question was being exploited at Westminster, with rhetorical flourish and with the object of tying the hands of the government in raising current funds, the busy pamphlet press carried forward the controversy with keener weapons of analysis and a closer scrutiny of theoretical niceties. In the writings of a remarkable group of men of affairs we are able to trace a well-defined continuity of doctrinal development, which culminated in strikingly formal statements of fundamental principle and hotly contested suggestions for immediate policy. While the general drift of these opinions is fairly familiar to modern economists,[9] there are certain phases of them which have been commonly overlooked or misunderstood. There is evident in the course of contemporary discussion a progressive narrowing of vision and of emphasis which gave plausibility to practical proposals which require fresh scrutiny. Particular pains will be taken to show that, behind the bold principles and cogent admonitions of this so-called "bullionist" school of writers, there is discernible the bias of personal interests which distorted their analysis to a degree apparently unsuspected by many leading commentators who have held up their writings as models of scientific method and financial acumen.[10]

The substance of the theories which ultimately crystallized into the "bullionist" doctrine was stated in compelling form by Walter Boyd, an international financier and public loan contractor who, in January 1801, addressed an open letter to William Pitt.[11] This was a time of great agricultural dearth, and unusually high prices, not only of provisions, but of the precious metals and foreign bills of exchange. In these indicia, taken together, Boyd believed that he saw definite evidence of excessive currency, which he traced directly to the Bank of England, upon whose directors he laid the entire responsibility. Since the abnormal conditions had lasted for many months, the inference was plausible and not easily

[9] See, for example, J. H. Hollander, "The Development of the Theory of Money from Adam Smith to David Ricardo," *Quart. Jour. Econ.*, May 1911.

[10] Cf., e.g., McLeod, *Theory and Practice of Banking,* Vol. II; Sumner, *History of American Currency;* Andréadès, *History of the Bank of England;* Cannan, *The Paper Pound of 1797–1821,* a reprint of the *Bullion Report;* a recent American reprint of the same *Report,* with introduction by Stuyvesant Fish (New York, 1920); and Alfred Marshall, *Money, Credit and Commerce.*

[11] Walter Boyd, *A Letter to the Right Honorable William Pitt, on the Influence of the Stoppage of Issues in Specie at the Bank of England on the Prices of Provisions, and Other Commodities.*

contradicted, even tho Boyd could not adduce more than a meager showing of statistical data on the actual increase in the volume of circulating credit. But to show that responsibility rested wholly with the Bank, and that it was the Bank's issues which had exclusively originated the alleged inflation, required some definite reason. This Boyd found in the belief that the country banks were not legally enjoined from cash payment, and that they were in any case powerless to create credit "in excess of local demands." Should they attempt to do so, the local excess would be speedily and automatically reduced by demands for cash or Bank of England notes for use in other localities, such as London. "It may be therefore inferred," Boyd stated, "that no part of their issues can possibly remain in circulation beyond what the increasing prosperity and industry of the country where they circulate can fairly absorb or digest." Far from being instruments of inflation, the provincial bankers were represented as the suppliers of essential business capital; their increased issues would be always the result of more active trade or perhaps of their having more Bank notes available for their reserves. Such reserves, however, could never be enlarged, save upon the initiative of the central bank. This view formed the basis for a vast amount of subsequent theorizing.

Boyd's real attitude, however, was not one of special sympathy with the country banks so much as of deep personal resentment against the Bank of England. In 1796 Boyd's concern (Boyd, Benfield and Co.) had heavy commitments in contracting for the current government War loan. The market quotations for the public funds fell sharply at an awkward moment; while the Bank, in the midst of great financial confusion and strain, coldly resisted appeals for more liberal accommodation to the money market. In fact, Boyd refers explicitly and with bitterness to "the cruel circumstances in which I was then placed and those, still more dreadful, which have since occurred to annihilate my commercial existence in this country." Again, Boyd was perhaps induced to draw parallels between Bank notes as quasi-public issues and the French *Assignâts,* as his ramifying business connections had taken him to Paris during the Revolution and he had witnessed the chaos attending their rapid depreciation. It was wholly natural, then, for him to fall into such strong phrases in alluding to a specific portion of the English currency as "positive depredation" and "forced issue."

As a contractor to the government loans, Boyd had had in his charge the remitting of subsidy funds to the Austrian Emperor; he was a leading expert in foreign exchange practice, and could not but be cognizant of the effect of large foreign remittances upon the price of foreign bills and of specie. Yet he made no place for them as a factor affecting the exchange and bullion markets. It was "depreciation" alone which caused these abnormalities, as well as the high prices of provisions, and the increased burdens of government, all of which portended eventual discredit and collapse. Boyd implied in a curious way that the high paper prices of goods in England were not a causal factor in the distorted exchange and bullion prices, but rather a coincident.[12] He failed to analyze satisfactorily the precise relation between price levels and the exchanges; he left with his reader a possible impression that there was a *qualitative "depreciation"* of Bank notes which caused the exchange aberrations, and a *quantitative excess,* which acted to some extent independently upon local commodity prices. At any rate, he gave a curiously indefinite explanation of the forces actually affecting the foreign exchange market. Accordingly, in the matter of remedying the situation, Boyd could not offer a very definite program, but admonished the Prime Minister to give the entire matter his earnest consideration.

The thread of Boyd's discussion was immediately taken up by Henry Thornton, an eminent and highly respected London banker, having important connections in the provinces. While naturally sympathetic to the country banks, Thornton in his lengthy *Enquiry*[13] stopped far short of Boyd's condemnations of the Bank of England and made his more temperate references to that institution part of a remarkably incisive (tho awkwardly presented) analysis of monetary principles and current banking practice.

Thornton admitted and emphasized Boyd's contention that the Bank of England was the basis and ultimate controlling influence of the country's entire credit circulation, and he elaborated the notion with considerable skill. He evolved it from the fundamental principle of an equilibrium of currency value in commercially connected areas. Among countries on a gold basis Thornton showed that gold distributed itself through the action of currency expansion and contraction upon commodity prices; he advanced and brilliantly expounded the conception of a world-level in the purchasing power of gold. An outflow of bullion from a country and a turn of the exchanges against it would denote a

[12] He admitted that, should the degree of exchange deviation exceed that of domestic average price elevation, a stimulus to exports would be an incidental benefit. "If the increase of prices in the home market should, fortunately, not keep pace with the depression of the exchange [in foreign money], all our articles of production must feel the effects of the increased demand in the foreign markets in consequence of the diminished value of British money abroad" (p. 37).

[13] Henry Thornton, *An Enquiry into the Nature and Effects of the Paper Credit of Great Britain* (1802).

relative excess of currency which depressed its value below the level abroad. Hence, through an increase of imports and decline of exports, some gold would flow abroad and a new international price equilibrium would result. To Thornton, not Ricardo, belongs the credit of first stating this important principle in clear and convincing form.

These ideas were now applied to the case of the relative value of money in different areas of a single country, tho in the qualified manner of Boyd's one-way relationship—from London *to* the country, not *from* the country to London. If country bankers generally and simultaneously issued an "extraordinary quantity of notes," local prices would rise; the provinces would then tend to buy more in London; demands upon the local bankers for Bank notes and London drafts ("which is nearly the same thing") would reduce their working reserves and necessitate a local note contraction. It was implied that the remitted Bank notes and draft credits would not raise prices in London substantially higher than before. If, however, the Bank of England greatly expanded their issues and their credits to London houses, this would directly enlarge the reserve basis for new country circulation. This curious view continued more and more to dominate the literature championing immediate monetary contraction by the Bank of England, and its theoretical importance as a basis for such action has not hitherto been generally noticed. We shall comment upon its validity hereafter.

Thornton, however, refrained from the natural inference. While admitting that inflation was now *possible,* he defended the Bank and argued persuasively that the directors exercised such caution in their operations, and had so high a sense of public responsibility, that excessive issue not only was unlikely, but could be shown by the available data not to have occurred. The lending to the State had been, he thought, on a conservative and moderate scale. Hence it followed that an automatic preventive of general currency excess was actually in operation, even tho the Bank's operations were no longer limited by gold.

In applying the general principle of international values under conditions of inconvertible paper, Thornton's analysis was marked at times by brilliant insight, again by extreme clumsiness and vagueness of expression, and, in general, a failure to keep the cases of convertibility and inconvertibility clearly distinct. This was a failing whereby Thornton generated a long series of misunderstandings and cloudy controversy. There are passages in which the author implies that inconvertible paper, if rapidly expanded, will drive gold abroad and in this way cause the exchanges to deviate "unfavorably." The mechanism seems no different from that in the case of convertibility. A high price of bullion and foreign bills indicates local "excess" by indicating the outflow of bullion which always attends excess. This idea, which makes apparent proof of excess so universally applicable and so plausibly decisive, played a subtle part, as will appear below, in the resumption program of later writers, including Ricardo, who never attained a thoroly clear conception of the matter.

Nevertheless, Thornton did present (altho not in a context definitely specifying his assumptions) a striking statement of what has come to be called the "purchasing-power-parity" doctrine relating to conditions of irredeemable paper—a doctrine which ought in justice to be associated with his name. A persistently unfavorable course of foreign exchange, according to Thornton, registers such a divergence of (paper) prices above the normal international level that, in order to maintain the same relative volume of exports and imports, English exporters will receive more paper for their bills and foreign importers will obtain remittances payable in English paper money at a reduced rate, all of which tends to neutralize the high (paper) prices of British goods. London bills thus become cheap when quoted in foreign gold, and this, to use Thornton's own words, "will operate as an advantage to the foreign buyer of our commodities in the computation of the exchangeable value of that circulating medium of his own country with which he discharges the debt in Britain. . . . It will thus obviate the dearness of our articles; it will serve as a compensation to the foreigner for the loss which he would otherwise sustain by buying in our market."[14] If this be true, it follows that gold need not flow abroad to equilibrate the international level; the result is accomplished by variations in the exchange quotations and the paper price of specie, which will correspond roughly to those in the average relative prices of commodities. But in other parts of the book Thornton perplexes the reader by implying that exportation of specie will be involved as a result of such paper excess.

In contrast to Boyd, Thornton showed that the quotations of foreign exchange and bullion might be affected not only by the state of the currency, but by unusual foreign remittances. He called attention to the abnormally large importations of foreign foodstuffs to relieve the well-nigh famine conditions of 1800–1801; to the purchases of naval stores in the Baltic; and to the huge sums being spent abroad for purposes dictated by military necessity. But he submitted that such factors could not exert a permanent and continuing effect upon the exchange market;

[14] *Ibid.*, p. 201.

if abnormal deviations persisted for many years, they could only signify some currency inflation. Thornton doubted whether actually a sufficient time had yet elapsed to render it certain that the latter factor predominated.

Thornton was restrained from urging immediate limitations upon the Bank of England, not only because he believed the Bank's loans to the State were moderate and necessary and their merchantile discounts cautiously made, but because of his very real fear of the violent commercial disruption which any sudden contraction of circulation would create. Thornton emphasized again and again the lessons of the financial stringency of 1796, which he believed was unnecessarily aggravated by the Bank's course of action. Any attempt on the part of the Bank to regulate its extension of credit in strict proportion to its reserve he regarded as the result of a "merely theoretic" idea, which could have only unfortunate consequences for industry and trade in the existing critical state of affairs.

While Thornton was completing his treatise, a small group of liberal thinkers were preparing to launch the *Edinburgh Review.* Francis Horner, a rising young Scottish barrister, and several friends worked their way laboriously through Thornton's difficult pages and finally composed a concise summary and appreciative review, which was printed in October 1802, in the first number of the periodical. Horner carried the analysis forward at a number of points. Puzzled by Thornton's vacillation between convertible and inconvertible conditions of issue, Horner fought his way to what he considered a clearer statement of the whole matter. If paper is inconvertible and its quantity increased, general paper prices rise; this causes the value of gold to exceed the value of paper and "in order to preserve the same apparent rate of [foreign] exchange there ought to be a corresponding alteration of the commercial tables in which that rate is expressed." In other words, the abnormal quoted rates will be "nominal," and will indicate nothing whatsoever as to specie movements; indeed, the variations in these nominal rates are precisely the forces which obviate such dislocation in the relation of exports to imports as would otherwise occasion specie movements. At all events, the causation would run from higher prices to a compensating rise in gold and foreign bills (without movement of gold), not, as Thornton had occasionally implied, from higher prices of goods to a debit trade balance and a resulting export of gold to restore the international equilibrium.[15] Whether affairs had actually reached the stage where a high price

[15] "When an excess of paper money produces a nominal rise of prices, a nominal fall

of bullion had become a chronic condition, Horner was as uncertain as Thornton had been, and he concluded in the same tone of hesitant expectancy. But whatever the degree of possible inflation, he was struck by the fact that the restriction "should have been continued for more than five years without any depreciation of the paper from a failure of confidence"; this he believed to be a fact "which has falsified all reasonable prediction, and forms an exception to the most confident maxims of all former economists." This statement shows in a pointed way how a theorist of Horner's type, unacquainted with the practices and attitude of the business world, brought together the ideas of currency expansion and currency discredit—an association of ideas perhaps natural to a student of Continental experience and of opinions derived from the pages of the *Wealth of Nations,* wherein colonial experiences with "paper money" are so graphically described.

Contrary to the expectations of some, the Bank Restriction was continued during the short Peace of Amiens, and after the renewal of hostilities in 1803. This was not effected without the usual spirited opposition from the anti-War party in Parliament, who were at this time given support by Lord King, an extensive landed proprietor of somewhat reclusive and eccentric character, to whom the fall in the purchasing power of money rents seemed a far greater calamity than any change in the fortunes of France or England. Lord King spoke effectively and skillfully, and utilized in his argument the materials we have been examining. He later published the substance of his remarks in a clearly written pamphlet which commanded wide attention.[16]

Lord King extracted from the writings of Boyd, Thornton, and Horner the already well-defined ideas of the possible significance of exchange and price fluctuations and the passive nature of country credit; and he added such pertinent data as he could find on the Bank's note issue and the prices of foreign bills and specie (silver). His type of reasoning lent itself conveniently to such statistical treatment, since the easily available exchange rates or price of bullion alone served the purpose of proving "depreciation." Hence the term "bullionist" as a descriptive epithet applying to this entire group of anti-Bank-Restriction

of the foreign exchanges will always take place, and is a consequence of that steady excess of the market price of gold above its mint price which originated immediately in the excessive issue of paper." (*Ibid.*)

[16] King, *Thoughts on the Restriction of Payments in Specie at the Banks of England and Ireland* (1803). The Bank of Ireland suspended cash payments in 1798, and in the ensuing years a considerable aberration in the rates of exchange between London and Dublin had occurred. King used these facts to support his contentions regarding the British currency.

writers. And at the same time that King introduced what he believed convincing factual evidence, he discarded all the qualifications and alternative possibilities which Thornton and Horner had entertained; there could be but one causal principle—depreciation by excess; and what Horner had feared might yet be possible, King now regarded as unquestionable. Under existing conditions, he reiterated, there was no certain or determinate limitation to the supply of circulating credit: it was free to become a law unto itself. As the Bank, he found, had increased their circulation by as much as five millions in the seven years since 1797, he pronounced that institution a mischievous and irresponsible dabbler in accommodation paper. "The Bank directors," he affirmed, in ill-tempered invective, "have willingly accepted, and, it is most probable, have solicited, a continuance of this legislative interference. Instead of exerting themselves to perform their engagements to their creditors, they have shared larger profits among the proprietors of their stock; and there is no reason to believe that they will at any time resume their payments in cash, unless compelled by a discontinuance of the present Suspension."[17]

King appeared to see but little connection between the Bank's position and the carrying on of a comprehensive war. To be sure, he did notice the political factors capable of affecting bills and specie: "The necessity of great remittances, or an unusual expenditure on the Continent of Europe, will to a certain degree produce this effect: but as such causes of irregularity are occasional and temporary, it may be safely affirmed as a general rule . . . that an unfavorable exchange, long continued, is alone a decisive proof of a deranged and depreciated currency." Bank notes, in his view, were already so degraded as to be precisely comparable to the silver coins of King William and the fateful *Assignâts.*[18] Again we find the country bankers, despite their mushroom growth and unrestrained practices, duly eulogized and defended—on

[17] King, *Thoughts on the Restriction of Payments,* p. 12. As a matter of fact, the Bank had expressed a willingness to initiate resumption of payments at the time the Peace of 1802 was concluded.

[18] In the Goldsmiths' Library of the University of London is preserved Thornton's personal copy of King's *Thoughts on the Restriction of Payments,* in which, among Thornton's penciled notations, is one attributing to Walter Boyd the belief that *mere inconvertibility* of Bank notes occasioned their depreciation. Against this Thornton was now inclined to entertain the possibility of a moderate depreciation tho enlarged volume of circulation. Thornton, indeed, warmly endorsed King's belief that "an excess of paper is the great radical cause of a long-continued unfavorable exchange" as "a great and important principle," and admitted that in 1801–1802 there may have been "a somewhat too great issue of Bank of England notes." At the same time he pointed out that King's figures failed to show a point-for-point correspondence between specie and exchange quotations and the Bank's issues.

the ground that free competition among them tended absolutely to forestall the issuance of more than a "sufficient" volume of currency for local needs; each country issuer was checked, "if not by the public, at least by the interested vigilance of his rivals." On other grounds King exonerated the local institutions—which, of course, financed the agriculturists and corn merchants who paid his Lordship's rents: speculative operations in produce steadied prices, but could not elevate them for any time; and, further, the accommodation of the country bankers even to speculators was limited by the moderate size of their capitals! All of this King drew from his imagination rather than from the facts about him.

Passing over numerous lesser contributions to the discussion which followed, more or less ably, the same general line of argument, we may give attention to two other writers of the "bullionist" school, whose opinions had unusual influence and contain interesting features.

Mr. John Wheatley, of whose life we know practically nothing save that he resided in the provinces and was a close student of Adam Smith, published in 1807 an elaborate treatise on monetary principles and credit policy,[19] in which we find a bold attempt to harmonize the views of Thornton and Lord King with those presented in the *Wealth of Nations.* With an extreme rigidity and formal precision of statement, Wheatley attacked the currency problem with keen insight and no little originality. Several aspects of his work are notable from the point of view of doctrinal development.

First of all, Wheatley formulated the "purchasing-power-parity" idea relating to irredeemable paper in remarkably clear and cogent form. "If the paper be not convertible into specie at the option of the holder, and a relative excess of currency ensue from its over-issue, the course of exchange will prevent the interruption that would otherwise be effected in the general level, by maintaining the specie at the same value with the value of money in other countries, and reducing the paper to a discount in proportion to the excess:—in proportion as it elevated the prices of the country where it circulated above the prices in other countries. . . . Specie, therefore would bear a premium commensurate with the premium on a foreign bill, and, no longer participating in the degraded condition of the paper, would resiliate to its level and be maintained at the same value with the value of money in other countries."[20] Wheatley

[19] John Wheatley, *An Essay on the Theory of Money and the Principles of Commerce,* Vol. I.

[20] Wheatley, *An Essay on the Theory of Money,* p. 68.

saw all things in sharply defined outline: they were either black or white. Following King, he denied any possible effect upon exchange rates or specie of foreign remittances or unusual disturbance in the balance of payments. These rates and prices, under existing conditions, were *exclusively* controlled by the relative nominal price-levels in England and foreign countries.

In developing the practical bearing of this position, Wheatley followed out a line of reasoning which doubtless found inspiration in the *Wealth of Nations.* In discussing the financing of wars Adam Smith says: "The funds which maintained the foreign wars of the present century, the most expensive perhaps which history records, seem to have had little dependency upon the exportation either of the circulating money, or the plate of private families, or of the treasure of the prince. . . . The enormous expense of the late [Seven Years'] war, therefore, must have been chiefly defrayed, not by the exportation of gold and silver, but by that of British commodities of some kind or other. When the government . . . contracted with a merchant for a remittance to some foreign country, he would naturally endeavour to pay his foreign correspondent, upon whom he had granted a bill, by sending abroad rather commodities than gold and silver."[21]

Wheatley, therefore, argued in similar vein: wars *can* be financed upon a convertible currency basis and without unusual use of the precious metals in remittances; even should political expediency demand exceptional remittances, an inexhaustible store of gold and silver can be assured by the simple device of keeping British prices sufficiently below the international level to cause a plentiful supply of export bills in the exchange market to meet any demand for remittances drawn on the foreign balances. "If Mr. Pitt had . . . obstructed the excessive utterance of the paper with which the country was inundated, he might have caused the influx of money to any extent, at the same time that he was forwarding the succors, which, consistently with the real resources of this country, it was our duty to have given."[22]

This is a most rigid application of pure theory to the complicated circumstances of a major war. Under such circumstances a banking system is necessarily subject to unusual strains and unpredictable demands. An attempt to maintain normal specie payments in a nation dependent upon highly developed credit which rests upon a slender cash reserve cannot but expose that credit structure, and with it the military effort,

---

[21] Smith, *Wealth of Nations,* Bk. 4, Ch. 1, "Principle of the Commercial System."
[22] Wheatley, *An Essay on the Theory of Money,* p. 194.

to extreme and dangerous shocks. No one has ever devised a perfect method whereby the entire funds needed by the state in a great war can be raised wholly by such a conscription of private income as will involve no borrowing, no rise of prices, or no discouragement to essential productive energies and commercial activity. If public borrowing does occur, it always involves, not only a *diversion* of investment but some *creation* of fresh bank credit, directly or indirectly. To ensure such credit being available quickly when emergency arises, requires a flexibility in the financial institutions which cannot exist if their lending power is restricted by cash reserves that are constantly subject to depletion by the unusual commercial difficulties interposed by naval warfare, by alarms and hoarding among the masses of the people, and by the tactical machinations of an enemy cognizant (as Napoleon was) of the power of credit as a military weapon. Writers of Wheatley's type looked upon the currency problem narrowly and failed to grasp its connection with the state's financial efforts. Following the letter of Adam Smith too closely, they applied abstract reasoning on the basis of purely commercial mechanics to a situation rendered highly complex and abnormal by political considerations. Hence their facile assumptions as to the possibilities of convertible credit, and their failure to distinguish carefully between the workings of international exchange under conditions of convertibility and of inconvertibility. Hence, again, the confidence with which they could urge even moderate contraction in currency volume as a means of easily attracting gold and silver to the coffers of the Bank.

Wheatley, however, did display commendable originality and a firm grip upon realities in laying the blame for such needless expansion of British credit as existed where it mainly belonged—on the unregulated extravagance of country banking. Under war conditions it becomes more than ever important to exercise control over the extension of credit, and to strengthen the banks and coördinate them so that they work together for a common purpose and with all possible caution. It was in this direction that the British government displayed perhaps its greatest weakness; but doubtless for the very reason that no outstanding publicists proffered the proper counsel and advice. Wheatley's thinking on this point was clear and logical, but his voice was weak. Reversing Boyd's thesis as to the relation of country credit to London credit, he held that the Bank's issues were dominated in large measure by those of the country: "the quantity of paper of a higher denomination must in great degree be regulated by the quantity of the inferior means of payment."[23]

[23] *Ibid.*, pp. 194, 348.

Wheatley therefore recommended, in a very sane spirit, the reformation and strengthening of the entire British banking system as a prerequisite to restoring general convertibility, declaring that "none but chartered companies should be allowed the privilege of issue," and that there should be no issues below ten, or even fifteen, pounds.

This view of the country-bank situation seems to the present writer on the whole a proper one. London and the rest of England were not then, and are not now economic areas producing identical wares. If the price of iron or hops or wool rose in the provinces by reason of liberal credit accommodation to farmers and speculators, the high prices would be paid by buyers in London, who might borrow directly or indirectly from the Bank upon bills and notes drawn up in larger figures. It could not result in purchases from London of what London did not produce.[24] Also the use of Bank notes as local reserve and currency was by no means general, being practised mainly in the West Riding of Yorkshire. Again, the practice of rediscounting local paper with London houses was rapidly developing and made great liberality of accommodation possible in view of the general acquiescence in the City in the relief from specie payment. There was no definite limit upon the structure of credit which these private banks of London might pyramid on almost no reserve at all. The remittance of Bank notes to London did not, as in the years of normal currency, involve the reduction in their quantity through exchange for gold at the Bank; the notes merely passed through the London private banks and perhaps bullion dealers, and then became the basis for possible new advances *via* a correspondent firm to some inland district.[25]

[24] It is surprising to find even such modern writers as Alfred Marshall seemingly lending support to this old view. Cf. *Money, Credit and Commerce,* p. 62 n.

[25] Wheatley's views on the country banks were shared by many writers who did not accept the "bullionist" doctrines. T. R. Malthus, for example, in the 1803 edition of his work on Population pointed out the power of local issues to raise prices throughout the country; the local currency "being once absorbed into the circulation, must necessarily . . . throw great obstacles in the way of returning cheapness" (*Essay on the Theory of Money,* p. 404). See the evidence of T. Richardson, a London bill-broker, before the Bullion Committee; also J. Atkinson, *Considerations on the Propriety of the Bank of England resuming its Payments* . . . (1802).

Evidence in support of the above interpretations has been presented by the writer in a recent study of *British Prices and Business Cycles, 1779–1850* (Suppl. to the *Rev. Econ. Stat.,* October 1923). It was found that the quarterly cyclical fluctuations in the country notes *preceded,* or *synchronized with,* those of wholesale commodity prices, while the discounts of the Bank of England (a much more accurate measure of accommodation than their notes) almost invariably *followed* them. It is also shown in the study referred to that the Bank's loans to the State tended to expand when discounts were moderate, and *vice versa.* In other words, the Bank granted accommodation to the government during the War rather sparingly and according to the state of their mercantile accounts. They put the

The drift of the doctrine we have traced—that excess of inconvertible currency is accurately tested by the nominal rates of exchange and price of specie, and that contraction of bank circulation will permit unusual foreign debts to be financed (even in war-time) by depressing prices and causing a favorable commercial balance—was given its most influential, altho by no means its clearest, formulation in the writings of David Ricardo, one of the leading characters of his day on the London Stock Exchange. Beginning with a brief communication to the *Morning Chronicle,* on August 29, 1809, followed by replies to critics in the same columns and later by pamphlets on the subject, Ricardo argued

---

business interests foremost and assumed a primary responsibility for the maintenance of British trade and industry, which, in an essentially commercial war, was of vast consequence.

It will further appear from the appended Chart that the proportion of the total unfunded government debt carried by the Bank was, at any rate in the light of more recent European experience, not immoderate. Analysis of the Bank's accounts shows that the approximate volume of *notes* issued in advance to the State was insignificant, especially from 1805 to 1810.

British Unfunded Public Debt (Mainly Exchequer bills) in January Each Year, from 1794 to 1821 ————

Exchequer Bills Held by the Bank of England in January Each Year from 1794 to 1821 ---------

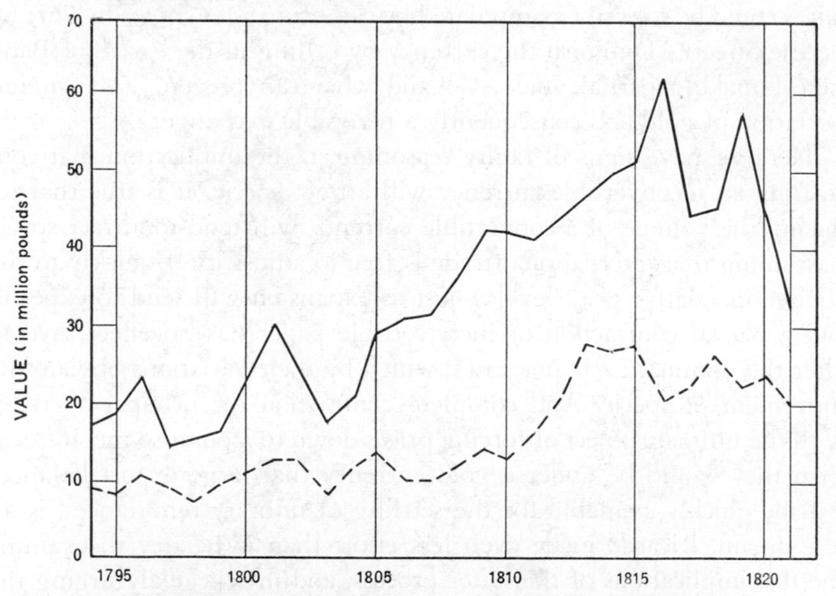

The total unfunded debt figures are for January 5th (*Parliamentary Papers, 1821,* Vol. XVI) and the Bank of England holdings of Exchequer bills for the date in January nearest the 5th, as given in accounts in possession of the writer. There are no figures for computing the average annual Exchequer bills outstanding from the Treasury.

the entire matter with all the rigid abstraction of King and Wheatley and with an unusual degree of emphasis upon the necessity of immediate action in restoring the Bank to a cash basis.

Making his first literary effort in the columns of the *Chronicle,* Ricardo pointed to the state of the exchanges not only as proof positive of Bank note "depreciation," but, in the manner of a fevered alarmist, as portending dire calamity. The general public "do not seem to be sufficiently impressed with the importance of the subject, nor of the disastrous consequences which may attend the further depreciation of paper. I am anxious whilst there is yet time, that we should retrace our steps and restore the currency to that healthful state . . . the departure from which is pregnant with present evil and future ruin."[26] Ricardo appears to have supposed that since the exchange and bullion deviations were due solely to inflation, the mere extinction of two or three millions of notes—even tho not convertible—would suffice to correct the entire situation. He aimed his policy consistently at the Bank, ignoring the rest of the credit mechanism (on the grounds of Thornton and King) and giving little attention to the non-commercial factors operating in the exchange market. Why consider these when international commercial balances could be so easily manipulated by canceling a few notes in Threadneedle Street? "Diminish the currency by calling in the excess of Bank notes: make a partial void . . . and what can prevent . . . an importation of gold and consequently a favorable exchange?"[27]

Here we have signs of faulty reasoning in the implication that contracting an inconvertible currency will attract specie. It is true that reducing the volume of a convertible currency will tend to attract specie (assuming that international trade is free to adjust itself quickly to the change in relative price levels) just as expansion will tend to expel it. But a partial contraction of inconvertible paper has no effect save to alter the nominal exchange rates, which by their variations obviate the movement of specie. And complete contraction of such paper credit, with the ultimate object of forcing prices down to a point so much *lower* than they would be under a gold currency that large export balances will be quickly available for the settling of military remittances, is an idle dream. Ricardo made even less effort than Wheatley to examine the full implications of the latter process, and in repeatedly urging the former he lapsed into the error of regarding the abnormal exchange quotations at the time as indicative of a drain of specie from the country.

[26] *Morning Chronicle,* August 29, 1800.
[27] *Ibid.,* September 14, 1800.

It is most interesting to notice that during these very years Napoleon was being deceived by the same misapprehension in his efforts to weaken the foundations of British credit by shutting the markets of the Continent against British exports. We are told that Napoleon eagerly studied the lists of exchange quotations and interpreted every new deviation in the Hamburg or Danzig rates as proof of more specie being drained from the Bank of England in lieu of cargoes of Manchester cottons and Jamaica sugar.[28]

Early in 1810 Ricardo set forth his views more fully in a pamphlet entitled the *High Price of Bullion a Proof of the Depreciation of Bank Notes.* He "proved" the depreciation in the familiar way, and again insisted that the evil was a matter "which yields to no other in importance."[29] If the currency were convertible, Ricardo argued, no amount of military remittances or foreign subsidies need affect the exchanges, because of the consequences of a lowered price level. And again we find him implying that specie was actually flowing out of England *because driven out* by excessive irredeemable paper. "Specie will be sent abroad to discharge a debt only when it is superabundant; only when it is the cheapest exportable commodity.[30] . . . If the Bank were to diminish the quantity of their notes until they had increased their value 15 per cent, the Restriction might safely be removed, as there would be no temptation to export specie."[31] All this is inconsistent with the purchasing-power-parity idea as set forth by preceding writers.

By assuming paper to be somehow debased, Ricardo could plausibly argue that foreign bills (payable abroad in gold) could be bought with Bank notes only at a high premium *because* gold in London was at a premium and this because the notes were debased. Actually the premium on *both* gold and foreign bills was in large measure due to the fact that

[28] Napoleon "believed that his Continental System had shaken the principal support of England's power; . . . he thought to succeed in ruining her credit, whose measure he wrongly sought in the capricious course of the exchange, and to exhaust the source of the subsidies which she could have given to the new coalition." Mollien, *Mémoires,* Vol. III, p. 237; quoted by Audrey Cunningham, *British Credit in the Last Napoleonic War* (1910).

[29] The tract was probably first thrown together several years before, as essentially a criticism (through the eyes of Horner and King) of Thornton's hesitant conclusions; it contains some evidence of Wheatley's influence, and, like Wheatley's *Essay on the Theory of Money,* refers to no political or economic events later than 1805. The main body of the tract was, in all probability, prepared prior to the articles in the *Chronicle* newspaper.

[30] David Ricardo, *High Price of Bullion,* p. 269. Ricardo's tendency to argue as if gold was actually being exported by reason of currency excess appears more strikingly in his subsequent *Reply to Bosanquet* (1811) and in his well-nigh interminable controversies with his friend Malthus. Cf. *Letters of Ricardo to Malthus, passim,* and the Appendix to the second edition of the *High Price of Bullion* (1811).

[31] *Ibid.,* p. 279.

the total demand for remittances (including subsidies) was exceedingly great. Putting it somewhat differently, Ricardo assumed that gold was still effective as a legal standard and could never itself *rise* in price in terms of paper. It was always paper that fell, not gold (or foreign money) that rose. This is the fundamental basis on which the alleged "proof" of depreciation, as the exclusive cause of exchange deviations, rested, and it is vitiated by the consideration that in an inconvertible system gold becomes a commodity, used chiefly in foreign payments along with bills; and that, far from being a fixed standard, to which all nations may "unerrinngly refer," it may become (especially under conditions such as existed at this juncture) an article subject to unusual fluctuations of demand and supply. What was purchased with paper in London was either gold or the use of a foreign balance, both of which were relatively difficult to obtain because of a current supply inadequate to extraordinary demands—as well as because purchased with British paper circulated in unusual abundance.

Ricardo endeavored to attribute the "fall" of paper sometimes to the Bank's deliberate and mischievous liberality in making loans (whether mainly to the state or to business was not made clear), and more often, and more subtly, to a mere inherent debasement in quality.[32] This could easily be translated, however, into "excess" by supposing that a contraction of the circulation (on the strict analogy of withdrawing part of a debased coinage) would improve its value. "Excess" would not, then, refer to an amount exceeding that which would assure a stable general price level, but, in the more special sense, to an amount exceeding the quantity that would maintain the price of gold at the mint price and the exchanges at par—even tho the foreign debt "equalled the largest subsidy ever given by this country to an ally." All this reasoning, it must be noticed, was in the direction of establishing the main point, that is, plausible ground for immediate contraction of the Bank's accommodation. Bank notes were somehow depreciated in terms of gold; contraction would remove the depreciation; hence they were also "excessive"; hence they were "depreciated by excess." Ricardo did not deduce the exchange deviations *from* domestic price elevation as Horner had done. The price-level changes were an incidental *result* of the "depreciation,"

[32] In Ricardo's subsequent treatise on the *Principles of Political Economy and Taxation* (1817), Ch. 7, he says: "By sending 130 good English pounds sterling to Hamburgh, even at an expense of £5, I should be possessed there of £125; what then could make me consent to give £130 for a bill which would give me £100 in Hamburgh, but that *my pounds were not good pounds sterling? they were deteriorated, were degraded in intrinsic value, below the pounds sterling of Hamburgh.*" (My italics.)

and were attributable to that cause to a degree not exceeding that registered by the direct and conclusive indices.[33] In this curious and subtle twist of ideas, as well as in his "proof" of "depreciation by excess," Ricardo's thought was a reversion to the superficial pronouncements of Fox or Boyd rather than an advance to new and clarified analysis.

Ricardo's central purpose, apparently, was to force the Bank to immediate resumption of payments; and in all his writings he manifested an extraordinary hostility and harshness toward the Bank. He charged the Bank directorate with having the arbitrary and dangerous power "of diminishing at its will the value of every monied man's property, and by enhancing the price of provisions and every necessity of life, injuring the public annuitant and all those persons whose incomes were fixed."[34] His bullion pamphlet was hardly more than a polemical tract directed against the Bank. So little significance did its author attach to the other banking institutions of the country that he even argued that one of the causes of the "excess" of Bank notes was the expansion of the country issues, which had thereby narrowed the field within which the Bank's issues could circulate; the latter overflowed, in other words, a contracted channel—a truly remarkable opinion.

Again, Ricardo appeared to have no constructive suggestion as to the proper relation of the Bank to the financing of the government's pressing needs. The possibility of immediate resumption having an embarrassing effect upon the Treasury's current operations seems never to have occurred to him. Since he professed not to see any causal relation between the heavy remittances abroad for army and subsidies (regarding which a very active member of London's great clearing center of current news ought certainly to have been well informed) and the issue of Bank credit to the state on Exchequer bills for the purchase of foreign exchange, he did not raise the question of the possibility of an immediate resumption draining the Bank of its reserve and forcing it quickly into the bankruptcy which had been so narrowly averted in 1797. What possible explanation, other than ignorance of the facts, can be given for a leading financial figure attempting to force a central bank into an obviously impossible situation at a critical stage of a great war? Why should Ricardo have seen the Bank in so different a light from that of the vast majority of merchants, bankers, and traders of London? How explain his persistent emphasis upon its supposedly enormous profits

---

[33] See Ricardo's evidence before the Committee on Resumption of Payments (1819) for a statement of this portion of his doctrine.

[34] *Morning Chronicle,* August 29, 1809.

and its "very dangerous power," which might "involve many thousands in ruin"? Why the striking similarity between Ricardo's attitude and policy and that of the Parliamentary Opposition? A study of Ricardo's environment will perhaps reveal an answer.

In Ricardo's day the membership of the Stock Exchange comprised two main factions: the contractors to public loans, who naturally took the bull side of the market, and the professional broker-jobbers, who took the bear side in order to derive profits on "continuations." This group borrowed money at five per cent (the maximum legal rate) from local and provincial bankers, and loaned it—*with no limit to the possible rate*[35]—to the public, who purchased government stock (the principal type of security traded in at this time) upon an installment or margin basis. There were but two places where loans upon the collateral of the public funds could always be obtained: (*a*) the stock-jobbers, and (*b*) the private banking house of Goldsmid and Co. Between the stock-jobbers and the Goldsmids there was no very cordial feeling, since the Goldsmids did not charge above five per cent on loans and were able greatly to extend this branch of the business because the Bank of England was becoming increasingly active in the line of mercantile discounts. The Bank was very unpopular among the Stock Exchange bears because, while it did no lending on stock collateral, it did, by increased discounts and the provision of a liquid rediscount market, enable the Goldsmids to obtain ample funds, which the smaller houses would otherwise have invested in bills, and to employ them in collateral loans.[36] This greatly reduced the power of the inner clique of exchange professionals, of which Ricardo seems to have been an acknowledged leader, to exact the former high level of continuation rates, sometimes netting 100 per cent annum, which formed the basis of their rapidly augmented fortunes. Benjamin and Abraham Goldsmid always stood ready, not only to loan upon the funds, but to purchase them, so that they formed an increasingly important support for the contractors who were all to often the victims of skillfully engineered price depressions soon after they had negotiated on a definite basis for the floating of a new war loan. This had been Boyd's experience in 1796. By depressing prices in this way (a process very easy under the loose Exchange rules of the time) the bear-jobbers bought in at a low figure and then sold

[35] See the evidence given by Ricardo and others to the Commons' Committee on the Usury Laws, in 1818.

[36] The banks in general preferred to have nothing to do with loans on public stock because of its erratic movements in price and the degree of manipulation known to be practised on the Exchange.

the stock for time, maintaining a high rate of interest on their advances and discouraging the conclusion of margin holdings by sustaining the depression of prices as long as possible. An Exchange contemporary of Ricardo, identified as J. Lancaster, tells us that, while the public loan agents were every day hustled and mocked on the floor of the House, "Milord David, the bear-general, like a commanding officer upon his own parade, may be observed walking up and down uninterrupted and earnestly persuading Mr. Shallow, that, by the price of bullion, or by what guineas fetch in France on the foreign exchanges, stocks, instead of 69, should be 49."[37]

The persistent attack on the Bank of England therefore promised a double advantage to the professional jobbers. It would affect the temper of the business community and depress security prices, and, secondly, it promised to restore the system prevailing in the early years of the War, by which outside funds were kept pretty well out of the hands of speculators in public stock. In this way the continuation-interest system within the House might be restored to full profitableness. The publication of a tract emanating from an influential source and calling for drastic credit contraction operated undoubtedly in the direction of creating anxiety, perplexity, and embarrassment. And "to coöperate with the Bullion pamphlet without," Lancaster tersely remarks, "stock was offered often within the House at 20 per cent or thereabouts under the price, on condition of the payment in guineas."[38] The price of the funds, in fact, fell abruptly late in 1810; the Goldsmids were placed in a desperate predicament, and one of the partners committed suicide.

Ricardo was not content to let the matter rest with the publication of a pamphlet, and, working through his friend Francis Horner, who now sat in the House of Commons, he began at once to agitate his program in Parliament. Horner managed to have a Committee appointed to canvass the subject of the high price of specie, the state of the exchanges, and other alleged signs of impending ruin, and "to report the same with their observations thereupon, from time to time, to the House." Horner headed the Committee, and was assisted principally by Henry Thornton (who was M.P. for Southwark) and William Huskisson, lately of the Treasury. Hearings were held and all three

[37] A rare tract entitled (in part) *The Bank, the Stock Exchange from the Times of Boyd to Those of Bowles* (1821), p. 56. Authorship attributed to J. Lancaster, in Halkett and Laing's *Dictionary of Anonymous and Pseudonymous Literature.* Much of the above account is drawn from this apparently well-informed "insider." The tract is in the British Museum collection.

[38] Lancaster, *op. cit.*, p. 47.

of these gentlemen collaborated in drawing up, by way of report, a "motley composition" which has ever since exerted an extraordinary influence upon economic thought.[39]

The Committee first called and examined witnesses, including prominent business men, bankers, bullion-brokers, and others. Most of them pointed out that the phenomena under consideration were natural and inevitable consequences of war-time conditions: the restrictions by the enemy upon commerce; the army financing and subsidies; the difficulties of making remittances owing to naval and military operations—all of which, with suspended cash payments, raised the paper price of bills and bullion. Few were inclined to admit that "depreciation" of Bank notes existed—the word suggesting to most of them, as to the public generally, the existence of open discredit. The Governors of the Bank were put through several grilling examinations, during which, carried rather too far by their convictions, they denied any possible connection between the amount of their issues and the prices of exchange and specie. They claimed that their methods of making commercial advances were calculated to meet the legitimate demands of conservative borrowers, and that under the circumstances they could better serve the country by cautious and judicious lending than by incessantly juggling their circulation to conform to the vagaries of the foreign bill market.[40]

The Committee, however, brushed aside all this evidence, and composed an essay on principles strictly in line with the "bullion" theory. Their introductory considerations are, so far as they go, eminently sound: that the quantity of the circulating medium has an important causal relation to prices; that inconvertible paper opens the door to abnormal possibilities and to abuse, with grave social and economic consequences. Some emphasis at this time upon fundamental truths was no doubt appropriate, in view of a professed inflationist sentiment which was beginning to crop up in various quarters. The great majority of the public, including Parliament, however, appear to have been in no dan-

---

[39] It is surprising to find the statement in Alfred Marshall's recent volume, *Money, Credit and Commerce* (p. 41), that "Ricardo was one of the powerful thinkers, who wrote the great Bullion Report of 1810." A similar error is made by Joseph French Johnson (*Money and Currency* [new ed.], p. 292) in stating that Ricardo was a member of the Bullion Committee. That Ricardo influenced very greatly the opinions contained in the *Report,* however, is undeniable.

[40] As Professor Foxwell says, "The directors considered that the loss of exchange and gold parity was a lesser evil than a general financial collapse would have been. . . . Their instinct was perhaps sounder than their reasons." (*Jour. Royal Stat. Soc.,* LXXXIII, 287).

ger of becoming adherents to radical proposals for "ideal standards" and for unlimited cheap credit as permanent institutions. The Restriction Act, moreover, had already definitely provided for the restoration of the gold standard within six months after the close of the War. But the Report of Horner's Committee, by its preoccupation with non-essentials, by the disregard of important evidence, and by practical proposals of the rashest character, instead of making essentially sound principles, and the desirability of effective precautions, better appreciated, aroused the indignation of loyal Englishmen. By twisting simple truth until it appeared ridiculous, the Report had the effect of giving the unsound-money party added encouragement and a new weapon.

In investigating the causes of the "high price of bullion" a Parliamentary committee might have been expected to examine the matter coolly as an urgent and practical problem in war finance, even tho the pamphleteers did not. How, for instance, might the current funds needed by the government be best obtained with the least inflation? how might the country's credit institutions as a whole be mobilized to meet the needs of the situation and strengthened against abuse?—All this did not seem to interest the Committee, who wished to study bullion. They proceeded to analyze the bullion and foreign exchange markets into two distinct entities, both divorced from any relation to the War. They argued that gold, notwithstanding the Suspension, was still the standard; hence it was paper which fell because degraded.[41] Gold, furthermore, had not risen in value on the Continent—a curious irrelevancy arising from the belief that gold was a stable international "standard" by which the value of paper could always be tested. As for the exchanges, the doctrine of a distinction between "real" and "nominal" deviations of exchange from par was further elaborated. A "real" deviation arose from the general balance of payments, that is, demand and supply of bills; a "nominal" deviation was that part due to an altered condition of the currency, as in the case of a debased coinage. The extent of "real" deviation, it was supposed, could always be easily measured; it never could exceed the costs of shipping specie. All else was "nominal" and registered "depreciation." This hypothesis, so plausible at first blush, is thoroly erroneous, since it involves slipping back to the idea of gold necessarily selling at the old mint price in settling international balances, when purchased in irredeemable paper which is not excessive or depreciated.

[41] A view given great emphasis also in the well-known pamphlet by William Huskisson, in which he sought to popularize the conclusions of the Committee.

When a country's currency consists of inconvertible paper, the balance of payments *alone,* acting upon specie and bills simultaneously (as alternative instruments of remittance) may cause deviations from the *original* (now inoperative) par to almost any extent—even, conceivably, without excess or price inflation in the domestic equation of exchange.

In attempting further to prove that commercial factors could not account for this divergence, the Committee utilized a set of hopelessly inaccurate "official" trade values based on seventeenth-century prices,[42] which happened to indicate a handsome favorable balance—on the convenient assumption that the values of all net imports from the Orient, as well as from all British colonies and plantations, went into the pockets of Englishmen. A calculation of the commercial balance with the Continent alone for a few years, by means of specially prepared "real" values, revealed a very scant "favorable" margin as compared with the corresponding official values. This table was relegated, without comment, to an obscure appendix (copies of which were not available to the general public for many months). On the balance of *payments* as a whole their researches yielded only meager results, largely for the reason that adequate data of the important items of military remittances were not obtained—even tho (or possibly because) one of the Paymasters-General, Charles Long, was a member of the original Committee.[43] In the absence of data, the Committee resorted to hypothesis: if the foreign payments of the State *had* created marked deviations from exchange parities, this could be only a very temporary matter, since foreigners, attracted by low prices of sterling, would forthwith begin to buy British commodities and thus immediately expand British exports, with the result of readjusting the balance of payments. It happened that many erstwhile foreign buyers had other preoccupations at the moment.[44] It should be said in justice to Thornton that he still appreciated the importance of the balance of payments; but in his contribution to

[42] See Part 1 of this study, *Quart. Jour. Econ.,* February 1924, pp. 228, 229.

[43] "Your Committee had hoped to receive an account of these [remittances] from the table of the House; but there has been some difficulty and consequent delay in executing a material part of the Order." Long resigned from the Committee shortly after his appointment, perhaps in preference to handing over to such a body the highly confidential information in his charge.

[44] "I suppose," Horner wrote to Dugald Stewart in November 1810, "it is with respect to the wages of labour and the pay of the army and navy that you wish we had spoken out more fully, and followed out the consequences of our reasoning. . . . But in first breaking the subject against the prejudices of a large portion of the English public, and against the arts of misrepresentation which Government and the Bank were sure to put in practice, it seemed more advisable to rest the argument upon those grounds with which it was most difficult to mix any topics of declamation." (*Memoirs of Francis Horner,* Vol. II, p. 39.)

the Report he somewhat modified his earlier opinions, stating that while the military situation had originally created the exchange deviations, the excess of currency prevented their improvement. He apparently had but meager information as to the amounts involved.[45]

The Committee attacked the Bank without grace or mercy. The directors were arraigned for having neglected the cardinal principle of sound banking in not regulating their issues strictly in accord with the prices of exchange and specie, a principle applicable only to a convertible system. The notes of the Bank were represented in the familiar way to be the foundation upon which the country circulation rested. Perhaps the most extraordinary single feature of the Report was its complete exoneration of the country banks, despite tremendous increase in their number and the grave abuses in their operations. They were praised for their helpful services to trade and industry, and Parliament was earnestly advised to leave their reckless career free and unmolested.[46]

There are several reasons, aside from Ricardo's influence, for the preoccupation of the "bullionist" writers with the *notes* of the Bank of England, and their scant attention to, and greatly misconceived notions of, the remainder of the credit system. One was the close association of the Bank with public finance, serving the ends of a War which was opposed in principle by some supporters of the deflation idea. Another was the fact that the figures of the Bank's accounts, which only gradually found their way into print by way of occasional Parliamentary Reports,

---

[45] R. G. Hawtrey, in reviewing Cannan's reprint of the *Bullion Report,* speaks of the Bullion Committee's "exposure of the Balance of Trade [*sic*] fallacy," and appears to regard that principle as merely an erroneous popular notion: "Indeed, the fallacies against which the Bullion Committee contended are widely prevalent at the present time. They are confidently voiced by bankers, politicians, and others . . . who yet hardly seem to be aware that the Balance of Trade [*sic*] theory is not the last word of scientific thought." (*Econ. Jour.,* 1920, XXX, 91.) We must examine, of course, each case on its own merits; but a realization of the wide divergence between fact and supposedly enlightened contemporary opinion one hundred years ago may restrain us from dogmatizing about our present problems of international exchange and European currency.

[46] "I have no doubt," Horner wrote to T. R. Malthus in September 1810, "that, at no distant time, the evils, proceeding from the want of responsibility of the Bank, will get to such a pitch, as to force upon Parliament a recurrence to the old systems [gold standard]. I am only afraid that some mischief may be done in the mean time, by interfering unwisely with the country banks, and with that diffused and subdivided credit, afforded by their means, to the enterprises of small capitalists in remote parts of the country." (Horner, *Memoirs,* Vol. II, p. 36.)

William Leatham estimated the total country bank circulation in 1819 (after two successive periods of deflation had occurred) at £24,000,000. (*Parliamentary Papers, 1819,* Vol. III. Lord's Report, App. F11.) The Bank did not publicly press for reform of the country bank evil perhaps because it professed to be itself the "regulator" of the entire system. To confess that the system was at fault might have prejudiced one of the Bank's cherished traditions and its subsequent prestige when convertibility was restored.

very rarely included significant details of the assets, or of the important deposit item of the liabilities.[47]

In attempting to prove statistically that the Bank of England *had* actually issued excessive notes, the Committee found the data somewhat refractory, since during a period of twelve years the total issues had risen to the extent of £8,000,000, of which £4,500,000 were the smaller notes, which had mainly displaced coin. To reconcile supposed cause with observed result, they argued that the velocity of the circulation had been vastly increased. Scant attention was paid to the upward trend of the physical volume of British business.[48]

Much more than this, indeed, is insinuated in the Report, especially in certain passages fairly attributable to Francis Horner. There is a subtle implication that it was not, after all, the quantity of the notes, but something in their quality—their intrinsic acceptability—which was at fault. The slippery term "depreciation," altho accounted for on quantitative grounds, lent itself, as it did in the writings of Horner and Ricardo, all too easily to this other meaning. Occasional hints of similarity between Bank notes and *Assignâts,* and the hard-worked Ricardian analogies with debased coin, point to grave apprehensions in the minds of the Committee, which are revealed in a telling sentence in their conclusion: "A return to the ordinary system of banking . . . alone can effectually restore general confidence in the value of the circulating medium of the kingdom."[49]

The Committee's suggestions for practical policy (which they gave without having been asked for them) are most extraordinary. A return to cash payments they declared, even tho the War continued, and its scope enlarged, must be accomplished; preferably at once, but at most within two years.[50] It is needless to dwell upon the manner in which

---

[47] The notable Parliamentary investigations of banking affairs conducted in 1797 (Suspension), 1810 (*Bullion Report*), 1819 (Resumption Question), 1831–32 (Charter Renewal), and others since, furnish a mass of statistics, elaborately complete in some respects, but incapable of showing accurately either the variations in the Bank's loans to the government or the reserve. The figures for its discounts of commercial paper were withheld until 1832, when quarterly data since 1797 were published. (*Parliamentary Papers, 1831–32,* Vol. VI.) To the Bullion Committee, the Bank vouchsafed only a "proportionate scale" of their discounts, which the Committee were forbidden to divulge in their *Report.*

[48] Even assuming a *doubled* velocity, however, a net increase of £7,000,000 of effective large notes in twelve years could hardly be regarded in itself as a national menace.

[49] Cannan, *The Paper Pound,* p. 70.

[50] At this point again Thornton took a more moderate view; it is known that he disagreed with his colleagues in the matter of requiring the Bank to resume prior to the close of the War; his object (essentially nugatory) was to have the Bank regulate or vary the volume of its issues to conform with the rates of foreign exchange.

counsel so remarkable was received. The plausible arguments supporting it found ready acceptance in certain circles; but the Report immediately occasioned minute and pointed criticism from merchants and financiers.[51] The recommendations were negatived by a decisive majority in the House when the Report was debated in 1811; but not until the supporters of the government had unfortunately been led into very extravagant nonsense in their somewhat flustered efforts to meet a subtle indictment of the nation's credit and at the same time avoid divulging too much valuable information to the enemy. The most important immediate effect of the Report, at any rate, was to create a general fear of abrupt and arbitrary deflation, which contributed to precipitating, in 1810 and 1811, one of the most desperate commercial revulsions and financial panics ever known in England.

It is remarkable that while in 1809 Ricardo demanded a "partial void" in the currency to right the exchanges, in 1819, when resumption was under consideration, he admitted that resumption at the original mint price of gold (£3, 17*s.* 10½*d.* per ounce) was justifiable only because at the moment the deviation from par was, he thought, but four or five per cent. Had it been more than this small margin in 1819 he would have advised "devaluating" the pound to a new level, rather than deflation and par resumption.[52] Having become a landed country gentleman, Ricardo now hesitated to advocate a policy which would have reacted to the disadvantage of the agricultural interests, which had already suffered greatly in the price decline of 1816. Restoring a gold basis would remove the "depreciation" of five per cent and lower prices by only five per cent.

Summarizing the main theme of this discussion, it appears that essentially sound principles regarding the effects of *convertible* currency expansion upon commodity prices and rates of foreign exchange came to be applied by certain influential publicists to war conditions and *inconvertible* paper, without proper qualifications and without the slighest regard to existing political circumstances. Policies regarding the currency were proposed, which rested upon an exaggerated sense of the national importance of abnormal exchange rates, and upon an almost incredible

---

[51] The appearance of this *Report,* so strangely congenial to French hopes and designs, caused general satisfaction in Paris. "In the embarrassed state of her commerce with the Continent," observed the *Journal de l'empire,* "England having no other relief but the Bank discounts, the very day when the Bank shall be obliged to pay in specie, the presence of the Berlin and Milan Decrees will be felt in all its FORCE." (Quoted in the *Times,* September 21, 1810.)

[52] See his evidence in *Parliamentary Papers, 1819,* Vol. III.

misunderstanding of the Bank of England and lack of concern for its safety. While a currency immediately convertible into gold, and a policy of regulating banking credit according to the observed tendency of commercial forces to cause gold inflow and outflow, are both sound and important elements of financial principle under normal conditions, they necessarily become hopelessly impracticable in a major war of any duration. The insistence by certain interests at that time upon the regulation of credit by the Bank of England according to variations in rates of exchange and specie grew out of several misapprehensions: first, that the Bank of England was, under the prevailing conditions, still the ultimate source and prime manufacturer of credit; second, that the deviations in exchange and bullion from par were due wholly to readjustments involved in the impact of inflated currency upon the prices of staple commodities; and again, that a moderate reduction of the currency could attract specie from abroad. There is no doubt that the total currency was inflated, but the inflation was due far more to the excesses in country banking than to the operations of the Bank of England.

It is curious to reflect how well the fundamental principles of the Bullion Report, leaving aside the numerous errors of fact and inference, have been found, during the last half-century, to apply in the banking practice of advanced commercial countries *under normal conditions.* Had these same principles, however, been rigidly followed under the circumstances to which its authors believed they peculiarly applied, there would probably be no British Empire today.

21

*The Crisis of the Gold Standard**

By JOHN H. WILLIAMS

I

We have this year (1931) passed through the most acute international money crisis that has ever occurred in time of peace. The panic which began with the failure of the Austrian Kreditanstalt in May, forced the Hoover debt holiday and the freezing agreement on German short-time debts in June and July, wrecked the British Labour government in August and drove England from the gold standard in September, and then drained $738 million of gold from the United States by the end of October, has no parallel for speed and magnitude in the history of international finance. Coming two years after the beginning of the decline in business conditions, at a time when according to virtually all the professional forecasts recovery should have been well under way, these events produced profound bewilderment and dismay in all countries.

I do not pretend to be able to diagnose this depression. Though there are many plausible theories, there is very little agreement about the causes of the business cycle. There is reason to question whether economic changes unfold according to any pattern so definite as the term "cycle" implies. But we do recognize minor and major variations in economic conditions and have had experience of great world "conjunctures." Most frequently they have occurred after wars. The Napoleonic Wars were followed by such a period, the Civil War and the Franco-Prussian War by the long depression of the seventies. Indeed, the slump of the nineties seems the only one comparable in duration and severity which does not fit into this chronological sequence. As the current depression has unfolded we have ceased to regard it as a minor variation

* John H. Williams, *Postwar Monetary Plans and Other Essays* (New York, 1944), pp. 154–72. Reprinted by permission of Alfred A. Knopf, Inc. The author and the publishers of *Foreign Affairs,* in which the paper originally appeared, January 1932, have also given permission for the present reprinting.

consequent upon our stock market collapse—which seemed to be the majority opinion of American forecasters in the winter of 1929—and have come to view it as the culmination of certain deep-seated international maladjustments which had their origin in the war.

The greatest single change which has occurred since 1914 has been in the comparative international positions of the United States and England. From being the world's leading debtor we passed during the war to being the world's leading creditor. England's position has meanwhile become steadily weaker. It may take decades to work out all the implications of this revolutionary change and to make all the necessary international adjustments. Most of the larger world problems of today proceed out of it or have some intimate connection with it. England's creditor position in the nineteenth century had developed gradually, along with the development of a world economy involving the division of productive effort between the older industrial areas and the younger agricultural areas and the flow of accumulated savings from the former to the latter. The same circumstances which assigned to England the leading role in capital export made London the international money market and the Bank of England the administrator of the gold standard.

The international gold standard is based upon the assumption that the flow of gold makes an automatic correction of departures from equilibrium in international payments. This assumption is most valid when four conditions are fulfilled: (1) when there are no surplus gold reserves in the banking system and a loss of gold must mean a shrinkage of bank credit; (2) when there are no international capital movements, so that, on balance, exports of goods must equal imports and any excess of one over the other must induce a corrective flow of gold; (3) when unit costs of production are responsive to money price variations, so that when prices change in response to increases or decreases of gold, production and trade will respond to the movement of prices; (4) when international demand responds freely to changes in prices, so that a fall of prices will produce an increase in value of exports relative to imports, and contrariwise. Given these conditions, trade changes are corrected by the interaction of gold flow and prices.

It must be admitted that these conditions are never found fully and simultaneously developed and that there has never been that "automatic" working of the gold standard which the English Bank Act of 1844 was designed to insure. But there was a closer approximation to these conditions before the war than there is at present. At that time the chief qualification was in the flow of capital. A rise of prices in one country relative to others (such as in the absence of capital movements would cause increase of imports, outflow of gold, fall of prices, and thus an increase of exports to the point where exports again equal imports and gold flow ceases) may in fact attract capital from abroad. Rising prices usually mean rising profits, which attract capital, which in turn is likely to cause further rise of prices, and hence more profits, and hence more capital inflow. This cumulative movement is more apt to be accompanied by gold inflow than by gold outflow, and the gold inflow provides a monetary basis for still further expansion. Recent investigations of the prewar movements of gold show, in the case of both England and the United States, a clearly defined tendency for gold to flow inward during prosperity and outward during depression. Outstanding instances of the cumulative effects of prewar capital movements are the American boom which terminated in the crisis of 1873, and the Argentine boom which culminated in the Baring Panic of 1890; but in neither of these cases was the capital-importing country upon the gold standard.

Under prewar conditions, however, capital movements were less likely to produce serious maladjustments than has been the case under the conditions existing since 1914. The same conditions which attracted foreign capital attracted foreign products, particularly in the form of capital goods. Trade adjustment was thus to a large extent a simultaneous process rather than a sequence of steps. Foreign investment and foreign trade were not so much a cause and an effect as they were dual aspects of a single phenomenon. Gold flow would occur only when the balance of foreign investment was in excess of or less than the balance of foreign trade. But its effect when it did occur might still be cumulative rather than corrective. A flow of gold to the capital-importing country might produce credit expansion, rising prices, and a further inflow of capital, while producing in the capital-exporting country a more drastic, and at the same time less effective, curtailment of credit than the simpler theory had assumed. The Bank of England's discount rate policy, designed to protect the gold reserve, was an effective check upon the process in so far as a higher bank rate could discourage British foreign lending, attract outside short-term funds to London, and stop the outflow of gold by reversing the forces which caused it. Since the English banking system had in it very little slack, being operated upon a comparatively small reserve of gold and employing a very expensive form of currency in the Bank of England note, protection of gold reserves was the chief, and probably the only important, criterion of credit policy. The Bank of England's action was therefore prompt, and ordinarily effective. England was the leading exporter of capital, the free market for gold, the international discount market, and the international banker for the trade of other countries as well as her own. She thus held all the controlling elements of the situation in her hands, and her own monetary and trade position was such as to insure their prompt and effective use. The world was in this sense upon the sterling standard.

II

Postwar conditions have in various ways been radically different. It is often suggested that maldistribution of gold is the major cause of the depression and the recent monetary crisis. But it is necessary to account for the maldistribution. When England left the gold standard the United States had $5 billion of gold and France about $2.3 billion, out of a world total of about $11.5 billion. This is obviously maldistribution in some sense or other; it strikes one immediately as undesirable and abnormal. But it is less easy to say in just what sense it is abnormal; and this is particularly important when one considers how to change it. The French supply is relatively much larger than our own, but France has always liked to have a large supply. France is the European sink for gold. Her price level is comparatively insensitive to gold flow, so that she finds it much easier to attract gold than to expel it. It is indeed unfortunate that this should be the case, but it is not altogether a new problem.

It is said by European and American economists that our own gold policy has been chiefly responsible for the world's ills. We are accused of sterilizing gold. As Mr. Keynes put in 1924, the world's gold has been buried in the vaults of Washington. This view has gained wide support. It has become part of the viewpoint of the man in the street, a commonplace of newspaper financial gossip. The thesis has taken different and somewhat conflicting forms. Some writers complain of too much artificial "management" of the gold standard by the Federal Reserve System. When gold comes in, it is "offset" by open-market sales of securities by the Reserve banks, which decrease the reserves of member banks by as much as the new gold has increased them. When gold flows out, it is offset by open-market purchases of securities which replenish reserves. Our gold holdings are so large that the Reserve banks can afford to ignore the effect of gold movements upon themselves.

By offsetting the gold flow we keep our domestic price level stable and throw the entire strain of trade adjustment upon foreign price levels. Other writers complain of too little management. Our banking system makes such an economical use of gold that the gold flow exerts little effect on prices; therefore the Reserve banks, by appropriate open-market operations, should compel the gold flow to influence prices. But far from inflating credit to the limits of our gold we are said to have pursued a policy of price stabilization, or at best a policy of indifference toward the plight of other nations. Meanwhile our international creditor position exerts a pull upon the world's gold whenever our new annual exports of capital diminish. Thus more and more gold becomes buried in our vaults. Now we have reached the breaking point and have cracked the world asunder.

This is indeed a serious indictment, but I am not at all sure that either version of it is valid. The analysis so interweaves truth and error that they are not easy to unravel. We can all agree that something is seriously wrong, but not necessarily on what it is. That we have acquired and retained the gold is clear enough. Since 1914 we have increased our gold stock by about $2.5 billion. Much of it came during the war in part payment for our huge wartime exports; even more of it came in 1921–24. With Europe off the gold standard, and with European currencies depreciated and European capital seeking safety here, we were the only large market open to gold and the most effective bidder for it. In 1925–29 our gold holdings did not increase, though there were some rather violent inward and outward movements. From October 1929 to July 1931, we imported $573 million of gold.

During the depression the gold has come mainly from the young countries of the world, whose commodity prices have been acutely depressed at the same time that their inflow of capital has been cut off. The burden of interest payments and of imports has turned the foreign exchanges against them and drained off their gold, partly to the United States but chiefly to France. It is very interesting to note that these countries have lost gold not because, as in the orthodox theory, their price levels were high relative to those of other countries but precisely because the prices of their exports have been abnormally low relative to those of other countries. This is a striking example of the way in which our four qualifications, previously stated, can alter the simpler theory of the gold standard. The demand for agricultural products is inelastic. When prices fall sharply, the total value of exports is likely to decrease relative to imports, which consist of industrial products for which demand is more elastic. Since there is little or no diversification of production, these countries find it peculiarly difficult to curtail output. Meantime, interest on foreign debts must be paid. With prices falling, the debt payments entail a progressive increase in quantity of exports relative to value of exports, but increasing quantity depresses prices further. It becomes a case of indeterminate equilibrium, and gold flows out persistently until collapse ensues. Since 1928 the South American and Oriental countries, plus Australia and South Africa, have together exported over $1,250 million of gold. Australia and Argentina are off the gold standard, Canada has been on and off a number of times, Brazil has defaulted on her foreign debts, and all South American bonds have been at panic prices.

I would especially hesitate to lay this draining off of gold from the agricultural countries to any sins of commission or omission by our banking system, except of course in so far as it can be shown that our earlier gold management was responsible for the depression's getting started in those countries. A more straightforward explanation may be found within agriculture itself: revolutionary improvements in technique, restoration of European production lost in the war, increased Russian exportation since 1928, price-fixing schemes in copper, rubber, coffee, tin, and other products, not to mention the interesting experiments in this line by our own Farm Board, which have artificially protected high cost production and increased total output. All this has increased the difficulties arising out of the inelastic character of the demand for agricultural products. But even this explanation is not so straightforward as it seems, and agricultural economists are divided on whether overproduction preceded the fall of prices or the fall of prices preceded overproduction.

Banking statistics do not indicate that we have sterilized gold. The gold that flowed in before 1925 was used by our banks to pay off rediscounts which were swollen by the boom of 1919–20; but it also served as a basis for credit expansion, as loans and deposits increased substantially. After 1924 our gold holdings did not increase, demand deposits ceased to expand, but bank loans and time deposits continued to increase. For the period 1914–29 our bank deposits increased by over $35 billion or by fifteen dollars of deposits for every dollar of gold imported, and our gold reserves were less than 7 per cent of our bank credit. This is a more intensive utilization of gold than is found in any other country except England.

It is true nevertheless that we do not need all our present gold, in view of the economy of the Federal Reserve System. The phenomenal expansion of time deposits since the war, and the continuance of this expansion after 1925, when demand deposits ceased to grow, would suggest not unwillingness of our banking system to use gold but a saturation of demand for credit. As bank assets increased, the public carried an increasing amount of the resultant deposits as idle deposits. The alternative, if we do not fully utilize the gold ourselves, would be to push it out; but this is less simple, under recent world conditions, than it might appear. We have, in general, kept discount rates low and assisted foreign central banks by various credits and exchange transactions. We have drawn no gold at all from England since 1929. In 1927 we tried to force out gold. By lowering our bank rate we did succeed in pushing out the accumulations of the preceding five years, but the low money rates contributed to our stock market boom, which induced a new inflow of gold.

There is a vast difference between trying to expel gold and controlling a flow which is induced by economic conditions themselves. England's prewar task of administering the gold standard was simple in comparison with ours today. Some of our gold "management," for example, has clearly been directed toward inducing gold outflow by offsetting its effect on money rates and preserving the monetary ease essential for its continued flow. But if low money rates induce an increased domestic use of credit they may start a spiral of expansion, the last phase of which is inflow of the gold which flowed out at the beginning. We completed this full circle between 1927 and 1929. The problem of gold regulation by central banks has materially changed since the war. The world is more closely knit, and there is frequently a sharp contrast between the internal and external results of a change of bank rate. This fact has been felt in England and in Germany on many occasions in recent years. For example, the Reichsbank has found that when it put up its rate in order to decrease credit, short-time balances flowed in from abroad; and when it put down the rate in order to increase credit these balances went out again. Nothing could better prove that in the future central banking policy must be based upon closer international co-operation.

Since 1926 the world's gold has gone to France. At the end of that year the gold holdings of the Bank of France amounted to $725 million; on November 12, 1931 they amounted to $2,703 million, and there were besides some $535 million of sight balances abroad, which represent a claim on gold. These figures do not of course include the foreign balances of French private banks. In view of these figures it is rather fanciful to put the responsibility for maldistribution of gold upon the United States. The Bank of France gold reserves are today within $200 million of those of the Federal Reserve Banks, and a further conversion of French balances in New York would make them equal to ours. The French note circulation, the principal form of credit, is about $3,310 million, which means that there is almost 100 per cent coverage by gold and gold exchange. This indeed is sterilization of gold. Meanwhile England since 1925 has been struggling unsuccessfully to maintain the £150 million gold minimum recommended by the Cunliffe Committee, and Germany's gold reserve has ranged between $303 million and $666 million.[2]

Why this enormous drain of gold to France? The explanation is somewhat complex, but goes back to the fact that France stabilized the franc at too low a figure. The *de facto* stabilization was accomplished in December 1926. Prior to that time the franc had been depreciating rapidly, and got down at one time under two cents. Capital had been leaving the country. When Poincaré succeeded in stabilizing the franc at about four cents, confidence revived. French capital began to come back and foreign speculative capital was attracted by prospects of a rise in francs and French securities. At the same time the French price level remained low relative to outside prices, the balance of payments was favorable, and the export trade piled up increasing balances in foreign centers. The result was that France had difficulty in holding the franc down to the stabilization level and was compelled to buy foreign currencies. Thus she accumulated very large balances abroad, chiefly in New York and London. By the middle of 1927 the foreign-exchange holdings of the Bank of France exceeded a billion dollars.

But France had no intention of employing the gold exchange standard except as a step toward the gold standard itself. She therefore proceeded to convert her balances into gold with the object of bringing her reserves up to the prewar level, which had been almost two billion dollars. From 1927 to the middle of 1929 the Bank of France became the leading buyer of gold. French economists argue that up to this point the movement merely established a better balance of gold in the world, since in large part it represented the reclaiming of gold which had previously gone to the United States. But one significant difference from the prewar situation was that the drain exerted great pressure upon London, which was much less capable of protecting its reserves than it was before the

[2] On November 14, 1931 the Reichsbank's reserve, exclusive of credits owed to foreign central banks, was about $131 million.

war. Much credit is due the Reserve banks during this period for their assistance in relieving the strain upon London. By the middle of 1929 the Bank of France had about one and a half billion dollars of gold, the *de jure* stabilization of the franc had been accomplished (June 25, 1928), the foreign exchange holdings of the Bank of France had ceased to grow, and the Bank of France had ceased to purchase gold abroad.

But the French private banks continued their purchases. The French price level had shown no effect of the gold inflow, remaining stationary from 1926 to March 1929 and then beginning a gradual decline; the trade balance was still favorable to a gold inflow. Since 1929 it has been this private inflow that has been the source of disequilibrium in the world's distribution of gold. France has no adequate bill market, and the French banks have never leaned heavily on the Bank of France, which they regard as being somewhat their competitor. They increase their reserves by drawing on their foreign balances, and the Bank of France cannot refuse to accept gold from them so long as the gold standard remains in force. The corrections for this situation would be a rise of the French price level or an exportation of capital; but the French price level is remarkably insensitive, and until 1929 the export of capital was virtually prohibited by tax and other restrictions. In any case, the French people have not been interested in foreign investments. The result has been the continued accumulation not only of gold in France but of balances abroad. These balances, of course, are highly unstable. Together with the short-term foreign balances of other nations they have been a chief cause of the acute monetary disturbances of the present depression period.

III

The task of administering the gold standard belongs logically to the capital-exporting nations. One significant difference between the prewar and postwar periods is that formerly this role was assigned to England, not only by the monetary necessities of the case but also by the economic circumstances. Today this logical alliance is by no means so clear. The monetary situation assigns to the United States and France the role of preserving a proper balance in the world by the flow of capital. But France has long pursued the ideal of the self-sufficing nation and has neither the financial machinery, the business flexibility, nor the economic motivation which fits a nation for such a role. It is not possible to conceive a nation less fitted than France to hold the world's gold or administer the gold standard.

The foreign investment position of the United States contains some highly abnormal elements. We achieved our creditor position as a result of the war. In four and a half years we exported $1,150 million of goods in excess of our importations, an amount which equals the sum of our export surpluses from 1873 to 1914. We received part of the payment in a billion dollars of gold, another part by the return of our foreign-held securities and by various exchange-pegging loans, and the principal part in the form of credit advances by our government to the Allied governments. The Allies bought our goods with promises of future payment which they could not honor except as Germany supplied the means by reparation payments. Germany, lacking present capacity to pay, turned to the Allies' creditor. In so far as this system works at all we substitute one debtor for another. The German debts to us are private debts, the Allied debts and the reparation payments are public debts, so that the further result is an inextricable tangle of public and private debts. This is no doubt the kind of thing that Ramsay MacDonald calls "crazy economy." One aspect of it is the present conflict of interest among Germany's creditors, the French being reluctant to concede priority to private debts while this country and England are most concerned over private debts.

One of the larger aspects of this condition is that since 1914 the flow of capital has been, to a large extent, perverse. By prewar standards it would be called a flow of capital in the wrong direction; it is a flow of capital not from old countries to new countries but from new countries to old countries. Its purpose was not to develop productive capacities but to meet extraordinary war expenditure. Partly by reason of the processes involved in Europe's restoration of the gold standard, the capital movement has taken peculiar forms. We have exported capital to Europe on long term at high rates and imported short-term balances from Europe at low rates. Meanwhile England because of economic conditions has exported capital on long term, and because of her monetary requirements has imported capital on short term. As time has gone on, our own capital export has become increasingly short term in character, until the world's money markets have been saturated with short-term balances and a pronounced gap has developed between short-term and long-term interest rates. Nothing could better show the abnormality of much of the postwar capital flow, or the increasing distrust of it among bankers and investors. Given, then, a further and more severe shock to confidence in the present year, the consequences have been tremendous.

There is theoretical validity, I believe, in the view that a nation's capacity for payment can be developed by capital borrowing, even though the nation is not a young country, provided the process is spread over a long period, provided the burden of payment is moderate and definite in amount, and provided the borrowed capital is directed into productive employment. There is considerable evidence that Germany was responding in this fashion between 1924 and 1928—in the rise of real wages, the growth of savings, the expansion of output, and the lowering of costs by rationalization; though there is also evidence that the capital inflow was too rapid and too large and that some of it was extravagantly spent. On the whole, I am not convinced that Germany cannot in a more normal world pay reparations of moderate amount, though it is obvious that with a world price level one third lower than in 1928 she cannot by any means carry the burden imposed under the Young Plan. And I am unable to see how, prior to the restoration of normal business conditions, she can make any payments at all. Germany's difficulties today are similar in kind to those of any debtor country under conditions of acute depression. She is worst hit because her debt is greatest, but she is by no means unique in her position. On broader grounds I have from the start disapproved of reparations. Large, arbitrary payments of this sort are bound to distort the international economic structure. It is not primarily a question of whether Germany can pay, but whether the world can afford to have this sort of thing.

The abruptness and the abnormal character of the change in our international position, forced on us by war, raises questions regarding our ability to perform the functions of administering the gold standard as well as England did before the war. It is an interesting question whether, had there been no war, we should today be exporting capital on balance. Such a change would have come in time, without doubt, but it would have been accompanied by a change in the general conditions affecting external versus internal investment. Monetary equilibrium now requires an outflow of capital from this country, but investment is a matter for individuals, and it is by no means clear that individuals may not prefer domestic investment and be quite right in their decision. The boom of 1928–29 was of course an extreme case, but not without very great significance. Though the causes of such a boom are always complex, it grew, without doubt, out of the kind of economic progress and the general conditions of economic change that we associate with young countries rather than with old. It was a case of America reverting to type. We witnessed the paradox of large imports of capital coming into the country which, on monetary grounds, should have been supplying capital to other countries. The draining of foreign funds into our stock market seems, without question, to have been one cause of the depression.

We have seen in England the opposite aspect of the matter. British economists complain that capital which should go into home investment goes abroad. That any Englishman should make such an outcry is a striking commentary on how times have changed. Before the war of 1914 British foreign investment was quickly reflected in the export trade. Foreign investment meant more and cheaper food and raw materials and an increased market for British goods. As I have said, investment and trade were dual aspects of a virtually simultaneous process. The cumulative effects upon England were extremely beneficial. She was enabled to specialize at home in industries operating at decreasing costs as output increased, while developing abroad cheaper products of increasing cost industries. Armed with these advantages, and intellectually fortified by her doctrine of free trade as a universal and eternal truth, England played at will upon the economic world, with enormous advantage to it as well as to herself. The more capital she exported, the more she had for home investment. In this way she piled up capital and labor upon her small island, and earned excellent rewards for both.

England was the first user of mass production methods, but by exporting her capital, labor, and business men she put the world in a position to use her methods. Now younger nations, with superior resources, have outstripped her. England's trouble is in part a bad balance of productive forces, too much capital and labor for her resources. But in part it is the increased rigidity and immobility of her economic structure. In part, also, it comes from her wartime loss of markets—for example, the Oriental market for cottons, which in some cases no amount of improvement in production costs could probably now win back for her.

England stabilized the pound in 1925 at its prewar value. By so doing she assumed the full burden of her internal war debts, in contrast with the Continental countries which by currency devaluation were largely relieved of their internal burdens. It must be noted further that British industry likewise became saddled with the full weight of the fixed charges upon its heavy capitalization, in contrast, for example, with German industry, which by currency depreciation had largely freed itself from interest charges. It is sometimes contended, nevertheless, that England might have succeeded with her stabilization program had she pursued proper policies in subsequent years, though there seems to have been little agreement about what constitute proper policies under such conditions as England has had to face. A more correct statement, perhaps, is that the prewar sterling standard might have served tolerably well as a fair-weather postwar standard, but England has had very little fair weather since 1925 and very bad weather indeed since 1928.

Stabilization at the prewar figure involved some fall of prices, though it was not a great fall initially, and would not perhaps have proved serious had production costs been more flexible and had the general conditions affecting British foreign trade been less seriously deranged. Wages would not come down; in some cases technical equipment and methods proved inefficient and difficult to change. Labor has been immobile, both externally and internally. It does not leave the country and it does not move rapidly between industries within the country. The dole has intensified both evils, being based on the principle that the worker should have employment in his own type of occupation. Generations of employment in specialized industries unfit both capital and labor for other employment. Specialization in foreign trade industries creates the problem of unequal magnitudes as between industries. Once these trades are lost, the productive factors must shift into other foreign trade industries of equal magnitude or must migrate to other countries. There cannot, in the nature of the case, be domestic alternatives, and foreign trade alternatives do not present themselves full-blown. Meantime high wages, high taxes, and the dole constitute a tremendous burden upon capital. There thus develops a vicious circle. Foreign investment is preferred to home investment, but export trade does not respond because costs are high relative to foreign costs. Imports increase relative to exports. The increase of foreign investment and of imports throws domestic industry out of employment, which further decreases export trade, and further increases foreign investment as against home investment. The cumulative effects are just the opposite of those which existed in the prewar period. They have exercised, of course, an insistent pull on British gold.

There has been evidence since June of a better understanding of the world's problem and of a greater willingness to work it out. There is as much danger of overpessimism today as there was of overoptimism in 1928. The process of adjustment will no doubt be gradual, but it will proceed much faster if there is continuing evidence of a disposition to make mutual adjustments. England's suspension of the gold standard was economic nature's temporary cure for an impossible situation. It affords temporary relief by lifting prices, since costs will not decline; it should to some extent improve the trade balance and revive trade, and there is some evidence that this is happening. But it is not a permanent remedy. The most pressing problem at the moment is to relieve the uncertainties of Germany's position. The solution of gold maladjustments does not readily suggest itself. The problem will of course be less acute under more normal conditions. It is unlikely, if we make proper adjustments now, that the world will soon again have to face international movements of such speed and magnitude, or of such uneconomic origin and character, as we have witnessed since the war. The immediate problem is to restore normal conditions. The greatest single help of international character would be the further postponement and substantial reduction of war debts and reparations, along with the slow and orderly liquidation of German private debts. Looking farther ahead, I favor improving the gold standard rather than abandoning it in favor of some other standard. There is still much room for economizing gold and for improving the mechanism and control of international clearance. With war debts reduced and some of the abnormalities of international payment thereby removed, it should be possible by international co-operation to work out a better administration of the monetary standard.

SECTION III

Method

22

*The Tasks of Economic History**

By EDWIN F. GAY

I

It is a great honor, deeply appreciated, to be chosen first president of the Economic History Association. I cannot pretend to act as spokesman for this newly organized scientific group. I assume that I owe my present honor and responsibility partly to the number of years I have imperfectly taught economic history—and, I hope, stimulated some interest in it—and partly to your recognition of the principle of historical continuity. For I was a student under Schmoller at Berlin; he in turn was a pupil of Roscher (whose last lectures at Leipsic I heard); and Roscher, almost a century ago, was one of the first historical economists and the original formulator of a program for the new "school" of economics. I wish to recall to your attention these beginnings of our discipline in order to emphasize how the subsequent shift in its development has made us economic historians instead of historical economists.

There had been in the writings of Adam Smith and Malthus and of some of their Scotch and German predecessors much incidental use of economic history and of observation of contemporary economic life; but the tendency to abstract theorizing, admittedly taken over from the Physiocrats, continued increasingly predominant in England and on the Continent from the founding of modern Political Economy. The Historical School was a reaction against this tendency, and its first expression was highly critical of the method, fundamental assumptions, and results of the prevailing theory. Friedrich List was the mouthpiece for the rising nationalistic rivalry of Germany with England when he attacked the failure of the theorists to recognize historical relativity in the stages of national economic development and in the use of the pro-

* *Journal of Economic History,* 1941, I, 9–16, Supplement. Reprinted by courtesy of the New York University Press.

This paper was presented as the presidential address at the first annual meeting of the Economic History Association at Princeton, N.J., September 6, 1941.

ductive forces of a nation. Karl Knies, one of the profoundest of the critics, not only maintained the principle of historical relativity against the "absolutism of theory," but also insisted upon the continuity of historical development and the interaction of all manifestations of the human spirit, economic, legal, political, social and religious, during each period of history. In man's physical environment, he held, in the sphere of laws to which the growing economy must be adapted; but in the successive economic activities and institutions there are such differences as well as likenesses that only analogies may be discovered, not the working of laws. He rejects, therefore, Roscher's persistent analogy of economics with the science of physiology—a comparison later unduly insisted on by Schaeffle in his *Bau und Leben des Socialen Koerpers.* Knies preceded Hildebrand in castigating the "cosmopolitanism" and individualistic "atomization" that was both the underlying assumption and the half-avowed goal of the Free Trade School. While strongly emphasizing the rôle of the state and the community, and the immensely strong social disposition of man that originates and maintains those institutions, Knies especially inveighed against the defective psychology of those economists who based their entire deductive system upon the operation of one compelling motive, that of "desire for wealth," "hope of gain," or self-interest. Like the other historical economists, he demanded that the whole complex of motives and interests, varying among themselves in intensity at different occasions and times should always be taken into account by the investigator of any form of human behavior. The Historical School would not agree even with Bagehot's concession that perhaps the predominance of self-seeking motives might apply solely to English business circles of recent times. Always weighting heavily the social or aggregative tendency in men, the historical economists refused to eliminate the ethical element.[1] All members of the Historical School, but chiefly Roscher, stressed the importance of the comparative method as essential to the understanding of any people or institution. But Roscher warned that the method should be utilized with a great caution, a warning he himself did not often heed.

The historical economists of the mid-century, and to some extent their English successors, such as Cliffe-Leslie twenty years later, believed that they were inaugurating a new and much more realistic stage in the development of science. Knies prophesied for the second half of the

[1] Knies held that no ends, however beneficial, justify unethical means: "Even if from a sowing of dragon's teeth an armored power arises, it is a power that finds no rest until it destroys itself." (Karl Knies, *Political Economy from the Standpoint of the Historical Method,* p. 489.)

nineteenth century a change in doctrine comparable to that of the second half of the eighteenth century when the Physiocrats and Adam Smith supplanted the Mercantilists. But Knies, though he elaborated a full criticism of the old school and a set of directives for the new, never undertook to write a systematic treatise on economics according to the method he had prescribed. Perhaps his clear mind saw the formidable difficulties of execution and realized that the range of knowledge his prescription demanded was beyond the compass of one man of his generation. Hildebrand ventured to launch such a treatise, but after setting forth in his first volume a critical standpoint and an outline of what seemed to him the most important economic stages of barter, money, and credit, he failed in the many subsequent years of his life to fulfill the promise of a second volume. Roscher alone, the most learned and the most naïve of the three foremost founders of the Historical School, but not so acute and philosophical as Knies, spent a long, laborious life in revising and annotating in many editions the outline he had proposed in his inaugural dissertation of 1843. His four-volume work, besides affording, like Scotch haggis, much "fine, confused feeding" in its superabundant notes, presents as its formative concept the physiological parallel of an individual's life to the birth, youth, maturity, and decay of peoples. On this theme he played many variations in the form of economic stages for nearly all the activities of economic historical development. Some of these generalizations have been more fully stated by Roscher's successors, such as Schmoller, Karl Bücher and Sombart, but none has given the procedure the criticism it deserves. Roscher was not the first to construct these convenient, preliminary scaffoldings, but none before him, or indeed after him, built so many with such fervor. "Economic stages" are usable working hypotheses; they furnish rough overall characterizations of institutional change, but, in Roscher and his successors, they lack sufficient interrelation and causation. They usually lack adequate intervening steps between the stages and a compelling reason for making the ascent; therefore the scaffolding is left practically unscalable except by a leap of the imagination. And once the leap to the last or highest stage has been achieved, the imagination can soar no higher, for, unlike Jacob's ladder, the stages stop with the present which, it may be assumed, represents not only the last but the best in human progress.

Werner Sombart's *Modern Capitalism* is a good illustration of this tendency. In this last effort of the German historical school to set forth a theoretical exposition of economic history, Sombart studies in four volumes the stages of capitalism. In this instance, with his fascinating and often irresponsible generalizations and with great parade of learning, he has ingeniously reconstructed the intervening steps, but when the topmost plateau of *Hochkapitalismus* has been reached and surveyed, one is left to wonder what can lie beyond. Is it to be a gradual or precipitous decline and fall? Does the author, perhaps, see in the distance the classless, static Elysium of the Marxists, or is it the slave state of the Nazi new order?[2] There is danger that the "economic stages" may tend to be regarded not as merely scientific tools but as ends in themselves, and the temporary historical hypothesis may become a new "absolutism of theory."

II

In the next generation after Roscher, besides Sombart's work which did not try to cover the whole field, one prominent general treatment of economics was essayed by Gustav Schmoller, the last notable representative of the German historical economists. After ranging, during a long and fruitful life, from studies of German meat consumption in the sixteenth century to the institutional history of the seventeenth-century Hohenzollerns, from participating with one of his students in a gild history of Strassburg during the middle ages to initiating with his colleagues the *Verein für Social-Politik,* a series of valuable investigations of modern economic life, Schmoller finally, and I believe somewhat reluctantly, wrote the two volumes of his *Grundriss,* obviously based on his lecture notes and on his previously printed scattered papers. He told me once, a few years before he undertook this general summary, that he did not expect such a synthesis in his own life. "The great leaders of the preceding generation," he said in substance, "outlined the task and the method. Just as Darwin and other pioneers in scientific synthesis left to the next generations the detailed research that should amplify and test the preliminary generalizations, so the fathers of historical economics bequeathed to us the arduous labor of detail-investigation which is by no means yet done. Ultimately we, as specialists in this field, will be overwhelmed with the mass of facts, only partially digested, and we shall demand a new and truer synthesis. That will come quite normally, in its due time—perhaps in another generation or so." What made him change his mind, I do not know, but he must have regarded his final work as a provisional outline rather than as the synthesis to

---

[2] Cf. Leo Rogin, "Werner Sombart and Transcendentalism," *Am. Econ. Rev.,* XXXI, 493–512.

which he had looked forward. No one could realize more than Schmoller the enormous difficulty of such a task. He was oppressed by the mystery of the creative human spirit that moved behind the interlacing tangle of economic and social changes. Frequently at meetings of his seminar, after he had made one of his exciting suggestive commentaries on some student's paper, he would end, with an interweaving motion of his hands, by saying: "*Aber, meine Herren, es ist alles so unendlich compliziert.*"

Though conscious of the extreme complexity of the task set by the founders of the historical school in economics, he upheld to the end their program and aim of reforming the science and displacing the deductive theorists. His chief lecture course was on economics, not on economic history. While most of the *Forschungen,* the long series of studies mainly by his students under his editorial direction, were historical in character, the articles in his Journal, on the other hand, were largely economic. Unlike Knies and Hildebrand, he was not vociferously critical of his fellow economists of another persuasion, though he could answer vigorously when attacked. But he looked with distrust upon the subjective analysis of the Austrian School, and he regarded Marshall's method, despite its realism and refinement of theory, as still fundamentally inadequate. The social sciences he thought no suitable field for mathematical treatment except of the simplest kind and in but narrow applications, for man's impulses and social reactions normally produce too many variables of conduct for any calculus. Statistics, whenever economic activities are measurable, he welcomed in their widening scope as an invaluable auxiliary to historical research, but always his first question on scanning a statistical tabulation was: "What does all that mean?"—a query that included the source, sufficiency, and manipulation of the figures as well as their interpretation and relation to other cognate facts and theories.

We can now see that the full hopes of the historical economists have not been realized and are not realizable. Their criticism has helped to modify the "absolutism of theory," but their work has not displaced that of the "theoretical" school. The emergence of the historical school was justified a century ago. The narrowness of method and the obvious imperfection of results in deductive reasoning, especially of the then prevalent Ricardian type, invited correction; the rising tide of nationalism demanded a juster appreciation of the rôle of the state; the growth of abuses of unfettered wealth, of corporate and urbanized industrialism, created, as Sismondi had earlier realized, new problems for a heightened social consciousness; and the sweep of evolutionary doctrine after the mid-century offered alluring prospects for the conquest of opinion both for the historical dialectics of Marx and the somewhat less dogmatic generalizations of the historical economists. But the justification for the critical dogmatism of the historical economists has gradually disappeared. As the nineteenth century has moved on to the twentieth, economics has increased the range and depth of its contemporary observation; its use of the deductive method has become more guarded, its analysis more subtle and in the hands of such masters as Wesley Mitchell inductive research has notably developed; its viewpoint has become less individualistic and more social; its active present dissensions and doubts, unlike its past complacency, are evidence of vitality and growth. Meantime, especially outside Germany, the historical economists have given place to the economic historians. Germany has been producing regional and local economic histories, such as Gothein's admirable economic history of the Black Forest, or histories of industry, and good work in all the minor branches of economic history, but there has been no outstanding comprehensive economic history of the German people. Lamprecht's *Deutsche Geschichte* does not fill the gap, since it is an ambitious attempt at social rather than economic history. Such works as those of Levasseur, Pirenne, and Cunningham were produced in countries under the sway of the general nineteenth-century historical movement, not primarily of the German historical economists. Outside Germany, economic studies of economic ideas, activities, institutions, places, prices, and periods have also abounded. Outside Germany, economic historians like Ashley have proclaimed that economic history should make no effort to compete with economics. It only wished, said Ashley, to be let alone.

III

Today, we can go a step farther. The economic historian disclaims with Ashley any ambition to compete with the economists, but he does not desire to stand alone. He wishes to cooperate with all the social sciences and especially with economics. In method he is linked to history, in general purpose to all the social sciences, but in origin and specific objective, the understanding of man in economic life, he is closest to economics. Full cooperation, however, is not yet easy or intimate, and one of the first tasks of the economic historian today is to open the way to a more complete connection of the two disciplines. Perhaps the theorist, with a lingering memory of former criticisms and competitions, still regards the historian as intrusive. Perhaps he thinks him necessary only to supply a perfunctory introduction or an occasional footnote. The two disciplines should have more community of training, interest, and awareness of interdependence. The tentative generalizations of the economists give foothold and insight to the economic historian, and in turn the perspectives of the economic historian help in the valuations of the economist. If, for example, careful historical investigation, armed with the qualitative tests that recent research into business cycles can provide, should show that "random perturbations," such as plagues, famines, and wars, cannot fully account for the recurrent fluctuations of the west European credit economy since at least the sixteenth century, in other words, that business cycles are not so recent as the economist supposes, then perhaps long-persisting factors must receive more weight in cycle theory than those of later origin. An adequate equipment with two skills, that of the historian and the economist, is not easily acquired, but experience shows that it is both necessary and possible. In other longitudinal sections from the general fabric of history, such as legal history, the task has been partly accomplished. Pollock and Maitland's *History of English Law,* most of which Maitland wrote and Pollock checked, gives an outstanding example of the co-working of the masters of two disciplines.

IV

I do not know the answer to another difficult problem of the economic historian. It is his task to keep abreast of the entire advancing front of the social sciences, but his knowledge must be superficial or casual until more satisfactory means of inter-communication are established. It is one of the great but inevitable defects of specialization that the deeper the trench—and the specialist must dig deep—the less the whole terrain can be surveyed. Liaison officers and reliable runners are needed. Yet the need for such information and assistance from every sector of the front is urgent and will become more urgent as the world presses closer about us. Economic history is more than a longitudinal cut through the whole fabric of history; my former analogy is imperfect. It would be truer to compare it with the dissection from a living body, all of whose reactions, physical and psychical, must be watched by the surgeon. Man, the social animal and the moral demi-god, is both formed by and forms all social groupings; he receives and originates all those ideas, old and new, which make his life and his civilization. Family, community, state, party, class, sect, tradition, law, and morals mould his striving ambitions, and all with different force at different times and places. Economists, political scientists, jurists, sociologists, social psychologists, philosophers all are studying this creature; politicians and warriors are manipulating him. No longer do peoples live and perish in secluded vales of history or pre-history; no longer do ideas or ideals percolate slowly from group to group. Now waves of emotion span the planet, common purposes animate continents of men arrayed against one another in immense masses, conspirators plot by radio around the world, statesmen consult in mid-ocean.

This shrinking of our world is due to the natural scientists and technicians, but they cannot be held responsible for the use or misuse of the economic, social, or political consequences. We cannot shift the blame nor stop the process of change. The social scientists, together with their fellow clerks, in state and church, in the press and literature, in what they have said and done and in what they have left undone, are responsible for much of the past and the present and more responsible than ever for the future. In the first world war and in this, its continuation, the social scientists were and are called to action, their advice listened to (though not always heeded) as in no other periods of social stress. With all their limitations of means and knowledge they must pool their resources, if they hope to help effectively in war and in the hard following time of peace. They face the problems of statesmanship, the right union of justice and force as between nations or combinations of nations, and they face the problems that are seething within states. How define, for example, the firm but elastic line between the necessary increase in the authority of the state and the equally necessary maintenance of free zones of personal judgment and private enterprise? In these human group relations it is almost never a question of "either—or," but one of "more—or—less," and the reconciliation of minds to the continually shifting social adjustments. The students of man in society and of man as a personality want to help in these problems, and we believe that they will find ways to join their efforts. Possibly none among them can estimate more truly than the economic historian the magnitude and weight of the forces that have been undermining the social structure in the past, or the time and patience, understanding and goodwill that must go into the rebuilding of the future. The economic historian knows something of the long trends of the productive energies and social pressures that have brought us where we are. The statesmen who are to guide the future should use that knowledge. It is one of our major tasks to see that he does.

23

*Economic History as a Discipline**

By SIR JOHN CLAPHAM

Economic history is a branch of general institutional history, a study of the economic aspects of the social institutions of the past. Its methodological distinctiveness hinges primarily upon its marked quantitative interests; for this reason it is or should be the most exact branch of history. But it is often difficult or even impossible to introduce quantitative treatment into the institutional study of the subject. Thus for all but the most modern period the absence of statistical material may make only very rough and uncertain quantitative treatment possible. Even such simple questions as the membership of guilds or early trade unions, the sizes of villages and towns and the ratio of wage earners to non-wage earners in industry at different dates often defy accurate answer.

It would not be difficult to give some simple aspects of institutional history a more quantitative and graphic treatment than they have generally received. Maps of England in 1300, 1400 and 1500, marking the principal towns at each date and indicating those which are known either to have had well developed craft guilds or not to have had them and those about which information is lacking, might prove most instructive. So might maps based on *Domesday* and the Hundred Rolls of Edward I, indicating those villages which appear to have coincided with the manor and those which do not. Such elementary quantitative statements, which could be made more easily for mediaeval England than for most countries because of the relative perfection of the English records, can, however, only touch the externals of institutions and illustrate the frequency of institutional types. In the study of institutional organization and function quantitative methods are usually inapplicable and the method of economic history differs in no way from that of history in general.

Should the records happen to be abundant, quantitative treatment of

---

* *Encyclopaedia of the Social Sciences,* Vol. V (New York, Macmillan Co., 1930), pp. 327–30. Reprinted by courtesy of the Macmillan Co.

the economic aspect may become possible and very fruitful. *Domesday Book,* a tax book with some of the features of a census, is primarily an economic and only incidentally a legal and institutional record. From the "valets" of *Domesday* an almost exact "business" statement has been worked out (see Corbett, in *Cambridge Medieval History,* vol. v, ch. xv) of how William of Normandy assigned the shares of England, taken over as a going concern. It was to the abundant business records of English landowners (bailiffs' accounts, etc.) that the quantitative method in mediaeval history was first applied on a large scale by Thorold Rogers; it provided series of price, wage, crop yield and other statistics over long periods. The quantitative method is still being applied and the records have still much to furnish. For some countries, e.g. Spain, the comprehensive study of price records has only recently begun.

For handling the records of the economic history of the ancient, mediaeval and early modern world the necessary training is mainly that of the general historian—the linguistic, epigraphic and palaeographic knowledge appropriate to the age and country studied. For the ancient world epigraphic knowledge is particularly important because the literary sources contain little precise economic information. It is only to the study of the most recent history, that of the last century and a quarter and particularly of the last half century—the age of census and other official statistics—that methods requiring any but the most simple statistical knowledge can profitably be applied. But the study of price history for any period for which records are reasonably abundant, i.e. for any period since the twelfth century, requires familiarity with contemporary methods of price inquiry and with the elementary principles of index numbers. For the most recent period a fairly complete statistical equipment is necessary, because the abundance and variety of the statistical material permit the application of some of the more refined statistical methods. This work tends therefore to fall into the hands of the inductive economist, who is only secondarily a historian.

Every economic historian should, however, have acquired what might be called the statistical sense, the habit of asking in relation to any institution, policy, group or movement the questions: how large? how long? how often? how representative? The requirement seems obvious; but a good deal of the older politico-institutional economic history was less useful than it might have been through neglect of it. The latifundia were not so representative of Roman economic life in the early part of the first century B.C. as historians once supposed. Many theories of urban origins which have found support among continental scholars break on the question "how representative." The manorial map of England might put the manor village in its proper place. The political importance that has sometimes been assigned to the English trading companies of the sixteenth century has been greater than is warranted by their economic importance as understood at present. American scholarship has reduced the economic hardships inflicted by the old colonial system to their proper and rather limited size. Many accounts of the industrial revolution in Great Britain would hardly suggest that in 1830 only one person in eighty worked in a cotton mill: they omit to state clearly "how many."

Neglect of the question "how representative?" vitiates most of the schemes, made particularly by German scholars, for scheduling states in economic development. Such schemes besides concealing the variety of history may confuse logical with temporal succession. The most general of them was that of Bruno Hildebrand, which postulated the sequence of natural economy, money economy and credit economy ("Natural-, Geld- und Kreditwirtschaft" in *Jahrbücher für Nationalökonomie und Statistik,* vol. ii, 1864, p. 1–24). Its drawback when applied to history has been that the labeling of an age as one of natural economy may easily lead to neglect of evidence for the coexistence of other types of economy. Thus prolonged research and controversy have been required to establish the fact that the early Middle Ages in northern Europe were not ages of pure natural economy. Moreover, the term natural economy may cover both exceedingly simple and very complex economic systems. Exchange in ancient Egypt was predominantly that of goods for goods; but Egyptian civilization had little in common with that of primitive Germany or of primitive modern societies in which money is unknown. And since, except in prehistoric and in the earliest historic times, money using and non-money using societies have always existed side by side, since remnants of natural economy have long survived and still survive in money using communities, and since credit in some form appears at a very early stage in most civilizations and never completely dominates any, the assignment of a particular age or even of a particular society in that age to one or other of the stages becomes a delicate problem of fact and of degree scarcely worth attempting.

Similar but more destructive criticism applies to the stage scheme of Karl Bücher (*Die Entstehung der Volkswirtschaft,* 1893), based on that of Schönberg of 1867 ("Zur wirtschaftlichen Bedeutung des deutschen Zunftwesens im Mittelalter" in *Jahrbücher für Nationalökonomie und Statistik,* vol. ix, p. 1–72, 97–169), with its succession of self-sufficient domestic economy, in which there is no exchange but every household meets all its own needs; town economy, in which the goods pass directly from producer to consumer and from countryman to townsman; and national economy, in which intermediaries between producer and consumer appear. Bücher claimed that the whole course of economic development, at least for the peoples of central and western Europe, could be brought under this scheme. But it most certainly cannot. It is impossible to distinguish such stages with precision in the history of those peoples; and the first two are arbitrary conceptions not corresponding to any known group of historical facts, although it is easy to find places and periods in which most households have been comparatively self-sufficing or in which the simple intercourse between small towns and the surrounding country has been dominant. Although stage schemes have furnished convenient categories for the classification of economic phenomena and have provided scholars with Max Weber's "ideal types" with which the varied reality may be contrasted, they have done more harm than good to the study of economic history. They may be specially harmful when history is being summarized for the use of students.

The inevitable breaking up of economic history into periods for convenience of study and teaching has some of the dangers of the stage schemes, if period and stage are unduly identified or if the period specialist loses perspective through relative ignorance of what went before and came after the age of his choice and so is unable to select for special attention those of its features which are of the greatest general significance. These are the ordinary dangers of historical periodization and specialism. The tendency of economic history to take over ready made the conventional divisions of general history has at times produced unfortunate results but need not do so. Clear dividing lines purely economic in character do not exist or at least have not yet been generally agreed upon. If periods are recognized as simply slices of time, within which some particular economic phenomenon—slavery, economic feudalism, early capitalism, corporate capitalism—may be of special importance but not necessarily to the exclusion of phenomena of other types, their study has no serious drawback. It is, however, probably even more important in economic than in other branches of history that period study should be associated with adequate study of the contemporary world, the *terminus ad quem*.

Stage schemes in economic history were devised mostly by members of the German historical school of economists, who attempted to substitute, as it were, historical generalization for economic theory. Most scholars are now agreed that such an attempt failed even in the hands of Schmoller. The central problems of economic theory, although they may be stated in terms of some particular historic phase, are in essence independent of history. In theoretical discussion it is necessary to isolate forces and factors in a way which history does not permit. Even more important than this independence and the necessity for abstraction is the fact that the absence from all history, except that of the latest statistical age, of enough trustworthy sequences of ascertained facts makes impossible the exact treatment at which theoretical inductive economics aims. Even the statistical age has not yet supplied nearly enough tested sequences of facts for the economist's needs, and the necessarily defective historical record will scarcely satisfy him. For example, there can be no exact discussion of English unemployment before 1886, when certain trade union statistics were first issued. There are countries in which such exact discussion is hardly possible even yet. Generalizations about the unemployment complained of in Shakespeare's *Henry VIII* (act i, scene 2) or even about that in Lancashire at the time of the American Civil War will give the contemporary economist little help. The historian recognizes that except in price history and other quantitative sections of his work his results will be on a lower plane of truth than that to which the fully equipped inductive economist may conceivably attain. It remains true, however, that some parts of economic theory, such as the succession of industrial types, the evolution of money and the problem of population, are or purport to be generalizations from history.

The relation of economic history to social history is much closer. It is true that with certain aspects of social history the economist as such is not concerned, unless he is in a position to trace the play of economic forces upon them. For example, his interest in costumes, manners, recreation and non-economic ideals may be limited only to such aspects as the clothing of India in Lancashire cotton, the aping of the millionaire, the professionalizing of games and the commercializing of ideals. But as the main concerns of society are and always have been economic, by far the greater part of social history, it may be argued, is simply economic history. As a critic of particular social histories the economist's main question will tend to be "is this representative." The social historian may with fairness reply to such criticism that he deliberately studies society at leisure with more care than society at work, because in the spiritual history of mankind the important matter is the use made of time saved from the plow or the machine. To this there is no conclusive rejoinder; but plow and machine remain important and representative. The economic historian, on his side, can hardly afford to be ignorant either of non-economic social history or of general history. If he is, he will almost certainly mistake the importance of the economic factor in any group of historical factors. It is unfortunate that the progress of specialization tends to increase rather than reduce this risk.

The links between economic history and human geography as now studied are similarly close. Although in the strict statistical or institutional treatment of economico-historical problems geographical considerations may be irrelevant, they obviously are relevant to the wider economic history which would trace the evolution of societies getting their living in particular environments and altering those environments in the process. How far and in how much detail geographical description should be introduced into economic histories depend on the scale of the work and the amount of knowledge which may reasonably be expected of the typical reader. The geographer must describe; the historian may often assume. But it should be said that economic history as hitherto written has much more often suffered from neglect not merely of geographical description but even of essential geographical considerations than it has erred by incorporating too much geography. It would be easy to cite agrarian histories which almost ignore climate and soil. The modern school of anthropogeographers, on the other hand, makes full use of the conclusions of economic history and sometimes even writes it, although with a geographical bias (e.g. Brunhes and Deffontaines' *Géographie humaine de la France,* 2 vols., [1920–26]). It is much to be desired that there should be a closer union between the two studies. The inevitable overlap at this or any other margin is not dangerous: it is at the overlapping margins of disciplines and sciences that the most important discoveries are usually made.

24

*A Plea for Theory in Economic History**

By ELI F. HECKSCHER

Controversies regarding method are almost always barren. But it may none the less be useful to recall for one moment the fierce antagonisms which were roused in the last quarter of last century, especially in Germany, over the comparative virtues of historical and theoretical treatments of economic phenomena. It will be remembered that the school headed by Gustav Schmoller in Berlin, partly on principle but even more in practice, wanted to throw overboard the theoretical study of economics which had dominated the field for at least a century before, wanting to substitute for it a collection of facts from different ages, studied without any preconceived ideas as to what was to be learnt from them.

From these painstaking and extensive efforts surprisingly little has emerged in the shape of contributions to our insight into the working of economic life. To prove this, it may be enough in this place to point to the complex problems of war and after-war economy. These might have been expected to afford a particularly wide scope for a treatment on the lines of the so-called historical school, mixed up as they were with all sorts of political and social issues. But as a matter of fact practically all scholarly contributions to them have been the work of theoretically trained economists, making extensive use of their training in its application to the matter in hand. The natural consequence of this has been that theory has become dominant again in the study of economics, not only in America, Britain, Scandinavia, Holland and other countries, where it had never been given up, but in Germany also.

Now, it would be easy to draw the conclusion that this simply points to a cleavage, a natural and necessary distinction, between economics proper and Economic History; and this view appears to be widely held.

---

* *Economic History* (Suppl. to the *Economic Journal,* 1926–29, I, 525–34. Reprinted by courtesy of Eli F. Heckscher and Macmillan, London.

This paper contains an address delivered before the International Historical Congress at Oslo, Norway, in August 1928, with a few alterations.

To all appearances there is also a great deal to be said for it, in so far as Economic History means the study of the causes of economic developments, the study of the reasons for changes in the body politic, on the economic side as on all others. Even there a very great deal is to be learnt from economic theory, as the following will indirectly show; but that the study of economic development is something distinct from the study of an actual economic situation is none the less true, and it must be added that the treatment of social evolution as subject to historical laws has so far proved of small value. In this respect the non-theoretical treatment of history has lost no ground; and this must by no means be lost sight of.

But it is quite otherwise with regard to the explanation of economic phenomena "in being," *i.e.,* as considered in existence at a particular time. To argue for separating the method of such a study when it applies to earlier ages from that which is used for the problems of to-day is certainly not admissable without actual proof. It would mean, either that the economic conditions of earlier times were fundamentally different from those of the present day, or that economic theory had been created with an exclusive regard to the more or less ephemeral characteristics of the present age. On the former supposition, it might be asked to what use the study of Economic History could possibly be put; in the latter case it would point to a narrowness in the concepts of economic theory which would be far from satisfactory. If, on the other hand, both suppositions are wrong, it is difficult to escape the conclusion that economic theory can be of value to the understanding of economic phenomena at all stages of human development; and as a matter of fact they *are* both wrong, as the following will show. It is therefore necessary to repudiate the idea of economic theory and Economic History as belonging to different stages of human development; they are both essential to an understanding of all periods of history, including the present one.

This relation of theory to the study of history is not peculiar to the field of economics. On the contrary, it is necessary to historical study to base itself all along the line upon what has been found with regard to the general character of those phenomena which are studied. To take a parallel as remote from economics as possible, the study of the history of war has always been found to stand in need of a knowledge of tactics and strategy. The battles and campaigns of Alexander, Hannibal, Cæsar, Charles XII and Napoleon, as well as the history of naval war at different periods, have been studied on the same lines as those of our own day. And this essential unity in the treatment of warfare has been found to exist in spite of the fact that war has from some points of view been revolutionised through the use of powder and of steam.

As to economics, this necessary unity in the problem, irrespective of time and space, is considerably greater than is the case with war. It is here, if anywhere, a question of *nécessités permanentes;* for the basis of economic life and consequently of economic theory is practically universal and all embracing; it is the necessity for "making both ends meet." Economy is not a particular branch or department of human life, as is often believed; it is an aspect of almost all human activities, or those activities as regarded from a particular point of view. The name "economy" and that of the science relating to it, economics, aptly describes the point of view; for οἰκονομία, housekeeping, presupposes an insufficiency of resources; without such an insufficiency there would be no need for housekeeping. The insufficiency of human resources for satisfying the total wants or requirements felt and put forward by man, the "scarcity" of commodities and services, is at the root of almost everything which we call economics. The fundamental concept of economic theory, in accordance with this, is the relation between wants and the means for their satisfaction, between demand and supply. From this flows the necessity of limiting the demand to the available amount of goods and services, as well as the efforts made to direct those goods and services into the channels which are considered best able to satisfy such wants as make themselves felt. The results falling to different groups and individuals constitute their incomes. In so far as the results are achieved through barter or exchange, a new, particularly important set of problems emerges, and primarily the questions of money. The views entertained upon the interplay of all these complicated factors constitute economic opinion or ideas.

It is now made clear for what reason the economic problem must be *fundamentally* the same in all ages. If goods and services are insufficient for satisfying everything which man is asking for at the present time, it was only to be expected that such must have been the case in earlier ages, when the supply of them was far smaller, when man had not learnt one-tenth of what he knows now about his ability to direct his efforts to the purposes desired. True, human wants, as actually felt, were also much smaller in past ages, so that there is no absolute necessity for the scarcity or insufficiency to have made itself felt in those days. It is enough to state that as a matter of fact it did, and that there would have existed no economic problem if it had not.

On the other hand, the solution of the basic problem of economic life, the adjustment between demand and supply, may differ enormously and has done so. Even important concepts of an economic theory intended to explain modern conditions will therefore have to be discarded when remote ages are concerned; *e.g.* the price system, which is now in some quarters looked upon as the central body of economic doctrine, is often meaningless with regard to earlier times, because prices—or at least prices alone—were not used as the engine for equalising demand and supply. But if other means were made use of instead, this does not affect the fact that the adjustment must have taken place; and the character of this process will then have to be studied on the basis of general economic theory. For most periods of known Economic History the changes necessary in the usual theory are not fundamental, however. Especially in the field of money, which constitutes from some points of view the favourite playground of economic theory, and which is at the same time calling for the lion's share of the attention of economic historians over some twenty-five centuries, there are few problems upon which the generally accepted theory is unable to throw some light.

It has been said, *e.g.* by the well-known German scholar Bücher, that the different character of economic life in different ages calls for a particular set of economic concepts for each successive age, one for "household economy," another for "town economy," and a third for "national economy." But it is difficult to see the advantage of such a curious procedure. Economic life, like human life in general, is not "transmuted" from one perfectly consistent set of relations to another, but changes, on the contrary, uninterruptedly in time and space, is never altogether the same in one year as in the next, in one place as in the neighbouring one. The creation of hard-and-fast lines between different periods is therefore in itself distinctly unfortunate and must not be made unless it is indispensable. And this is not at all the case with economic theory. For even if it is intended exclusively for modern conditions, theory must not limit itself to one particular set of circumstances. If the theory starts from abstract and consequently unreal conditions, these premises must in the subsequent study be modified now in one direction and now in another, in order to make them suit actual facts. There is not the slightest reason for giving up this method when the facts of previous ages come to be studied. There may be a difference in degree, but there certainly is none in character, between what is done with regard to modern and what should be done for earlier economic problems.[1]

[1] EDITOR'S NOTE: In a later article Heckscher defined economic history in such a way as to draw the full consequences of the above position. He wrote: "The object of

Coming now to a more concrete discussion of what economic theory can do for Economic History, this will be found to depend to a great extent upon the task which historians are setting themselves. Historians not seldom think they have done everything which can be expected from them when, by the aid of auxiliary sciences and historical criticism, they have ascertained their facts and have presented them. If this view, the reasonableness of which does not now concern me, is held, the use of economic theory is necessarily limited; for it cannot be used as a substitute for historical criticism. A good deal can be learnt from it even for such problems, however; for theory is in a great number of cases able to create a strong presumption for or against the existence of alleged facts. It may appear dangerous for an economist, who lives long after the time in question, to claim such a superior knowledge; but the economist knows how difficult economic facts are of observation and what sorts of mistakes are usually made; and as a matter of fact the historian does not fail to do the same thing in other cases. To quote MM. Langlois and Seignobos in their well-known book, *Introduction aux études historiques:* "Historiquement le diable est beaucoup plus solidement prouvé que Pisistrate: nous n'avons pas un seul mot d'un contemporain qui dise avoir vu Pisistrate; des milliers de 'témoins oculaires' déclarent avoir vu le diable. . . . Pourtant nous n'hésitons plus à rejeter le diable et à admettre Pisistrate."

But no doubt the value of economic theory increases enormously when the work of historians is carried further than the stating of external facts; for its most important use refers to the *choice* of facts and the *explanation* of them.

As to the choice of facts, it is a remarkable thing that a very great, perhaps even the greater, part of what is commonly called Economic History is something else, such as social, legal, political or otherwise institutional, or, on the other hand, technological, history. A study of numismatics is something quite different from that of the functions of money in economic life; the history of banking, of iron, of shipbuilding, of agriculture, may be absolutely non-economic, if it is not concerned with the part played by these different activities in their relations to demand, if not studied from the point of view of their inter-relations with

economic history is to show how scarce or insufficient means have been used for human ends throughout the ages; how the character of this problem has changed or 'developed'; what these situations and changes in them have been due to; how they have reacted upon other sides of human life and human society. As far as I can see, this covers the whole field, and nothing but the field, of economic history." ("Quantitative Measurement in Economic History" *Quart. Jour. Econ.,* 1939, LIII, 167).

the other factors of economic life. For, as I have said already, economics is not concerned with any particular set of external facts, but with a particular point of view upon almost all human activities. Consequently, the history of, say, the Socialist party is no more necessarily economic than that of the Conservative party. The history of class conflict, in which Marx saw the true meaning of all history, is not necessarily a problem of Economic History, as class antagonism can have many reasons besides economic ones. And the notorious dictum of Feuerbach, *der Mensch ist was er isst,* "man is what he eats," is not an economic but a physiological conception of history.

It is perhaps even more important to point out that the legal or social character of institutions is distinct from their economic character. A very significant instance of the want of clearness on this point is the study of the rise of towns in the early Middle Ages. For it has usually been taken as a criterion of a town that it is a place having a sort of charter, a certain system of law, a certain form of administration. As a matter of fact, a town in the economic sense—or in any economic sense—may have been lacking in all these legal or institutional characteristics; and, on the other hand, hundreds of places have had those characteristics without differing economically in any way worth mentioning from the rest of the country. Scholars having made these distinctions imperfectly clear to themselves have been led to discuss town charters as if they were concerned with the rise of actual towns, though those charters would have proved rather an insufficient livelihood for the inhabitants.

In the same way, the study of the manorial, or *hofrechtliche,* origin of crafts and the legal status of the craftsmen have been discussed as problems of Economic History, though they may have been more or less unimportant to the economic character of mediæval industrial life, and were in any case only indirectly concerned with it. This constant unwillingness to distinguish between economic and legal or institutional history has been a rather serious limitation on the value to Economic History of important contributions made by the well-known German scholar von Below; his studies are with few exceptions institutional and very often not economic, even when he believes them to be. In the same way, Sir Paul Vinogradoff a few years ago complained of a recent Economic History of the Middle Ages because it did not contain more of legal history than it did; the obvious answer is, that it had no business to.

Of course this must not in the least be construed as a disparagement of the non-economic sides of history; it is solely intended to point out that Economic History has a distinctly circumscribed object of its own, which cannot be fulfilled if it is constantly set aside for aims belonging to other departments of historical study.

It is only natural that this danger should exist; for Economic History has an object and materials which are usually more intangible than those of other branches. How coins have been minted, iron smelted, or corn sown, are concrete problems, not always easily solved, it is true, but still belonging to something external. Laws and institutions have not got the tangible character of technological processes; but they are none the less usually embodied in *ad hoc* produced things, put upon paper and so on. But while economic facts are always internal, human, or psychological, like institutions, it has usually been nobody's business to put them on paper. They constitute the relations between supply, which is partly tangible (commodities) and partly not (services), and demand, which is altogether intangible; these relations come to light through prices, incomes and so on, all of them things which have no generally accepted embodiment and are even extremely difficult of presentment in their totality. It is therefore greatly to be feared that Economic History, of which so much has been expected, will be unable to do the work allotted to it unless a clear view is gained of what it really means, which sort of facts it has to work upon.

So much about the choice of facts. In the explanation of facts the use of economic theory is even more indispensable. A few instances must suffice, selected more or less at random.

A problem common to most periods of known history—which I have treated in Swedish at different times and hope to be able to come back to—is the view entertained with regard to the desirability of "plenty" or "scarcity" of commodities existing in a country, "love" or "fear" of goods. Broadly speaking, the former, the "love" of goods, resulting in a tendency to favour imports and hamper exports, dominated the periods of natural economy, because under those conditions it was clear to the meanest capacity that you could not gain by giving much away and getting little back. But the introduction of money, though of enormous importance as a means of facilitating exchange, at the same time complicated economic relations more perhaps than anything else has done, and thus concealed from view the fact that the real reason for giving goods away was the need for having goods—not money—back. The consequence was that tendency and policy which is usually called mercantilist, though it has survived mercantilism and is still a power in the world.

These very ideas of natural and money economy stand in need of much more economic analysis than they usually receive at the hands of historians. Money is an instrument of exchange, and the first question consequently must be, whether, or rather, to what an extent, exchange is taking place at all; this is the fundamental distinction. If exchange *is* taking place, the second problem will be, whether it is a direct one, *i.e.* barter of goods and services against goods and services, or an indirect one, introducing a particular sort of goods which neither of the parties to the exchange wants, as an intermediary between those which they do want. In the second case, that of indirect exchange, there are also two very important cases to be distinguished, that of all sorts of common goods used as intermediaries, and that of one particular commodity serving as a generally accepted intermediary. Only in the last-named case have you got money economy; natural economy is a concept covering both barter (direct exchange) and indirect exchange through the aid of promiscuous common goods—non-exchange, lastly, remaining outside both concepts. All these types of economy are historically important, and it would be easy to exemplify them from different stages of human development—that of an indirect exchange without the use of money, for instance, from the history of Sweden in the sixteenth century. But unless theoretically trained, the student of Economic History will be unable to look out for the problem at all.

To take another instance. In the years following the World War attempts were made to elucidate the Economic History of the Later Roman Empire by showing the existence at that period of "scarcity" and "high prices," as a parallel to the problems of the years 1914–18; this was even considered as one of the principal reasons for the decline and fall of ancient civilisation. But the whole of this reasoning lost its force through an inability to distinguish between a rise in general prices, almost always caused by changes in monetary conditions, and a rise in particular prices for important commodities, like food, of which the supply had diminished. Earlier explanations of that same phenomenon, the decline of ancient civilisation, have suffered even more from a want of economic insight; perhaps the most astonishing being that which explains the ruin of the work of centuries through the interesting fact that the Empire became too great to have a foreign trade—as if trade lost its usefulness because both parties to it belonged to the same State! Elementary misunderstandings of a more or less mercantilistic character are among the most common in the study of Economic History.

An often-recurring problem is the consequence of interference with prices and even more with wages. If the result is reached that, say, assessments of wages, as they have been practised for thousands of years, have been depressing or raising the payment of workers as compared with what it was before, it is necessary not to stop at that point but, on the contrary, to try and find out how such a system could have been reached. As the supply and the demand for labour were—presumably—uninfluenced by wage assessments, it is truly remarkable that the price could have been changed. Taking the best-known of these instances, the measures intended to prevent the workers from profiting from the Great Plague about the middle of the fourteenth century, how were farmers prevented from competing for the supply of labour, which had diminished as a consequence of the Plague? Before this is discussed, no true explanation has been given. Or take the parallel case of "customary" rents. If landowners really were, or felt, bound not to increase rents even when the demand for leases exceeded the supply at these rents, in what way was the choice effected between those wanting to take the same lease and of which only one could get it? To state that legislation or custom has been effective in cases like these is really saying nothing; for the economic problem must still be solved.

Or take another case, that of the influence upon the balance of trade of one measure or another, resulting in an excess of imports or exports. The important thing is of what that external result is a picture: in what way the excess of imports was effected or paid for or payment was received for the excess of exports, either through a flow of precious metals, a change in shipping or other services, or international credits. The change in the balance of trade in itself tells us nothing of economic relationships.

It is quite true that our knowledge of facts is very often too incomplete to admit of a clear answer to what constitutes the real economic meaning of what has happened. But even in that case it is necessary not to stop at a so-called fact which is meaningless in itself; what explanation it really points to must be investigated, and often it will be found out that the sources will yield all the knowledge wanted, if only properly questioned. It is the lack of that questioning which is most usually at the bottom of the difficulty. Without the aid of economic theory, economic historians usually lack what is called the "heuristic principle," *das heuristische Prinzip.*

As I have said already, monetary problems are the most important field of all for a use of economic theory in the service of history; fortunately it can be added that it has also been more extensively applied to these subjects than to most. But still much remains to be desired. This is perhaps even more the fact with regard to the relations between money and capital, a problem which presents great difficulties in most ages. A special warning, I think, is necessary against the promiscuous use of the concept of "capitalism"—*das Wort das sich immer zur rechten Zeit einstellt, wo volkswirtschaftliche Begriffe fehlen,* to adapt a famous phrase from the *Faust* of Goethe. By this it is, of course, not intended to infer that some rational and distinct meaning cannot be expressed through the word "capitalism," but simply that it is far too often made an excuse for muddled thinking.

If space admitted, it would be very tempting to go more deeply into the use of economic theory in the service of history. But I hope to have made good my thesis that no Economic History worthy of the name is possible without it.

25

Introduction to Arthur Spiethoff

By FREDERIC C. LANE and JELLE C. RIEMERSMA

One might infer from Heckscher's observations that economic theory is, as it were, something given, a conceptual apparatus to be used by economic historians after it has been constructed by theorists. A moment's reflection raises important problems. In the first place, a number of different economic theories have been developed; there exists not just one theory. A wide range of theories, from Smith to Keynes and Schumpeter, shows the fecundity of the deductive imagination. But the situation is made even more complicated by a second consideration: the historian, not the theorist only, can take part in the development of economic theory. The historian's contributions might conceivably alter the conceptual framework of economics, and it is this possibility which has strongly occupied the minds of many economists in Germany, from Roscher to Spiethoff. They are close to the French positivist tradition in their emphasis on induction, but we will see that the theoretical structure which they tried to build was in some respects decisively different from that of the positivists.

Following the lead of Auguste Comte, not only did positivist writers claim that historical studies should affect theoretical construction, but they wanted theory to be simply derived from historical studies. Theory was to be nothing but a body of generalizations from empirical data. Under the influence of Durkheim and his school the tenets of positivism underwent considerable methodological refinement. Around 1900 positivitism dominated French intellectual activity, and to some extent that of the Anglo-Saxon world.

In Germany, in contrast, Comtean precepts were never widely accepted. The humanistic and other particular aspects of the historical disciplines were defended not only by the historians themselves, like Eduard Meyer, but also by an important group of philosophers following Wilhelm Dilthey. These men criticized the very foundations of positivism; at the same time they made a constructive attempt to formulate an alternative way of organizing the data of social and historical knowledge, to supplement the generalizing and abstracting approach advocated by the positivists. The Dilthey school made a distinction between *Naturwissenschaften* and *Geisteswissenschaften.* Whereas the natural sciences had primarily made it their task to find empirically valid abstractions and generalizations, the cultural sciences would have to use concepts that described unique particulars. The method of the cultural sciences, the *geisteswissenschaftliche Methode,* was modeled by analogy from the way materials were presented by traditional historiography. In the works of Ranke and other great historians the material had not been organized as a manifestation of general "laws of history," but selected and presented as a series of unique and historically important phenomena. The subject matter of history was presented in concrete detail, and data were grouped together under such unique "concepts" as "The French Revolution" or "Frederick the Great." Without selection and organization, the task of historiography would evidently have been impossible; some kind of conceptualization had therefore always been implicit in historical work. It was the achievement of Dilthey, Windelband, and Rickert to give a clear expression of these silently accepted principles. Rickert, with a somewhat dogmatic insistence, wrote: "Historical laws are not just more or less difficult to find—the very concept of historical law carries an inner contradiction. Historical and nomothetic science are mutually exclusive."[1] The full significance of this outlook can be understood only in connection with the whole philosophical tradition of German idealism, a tradition which was different from that which shaped the conceptions of French and Anglo-Saxon social scientists and economic historians.[2] This idealist philosophical background has determined the basic concepts and terms of men like Weber, Sombart, and Spiethoff—much as they may differ among themselves. Thus, when one reads Spiethoff's paper immediately after the contributions by Clapham and Heckscher, one feels transplanted into a different world with different preoccupations. The Anglo-Saxon tradition of economic historians has kept theory and history apart, as separate disciplines, while Spiethoff argues in favor of a discipline in which theory and history interpenetrate.

Ever since the 1840's German scholars have been attempting to rebuild economics upon a historical foundation. In Edwin F. Gay's address

[1] Heinrich Rickert, *Die Grenzen der naturwissenschaftlichen Begriffsbildung* (2nd ed., Tübingen, 1913), p. 257.

[2] Talcott Parsons, *The Structure of Social Action* (Glencoe, Ill., Free Press, 1949), Ch. 13, "The Idealistic Tradition," especially pp. 437–87.

the main representatives of these historical schools of economics have already been mentioned. At this point it suffices to point to those aspects of their contributions which foreshadow the later work of Arthur Spiethoff.

Roscher's *Grundriss zu Vorlesungen über die Staatswirtschaft nach geschichtlicher Methode* (1843) was one of the starting points of methodological discussion. The author criticized the abstract character of classical economics; this science, since the days of Ricardo, had tended to become a purely deductive discipline. Roscher proposed a return to empirical data and historical evidence. In practice, however, his departure from current theory did not go beyond the supplementation of theory with historical examples. He constructed neither a basically new method nor a new conceptual framework.

A second and more decisive step was taken by Bruno Hildebrand, who, noting the static and timeless character of the laws of classical economics, wanted to revise these concepts in such a way as to account for historical change. In the introduction to *Die Nationalökonomie der Gegenwart und Zukunft* (1848) Hildebrand proposed "to transform political economy into a theory of the laws of the economic development of nations." He argued that the historical character of these economic laws contrasted with the regularities of the physical sciences which are truly independent of time and place. In 1863 Hildebrand became the founder of the important journal *Jahrbücher für Nationalökonomie und Statistik;* the first volume contained programmatic articles by the editor in which he urged the use of historical materials in economic science and again stated his views about the time-bound character of economic life.

The writings of Karl Knies fall approximately in the same period as Hildebrand's main publications. Although Knies had a penetrating insight into methodological issues and raised important questions, his immediate influence was rather limited.[3] His style was highly involved, and his leading ideas were ahead of the times. Only much later would the program for a purely historical theory come closer to its realization. In his main methodological work, *Die politische Ökonomie vom Standpunkt der geschichtlichen Methode* (1853), he went so far as to deny the existence of economic laws of whatever kind, even of Hildebrand's developmental laws.

In the closing decades of the nineteenth century German economics

---

[3] Edgar Salin, *Geschichte der Volkswirtschaftslehre* (2nd ed., Berlin, Springer, 1929), pp. 85–86.

came under the strong influence of a man who argued for a purely inductive and historical approach: Gustav Schmoller. During his professorship at Strassburg and later at Berlin, Schmoller and his disciples vigorously assembled materials for monographs on what we would call economic history. The purpose of this work was to create the basis for a new kind of economic theory, and these men regarded themselves as economists rather than historians. What kind of theory did they try to build? This abstract question was left without definite answer while Schmoller and his school continued their detailed investigations and partial syntheses.

Methodological controversy flared up suddenly as a result of the sharp criticism of Schmoller's methods by Carl Menger. The great Austrian economist published in 1883 his *Untersuchungen über die Methode der Socialwissenschaften und der politischen Ökonomie insbesondere.* He did not deny that a certain kind of law—namely, "empirical law"—could be derived from historical evidence, but he vigorously criticized the view, held by the historical school, that such "empirical laws" were the substance and the most important concern of political economy. Thereby Menger defended an autonomous and clearly separate sphere of exact economic theory against the encroachments threatened by historical study. In his opinion, the historians who used the inductive or "realistic-empirical" approach were unqualified to engage also in the purely deductive or "exact" approach practiced by the economist. Menger also objected to another facet of the method of the historical school: its adherents had tended to regard all social phenomena as interdependent. They had not made sharp distinctions in their treatment of economic, legal, political, and psychological phenomena but had dealt with all these phenomena in one and the same study. According to Menger, this procedure was unjustified. It blurred the boundaries between scientific disciplines and therewith invited dilettantism. Menger held that any scientific pursuit requires the isolation of a specific kind of phenomena, and he argued in particular for the clear separation of economic from other kinds of human action. The consequence of this view was the autonomy of economics as a separate science.

Menger's accusations were not to remain unchallenged; they had raised fundamental issues which demanded clarification, and they had attacked one of the leading figures in German academic life. Schmoller answered his critic by means of a review in his *Jahrbuch* of Menger's *Untersuchungen.* The review is of considerable interest as a clear-cut statement of the methodological views of the historical school, and particularly those of Schmoller himself. The fundamental idea was the following: "Traditional political economy, after having achieved important results, lost its vigor and vitality because of a too strong tendency to distill its results into abstract schemes devoid of any real content. It is useless to persist in this preoccupation with abstractions . . . ; what is needed is a radical change of approach which would be the start of a new and entirely different method of studying things. The achievements of the historical school to the present day, in so far as they have lasting value, are indeed based upon the foundations of traditional economic theory. It is also true that political economy will enter a new period of fruitful development. But this will happen only through the utilization of the whole body of historical, descriptive, and statistical material which is now being assembled, not through the continued distillation of the abstract dogmas which have been distilled a hundred times before."[4]

Schmoller's review was countered by Menger in a series of imaginary letters, called *Die Irrthümer des Historismus in der deutschen Nationalökonomie* (1884). Here Menger restated his position with utmost vehemence: "The erroneous assumption that political economy could be reformed simply by connecting it with historical knowledge—this is what the application of the false dogma of 'Historismus' means in our field—was doomed to failure from the start. Any science can be reorganized only from the inside, from the center of its own sphere of ideas. Reform must be the work of students who are immersed in the problems of their own discipline. Political economy will not be lifted from its present low state by historians, mathematicians, physiologists, or those who blindly follow the example of those disciplines. The transformation of political economy can begin only with ourselves, with the scholars dedicated to this particular science. Other disciplines and their representatives will be able to supply us with fuller insights into their particular problems, and they will bring their own achievements to greater perfection. In so far as they are significant for the development of our science, we will make a careful and grateful use of these results, whether they derive from historical inquiry, from statistics, psychology, logic, or technology. However, in the future we must firmly refuse any interference with economic science that aims to reform it through ap-

---

[4] Gustav Schmoller, "Zur Methodologie der Staats- und Socialwissenschaften," *Jahrbuch für Gesetzgebung, Verwaltung, und Volkswirtschaft im deutschen Reich,* 1883, Vol. VII, pp. 965–94, especially p. 978.

plying extraneous methods and viewpoints. If that is not done, German economic thought will, after yet another half-century, again face a period of disillusionment."[5]

"How has the German historical school of political economy developed? Theory! Then theory embroidered with historical and statistical notes, interspersed with historical excursions! Finally, mere notes and historical excursions, with the pretense of theory! Further progress in this direction hardly seems possible."[6]

By a curious coincidence, Schmoller's review of Menger's *Untersuchungen* had been accompanied by his review of another work of profound methodological significance. This milestone of German methodological reflection was Wilhelm Dilthey's *Einleitung in die Geisteswissenschaften,* a philosophical work that advocated an approach of which we have already indicated some fundamental aspects: the *geisteswissenschaftliche Methode.* In spite of the fact that he admired Dilthey, Schmoller never incorporated the new conceptions in his own theoretical work. Only with Max Weber and Werner Sombart did the method find explicit application in economic history, resulting in such concepts as "ideal types" and "economic systems."

In Schmoller's methodological discussions he spoke characteristically of "persistent directions of development" and "regularities," rather than of "laws." The latter term was avoided for reasons of expediency and scientific modesty: Schmoller thought that economic science was not sufficiently advanced to allow the formulation of "laws." Before that stage could be reached, historical knowledge would, in his opinion, have to be enriched by the careful accumulation and analysis of masses of empirical material.[7]

The economists and economic historians who were influenced by the *geisteswissenschaftliche Methode* also avoided the term "laws" in favor of other expressions, but they did so for a different reason. Schmoller's reason was practical, one might say, and determined by the actual condition of the social sciences in his own day. An author like Max Weber, however, rejected the term "laws" because he envisaged a basically different method of conceptualization through the use of "ideal types." This was a new departure, starting from a revision of the principles of methodology. While Schmoller still tried to generalize on the basis of

---

[5] Carl Menger, *Die Irrthümer des Historismus in der deutschen Nationalökonomie* (Vienna, Holder, 1884), pp. iv–vi.

[6] *Ibid.,* p. 50.

[7] Gustav Schmoller, "Volkswirtschaft, Volkswirtschaftslehre, und -methode," in *Handwörterbuch der Staatswissenschaften,* Vol. VIII (3rd ed., 1911), p. 488.

historical evidence, Weber's "ideal types" transcended historical experience and were, to some extent, deliberate mental constructs formed by the historian or social scientist. Schmoller's attitude toward these mental constructs was critical; he wrote: ". . . While Weber, through his theoretical excursions, has greatly enriched the concepts and methods of history and social science, I would nevertheless like to point out that he combines within his 'ideal types' too great a variety of concepts. . . . Here Weber throws together concepts which have the character of classifications with a different kind of concepts that have the character of ideals. When he declares all his 'ideal types' to be utopias, both Bücher and I must defend ourselves against confusing our concept of the 'town economy,' for instance, with the kind of concepts represented by the utopias of the socialist or of the Manchester school."[8]

This statement, written in 1911, finds support in the careful analysis of Weber's theory by Alexander von Schelting, a decade later. According to this author, Weber uses the concept of "ideal types" in two different senses.[9] Sometimes it means the description of a pattern of action that occurred at a specific time and in a specific place—for instance, "primitive Christianity" or "the medieval town economy." But at other times it refers to patterns that have no necessary counterpart in history. This meaning is indicated by the word "utopia," against which Schmoller reacted; Weber emphasized and greatly elaborated this particular aspect of the "ideal-type" concept. In our present discussion, when we mention "ideal type," we mean henceforth this second meaning of the term. A good example of such a "utopia" is the conception of a harmonious interplay of enlightened self-interests, described in the kind of economic theory developed by Adam Smith and his followers. About this conception Weber wrote: "Abstract economic theory exemplifies the kind of synthetic constructions that are usually called 'ideas' of historical phenomena. The theory gives an idealized picture of the occurrences in the commodity market under the conditions of an exchange economy, free competition, and strictly rational conduct. With regard to its contents, the construction has the character of a *utopia.* By the exaggeration of certain elements in observed reality this *utopia* originates in the scientist's mind. . . ."[10]

---

[8] Schmoller, "Volkswirtschaft, Volkswirtschaftslehre und -methode," *loc. cit.,* p. 468.

[9] Alexander von Schelting, "Die logische Theorie der historischen Kulturwissenschaft von Max Weber und insbesondere sein Begriff des Idealtypus," *Archiv für Sozialwissenschaft und Sozialpolitik,* Vol. XLIX, pp. 726–31.

[10] Max Weber, *Gesammelte Aufsätze zur Wissenschaftslehre* (Tübingen, Mohr, 1922), p. 190.

The "ideal type," as appears from this passage, is a model or a construct; and yet it is unlike the abstractions encountered in the natural or exact sciences. It is not a generalization from experienced reality but rather resembles an ideal picture with which the historian can compare actual historical situations or patterns. Thus, in Weber's use of the concept, the "ideal type" is frequently a means, not an end, of the investigation. It serves as a tool, a standard of comparison, which helps to bring order into the chaos of descriptive historical materials.[11]

The construction of ideal types depends on the scientist's vision of historical patterns as totalities. This vision is indicated by the German word *Verstehen,* if used in the sense of the *geisteswissenschaftliche Methode.* As an English equivalent, be it a rough one, we might use "understanding." What does it mean if a historian "understands"? The English philosopher and historian R. G. Collingwood writes: "The historian, investigating any event in the past, makes a distinction between what may be called the outside and the inside of an event. By the outside of the event I mean everything belonging to it which can be described in terms of bodies and their movements: the passage of Caesar, accompanied by certain men, across a river called the Rubicon at one date, or the spilling of his blood on the floor of the senate-house at another. By the inside of the event I mean that in it which can only be described in terms of thought: Caesar's defiance of Republican law, or the clash of constitutional policy between himself and his assassins. The historian is never concerned with either of these to the exclusion of the other. . . . He is interested in the crossing of the Rubicon only in its relation to Republican law, and in the spilling of Caesar's blood only in its relation to a constitutional conflict. His work may begin by discovering the outside of an event, but it can never end there; he must always remember that the event was an action, and that his main task is to think himself into this action, to discern the thought of the agent."[12]

The historian seeks to understand events and situations in terms of thought. Dilthey was therefore in accord with historical practice when he maintained that the cultural sciences should use concepts that reflected the thought and attitudes behind human actions in history. "Ideal types" —for instance, the harmonious interplay of self-interests in competitive markets—are concepts of this kind; we can imagine ourselves in the

[11] H. H. Gerth and C. Wright Mills, *From Max Weber: Essays in Sociology* (New York, Oxford University Press, 1946); Introduction, p. 60.

[12] R. G. Collingwood, *The Idea of History* (London, Oxford University Press, 1946), p. 213. See also pp. 63–67, 170–76, 205–31.

position of competitive agents and predict our reactions to changes in the market conditions.

The full meaning of the *verstehende Methode* can be grasped only after a study of German methodological thought and its application in the works of historians and social scientists. One should guard against a too strongly psychological interpretation of the approach. Theodore Abel, for instance, defines *Verstehen* as "analyzing a behavior situation in such a way—usually in terms of feeling states—that it parallels some personal experience of the interpreter."[13] Social scientists and historians have sometimes been guilty of unscientific, psychologizing explanations. But it must be acknowledged that Weber's use of *Verstehen,* through the "ideal-type" method, is an attempt to get away from those subjective interpretations as much as possible. He did not confront the data with his own experiences and motivations but compared them with sharply and explicitly defined models, in the form of "ideal types." These utopias, as he called them, might be deliberate constructs, but they were not simply deducible from the observer's "feeling states." The thought, purposes, and motives which Weber considered important for "understanding" historical situations are those of the historical agents themselves. They are purposes which the historical actors have in common with other members of the social groups to which they belong—class, generation, nation—and which can be inferred objectively from their manifestations. German scholars have used the term *objektiver Geist* for such shared thoughts and motives; strictly individual thoughts and motives, on the other hand, fall into the realm of *individueller Geist.* The latter are expressly excluded by Max Weber, as being irrelevant for "understanding."[14]

Perhaps the most impressive embodiments of the *verstehende Methode* in the social sciences are Weber's *Wirtschaft und Gesellschaft* (posthumously published in 1925) and Sombart's *Der moderne Kapitalismus* (1902; greatly enlarged edition in 1916). The former is an attempt to deal with the social, political, and economic structures of all times and peoples; the latter deals comprehensively with the whole history of European capitalism.

Sombart's debt to the Dilthey school is evident in his emphasis on the unbroken totality of cultural life. Against Bücher he argued that forms of economic life cannot possibly be characterized and distin-

[13] Theodore Abel, "The Operation Called *Verstehen,*" *Am. Jour. Soc.,* 1948, LIV, 211–18. See p. 218.

[14] Max Weber, "Über einige Kategorien der verstehenden Soziologie," in *Gesammelte Aufsätze zur Wissenschaftslehre* (Tübingen, Mohr, 1922), pp. 403 ff.

guished by a single analytical criterion; a number of aspects rather than just one should be taken into account. In a widely read series of essays that appeared in 1893 under the title *Die Entstehung der Volkswirtschaft,* Bücher had separated the "household economy" of antiquity, the "town economy" of the later Middle Ages, and the "national economy" of modern times as three distinct stages (*Stufen*). The stages were distinguished according to the criterion of the "distance" between producer and consumer. This procedure, in Sombart's opinion, was unjustified because it was too mechanistic.[15] For the same reason Sombart objected to Hildebrand's formulation of the stages of a "natural," a "money," and a "credit economy."[16]

A more complex criterion, consisting of a number of indices rather than of a single one, was, in Sombart's view, necessary to make adequate distinctions between patterns of economic life. In *Der moderne Kapitalismus* he separated periods of European economic history by focusing on three characteristics: the technique, the organization, and the spirit of economic activity (*Wirtschaftsgeist*). Karl Marx and Gustav Schmoller had already taken technique and organization, respectively, as representative of an economic period. The specific contribution made by Sombart is the application of the *Wirtschaftsgeist* concept. The economic mentality or *Geist* is not merely an empirical datum but also a creative potentiality. According to Sombart, "to write the history of modern capitalism is to describe how in the course of centuries the idea of the capitalist system is changed into a reality; it means to describe how the economic life of the peoples of Europe develops itself, in all its branches, from the new spirit."[17]

The conception of a *Wirtschaftsgeist*, characteristic of an economic pattern, derives from idealist philosophy. *Objektivierter Geist* is the objectification, in artifacts and institutional patterns, of the ideas and attitudes of people in certain historical periods. *Objektiver Geist*—defined earlier—and *objektivierter Geist,* taken together, have much the same meaning as the term "culture" in the usage of Anglo-Saxon anthropologists, namely, the sum total of beliefs, habits, artifacts, and institutions of a certain society.[18] The creative development of a "spirit" in human

[15] Werner Sombart, *Der moderne Kapitalismus* (1st ed., München and Leipzig, 1902), p. 54.

[16] On stages see: Gertrud Kalveram, *Die Theorien von den Wirtschaftsstufen,* Frankfurter wirtschaftswissenschaftliche Studien, Heft 1 (Leipzig, Hans Buske, 1933).

[17] Sombart, *Der moderne Kapitalismus,* Vol. I, (2nd ed., München and Leipzig, Duncker and Humblot, 1928), Pt. 1, p. 330.

[18] Werner Sombart, *Die drei Nationalökonomien* (München and Leipzig, Duncker and Humblot, 1930), p. 166.

history had been the theme of Hegel's philosophy of history, and the consequences of this philosophy deeply influenced later developments in German methodological thinking. Talcott Parsons has described these consequences as follows: "Instead of being tested by and for itself an individual human act . . . tended to be interpreted as a mode of expression of a 'spirit' (Geist), sharing this quality with multitudinous other acts of the same and of other individuals. Thus to Hegel human history was the 'objectification' of the single unitary *Weltgeist.* The result of this tendency was to arrange human activities in relation to comprehensive 'collective' or 'totality' patterns. . . . The unifying concept under which empirical data were subsumed was not that of a general 'law' or analytical element, as in the positivist tradition, but rather a particular, unique *Geist,* a specific cultural totality clearly distinct from and incommensurable with all others."[19]

The "economic systems" which Sombart proposed to substitute for Bücher's "stages of economic development" are, indeed, totality patterns, each characterized by a particular technique and organization and, above all, by a particular spirit. Should we regard these "systems" as exemplifying Weber's "ideal types"? Were they mental constructs, especially devised to deal in an empiric and comparative fashion with the transformation of European economic life? Sombart himself answered in the affirmative; but his volumes present his "system" as if it were a replica of reality rather than just an idealized model. Sombart's conceptualization is constructed on the basis of concrete evidence from one particular historical situation, namely, Europe in medieval and modern times, envisaged as one cultural entity.[20]

Arthur Spiethoff proposes the term "real type" for a totality pattern that is as close as possible a representation of some historical reality.[21] With Spiethoff, the method of the German "historical economists" has been carried to a new level of refinement. The author, for years Schmoller's assistant and later editor of the *Jahrbuch,* had a real interest in pure economic theory and did important work on business cycles.

---

[19] Parsons, *The Structure of Social Action,* p. 478.

[20] See Sombart, *Der moderne Kapitalismus,* Vol. I, (2nd ed., 1928), Pt. 1 p. 23: "Thus the various 'economic systems' which have been dominant in the eleven centuries from 800–1900 had to be determined, and, to begin with, they had to be described ideal-typically, as pure concepts." Parsons, in *The Structure of Social Action,* p. 496, has commented: "However much Sombart may emphasize the abstract theoretical character of his concepts, the fact remains that their reference is individual and historical and not analytical and general."

[21] Arthur Spiethoff, "Anschauliche und reine Theorie," in *Synopsis. Festgabe für Alfred Weber,* Edgar Salin, ed. (Heidelberg, 1948), p. 571.

At the same time he continued Schmoller's quest for a solid empirical foundation, and his theories are built in the closest proximity to historical evidence. Spiethoff's conceptualization has elements in common with Weber's and Sombart's conceptual framework, but differs from it in important points. The "real types" do not contain the deliberate exaggerations of Weber's "ideal types." Specifically, Spiethoff proposes that Sombart's "economic systems"—an application of the "ideal-typical" approach—be replaced by a new concept, the "economic styles." Unlike Sombart's "systems," the "styles" do not necessarily have logical unity. A "style" cannot be deduced from certain fundamental principles; its internal coherence depends on a unity of form that can be seen, that is visually evident, like the internal unity of a work of art. Art history had, of course, been using the concept of "styles" to characterize historical periods, and unity of form in works of art suggested a similar unity of form in economic life. Thus an "economic style" (*Wirtschaftsstil*) is a representation of the form that economic activity takes in a certain historical situation; and, in Spiethoff's view, all the essential elements, or uniformities, of the actual and concrete situation must be represented in order to make the "economic style" an adequate concept.

Although Spiethoff is not opposed to deductive or pure theory, he is more interested in an inductive kind of economic theory that describes and analyzes patterns of economic action. His theory may therefore be characterized as an "economic Gestalt theory." Fritz Redlich has chosen this phrase as the best translation of what Spiethoff calls "anschauliche Theorie."[22]

[22] [NOTE BY FRITZ REDLICH: A literal translation of *anschauliche Theorie* being impossible, as everybody will agree who knows both languages, its intrinsic meaning and the intention of the scholar who coined the term must guide in the choice of an English counterpart. As the picture unfolds, the reader will see that Professor Spiethoff's method of *anschauliche Theorie* aims at reflecting the totality of whatever phenomenon is the subject of theoretical analysis. The totality of phenomena, however, is also emphasized by the Gestalt idea, now generally known through the work of the Gestalt psychologists. Under these circumstances, the translator decided to choose "economic Gestalt theory" to paraphrase the original German term, the more so since it seemed advantageous to use a phrase that was not already used in any conflicting sense in everyday language or in established economic theory.

Of the German term, Spiethoff himself says (*Synopsis,* p. 648 n.): "The first to describe the method of what is here called *anschauliche Theorie* was Joseph Schumpeter in Schmoller's *Jahrbuch,* 1926, Vol. L, p. 377 n. He did so by citing my business-cycle theory as an example. Later Edgar Salin gave that kind of theory a specific name, *anschauliche Theorie,* first in a review article on Sombart's *Der moderne Kapitalismus* in *Weltwirtschaftliches Archiv,* 1927, XXV, 314 ff., and again in his *Geschichte der Volkswirtschaftslehre* (3rd ed., Bern, 1944), pp. 145 ff. Ever since the beginnings of economics there has existed realistic, 'concrete' theory, and, lest our tools get in confusion, we must always be very careful in creating new terms. On the other hand, a new term has the advantage of preventing fruitless discussions, resulting from the confounding of different

A concrete example of *anschauliche Theorie* is Spiethoff's own study of business fluctuations.[23] Unlike most presentations of a theory of the business cycle, Spiethoff's treatise does not culminate in pointing to a crucial causal factor such as monetary expansion, harvest fluctuations, or underconsumption. The author does not deal with the economic cycle as a separate phenomenon that can be studied in isolation. He emphasizes the "wholeness" of the historical situation within which the fluctuations occur, and his analysis concludes by indicating a flexible plurality of causal factors all of which are historically conditioned, as elements of a prevailing economic pattern. Spiethoff's study called "Krisen" contains a sequence of deductive and inductive sections; deduction is controlled by historical fact. Thus the study contains a long empirical treatment of the whole history of business cycles since the sixteenth century; the characteristics of economic fluctuations are shown to be dependent on the historical circumstances of different periods. The description of various types of cycles is of particular interest to economic historians. The treatise ends with a model describing the stages of the typical business cycle of fully developed capitalism in general terms. At this point Spiethoff comes relatively close to what is usually conceived as business-cycle theory. But Spiethoff's model, in accordance with his methodological aim, "has been formed in the closest proximity to historical experience."[24]

The following pages contain representative parts of Spiethoff's methodological writings. The opening sections give the distinctions between pure economic theory, economic Gestalt theory, and economic history. They are followed by Spiethoff's analysis of specific concepts and by a discussion of "ideal types" and "real types."

---

concepts covered by the same term. While Salin, when he framed the term *anschauliche Theorie,* was not guided by epistemological considerations, he intended to distinguish theory in the Greek, and especially in the Platonic sense—a conception adopted by German scholars—from theory in a stricter, technical, rational sense."]

[23] Arthur Spiethoff, "Krisen," in *Handwörterbuch der Staatswissenschaften,* VI (4th ed., Jena, 1925), pp. 8–91.

[24] Spiethoff, "Krisen," *loc. cit.,* p. 38.

26

*Pure Theory and Economic Gestalt Theory; Ideal Types and Real Types**

By ARTHUR SPIETHOFF

Editor's Foreword

The following selections from Spiethoff's methodological writings have been translated by Dr. Fritz Redlich. To transpose the spirit of the argument, it has been necessary in some instances to depart from the original wording. Professor Spiethoff has read the present translation and has given his full approval.

I. ECONOMIC GESTALT THEORY AND PURE THEORY: THEIR PURPOSE AND METHOD[1]

History deals with unique and singular phenomena which it describes, explains, and tries to understand.[2] Theory, on the other hand, is interested in uniformities. Only those phenomena which present uniformities are therefore liable to theoretical treatment. It would be impossible to give a theory of business cycles if each upswing and downswing was different from any other and resulted from specific causes. If they had no recurring elements or uniformities, business cycles would be similar to wars and earthquakes; they would be mere accidents, impinging upon economic life, rather than part and parcel of a certain economic style.

---

* Parts I, IIA, and IIB consist of selections from Arthur Spiethoff, "Anschauliche und reine volkswirtschaftliche Theorie und ihr Verhältnis zueinander," *Synopsis. Festgabe für Alfred Weber,* Edgar Salin, ed. (Heidelberg, 1948). Parts III and IV are taken from an unpublished essay, a part of which appeared in the *Journal of Economic History,* 1952, Vol. XII, No. 2, pp. 131–39.

Reprinted by courtesy of Arthur Spiethoff and of Verlag Lambert Schneider, G.m.b.H., Heidelberg.

[1] *Synopsis,* pp. 569–72.

[2] [TRANSLATOR'S NOTE: The reader should be aware of the distinction between "explaining" and "understanding," a distinction to which German social scientists have given much thought. A phenomenon is "explained" by showing its causal relationships with other phenomena, taking "cause" in the scientist's sense. A phenomenon is "understood" by uncovering the motives of the human agents who brought it into existence.]

Social reality is bewilderingly full of singularities, so that uniformities do not stand out. Uniformities are made accessible for research only through a process of abstraction and isolation; a phenomenon must be seen within a certain frame of reference and in only those relations with other phenomena that equally appear within the frame. Dependent on the method of abstraction and isolation which is used, it is possible to distinguish pure economic theory and economic Gestalt theory. Pure theory emphasizes the isolation of specific phenomena and their relations to other isolated and specific phenomena; other relations which may also exist are disregarded. It is interested in isolated phenomena, not in the innumerable concatenations that in reality link them together. Attention is focused upon specific phenomena and relations, selected with the aid of a given frame of reference and manipulated for research purposes without regard for their location in a "total" situation. This may even lead to the study of phenomena that have not been observed but are merely assumed; in this case the object of research is an arbitrary or nonempirical model. Pure theory starts from data which have an axiomatic character, and conclusions are reached by a process of logical deduction: the student draws conclusions about effects by taking given data as causes. As a matter of principle, in the strictest version of pure theory, conclusions are reached without any control through comparison with reality. Professor Vleugels has characterized the results of pure theory as the offspring of a "logical genesis," which proceeds according to certain "laws." Assuming correct procedure, its results are therefore necessarily "right." The value which the results have for the explanation of economic reality depends on the way the problems are posed and upon the fruitfulness of the underlying assumptions.

In the case of economic Gestalt theory the situation is very different. This theory aims at the closest possible approximation to observable reality. It goes without saying that economic Gestalt theory cannot deal with reality as a whole. In that case it would lose sight of the uniformities, being confronted with the overwhelming multitude of historical singularities and their interrelations. It would cease to be theory. However, economic Gestalt theory considers the maximum number of relations in which the phenomenon to be investigated actually occurs, provided that those relationships are uniform in character. By a process of induction, economic Gestalt theory arrives at discrete species of phenomena whose characteristics are the data from which it starts. It does not propose to deal purely and simply with relations between rigorously specified phenomena; on the contrary, its purpose is to consider all phenomena that actually and *uniformly* impinge on the one which is the center of attention. Consequently, the selection of phenomena is not determined by looking only at relationships that have been defined in advance, but by the goal of embracing *all uniform* and *essential* relations that occur in a given situation of economic reality. Essential are those phenomena which appear to be causes or conditions of the one under investigation or indicative of those causes and conditions. The ultimate goal of economic Gestalt theory is a replica of reality.

In this procedure the Gestalt theorist continuously verifies his theory by observations of economic reality; hence his method is not to be characterized as a "logical genesis" from data given in advance. The data which he uses are obtained by empirical research. Like pure theory, economic Gestalt theory makes use of abstraction and isolation, but in a different way and in a different spirit. Its abstractions are formed in such a way as to leave out only the irregular and the inessential. Everything that is both uniform and essential is included as completely as possible.

One may therefore characterize pure theory and Gestalt theory as being located on two poles of the *globus intellectualis.* To distinguish them according to the degree of abstraction, as has been done, is not sufficient. This would imply that one kind of theory shades into the other. In fact, while both theories engage in abstraction and isolation, each does so in a specific way and spirit; and it is impossible to blend theories that are fundamentally different in character. Even when pure theory keeps abstraction at a minimum and works with models that are not arbitrary but empirical, it manipulates its data in line with specific questions which the student has formulated in advance. Economic Gestalt theory, on the other hand, derives its data from reality by abstraction from time-conditioned singularities. Whatever the degree of abstraction, the data for economic Gestalt theory are *actually existing* uniformities, not subject to modifications by particular research interests. The situation is similar in regard to isolation. In pure theory isolation is arbitrary; the student isolates whatever he wishes to explore. But in economic Gestalt theory the student isolates what is uniform and essential in its concrete framework of concatenations. The degree of abstraction and isolation is undoubtedly different in both cases, but the difference is overshadowed by the more fundamental contrast regarding the subject matter of research. This fundamental difference must be summarized as follows: pure theory isolates arbitrarily selected phenomena that are manipulated for the purpose on hand; economic Gestalt theory isolates the sum total of actually existing uniformities, everything that is essential in relation to a given phenomenon.

IIA. ECONOMIC GESTALT THEORY AS DISTINGUISHED FROM ECONOMIC HISTORY: ALFRED WEBER'S TREATMENT OF THE FRAUEN-HAUSINDUSTRIE

In the preceding section economic Gestalt theory has been distinguished from pure theory; now it must be differentiated from economic history. Economic Gestalt theory is theory in the true sense, because it aims at making statements of broad applicability. While it attempts to approximate reality, it does not deal with historical singularities that are subject to *ad hoc* explanations.

Economic Gestalt theory deals with economic reality, and it therefore is concerned with such subjects as economic "styles" (patterns of economic life), mass phenomena, or institutions. It deals not only with economic phenomena that have a material substratum but also with economic ideas, motives, and goals. Thus economic Gestalt theory describes and analyzes discrete and uniformly recurring species of economic phenomena that exist or have existed in space and time. Through this analysis of reality a kind of knowledge with broad applicability is obtained.

Whenever an economic institution subject to temporal change is studied by the methods of economic Gestalt theory, the border line between this theory and economic history becomes fluid. Then it depends on the emphasis of the study on which side of the fence it belongs. If the emphasis lies on uniformities that are common to various representations of the institution that are being studied, the result may belong to the realm of theory. On the other hand, if the study deals mainly with the ways in which the institution has come to life, with the unique aspects of these cases and their differences, the result undoubtedly belongs to analytical economic history. Alfred Weber's treatment of the urban putting-out system making use of female labor is a good example of a border-line case; I regard it as analytical economic history using the methods of economic Gestalt theory.[3]

During the course of his research,[4] Alfred Weber found that production under the putting-out system—at one time there existed three different forms of this system—was, from the beginning of the eight-

[3] To replace paragraph 2 of p. 589, the preceding paragraph has been inserted by the translator, with the approval of Professor Spiethoff.

[4] Alfred Weber, "Die Hausindustrie und ihre gesetzliche Regelung," *Schriften des Vereins für Sozialpolitik,* Vol. LXXXVIII (Leipzig, 1900), pp. 12 ff.

eenth century on, losing importance compared with other forms of industrial organization. The putting-out system was definitely a backward form of industrial production after the middle of the nineteenth century, but nevertheless it achieved a new growth in the urban Frauen-Hausindustrie. How can this strange fact be explained?[5] As a matter of fact, an interpretation was achieved by testing an intuitive hypothesis which proved to be useful also in explaining the survival, in competition with the factory, of one of three forms of Hausindustrie. The explanatory principle was derived from the observation that there was a kind of labor supply for which no demand existed except in the Frauen-Hausindustrie.

To prove the correctness of his hypothesis, Alfred Weber investigated a wide segment of social and economic history, as well as demographic and industrial statistics. In old trade centers and in seats of government administration, female labor, as social and economic history showed, was traditionally employed in domestic services and as occasional help (such as cleaning women and washerwomen) by families in the higher-income brackets. In the new industrial centers of the nineteenth century the supply of female labor became much larger, and the traditional occupations could not absorb what was available. Moreover, industrial statistics are available to show that the dominant industries in modern urban centers have grown from industries that employed male labor and that those industries continued to use men only. Population statistics were used by Weber to show that overseas emigration after 1850 carried away mostly men; only one-third of all adult emigrants who left were women. The resulting surplus of women migrated to the big cities. In those cities more than anywhere else, according to the findings of social history, women belonging to middle-class families came to join the ranks of working-class women who hunted for employment. An oversupply of female labor in the big cities, in varying degrees, was the consequence of these population movements. If one compares successive occupational and industrial census reports, it is evident that there was an increase in female labor. In particular, the number of women who could not find work in traditionally female occupations was increasing. The course of industrial history shows that cheap female labor has tended to be bound to specific locations; therefore, industries which were anxious to tap the supply had to migrate to these locations. But this was

[5] Alfred Weber, "Die Entwicklungsgrundlagen der grosstädtischen Frauen-Hausindustrie," in *Schriften des Vereins für Sozialpolitik,* Vol. LXXXV (Leipzig, 1899), Pt. 2, pp. xiii ff.

impossible for highly developed, capital-intensive industries which by their fixed investments were already tied to certain other places. Only those industries could be moved which could organize production under the putting-out system. Thus the concentration of otherwise unemployable female labor in big cities resulted in the rise of an urban Frauen-Hausindustrie.

IIB. CAUSAL ANALYSIS AND INTUITIVE HYPOTHESES[6]

The foremost and principal task of scholars is the search for causes. In economics two kinds of causality are to be considered: objective causality and motivational causality (*Sachkausalität* and *Motivkausalität*). In dealing with objective causality—which may also be termed "mechanical"—a phenomenon is seen as caused by objective factors; it is "explained," in the narrower sense of the term. Having found the "cause" of a phenomenon, one can proceed to the next step, which is to find the cause's cause, and so on, ad infinitum. For practical reasons it is advisable to stop the investigation, once the search for causes leads into the domain of another science; otherwise it is in danger of becoming dilettantic. Motivational causality, on the other hand, implies causal imputation: economic activities are seen as the result of or caused by certain motives. The word "motive" means the totality of mental activities behind human action. The latter kind of causality lies at the root of the method called "understanding" or *Verstehen.* While there are certain scholars who reject, as a matter of principle, the idea of investigating human motives, others definitely demand this uncovering of the motivational background.

When the economic Gestalt theorist aims to give an "explanatory" or "causal" description of a species of phenomena, he uses two procedures: causal analysis and the verification of intuitive hypotheses (*Erklärungseinfall*). Causal analysis belongs to the inductive method, implying a search for causes and conditions. The discrete species of phenomena which must be explained is subjected to a process of investigation—observation being followed by analysis—in which uniformities are brought to light. Subsequently, he tries to establish links between that species of phenomena and the theoretically discovered uniformities, until enough data have been accumulated to justify the conclusion that these links are generally existent. Then the species of phenomena, considered as an effect, has been linked to certain causes and conditions. However, this direct approach of causal analysis is successful only if the

[6] *Synopsis,* pp. 616–20.

fabric of causes and conditions is untangled with relative ease; and for this the interweaving of threads must be easily recognizable. If the causal nexus is complicated, the scholar must be favored by fortunate circumstances if causal analysis is to be successful.

In complicated interrelationships, decisive uniformities can be found, and causal analysis applied, only in an indirect fashion. By means of observation one may elicit intuitively perceived relationships. From an intuitively grasped hypothesis one may deduce what causes and conditions could lead to the species of phenomena which have to be explained and which are therefore viewed as "effects." Of course, the "causes" that are thus deduced are only tentative; true causes must be verified by empirical research. The original determination of causes depends, methodologically speaking, on deduction; the step-by-step verification of the argument, by means of empirical research, is induction. Actually, theoretical deduction and empirical induction go hand in hand in the task of explanation. A subject of investigation can be approached with a hypothesis; with its help an over-all picture of the possible relations among the phenomena under consideration is constructed. It is also possible that factual research rather than intuition leads to the initial discovery of interrelations and the formulation of imputed causes. Speculative deduction is indispensable; but no logical method exists which by itself would be sufficient to result in an intuitive hypothesis. In later stages of the investigation, empirical research and theoretical considerations mutually influence each other.[7]

III

In his eternal quest for periodization of history, the analytical economic historian will find the theoretical concept of "economic style" a very useful kind of model. The model reflects what can be characterized as a *Kausalzusammenhang:* it mirrors a system of elements held together by interaction, and at the same time reflects a specific set of economic institutions which are at the root of that system of interacting

[7] End of the selections from *Synopsis.* [TRANSLATOR'S NOTE: The sections which follow are a direct continuation of Spiethoff's article, "The 'Historical' Character of Economic Theories," *Journal of Economic History,* 1952, Vol. XII, No. 2, pp. 131–39.

Why the word "historical" is put between quotes can perhaps best be realized from the way in which Spiethoff uses it in the present argument. Here the word has wider connotations than in Anglo-Saxon usage. Many phenomena that at first sight, and without further analysis, appear to be nonhistorical are in fact part of a unique and temporary set of conditions. Thus, as Spiethoff shows, a good deal of economic theory is "historical" in character. Its concepts would be irrelevant and inapplicable were it not for the existence of unique patterns of economic life for which the author coined the term "styles."]

elements. This set of institutions may be real (that is, one that exists or one that has existed or one whose coming is anticipated), or it may be imaginary and constructed for the purpose of mental experiment only.[8] Consequently, one has to distinguish between the following types of economic style models:

Type 1. The model which mirrors a real institutional situation, and is arrived at by economic Gestalt theory.
Type 2. The model in pure theory arrived at by abstraction from reality.
Type 3. The model in pure theory which has no counterpart in reality.
Type 4. The model envisaged by statesmen or utopians to be realized in the future.

In the following two sections of this paper these four types of style models will be analyzed in order to show their logical character. They are not individualizing concepts covering only one actual or hypothetical pattern of economic life; on the contrary, they are of a general character. In relation to any specific pattern, such as capitalism or communism, the concept of economic style is of a generic nature (generic in the sense that it is a formulation of the traits common to a class of phenomena). The concept points to a specific pattern of economic life characterized by a set of unique institutions.

Type 1. In order to deal with "historical" reality by using as a tool a style model of type 1, it is necessary to master "historical" differences. This must be achieved by a mental process, for the concrete counterparts of the style models do not exist in particular years in a pure state. Moreover, as must be stressed, the economic style is not a descriptive concept, it is a model.

This model has been criticized by historians who are so engrossed in studying unique historical processes that they are suspicious of any generalizing concept and of any research of a generalizing nature. Georg Weippert[9] tried to overcome their objections by showing the epistemological basis of the disagreement between historians, on the one hand, and sociologists and other researchers, interested in theory and general results, on the other. The concept of economic style and other similar concepts stress similarities and uniformities. Historians often try to break them down; they even try to demonstrate that these concepts are absurd, by pointing to exceptions and contradictions. This must be regarded as

[8] Hans Ritschl, *Theoretische Volkswirtschaftslehre,* Vol. I (Tübingen, 1947), pp. 110 ff.

[9] "Zum Begriff des Wirtschaftsstiles" in *Schmollers Jahrbuch,* 1943, Vol. LXVII, pp. 440, 441. Weippert operates with the distinction of *"personaler," "objectiver,"* and *"objectivierter" Geist.*

an error. It cannot be doubted that the concept of economic style and other similar concepts criticized by historians mirror a unity of form which is real and characteristic of the objectifications of the human *Geist* which come into existence during certain periods.[10] The criticism of the historians is predicated on the tacit assumption that a generalizing concept, such as "economic style" or "economic system," can be correctly used only if all the data can be subsumed under the heading in question. But this is a logically unwarrantable demand. It is characteristic of the concept of economic style that it takes exceptions for granted.[11] Exceptions and contradictions—the impossibility of subsuming all facts under certain general concepts—do not prove that such general concepts are untenable nor, in our particular case, that the concept of style must be one of abstract logic. When one can prove that the greater number of cases of a particular phenomenon show uniformities, and especially unity of form, one can make such unity of form the subject of research, and one is entitled to frame generalizing concepts as tools for that end. Incidentally, one can speak of a set of institutions as the dominant pattern and disregard statistical measurement if certain manifestations [actions] of an élite have become very influential, while at the same time the principles of older institutional forms lose their power. So far Weippert!

The style model of type 1 is not simply derived from experience, but is predicated on intimate knowledge of economic reality. Its aim is to mirror economic life as a specific set of economic institutions, economic life in its concreteness. Whatever is properly claimed as a specific characterizing element of the style in question must be, or must have been, essential in the institutional situation mirrored by the model. If, for example, one wants to determine the economic style of medieval economy, one must know the motivation of the men who were active in the economic life of the era. Since the concept of style aims to reflect economic

---

[10] [TRANSLATOR'S NOTE: The reader may find the following explanation helpful. *Geist* is an over-all name covering in German those mental activities which are characteristically human. They include the perception of meanings and abstract ideas, evaluation, dealing with what transcends the individual, and understanding. *Geist* finds its expression especially in creative intelligence. It is in the realm of *Geist* that men are able to comprehend shared meanings of the relations between people and between people and objects, which is a distinctly human characteristic. The human *Geist* can become apparent through manifestations and objectifications. An objectification implies that the result of such mental activity has become embodied in a material object so that the result can be communicated without personal contact.]

[11] [TRANSLATOR'S NOTE: Sombart has shown in relation to his "economic systems" that numerous such exceptions are relics of older patterns or precursors of a coming one, consequently that they are far from disproving the validity of the style concept.]

reality, the student using the concept cannot evade critics who argue that a feature which he considers characteristic of a particular style is not in fact characteristic. He is not entitled to seek refuge behind the claim that the style concept is a theoretical rather than a historical one.[12] In view of the goal, a model of type 1 cannot be arbitrary. In order to master theoretically actual economic life in the present or in the past, we need models which reflect without exception all the essentials of concrete patterns of economic life, and we need as many style models as there are essential differences which we discover. Consequently, it is our task to find in the ever-changing and varying stream of economic life specific forms and specific uniformities, and the concept of economic style is the tool for that end.

The concept of any specific economic style arrived at by economic Gestalt theory is a "real type." Although it is a model, it is not an ideal type in Max Weber's sense. Max Weber[13] used the ideal type as a tool for the diagnosis and identification of individual historical phenomena. He was especially interested in the formulation of concepts, and he distinguished between generic and ideal-typical concepts. Unique historical phenomena can be confronted with the latter kind of concepts, in order to be categorized and understood.[14] The border line between generic and ideal-typical concepts is fluid, as Weber knew. His ideal type is a construct from elements abstracted from concrete reality, elements which within a given period and in certain places are more or less frequent and which in certain times and places may even be absent. These elements are "put together to form a unified conceptual pattern. This involves a one-sided exaggeration (*Steigerung*) of certain aspects of the concrete reality, but is not to be found in it."[15] The historian, when

[12] An example of such a nonpermissible evasion of justified criticism is Karl Bücher's discussion with Georg von Below in the Introduction to the second edition of *Die Entstehung der Volkswirtschaft* (Tübingen, 1898). Bücher did not understand the difference between a model of what is here described as type 1 and a model here described as type 2. His was a model of the former type, and consequently it was subject to that criticism which von Below leveled against it.

[13] "Die Objektivität sozialwissenschaftlicher und sozialpolitischer Erkenntnis," *Archiv für Sozialwissenschaft und Sozialpolitik,* 1904, Vol. XIX, pp. 22 ff.

[14] [TRANSLATOR'S NOTE: Alexander von Schelting in "Die logische Theorie der historischen Kulturwissenschaften von Max Weber und insbesondere sein Begriff des Idealtypus," in *ibid.,* 1921–22, Vol. XLIX, has shown that Max Weber's concept actually includes two heterogeneous categories of generalizing and individualizing concepts, as Talcott Parsons, following von Schelting, puts it in *The Structure of Social Action* (New York, 1937), pp. 604 ff.]

[15] Max Weber, "Die Objektivität," *loc. cit.,* p. 65. [TRANSLATOR'S NOTE: This passage has been transposed by Parsons, *The Structure of Social Action,* p. 603. The translator has adopted Parsons' formulation which is to be found within the quotation marks. Sometimes the meaning of the "ideal type" is clarified by saying that it is something like a "utopia."

using an ideal type, compares it with particular and concrete manifestations of reality; his aim is to discover the extent to which reality deviates from the ideal picture. For example, in studying the conditions in a particular medieval city, he shows to what extent they correspond to the ideal type of a "town economy." Max Weber stressed that for the exploration and presentation of certain subjects the concept of "town economy," if applied with caution, is definitely useful. On the other hand, he warned[16] against confounding theory and history. This confusion might arise if those conceptual pictures were considered standing for the realities of the subject, or if the description of a historical process were forced into a mold which does not fit, or, finally, if such concepts were treated as forces determining historical development. Alexander von Schelting has emphasized that Max Weber did not invent the use of the ideal type; it was widely used by theorists before him. According to von Schelting, Weber's achievement lay in the discovery of its specific logical character.[17] This statement holds true only for the ideal type as a tool of pure theory. For the purpose of dealing with unique historical phenomena, Weber really discovered the ideal-type concept as a new tool of which he strongly advocated the application. But is the ideal type really suitable for that purpose, and does it have advantages over other tools?

In order to answer this question, we must inquire into the significance of one-sided exaggeration (*Steigerung*), a *modus procedendi* which we mentioned as a characteristic of the ideal-typical method. One-sided exaggeration is justified only when one deals with a particular instance, in which the side in question is but weakly developed. But if for methodological reasons one has to exaggerate a certain aspect beyond the degree to which that aspect is commonly represented in the phenomenon under investigation, the ideal type is hardly to be recommended for the elucidation of concrete phenomena. And this is our goal. The historical phenomena which it should comprise do not fit a theoretical frame constructed by deliberate exaggeration. With the help of an ideal type we can undoubtedly ascertain how far reality is removed from the

This is true in so far as both ideal type and utopia are somewhat remote from reality. But a utopia is a thought-construct which stirs to action; it represents an ideal for which some people strive, while an ideal type is devoid of implications for social action and is nothing but a scientific tool. Walter Eucken has pointed out that ideal types are not, like genuine utopias, contrasted with existing conditions but are "got from the actual economic world and [serve to] help us understand it." *Foundations of Economics* (Chicago, 1951), p. 173.]

[16] Weber, "Die Objektivität," *loc. cit.,* p. 69.

[17] Von Schelting, "Die logische Theorie," *loc. cit.,* pp. 623, 624.

ideal picture, as Max Weber suggested. Or, to put it differently and by way of an example, if "town economy" is an ideal type, there is, in reality, no town economy; there are only institutional situations approaching that ideal type. Max Weber saw this clearly and therefore identified the ideal type with a "utopia"; but this identification does not establish its superiority as a tool for the historian, and especially for the economic historian. The advantage may lie in the greater ease with which an ideal type can be constructed: arbitrary elements can be used for building-stones instead of elements that are derived from empirical material through a process of painstaking investigation. Instead of aiming at the total situation, one searches for "interesting" elements. However, this argument should not be decisive. Alexander von Schelting characterized an ideal type as the mental perfection of what in reality exists only in tendency. In his opinion, the social scientist builds ideal types in order to obtain fixed points of reference in the perpetual flow of history.[18] Is it a good idea to use a "utopia" as a fixed point of reference? It seems to me that a "real type" would do much better service; for a "real type" originates in the mental process of separating recurring social phenomena from their unique particulars or, if you prefer, of cleansing those phenomena of their unique features. Thereby one avoids the pitfall anticipated by Max Weber of using ideal types as molds into which to force historiography. Actually, many authors have succumbed to that danger. This discussion has been presented to make it clear beyond doubt that the concept of economic style does *not* permit any one-sided ideal-typical exaggerations.

In devising a real type, such as economic style, just as in constructing an ideal type, the student puts together dispersed and often hidden individual phenomena. By putting them together they are made clear, and the tool "economic style" is sharpened. But the spirit behind the procedure that is used in elaborating a real type is distinctly different from that behind the procedure used to construct an ideal type. In the former case there is no one-sided exaggeration, but a painstaking analysis of the concrete reality; the analysis aims to find causal elements essential for the particular style whose model must be elaborated.

Elements *not uniformly* present in reality are considered only if they are not rare exceptions. Rare phenomena can be disregarded by the designer of a real type: they do not represent essentials. The designer of an ideal type, in contrast, may not be able to follow that procedure. He

---

[18] Von Schelting, "Die logische Theorie," *loc. cit.*, pp. 711, 719.

may have to exaggerate rare phenomena, because, from his point of view, they are essential for his construct.

At this point it becomes necessary to discuss whether or not an ideal type reflects the essentials of a historical reality; it depends on the insight of the scholar who designed the particular ideal type rather than on the logical character of the ideal type itself. In view of what actually may be embodied in those concepts, Max Weber went too far, of course, when he denied that the essentials of a historical reality are reflected in an ideal type. Obviously, individual "historical" phenomena are not selected at random; this would make no sense. The designer of an ideal type certainly selects phenomena essential to the Gestalt of a total "historical" situation. It seems to me that this procedure is necessary if one really intends to characterize individual "historical" phenomena with the aid of ideal-typical concepts.

Sombart,[19] for one, used the procedure in this way, and even the exponents of pure theory do not share Max Weber's reluctance to consider ideal types as reflecting the essentials of phenomena.[20] These authors frequently aim to reflect the essentials, and other elements of economic reality, in their concepts and theorems. To quote Schumpeter:[21] "No doubt, our picture is only a schema. But it is a schema which is linked to reality by an unbroken analytical chain. This analysis has selected what seems to be essential of the economic process while it has left out what is neither a causal factor nor essential. Therefore, we are entitled to expect that it reflects all the characteristic features of economic life."

To be sure, Max Weber himself at times approached this point of view.[22] While he rejected the proposition that the ideal type reflects the essence of a historical phenomenon, he claimed that it presents basic ideas embodied in cultural phenomena. While discussing the possibility of an ideal type of capitalistic culture, he made what amounts to essentially the following statement: It is certain that numerous ideal types (utopias) can be designed that are all different and yet may all claim

---

[19] *Synopsis,* pp. 653 ff.

[20] [TRANSLATOR'S NOTE: Spiethoff seems to touch here upon a problem which has been discussed in America by A. N. Whitehead and Morris R. Cohen, by the former under the head of "fallacy of misplaced concreteness"; by the latter under the label of "reification" of theoretical systems.]

[21] *Theorie der Wirtschaftlichen Entwicklung* (2nd ed., München, 1926), p. 77. [TRANSLATOR'S NOTE: The passage is to be found in Ch. 1, Appendix, which has not been included in the English edition; see *The Theory of Economic Development* (Cambridge, Mass., 1934), Preface, p. xii.]

[22] "Die Objektivität," p. 66.

to represent the idea of capitalistic culture. All those claims may be justified in the sense that each utopia contains certain existing characteristics of our culture, which it combines in an ideal picture. The phenomena which interest us derive that interest (on which rests their importance for our culture) from very different value attitudes. Just as there are different points of view from which we may regard certain phenomena as important, there are also different principles that can be applied in selecting elements to be embodied in an ideal type.[23] So far the *modus procedendi.* To the question of how the basic ideas of cultural phenomena can be found, Max Weber answered: significant traits, characteristic of an actual culture, are brought together in an ideal picture. For that purpose all traits may be used which interest us because they are related to a value premise.

At this point a decisive difference between an ideal-type and the real-type economic style becomes evident. While there may be numerous ideal types possible to picture the capitalistic way of economic life, there can be only one real type of the capitalistic economic style. There is only one purpose that guides the selection of characteristics to be combined in that real type: completeness of the causal elements. Which those elements are is not a matter to be settled once and for all. They may vary according to the progress of research. But one thing is settled, namely, the point of view from which the elements are selected. To sum up, economic style models of type 1 are not ideal types, they are real types, which aim at reflecting historical reality.[24]

The concept of economic style is not built for the use of [positivistic] historians who wish to picture the events of economic history in their uniqueness. On the other hand, it is not a construct like the deliberately unrealistic models of pure theory. A real type reflects a specific pattern of economic life and embodies its essential properties. The concept of economic "style," type 1, being a product of economic Gestalt theory,

[23] [TRANSLATOR'S NOTE: For the understanding of this passage it might be useful to point to Max Weber's opinion that the actions and achievements of human beings are embodiments of values. Our interest in them is directly determined by their relevance to values. "It is this relevance to values (*Wertbeziehung*) which constitutes the selective organizing principle for the empirical material of the social sciences." (Parsons, *The Structure of Social Action,* pp. 592, 593.)]

[24] This is also Sombart's aim, as indicated before. He embodies it in a concept which he calls "economic system." In designing economic systems he uses the method of abstracting the essential characteristics from historical reality and embodying them in a concept. See *Der moderne Kapitalismus* (1st ed., Leipzig, 1902), p. xxii, and *Schmollers Jahrbuch,* 1920, Vol. XLIV, p. 1033. Sombart calls *Wirtschaftsepoche* the period in which an economic system was actually realized; *Ordnung des Wirtschaftslebens* (Berlin, 1925), p. 30. See also Edgar Salin, "Hochkapitalismus," *Weltwirtschaftliches Archiv,* 1927, Vol. XXV, p. 324.

uses as data characteristic features of a pattern of economic life; in contrast, the "systems" that are concepts in pure theory are logical constellations, and they use data in a different way. In both cases the result is meaningful knowledge. In contrast to the procedure of pure theory, however, the data of a style (the specific properties of the pattern under investigation) cannot be arbitrarily selected, since the style concept belongs in the realm of economic Gestalt theory.

The specific characteristics selected for the determination of a style model of type 1 serve the function of elucidating why that specific pattern of economic life came into existence and persists; they are meant to explain causally the working of a concrete pattern of economic life. For the determination of a style model of type 1 the basic principles of economic Gestalt theory are applicable: first, statements must be as close to reality as possible, so that hypothetical elements and imaginary constructs are excluded; second, selective choice is not permissible, all important elements must be taken into consideration. It does *not* matter whether or not the elements, put together, form a *logically consistent* body of knowledge. The ideal of consistency plays no role in the selection of what appear to be the characteristics of a style. A spirit of realistic accuracy must determine the selection. The combination of those elements in a model will nevertheless appear meaningful when those characteristics go together in reality.

Economic style models of type 1 reflect specific patterns of economic life, what I have called *Arteigenheiten.*[25] The economic style is a generalized model; at the same time it represents a Gestalt. Numerous characteristics are therefore needed to circumscribe its specific nature (*Arteigenheit*) and to distinguish one style from another. Moreover, as mentioned above, these characteristics are meant to lead to a causal explanation; this principle has been taken over from those of my predecessors who designed the economic "stages." The construction of a "style" is similar to the making of a representative replica.[26] As a rule, one delimits discrete species of economic life (*Arteigenheiten*) by observing uniformities and by determining theoretically which of the uniformities are essential, i.e., of a causal nature.[27] Essential uniformities emerge as the results of research; these characteristics are not arbitrarily selected in advance to form the basis for research. Especially, they are not selected to suit a preconceived theoretical system. All uniformities

[25] *Synopsis,* p. 606. *Arteigenheit* connotes a discrete species of phenomena.
[26] *Synopsis,* pp. 637 ff.
[27] For details, see *Synopsis,* pp. 594, 616.

that characterize an economic style are causal except for one characteristic that is descriptive: this refers to the course[28] which economic life typically takes (stationary or progressive or cyclical).

Characteristics are found through observation, through deduction, and through the search for possible causes. Thence one arrives at a specific style model by the separation of elements and causal analysis practiced in economic Gestalt theory.[29] The specific pattern of economic life is studied as closely and in as much detail as possible to find a maximum of uniformities and causal relationships. But the uniformities that are derivative are later eliminated. If a uniformity is derived (that is, reducible to another uniformity), it is not the ultimate causal factor in the institutional complex under investigation. On the other hand, if the investigation leads again and again to the same primary uniformities, the latter presumably are causal characteristics.

The search for causes uses special methods if the object of research is a particular aspect or a part of a total situation. Then the scholar starts from a meaningful conception which embodies his preliminary impressions of the interplay of the pertinent phenomena, their causal relations, and the essentials determining the Gestalt of the total situation.[30] He will aim at a minimum of characteristics, and for this purpose he will preferably select those which can be proved to be the causes of others. This method is different from that once applied by the designers of economic "stages." They relied on one typical property to characterize a "stage," which criterion was the starting point of elaborate description. In this description they did not aim at a minimum of distinguishing traits, but they presented as many as possible. In my method the presentation of the characteristic features of a "style" is always open to improvement. On the basis of new observations the number of characteristic features may be increased; but it may also be decreased through improved analysis.

The economist who starts out to design an economic style model of type 1 may be confronted with a lack of the kind of information he needs, because no historian has yet provided this material. In historical descriptions and analyses just the kind of things that are essential for his purpose may be lacking. The theorist who uses historical descriptions always has difficulty in finding the answer to his very special ques-

[28] *Schmollers Jahrbuch,* 1932, Vol. LVI, p. 917.

[29] *Synopsis,* p. 595.

[30] [TRANSLATOR'S NOTE: See the very similar description of sociological procedure by Robert Angell in Social Science Research Council Bulletin 53 (New York, 1945), p. 179.]

tions. On the other hand, as must be stressed once more, to determine an economic style model of type 1, characteristics cannot be selected in advance of a knowledge of empirical material. This material may be supplied by historical studies. History is therefore charged with new and very important tasks; and it comes to depend on the co-operation of economic theorists whose questions the historian is expected to answer. Scholars who wish to work on style problems must be familiar with economic theory as well as with historical method. A scholar like Werner Sombart was eminently fitted to determine style characteristics after he had completed the second edition of his monumental work on *Der moderne Kapitalismus.* Similarly qualified were the earlier theorists of economic "stages," who, for their time, were very capable in dealing with past and present economic life. Recently H. Bechtel and A. Müller-Armack have worked in the field.

Before leaving the discussion of economic styles of type 1, elaborated by economic Gestalt theory for the purpose of reflecting economic reality, a word must be said about their logical character.[31] An example may serve for that purpose: "the medieval town economy of Nürnberg" is an individualizing concept and therefore *strictly historical* ("strictly historical" meaning that the concept covers a unique case only). In contrast, the concepts of "the ancient town economy" or "the medieval town economy" are generalizing concepts of a "historical" character. They are "historical" in spite of their generalizing nature because the distinguishing complex pertains only to a limited number of individual cases. "Town economy," pure and simple, is a generic term with respect to "ancient town economy" and "medieval town economy," being at the same time also a generalizing concept of historical character. But, as can readily be seen, the historical element progressively vanishes. Generalizing concepts of a historical character can be exaggerated and made into ideal types if the scholar wants to do so, but in that case they cease to be historical concepts. If a scholar formulates generalizing concepts by using the ideal-typical principle of exaggeration, he should make clear beyond doubt that he works with ideal-typical and not with real-typical models. If we speak without reservation of the economic style of "the town economy," we use a generalizing concept of historical char-

[31] Heinrich Rickert, *Die Grenzen der naturwissenschaftlichen Begriffsbildung* (5th ed., Tübingen, 1929) pp. 438 ff; Weber, "Die Objektivität," *loc. cit.,* pp. 64 ff; von Schelting, "Die logische Theorie," *loc. cit.,* pp. 701 ff; Bernhard Pfister, *Die Entwicklung zum Idealtyp* (Tübingen, 1928), *passim* (this book is unduly neglected); Georg Weippert, "Die idealtypische Sinn- und Wesenserfassung und die Denkgebilde der formalen Theorie," *Zeitschr. f. die ges. Staatswiss.,* 1939–40, Vol. C, pp. 257 ff.

acter. Designed by real-typical methods, it is meant to serve as a tool of economic Gestalt theory. If it were to undergo an ideal-typical exaggeration, it would cease to be a real type, a concept of economic Gestalt theory.

IV

Style Model of Type 2. Style models of pure theory, which are obtained by the quite permissible procedure of abstracting from concrete reality, may be designed for heuristic purposes. They are the kind of models envisaged by Ritschl,[32] useful in elucidating style models of type 1. From a style model reflecting a historical reality the student derives a more abstract model representing a constellation of data which is logically deducible from certain premises. A style model of type 2 represents "historical" pure theory, in contrast to style models of type 1, which belong to the realm of "historical" economic Gestalt theory. Heuristic style models are very important and even indispensable for the scholar who works with style models of type 1. The most important example of a style model of type 2 is the classical style model of the capitalistic economy, specifically in Ricardo's conception.

Style Model of Type 3. One can, of course, design style models by arbitrarily combining elements for the sake of pure mental experiment. Such models can be compared with geometrical figures; they belong in the realm of abstract logic. Helmut Arndt,[33] who suggests that economic theory should investigate all conceivable patterns of economic life, regardless of whether they ever have been or will be realized, would have to use models of this kind. There is no serious objection to his proposal to investigate all possible uniformities in economic life (although it is hardly feasible), nor can there be any objection to the use of tools of that character.

Models of type 2 and 3 have in common that they belong in systems of pure theory.

Style Model of Type 4. Such models may serve to elucidate the possibilities and also the dangers of a desired set of economic institutions. Until recently, the desired socialist economy of the future has not been subjected to a style analysis. Such an analysis is possible by methods of pure theory as well as by economic Gestalt theory. Socialist economists have usually spent their energy on exposing and criticizing the

---

32 Ritschl, *Theoretische Volkswirtschaftslehre,* Vol. I, pp. 110 ff.

33 *Über die Voraussetzungen des Marktautomatismus, Gedanken über die Möglichkeit einer krisenfreien Weltwirtschaft* (Heidelberg, 1947), pp. 300 ff.

capitalist style. The discussion took a turn for the better when Ludwig von Mises published his critical appraisal of socialism.[34] Recent works by Joseph Schumpeter[35] and Alfred Weber[36] (who take a more positive attitude toward socialism) are masterpieces of this important kind of investigation. Because of the present trend toward socialism, such research has become of the greatest political importance and urgency; the more so since other economic conceptions are advanced at the same time, like a new liberalism by Walter Lippmann[37] and Wilhelm Röpke.[38] Arndt's previously cited book belongs to the same type of literature.

In all these cases the style model under investigation reflects a possible and desired reality, not a reality which was or is in being. But the style model used is *not* an arbitrary construct without connection with reality. This is what distinguishes the style model of type 4 from that of type 3. That it is not designed for heuristic purposes distinguishes it from models of type 2. The model of type 4 aims to reflect a coming style, considered capable of existence and desired for certain reasons. This gives the model its specific character and its flavor of nearness to reality, even though it is a reality not yet achieved. Models of type 4 are tools for research on political possibilities, a field in which economists will have to take an interest.

Of course, a desired economic situation can be investigated also with the help of models of type 2—models designed and analyzed with the methods of pure theory. Heinrich Dietzel[39] has pointed out that the Physiocrats and the early English classical economists could not adopt any method except that of deduction. An economic system based on competition was nonexistent apart from the imagination of classical economists, and its working could therefore be determined only by deduction from certain premises. Thus early economists presented what one might call a "hypothetical" style model of type 4, using the methods of pure theory. Their *modus procedendi* contrasts with that used by Schumpeter and Alfred Weber, who elaborated what might be called a "realistic" style model of type 4, by methods of economic Gestalt theory.

---

34 Ludwig von Mises, "Die Wirtschaftsrechnung im sozialistischen Gemeinwesen," *Archiv für Sozialwissenschaft und Sozialpolitik,* 1920–21, Vol. XLVII, pp. 86 ff; *Die Gemeinwirtschaft, Untersuchungen über den Sozialismus* (Jena, 1922).

35 *Capitalism, Socialism and Democracy* (New York and London, 1942).

36 *Freier Sozialismus, ein Aktionsprogram* (Heidelberg, 1946).

37 *An Inquiry into the Principles of Good Society* (Boston, 1937).

38 *Civitas humana* (Zürich, 1944).

39 Heinrich Dietzel, *Theoretische Sozialökonomik* (Leipzig, 1895), p. 104.

Georg Weippert[40] stresses correctly that a "possibility" which has been proved in a mental experiment (ideal possibility) is not the same as a corresponding possibility in actuality (real possibility).[41] In order to determine whether an economic style which has been recognized as "possible" by mental experiment is also possible in reality, additional research is necessary. One must find out whether the requisite conditions of the proposed style are in existence, and one should know which conditions must be created first, by political means, for instance. Only a far-reaching and penetrating analysis of a historically given situation can determine whether or not a given possibility is real. It is a matter of economic theory to determine ideal possibilities; it behooves the statesman to investigate both ideal and real possibilities. The practical realization of an economic pattern whose possibilities are recognized is, of course, not a matter of science; political power, social realities, and psychological reactions must be taken into consideration.[42]

If an all-inclusive economic theory is desired, it must be prepared in such a way as to embrace a number of "historical" style theories belonging to the realm of economic Gestalt theory. In order to attain our goal, we would also need "pure" style theories, paralleling the Gestalt theories. For this reason style models of type 2 are indispensable and style models of type 3 may be a great help. While style models of type 4 do not strictly belong to economic theory, they are supplementary. They may be of a certain importance for elucidating styles that were or are in existence; and, if the envisaged pattern of economic life becomes a reality, the findings would *ipso facto* be part and parcel of an all-embracing general economic theory. In that case scholarly work devoted to the investigation of a style model reflecting a possible institutional reality would be preparatory to genuine economic theory and would have to be adopted.

Some scholars have objected to style theory because it disregards too many traditional theoretical problems and generally accepted answers, which nevertheless remain indispensable in economic research.[43] My answer is that style theory is important as a separate kind of theory which through its close relation to reality is important not only for research in economic history but also for the formulation of economic policy.

---

40 "Zum Begriff des Wirtschaftsstils," *loc. cit.*, pp. 141, 142.

41 See Nicolai Hartmann, *Möglichkeit und Wirklichkeit* (Berlin, 1938).

42 Incidentally, Weippert doubts if one should use the term "style" for our models of types 3 and 4. I cannot recognize his objections as valid.

43 Carl Brinkmann, *Wirtschaftstheorie* (Göttingen, 1948), p. 20.

27

Introduction to François Simiand

By JELLE C. RIEMERSMA

François Simiand in his methodological writings opposed the strongly deductive approach of theoretical economists, and in this respect he shared a major preoccupation with the German adherents to a *geisteswissenschaftliche Methode.* But here the similarity ends. A comparison between Spiethoff's and Simiand's writings will reveal a basic contrast. Spiethoff, like his precursors Sombart and Weber, tended to regard patterns of economic life as unique totalities, occurring at a certain moment of history. While these German authors were strongly concerned with empirical verification and validity, they did not model their investigations of human conduct on the example of the natural sciences. Simiand, on the other hand, continued the tradition of French positivism in which the facts of human history are regarded as similar, epistemologically speaking, to the facts of the natural sciences. In the second place and in close connection with this first postulate, Simiand analyzed concrete historical situations into abstract elements. He was not interested in the "wholeness" of a historical pattern, which the German school had expressed by the term *Ganzheiten.* From his positivist viewpoint, particular events or unique phenomena were outside the boundaries of science. Consequently, his method had no definite place for unique concepts comparable to Spiethoff's "styles" or to Sombart's "systems."[1]

How did the French positivists and, in particular, the Durkheim school, to which Simiand belonged, propose to attain objectivity in the social sciences? Their object of study was formulated in terms which remind one of the concept of "culture" in modern anthropology. According to Halbwachs: "What makes scientific results objective is that

---

[1] In dealing with human history he reduced unique events to a concurrence of causal chains or laws, or he regarded them as a residue of unexplained phenomena which would be reduced in the further advance of science. Cf. François Simiand, "La causalité en histoire," *Bulletin de la Société française de philosophie,* 1906, VI, 249–50.

they appear independent of our own action and spontaneous thought. They present regularities of coexistence and succession which we have no power to change. . . . In the domain of social facts, therefore, everything is objective that comes to us from society: legal rules, religious dogmas, forms of property, exchange procedures, and the like. This complex is distinct from my individual will, and it can be isolated from my will by a process of abstraction. In this way it is possible to arrive at social facts."[2] As is evident from this passage, the observer or student of human conduct is here placed entirely outside the human situation which he studies. In contrast, the method called *Verstehen,* in German social science, implies a certain involvement of the observer in the situation.

For practical purposes, it is important to realize that the followers of Émile Durkheim engaged in the study of social phenomena by splitting a total pattern or situation into separate elements which they called "indices." The reason behind this procedure is that a social science following the example of physics must necessarily pay great attention to exact comparison and measurement; and measurement is possible only if specific elements are singled out from a total pattern or situation.[3] Outstanding examples of this analytical approach are Durkheim's study of suicide and Simiand's study of wage fluctuations. These works begin with a very careful elaboration of definitions in relation to the problem to be explained; rigorous definitions serve as the starting point for quantitative measurements or comparisons. To give a scientific interpretation based on empirical data, one must, "in the words of Descartes, [find] the way in which they are scientific, that is to say, . . . discover in them some objective element that allows an exact determination."[4]

The isolating empiricism of the French positivists was in constant danger of overemphasizing the explicit and measurable phenomena in society and consequently of overlooking less accessible but equally important facts. Durkheim attempted to guard himself from this pitfall by regarding the explicit phenomena merely as manifestations of underlying social realities; he drew conclusions about the real determinants of social change only after a great many empirical variables had been studied. Thus, in *The Division of Labor in Society* (1893), legal trans-

[2] Maurice Halbwachs, "La méthodologie de François Simiand. Un empirisme rationaliste," *Revue philosophique de la France et de l'étranger,* 1936, CXXI, 281–319, esp. p. 285.

[3] Émile Durkheim, *The Division of Labor in Society,* translated by George Simpson (Glencoe, Ill., 1949), p. 36.

[4] *Ibid.,* p. 36.

formations were used as an "index" for more basic changes in society, particularly changes in social solidarity. None of the separate variables could by itself provide conclusive evidence. Only by studying the total complex of social variables, according to Durkheim's principles, was it possible to give the exact explanation of a social phenomenon. Simiand's empirical work shows that he used the same cautious approach.

Simiand's interests ranged from problems of methodology—he had considerable philosophical schooling—to statistics, economics, and sociology. His main work in economic history is a voluminous study of wage fluctuations, particularly of the long waves occurring in France after the Revolution. This study found its starting point in his dissertation, dealing with the wages of coal miners (1904). It was continued until the appearance of the three volumes of *Le salaire* (1932). The work surveys a tremendous number of economic and other social facts for the purpose of getting an insight into the causes of increasing and decreasing wages.

In the Preface, Simiand stated: "The method which I have attempted to apply here upon the subject matter of economics, simply consists of the essentials of the method which has resulted in the present successes of the natural sciences, that is: the experimental method."[5] The use of the word "essentials" in this sentence suggests that Simiand did not adopt the method of the natural sciences in its entirety. The term "experimental method" in his work acquired a particular meaning. Obviously, the study of wages could not be made in a laboratory under carefully controlled conditions. To Simiand the "experimental method" meant simply the use of data derived from historical documents in a systematic way, according to explicit, one might almost say mechanical, procedures. Rigorous definitions of wages, prices, industrial concentration, and other variables were followed by masses of quantitative data; their changes in time were subjected to statistical analysis. By correlation studies the general and immediate determinants of the central variable, namely, "wages," were separated from the other and more remote determinants. The procedure of elimination was analogous to, but not identical with, experimentation in the physical sciences.

Simiand was not contented with an explanation unless he had tried out a sufficient number of possible alternatives to show that his conclusion was unavoidable in the light of the evidence. He thought that if this stage in the investigation had been reached, all observed correlations would be deducible from a small number of general propositions.

---

[5] François Simiand, *Le salaire* (2 vols., Paris, Alcan, 1932); cf. Vol. I, p. x.

Thus Simiand was seeking a theory which had not only empirical validity but also logical unity and coherence. Robert Marjolin has summarized the matter as follows: "Simiand is not content to be merely a historian; he maintains that the contingent relationships which he has succeeded in establishing by means of statistical analysis lead on to a system of universal and necessary relationships. Not only does he establish the necessity and universality of each proposition, but he goes further and aims at conferring these attributes upon the system itself; he aspires to bring together, within a single causal nexus, the various observable series of causal relationships. Hence a monism which is not without certain difficulties."[6]

The difficulties or limitations of this monism are twofold. In the first place, Simiand was compelled to recognize at certain points of his works the influence of historical accidents or intrusions which were not explained by his theory but remained exogenous. His causal analysis showed, for instance, a decisive influence on the price level from the side of the money supply. (The price level, in turn, was shown to be a decisive factor in wage fluctuations.) Now the money supply depended on occurrences which could not be characterized otherwise than as sudden intrusions or "releasing factors"—for instance, the discovery of new gold mines or the issue of fiduciary money by the state in case of war.[7]

A second and most important factor, comprising some "antécédents immédiats et réguliers" in the rise and fall of wages, was the psychological behavior of the workers and the employers. In the course of his interpretation of wage fluctuations, Simiand postulated a type of *homo oeconomicus.* He discovered the interesting fact that economic conduct was determined not so much by real rewards as by the monetary expression of these rewards. Important also was the tendency of wage earners to keep their daily compensations, in money terms, on a constant level.[8] In important aspects, Simiand's *homo oeconomicus* differed from the rational agent of classical theory. The bundle of tendencies which Simiand postulated in his "economic man" was more than a combination of tendencies to maximize value and to minimize effort. Moreover, this type was not deduced from general psychological assumptions but was derived from a methodical analysis of a great mass of observations.

---

[6] Robert Marjolin, "François Simiand's Theory of Economic Progress," *Rev. Econ. Stat.,* 1937–38, V, 159–71, esp. p. 159.

[7] Simiand, *Le Salaire,* Vol. II, 524–27.

[8] *Ibid.,* Vol. II, 496–97, 500–505.

Simiand carefully distinguished between the psychological characteristics of laborers and those of employers; instead of making psychological tendencies universal, he pointed to their historical, society-bound character. "This *homo oeconomicus,* derived from our objective scrutiny of the facts, appears to us in the first place as a result of economic evolution. . . . The concept describes not a spontaneous drive of individuals in general, the same in all times and all places, but a social reality formed by the facts and elements of a particular society under particular conditions."[9]

In Simiand's empirical work quantitative measurement serves as the foundation for all conclusions. Yet, in the final analysis, the empirical materials are interpreted by means of psychological determinants and historical events. Where Simiand speaks of "social realities," he introduces, in accordance with the Durkheim tradition, certain configurations of customs, institutions, and religious beliefs which are qualitatively rather than quantitatively distinct. He approaches the "system" or "style" concept, or even the *Wirtschaftsgeist* utilized by Sombart to characterize periods in economic history. It is true that the German authors devoted relatively little attention to statistical measurement and analysis and that they were concerned with patterns rather than trends. But, in spite of the different terminology and technique, Simiand's methods and conclusions are ultimately anchored in social and historical realities similar to the ones conceptualized by the German school.

To sum up, Simiand's studies introduced, at crucial points, particular events or psychological and cultural determinants. The strongly naturalistic approach which Simiand employed needed supplementation by exogenous factors which were not themselves open to quantitative research and interpretation. The study of such factors, the primary concern of historical study as traditionally conceived, did not become superfluous. The main effect of Simiand's work was to make historians more aware of the possibilities of statistical research.[10] The study of French prices and wages, particularly in the works of Labrousse, Lefebvre, and Chabert, can be regarded as a continuation of Simiand's life work.

[9] *Ibid.,* Vol. II, p. 500.

[10] Marc Bloch, "Le salaire et les fluctuations économiques à la longue période," *Revue historique,* 1934, CLXIII, 1–31; esp. p. 31.

28

*Causal Interpretation and Historical Research**

By FRANÇOIS SIMIAND

Editors' Foreword

This discussion of the problems of cause and effect in history begins with an indication of certain unscientific habits of thought in traditional historiography. Simiand then gives a number of positive precepts of historical method. In an ensuing debate the historian Cantecor discusses the merits of Simiand's approach.

J. C. Riemersma is responsible for the translation.

I

It would be in order, at the present moment, to get rid of certain mental habits which deserve our condemnation. Borrowing Bacon's metaphor, they may be called "the idols of the historical tribe." Without delay we should fight these habits; the following may serve as examples:

1. "The political idol" is the predominant study of the facts of war and politics. As a result of the perpetual preoccupation with political history, historians ascribe too much importance to this category of events, and, since accident and contingency are perhaps more important here than elsewhere, their studying them exclusively retards the rise of a truly scientific attitude. "The political idol" obstructs the systematic elimination of contingent influences; regularities and laws seem inconceivable or difficult to attain. Political facts should not be ignored, but they should be removed from the altogether unjustified position of

---

* Passages from two separate papers:

1. "Méthode historique et science sociale," *Revue de synthèse historique,* 1903, VI, 154–57.

2. "La causalité en histoire," *Bulletin de la Société française de philosophie,* 1906, VI, 246–52, 262–72.

3. *Ibid.,* pp. 279, 282–83.

Simiand's few footnotes have been omitted. The translator has added a number of explanatory notes.

eminence which they maintain even in other branches of historical study.

2. "The individual idol" is the deeply rooted habit of regarding history as a history of *individual persons,* not as a study of *facts.* Thereby one is customarily led to arrange and assemble research data in connection with a particular person, not in connection with an institution, social phenomenon, or relationship. Suppose a certain Pontchartrain has the good fortune of being, first, councilor of the Parliament of Paris and then successively president of the Parliament of Brittany, intendant, comptroller-general, state secretary of the navy, director of academies, and chancellor of France. The custom is to study Pontchartrain *and* the Parliament of Paris, Pontchartrain *and* the provincial Parliaments, Pontchartrain *and* local administration, Pontchartrain *and* financial affairs, *and* the navy, *and* literature, *and* the church. None of those one-sided investigations, without direct reference to institutions, without adequate setting, and without distinctions imposed by the nature of things, will lead to a full and useful knowledge about any of the considered institutions, every one of which is more significant than the whole personality of Pontchartrain. Even in dealing with a man like Colbert it is not certain whether the biographical and individual approach is the best and the most scientific. Why not, in principle, prohibit such institutional studies, occasioned by a secondary person; why not demand the study of the institutions themselves? And, finally, why not eliminate altogether, at least from scientific history, those researches devoted to nothing but the biography of some remote and insignificant cousin of a great man? Let us dispatch those studies to the field of anecdotic history and the historical novel, where they may join the "case of the necklace" and all the "families of Napoleon"—as long, at least, as we do not have adequate studies about the state of industry and agriculture in the time of Turgot and know next to nothing about French economic life during the Revolution and the Empire. We must sacrifice one kind of work or the other; there is not enough time and personnel to do both.

3. "The chronological idol" is the habit of losing oneself in the search for origins and in investigations of local or temporal peculiarities rather than studying and understanding first the "typical" or normal phenomena in a society or epoch. Instead, historians should follow Ashley, for instance, who in his study of the manorial system began by investigating its fully developed form; this "type" could be isolated and

defined best in the central and southern counties of England in the twelfth century. Only *then* did Ashley go back to the origins which might explain the system, and afterward he extended his study to the less clear forms in other counties.

"The chronological idol" causes all periods to be regarded as equally significant; history is considered an uninterrupted scroll, each segment of which has an equal claim to attention. Thus the historian fails to observe that one period is more characteristic and more important than another; he does not see that certain "crucial" phenomena merit deeper study, while the repetitions of a known type of phenomenon are uninteresting and a rather sterile ground for further research. To sum up, this "idol" consists in regarding all facts and all moments as equally worthy of attention and as susceptible to one and the same kind of study.

There is perhaps no criticism more likely to shock traditional historical scholarship. We must insist, however, because the point of method is of cardinal importance. And we must show that, without knowing it and consequently with many errors, traditional historiography has already accepted our criticism and constantly applies it. Why is it that present-day historiography proceeds less confidently than that of the last century, if not because the historian now feels it is necessary to know what came afterward before he can understand what came earlier, appreciate its importance, and discern its elements? Why is it that a good deal of historical work is devoted to the study of the *origins* of an institution or a people, if not because the later state of existence of that institution or people suggests the question to the historian's mind? What is described as an earlier phenomenon is always chosen, sifted, and elucidated with the purpose of making intelligible that which came afterward. We should have a clear conception of this necessary procedure and thus apply it better, more methodically and rigorously, than historians have done so far. Instead of formulating our questions haphazardly and on the spur of the moment, we should prepare the framework with which we approach the past by first establishing a well-defined complex or a "type" which can be found in the period with which we propose to deal. Only after this preparation can we study earlier phenomena that might explain them genetically.[1] Instead of unrolling the tissue of pure chronology indefinitely and me-

[1] A "genetic explanation" consists in fitting a fact or institution in a temporal chain of unique concepts or particulars, a continuous sequence of change from certain "origins."

chanically, we should search for explanatory groupings with an objective coherence. Mere chronological arrangement, as we have seen, is not a genuine organization of the data; this kind of interpretation is to be accepted only in the absence of other possibilities. For the understanding of real relationships, even those of succession, one must know the normal and complete phenomenon before one tries to discover particular variations, exceptional cases, or undifferentiated embryonic stages.[2]

II

I have set myself the task here of outlining a theory of causality in historical phenomena which will be as impersonal and as independent of any specific metaphysical thesis as possible. My aim is to bring out a conception of causality similar to the one which in the natural sciences enters even into the detail of everyday work and which serves to form the very backbone of scientific research. And I readily admit that such an investigation has a practical purpose. It is difficult, I believe, not to be amazed by the enormous mass of historical work that is produced nowadays and the lack therein of truly scientific results. There is no absence of philosophies of history, of general propositions on the explanation of historical phenomena, theses on the role of the individual, on historical determinism, and on the factors of human evolution. What is wanting, however, is a body of precise methodological rules, applicable in the daily practice of interpretation and analysis. I would like to succeed in formulating rules of this kind in connection with the determination of causes.

1. I will take my departure from Bernheim's exposé of the problem in his *Lehrbuch der historischen Methode.* Among recent historians who have dealt with methodology, Bernheim seems to me to have made the clearest and most rigorous statement of the problem. He definitely regards history as a science. He moves away from the conception of history as purely story-telling, from narrative or literary history, as well as from the conception of normative and moralizing history. Like every other science, history aims essentially at explanation.

2. But this explanation has a unique character by the very nature of the subject of historical inquiry. History aims at knowledge of human facts in the past. It is true, Bernheim thinks (and here he speaks contrary to certain historical methodologists who take a more exclusive view), that these facts of the human past can be studied, and quite

[2] End of the passage in *Revue de synthèse historique,* 1903, VI, 154–57.

legitimately, in a way for which the natural sciences serve as the model. In other words, Bernheim agrees that causal relations can be established among those facts, analogous to the causal relations found in the natural sciences; in the one subject matter as well as in the other one can proceed by means of abstraction and isolation, and he therefore justifies the existence of the social sciences. But, Bernheim argues, in dealing with the facts of past human existence, history has quite a different purpose; it searches for the "individual" and "concrete" in those facts and accounts for their concrete succession; the facts are interlinked by their own sequence. Because of this separate purpose, history takes a unique position among the sciences: all the other sciences try to discover the "general." And yet history is not an art, according to Bernheim; it is a science, but a science with a particular method of interpretation.

3. This contrast derives not only from the perhaps greater complexity of historical phenomena or from the greater role played by what is, scientifically speaking, chance or accident. It derives from an essential difference between the kind of causality found in the positive sciences and that which exists in history; the difference results from the fact that the task of history is to study and explain psychological processes. Within a particular, concrete psychological process it is impossible to find the constant forces—analogous to the forces of nature—a combination of which will explain a particular complex. No laws can explain its occurrence. The laws of psychology cannot explain the content of a psychological process any better than the laws of logic can explain the actual content of an argument. The psychology of a man is not the same as his history. The ultimate reason why the one cannot possibly be deduced from the other is not only the intervention of free will but also, more generally, the fact that the same external stimulus may give rise to different psychological reactions. The second time the reaction may be different from what it was the first time; and the difference may be due solely to the fact that there *was* a first time. In psychology, therefore, the same cause does not produce the same effect, and the conception of causality is different from that used in the natural sciences. In the latter the causality principle implies essentially the constant use of the formula: "The same causes produce the same effects." (So far Bernheim's argument.) Before entering upon our criticism we might remark that the last part could be stated more correctly: The principle that "the same causes produce the same effects" cannot be applied in psychology, not only for the reason that similar causes may produce different effects—although even this is quite contrary to our sense of rea-

soning—but also because the same cause never returns in the full concreteness of psychological life.

This is the standpoint to be adopted by a consistent historian if he wants to contrast the well-known kind of causality of science with a separate historical causality. In line with the present inquiry, I must omit a scrutiny and a separate discussion of the metaphysical assumptions upon which Bernheim's argument is based. I must ask only whether this position is tenable for any kind of history that claims to be interpretative and scientific. To answer the question, I will formulate successively two hypotheses, each of which could also stand by itself, pertaining to the nature of the "individual" and the "concrete."

4. (*a*). On the one hand, one may regard the "individual" or "concrete" phenomenon as compounded of simpler elements, as the converging point of separate causal sequences whose coincidence is relatively contingent. The resulting phenomenon is always relatively predictable, if not absolutely. However, this meaning of the "individual" and "concrete" is not unique to the field of psychology; it occurs in that of any other science. That which Bernheim mentions as the characteristic of a psychological reaction, namely, the peculiarity of an effect of a given cause, exists also and almost to the same degree in biology and even in physics. Today my stomach does not react to a certain kind of food in the same way as it did yesterday; and again we remark that the earlier reaction is the very reason why it acts differently the second time. Probably this anatomic and physical "I" has never existed before and will never exist twice in the same state; its existence is momentary. Our earth probably will not have two carboniferous periods.

Xénopol, the historian and methodologist, recognized this objection, and he criticized Bernheim for arbitarily restricting unique phenomena to the field of psychology. But, on the other hand, Xénopol himself was rather arbitrary in his contrast between "sciences of succession," dealing with sequences, and "sciences of repetition." The iron bar which is expanded by heating is certainly, by virtue of my experiment on this earlier day, not identically similar today to the one I had yesterday. Here we have, as in any other field of investigation, an "individual" which is never repeated identically. In physics and chemistry we forget this as a rule, because our minds have in these fields long been accustomed to search only for the general; we are not interested in particulars. In the domain of biology the same evolution becomes more and more complete; it suffices to compare, for instance, the place of teratology in a treatise of Ambroise Paré with the space which the same subject occupies in a modern handbook.[3] Undoubtedly we can conceive of the possibility that a similar mental orientation toward the general will be developed in human affairs. But that does not answer our question.

Our minds are more inclined to investigate the individuality of human beings, or of a particular man, than the individuality of a sheep or an iron bar. We find reasons to do the former, not the latter. It may be a quite legitimate, generally accepted, and enduring curiosity which prompts us to explain a particular "individual" rather than the general elements which it contains; but the question is, by what kind of causal relation can we possibly arrive at an explanation of the individual? I can think of only two possibilities. Either the explanation of the individual is a limiting case, that which remains if, through the combination of various levels of abstraction and known causal relations, the field of the unforeseen has been progressively restricted. Ultimately the method of residues may allow us to interpret these remnants of particularity. Even if the inexplicable can never be reduced to zero, one thinks of it as indefinitely reducible. But in this procedure we evidently are using a kind of causality concept similar to that of the natural sciences, whether the field be psychology, biology or geology. Or the unique phenomenon will be considered in itself; since, theoretically, one single experience suffices to establish a causal link, theoretically I can discover the cause of this unique phenomenon. However, will the established causal relation be of a new kind? I admit that this cause or this complex of causes and conditions has never before been encountered and will never recur in exactly the same fashion. But it is more important to know whether the same phenomenon would be reproduced, supposing that the cause *did* recur. Phenomena of this kind may be unique without being "individual"; our knowledge of them depends on their conceivable recurrence rather than on their actual recurrence. Are we not confronted with this problem in the case of an eclipse or the passage of a comet, each manifestation of which, with all accompanying regularities, would, strictly speaking, be the only one of its kind? We can assert, however, that the same concatenation of causes would necessarily be linked with the same phenomenon, if it ever appeared again. Such a law or statement may be practically useless. It is not even sure that it could be adequately established in the field of

[3] Ambroise Paré (1510–90) became famous as a surgeon in the French army. He wrote a number of works on medicine; in 1573 appeared his book, *Des monstres tant terrestres que marins,* to which Simiand seems to refer. Teratology is the science of monsters and monstrosities.

our subject; but, as long as it is not established, no explanation has been given. Theoretically it is possible. And the resulting explanation is of exactly the same type as the causal relations of the natural sciences.

5(*b*). But one may conceive of the "individual" as not or not entirely reducible to a complexity; one can regard it, at least in certain cases, as a spontaneous and original creation which must be absolutely unforeseeable. Let us observe, first, that, even in this meaning of the word, the "individual" is not necessarily restricted to the field of psychology. Certain philosophies see an element of spontaneity in the organic and even in the inorganic world; and our science does not necessarily have to exclude this possibility. Thus we are able to deal with the problem of human freedom not as a separate issue but as a problem connected with spontaneity in general.

The extent to which spontaneous influences are operative is a metaphysical question which, given the objective of this study, must be left aside. Assuming that there is a spontaneity in "individual" phenomena which a certain body of knowledge attempts to explain, our question is to determine the nature of this explanation. Bernheim tells us it is characteristically regressive, while an explanation by means of the causality principle of the natural sciences would be progressive. Only after a phenomenon has occurred can one gradually try to discover explanatory factors. Once the synthesis has been achieved, the historian may unravel its elements by a procedure of regression; the uniqueness of the phenomenon (which prevents its reproduction at the will of the scientist) prevents the opposite course. But this does not solve the problem. Suppose the observed phenomenon results from an original synthesis or conjunction of separate elements. The elements, whether they are discovered after the fact or before, do not explain their unique combination, since they derive their significance only from the accomplished synthesis. Something similar is said in the classical analysis of free will: the impulse which ultimately gains the upper hand in the struggle of motives does not win because it is the strongest, but it is the strongest because it has won. After a regressive or progressive analysis we still need to know how the factor of spontaneity explains the synthesis for which it is the presupposition. This factor cannot be analyzed, since we would then return to the view that the "individual" is a complexity. I think two possibilities exist. The synthesis or spontaneity may be "explained" in the same sense in which a symphony "explains" or expresses a mood, or a painting "explains" or represents a landscape. One performs in that case no analytical operation that can be reduced to objective rules; one makes use of intuition or inspired choice, at least to a certain extent, and from an objective point of view this is arbitrary. Whether this mental procedure is satisfactory, whether it is a makeshift instead of an ideal—for our purpose it is sufficient to consider whether an explanation of this kind can be called scientific without an intolerable confusion of terms and whether it is not indisputably much closer to art than to science. Thus one either enters the realm of art or one remains in the field of science and objective knowledge; but in the latter case it is obvious that research in the proper sense can explain everything but that small or large element of spontaneity and original synthesis which we assume to exist in the individual. Scientific research must tend to circumscribe the domain of spontaneity in order not to enter it; this domain is segregated from the only true field of science: that in which regular causes are operative.

To sum up: whatever metaphysical position we have assumed, without having to pronounce ourselves in favor of one or of the other, and by attributing to history, in accordance with its own methodologists, the task of increasing our knowledge and interpretations of the individual and concrete aspects of the human past, we have not been able to find the new and appropriate principle of causal explanation which historical methodologists tried to establish. The explanations arrived at by history, even in the domain of the individual, seem to be reducible, in one form or another, to the kind of explanation utilized in the natural sciences; the alternative is an explanation that enters the domain of art or one that cannot exist.[4]

III

1. Precisely because the historical method proposed by the historians themselves seems to us inexact and illogical, while their practice is uncertain and unconscious of its own tendencies, we are faced with the urgent necessity of finding means by which historical study may yield the results of which it is inherently capable. It would be a great help if we could provide historical work with some simple and rigorous precepts which would automatically, as it were, lead to the establishment of causal relations that are truly explanatory. Such are the rules I will try to formulate. To be immediately and generally applicable, these rules must be independent of any fundamental belief about the nature of historical phenomena or even about the nature of historical science.

[4] End of passage in *Bulletin de la Société française de philosophie,* 1906, VI, 246–252.

In other words, these principles must have a purely formal character. I will imply only one single postulate—but the historians will be the last to dispute its validity—namely, that the kind of knowledge sought for is factual and not a priori. If this is agreed on, I think I can reduce the method for the discovery of true causal relations in history to two propositions, followed by two corollaries; all four propositions being of a purely formal kind (A, B, C1, C2).

The first rule I would state as follows:

A. *Define, in general terms, the specific effect* that must be explained. I do not ask, at this point, that the historian should in principle abstain from objects of study that are particular or individual phenomena. But, instead of, as usual, being satisfied with naming this object by a vague generic term accompanied by particulars of time and place or by a completely individual or concrete designation (the Revolution of 1848 in France, the repeal of the Corn Laws in England), the historian should search for a definition which in itself would already represent a scientific analysis. Such a definition, established by successive approximations, by gradual advancement, would focus on the relations to be considered: "the overthrow of a government by a small group of opponents"; "the overthrow of an unpopular government by a small group of opponents who take advantage of this or that factor"; "the abolition of a law which hurts the interests of an economic sector which has this political power, an abolition that benefits that economic category, which may be defined in this way"; and so on.

Thereby the one great merit of the historical spirit, namely, the conception of the facts of the human past as objective and positive realities, encountered always in their particular manifestations, would be preserved. And one would avoid the danger into which at present historians themselves often fall: in advancing to what are called "general" views, they enter into arbitrary abstractions that are too far removed from reality. It must be shown that "generality" and "precision" do not exclude each other, that within a concrete phenomenon elements of a more general character may be isolated, and that one arrives at a correct definition and adequate knowledge of it only through such a procedure. It is not necessary, in my opinion, to renounce from the outset any interest in the characteristics of time and place. Phenomena should, however, no longer be defined by those characteristics alone; the obligation to define phenomena in another way would reduce local and temporal characteristics to their true meaning and importance. This importance resembles that which the indication of the place and sometimes the date has in the case of a mineralogical sample or of a plant or animal specimen.

3. The second rule would require a clear distinction between cause and condition. I would formulate it thus:

B. *Among the various antecedents of a phenomenon, the one which is linked with it by the most general relation is the cause.*

The confusion of causes and conditions is not the prerogative of history. Even a logician like Mill has not made a clear-cut distinction. Reconsidering the example given by Mill (a stone thrown into the water sinks to the bottom), one observes that he can name any antecedent whatever as a cause or as a condition, for the simple reason that he does not explicitly state precisely which phenomenon he is studying (our rule A): "the fall of a body," "the fall of a body in a liquid," and so on. If this is done, if the phenomenon is specified, then one of its antecedents can be linked with it by a more general relation than any other antecedent; and this one will be the cause of the phenomenon. In history, where, as we have seen, the considered phenomena are as a rule very complex and badly defined and where a plurality of antecedents can be linked with the same fact, the situation is even worse than in other sciences. Either the historian chooses a cause among the antecedents in an entirely arbitrary fashion, or he forgets the distinction between cause and condition altogether. This situation most directly obstructs the discovery of causal regularities. I believe that the rule I indicated suffices to avoid any arbitrariness and vagueness in distinguishing between cause and condition. In one of Seignobos's works on method the following passage is characteristic: "When by setting fire to a powder charge, someone explodes a massive rock [it is possible to say that] the rock, the powder, and the fire all are equally to be considered as causes and conditions." In another context I have paralleled this statement with Seignobos's explanation of the Revolution of 1848 as an "accident." "The Revolution of 1848 which led to the practice of universal suffrage, which prepared the national unity of Central Europe, and which led to the organization of the Socialist and Catholic parties was the work of some democratic agitators who were helped by Louis-Philippe's lack of courage." Let us apply our rule: If we consider the explosion as the central phenomenon of the blowing-up of the rock (and not another phenomenon, such as the way in which the stone is fractured or the effects of the explosion), then we easily perceive that the antecedent "rock" is only by a very particular relation linked to the consequent "explosion." Explosions occur in the absence of rocks, and vice versa; similarly, not every fire is connected with an explosion, and, conversely, there are explosions which are independent of heating by fire: some are produced by a shock. Even the powder is not the most general determinant of the explosion, since it is possible to find other kinds of explosive. Advancing in this way, we finally discover that "the sudden expansion of gases" is the antecedent linked to the phenomenon "explosion" by the most general relationship. Thereby we arrive at a cause in the proper sense, namely, the expansive force of gases. It is clearly impossible, to take the other case, to connect the phenomenon "revolution" with the presence of small groups of agitators, as a causal factor, even when their presence coincides with the discouragement of a king. In other places and periods the same combination of circumstances has not led to a revolution, and, conversely, revolutions have occurred in the absence of these antecedents. Without great difficulty we recognize also that the coming of universal suffrage or, more generally, a change in voting rights, the unification of national states, and so on, are not connected by a general proposition to the phenomenon called "revolution," or vice versa.[5] Since these arbitrary and unproved "causes" are inadequate, we must always try to find the particular antecedent which, by a statement more general than any other, can be linked with the phenomenon selected for study; and this phenomenon must be defined with precision.

The distinction can be put in another form: *Conditions are those antecedents which can be replaced by others, while the cause is not, or is least of all, replaceable.* The explosive may be surrounded by massive rock, by wood, earth, or masonry: in all cases the phenomenon "explosion" can occur in the same way. Whether the detonation is effected by a flame, by a shock, or, for certain explosives, by the mechanical displacement of substances, the phenomenon produced will be similar. If, then, a "sudden expansion of gases" occurs in all these cases and cannot be replaced by another phenomenon, this antecedent may properly be called "causal," in preference to those that may have substitutes and that should be called, in any particular case, the conditions. I must im-

[5] A true causal relationship, for Simiand, is a proposition of the type: "if A, then B." He calls A the cause of B if it can be empirically established that the above proposition is *general,* i.e., whenever A is present, B is present also. Moreover, it must be established that, in the absence of A, B does not occur. In other words, the relation between A and B can be converted; whenever B occurs, A is present. This implies the postulate of "causal monism" (Bloch); the same effect B cannot be the outcome of various causes A, A′, A″, and so on. (See, for the conversion of propositions, i.e., the transposition of subject and predicate, W. S. Jevons, *Elementary Lessons in Logic* [London, Macmillan & Co., Ltd., 1946], Lesson X.)

mediately add that the causal character of an antecedent cannot be established in the absolute sense. It is determined by comparison and from a certain point of view. Moreover, the distinction itself between cause and condition is merely relative. A condition is often a cause in the second degree, the cause's cause. That particular aspect of a phenomenon which is the center of attention and the kind of knowledge on which the point of view of the observer depends determine whether one antecedent is to be called "cause" and another "condition," or vice versa. To a medical student an epidemic will seem to be caused by the propagation of a microbe; as conditions he will regard uncleanliness, promiscuity, and bad health, all in turn the results of pauperism. For the sociologist and philanthropist pauperism will be the cause, and the biological factors are conditions. This relativism is very evident in the phenomena dealt with by history, which are not only very complex but ordinarily also badly defined. The more reason to advocate a distinction between cause and condition! This rule is a means of analyzing a phenomenon with regard to specific elements therein and with regard to the points of view from which they can be observed, leading to different kinds of causal relations. Only by using this procedure can one systematically avoid arbitrariness and confusion.

4. This analysis can be made easier by applying two complementary rules, corollaries of the preceding, which we will try to elaborate.

C1. The first rule demands that we would *always make explicit the immediate antecedent.* The reason why one often fails to see causal regularities and ends up with arbitrary or purely accidental causes, or with statements that have no scientific character, is that one overlooks or fails to analyze the many intermediary steps between the phenomenon which serves as an explanation and the phenomenon which has to be explained. This mistake is apparent in several of the examples given earlier. History tends to resemble knowledge of the common-sense variety, which is not, properly speaking, scientific. Certain historical methodologists are the first to admit it; they even accept this aspect of history as a definitive characteristic of the discipline. Historical interpretations resemble common-sense generalizations of the type: "When one catches a cold, one gets a nasal infection." Let us regard it somewhat closer: the scientific inadequacy of such a statement results from the fact that it does not isolate all intermediary stages between antecedent and consequent. Among these intermediaries one could establish well-defined and properly scientific relations (coldness, congestive effects of cold on tissues, on specific tissues, the mucous membranes, resulting in secretions of those membranes, and so on). Something similar could be done with the generalizations with which so-called "interpretative" history is too easily satisfied.

C2. The second corollary leads to the rule: *Always try to establish the kind of explanatory proposition of which the converse is also true.*[6] This means, in final analysis, that the causality principle applies not only in the form "the same causes produce the same effects" but also in the form "the same effect must have the same cause." While the first statement can be deduced from the customary formulation of the principle of causality, namely, that "every phenomenon has a cause," the second cannot. Nevertheless, there are good reasons to make it a legitimate principle; and, in fact, it is at present being used in the natural sciences. For instance, this principle is applied when the chemical composition of the sun is determined by analysis of its spectrum [through a comparison with the known spectra of chemical elements on earth. One infers from the existence of similar effects—similarities between the spectrum of the sun and the spectra of certain elements on earth—to similar causes: the existence of those same elements on the sun]. The use of this principle is justified only if one has arrived at a genuine cause, not just a more or less proximate condition; more especially, it is imperative to isolate as carefully as possible the immediate antecedent. In historical inquiry, at least in its initial stages, this can hardly ever be achieved, and the manipulation of our second rule is a subtle and difficult process. For these reasons I present the requirement of reversibility cautiously, as merely an ideal of perfection. While historical studies should approximate the ideal, they cannot achieve its realization in all cases or in the early stages of investigation. The rule can be shown to rest on an application of the logician's principle of parsimony.[7] In that case it will be valuable in raising useful suggestions, doubts, and questions. For instance, some of the remarks and objections we made earlier have been suggested by it.

5. These four purely formal rules, two principal propositions and two corollaries, seem to me adequate in directing historical research

[6] Thus, according to Simiand, a cause must be a necessary as well as a sufficient reason, so that it is possible to conclude from the effect to the cause as well as from the cause to the effect.

[7] The principle of parsimony in logic (Occam's razor) states that one should not introduce more hypotheses than are necessary. Simiand argues that, if we cannot explain an effect by a single cause but only by a multiplicity of causes, then scientific analysis has not advanced far enough. A redefinition of the effect or a deeper penetration into its causal connections must lead, in his opinion, to the establishment of a single convertible cause-and-effect proposition.

toward a more satisfactory causal analysis. I would like to show briefly how their consistent use would lead to the abandonment of the illusory or inadequate explanations that usually are the final results of historical studies, and how this practice would supply a basis for some methodological precepts which, up to now, have been established in a different way.

(*a*). They will in the first place dispel the common illusion that by telling the story of what happened earlier one somehow *explains* what came afterward; it is often assumed that to some extent a chronological sequence in itself can make successive facts comprehensible. In spite of their denials, and perhaps without suspecting it, historians are constantly trying to make history backward. When at a given moment an institution, class, or family becomes important, the historian tries to discover its origin. This does not mean that he looks for the causes and conditions that would explain its birth, formation, and development. He is usually satisfied with observing that the *Parlement* of Paris, before it was organized in a certain form by Philip the Fair, existed in such and such a form in the reign of Saint Louis, in another form under the early kings of the house of Capet, and so on. He describes how a communal charter was the precursor of other charters and how it was itself established in the wake of certain particular events. He shows that the House of Hohenzollern "had its cradle" in some minute feudal domain, that the *Markgraf* became elector, the elector became king, and so on. When the working classes begin to occupy a significant place in modern life and thought, the historian promptly tries to discover what the workers did in a certain century of the past and is pleased with the discovery that there *already* were strikes in the sixteenth or fourteenth century and that there *already* was a social question. The examples could be multiplied. In what sense do they explain anything? Behind them there is a scientific conception, the idea of evolution: successive facts are not without interconnections. This idea remains sterile, however, because it is being kept altogether vague and also because the historian fails to realize that a succession or evolution explains things only if it is itself seen as dependent on a certain law. Similarly, in the study of crime the antecedents of the criminal—for instance, the qualities of his ancestors and the character of his environment—are meaningless if one does not consciously or unconsciously adhere to some theory about criminal psychology, hereditary influences, or environmental factors. A historian who tries to explain a fact or institution by preceding facts, through a step-by-step ascent toward early forms and origins, only explains things if he is in possession of a valid theory about the sequence or development of institutions. Nowadays, as a result of an inadequate analysis of what he is doing, the historian usually makes no distinction between the simple description of a sequence and a statement about a development. The application of our rules of method would force him to analyze the proposed explanatory factors and would inducc him to formulate these factors in general terms. Then he could differentiate between mere antecedents and genuine causes, and, seeing the uselessness of most investigations in these directions, he would give to chronology and the quest for origins a more limited value.

6(*b*). If our rules were applied, the human individual would not figure as a cause, neither in the form of a person nor in the collective manifestation as in a party. Our first corollary would superficially seem to point in the opposite direction: Do we ever arrive at anything else but human individuals as immediate antecedents? Actually, as our rules will show, the individual is never the immediate antecedent in the proper sense of the term. When a law wanted by Peel or Gladstone is passed, these concrete individuals are not the immediate antecedents connected with this legal measure by the most general relation: the same antecedent does not have this result in other cases. Other laws which they want are not passed by the legislature. The most general and precise immediate antecedent is that element in Peel or Gladstone which differentiates the case in which their law is passed from that in which it is unsuccessful. This element, which can be abstracted from the concrete individual as a whole, coincides with the effect when it occurs and is absent when the effect does not occur. In other words, the complete human individual is at most a condition; a certain abstract element of the individual is the immediate antecedent really capable of explaining the effect. When searching for the precise and general antecedent of some phenomenon according to this precept, one will often see, I believe, that the individual person or party merely allows regular and real causes to do their work. Action by individuals effects, at most, the release of a bundle of causal regularities—and even this effect is not necessarily contingent and spontaneous. The individual is often replaceable in this limited role: if this particular person or party had not appeared to release the cause, some other one would in all probability have done the same thing. Thus the "individual" as such is rather unimportant in producing the effect.

7(*c*). The application of our rules also eliminates "imitation" and "fashion" as causal factors, a kind of explanation too often used by historians and even by sociologists. Just try to generalize an explanatory proposition of this kind; it is clearly impossible, because one fashion succeeds, another fails; one imitation occurs, while another remains undeveloped. The element "fashion" or "imitation," the same in either case, evidently does not explain the difference between success and failure and cannot therefore be the cause of the phenomenon. Fashion or imitation, once eliminated as causes, may, however, often reappear as conditions.

8(*d*). Our rules would also eliminate human ideas and purposes as causal antecedents. In other words, teleological explanations are excluded. One will admit that imputed or even observed human ideas and purposes cannot by a general relation be linked with the phenomenon to be explained. The idea or purpose may be absent or different in some of the cases; it does not occur as a really immediate antecedent; and the proposition which links it with its effects cannot be converted. At best, ideas and purposes are conditions rather than causes. The rules of excluding any explanations based on human ends and purposes should be made more precise, as follows: (i) *Tendencies* can still be regarded as valid explanations or causes, at least if these tendencies are established objectively, in the way in which other explanatory antecedents are established. (ii) While teleological explanations are excluded, the explanation by *function* is something different. It is often forcefully suggested by the facts and is quite legitimate, particularly in the realm of human and social phenomena. (iii) Teleological explanations, having been banished from the natural sciences as manifestations of anthropomorphic reasoning, would, according to some authors, still be permitted in the realm of human facts because man is the center of those phenomena. One should be careful: we may easily take an anthropomorphic view of human phenomena themselves, assuming that things are as we believe them to be. Thus we "explain" things by our own ideas about them. This anthropomorphic view is bound to disappear, not only in the natural sciences, but also in the social sciences, through the application of our rules.

9(*e*). We will also exclude the explanation by general psychological factors, readily used by historians who advance to so-called "general" considerations. If we demand that causal relations be general and precise and if we try to approximate the condition that their converse should be true, then we perceive that these factors are not the immediate antecedents which in a real sense explain the phenomena under consideration. They may be the cause's causes, conditions linked with the phenomenon by a number of intermediary steps. The sexual drive, for instance, determines the form of marriage in the same way in which the force of gravity determines the circulation of the blood or in the way in which the elasticity of matter determines the movements of the heart. To explain the form of marriage, the circulation of the blood, the movements of the heart, the corresponding sciences no doubt *imply* the existence of those general factors, which are recognized as conditions; but they have not accomplished their task by doing so. Any explanation in the proper sense points to the immediate antecedent of the phenomenon, usually of the same order as the phenomenon itself (for instance, a social phenomenon is to be explained by another social phenomenon).

10. The application of the experimental method has been said to encounter certain obstacles in the domain of social phenomena; I will indicate how our rules suffice to overcome these obstacles. I am thinking particularly of John Stuart Mill's well-known argument that the social sciences would not be able to establish rigorous cause-and-effect propositions. He takes as an example, one will remember, the question of the influence of free trade on the wealth of nations. It seems to me that Mill's difficulties result not so much from the social nature of these phenomena as from their being badly chosen. In any other field where problems could be posed in this way and in similar terms, the same logical doubts would be encountered. Mill's argument could be equally applicable if one asked the question: "Is a vegetarian way of life conducive to health?" Nobody would conclude [from the impossibility of solving this question] that in biology rigorous causal relations could not be established. Mill, instead of taking something as vague and complex as the wealth of nations, should have taken a more precise phenomenon; he should have attempted to find immediate causal connections instead of a distant connection consisting of a series of unanalyzed intermediary steps. Suppose he had proceeded in this way and had posed the problem as follows: Is the system of free trade accompanied by fluctuations in the prices of the particular products that are being exchanged? Then his logical argument would probably be invalidated. [In the case of such a problem], dealing with a specified phenomenon of which the number of immediate antecedents is probably limited, one would find empirical data of sufficient number and quality to allow a negative and even a positive proof of the influence of certain causes. The proof would be as reliable as are the proofs in the natural sciences whose capability of establishing causal relations Mill does not dispute.

11. Our formal rules, which nobody can refuse to try on a priori grounds, have by their application led us to establish all the methodological propositions which are needed in a truly explanatory historical science. Sometimes quite legitimate and fruitful attempts have been made to establish the same propositions in a more direct and appropriate fashion. But I thought it would be in order, as well as useful, to present them here as the consequences of certain minimal hypotheses that are applicable more generally than in history alone. If only for the sake of experiment, one may follow our rules without being forced to choose among the various philosophical and metaphysical theses that are struggling for the possession of this domain. I merely ask the methodical application of these few precepts; I am confident that they would automatically lead to a scientific determination of causes.[8]

III

CANTECOR: The rules which Simiand proposes to us in his conclusions seem to me quite acceptable. I will point out, however, that they are a little too general. As stated, they could be applied to every science of facts. But historical facts surely have characteristics of their own. They therefore require special precautions for their explanation; they present their own kind of difficulties; their interpretation raises various delicate problems. In this meeting we expected to hear an exposition and discussion of precisely those problems, difficulties, and precautions which are connected with the search for *historical* causes. . . .

SIMIAND: . . . If I have not occupied myself with determining particular precepts for the study of history as opposed to the study of the positive sciences, the reason is my fundamental conviction that those particular precepts do not exist. Here I leave aside the technique which is expounded, quite adequately, in existing manuals of methodology. I firmly believe that history, not in the sense of an auxiliary discipline and the grouping of materials, but as an autonomous science complete in itself, has no reason for existence and is bound to disappear: it has no explanatory method of its own.

CANTECOR: Your statements seem to reveal a tendency to reduce history to sociology. Nevertheless, we have here two kinds of study which are essentially different. Reality manifests itself as a system of particular facts. One can undertake to search for the general laws which produce them: this is the work of science. One can also undertake to

[8] End of the passage in *Bulletin de la Société française de philosophie*, 1906, VI, 262–72.

enumerate these facts by themselves, to locate, to characterize and to explain them one by one, and to give an account of their particularities and their singular location in time: this is the work of history. It is true that your purpose is to show how one can explain the particular; but somehow, fascinated by scientific procedures which you would like to transplant to another domain, you go so far as to misjudge the special conditions of this [historical kind of] study. You seem inclined to relate certain categories of events, as a whole and in an approximate way, with known laws of a general character, and you tend to neglect the particular aspect of facts as well as unique circumstances. You do not account for the particular characteristics, and you exclude unique circumstances as causes. On the whole, your conception of history remains vague.

SIMIAND: Whether the application of my precepts of method must lead history in the direction of sociology is a question which experience will answer. It will certainly become apparent that the human facts studied by history are, above all, social facts. But I believe that this postulate is not a priori implied in the observations which I have presented today. You distinguish and contrast two kinds of problems: one belonging to sociology and the other to history. I confess that I do not recognize that distinction. I see, if you wish, static problems dealing with situations and dynamic problems whose purpose it is to interpret changes and evolutions. Both kinds of problems may begin with the observation of phenomena that several situations or several changes have in common. Descending more and more toward the particular, both kinds of problems may ultimately apply to the interpretation of a *single* situation or change. But this creates neither two methods of interpretation nor two different sciences; it only creates two levels or, at most, two directions of interpretation. The central thesis which I maintain is that in both kinds one uses the same type of causal relation.[9]

[9] End of the passage in *Bulletin de la Société française de philosophie,* 1906, VI, 279, 282–83.

29

Introduction to Marc Bloch

By JELLE C. RIEMERSMA

The debates on the scientific status of historiography, of which the discussion between Simiand and Cantecor may serve as a sample, did not end in a reconciliation or a definite conclusion. Historians, for practical as well as philosophical reasons, did not adopt the rigorous rules advocated by positivist authors. But it is noteworthy that the principles of historical method were subjected to a new scrutiny and that historians were at least willing to give men like Simiand a careful hearing.

In the works of one of the most brilliant French economic historians, some decades later, a method of inquiry and presentation was employed which reveals positivist influences. Marc Bloch's investigations were based on principles which derived from Durkheim's sociology as well as from the precepts of traditional historical method. It is true that Bloch's method does not consist in the application of rigidly prearranged procedures, as exemplified in Simiand's *Le salaire.* But he did regard history as a discipline which should use more precise methods of interpretation than it had thus far employed.[1]

Bloch's criticisms of historical interpretation resemble the ironic comments given by Simiand; both authors wanted to replace commonsense explanations by methodically discovered "real causes." The following comment shows Bloch's attitude toward authors writing narrative history: "Is it a matter of finding out whether some human action has really occurred? Then research is carried on with endless care and criticism. Do they proceed to the reasons for the action? The least semblance of an explanation satisfies them. As a rule it is based on one of those proverbs of common-sense psychology which have neither more nor less validity than their opposites."[2] The customary haphazard way

[1] Marc Bloch, *Apologie pour l'histoire ou métier d'historien* (Paris, Colin, 1949), p. xiv. This is a fragment of a planned book on method, which remained unfinished because of Bloch's death in 1944.

[2] Bloch, *Apologie,* p. 102.

of formulating the results of historical inquiry should, in his opinion, be replaced by a more analytical and methodical approach; *une entreprise raisonnée d'analyse.*[3] The *Annales d'histoire économique et sociale,* edited by Marc Bloch and Lucien Febvre, aimed to stimulate this kind of historiography. The journal also gave great attention to the interconnection of cultural phenomena and to problems which covered a wide geographical and temporal range. By focusing on problems which demanded the co-operation of workers from various disciplines and nationalities, the editors fought the tendency to compartmentalize scientific pursuits. The ideal of the *Annales* was to create *une histoire plus large et plus humaine.*

In so far as they were explicitly stated, the methodological precepts of this new history are contained in Bloch's *Apologie,* an unfinished treatise which, in the author's own words, expresses the thoughts of a historical craftsman rather than the speculations of an epistemologist. Characteristically, Bloch's expressions of indebtedness refer to historians like Michelet, Pirenne, Maitland, and Fustel de Coulanges. The institutional and sociological interests of the historians whom he admired recall the influence of Stubbs on many English historians. Fustel de Coulanges, for instance, defined history in the following terms: "History is not the accumulation of all sorts of events which have occurred in the past. It is the science of human societies."[4] Bloch remarked that his *Apologie* could be regarded as a commentary on this definition.[5]

The application of this concept of history led to formulations of a kind exemplified by the following section in his study of French agrarian institutions: "The peasant's system of property was tenaciously maintained. This preserved a continuing tradition in the design of the landscape, saved communal practices from modernizing influences, and resulted in making technical advances very slow. In turn, the system of property was based, juridically speaking, on the customs of the *seigneurie.* Economically, the system derived its origin from the abundance of land and the scarcity of men, in a time when royal courts did not yet sanction the tenants' rights."[6] In this analysis the system of property is considered a cause determining other "social facts," namely, the external appearance of the landscape and the slow advance of technology. The cause itself is presented as depending on historical

[3] *Ibid.,* p. xiv.
[4] *Ibid.,* p. 110, n. 4.
[5] *Loc. cit.*
[6] Marc Bloch, *Les caractères originaux de l'histoire rurale française* (Oslo, 1931), p. 251.

facts, which, as he remarks, will be seen differently according to whether one takes a juridical or an economic point of view. Bloch differs from Simiand in being opposed to "causal monism," i.e., the reduction of all observed phenomena to a single ultimate cause or set of causes.

The term "social fact" belongs to the Durkheim tradition.[7] Perrin has remarked that, of all the disciplines which contributed to the shaping of Bloch's thought, Durkheim's sociology was the most efficacious.[8] Like Durkheim, he argued that historical explanations should go beyond the search for precursors or origins.[9] It is true that Bloch, being primarily a historian, took account of the role of unique circumstances or precipitants; but his main preoccupation was the study of stable sets of social and cultural conditions.

Bloch's preoccupation with the study of social structures can be explained to some extent as a consequence of his concern with scientific rigor. On the whole, historians had previously tended to direct their efforts toward the discovery of unique precipitants, for which the evidence was often inconclusive. Bloch held that statements about the more permanent substratum of social life were much less affected with uncertainty. "The only causes which are often made uncertain by the psychological makeup of witnesses are the most immediate antecedents. A great event can be compared with an explosion. Under what conditions, precisely, is the molecular shock produced which is required to set off the sudden expansion of the gases? On this point we must frequently acquiesce in our ignorance. But the composition of the exploding mixture is quite susceptible of analysis. . . . [Similarly] the inner recesses of human destinies, the changes in mentality, in techniques, and in the social and economic structure . . . are hardly subject to the infirmities of momentary observation. Voltaire already recognized that through a fortunate coincidence the deepest things in history are also the most certain."[10]

Social facts are, in a sense, psychological facts. But, when Bloch used the word "psychological," he did not refer to universal human drives or instincts. He meant rather the peculiarities in the ideas and attitudes of a people, a particular society, or a particular historical

---

[7] Émile Durkheim, *Les règles de la méthode sociologique* (9th ed., Paris, Alcan, 1938), Ch. 1: "Qu'est-ce qu'un fait social?" Cf. Bloch, *Apologie,* p. 23: "Above all, we have learned to enter more deeply into the analysis of social facts."

[8] Charles-Edmond Perrin, "L'œuvre historique de Marc Bloch," *Revue historique,* 1948, CXCIX, 161–88, especially pp. 183–84.

[9] Bloch, *Apologie,* p. 5. Cf. Durkheim, *Les règles,* p. 144.

[10] Bloch, *Apologie,* pp. 48–49.

period. The following passage may serve as evidence: "The virus of the Black Death was the primary cause of the depopulation of Europe. However, the epidemic could propagate itself with such speed only because of certain social, that is, basically mental, conditions. And its moral effects can be explained only by the peculiar predispositions of collective sensitivity."[11] The search for "collective sensitivities" is an important part of Bloch's approach. He was not content to study merely the externals of human behavior, he also tried to discover the meaning behind the actions. This was not the same thing as finding the explicit purposes of the historical agents themselves. According to Bloch, planned action and clear motivations were often less historically important than actions determined by seemingly absurd, dimly realized, or unexplained ideas. An example is the idea of the magic power of kings, "thaumaturgic kingship," the theme of one of Bloch's earlier books.[12] This idea enhanced royal prestige and power through a long period of medieval and even modern history. But, except in a few instances, there existed no deliberate scheme to impose the idea upon the subjects; it should rather be regarded as a manifestation of social attitudes or "collective sensitivities."

The study of history was for Marc Bloch a personal confrontation with sources. "One word, after all, dominates and illuminates all our studies: the word 'understanding.' To study history . . . is to be confronted with the infinite variations of human conduct. It is a perpetual encounter with various kinds of men. For the sake of life itself, and for that of science, everything can be gained by making the meeting fraternal."[13] He demanded of the historian a constructive imagination, an ability to see the "wholeness" of cultural patterns and historical situations. His inspiration came from Michelet and Fustel de Coulanges. "Suppose," the latter wrote, "that a hundred specialists divided among themselves the past of France, in separate allotments. Do you believe that in the end they would come out with a history of France? I doubt it very much. The links connecting the facts would be lacking, and these interlinkages are themselves a historical truth."[14] The aspect of history which Fustel de Coulanges indicated by "links" was expressed by Michelet as a "great vital movement" in which the facts are embedded. Bloch's method implies a similar conception. However, instead of per-

[11] *Ibid.,* p. 101.

[12] Marc Bloch, *Les rois thaumaturges. Étude sur le caractère surnaturel attribué à la puissance royale particulièrement en France et en Angleterre* (Strasbourg, 1924).

[13] Bloch, *Apologie,* p. 72.

[14] Fustel de coulanges, as quoted in Bloch, *Apologie,* p. 78.

ceiving and describing the relations among historical phenomena in a unified vision, Bloch was concerned with "causes"; and the causes which interested him most were the enduring social structures and "collective sensitivities."

In the search for causes, Bloch used the comparative method. This method is a systematic and explicit way of explaining historical phenomena by showing their interrelations. Durkheim stated the essentials of the comparative method in the following words: "We have only one means to demonstrate that one phenomenon is the cause of another, namely, to compare cases in which the two phenomena are simultaneously present or absent, and to discover whether their variations in those various sets of circumstances allow the conclusion that one depends on the other. When the two phenomena can be produced artificially, at the will of the investigator, we have the experimental method in the proper sense. When, on the other hand, the facts cannot be produced at will but have to be studied as spontaneous occurrences, the method is called indirect experimentation or the comparative method."[15] This basic idea will be elaborated, with many illustrations, in Bloch's paper on the comparative history of European societies.

[15] Durkheim, *Les règles,* p. 153.

30

*Toward a Comparative History of European Societies**

By MARC BLOCH

Editor's Foreword

The argument of this paper can be outlined as follows:

A. Introduction: the purpose of the paper and a definition of the comparative method. (In Bloch's subdivision Parts I and a section of II)
B. Comparison of unrelated societies (most of II)
C. Comparison of related societies
  1. To discover important and hitherto unobserved developments (such as the enclosure movement in France, III)
  2. To discover causes of those developments and their similarities
     i. Of those caused by the influence of one society on another (such as the Visigothic and Carolingian monarchies, IV)
     ii. Of those related to the same general causes (such as the rise of Estates in many European countries, V)
  3. To discover the causes of different developments in spite of similar origins (English *villainage* and French *servage,* VI)
  4. To discover the separate origins of certain elements in mixed societies (patterns of agrarian organization reflect various ethnic origins, VII)
D. Conclusion: essentials and prerequisites of the comparative method (VIII)

The translation was prepared by J. C. Riemersma.

I

My very first words should prevent an ambiguity. I do not pretend to be the discoverer of a new universal remedy, because such a pretension would be slightly ridiculous. The comparative method will accomplish great things, and I consider its perfection and general use one of

* "Pour une histoire comparée des sociétés européennes," *Revue de synthèse historique,* 1928, XLVI, 15–50. Notes have been added by the translator; the author's own footnotes were omitted. Reprinted by courtesy of M. Etienne Bloch.

The paper was presented as an address at the International Congress of Historical Sciences, Oslo, Norway, August 1928.

the most pressing needs of present-day historical science. But the method is not capable of solving everything—there are no magical cures in science. Moreover, there is no need to invent the comparative method. In several social sciences the method has long earned its spurs, and its application in the history of political, economic, and legal institutions has often been recommended. It is quite evident, nevertheless, that most historians have not been thoroughly converted. Scholars often express polite approval, and then go back to work without changing their habits. Why? Without any doubt, the reason is that historians are easily led to believe that "comparative history" is a chapter of the philosophy of history or of general sociology. It is evident that the empirical historian will never practice either of the two disciplines, although he may, according to his state of mind, grant them admiration or a skeptical smile. The historical specialist asks for a method which is a technical instrument, generally used, easily manageable, and capable of giving positive results. The comparative method is precisely such an instrument; but I am not sure that this has been sufficiently demonstrated. I believe that this method can and must penetrate monographic studies. Its future is at stake, and therewith perhaps the future of historical science as a whole. I would like to clarify for you, and with your help, the nature and applications of this excellent tool. Some examples will illustrate the main services which one may rightly expect from the method. Finally, some practical means of facilitating the comparative approach will be suggested.

Speaking for a public of medievalists, I will draw my examples primarily from the period which is usually called the "Middle Ages"—rightly or wrongly. The following observations would, of course, be equally applicable—*mutatis mutandis*—to European societies of the so-called "modern" period. Therefore, I will also occasionally allude to the latter period.

II

The term "comparative history," now in current use, has had the fate of almost all common words: shifts in meaning. We will leave aside certain usages of the term which are definitely wrong; but, even apart from such errors, an ambiguity remains. In the social sciences the term "comparative method" is generally used in such a way as to include two very different intellectual procedures. Only linguists have made a sustained effort to keep these two meanings carefully apart. Now it is our turn, as historians, to make a precise distinction.

In the first place, what does it mean if a historian "compares"? Without any doubt it means this: he selects two or more phenomena which appear at first sight to be analogous and which occur in one or more social milieus. He finds out how these phenomena resemble or differ from one another, traces their evolution, and, as far as possible, explains the similarities and differences. In order to have historical comparison, two conditions must be fulfilled: a certain similarity or analogy between observed phenomena—that is obvious—and a certain dissimilarity between the environments in which they occur. If I study the landholding system of the Limousin region, for instance, I will constantly compare fragments of evidence drawn from the records of this or that *seigneurie*. This is comparison in the common sense of the word, but, nevertheless, I do not think that I engage here in what is, technically speaking, comparative history; for the various objects of my study are all derived from parts of the same society, a society which in its totality forms one large unit. It has become common practice to reserve the term "comparative history" almost exclusively for the confrontation of phenomena which have occurred on different sides of the boundary of a state or nation. Political and national contrasts are indeed the most striking and immediately evident of all social contrasts. But, as we shall see, this restricted conception of the comparative method is a rather gross simplification. Let us therefore use here the notion of a "difference of environment"—a notion which is more flexible and more precise.

All forms of the comparative method have in common the procedure of comparison defined above. Depending on the field of inquiry, there are two altogether different ways in which the method can be applied, different both in principle and in results.

First case: the units of comparison are societies far removed from one another in time or space. Analogous phenomena observed in these societies cannot be explained, therefore, by mutual influences or by a common origin. Such a comparison is exemplified by the confrontation of the Greek and Roman civilizations of ancient times with presently existing primitive societies. This application of the comparative method has become common since the days of Father Lafitau, S.J. (1724), who invited his readers to "compare the customs and manners of American savages" with those of "the earliest times." Within the relatively advanced civilization of the early Roman Empire one ritual stood out like a strange and cruel discrepancy. Very near Rome was a little temple of

Diana on the beautiful shores of Lake Nemi. Anyone could become a priest of this temple, but only after fulfilling one specific and inescapable requirement: he had to kill the priest whose place he intended to take. "If we can show that a barbarous custom, like that of the priesthood of Nemi, has existed elsewhere; if we can detect the motives which led to its institution; if we can prove that these motives have operated widely, perhaps universally, in human society, producing in varied circumstances a variety of institutions specifically different but generically alike; if we can show, lastly, that these very motives, with some of their derivative institutions, were actually at work in classical antiquity; then we may fairly infer that at a remoter age the same motives gave birth to the priesthood of Nemi."[1] Here we have the starting point of the immense inquiry of *The Golden Bough,* a most famous and illustrative example of a study based upon evidence from all parts of the world. Such an application of the comparative method has rendered various and important services. It has done so especially for the study of Mediterranean antiquity. Humanistic education had accustomed us to regard Hellas and Rome as much too similar to ourselves. The ethnographers and their comparisons, by a sort of mental shock, restored the sense of a contrast between ourselves and the ancients. Thereby we regained that peculiar sense of the exotic which is a prerequisite for a sound understanding of the past. Other benefits of the comparative method in the grand manner are of a more general nature. Gaps in documentation may be overcome by hypotheses based on analogies, comparisons may suggest research in new directions and, in particular, may explain many "survivals" which hitherto had remained strange and unintelligible. By "survivals" I mean customs which are retained and crystallized in a milieu entirely different from (and later than) the psychological enviroment in which the customs originated. Such phenomena would appear bizarre and inexplicable, were it not for the existence of similar traits in other cultures which allow precise reconstruction of that vanished social environment; the ritual murder of Nemi is a case in point. This comparative method on the grand scale can be summarized as essentially a procedure of interpolation of lines of development. The basic postulate of this method, as well as the conclusion to which it constantly returns, is the fundamental unity of the human spirit or, if you wish, the monotony and astonishing poverty of

[1] James G. Frazer, *The Golden Bough: A Study in Magic and Religion,* Vol. I (3rd ed., London, Macmillan & Co., Ltd., 1911), p. 10.

human intellectual resources during the course of history. This poverty is most evident in the ages when, in a first crude attempt, primitive humanity elaborated a philosophy of life (Frazer).

There exists another application of the comparative procedure: that in which the units of comparison are societies that are geographical neighbors and historical contemporaries, constantly influenced by one another. During the historical development of such societies, they are subject to the same over-all causes, just because they are so close together in time and space. Moreover, they have, in part at least, a common origin. This second form of the comparative method corresponds, within the historical discipline, to the approach of comparative linguistics (dealing with one related group of languages, for instance the Indo-Germanic). The comparative method in the grand manner, on the other hand, would correspond approximately to general linguistics, which deals with all human languages. From the scientific point of view the method with the more restricted outlook appears to be the most promising; this holds for history as well as for linguistics. The latter method may arrive at more precise and less hypothetical conclusions, because its classifications can be more rigorous and critical. At least, this is what I will try to show. The comparison of various European societies which I intend to suggest to you belongs to this latter methodological category. I will direct attention to adjacent and contemporaneous societies of western and central Europe which derived, if not from one origin, at least from a limited number of common origins.

III

Before phenomena can be interpreted, they have to be discovered, and the utility of the comparative method is first evident in this basic step. But someone might ask: "Is it really necessary to make so much work for oneself to 'discover' historical facts? Facts are knowable only through documents. Is it not sufficient just to read the texts or monuments to bring the facts to light?" Without doubt, but one must know how to read. A document is a witness, and, like most witnesses, it does not talk unless it is questioned. The difficulty is how to prepare the questions. Here, precisely, comparative study gives the historian—who is always in the position of a *juge d'instruction*—the most precious aid.

Very often, this is what happens: In some society a phenomenon has had widespread consequences which can be recognized clearly, particularly if there are political repercussions which almost always are reflected in historical sources. Therefore, any historian, unless he is afflicted with blindness, will observe the phenomenon in question. In an adjacent society, however, quite a different state of affairs may prevail. It is possible that our phenomenon has a parallel elsewhere, resulting in equally widespread and important consequences. But these effects are not immediately recognizable, because of the state of our documentation or because of a different social and political framework. This does not mean that the effects are less important. They are only less obvious, they remain, so to speak, on a deeper level. Some diseases of the body fail similarly to produce clear-cut symptoms immediately, yet linger on for years without completely revealing themselves. Even if ultimately the effects become quite evident, the disease itself can hardly be recognized: the observer cannot link the presently visible symptoms with the original disease because the causal factor occurred in a distant past. Would such a situation be purely hypothetical? The opposite is true. To demonstrate this, I have to take an example from my own investigations. It is with some regret that I bring myself into the scene, but, since historians do not as a rule take the trouble to publish their gropings and errors, the literature does not give me any case which I could substitute for my personal experience.

One of the most striking phenomena of the agrarian history of Europe is the extensive *enclosure movement.* We indicate by this name the agrarian transformation which occurred in England between the early sixteenth century and the first years of the nineteenth. In its essential aspects, it can be defined as the disappearance of collective servitudes and the individualization of agriculture. The movement took two forms: enclosure of wasteland and enclosure of the arable land. At present we will restrict ourselves to the enclosure of the arable. At the beginning of the transformation we have a system in which the cultivated fields are open to pasturage immediately after harvest time. At that moment the arable became the object of common exploitation by the village community as a whole. The very rhythm of agriculture, the time of sowing and the period of ripening, was determined by the fact that the fields were to be used as pastures. Thus the rules and regulations which determined the methods of cultivation were devised to protect the interests of the community as a whole. At the other end of the development, after the enclosures have been accomplished, the situation is entirely different: a system of pure private property prevails. This great transformation is quite of a sort to attract and retain our attention. During its whole history it stirred up violent polemics. A major part of the relevant documents are readily accessible—for instance, the Acts of

Parliament and the official inquiries. The enclosures have also many ties with political history. They were promoted by the rise of Parliament in which the great landowners exerted considerable influence; and, by a reverse effect, the enclosures contributed to the consolidation of the power of the gentry. Both colonial expansion and the industrial revolution—the two most evident facts of English economic history—seem to have been facilitated by the enclosure movement. (Some scholars have expressed doubts on this point, but for our purposes it suffices that the matter has been a subject of discussion.) Not only were the enclosures influential in affecting social circumstances—always very difficult to unravel—but they even affected the external appearance of the landscape. The English countryside, formerly open as far as the horizon, became covered with walls and hedges. Thus it is no wonder that even the most elementary textbook on English history should devote some space to the enclosures.

Now let us open a book on French history, which, alas, may even be an economic history. We will not find the slightest allusion to a movement of this kind. Nevertheless, it has occurred. Especially owing to the work of Henri Sée we begin to discern its existence, but we cannot yet estimate its extent. Moreover, we have as yet no clear idea about the differences between the rather similar and yet divergent evolutions of French and English society. For the time being, this problem of differences must be postponed. We are still concerned with the discovery of the phenomenon. In the comparative approach, in the proper sense, the observation of differences comes second.

Remarkably enough, the disappearance of collective servitudes has up to now been noted in France only during those periods and in those regions where it was, as in the English case, easily recognizable by its reflection in official documents. Such texts are the *édits de clôture* of northern France in the eighteenth century and the inquiries which preceded or followed them. The same agricultural transformation, nevertheless, occurred in another region of France, namely, the Provence. Nobody, as far as I know, has observed that it also occurred in this region, even at a rather early date, in the fifteenth, sixteenth, and seventeenth centuries. The movement here probably had deeper and more important consequences than in most of the more northern regions, where the phenomenon has been studied many times; but in the Provence, unfortunately, the transformation occurred at a time when the thoughts of authors and administrators were not yet concerned with economic and agricultural questions. Moreover, it did not change the appearance of the landscape. The abolition of collective servitudes did not result in the construction of barriers or fences between fields, and therefore it could easily pass unnoticed.

Were its results the same in the Provence as in England? For the moment I do not know. I have strong doubts whether all the characteristics of the English transformation would be found to have repeated themselves on the Mediterranean coast. On the contrary, I am impressed by very special traits of the Mediterranean phenomena in which the agrarian organization was quite different from that in the north. Consequently, no redistribution of fields or reallotment, as occurred in England, took place in the Provence. Moreover, there are some peculiar economic practices, like the *transhumance,*[2] which lead to social conditions without English parallel; for instance, the antagonism between *nourriguiers* (rich stockbreeders) and other classes of the population. Despite such differences, it is remarkable that a Mediterranean region shows evidence of a phenomenon which thus far has been regarded as occurring only in higher latitudes.

It is not very difficult to observe the phenomenon in the Provence. Fairly numerous texts, if studied with some attention, permit us to follow its traces. Such documents are the county statutes and municipal deliberations, and, furthermore, we have the lawsuits whose length and intensity are evidence of the clash of important interests. But it is necessary to think of looking for these texts and to compare one with the other. My achievement in this respect is hardly due to the fact that I am particularly familiar with local documents; the opposite is true. Scholars specializing in Provençal history are much better acquainted with them than I will ever be. Only those scholars will really be able to exploit the quarry of material which I have indicated. If I have an advantage over the specialized local historians, it is a modest and altogether impersonal one: I have read books on the English enclosures and on analogous rural revolutions in other European countries, and the contents of those books has been absorbed into my thinking. The matter can be summarized by saying that I have used a powerful magic wand, namely, the comparative method.

IV

Consider, now, the interpretation of the phenomena.

The most obvious service which an attentive comparison of different

[2] *Transhumance:* seasonal migrations of cattle herds from the lowlands to the mountain meadows and back.

and neighboring societies can provide is that it enables us to discern the influences which these societies exert upon one another. Without doubt, careful study would reveal transmissions of cultural traits among medieval societies which have hitherto remained somewhat obscure. The following example may provide a working hypothesis.

Compared with the immediately preceding Merovingian monarchy, the Carolingian monarchy appears to have absolutely new and original characteristics. In their relation to the church the Merovingians had always been mere laymen. The Carolingians, on the other hand, received at their accession to the throne the mark of sanctity; Pippin and his descendants were anointed with holy oil. Of course, the Merovingians, like the people in general, had been adherents of the Christian faith. While they had dominated, enriched, or exploited the church from time to time, they had never seriously attempted to make political power into a devoted servant of Christian ideals; with the advent of the Carolingian dynasty this was changed. It is true that the Carolingians, in the period of their power, regimented the clergy and utilized church property for political purposes. But at the same time they clearly considered themselves responsible for the rule of God's law on earth. Their legislation had essentially a religious and ethical character. A short time ago I chanced to read a decree of the Wahabite emir of Nedjed, and I was struck by its resemblance to the pious reading of the capitularies. The Carolingian court sessions, surrounding the king or emperor, are hardly distinguishable from church councils. To mention a final characteristic, the personal relations between lords and vassals under the Merovingians occupied only a marginal position in the legislation of the realm. Despite their actual importance, such protective relations (*liens de dépendance*) had traditionally been ignored in the legal code. The Carolingians had quite a different policy: ties of personal dependence were officially recognized and sanctioned. The cases in which a vassal could abandon his lord were clearly defined. Personal relations of protection were used in Carolingian policy as a means of preserving and consolidating the public order. The peace of the realm, almost impossible to achieve, was always the ideal for which the dynasty was striving. A capitulary of 810 gives a short and eloquent formulation of this social policy: "Ut unusquisque suos iuniores distringat ut melius ac melius oboediant et consentiant mandatis et praeceptis imperialibus."[3]

[3] "Let everybody keep his inferiors under control in order that the latter may obey and consent to the imperial mandates and precepts." (Cap. No. 64, c. 17, edited by Boretius.)

A careful observer would find even in Merovingian Gaul some evidence of those characteristics which we have presented here as Carolingian. It is, nevertheless, no exaggeration to say that the Carolingian state appears to be an entirely new and original creation, at least if one looks only at the historical evidence for Gaul. Let us now look across the Pyrenees, however, and similar characteristics will be seen. Since the seventh century the Visigothic kings had received the sacrosanct unction, in Erviga's words. The Visigothic monarchy was strongly religious and attempted to realize the triumph of the church orders by means of state action. In Spain church councils merged with political assemblies. Since ancient times the laws of the Visigothic kings had defined and regulated the ties between lord and vassal, and there existed a tendency to base the military organization upon such interpersonal relations. All this strongly resembles the Carolingian system. It is, of course, not difficult to discover differences as well as analogies. The main difference is that the early Carolingians dominated the church, while, conversely, the church dominated the seventh-century Gothic kings. Nevertheless, the resemblances are very remarkable. Should they be regarded merely as the effect of similar causes which on both sides of the Pyrenees worked in the same direction, the nature of those causes remaining to be discovered? Or, in regard to the definitely earlier appearance of the Visigothic traits, should the Visigothic system be regarded as the historical example of the Carolingian monarchy? A certain conception of kingship and certain ideas on feudal relations first appeared in Spain and were embodied there in legislative texts. Should we assume that these conceptions were consciously taken over by the environment of the Frankish kings and by the kings themselves? Only after a detailed inquiry would we have the right to answer this question. The main objective of the inquiry would have to be the discovery of the channels through which Visigothic influence could penetrate into Gaul. Some universally known facts appear to make the hypothesis of an influence rather probable. There undoubtedly existed a Spanish *diaspora* in the Frankish kingdom during the century following the Arabian conquest. The fugitives *de partibus Hispaniae* who had been settled in Septimania by Charlemagne and Louis the Pious, were mostly people of low social standing. But some of them belonged to the higher classes (*majores et potentiores*) or to the priesthood. These persons would be familiar with political and religious customs of the country which they had been compelled to leave. A few Spanish refugees had brilliant careers in the church of Gaul: Claudius of Turin and Agobard of Lyons. The latter was a proponent of legal unification, an idea which he could have observed in reality while he was still in Spain. Above all others, Theodulf of Orleans should be mentioned; he was the earliest to arrive and also doubtless the most influential of all Spanish immigrants. Spanish collections of conciliar decisions affected Carolingian canon law. The existence of this influence is undeniable, even if its importance remains to be specified. Once more, I do not claim to have solved the problem; but I hope you will concede that it deserves to be stated. And it is by no means the only one of its kind.

V

"Historical similarities," Renan wrote in connection with Christ and the Essenes, "do not always imply influences." Upon careful examination it appears that many similarities cannot be reduced to imitations. And these cases are the most interesting ones, it seems to me, because they can be helpful in the discovery of causes. In the exhilarating, never-ending search for causes, the comparative method may again render invaluable service. It may lead historians to track down real causes, and, to begin with a more modest but undeniable advantage, it may guide them away from kinds of research which would lead only to a dead end.

Everyone has heard of the so-called General and Provincial Estates of France in the fourteenth and fifteenth centuries. Here I am using the convenient words "General" and "Provincial" in their roughly defined but generally accepted meaning. There is, of course, a whole series of gradations between General and Provincial Estates. I also grant you that General Estates in the true sense have practically never assembled and that during a long period of history no fixed provincial boundaries were in existence. In recent years a considerable number of monographs have been written, dealing with the subject of Provincial Estates, especially the Estates of the great feudal principalities. No doubt these monographs have required great effort on the part of historical scholars. Especially for the earlier periods the documentation is very sparse and unrewarding. Many important refinements of historical knowledge have resulted from such meritorious investigations. But, unfortunately, all authors have been tripped up at the very beginning of their work by a methodological difficulty. The problem which they did not clearly recognize and which they were unable to solve is the problem of "origins." This term is current among historians, but it is ambiguous. As commonly understood, the study of origins combines two intellectual procedures with different principles and applications. On the one hand, one may inquire about the more ancient institutions, such as ducal or county courts, from which the Estates derive as a sort of development. This is a quite legitimate and necessary inquiry. In the second place, however, we need another investigation to explain, in any given time, the spread and the new importance of the ancient institutions and their transformation into Estates, that is to say, into assemblies endowed with political and particularly financial functions not possessed by their precursors, assemblies aware of their power with respect to the sovereign and his council, a power which is perhaps of subordinate importance but which nevertheless is distinct and represents, in extremely varied combinations, the various social forces in the realm. Revealing the germ of a historical development is quite a different thing from uncovering the causes of germination. Will we ever discover the latter if we stay within the boundaries of Artois (in case we are concerned with the Artesian Estates), within Brittany (in dealing with the Breton Estates), or even if we content ourselves with surveying the whole of France? Certainly not. Proceeding in this way, we will only get lost in a bewildering maze of local facts, to some of which we will attribute a quite disproportionate importance. And, on the other hand, essential aspects will inevitably be overlooked. A general phenomenon must have equally general causes. Now the phenomenon described as the rise of Estates is certainly a phenomenon which occurs all over Europe. The *États* in France, the *Stände* in the German territories (the two terms are curiously akin in meaning), the *Cortes* in Spain, and the *Parliamenti* in Italy all arise at about the same time. Even the evolution of the English Parliament, originating in an extremely different political milieu, is conditioned by needs and movements of ideas analogous to those operative in the rise of what the Germans call the *Ständestaat.* I hope you will not misunderstand me. I fully recognize the great utility and importance of local monographs, and I certainly do not require their authors to transgress the proper limits of their studies in order to solve the great European problem which has been indicated. On the contrary, we ask them to realize that none of them, working separately, is able to provide the solution. They can, however, point out the social and political circumstances which precede or accompany the rise of Estates in a particular region and which seem to be of such a kind as to be provisionally classed among the possible causes. In this inquiry the local historian can be guided by results which have already been obtained in other regions

In other words, he will profitably make use of some comparative history. Over-all comparison can only come afterward; it would be vain without such preliminary local studies. On the other hand, monographs become important only because the comparative method can elicit from the chaotic multiplicity of circumstances those which were generally effective—the real causes.

Other examples could, of course, be found without difficulty. German historians studying the formation of "territorial states" have regarded them too often as a specifically German phenomenon. These territorial states were formed during the twelfth and thirteenth centuries within the Holy Roman Empire, and gradually they absorbed a great part of the central power. Why should the study of this phenomenon be isolated from the study of the strengthening feudal principalities in France?

Another problem in which the comparative method may give help to local historians is the evolution of the nobility. In the late Middle Ages and at the beginning of the modern period the revenues of lords were dwindling: money rents, as a result of depreciations, diminished in real value. In that period the nobles became for the first time aware of the perilous impoverishment of their fortunes. This danger is recognized and fought in all countries, although with different devices and with unequal success, depending on the region. One method was the increase of "casual obligations" resting upon the tenants. This could be done if customary usage had not yet rigidly established the extent of such obligations (*fines* in England). Another method was the substitution of payments *in natura* for money payments, wherever it could legally be done, which made revenues proportional to the harvest; hence the expansion of *métayage* in France. Lastly, tenants could be deprived of their holdings by force; and this dispossession occurred in different ways, depending on the region (England, eastern Germany). It is clear that a general effort existed to increase the rents, but the method applied varied considerably and the success of the outcome varied even more. A comparison of national environments, then, reveals remarkable differences (we will soon see that this is an important aspect of the comparative method), and at the same time we can observe a common impulse behind the wide variety of effects. The plight of the nobility is a European phenomenon, to be explained by European causes only. One cannot explain the *Gutsherrschaft* in Mecklenburg or Pomerania simply by facts derived from these regions. Neither can the land accumulation in the hands of the English squirearchy be explained from English materials alone. Such efforts result in empty speculations and are a waste of time.

VI

The comparative method has often suffered from a certain misunderstanding. Too often it is supposed that the method has no other purpose than hunting out resemblances. It is therefore commonly accused of being content with forced analogies, even of inventing such analogies by arbitrarily postulating some kind of necessary parallelism between various social developments. Whether these accusations are justified is not our present concern. If it really did those things, the method would be a distortion of its true self. Correctly understood, the primary interest of the comparative method is, on the contrary, the observation of differences, whether they are original or the results of divergent developments from a common origin. Recently Antoine Meillet published a treatise "describing the particular characteristics which distinguish the development of the family of Germanic languages among the languages of the Indo-European branch as a whole."[4] At the beginning of this work, Meillet argues that it is one of the essential tasks of comparative linguistics "to show clearly the originality—the unique characteristics—of the separate languages." Something similar holds for comparative history: it should analyze and isolate the "originality" of different societies. Is it necessary to add that a more delicate undertaking can hardly be imagined, or a task which more strongly demands methodical comparisons? To observe an over-all contrast is not enough, one should also elaborate specifically in what respects the two objects under observation are dissimilar. Such an elaboration is much more demanding, but also more interesting, than the mere perception of a contrast; it evidently presupposes that the two phenomena have to be observed alternatively.

First, the ground has to be cleared from pseudo-similarities which often are suggested by the use of certain words (homonyms). Some of them are extremely treacherous.

How often have English *villainage* of the thirteenth, fourteenth, and fifteenth centuries and French *servage* been treated as similar phenomena! Certainly, a hurried observer would easily believe that points of resemblance exist. From the thirteenth to the fifteenth century, legal terminology and public opinion regard both *villains* and *serfs* as human beings without "liberty." In some Latin texts the common term *servus* is used. The English writers who express themselves in French do not

[4] Antoine Meillet, *Caractères généraux des langues germaniques* (1917).

hesitate to translate *villain* by *serf*. Both concepts were often associated with Roman slavery, known to erudite persons. Nevertheless, the analogy is superficial, because in different periods and regions the concept of "nonliberty" has varied greatly in meaning. *Villainage,* as a matter of fact, is a uniquely English institution. In a classic work, Vinogradoff has demonstrated the connection of *villainage* with the particular political environment in which it originated.

As early as the second half of the twelfth century, thus much earlier than their French neighbors, English kings succeeded in extending the jurisdiction of royal courts throughout the realm. But the rapid advance of royal power had its disadvantages. Royal judges had to respect the existing boundary line between public and private power; they were unable to transgress it before the very end of the Middle Ages: the constitution of society made it impossible for them to intervene between the lords and those who held their lands *in villainage.* Specifically, *villainage* implied the payment of a rent and the fulfillment of labor services by the tenant. Both duties were determined by the custom of the *manor* (i.e., the English equivalent of the *seigneurie*). There were, according to their origin, various kinds of tenants. Some were regarded as free. These tenants depended upon their lord only because of their tenure, their belonging to the *villa.* They were *villains* in the proper sense of the term. The others—*servi, nativi*—were bound to the lord by personal and hereditary ties in which the people of those times saw a mark of servitude. But both kinds of tenants, whatever their traditional status, were kept outside royal jurisdiction: in their relations with the lord (only in those) both remained absolutely beyond the competence of state courts. Consequently, the Common Law of the realm, elaborated and applied by the royal tribunals, failed to reach those tenants. As a result of this pitiful lack of legal protection, common to both groups, *villains* and *nativi* merged into one single class, in spite of earlier differences. The new class was, of course, heterogeneous in composition and could not easily be defined by legal experts. Soon the lawyers agreed, however, to call "free" only those persons whom the royal courts protected against everybody.

The development of this new conception of "freedom" is evident from legal terminology. The *villain* of former times, in the old sense of "tenant," ceased to belong to the class of *liberi homines* and was merged with the hereditary *servus* or *nativus,* who was equally deprived of recourse before the king's courts. The two words *servus* and *villain* came to be treated as synonymous, and this transformation is complete around

1300. At the same time, certain obligations which formerly had appertained to the servile class were gradually imposed upon the villains, especially rights relating to marriage. Originally such restrictions rested only upon the traditional *servi* and their descendants; now they extended their influence, at least in numerous manors, over the class of villains as a whole, taken in the new sense. A kind of "contagion" occurs which is not uncommon in medieval societies; in England it was particularly easy. Without doubt, the assimilation of the free into the servile class was an abuse of power, but the victims could not possibly voice an effective protest, since, by definition, they could complain only before a manorial court, that is, before the very beneficiaries of the abuse.

Very soon villainage was regarded as hereditary, as serfdom had been in earlier times. It was a characteristic of the period to make social status hereditary. In England there was a particular circumstance which precipitated the development: sometimes a high personality would receive a landholding *in villainage.* Whoever the tenant might be, this meant that certain burdens and disabilities rested upon the land. The man receiving the tenure would be aware of those disadvantages, particularly about the lack of protection from the royal courts with respect to the lord of the manor. Nevertheless, it was impossible to throw the recipient, who might occupy a high social position, into the unfree class. As a solution a distinction was introduced between the status of the land and the status of the man. *Villain* status was given to the descendants—to all the descendants—of the original tenants; and as a result a closed, humble caste was created. The new caste was defined by its particular legal aspect, which lawyers often expressed as follows: "the *villain* is a serf or slave (*servus*) in relation to his lord." This meant that nobody could intervene between villain and master, not even the king.

In France nothing of the kind took place. Royal jurisdiction advanced much more slowly, and the way in which this occurred was quite different. There were no great legislative ordinances, like those of Henry II in England. No strict classification was established with respect to the means of bringing suits before the royal courts (the English writs). The officials of the French king extended their influence by a series of intrusions, here earlier and there later, in a rather unsystematic way. Royal jurisdiction advanced step by step; case after case was drawn into its orbit. The process was slow and not guided by any theoretical plan, at least in the beginning. For that very reason royal influence penetrated more deeply into French institutions than in their English counterparts.

Seignorial or manorial jurisdiction constituted a complex of powers derived from various sources. It was applied to different groups, such as military vassals, bourgeois, free tenants, and serfs. [The difference between France and England lay in the way in which cases were classified.] The French monarchy regarded the groups of subjects mentioned above as one whole, but some cases were left to seignorial jurisdiction while others were to be judged by royal officials. For some cases there existed a right of appeal, while in other cases this right was absent. But, among the lord's subjects, no basic distinction was made between different kinds of people. [Instead of people, cases were distinguished.] The royal judge therefore gradually slid himself in between lord and tenant, and there was no reason to merge the free tenant—who, like his English counterpart, was called *villain*—with the *serf.* Until the end of the system the two social classes remain in existence as separate categories.

Let us summarize the matter. Legally speaking, the French *serf* of the early twelfth century and the English *servus, nativus,* or *theow* of the same period had the same position in society. They are two aspects of what could rightly be treated as one and the same institution. Then *villainage* appears in England, and the whole parallelism breaks down. In the fourteenth century the French *serf* and the English *villain* or *serf* are quite different classes. Is it still worth while to compare the two? Certainly, if only one mentions the contrasts which resulted from a strikingly different development in the two countries.

We may now enter into a more detailed comparison. Even medieval lawyers were not always able to draw a clear line between the various kinds of real rights. In the English manor of the thirteenth and fourteenth centuries such rights existed in bewildering diversity. Particularly it was necessary for the lawyers to know the distinction between the rights appertaining to *villain* tenures and the rights, also very complicated, which accompanied free tenures. Fixed and definite criteria were absolutely necessary, otherwise it could not be decided which lands and consequently which tenants remained outside the sphere of royal jurisdiction. What were the attributes of a person, or of a piece of land, which led to a relinquishing of royal jurisdiction?

In unraveling those questions, the lawyers sometimes drew a line on the basis of the kind of services with which the land was burdened. They constructed the notion of *villain services.* In the lawyers' opinion, the obligation to agricultural labor was an indication of *villain* status if a large number of working days was required. An even more important indication was an indeterminancy either in the number of these working days or in the tasks to be performed, those matters being left to the lord's discretion. The duty of fulfilling the tasks of village chief, the reeve in England, was generally also considered as affecting the liberty of those who were burdened with the obligation. The function of the reeve resembled that of the *starost,* familiar to us from Russian novels. The task was heavy and obligatory, depending on the terms of tenure.

When English legal theorists and lawyers constructed these legal norms, nothing new was invented. They drew from a long tradition of ideas, slowly developed and vaguely defined, which were current in English and Continental societies during the Middle Ages. It is an old human tendency to regard agricultural labor as somewhat incompatible with freedom. During the barbarian epoch, for instance, agricultural labor was described as *opera servilia.* The other conception—namely, that an indeterminancy of obligatory services distinguished the *servus* from the free tenant—is also of ancient date. The idea derives from the contrast of slavery and colonate in Roman times; it was quite influential in Carolingian Gaul and Italy; and it never disappeared altogether. Even in Capetian France, the mere fact that a peasant's obligations were limited to fixed proportions was commonly designated by the word *franchises,* and this certainly did not mean the abolition of such services! In many regions of Germany the performance of special services independent of the general load of forced labor was the burden distinguishing the unfree. Such demands, made by the arbitrary decision of the lord, in England were restricted to the duty of acting as reeve. In France, finally, the association of undefined obligations and unfree status has left only some traces, particularly in twelfth-century texts. Here the idea was less current, and it never became embodied in precise legal constructions. It is true that in thirteenth-century France the idea that agricultural work degrades was used to draw sharper distinctions between social classes. But it did not establish the line between the free and the unfree, as had been the case in England; it was utilized as a means of differentiating the nobility from the mass of nonnobles. Henceforth, the nobility was forbidden to act at variance with its rank in society (*déroger*), and manual labor was considered one form of self-debasement. Yet the category of nonnobles contained an increasingly large number of people who were generally regarded as free. In France as well as elsewhere the nonfree were, indeed, sometimes differentiated on the basis of particular services which they had to perform. Popular sentiment must have had a tendency in this direction. Toward the beginning of the thirteenth century some tenants in Gonesse, near Paris, are treated by their neighbors as if they are serfs. The alleged reason is that they perform special services, especially the dishonoring duty of escorting prisoners. The insulted tenants obtain a royal confirmation of their legal freedom without difficulty, and their liberty is put beyond dispute. Moreover, no French theorist, lawyer, or judge ever used the criterion of special services in order to define the serf. We are faced, consequently, with a very suggestive case of contrasting societies: France and England. Analogous ideas and tendencies exist in both countries, but in the former the ideas remain indistinct and deprived of official recognition, submerged in the diffuse mass of sentiments and ideas called "public opinion," while in the latter country they are subject of a considerable development and of legal crystallization.

The history of social classes in the Middle Ages may detain us a little longer. No subject could reveal deeper contrasts between different regions. The discrepancies may even be inexplicable, and in that case we must remain satisfied with a mere mentioning of the facts.

To begin with, let us consider western and central Europe in the tenth and eleventh centuries. The idea that birth creates inequalities among men—an idea common to all periods of history—is at the time not altogether absent from men's minds. For instance, Charles of Lorraine, the legitimate heir of the Carolingians, in 987 is excluded from the succession to the French throne. Archbishop Auberon justifies this exclusion by the argument that the pretendent has married below his rank with a woman from the vassal class. (Instead of Auberon, it is perhaps more accurate to mention the chronicler Richer, who states that Auberon is the author of a discourse containing the above argument. If it was composed by the chronicler himself, the argument still serves as evidence for the ideas of the period.) The implication is that no knight would have accepted willingly the son of a serf or villain as his equal. Let us make no mistake, however: heredity played as yet a minor role in the creation of rights. Society did not yet consist of a hierarchy of castes which were distinguished by blood; it should be conceived rather as an intricate bundle of groups, each of which was held together by ties of personal allegiance (*relations de dépendance*).[5] These relations of subservience and protection were considered very important. The same case of Charles of Lorraine may serve as an example. Spontaneously Auberon's argument takes a turn which reveals the contem-

[5] A vassal of a very important lord could derive social standing from his personal relation to "his" lord. Lowly birth could be overshadowed, as a status-determining factor, by a connection with this particular lord.

porary views. To be sure, the bishop begins by reproaching the prince with his misalliance: "He has married in the vassal order with a woman far below his rank." But immediately the bishop remembers that the father of the woman had served the dukes of France, and adds: "How could this great duke [Hugo Capet] have consented to see this woman upon the French throne—a woman taken from the ranks of *his own vassals?*" Note that the question is hereby brought into the personal sphere.

Servility in itself was regarded in theory as strictly hereditary, but actually it was not yet altogether incompatible with knighthood. As regards the legal status of free men, it is true that it varied with the region, with the type of contractual ties among men, and with social status. But it was not dependent on birth. Then, in the twelfth and thirteenth centuries, ideas and laws undergo inconspicuous but very important changes. The strength of personal relations dwindles, and the custom of *homage* is gradually transformed into an empty ceremony. The serf (*homme de corps* in French) is no longer thought of as "a man" of his lord but as a member of a lowly class. In all regions numerous social strata make their appearance, each with its own rules. Everywhere the new classes are based upon heredity. But what differences in the complexity of the development! In England *villainage* becomes solidly established, and this is almost the only new class in the new sense; there is no differentiation in legal status among free men. In France a scale of ranks exists, at the bottom of which we find *servage.* The members of this group from now on can no longer become knights. At the top we find the nobility, which gradually differentiates itself from the rest of the population by a series of particular traits, sometimes simply survivals from ancient manners and customs. These characteristics lead to differences in private law, criminal law, and fiscal law. In Germany, finally, the hierarchical idea shows an enormous fecundity from the thirteenth century on. In France the serfs who achieved knighthood (*serfs chevaliers*) had vanished as a class because of the crystallization of class sentiments; the same kind of people in Germany became the nucleus of a new and well-defined social category. In southern Germany they even give rise to two new social categories. The nobility as well as the serfs are differentiated into a number of layers. Not all nobles are *ebenbürtig* (of equal birth), and *connubium* (intermarriage) could occur only within the fixed boundaries of rank. Such social practices inspired the lawyers to construct the well-known *Heerschild* theory. They imagined a sort of ladder, on the rungs of which the social groups had their fixed place. Thereby a classification of higher society had been achieved, and whoever belonged to one of the upper groups could not, without self-abasement, accept a fief from someone belonging to a lower category.

Our example presents neighboring and contemporaneous societies, evolving in the same direction toward a greater importance of hierarchization and heredity. But there are differences of degree in the course and in the results of the evolution. These differences are so striking that they almost may be regarded as fundamental: they reveal opposite tendencies in the observed environments.

Another type of divergent evolution is easier to recognize, although it may be equally difficult to explain. Two neighboring societies may have common institutions, but in the course of history these institutions persist in the one country while they disappear in the adjacent territory. A good example is the evolution of the *mansus.* In Carolingian times, the soil held by the tenants of a *seigneurie* was for the greater part divided into *manses.* This was customary in the region corresponding to present-day France and also in the country which later would be called Germany. While the name *manse* was current in Romance territories, the Latin word *mansus* was usually translated into German by *hufe.* On the same *manse* several families of cultivators often lived together, but in the eyes of the lord the *manse* was a unit. Rents and services weighed not upon separate fields or buildings but upon the unit as a whole. The *manse* was the indivisible cell of agrarian organization, and it could never be split up into parcels. When we look at France around the year 1200, we find the situation changed. The word *manse* no longer designates a cadastral unit. In the Romance forms of *meix* or *mas* the term has different connotations. These words signify the house, the center of rural activity. The writers of charters no longer measure the extent of a lord's domain by the number of *manses* which it contains. The *censiers* (rent lists) received by the lord no longer simply enumerate the *manses:* the lists mention in detail the separate fields or, at any rate, separate individuals. This means that there are no longer tenures of a fixed and well-established form. The acreage, the vineyard, and the garden can be divided among different heirs or buyers; each one is an independent entity. In Germany, on the other hand, the *hufe* persists as an indivisible whole. Its fragmentation is prohibited, and it remains the basis for the allocation of rents and services in most lords' domains. Certainly, here too the *hufe* disappears, but this happens very slowly and often more in name than in fact. German lords attempt by various methods to maintain the principle of indivisible tenures, even up to the end of the manorial regime. These efforts seem to be almost absent among their French neighbors. The contrast is probably of ancient origin, since from sources of Charles the Bald's reign the disintegration of the *manse* is attested for western Gaul. The reasons for this disintegration I will not even try to scrutinize. You will agree, however, that a rural history of France or Germany which ignores the problem would be guilty of an essential omission. Looking at either of the two countries, the death of the *manse* in one case and its persistence in the other would not present a problem. It could easily be regarded as natural, and an explanation would seem superfluous. Only comparison reveals that the problem exists. A great service indeed! Is there anything more dangerous for scientific inquiry than the temptation to regard all things as natural?

VII

Antoine Meillet rightly proposes the discovery of the distinctive genius of different languages as one of the major tasks of comparative linguistics. But it should be remembered that the original effort of the discipline had another aim, namely, to determine genetic relations between languages and to find so-called "parent languages." As a result, the family of Indo-European languages was defined. Indo-European itself, at least in its basic characteristics, was reconstructed by means of hypothetical but nevertheless rather safe conjectures. These are impressive achievements of a discipline based entirely upon comparison.

Social history, in using the comparative method, is in a more difficult situation. A language is a unified and well-defined structure, but the opposite is true of whatever system of social institutions we may study. The problem of linguistic affiliations is therefore relatively much simpler. "Up to now," Meillet writes, "no case has been encountered in which we were forced to assume that the morphological system of a given language results from a mixture of the morphologies of two separate languages. In all observed cases there exists one continuous tradition of one particular language." The common way of perpetuating the tradition is the transmission of a language from the older to the younger generation. Gradual linguistic changes may also occur. Suppose, however, that at a given moment scholars discover examples of that still unknown phenomenon: genuine linguistic mixtures. Then, as Meillet writes, "linguistics must work out new methods." This terrible difficulty of "mixtures," which, if encountered in the case of languages, would be capable of embarrassing even the most self-confident of the social sciences, is very frequently suggested by the facts of the history of social institutions. True, the French language was subject to important German influences which affected its pronunciation as well as its vocabulary; but, nevertheless, French remained clearly a descendant of the kind of Latin spoken in Roman Gaul. French is the result of a linguistic transformation which was involuntary and to a large extent unconscious; but the descendants of the German tribes who took over Romance dialects made a genuine change from one language to the other. Social transformations are quite different. Nobody would venture to present French medieval society as a mere transformation of its Gallo-Roman precursor. Comparative history may reveal hitherto unnoticed interconnections between human societies, but it would be excessive optimism to expect that it would lead to the discovery of fragments of an ancient and hitherto unknown parent society.

In exceptional cases, however, comparative study enables us to demonstrate the existence of ancient affiliations between historically quite different societies. It would, of course, be very dangerous to conclude that such societies derive from a common origin, but some kind of common culture in a remote period can be recognized. An example is provided by the history of agricultural customs. Various scholars have attempted, with the help of agrarian customs and their geographical distribution, to reconstruct an ethnic map of Europe in the age preceding the existence of written records. The great effort made by Meitzen is generally known. Everybody agrees at present that the attempt ended in failure. Without entering into details, it will be useful to indicate briefly the methodological errors which led to this unfortunate outcome. First, Meitzen confused different kinds of facts which should have been kept clearly separate, for instance, the pattern of residence and the form of the fields. Second, many phenomena were regarded as "primitive" or "original," despite the fact that they had been observed in recent historical periods. Meitzen failed to recognize that these phenomena could be the outcome of relatively recent transformations. Third, the author studied mainly material facts and neglected the ideas and customs of which material circumstances are often the concrete embodiment. Fourth, he considered as ethnic components only historically attested groups, such as Celts, Germans, and Slavs. All these groups were relative newcomers in their habitats, and Meitzen therefore deliberately disregarded the influence of the substratum, to use a linguistic term. Nothing justifies the assumption that the anonymous original populations were annihilated by the invasions or that they totally abandoned their ancient customs.

From these errors an important lesson can be learned. The inquiry should not be abandoned, but it should be conducted in a more critical spirit and with a better method. At the outset we must point to a few facts. Immense areas of Europe are covered by rural territories consisting of narrow fields, without fences or enclosures. This pattern existed in England, northern and central France, almost the whole of Germany, and doubtless also in a large part of Poland and Russia. It is to be contrasted with quite different agrarian patterns: the almost square fields in the French Midi, and the enclosed fields in the western parts of France and England. The agrarian map of Europe does not at all coincide with its political and linguistic maps, and the agrarian may be older than the other two. While such a conjecture may be made, we will restrict ourselves for the present to recalling the facts rather than explaining them. If we limit ourselves now to the remarkable distribution of long and open fields (and scattered holdings) over quite different societies, it is evident from the outset that various explanatory hypotheses must be tried out: not only that there was a primordial community of culture, but also that there were technical procedures which radiated from an original center and were borrowed by neighboring societies. Nobody will ever account for the English open field, for the German *Gewanndorf,* and for the French *champs-ouverts* by merely studying England, Germany, or France separately.

Comparative history, therefore, demands most insistently that we abandon obsolete topographical compartments in which we pretend to enclose social realities; they are quite unfit for the contents which we force into them. A well-esteemed scholar some time ago wrote a whole book on *The Templars in Eure-et-Loir.* This naïve attempt may evoke a smile; but are we really so much better? As historians, do we not almost constantly fall into the same trap? It is true that the French *départements* rarely are transposed into the Middle Ages. But how often are present state boundaries used as a convenient framework for studies of past legal or economic institutions? Here we make a double mistake. In the first place, we are guilty of a glaring anachronism. A blind faith in a kind of vague "historical predestination" makes us attribute a particular significance to those lines drawn on the maps. Such lines have no prenatal existence, before the complex forces of war and diplomacy crystallize them. In the second place, another fundamental mistake is made. If a scholar is methodical enough to utilize the political, administrative, and national framework of the period with which he deals, he still encounters the difficulty that social phenomena do not always make a halt at the same boundaries, and political boundaries have no particular significance in this respect. It is generally known that the boundary or marginal zone between the dialects called *langue d'oil* and *langue d'oc* does not coincide with any political frontier. The demarcation line of *langue d'oil* on the German side does not follow the boundary of a state or *seigneurie,* and the same observation can be made for many other cultural traits. To study "French medieval cities during the period of the revival of towns" is to confuse in one vision two subjects which differ in every respect but in name. While the traditional Mediterranean cities (*oppida*) are centers of an agricultural countryside, inhabited by powerful landholders and *chevaliers,* the towns in the rest of France are mainly inhabited by merchants, who are responsible for their renewal. Would it not be an arbitrary decision to separate such towns from their counterparts in the German Rhineland? Another example is the *seigneurie* in medieval France. Any historian who had begun the study of the *seigneurie* north of the Loire would feel himself in a strange country when confronted with *langue d'oc* texts; he would feel himself quite at home, on the other hand, when studying documents from Hainault or from the Moselle region.

For each aspect of European social life, in each historical instant, the appropriate geographical framework has to be found. The boundaries are to be determined from the inside rather than from the outside. Only in this way will we at last escape from artificial divisions. This means arduous research, cautious procedures, and a great deal of trial and error. But to shrink from the task would be a sign of laziness.

VIII

Practically speaking, how should we proceed?

Undoubtedly, comparisons are valuable only when they are based upon factual studies which are detailed, critical, and well-documented. It is equally evident that, human capacity being what it is, primary studies must not be of too great geographical or chronological scope. Comparative work in the proper sense will be the task, unfortunately, of only a small group of historians. Nevertheless, it deserves some organization and certainly a place in the university curriculum. But let us not deceive ourselves: comparative studies can advance only very slowly, since in many fields the preliminary monographs are largely lacking. The old maxim remains true that a day of synthesis requires years of analysis. But too often the maxim is cited without its necessary corrective: analysis can be used for synthetic purposes only if it intends from the outset to contribute toward such an ultimate synthesis.

Authors of monographs have the duty to read what has been written by their precursors in the study of analogous subjects, not only of their particular region or adjacent territories—this is almost always done—but also of more distant regions, even of those belonging to different national or political units. This wider context is too often neglected. I venture to add: monograph writers would be well advised to study not only general handbooks but, if possible, also detailed monographs on distant regions. The latter are much more rich and lively than the broad surveys. This kind of background reading will suggest questions with which material on a given region can be approached, and hypotheses which may guide research until the discovery of new facts makes it necessary to correct or discard them. Such a procedure will save the scholar from attributing excessive importance to local pseudo-causes and, at the same time, will develop his sensitivity for specific differences.

I have pleaded here for a preliminary investigation of the existing literature. Historical scholars will find that this is not an easily traveled road. I will not occupy myself in detail with the material obstacles. But we may as well realize that they are considerable. It is an arduous task to assemble the bibliographical information, and it is still more difficult to get hold of the works themselves. A fast-working and efficient interlibrary loan service, including certain great nations which thus far have jealously guarded their treasures, would be extremely desirable. This practical aid would contribute more to the future of comparative history than a great deal of clever advice.

But the main obstacle is of an intellectual nature, and it derives from working habits which can be reformed. A linguist who specializes in one language will not find it difficult to gather data about the general characteristics of another language if he needs such information. In any grammar he will find the facts presented in categories which resemble the ones he uses in his own field. The general formula is the same. How much more unfortunate is the historian! Suppose that he is familiar with French society and that he wants to confront one of its particular aspects with the counterpart in, for example, Germany. If he reads some works devoted to the latter country, be it the most elementary manuals, he suddenly feels himself groping around in a new world.

Is the language responsible? Yes and no. Language differences as such do not prevent an almost exact correspondence between two scientific vocabularies. Of such correspondences the natural sciences give numerous examples. Rather, the serious difficulty is that, in going from German to French historical works, the words do not "cover" each others' meaning. How can the German word *Hörige* be translated into French? Or, conversely, *tenancier* into German? Several translations are possible, but they are either paraphrases (*Hörigen = les dépendants de la seigneurie*) or rough approximations (*Zinsleute = tenanciers* but of a very particular kind). A descriptive sentence as I proposed for *Hörigen* is moderately useful, but not commonly used. The lack of correspondence between the meanings of historical terms might be explained as a result of a stubborn adherence to terms commonly used in the Middle Ages. Then the discrepancy would have a historical basis and could be accepted. But such an assumption is absolutely wrong! Most discordant terms are the creations of historians who made up new words or changed the meaning of old ones. Rightly or wrongly, we have created technical terminologies. More or less unconsciously every national tradition of historians has elaborated its own vocabulary. Nobody has paid attention to neighboring schools, with the result that in European history a Babylonian confusion prevails. Great danger of misunderstanding threatens the inexperienced student, and, of course, every scholar becomes inexperienced as soon as he leaves his special region or nation. I have known a scholar who studied the *Mark,* as it is called in German history books (an area which several villages cultivate in common). He had studied this phenomenon in an originally Germanic country, and I had the greatest difficulty in persuading him that similar practices existed and still exist in many countries outside Germany. For instance, he did not believe that it existed in France, since French history books have no special word for this kind of collective agriculture!

Discordant terms are symptoms of a basic lack of harmony. Different schools of historiography almost never ask the same questions, and this holds whether one studies the works of French, German, Italian, or English scholars. As an example of this perpetual misunderstanding I have mentioned above the subject of agrarian transformations, but the examples could easily be multiplied. Witness the subject of *ministérialité,*[6] which has been completely neglected in descriptions of medieval society in France and England, or the subject of legal rights, which are classified differently in every country. If a historian asks himself whether some institution or event has a parallel outside the past of his own

[6] Marc Bloch, "Une problème d'histoire comparée: la ministérialité en France et en Allemagne," *Revue historique du droit français et étranger* (1928).

country, perhaps with modifications, he is often unable to satisfy this legitimate curiosity. If he finds nothing on the subject in the works consulted, he will still have doubts whether the silence means the absence of parallel instances or whether a great problem has been overlooked.

At this congress, I believe, much eloquence will be devoted to the conciliatory role of history in bringing different nations together. You need have no fear that I will improvise upon this delicate theme. Comparative history, in my opinion, is purely a scientific pursuit without practical ends, which merely attempts to extend our knowledge. Yet, what about a reconciliation of terms and basic questions? Let us address first the authors of general handbooks. Their role in providing information and guidance is crucial. For the moment, we will not ask them to abandon the national compartments in which they usually enclose themselves. In this respect science can only gradually achieve a better adaptation to reality. We merely ask handbook writers to remember that they will be read in countries other than their own. The plan, the basic questions, and the terminology of their general works should be inspired by analogous works produced elsewhere. This suggestion is similar to that which I have already given to authors of monographs. In this way, by mutual co-operation, a common scientific language may evolve which comprises both a collection of symbols and a classificatory order. Comparative history may then become more easily known, and it will also be better served by monograph studies. The latter will be greatly stimulated. Monographs are the prerequisites of comparative studies, but they would lead nowhere if the synthetic approach were absent. Let us by all means end the misunderstandings which exist among the various national schools of historiography. A dialogue between deaf people, each of whom answers with complete disregard for the other's questions, may be a standard device of comedy and draw laughter from a susceptible public, but it hardly deserves recommendation as an intellectual activity.

31

Conclusion

By FREDERIC C. LANE

Among the themes presented in the foregoing selections, the one that seems most worth commenting on in this conclusion is the contrast between a theoretical interest and a historical interest. Like most of the other issues concerning method in economic history, this contrast affects all knowledge about human action, but it is particularly important in our discipline because economic history depends, as its very name suggests, on the interaction of the two interests. Moreover, I believe it is a practical help to anyone undertaking a study in economic history to recognize that the theoretical interest and the historical interest, although often combined in the same individual, produce different results.

In his discussion of the comparative method it is apparent that Marc Bloch is interested in the particular instances examined, not merely as examples, but as interesting and worthy of study in themselves. Therein he reveals himself as basically a historian. A most eloquent formulation of this interest can be found in Clapham's inaugural lecture: "If the economic historian has his modesties in presence of the pure economist he also has his pride. He is proud because, by definition as a historian, he is one to whom the tangled variety of human life is attractive in itself; one who will study alterations in the tangle for the love of it, even when his information is such that he can never hope to pick out with assurance the forces at work, or measure exactly the changes brought about by the aggregate of them between dates x and y."[1] The selections from Arthur Spiethoff serve equally to make evident that from the historical point of view a knowledge of particulars, or some segments of the past, is worth while in itself. On the other hand, what I here call the "theoretical interest" aims at finding generalizations and leads to the feeling that intellectual progress consists in perfecting generalizations, that every body of knowledge advances by being formulated more and more in general terms.

[1] John H. Clapham, *The Study of Economic History* (Cambridge, Eng., 1929), p. 34.

Few people will deny that generalizations are to some extent desirable. The wish to know some particulars about the past is quite as strong, however, as the desire to generalize. I think it should be granted that a knowledge of particulars is justified as an end in itself. Certainly our wish to know about the American Revolution is not based merely on a desire to generalize about revolutions, nor do we wish to know about campaigns of the Civil War merely in order to be able to formulate general rules of strategy and tactics. Both interests—the historical interest in particulars and the theoretical interest in reaching generalizations—are to be accepted as each being independently worth while.

Since I will be referring so often to the "particular" and the "general," I offer an illustration to make clearer what I have in mind. Consider the following series of statements, the accuracy of which is at the moment irrelevant. Assuming that they were all equally accurate, which would be of most interest? Which would be the most important contribution to knowledge?

Example A

1. In 1300 Carrefour had a population of 1,000, its manufactures were sold to the immediate neighborhood only, and it contained 20 distinct crafts. In 1800 its population was 500,000, its manufactures were sold to distant markets, and it contained 2,000 distinct crafts.
2. An increase in specialization among industrial workers occurred in Europe between 1300 and 1800 as a result of the increase in the size of cities and the extension of their market areas.
3. The extent of division of labor depends on the extent of the market.

Obviously, the last statement is the one of most importance to anyone with theoretical interests. On the other hand, a person dominated by a historical interest will find the first or second statements the more interesting and consider them, if true, additions to the body of knowledge, which is his primary concern. As the contrast between the first and second sentences makes clear, the amount of generalization is a matter of degree, and there are many intermediate degrees of generalization, just as there are many shades of grey between black and white. Theoretical thought seeks truth with the maximum possible generality. Historical thought seeks truths that are of limited generality; it is, comparatively speaking, interested in particulars for their own sake. This difference in objective is no reason to call either type of thought inferior to the other. They spring from different interests, from different aspects of the desire to know.

Each type of thought makes use of the other. The theoretical draws on the knowledge of particular cases in order to discover general principles; the historical draws on theory in order to understand particular cases. But when they are thus helping each other, the contrast in their basic goals persists. To the theorist, particular historical cases are merely means to his end and have no real interest except in so far as they help him improve his generalizations. To the historian, the generalizations of the theorists are a means which interest him because they help him find out what he wants to know about particular past events.

In studying occurrences in the physical universe, theoretical interests generally dominate. For example: At 11:00 P.M. on January 16, 1943, the newly built steel tanker "Schenectady," while at its outfitting dock at Portland, Oregon, split across the deck and down both sides. The cracking of the steel was, like an eruption of a volcano, an individual historical event, a particular incident in time and place. A committee of engineering experts immediately conducted an investigation of the accident, and their report was an example of historical inquiry concerned with explaining, not human action, but a purely physical occurrence. They recorded the temperature and the change in temperature which occurred immediately before the cracking, the quality of the steel, the point at which the fracture began and the direction in which it proceeded, and the relation of the position of the fracture to the structure of the ship. All these particulars were noted in an effort to determine the causes of the fracture, the causes of this particular historical event. The search for causes was guided by some general theories about the nature of steel and the effects of welding on steel. The engineering experts, in their professional capacity, were interested in the particular historical event, the cracking of the "Schenectady," only in so far as its history would enable them to add to their general knowledge of the behavior of steel in ships. When on March 29, 1943, another tanker, the "Esso Manhattan," built in a quite different shipyard, split entirely in two on a calm day at the entrance to New York harbor, they were presented with another case study for the testing of their theories. All these cases, because entirely unplanned, I will call in a special sense "accidents." While studying the accidents, the experts planned to attach gauges to certain ships to measure stresses under various conditions; well-planned case studies of this kind are called "experiments." Statistics were compiled concerning the time, place, and characteristics of all fractures, even quite minor ones, in any of the thousands of welded ships in operation. As a result, then, of various kinds of historical study —general statistical surveys and closer examination of a few particular

cases, some unplanned "accidents" and others planned "experiments"—new generalizations applicable to the problem were developed and in later years were applied to ship design and the setting of specifications for steel plate. From the point of view of engineering science or applied physics, the cracking of the "Schenectady" became merely one of many cases to be studied comparatively. Scientists were interested in the general conclusions concerning the effects of heat and cold on the crystalline structure of steel; the naval architects were interested in conclusions that would affect the design of ships and the writing of steel specifications. These conclusions were revised again and again in the light of new experience, while the particular event that had occurred at Portland, Oregon, on January 16, 1943, passed into "history."

When a science is based on experiments, that is, on the study of events which the scientists planned and can cause to happen again, the setting of a particular case in time and place becomes so unimportant that it is easy to forget entirely that historical records of particular events, namely, of the experiments, lie at the foundations of these sciences. In the natural sciences with a more descriptive character, such as geology, the description of past occurrences as such, of the unplanned events which I have called "accidents," is of more evident importance.

Whether the cases studied be human actions or physical events, the methods used in studying them are subject to the same logical requirements if the theoretical interest is to be served. To a large extent the methods used in compiling and analyzing the laboratory notebooks that are the historical records of the natural scientist can and do serve as models for those students of human behavior whose method is determined by their theoretical interest. Simiand's method is an example.

To be sure, even those students of human affairs whose interests are theoretical differ from students of the physical universe in one important respect: they tend to formulate generalizations in terms of human motives, interests, and attitudes. The theoretical interest does not necessarily exclude an interest in human motives, attitudes, and institutional patterns. On the contrary, even Simiand, in making generalizations about "social facts," included attitudes as an essential ingredient of these "social facts."

What are the consequences of this difference between natural scientists and students of human affairs? In answering that question, it is desirable to distinguish between verification and discovery. (1) Are generalizations about human conduct subject to different criteria of truth, to different logical standards in verification, than those applied

in the study of the physical universe? My answer is "No." We may know by inner experience something about the human nature which is the subject of our generalizations, but this does not make it less necessary to apply the rigorous standards of verification developed by natural scientists. It makes it more necessary; for individuals differ as to their internal experience and accordingly are biased in one way or another. (2) When generalizations are first conceived, they are unproved hypotheses that come to the mind as flashes of insight. Some are sound, most of them are erroneous. Natural scientists recognize the importance of these "flashes of insight" quite as much as do the students of human affairs. We know little of this mental process, but it seems to me that the kinds of generalizations we make about human affairs are necessarily influenced by what we know of human nature from inner experience. Probably the influence is beneficial, and to that extent the student of man has an advantage over the student of physical things. But, for those with theoretical interests, this disadvantage is more than counterbalanced by the disadvantage already mentioned, namely, that our inner knowledge of human nature makes it very much more difficult to be entirely logical and accurate in testing and discarding the enormous output of "insights" which will not stand the test of verification.

In placing so much stress on verification, I may seem to deny the value of the sort of generalizations which cannot be verified. Unverifiable generalizations are exactly the kind which many readers of economic journals may, with some justification, associate with theoretical interests. There is, of course, a large output of economic theory which makes no claim that it can be verified by case studies, statistics, experiments, or any other empirical procedure. Indeed, some theorists claim that logical consistency is the one and only test of all generalization. Their activity seems to me comparable in many respects to that of mathematicians; they are concerned with ways of finding the logical consequences of certain assumptions, whether or not the conditions described in the assumptions exist, have existed, are likely to exist, or are utterly unlikely ever to exist. Economic theorists have approached most closely to the mathematicians in their methods, but such social theory as that produced by Max Weber in certain parts of *Wirtschaft und Gesellschaft* is similarly an elaboration of logical possibilities. As Spiethoff says, it is also pure theory. The usefulness of pure theory in building a body of knowledge about human affairs seems to me as undeniable as the usefulness of mathematics in our knowledge of the physical universe. But, to avoid misunderstanding, I must repeat that

I have been using the expression "theoretical interest" to designate, not pure theory only, but all effort aimed at a maximum amount of generalization. I have had in mind particularly the effort to combine as much generalization as possible with conformity to fact. Scientists who make this effort and those in whom the historical interest dominates have a common interest in historical case studies.

What, then, is the method appropriate to a study of historical events under the guidance of a theoretical interest? In spite of the fact that it is dealing with human nature, the study is comparable in most respects to a scientific or engineering study of an "accident." In describing the events, the investigator selects aspects which seem likely to make it fit into some general category (for example, the category of prices or price levels); he seeks other concurrent events which there is some reason to think may occur in some general relation to the kind of event being described (for example, depreciation of the currency or population growth) and examines the relations of the various events to see whether an available generalization, such as the quantity theory of money, is confirmed or whether it needs modification in view of the new facts, and, if so, how. A theoretical interest in economic history calls for a selection of "test cases" by standards as near as possible to those used in experimental sciences. It calls for a continual use of the comparative method both in selecting new cases for study and in interpreting the results of each new case examined.

Are different methods appropriate for the investigator dominated by historical interests? He starts with a particular event (such as the American Revolution) in the center of his attention, but he, too, has some ideas about general causal relations. He, too, selects for description aspects of the event which classify it under known general categories, and he describes attendant circumstances which seem causally relevant. His selection of characteristics and circumstances depends on what general theories he has explicitly or implicitly in mind concerning events of that type. As an example, reconsider Collingwood's reference to the killing of Julius Caesar. The historian who describes it by using such words as "dictator," "Senate," "assassination," "republicanism," is thereby stating aspects of the event that place it in certain general categories. In so far as relevant generalizations about human behavior available in the general body of knowledge of his time are known to him, the historian uses such generalizations as aids in framing his description.

But, in regard to the choice of topics and the range of the investigation, there is a contrast between the procedures dictated by historical and theoretical interests. If the dominant interest is theoretical, then the investigator, in asking himself what he should investigate, starts thinking about some general relation, such as that between a rise in prices and an increase in the quantity of money; asks himself whether there are any cases to the contrary or whether the relation is the same in all cases; hits on a case in which it seems superficially that the relation is unusual, for example, a country in which there occurred during some period a large importation of precious metals without a comparable rise in prices; and inquires into the special circumstances of that case. Perhaps he finds evidence of increases in population and in the velocity of the circulation of money. His findings may suggest a slightly more sophisticated form of the quantity theory of money. Following up his theoretical interest, he would turn next to other cases of increase in population, cases which occurred with or without increasing velocity of circulation. He would compare the many cases, seeking to find what general statement could be made that would be true of all of them. His standard in selecting new cases to study would be their value in enabling him to frame a statement with a maximum possible amount of generality.

When the dominant interest is historical, however, the investigator starts with a question which is, to some extent at least, tied to a particular time and place, such a question as: How did London become the financial center of the world? He is interested in the historical question for itself, not because answering it will make possible a generalization applicable to other cases. He begins looking for attendant circumstances that seem causally pertinent to his problem—for example, the pattern of trade or the financing of wars or the location of gold production. His selection of these circumstances as pertinent to his problem implies, at least, some general theories about the relations between financial settlements, on the one hand, and trade balances, government finance, and flow of precious metals, on the other. To evaluate the circumstances and give a causal explanation of the rise of London as a financial center, a historian needs to know what the best generalizations are which the theorists have attained. But, since one man cannot do everything, a historian is less concerned with changing these generalizations than he is with applying them for the solution of his problem. If his theme is the London money market, he will not desert it for the sake of making case studies of other money markets, not unless his historical interest weakens and a theoretical interest takes the upper hand.

Historical interest is thus a consumer, rather than a producer, of broad generalizations. Only by giving second place to his historical interest can an investigator let his research be directed into the paths necessary to test a generalization, modify it according to new findings, test its new form, and present as the fruit of his labors a new or improved generalization, more universally applicable. Consequently, the historian does not basically bear the responsibility for the quality of the generalizations which form our knowledge about human action in general. He does not bear the producer's responsibility for the quality of the generalizations in use. But he does have a consumer's responsibility for the quality of the particular products he uses. He deserves to be reproached, if he treats as sound, generalizations which have proved unsound. He needs to know the best of the theoretical thought of his time, and the investigator dominated by historical interest in economic events needs to know especially what his contemporaries with theoretical interests are thinking about economic behavior.

What most historians actually do most of the time is to use the generalizations which they find more or less explicit in the sources from which they construct the record. Perhaps there is less of that in the study of events that are so recent that we do not ordinarily think of them as historical, as was the cracking of the "Schenectady" for the investigating committee, but which are historical in the sense that they occurred once and for all in a definable time and place. Since our contemporaries are the sources of information on such events, however, we are quite likely to be affected by their general ideas, their theories. In examining the more distant past, a historian spends so much time working with the sources closest to the event that he can hardly fail to have in mind the general ideas there expressed—expressed even in the terms in which events are described—and to have no other generalizations to guide him unless he makes a deliberate effort to discover what generalizations about human behavior have been produced by the most recent thinkers on the subject.

Is it sound practice to introduce into the examination of past epochs general theories based on modern studies of society? Many of my historical colleagues seem to deny it; many passages in Collingwood's attack on the positivist methods in history seem to deny it. A history which consists essentially of reliving the past has no place for such theories, it is said. But Collingwood himself, when at work as a historian of Roman Britain, uses generalizations concerning the relation between methods of cultivation and the shape of the fields; and I doubt whether he would maintain that those generalizations were part of the thoughts of the Britons of Roman times. I see no reason why the study of money and prices in the sixteenth century A.D.—or in the sixth century B.C., for that matter—should be limited to aspects of events which were recognized by the people of the time. A good causal analysis of a past event should consider not only what the contemporaries thought was causally relevant but also causes which contemporaries knew nothing of but which are suggested by the modern body of knowledge about human affairs.

Nevertheless, historical interest leads to a living with the sources, and the investigator, trying as best he can to penetrate beneath deceptive rationalization, enters as far as possible into the attitudes and thoughts of those about whom he writes. Consequently, when faced with the problem of deciding which facts to present, of deciding, that is, what events are causally relevant to one another, he proceeds mainly by setting forth what was thought relevant by the people about whom he is writing. It would be a mistake to leave that out. The main interest now attached to the cracking of the tanker "Schenectady" is the human side of the event, the alarm it caused at the moment and the accusations exchanged by shipbuilders and steel manufacturers.

Generalizations in history and social science are, as we have seen, generalizations about human conduct. In framing them, we use our ability to participate in thoughts and feelings common to men generally. The use of what Germans have called *Verstehen* is indispensable, unavoidable, I think, in any striving toward general knowledge of human action. (And the process of striving to relive the past has other values; it can be justified on grounds that would be irrelevant here.) But a result of thus approaching events "from the inside" is to suggest to anyone of lively imagination a large number of conflicting generalizations. Distinguishing between the true and the false raises many difficulties, some of them basic problems of methodology which are still in dispute.

It must be admitted, therefore, that most causal explanations given by historians, even those given by as intelligent, widely informed, and careful a historian as Marc Bloch, have a very weak foundation in general theory. This is particularly true in regard to what Marc Bloch has called "particular causes," that is, the causes of differences in development when the two cases being compared are cases within the same general culture. An example is his description of the different combination of circumstances in England and France about the year A.D. 1100 and his explanation of the differences in social structure that appeared later when hereditary classes became more firmly established. Because the civilizations of France and England were of common origin, the differing circumstances in the two countries were relatively few. Yet they were enormous compared to the differences which an experimental scientist has to take into account when he analyzes and seeks a "particular cause." A chemist who put different combinations of substances into two test tubes and wrote in his laboratory notebook a comparative history of what happened when the test tubes were heated would be seeking a particular cause, namely, the cause of the difference in events in the two cases. In setting up his experiment, the chemist can create a degree of similarity between the cases which makes analyzing the cause of the difference relatively easy. The historian cannot thus simplify the difference between the cases being compared, and therefore descriptions of these differences occupy a prominent place in the historian's search for particular causes.

Moreover, the historian's interest compels him to seek particular causes even if he knows no general principles which can be applied to the case in question. According to the general logical theory of causality, a causal explanation is not well-founded unless the particular event or circumstance which is treated as the cause can be identified as a member of a general class of events or circumstances about which we have some general knowledge from other cases. The chemist's causal explanation of the different reactions in his two test tubes will be framed in terms of general categories, namely, chemical elements. The validity of the chemist's explanation depends on its being in accord with other cases and with the established knowledge concerning the properties of the chemical elements involved. The historian does not usually have a similarly well-developed system of classification to apply or knowledge of the pertinent general relationships. Although the economic historian is probably better off in this respect than the social historian, both are working in relative darkness. Nevertheless, it is part of the historian's function to explain as best he can, in the light of the inadequate general knowledge available to him, particular differences in historical development.

In the foregoing pages I have been concerned with analyzing the divergence of the historical and theoretical interest. For an economic historian to understand what he is doing, it is important that he recognize this divergence in lines of interest and recognize that both lines are worth-while ways of extending human knowledge. Many investigators start off on one line and then switch over to the other without fully realizing that they have changed their objective. They may start to test the truth of the hypothesis suggested by Max Weber's work, namely, that religious attitudes determine economic organization, or Marx's that economic organization determines religious attitudes; pick a particular case to work on, such as religion and business in the Netherlands in the sixteenth century; and end up more interested in the particular case than in the generalization with which they began. They may start out seeking a general proposition concerning factors producing change from one form of industrial organization, such as the putting-out system, to some other form, such as the factory system; pick a particular case to work on, such as the French cotton textile industry in the nineteenth century; and end up by writing a history of that industry, bringing in and explaining, as far as possible, a variety of the characteristics which that industry developed during the century—all of which is as it should be in a work dominated by historical interest in that particular historical "individual," the French textile industry of the nineteenth century, but which distracts the investigator from choosing and analyzing cases comparatively, as he should do if his dominant purpose is to discover valid generalizations. His final product should not be condemned, then, on the grounds that it fails to arrive at any clear-cut theoretical result, unless, of course, he fails to realize how his aim has changed and presents his work as if it were a theoretical study. Similarly, the investigator whose examination of historical particulars is limited to those which for him have theoretical significance should not be reproached for having failed to include "all sides of the story," provided that he has included those pertinent to his theoretical inquiry, and provided, of course, that he does not claim that he has presented the whole history of an event when in fact he has studied only the side pertinent to the generalizations in which he is interested.

Although I wish to insist, above all, on the consequences of the difference between the desire to generalize and the desire to know about historical events, I must turn now to consider some consequences of the fact that the difference is a matter of degree. As illustrated by the series of sentences offered as examples at the beginning of this discussion, economic history as presented in the basic manuals on the subject emphasizes mainly statements of an intermediate degree of generality, such as the statement that the variety of specialized occupations multiplied in the growing cities of Europe in the nineteenth century because of the extension of their markets. These are historical statements because they apply to a particular time and place. They are also general statements that summarize certain observed uniformities in the occurrences within that time and place. Because of their degree of generality, it is conceivable that they should be called "theories." They form a part of what Spiethoff would call *anschauliche Theorie,* although to satisfy his conception they have to be part of a general pattern or Gestalt embracing the essential causal relationships. How to determine what is "essential" seems to me the difficult point in his methodology, but I cannot probe that point here. The question that interests me is this: Are these "historical generalizations," as I will call those of this intermediate degree of generality, worth while because they are steppingstones to broader generalizations? Or are they worth while in themselves, that is, because they satisfy the historical interest? I believe the latter.

How far is the historical interest to be satisfied by historical generalizations and how far is it to be satisfied only by relatively very specific statements? To weigh the question in more specific terms, consider another series of statements of varying degree of generality somewhat more elaborate than that introduced at the beginning of this discussion.

Example B

1. In March 1440 the Senate of the Venetian Republic voted to charter four great galleys to carry specified cargoes to London and Bruges.
2. Nearly every year in the fifteenth century the Venetian government sent three to five galleys for the transport of high-priced cargoes on voyages to the English Channel.
3. In the later Middle Ages the Venetian government sent merchant galleys to all the main seaboard trade centers of the Mediterranean and western Europe to assume the safety of precious cargoes.
4. Medieval city-states made most elaborate provision for those branches of trade affecting most the income of the government, the supply of precious metals, and the food supply.
5. Governmental action in regard to commerce is always most intense on those exchanges which are believed to affect the income of the government, and the supply of food and of military stores, and the conditions of the currency.

Here, as in the earlier example, the last statement is in such general terms that a person dominated by historical interest will consider it, even if true, a less valuable contribution to knowledge than one of the preceding statements. But which preceding statement? If the value of statements 1–4 does not lie in their enabling us to arrive at the final most general statement, or some better generalization on the same theme, how decide which of the preceding statements is of most importance? Having rejected the proposition that, of two statements of equal validity, the more general is always the more important, are we without any criterion of relative importance? Is there no way in which to draw the line, then, between history and antiquarianism?

Logically, I do not think there is any general universally valid answer. Because of the nature of our culture, certain historical generalizations are esteemed of interest in themselves. Any general statement about why industrialism increased in the early nineteenth century and how it affected the family or social structure is, if true, worth while, whether or not it is a steppingstone to some statement about the nature of industrialism which is of so sweeping a character that it will apply also to the twentieth century. The worker in economic history, whether graduate student or director of a research institute, takes his interests from daily converse with other participants in our culture. The striving to attain a maximum of generalization is one characteristic of that culture; the effort to know about man's past is another prominent feature. He therefore encounters certain historical generalizations as well as universal generalizations; and, according to his bent, he can consider either one the means, the other the end.

Perhaps some readers will deny that either is justified in its own right and will argue that a third interest, the desire to predict, is and should be stronger in our culture than either the effort to generalize or to wish to know particulars about the past. Many people believe that prediction is the essence of science, that attempts at prediction should dominate all study of human affairs, and that the rules for acquiring and organizing knowledge should be shaped accordingly. How far knowledge can be so organized is too large a question to be examined here, but it is my impression that efforts by social scientists to predict what will really happen next in the continuing stream of history have not been notably successful. The will to construct a systematic body of knowledge enabling us to predict social developments is based on faith, therefore, not on the amount of success already attained in making such predictions. Concern over ability to predict has been increasing in economic history, but it still shares the field with the two rival interests we have examined, the theoretical and the historical.

Biographical Appendix

Biographical Appendix

MARC BLOCH (1886–1944) studied history and geography at the École Normale Supérieure in Paris. He published his doctoral dissertation on medieval history in 1920 (*Rois et serfs. Un chapitre d'histoire capétienne*); in 1919 he had been appointed professor of that subject at the University of Strasbourg. From 1936 on, he was professor of economic history at the Sorbonne. During the years 1939–40 he served in the French army, as he had in World War I. He returned to historical work in 1940. When in 1943 the Germans occupied the so-called "zône libre" he could not continue teaching because of his Jewish origins and because of his activities in the Résistance in 1941 and 1942, at Montpellier. After 1943 he devoted himself entirely to the Résistance. He was shot by the Germans on June 16, 1944.

An important journal of economic and social history was founded in 1929 by Marc Bloch and Lucien Febvre: *Annales d'histoire économique et sociale.* Many of Bloch's articles, reviews, and notes can be found in its volumes. He published the following books: *L'Ile de France. (Les pays autour de Paris)* (1913); *Les rois thaumaturges* (1924); *Les caractères originaux de l'histoire rurale française* (1931); *La société féodale* (Vol. I, 1939; Vol. II, 1940). A bibliography of his writings is contained in Lucien Febvre, "Marc Bloch et Strasbourg," in *Mémorial des années 1939–1945, Publications de la faculté des lettres de Strasbourg,* fasc. 103 (1947), pp. 190–93; see also Charles-Edmond Perrin, "L'œuvre historique de Marc Bloch," *Revue historique,* 1948, CXCIX, 161–88, and G. Debien, "Marc Bloch and Rural History," *Agricultural History,* 1947, XXI, 187–89.

SIR JOHN CLAPHAM (1873–1946), English economic historian, began his career as a student of history at the University of Cambridge, where he studied under Acton, Marshall, and Cunningham. He became professor of economics at the University of Leeds (1902) and returned some years later to Cambridge, where he was appointed senior tutor in economic history. In 1928 Clapham became the first professor in this subject at the University of Cambridge. He played an important role in the Economic History Society. He laid the plans for the *Cambridge Economic History,* of which the first volume appeared in 1941 under the editorship of himself and Eileen Power. He had retired from teaching in 1938.

Main works: *The Woollen and Worsted Industries* (1907); *The Economic Development of France and Germany, 1815–1914* (1921); *An Economic History of Modern Britain* (3 vols., 1926, 1932, 1938); *The Bank of England: A History* (2 vols., 1944). One will find a bibliography of his writings in the obituary by M. M. Postan, "Sir John Clapham," *Economic History Review,* 1946, XVI.

ARTHUR H. COLE (1889–), since 1933, has been professor of business economics at Harvard University. After his graduation from Bowdoin College he studied economics at Harvard University under Edwin F. Gay. He obtained the doctoral degree in 1916, was appointed tutor, and subsequently professor of economics at Harvard University. Since 1929 he has been librarian of the Baker Library, Harvard Business School. He was editor of the *Review of Economic Statistics* (1935–37); associate editor of the *Journal of Economic History* (1943–46); since its inception in 1940, he has been chairman of the Committee on Research in Economic History (Social Science Research Council); and since 1948 he has been executive director of the Research Center in Entrepreneurial History, Harvard University.

Main works: *The American Wool Manufacture* (1926); (with W. B. Smith) *Fluctuations in American Business, 1790–1860* (1935); *Wholesale Commodity Prices in the United States, 1700–1861* (1938); (with H. F. Williamson) *The American Carpet Manufacture* (1941); and *Measures of Business Change: A Baker Library Index* (1952).

RAYMOND ADRIEN DE ROOVER (1904–) has specialized in the history of medieval business organization and finance; he is at present professor of economics at Wells College, New York. After graduating from the Institut Supérieur de Commerce in Antwerp (1924) he became accounting expert and member of the staff of a large Belgian steamship company, the Agence Maritime Internationale. Later on he studied business administration and history at Harvard University (M. Bus. Ad., 1938), and economics at the University of Chicago (Ph.D., 1943). Main works: *Jan Impijn. Essai historique et technique sur le premier traité flamand de comptabilité* (1928); *The Medici Bank, Its Organization, Management, Operations, and Decline* (1948); *Money, Banking, and Credit in Medieval Bruges* (1948); *Gresham on Foreign Exchange* (1949); also several articles.

LUIGI EINAUDI (1874–) was elected President of the Italian Republic in May, 1948. He studied economics at the University of Turin and was professor of public finance at that university from 1902 to 1943. He also taught economics and public finance at the School of Engineering in Turin and at the Bocconi University of Milan. His main contributions lie in the fields of finance, taxation, and social policy. He became in 1901 an editor of *La riforma sociale,* a journal devoted to the scientific study of social and economic problems and to social reform. Between 1908 and 1935 he was director as well as editor. In 1936, with the termination of *La riforma sociale,* Einaudi founded a new journal, *Rivista di storia economica.* He has fulfilled a large number of official functions; in 1946 he became governor of the Bank of Italy.

The vast number of works he has written can be surveyed in the bibliography by Anselmo Bernardino, *L'opera di Luigi Einaudi, Saggio bibliographico* (Padova, 1950). Of interest to the economic historian are particularly: *Un principe mercante* (1900), *La finanza sabauda all'apprirsi del secolo XVIII e durante la guerra di sucessorio spagnuolo* (1907); *La guerra e il sistema tributaria italiana* (1927); *La condotta economica e gli effetti sociali della guerra italiana* (1933); *Saggi sul risparmio e l'imposta* (1941); *Lezioni di politica sociale* (1949). He edited *Paradoxes inédits de M. Malestroit* (1939).

EDWIN F. GAY (1867–1946) was a major influence in making economic history an established discipline in American universities. After graduating from the University of Michigan he spent a number of years at European universities and in private reading, concentrating first on medieval and ecclesiastical history and later, under Schmoller's guidance, on economic history. He received the doctoral degree at the University of Berlin with a dissertation on the English enclosures: *Zur Geschichte der Einhegungen in England* (1902). During the same year he was appointed instructor in economics at Harvard University, where he was later for many years professor of economic history.

During World War I, Gay participated in the work of government agencies; at the end of the war he was director of the Central Bureau of Planning and Statistics. Within the world of learning he inspired, planned, or directed over the years various educational and research institutions—among others, the Graduate School of Business Administration at Harvard University and, with Wesley C. Mitchell, the National Bureau of Economic Research. Gay was active in the establishment of the Committee on Research in Economic History and of the Economic History Association, of which he was the first president. From 1928 to 1932 he was editor of *The Journal of Economic and Business History.* In 1932 appeared a memorial volume in his honor, under the title *Facts and Factors in Economic History.*

N. S. B. GRAS (1884–), has been professor of business history at Harvard University since 1927. He was graduated from the University of Western Ontario, and in 1912 he obtained his doctorate at Harvard. After teaching history at Clark University (1912–18) he became professor of economic history at the University of Minnesota. After his return to Harvard in 1927 he became editor of the *Harvard Studies in Business History.* Since 1947 he has been president of the Business History Foundation.

Main works: *The Evolution of the English Corn Market* (1915); *The*

Early English Customs System (1918); (with Ethel Gras) *The Economic and Social History of an English Village* (1929); *Industrial Evolution* (1930); *The Massachusetts First National Bank of Boston, 1784–1934* (1937); and *Business and Capitalism* (1939).

EARL J. HAMILTON (1899–), during 1950–52 president of the Economic History Association, is professor of economics at the University of Chicago. He was graduated in 1920 from Missouri State College and obtained the doctor's degree at Harvard University in 1929. Afterward he became successively professor of economics at Duke University (1929–44), Northwestern University (1944–47), and the University of Chicago (1947–). Since 1948 he has been editor of the *Journal of Political Economy.*

His main interest has been the study of secular movements of prices and wages; he spent a number of years working in the archives of Spain, France, and other European countries to obtain the data required to put these studies on a firm empirical basis. He has also done research in a number of Latin-American countries on similar problems.

Main works: *American Treasure and the Price Revolution in Spain, 1501–1650* (1934); *Money, Prices and Wages in Valencia, Aragon, and Navarre, 1351–1500* (1936); *War and Prices in Spain, 1651–1800* (1947); *The First Fifty Years of the Bank of Spain* (1949); *El florecimiento del capitalismo y otros ensayos de historia economica* (1948).

OSCAR HANDLIN (1915–) studied American social history at Harvard University, specializing in the development of economic forms and of social groups in the United States. His doctoral dissertation, *Boston's Immigrants* (1941), was awarded the Dunning Prize of the American Historical Association. He has since written extensively on the history of the American people; his more recent works include *This Was America* (1949) and *The Uprooted* (1951).

Mary F. Handlin studied political science at Columbia University and at the London School of Economics. In addition to the article reprinted here, Mr. and Mrs. Handlin have collaborated on *Commonwealth: The Role of Government in the American Economy* (1947); *Danger in Discord* (1948); "Revolutionary Economic Policy in Massachusetts," *William and Mary Quarterly* (1947); "Origins of the Southern Labor System," *ibid.* (1949).

ELI F. HECKSCHER (1879–), historian and economist, studied at the University of Uppsala; in 1907 he obtained his degree and an appointment at the University of Stockholm. With the establishment of the Handelshögskolan (1909), Heckscher was appointed its professor of political economy and statistics. In 1929 he became director of the Ekonomiska Historiska Institut. Heckscher brought economic history to academic recognition in Sweden. He became professor of the subject at the University of Stockholm in 1937. He retired in 1944.

Heckscher took a strong interest in issues of social policy, participating in economic discussions in the 1920's as a contributor to the leading newspaper, *Dagens Nyheter.* In 1926 he served on a government committee on unemployment.

His works and articles have been listed in *Eli F. Heckscher's Bibliografi, 1897–1949,* E. Söderlund, ed. (1950). His main works are: *Världskriget Ekonomi* (1915), *Svenska Produktionsproblem* (1918), *Gammal och Ny Ekonomisk Liberalism* (1921), *Kontinentalsystemet* (1918; in English translation, 1922), *Mercantilismen* (2 vols., 1931; in English translation, 1935); *Industrialismen* (1931); and his unfinished *Sveriges Ekonomiska Historia från Gustav Vasa,* a monumental work in many volumes. Together with B. Boëthius, Heckscher edited *Svensk Handelsstatistik, 1637–1737* (1938).

LELAND H. JENKS (1892–), at present professor of sociology at Wellesley College, obtained his doctorate in history at Columbia University in 1927. His main works are *The Migration of British Capital to 1875* (1927); *Our Cuban Colony: A Study in Sugar* (1928).

FREDERIC C. LANE (1900–) graduated from Cornell University in 1921 and subsequently studied at the universities of Bordeaux and Vienna (1923–24). In 1930 he obtained his doctor's degree at Harvard University with a dissertation on *Venetian Ships and Shipbuilders of the Renaissance* (published 1934), and in 1944 published *Andrea Barbarigo, Merchant of Venice.*

Since 1946 he has been professor of history at the Johns Hopkins University. He has been editor of *The Journal of Economic History* (1943–51). As historian of the United States Maritime Commission, he wrote *Ships for Victory* (1951).

GINO LUZZATTO (1878–) is at present head of the Graduate School of Business in Venice, where he teaches economic history. After obtaining his degree at the University of Padua in 1898 he was successively appointed at institutions of learning in Bari, Trieste, and Venice. He became a member of the Accademia dei Lincei and financial councillor of the city of Venice.

A bibliography of his writings can be found in a memorial volume which appeared in 1950: *Studi in onore di Gino Luzzatto,* Corrado Barbagallo *et al.,* eds., Vol. I, pp. ix–xx. Important works: *I banchieri ebrei in Urbino*

(1903); *La cronica di Dino Compagni* (1904); *I servi nelle grandi proprietà ecclesiastici dei secoli IX e X* (1909); *Storia del commercio dall'antichità al Rinascimento* (1914); *I prestiti della Repubblica di Venezia* (1929); *Storia economica dell'età moderna e contemporanea, I: L'età moderna* (1932), *II: L'età contemporanca dal 1700 al 1894* (1948); *Storia economica d'Italia,* Vol. I (1949). See also his articles: "Les banques publiques de Venise (siècles XVI–XVIII)," in *History of the Principal Public Banks,* J. G. van Dillen, ed. (1934); "Les noblesses: Les activités économiques du patriciat vénétien, X–XIV siècles," *Annales d'histoire économique et sociale* (1937).

GARDINER C. MEANS (1896–) has been director of the Committee for Economic Development since 1943. After obtaining his doctorate in economics at Harvard University he served on a number of government agencies. From 1935 to 1939 he was director of the industrial section of the National Resources Committee, while from 1939 to 1940 he was economic adviser of the National Resources Planning Board.

Main works: (with J. C. Bonbright) *The Holding-Company—Its Public Significance and Its Regulation* (1932); (with A. A. Berle) *The Modern Corporation and Private Property* (1932); *The Structure of the American Economy* (1939).

WESLEY C. MITCHELL (1874–1948) was an economist with strong empirical interests, whose main contributions were made in the fields of monetary theory, monetary history, and business cycles. After graduating from the University of Chicago he studied in Halle and Vienna (1897–98). He obtained his doctorate in 1899 with a dissertation under the title *History of the Legal Tender Acts* (1903). In the following years he lectured in economics at the University of Chicago (1900–1912), and at Columbia University (1913–19 and 1922–44). From 1919 to 1931 he was director of the New School for Social Research. He also was chairman of the President's Research Committee on Social Trends (1929–33), director of research, National Bureau of Economic Research (1920–40), and fulfilled a number of other important functions.

Main works: *A History of the Greenbacks, with Special Reference to the Economic Consequences of Their Issue, 1862–65* (1903); *Gold, Prices, and Wages under the Greenback Standard* (1908); *Business Cycles* (1st ed., 1913); *History of Prices during the War. International Price Comparisons* (1919); (with W. I. King, F. R. Macaulay, O. W. Knauth) *Income in the United States, Its Amount and Distribution, 1909–1919* (1921–22); (with Arthur F. Burns) *Measuring Business Cycles* (1946); *What Happens during Business Cycles* (1951).

JOHN U. NEF (1899–) is the present chairman of the Committee on Social Thought at the University of Chicago. Since 1935 he has been professor of economic history at that university. He obtained the doctor's degree at the Robert Brookings Graduate School, Washington, D.C., in 1927, after having graduated from Harvard University.

Main works: *The Rise of the British Coal Industry* (2 vols., 1932); *Industry and Government in France and England, 1540–1640* (1940); *War and Human Progress: An Essay on the Rise of Industrial Civilization* (1950).

ARMANDO SAPORI (1892–) is professor of economic history at the University of Florence and at the Bocconi University of Milan. He has filled the post of city councillor of Florence and is a Senator of the Italian Republic. His main interest lies in the field of medieval economic history; a number of his important articles have been published in one volume under the title *Studi di storia economica medievale* (1941). His other works include *La crisi delle compagnie mercantili dei Bardi e dei Peruzzi* (1926); *Una compagnia di Calimala ai primi del trecento* (1932); *I libri di commercio dei Peruzzi* (1934); *I libri della ragione bancaria dei Gianfigliazzi* (1946); *Mercatores* (1941).

GUSTAV SCHMOLLER (1838–1917) studied at the University of Tübingen (1857–61) and wrote his doctoral dissertation on the economic ideas of Protestant reformers. He became professor of social and political sciences ("Staatswissenschaften") in Halle, moved in 1872 to Strasbourg and in 1882 to Berlin. He led an extremely productive seminar, the research papers of which were published in the *Staats- und socialwissenschaftliche Forschungen.* In 1880 Schmoller became editor of the *Jahrbuch für Gesetzgebung, Verwaltung, und Volkswirtschaft im deutschen Reich,* which came to be known as *Schmollers Jahrbuch.* It served as a rallying point for the "younger historical school" and was one of the main early journals in economic history.

Schmoller was not a secluded academician but joined a group of German scholars, mainly economists, who were known as "socialists of the chair." These men, among whom were Wagner, Conrad, and Brentano, intended to utilize social science in guiding a positive social policy on the part of the state. In 1872 they formed the Verein für Sozialpolitik, an association for research in the social sciences, which also was quite influential in shaping German social legislation. Schmoller was one of the founders of the Verein and later became its leader.

Main works: *Zur Geschichte der deutschen Kleingewerbe im 19. Jahrhundert* (1870); *Die Strassburger Tucher- und Weberzunft* (1879); *Zur Literaturgeschichte der Staats- und Sozialwissenschaften* (1888); *Umrisse und Untersuchungen zur Verfassungs-, Verwaltungs-, und Wirtschaftsgeschichte besonders des preussischen Staates im 17. und 18. Jahrhundert* (1898) (the first chapter of *Umrisse* was translated by W. J. Ashley under the title *The Mercantile System and Its Historical Significance* [1896]); *Grundriss der allgemeinen Volkswirtschaftslehre* (2 vols., 1901–2). An extensive bibliography of Schmoller's writings can be found in the article, "Gustav von Schmoller," *Handwörterbuch der Staatswissenschaften,* Vol. VII (4th ed., 1926), pp. 252–53.

NORMAN J. SILBERLING (1892–1942) obtained his doctorate from Harvard University with a dissertation on "The History of Theories of Money and Credit from Adam Smith to J. S. Mill" (unpublished). He subsequently taught at Stanford University. As an economist, his main interests lay in the field of economic fluctuations and their empirical treatment. His extensive researches found embodiment in *The Dynamics of Business* (1942).

FRANÇOIS SIMIAND (1873–1935), French economist and statistician, studied at the École Normale Supérieure under Lévy-Bruhl, and in 1896 he graduated in philosophy. In 1904 he completed his doctoral dissertation, *Le salaire des ouvriers des mines en France.* He taught economic history, statistics, and the history of economic doctrine at the École Pratique des Hautes Études (1910–35). From 1923 to 1934 he occupied the chair of political economy—in which position Jean-Baptiste Say had been his illustrious predecessor—at the Conservatoire des Arts et Métiers.

Simiand published a number of articles on method and on inductive economics in *L'année sociologique,* in *Revue de métaphysique et de morale,* and in other journals. His books are: *La méthode positive en science économique* (1912); *Cours d'économie politique* (3 mimeographed vols., 1929–31); *Recherches anciennes et nouvelles sur le mouvement général des prix du XVI*e *au XIX*e *siècle* (mimeographed, 1932), and, finally, the embodiment of his main researches, *Le salaire, l'évolution sociale et la monnaie* (3 vols., 1932). See for a bibliography of his writings: Basile Damalas, *L'œuvre scientifique de François Simiand* (1943).

WERNER SOMBART (1863–1941), German economist and economic historian, devoted his main attention to the empirical study of economic activity, particularly the study of capitalism as a historical phenomenon. He was a student of law and political economy at the universities of Pisa and Berlin and obtained the doctoral degree with a dissertation on Italian agricultural conditions, *Die römische Campagna* (1888). For a few years he was a councillor of the Bremen Chamber of Commerce; subsequently he was appointed professor of political economy in Breslau (1890–1906). He later became a professor at the Handelshochschule in Berlin (1906–17). In 1917 he succeeded the great economist Adolf Wagner at the University of Berlin, from which position he retired in 1931.

Main works: *Sozialismus und soziale Bewegung im 19. Jahrhundert* (1896); *Die deutsche Volkswirtschaft im 19. Jahrhundert* (1903); *Der moderne Kapitalismus* (1st ed., 1902; greatly enlarged edition, in several volumes, 1916). Separate aspects of the problem dealt with in this central work were treated in *Die Juden und das Wirtschaftsleben* (1911); *Der Bourgeois* (1913); and other books. Its methodological implications were set forth in *Die drei Nationalökonomien* (1930). See, for details on Sombart's life and work, M. J. Plotnik, *Werner Sombart and His Type of Economics* (1937), with bibliography. More bibliographical information can be found in *Handwörterbuch der Staatswissenschaften* Vol. VIII (3rd ed., 1911), pp. 553–54.

ARTHUR SPIETHOFF (1873–) studied economics and political science ("Staatswissenschaften") at the University of Berlin. He obtained his doctorate with *Beiträge zur Analyse und Theorie der allgemeinen Wirtschaftskrisen* (1905). He was assistant to Gustav Schmoller (1899–1908) and became, successively, lecturer in Berlin, professor of economics in Prague, and, finally, professor of political economy in Bonn (1918–39). After Gustav Schmoller's death Spiethoff became one of the editors of *Schmollers Jahrbuch* (1917–22); from 1924 to 1939 he was sole editor.

A large number of studies testifies to Spiethoff's interest in the theory of economic fluctuations. A comprehensive statement of his cycle theory is the article, "Krisen," in *Handwörterbuch der Staatswissenschaften* (4th ed., 1924). Other articles can be found in Schmoller's *Jahrbuch für Gesetzgebung, Verwaltung, und Volkswirtschaft im deutschen Reich,* of the years 1902, 1903, 1909, 1918, 1919, 1920. A bibliography of earlier writings can be found in the *Handwörterbuch der Staatswissenschaften* Vol. VIII (3rd ed., 1911), p. 685. Economic problems of housing were treated in *Boden und Wohnung* (1934). His methodological position is represented by the articles of which selections have been printed in the present volume, and by "Die allgemeine Volkswirtschaftslehre als geschichtliche Theorie. Die Wirtschaftsstile," Schmoller's *Jahrbuch für Gesetzgebung, Verwaltung und Volkswirtschaft,* Vol. LVI (1932–33); see also "Gustav von Schmoller und die anschauliche Theorie der Volkswirtschaft," Vol. LXII (1938), and "Anschauliche und reine volkswirtschaftliche Theorie und ihr Verhältnis zueinander," *Synopsis, Festgabe für Alfred Weber* (1948).

ABBOTT P. USHER (1883–), economist and economic historian, is at present professor emeritus at Harvard University. After his doctorate at Harvard University (1910), he taught at Cornell and Boston universities.

In 1922 he returned to Harvard University as professor of economics. Main works: *The History of the Grain Trade in France, 1400–1710* (1913); *An Introduction to the Industrial History of England* (1920); *A History of Mechanical Inventions* (1929); (with Witt Bowden and Michael Karpovich) *An Economic History of Europe since 1750* (1937); *The Early History of Deposit Banking in Mediterranean Europe* (1943).

JOHN H. WILLIAMS (1887–) is at present Nathaniel Ropes professor of political economy at Harvard University. He graduated from Brown University and obtained the doctoral degree at Harvard in 1919. He has taught economics at Harvard, Princeton, and Northwestern universities. His functions include those of contributing editor to the *Review of Economic Statistics* (1921–25), dean of the Graduate School of Public Administration, Harvard University (1937–47), and vice-president of the Federal Reserve Bank of New York (1936–47), of which at present he is economic adviser. In 1951 he was president of the American Economic Association. In the same year appeared a volume of essays in his honor, under the title *Money, Trade, and Economic Growth*.

His main works are: *Argentine International Trade under Inconvertible Paper Money, 1880–1900* (1920); *Annual Studies of the Balance of Payments of the United States* (1919–23); *Postwar Monetary Plans and Other Essays* (1944).

CHARLES H. WILSON (1914–) studied at Jesus College in the University of Cambridge; after graduating, in 1937, he went to Amsterdam to study Anglo-Dutch economic relations in the seventeenth and eighteenth centuries, in collaboration with the late Dr. J. C. Westermann. In 1938 he was elected a Fellow of Jesus College, Cambridge, and in 1945 became director of studies in history, university lecturer in history, and bursar of the college. Publications: *Anglo-Dutch Commerce and Finance in the Eighteenth Century* (1940), and several articles on mercantilism and business history.

Index of Names

Index of Names [1]

[1] Italicized numbers indicate either the beginning page of an article included in the present volume, or the beginning page of a section (introduction or biography) dealing with its author.

This book has been set on the Linotype in 12 and 10 point Garamond No. 3, leaded 1 point. Chapter numbers are in 24 point, and chapter titles in 18 point Bell italics. The size of the type page is 27 by 45½ picas.

Date Due